Hanna-Barbera: A History

Hanna-Barbera:
A History

JARED BAHIR BROWSH

McFarland & Company, Inc., Publishers
Jefferson, North Carolina

Library of Congress Cataloguing-in-Publication Data

Names: Browsh, Jared Bahir, 1985– author.
Title: Hanna-Barbera : a history / Jared Bahir Browsh.
Description: Jefferson, North Carolina : McFarland & Company, Inc., Publishers, 2022 |
Includes bibliographical references and index.
Identifiers: LCCN 2021046061 | ISBN 9781476675794 (paperback : acid free paper) ∞
ISBN 9781476644202 (ebook)
Subjects: LCSH: Hanna-Barbera Productions—History. | BISAC: PERFORMING ARTS /
Animation (see also Film / Genres / Animated)
Classification: LCC NC1766.U52 H3633 2021 | DDC 791.45/340973—dc23/eng/20211109
LC record available at https://lccn.loc.gov/2021046061

British Library cataloguing data are available

ISBN (print) 978-1-4766-7579-4
ISBN (ebook) 978-1-4766-4420-2

Front cover image © 2022 Shutterstock

Printed in the United States of America

*McFarland & Company, Inc., Publishers
Box 611, Jefferson, North Carolina 28640
www.mcfarlandpub.com*

To Mommy, from your Boo Boo

Table of Contents

Introduction:
Animation, Culture,
and the Legacy of a Partnership

Why Hanna-Barbera?

More than eighty years ago, Joseph Barbera arrived in California, enticed by the warm weather and a nearly 50 percent raise from his salary at the East Coast studio to leave Terrytoons for Metro-Goldwyn-Mayer's new cartoon studio. Fred Quimby was hired to start a new animated film studio after budget disagreements amidst the Great Depression led MGM to end their relationship with Hugh Harman and Rudolf Ising. Quimby and MGM were offering $87.50 a week and one-year contracts to lure animators from competitors like Harman-Ising, Fleisher, and Disney.[1] Soon after Barbera started at MGM, his desk was placed across from William Hanna, beginning an animation partnership that would span six decades and result in the production of thousands of hours of cartoons and the creation of dozens of iconic characters across multiple media. From *Tom and Jerry* to *Scooby-Doo*, the duo and their studio are responsible for providing entertainment for audiences across several generations around the world.

The content produced by Hanna and Barbera, who maintained a strictly professional relationship, and their studio led to seven Academy Awards, eight Emmy Awards and billions of dollars in profits from distribution and merchandising; however, they have been overshadowed in the construction of animation history by Warner Bros. and especially Disney, even though they produced more hours of content than either of the other studios between their first *Tom and Jerry* cartoon in 1940 and the death of William Hanna in 2001.[2] After their success as directors of the *Tom and Jerry* series, they maintained control of their own studio for 44 years, one year longer than Walt Disney oversaw his eponymous studio. Also, unlike Disney, Hanna and Barbera were true animators throughout their careers, with consistent hands-on involvement with the content credited to their names.[3]

Taking a Backseat to Disney, and the Importance of Context in Media Production

Because animated characters and their cartoons are often considered ageless, animated content is often overlooked as a reflection of the ideologies of the time of its dissemination, particularly the dominant ideologies connected to hegemonic formations within society. Whether it is animation's reputation as a genre for children or the perception that cartoons are low brow, animation's cultural connections and influence have often been ignored in academic analyses, particularly beyond the content produced by the seemingly omnipresent Disney. As a result, Disney and children's cartoons receive most of the analysis related to representation of race, gender, and sexuality, which often ignores the rest of the industry. No one analysis can cover the entirety of an industry that spans three centuries; however, the relatively limited research outside of Disney or children's animated content has led to narrow focus related to analysis and understanding of not only animation's place in American culture, but also how the industry has typically supported dominant ideologies as white heterosexual males dominated the production of animation throughout the 20th and 21st centuries.[4]

This consistent downplay of the contribution by the duo to the animation industry and art form is not only significant because of the amount of content produced, awards won, or profits made, but also because their careers spanned many of the most significant political and social milestones of the 20th century. From the tail end of the Depression through the aftermath of the events of September 11, 2001, the animators disseminated content with society-altering phenomena like World War II, the Cold War conflicts, various Civil Rights movements, and the rise of globalization occurring outside of studios responsible for producing animation. Hanna-Barbera also endured numerous changes within the film and television industries that claimed dozens of studios and series as the visual media industry quickly grew after the Second World War ended in 1945.[5] The lack of historical review and analysis is especially confounding considering their characters continue to be profitable and appear in various media, including the 2020 film *Scoob!* as an attempt to launch a Hanna-Barbera cinematic universe similar to what Disney and the current owner of Hanna-Barbera's properties, Warner, has done with their comic properties, Marvel and DC, respectively.[6]

No piece of culture is produced in a vacuum, and the societal context within which content is created and sold needs to be considered when it is analyzed. Doing so not only reveals more about what influenced the content, but it enables culture to become a common lens through which we consider various societal issues and phenomena. This includes the visual representations and rhetoric supporting dominant, often oppressive ideologies. Examining a pair of white male heterosexual content producers whose careers both cross numerous American societal touchstones and also parallel the establishment and growth of neoliberalism can reveal how white male patriarchal capitalism has been represented and communicated not only in a unique genre like animation but in the larger television and media industries. The aim of this project is to go beyond a detailed history of an under-analyzed animation studio and reveal the evolution of how dominant populations and ideas have both represented themselves and others in content throughout most of the 20th century, linking Hanna and Barbera's productions with the principles that form neoliberal American ideology throughout this time.[7]

Drawing a Distinction: What Makes Animation Unique?

Animation has been treated like a niche content style or genre since its introduction toward the end of the 19th century. As live-action films got longer, with more detailed plots, increased run times, and emerging stars through the first two decades of the 20th century, animation continued to be a novelty used to amuse, or distract, audiences for a short time with moving drawings. Though animation stars may have started to emerge by the 1920s, it was another decade before any studios even attempted to produce full-length features, and even then these longer films were often standalone adaptations of literature and did not produce the stars like Mickey and Bugs who were featured in the more common animated short films. Shorts from studios like Disney and Warner Bros. ran before and between live-action features adding to the perspective that animation was a novelty; however, as popular series like *Merrie Melodies* and *Silly Symphonies* were created, more viewers recognized animation as a legitimate form of entertainment and popular culture as evidenced by Mickey Mouse's meteoric rise in the 1930s.[8] Studio executives recognized this growing popularity of animation, funding production, but these executives also continued to be critical of the expense and financial return from animated films. This attitude was still present after World War II even with the development and growth of television, leading to a dearth of animated content outside of weekend mornings through the 1980s, after a brief period of experimentation with prime time animation in the late 1950s and early 1960s. Popularity of cartoons among younger audiences also led to animation being marketed mainly to children in the decades after World War II, limiting the subject matter animators could approach in their films and programs.[9]

This perspective may have presented obstacles for animators to get their content produced and disseminated, however, it also allowed animation to avoid the same scrutiny and oversight from executives as live-action television. Animators did face frequent public scrutiny especially as animation found its way onto television screens. Until recently, most of the criticism the animation industry faced was based on violence or exploitative marketing, with many ignoring the way individuals and groups are represented in cartoons. Like many types of popular media, the majority of animated content supports the ideologies of the time, but some animators took advantage of the lack of oversight to include occasional subversive content in their productions.[10] For example, Hanna-Barbera's overall output supported traditional white male neoliberal ideologies, but there were clear feminist messages in some of the programs, particularly in the late 1960s and early 1970s as the second wave of feminism reached its peak.[11] These moments of resistance need to be recognized alongside the vast amount of content that supports white male capitalist heteronormative ideologies as critical animation studies continues to expand. The research must go beyond recent works and popular companies, like Disney, to see how the industry has evolved and its messages have adapted to the societal conditions at the time of production and dissemination so we have a complete critical history of animation as a foundation for work on contemporary content.

Ownership and Control

Another feature unique to animation is the control producers maintain over the product. Unlike live-action media, which is typically reliant on the availability of actors, locations, and technologies, animated content is completely created by animators and producers, giving them the ability to manipulate the content and characters in infinite ways. Mickey Mouse has never asked for vacation, a bigger salary, or to pursue passion projects, making him the perfect contract star to market both on the screen and in ancillary markets.[12] Even with several changes in his design, the character onscreen has not aged a day since his debut in 1927, giving the rodent cross-generational appeal experienced by very few figures outside of literature, religion, or politics. Although characters may be tweaked, they remain recognizable, and more importantly, profitable across generations. Also, unlike live action, the content is more easily remastered to mask the age of the content from newly emerging audiences. The characters of Hanna and Barbera's first popular franchise, *Tom and Jerry*, continue to appear in new cartoons, including a 2021 feature film and spin-off series, over 75 years after they debuted.[13] Producers also can set the film or program in any location or time period without permits or special effects, providing opportunities for parody, violence and fantasy not available to live-action producers. In the same season Hanna-Barbera produced action-adventure, science-fiction, adult sitcoms, children's comedies, and historical animated programs.[14]

Even with this flexibility, producers are limited by both the higher budgets and longer production schedules animation typically requires creating a lag between the subject matter included in the content and when it is actually disseminated to the public. This delay can help maintain past ideas and messages, since they are being reintroduced in the content that was developed years ago or pushed producers to select broad topic or adaptations, like fairy tales, to avoid issues posed by changes in perspective or trends over time. The time period the content was produced will always influence the content some, but the "timeless" stories that serve as inspiration for animation prevents the content from becoming stale or uninteresting, similar to how literature like Shakespeare survives across centuries. This is especially important when considering so much of the animation audience has long been children, who carry older ideologies they are exposed to in this animated content as they grow up.[15] Animation is also even more derivative than other types of media, with a small, insular group highly influenced by successful content of the past producing a large portion of animated content consumed by audiences.[16]

Increasing the power of these messages is the fact that children enjoy re-watching content they are familiar, which helps reinforce these ideas, particularly as media found its way into the home and became more mobile and ubiquitous. This trend continues today as streaming and on-demand services have made it easier to meet children's demands to watch the same show over and over wherever they are. Although Hanna-Barbera was the most prolific producer of animation through the 1960s, 1970s, and 1980s many of its series, like *The Jetsons*, only ran for a season when originally produced and gained popularity through repeated reruns on weekend mornings, reinforcing the capitalistic messages that will be discussed further in Chapter 3. In fact, most of these shows only ran for a season and were replayed constantly for decades. If there are ideological messages in this content, then audience members across numerous generations have been exposed to them repeatedly as reruns continued to appear on television and are now available on-demand through cable and streaming services.[17]

Imitation Is the Sincerest Form of Ideological Maintenance

Animation is largely an imitative genre, using the audience's familiarity with other content, figures, and culture for subject fodder. As discussed above, because animators need to create all of the visuals and dialogue, they need to rely on culture, characters, and tropes the audience is already familiar. This often creates a delay between the introduction of the representation or ideology and the time it finds its way into animated content, which is exacerbated by the long production times for animated films and programs. This can result in maintaining or reintroducing older ideologies, keeping them in the public consciousness. For example, *The Flintstones* was clearly inspired by *The Honeymooners*, a show that ended five years before the Stone Age couple premiered, carrying over the tropes, ideas, and even some storylines from the popular 1950s sitcom.[18] Considering children often re-watch the same films, programs, and episodes they are especially vulnerable to these less progressive ideologies.[19]

Animation's beginnings can be traced back to vaudeville, and many of the features it adopted from the popular variety shows of the 19th century are still present today. This includes the consistent presence of slapstick humor, music, and the reliance on stereotypes, especially in the minstrel-inspired blackface characters featured in vaudeville performances, and later, animated content. As early forms of American performative popular culture, vaudeville shows and then films were often white audiences' only interaction with people of color, through the representations on stage or screen, with animation continuing the damaging ideas about non-white populations popularized in minstrel shows and vaudeville.[20]

Animation also often finds inspiration within its own industry, as financial commitment leads producers to avoid risk and ensure certain ideas or formulas work before including them in their productions. The same characters, series, and even stories reappear consistently through the history of animation for this reason. For example, the first full-length animated feature was produced three decades after the first live-action full-length feature since no animators wanted to take the risk, but after the success of Disney's films, other studios eventually produced their own full-length animated films hoping to replicate the success of *Snow White and the Seven Dwarfs*.[21] It is also not a coincidence that during the Golden Age of Animation the most popular characters across animation studios were animals, with rabbits, mice, cats, and ducks becoming cartoon stars across various series and studios.[22]

The inspiration for imitation also comes from literature and live-action film as many animated films used the flexibility discussed above to adapt works and parody popular figures and culture. Although this has helped audiences connect with the content due to their familiarity, it has also historically held back animation from being truly progressive, particularly in its representations, until recently.[23] If the character that is created is meant to imitate white men, like Art Carney or Jackie Gleason, the character is going to sound white and ultimately represent some level of whiteness. The same goes for the content, which is not only mainly produced by white heterosexual males, but also represents the white heterosexual experiences that have dominated mass media content since the beginning. Even if the imitation is parody, like *The Flintstones*, it still satirizes older ideologies through traditional visuals or subject matter. They may be finding humor in the conspicuous consumption or suburbanization taking place in America, however many people, particularly children, may miss the commentary, and it is still presented through a traditional male-led nuclear family living a neoliberal lifestyle, messages which will be explored further in Chapters 9 and 10.[24]

Animation's long maintained relegation as a niche genre did not prevent animated content, characters, and franchises from financial success and widespread popularity. Mickey Mouse continues to be the face of one of the largest media conglomerates in the world, which built its empire around animation before expanding its holdings in recent decades. Recent Disney/Pixar animated films like *Zootopia*, *Finding Dory*, *Toy Story 3*, and *Frozen* have all easily surpassed one billion dollars at the box office, and five of the top twenty-five highest grossing films are animated features, which is remarkable when consider less than ten percent of films released widely in the United States are animated films.[25] Since the Golden Age of Animation, which began in the late 1920s, the international market has been extremely profitable for American animators, with the majority of box office earnings coming from outside of the United States. In fact, over two-thirds of the box office grosses of *Zootopia*, *Frozen 2*, and Dreamworks' *Minions* were earned overseas, as animated films and characters often have cross-cultural appeal, can be dubbed into different languages, and are easier to adapt to different customs and sensibilities depending on the market. International considerations may broaden the subject matter to appeal to audiences across borders, but since most animation is still produced in the United States, this content often also communicates American and Western ideologies throughout the world. The financial success of these films alone are enough evidence of their cultural impact, and why they need to be examined more critically.[26]

Critical Animation Studies

Every day for two years after my mom picked me up from daycare we would watch Dumbo with a plate of crackers and a giant glass of apple juice. When I was really good, she would take me to McDonald's and I would get a Happy Meal with a stuffed ornament from the film *Oliver and Company*. I was the Boo Boo to her Yogi Bear, earning the nickname because I was always by her side. These memories, some of which are over 30 years old, have remained not only because of the emotional attachment, but the popular cartoons that I have connected with the experiences that continue to remain publicly visible due to their immortality. Considering new families often get Mickey Mouse or other items featuring popular cartoon characters when a child is born, this emotional attachment often begins at birth and is passed down from one generation to another. This attachment, which also occurs with other culture like sports, creates strong connections between fans and the content. This also obscures the ability for consumers to see the content objectively and recognize the ideological messages contained in the culture, making critical engagement with content like animation from both inside and outside the academy so important, as critics and scholars work to make those who are exposed to the culture aware of what ideologies are being reinforced or maintained.[27]

The perception of animation as a niche genre of media has greatly influenced research on both content and the industry with scholars across disciplines engaging with animation, but historically many of these researchers will study a single phenomenon before moving to another content area. They are often disciplinary tourists who may have the theoretical background to contribute to the research, but often lack the contextual or historical background in animation to fully understand the topic they are analyzing. Although these shortcomings have limited scholarship exploring animation in some areas, they have also presented opportunities to make critical animation studies a truly interdisciplinary field as these varied areas of research continue to influence how the content and business of animation is approached as more people try to under the impact of animation, and other popular culture, has on our society.[28]

Even as animation studies separated itself as a unique discipline over the last decade, its relationship with media studies, particularly television studies, is undeniable. As Wartella and Reeves note, research eras and focuses within media studies have often been connected with particular media. Although the foundation of the animation industry is planted firmly in film, and until recently a large portion of animation research examined popular animated film, the episodic and serial nature of animated content and the fact that the majority of animated content is now produced for, and consumed through, television, the emergence of television studies since World War II has greatly contributed to the evolution of the theories and methods necessary for the critical engagement with the content and industry.[29] The careers of Hanna and Barbera and the growth of their studio run parallel to the development of both television and animation studies, which presents opportunities to both critically engage with their content and company, while also exploring the historical context of the cartoons along with the evolution of ideological and representational research within the field. Also, much of the analysis of the media past and presence can be applied to animation considering the industry's reliance on imitating and satirizing other culture and society.[30]

Throughout the development of media and television studies there have been several approaches as researchers from a number of fields and disciplines recognized that the influence of culture and media and the role it plays in society could not be ignored, even if the content was considered "lowbrow" compared to the "high art" in museums and books. The social science approach to media research truly emerged in the 1930s, although concerns over children's literacy produced some early institutional research at the turn of the century and anecdotal evidence has been recorded since the 18th century.[31] This early research on media directed toward children largely attempted to confirm fears about the possible corruption of young (white) children consuming this content; however, this type of research on the dangers of media exposure, particularly among the younger audience, has greatly impacted animation research especially since the 1950s as animation developed the reputation of being a genre for children.[32] General media research before and during World War II, like children's media research, largely focused on effects of consumption with a significant portion of the concern over propaganda and persuasion, especially the ideological warfare connected to Nazism and the eventual American reaction to Aryan nationalism.[33] Scholars like Paul Lazarsfeld focused on the effects of consuming media as the airwaves became another battlefield during the War. With Elihu Katz, Lazarsfeld later constructed the two-step flow of communication that contemplated the role of community in filtering and disseminating information from the mass media and also described the possible narcotizing dysfunction of the media with Robert Merton, where the audience becomes apathetic to issues that the mass media inundates them with, so even if the consumer has concerns about content or misrepresentations they rarely act because they are paralyzed by the flood of ideas presented by the media, and those who are not conscious of these messages continue to be exposed without resistance.[34] This flood has only increased the last two decades due to technological advancement and increased access through digital platforms and devices.[35]

The recognition that media like radio and newspapers could contain both explicit and subliminal ideological and representational information helped raise awareness of the power embodied in culture and media, but the focus on effects led to broad conclusions and limited intervention into the motivations and processes behind the creation and production of this content. The Cold War revitalized this type of effects research, as the ideological war between the USSR and United States led to new strategies in creating and disseminating propaganda.[36] As the Cold War conflicts dominated news coverage, and Westerns and police shows filled the schedule, federal funding for research on the effects of violence on television was greatly increased in the late 1960s. Scholars like George Gerbner helped to move this research forward by going beyond individual effects to note the narrative structure of the media even across programs and networks. Gerbner noted that connections between violent media and aggressive behavior is not based on exposure to any individual show or scene, but rather that consistent inundation of violent images into the consciousness of the public creating, or cultivating, a "mean world syndrome" among heavy media and news consumers.[37] This research on news media and consumption was also influenced by already established journalism departments, whose scholars' contributed to knowledge about how news and information is produced and disseminated to a mass audience.[38] Herbert Gans called for more mass media research in 1972, further motivating scholarly work on the influence of media on ideology. During the 1980s, Gerbner noted that television continued to expand its role as the central storyteller in society, and that the audiences' understanding of the world was being influenced by the fact that television continues to include certain groups or ideas while clearly excluding others. This occurs for a variety of reasons, but typically results in reinforcing the status quo and maintaining hegemonic structures that support white male heteronormative capitalist ideology.[39] Although television and animation studies has separated itself from a purely quantitative and experimental approach that defined this early social science—inspired research into media and television, this sociological influence is more evident in television studies than other related disciplines like film studies, which has historically focused on the content while compartmentalizing the context. The social science influence and positivist approach also helped to legitimize the field as scholars in other disciplines questioned the necessity of studying low or mass culture while this research helped prove that television is socially, politically, and culturally relevant.[40]

Another approach that has contributed to the theories and methods of television and animation studies comes out of the humanities, particularly communication studies. Early examinations of television and animation from this perspective often focused on criticism about the quality and relevance of television content. The research throughout the 1960s and 1970s from communication scholars supported the criticism television faced from segments of the public and politicians. Federal Communications Chair Newton Minow called television a "vast wasteland" and criticism originating from the humanities warned of the pointlessness of the so-called idiot box.[41] For television studies, the emergence of scholarly fields concerned about understanding the experiences of marginalized groups led scholars and activists to push for consciousness and equality help to guide television and media studies away from pure criticism with increased focus on offering solutions.[42] As scholars deconstructed Renaissance artists and classical music, they also had a new respect for "low" or popular culture as a source of important information about understanding its role in society. Mass exposure to this content produced for a broad audience made it a fertile ground for research about how constructions and ideologies are unknowingly reinforced by those producing and consuming it.[43]

Rhetorical studies deriving from communication studies did not regularly produce analyses of popular culture until the 1970s, after television studies began to establish itself in various academic departments and cultural institutions like the University of Texas–Austin, the Museum of Broadcast Communication in Chicago, and the Paley Center (originally the Museum of Radio and Television). This rhetorical turn in U.S. television and popular culture research came well after Cultural Studies was established in the UK, whose scholars' research on "low art" also predated humanities' eventual recognition of the possible ideologies contained in popular culture. Richard Hoggart's establishment of the Centre for Contemporary Cultural Studies (CCCS) at the University of Birmingham in 1964 further legitimized television and popular culture scholarship. As Stuart Hall took over the center in 1968, Britain was experiencing social tensions that led to the establishment of the Media Group within the center that examined representations and ideologies contained in journalistic content, eventually transitioning from focusing exclusively on "hard news" to popular culture in later research. The work of scholars like Raymond Williams, who like Katz and Lazarsfeld was critical of the notion of the passive audience who mindlessly absorb media content, helped legitimize mass media analysis. Hall's "Encoding and Decoding in the Television Discourse" in 1973 contributed media scholarship by describing the agency of the audience and the role of culture in its everyday lives.[44] This analysis focuses more on the encoding of ideology in content; however, the qualitative, ethnographic work of those within the CCCS continues to influence audience studies. Considering the neo-Marxist influence within the Centre, it is not surprising that much of the focus on the construction of text and content came from a political economic perspective examining the influence of institutions like media corporations and government agencies on the production and dissemination of culture, which will be the approach taken in analyzing the work of Hanna-Barbera.[45]

The complexity of the industry formed around culture was explored by the Frankfurt School as it utilized historical materialism popularized by Karl Marx to examine society to try to illuminate the conditions necessary to force social change. Theodor Adorno and Max Horkheimer were especially critical of the exploitation of culture for the sake of both profit and ideological control of the masses. Although the work of scholars, like those from Cultural Studies, disagreed with Horkheimer and Adorno's negative perspective about the worth of popular culture and that its sole purpose was to undermine reputable art, "The Culture Industry: Enlightenment as Mass Deception" is still a foundational piece for scholars who critically engage with media and culture by looking at the larger industries and systems that are in place to mass produce and distribute content.[46]

In 1976, Horace Newcomb released the edited collection of what was considered one of television studies' foundational writings, *Television: The Critical View*, creating a comprehensive text as television scholars formalized the field. As this organization within the discipline was occurring, feminist and critical race scholars were finally recognized for the work they had been conducting for decades as they criticized the constant misrepresentation of marginalized groups in content and the lack of influence in the production of media.[47] Theories and methods coming from Women's Studies, Ethnic Studies, and Marx-inspired scholarship opened "high art" to criticism concerning representation and rhetoric contained within this content, which was seen as exemplifying true creativity, placing it above critique for many scholars.[48]

As white, mostly male researchers focused on the white masses and the culture and content consumed by white audiences, scholars and thinkers like W.E.B. Du Bois, Frantz Fanon, and James Baldwin criticized the role of culture from the West with content frequently misrepresenting populations of color which contributed to their discrimination by consistently and repeatedly reinforcing white supremacy. Feminist and intersectional scholars were also strongly critical of the role of popular culture in oppressing those that fall outside white male heteronormativity, and the 1970s and 1980s saw an increase of these scholars in the academy, which includes Charlotte Brunsdon, Gloria Anzaldua, bell hooks, and Patricia Hill Collins.[49] These interventions are often overlooked in media programs, especially in introductory courses, often pushed to topics classes in these schools and college; however, concentrations like Africana and Ethnic Studies have made up for some of this oversight in their own programs, reinforcing the impact culture and mass media have on identity and the experience of individuals and groups, particularly outside the dominant group(s).

By the mid–1990s, longer and more critical scholarly work in television and animation studies began to appear in book form as scholars explored media content and companies as the industry consolidated and conglomerates were formed. Disney was frequently the focus of these critical analyses, bringing more attention to animation as those inside and outside of the academy recognized that one of the largest media companies in the world was built on animation that reflected dominate ideologies throughout its history.[50] This scholarship enabled animation studies to begin the process of establishing itself as its own critical field, buoyed by the formation of the Society of Animation Studies in 1987 by animation historian Harvey Deneroff when he was a graduate student at the University of Southern California. Disney commanded most of the focus over the first decade of formal animation studies; however, research has quickly expanded to examine other producers and content.[51]

Considering animation is also an art form, the technical aspect of the genre cannot be ignored. The technical determinism championed by Marshall McLuhan and film studies was dismissed by scholars like Raymond Williams; however, it is clear that the technical aspects of producing animation have influenced the production and consumption of animated content.[52] The high costs associated with creating animation have long been a barrier for media companies interested in producing animation or establishing cartoon studios, with the expectations of the audience reinforcing these standards of quality. These expectations were shifted as animation was produced specifically for television, but various technical and cultural standards influenced by the desire to reach broad, typically younger, audiences in television animation through the 1980s also led to limited attempts to disrupt the status quo related to the topics and representations presented in animation that had found a home on Saturday morning. With the broadest, and most affluent audiences being white, middle to upper class children, shows and advertisers almost exclusively catered to them in storylines and through the identities the characters represented in the programs.[53] Also, the explosion of animation from in the late 1980s was partially due to improvements in computer animation that allowed for quicker, more cost effective production.[54] Considering animated content has existed since the beginning of film at the turn of the 20th century, its development has not been determined by technology; however, it is not immune to its influence either.

Lastly, performance studies has also influenced animation and television studies recently, recognizing that the analysis coming from this field could be applied to drawn figures. Recent research has found audiences suspend reality while viewing animated content in the same way as they do during live-action media and that audiences see many animated characters like stars and celebrities rather than drawings on a paper or cel, an idea promoted by Walt Disney since the 1930s. With vaudevillian roots, theater and animation have interconnected histories, and the explorations into the practices, politics, and motivations of performance has helped expand the scope and introduce new approaches to analyze animated content and characters.[55]

Theoretical Foundations

With roots in several academic disciplines, there are innumerable theoretical approaches to examining animation, while also utilizing popular culture as a lens to view larger society. While other theoretical fields will provide guidance for analysis, this project will be informed by television studies, specifically the critical feminist, race, and intersectional theories that helped build the foundation of representational research in the late 1960s and 1970s. As Du Bois notes, those in power want to maintain white supremacy due to the "public and psychological wage" or entitlements that they have become accustomed to receiving due to their privilege and systemic racism against populations of color that provides an advantage for white populations that are present before they are born.[56] This is also true for gender and sexuality, as the maintenance of their constructions and the hierarchy contained within them privileges maleness and heterosexuality over other identities, which is supported both consciously and unconscious throughout all systems and structures in society. This is not only reinforced in politics and everyday interactions, but also through culture and media, which white males continue to control even as the industry has expanded exponentially since the late 19th century.[57]

In the influential work *Gender Trouble*, Judith Butler discusses how gender, and race, are constructions and to maintain various binaries and structures we are forced to "perform" our gender to avoid upsetting the social order that is built on certain gender roles and expectations. Historically, humans have learned the correct way to conduct themselves through the guidance of family, friends, and the social world around them.[58] As culture, like religion/myth and literature, developed and grew in society, it also acted as a tool to reinforce gender norms creating a moral need to fulfill expectations. Performances, first through theater and then through mass media like radio, television, and film, provided audiovisual examples of how those identified as male or female are supposed to act within various social worlds. The mass media acted as a propaganda tool to indoctrinate the audience to the correct practices and actions of the gender within the binary with which they are identified.[59]

As electronic mass media spread throughout the 20th century, white males positively represented themselves in both entertainment and informational media while misrepresenting the characteristics and experiences of others. Even with its foundations in legal studies, critical race theorists have recognized the psychological power of media images and representations in maintaining a white hegemony in America. Culture is not only a battleground to maintain white male supremacy, but when given the opportunity, can be one to resist it as well, which places equal importance on analyzing the production along with the finish product to understand the source of the ideology. The purpose of critical race theory is to analyze and challenge the racial orthodoxy we are inundated with in our lives, which includes revisiting the complex history of various domains within society, including culture, where the status quo is consistently reproduced for the collective conscious. Critical race theorists from Patricia Williams and bell hooks to Derrick Bell and Todd Boyd discuss the role of media and culture as a tool of persuasion that typically works to maintain the status quo, particularly in content that is disseminated to the masses through the mainstream media.[60] The constant and repetitive nature of television is a particularly efficient tool in reinforcing these ideas, especially as the medium also brought these ideologies into the home.[61]

Williams also helped develop an important theoretical field influenced by both critical race and feminist theories to offer intersectional analysis that is better equipped to examine the complex experience of individuals in society, critical race feminism. The field recognizes that no one operates within a society through one identity, rather, various constructions and experiences form identity, creating multifaceted individuals who also are forced to embody certain behaviors, or they will be corrected pushed down to a lower position in the societal hierarchy based on race, gender, or sexuality.[62] Although scholars were practicing intersectional scholarship for decades, Kimberle Crenshaw officially introduced the term to academia in the mid–1980s, challenging not only the previous research that often isolated constructed identities, if they recognized them at all, but also highlighted the multiple levels of discrimination non-male black, indigenous, and people of color face, which was often overlooked by the masculine focus of earlier critical race scholarship and feminist research that typically centralized the liberation of white middle-class women over other groups.[63] Considering women of color are both underrepresented *and* misrepresented throughout the history of animation, media, and television, intersectional and critical race feminist theories are integral when deconstructing the representations within the content, the motivations behind those representations, and the potential effect of reinforcing oppressive ideologies in this content.

Another related field, decolonial theory, also has both an analytical and practical element that aims to confront and separate ideology from the influence of coloniality and the colonial matrix of power.[64] The process of colonizing occurs physically and psychologically, with culture and media being used as weapons in this ideological warfare, particularly since World War I when the West, especially America, increased its economic and political globalization transitioning from imperialization mainly achieved through military force. Instead the focus became utilizing the soft power of cultural imperialism to maintain dominance over non–Western nations along with people of color within Western nations. Frantz Fanon has been particularly influential in understanding the psychological damage that occurs through various forms of coloniality, and how art and culture can reinforce ideology, particularly in content consumed by children as it is typically assumed that it is entertainment devoid of politics.[65] Edward Said also discusses this in *Orientalism*, as mass media works to standardize stereotypes for those considered as the "Others" by those who control the production and dissemination of the culture. These are typically white males from the West, who also act as gatekeepers to block the participation of those who are othered in the production of popular culture, limiting multi-faceted and informed representations of those that fall outside the white heterosexual male experience. The constant exposure to the dominant group's productions, and the ignoring of the colonized's culture, which is often appropriated and presented as the colonizer's, contributes to the idea that only Western experience represents civilization.[66] Chandra Talpade Mohanty's works, especially "Under Western Eyes: Feminist Scholarship" and "Colonial Discourse and Under Western Eyes Revisited: Feminist Solidarity through Anticapitalist Struggles," both add to the argument that Western influence through everything from military intervention and economic domination to the inundation of the colonizer's media are constantly working to oppress those outside of white western male supremacy.[67]

This separation, or apartheid, not only occurs in the production and dissemination of cultural or media content, but also in academia as well, which has limited non-white and non-male scholars in animation studies. As the field has grown over the last decade so has the diversity of those analyzing animation, but animation scholarship from critical race, feminist, and intersectional theorist both inside and outside the discipline continues to be limited, leaving an entire industry that has seen limited analysis through approaches or methods originating from these theoretical fields.[68]

Literature Review

Critical animation scholars continue to work to develop scholarly work, courses, and programs that examine animation's role in society as a unique cultural form. Topic classes that analyze Disney through the lens of feminism, or texts on the philosophy of *The Simpsons* have appeared in course catalogues for years, but analysis from animation scholars, rather than scholars from other disciplines examining animation, began to appear in larger numbers in the 1990s, with the last decade seeing the establishment of the *Animation* journal and the release of works that represent the foundation of the critical side of animation studies.[69] Like any interdisciplinary field, there are key works from other fields that have been integral in the development of critical animation studies, but it is also important to recognize the works that exemplify the unique analysis and perspectives the field can offer.

One of the best examples of this unique perspective is Nicholas Sammond, specifically his book *Birth of an Industry: Blackface Minstrelsy and the Rise of American Animation*. Released in 2015, *Birth of an Industry* examines the history of animation by looking at the environment in which the animation industry was established and expanded throughout 20th century. With roots in vaudeville and blackface minstrelsy, animation carried many of these ideologies and practices well into the Golden Age of Animation. Even as animation moved away from humor and storylines directly inspired by blackface minstrel performances, it still maintained white supremacist messaging by limiting representations of non-white individuals and groups, particularly African Americans, through World War II and beyond. The few times African Americans or characters of color did appear in animated content they were presented as stereotypically inferior beings with very little depth to the representation. In an industry that relies on formulas, imitation, and is averse to risk, breaking away from both the white male heterosexual domination in production of animation and the consistent misrepresentation of non-white, non-males, and the intersections of groups outside of white supremacy has been extremely difficult. What makes Sammond's intervention so integral is that his approach is informed by an entire career studying animation and media with a critical eye. This has enabled him to bring an understanding of the industry and audience that scholars from other disciplines rarely have when analyzing animation. The consistent inclusion of context in Sammond's work is also key when considering that many content and textual analyses originating from other fields often examine the content in a vacuum, or at least leave out information pertaining to the industry and the political economic environment in which the content is produced.[70]

Sammond has been working to build this field for over a decade. His first book, *Babes in Tomorrowland: Walt Disney and the Making of the American Child 1920–1960*, is another example of the interdisciplinary approach that centralizes American animation and the industry that often defines it. Using research that was conducted from the period explored, Sammond is able to link Margaret Mead's findings with strategies deployed by Disney to market to children, becoming integral in constructing ideas about what is an acceptable and healthy childhood for (white) American children. Sammond's research and understanding of both the animation and children's media environment during this forty-year period produces detailed descriptions about how emerging societal concerns concerning the way media consumption could affect children was utilized by Disney to produce "appropriate" media for children which parents enthusiastically encourage their children to consume over other content. Sammond also contends that the audience, in this case early to mid–20th-century children, influence media production much more than we realize. Consuming media clearly has an influence on children's lives and development, as evidenced by Disney's transgenerational popularity, but the influence also works the opposite direction with children's behaviors and tastes influencing media production and marketing as Disney's approach became a blueprint for media companies looking to create a loyal lifelong fan base around their productions, characters, and products.[71]

Sammond has utilized this type of analysis in journal articles as well, using methods from his books to examine representations of difference and language. In "Dumbo, Disney, and Difference: Walt Disney Productions and Film as Children's Literature" Sammond discusses how difference is represented as narrativized in animation, and how overcoming obstacles presented by this difference actually reinforces ideologies related to neoliberal individualism.[72] In another piece published the same year, "Who Dat Say Who Dat? Racial Masquerade, Humor, and the Rise of American Animation," Sammond provides strong evidence that representations in the visual media go beyond what we see and understanding how language and other features that the characters represent is integral when advocating for more sensitive and factual representations of non-white groups.[73]

Although he could be described as a general media or television scholar, Jason Mittell's ventures into television animation have been integral as animation studies has expanded its scope beyond just Disney and other cinematic animation. His piece "The Great Saturday Morning Exile: Scheduling Cartoons on Television's Periphery in the 1960s," from *Prime Time Animation: Television Animation and the American Culture*, edited by Carol Stabile and Mark Harrison, is a comprehensive political economic analysis of how various industry and policy factors, which lead to the utilization of Saturday morning, a time slot known as the ghetto of television, as a children's media haven, influenced the animation broadcast on all the networks. Although this type of analysis has been done in other media industries, like film, television animation, particularly general audience fare, had long been ignored and Stabile and Harrison's compilation helped to highlight the influence television animation, like from Hanna-Barbera's Cartoon Studio, has had on American media and culture. Mittell's piece in particular provides a template for conducting political economic analysis that make the relationship between production, business, and representation explicit.[74]

Mittell's scholarship exploring the business of television and how the industry organizes and defines itself helps supplements the large amount of research that continues to focus exclusively on content or technology without providing the political economic context for various decisions or trends. In *Genre and Television: From Cop Shows to Cartoons in American Culture*, Mittell explores the role of categorizing or organizing television programs by genre, which supports the industry's reliance on formulas. Mittell argues that genres are actually cultural categories that shape not only television content, but how the audiences see and approach the world, especially if they grow up in an environment inundated by television.[75] Mittell's *Television and American Culture* is arguably the most complete political economic contemporary deconstruction of the television industry and is used as a textbook in many television studies and media institution courses.[76]

The mere act of informing and contributing to more complete histories of various phenomenon and systems can easily be considered an act of advocacy, but Mittell's works often stop short of providing sharp criticism of the industry or, more generally, American culture. Robert W. McChesney's work provides a critical anti-capitalist eye that more directly connects the rise of neoliberal capitalism with the current structure and state of American media. His recent work has focused on the influence of capitalism on digital and social media; however, his 2004 book *The Problem of the Media: U.S. Communication Politics in the Twenty-First Century* is still a key intervention in the political economics of communication in America. McChesney argues that the media requires outside regulation because the industry is unable to regulate itself, which has resulted in a media environment where profits will always supersede any interest in providing a positive public service. McChesney's utilization of historical context while revealing the political economic motivations behind industry decisions strengthens the critical arguments he makes throughout the book and exemplifies the importance of recognizing the influence of business and policy decisions has on the content that is ultimately disseminated and consumed.[77]

Kevin Sandler, a top scholar in media industries has been extremely influential in examining animation outside of Disney, particularly Warner Bros. and Hanna-Barbera. Sandler edited *Reading the Rabbit: Explorations in Warner Bros. Animation*, also writing the Introduction and the chapter "Gendered Evasions: Bugs in Drag" providing a framework for studying identity in "classic" animation while also encouraging deeper research into Warner Bros. and other animation companies.[78] Sandler's work not only looks at the content, but the societal contexts and production, reinforcing the need to not study the content in a vacuum, recognizing the numerous influences on media and animation production. Sandler is currently working on a book about *Scooby-Doo*, a Hanna-Barbera show whose impact and influence on television animation and cartoon marketing has been largely overlooked since its debut in 1969, particularly considering the release of the full-length feature film *Scoob!* in May 2020, the first fully animated feature from the franchise produced for theaters.[79]

In any critical academic field that examines culture, histories that are approached as objectively as possible are extremely important in creating a common informational base for analysis. When exploring animation from the late 19th century through the mid- to late 20th century, Leonard Maltin's *Of Mice and Magic: The History of American Animation* and Michael Barrier's *Hollywood Cartoons: American Animation in its Golden Age* represent the most cited general history of the art, industry and institutions built around popular animated content and characters. Maltin's work focuses on the most popular content and the largest companies, including Disney, MGM, and Warner Bros. animation studios. As a more general film historian, Maltin is able to include context related to the larger film and entertainment industry, which is important considering Disney was the only animation studio established without an association with a larger film studio. *Of Mice and Magic* also includes discussions about the representations contained in the films and characters Maltin examines in his work.[80] As both a film historian and critic, Maltin has also conducted interviews and written shorter pieces that examine both past and present film and media, this includes interviews with figures like Joseph Barbera, providing invaluable information directly from those responsible for creating and producing the content and characters being examined in this study.

Barrier's work, which was published about twelve years after Maltin's last revision, helps supplement Maltin's work by including the histories of some of the overlooked studios in animation history that have impacted the development of the industry and art form. Barrier also includes more information about the producers of the films and how their presence and background influenced the cartoons they produced, which is necessary when trying to explain the motivations behind representations and ideologies that are reinforced by culture outside of animation. Although Barrier's historical examination ends in the 1960s, it still represents an extremely important and detailed explanation about why contemporary animation looks and operates the way it does, including the origins of many of the same characters and franchises that audiences of all ages still consume today.[81]

As discussed, Disney and popular contemporary franchises like *The Simpsons* have gotten the a significant portion of the attention within animation studies and from animation research originating from other disciplines, which is why it is important to recover and critically analyze historic information about companies like Hanna-Barbera; however, research by Jerry Beck, one of the few historians focusing almost exclusively on animation, has provided some foundation for research on the television animation duo and their studio. As Beck was working to become an animator, he received his start as a historian working as a research associate on the first edition of *Of Mice and Magic* with Maltin. Beck brings a unique perspective because he has also held numerous positions within the industry as co-owner of a film distribution company, specializing in international animation. He also served as president of Nickelodeon Movies, helping the network release their first animated feature film, and also served on the advisory board for Cartoon Network. He has written illustrated histories on both Hanna-Barbera and *The Flintstones*, combining his knowledge of animation history and art to compile a multi-layered review of the company and arguably their most popular franchise. Later in his career he assisted with archiving and producing compilations for MGM, including Hanna and Barbera's *Tom and Jerry* series, contributing historic commentary about the production and marketing of the studio's most successful animated franchise.[82]

Hal Erickson's *Television Cartoon Shows: An Illustrated Encyclopedia* complements both Barrier's and Maltin's work by focusing on the production of individual shows where as Barrier, Beck, and Maltin all compiled corporate histories for the most influential studios/companies from the Golden Age of Film Animation. Erickson's two-volume book includes entries for every syndicated and regularly scheduled animated program that appeared on American television through 1999. Erickson does dedicate more space to the more popular or well-known programs, making the argument that their popularity or infamy indicates more widespread consumption and impact, warranting more attention and detail. Considering that a significant number of animated television programs were co-produced by several studios or were at the very least influenced by the input of the networks, Erickson's approach reveals the complex process of getting an animated show on television and the frequent franchising and licensing involved in television animation that results in series being rerun for years after production to recoup the relatively high production costs for cartoons. Erickson's work also reveals how characters often appear on numerous programs after becoming profitable. Having information for all these shows in one place helps to connect the corporate dots in an insular industry.[83] Erickson previously produced *Syndicated Television Shows* in a similar style, which examined programs that were distributed through the syndication market, lending supplementary information as many Hanna-Barbera series and films were disputed through syndication throughout the company's history, especially after Financial and Syndication Interest Rules were enacted in 1970.[84] Other reference works like Jeff Lenberg's *Encyclopedia of Animated Cartoons*, David Perlmutter's *America Toons In: A History of Television Animation*, and David Mansour's *From Abba to Zoom: A Pop Culture Encyclopedia of the Late 20th Century* provide important background information about the shows, characters, and studios being examined throughout this piece.[85]

When looking at past work in this field it should be noted that the vast majority of animation and media historians are white, mostly heteronormative, males. This has clearly influenced the construction of the history similar to how the largely white male presence in writing traditional histories has led to overlooking or discounting the experiences of Black, Indigenous, and People of Color, those who identify as LGBTQ+, and the experiences of women both as producers and audience members.[86]

Recognizing the Words of the Subject

Compiling a history is a political act, regardless of how objective the historian attempts to be in research and writing. As we have learned through the white supremacy displayed in traditional American history, what is included and excluded can very easily change the reader's understanding of a phenomenon or event; however, when determining the motivations behind an action or production, using the words of those involved can strengthen arguments related to why various decisions were made.[87] Although there are limited detailed histories examining William Hanna and Joseph Barbera, they each wrote autobiographies that reveal important information about their careers, the development of their styles, their relationship, and the operation of their television animation studio. As autobiographies, some of the information needs to some skepticism, since most memoirs and life narratives written by or with the subject tend to avoid truly critical observations, however, taken together Barbera's *My Life in 'toons: From Flatbush to Bedrock in under a Century* and Hanna's *A Cast of Friends* complement each other and still act as primary resources about their experiences in the industry, particularly the decisions they made as animators and as the heads of their own studio.[88] As discussed earlier, revealing the backgrounds and viewpoints of those responsible for making the production and disseminating media, in this case animation, is integral in understanding how perspectives and ideologies are implanted in popular culture. Similarly, Iwao Takamoto's *My Life with a Thousand Characters* also provides a third party view of the animation duo by someone who worked with them for over thirty years and helped design some of their most popular characters.

Another key book that exemplifies a historical approach to culture that connects context with representations in television content is Sasha Torres' *Black, White, and in Color: Television and Black Civil Rights.* Torres' book is not only key since it examines a time period and movements in contrast to how it was represented at the time and compares that to what was actually happening in the communities throughout American society, but similar to this project and Sammond's *Babes in Tomorrowland*, Torres understands that the media-audience/society relationship is not a one-way path. The media instead reacts to what is happening in society, and vice versa, although society's effect on media tends to lag more than media's effect on society, especially when considering concepts or theories related to agenda setting.[89] Torres carries her analysis into the 1990s, discussing the role the Rodney King assault had on coverage of civil rights issues along with how contemporary media representations of Civil Rights work and demonstrations often supports a revisionist history that whitewashes the contributions and impact of various individuals and events of the movement. Looking at both news and entertainment media, it argues that early television often supported skepticism about (white) police while later television in the 1990s supported more reverence for law enforcement, which can be seen throughout television from the new to children's shows.[90]

Television came of age in 1960s and 1970s as technologies, formulas, and numerous events including the aforementioned Civil Rights Movement and Vietnam War helped the industry display both the medium's power as dramatic images, both fictional and real, were broadcast into living rooms across the country. Aniko Bodroghkozy's *Equal Time:*

Television and the Civil Rights Movement indirectly adds to Torres' analysis by focusing more on how the industry developed at this time, and how Civil Rights and other phenomenon at the time influenced how producers approached representing non-white people and characters, specifically African Americans. Splitting the analysis between news and entertainment programming, Bodroghkozy explores how both were forced to recognize the message of the Civil Rights and women's liberation movements, which is important considering there were only three national commercial networks at the time with the Public Broadcasting System debuting in 1969, absorbing National Educational Television after Congress passed the Public Broadcasting Act of 1967.[91] Even as producers were forced by societal progress to recognize different groups and their varied experiences, the white males, who represented the majority of producers, still struggled to sensitively and accurately represent the perspective of groups outside their own experience or background.[92]

Agency and Effect

Jennifer Barker is able to connect the representations in early animation with the continued struggle to accurately represent African Americans in contemporary content in her piece "Hollywood, Black Animation, and the Problem of Representation in 'Little Ol' Bosko' and 'The Princess and the Frog.'" Using these two films as bookends between the minstrel origins of animation and more recent productions, Barker also argues that within these franchises there is still room for the audience to create their own meaning and even use the content as a site of resistance. Jose Esteban Munoz discusses this navigation through the lens of queer theory in *Disidentifications: Queers of Color and the Performance of Politics* examining how those from marginalized groups are able to create their own meaning from content they consume, transforming a piece of art or performance to fit within their own experience or desires even when the producers and the content ignore their presence. Discussing these places of resistance recognizes the agency of the audience without making broad assumptions or conclusions connected to effect. Viewers of animation whose privilege is not supported by white male heteropatriarchy have historically created their own meaning, particularly when characters represents their experience or identity are consumed, like Speedy Gonzalez's popularity in Mexico in spite of the negative stereotypes the mouse embodies.[93]

One of the main obstacles for critical media/television/animation studies is describing the effects of media consumption, particularly as it relates to ideology and representations since revealing these effects risk new challenges to current societal hierarchies. Since the middle of the 1940s, effects research has tried to make broad claims about the influence of the media on people and groups, but much of this research has been lacking since the controlled experiments rarely replicated real-life consumption situations and other methods like media diaries were too dependent on the subject's constant participation and the subjects were vulnerable to uncontrollable outside variables. Also, this research has often focused on particular content and effects, like the influence of violent television on aggressive behavior, rather than larger ideological questions or identity constructions. However, with the influence of disciplines like Ethnic Studies and Gender Studies, more experiential research has been used as evidence, rather than focusing on providing evidence specific effects actually occur or working to prove media and culture has the same influence on all people and groups. Outside of the superficial walls of academia, James Baldwin has exemplified this type of experiential cultural work in essays and novels like *The Devil Finds Work*, but he is often left off of traditional syllabi because many disciplines and academics that critically analyze culture often see his work as not scholarly enough due to the lack of theoretical or conceptual engagement in his personal essays and other writing.[94]

Human-focused disciplines like Ethnic Studies and Gender Studies helped link theory and experience, and bell hooks exemplifies this work within media studies, particularly in *Reel to Real: Race, Sex, and Class at the Movies*. She argues that "identity is always about representation" when describing how people of color, particularly African American women, are represented in film and how that informs the way not only people interpret the intersectional experience of those often overlooked in media portrayals, but also how it informs the way they see themselves. hooks includes her own experience as evidence alongside the ideas and concepts she employs from critical race and feminist theories, utilizing the evidentiary power of experience while appealing to certain scholarly expectations related to theory and structure, making her work simultaneously appealing to scholars and accessible to non-academics. hooks' analysis also exemplifies intersectional media research, recognizing not only race and gender but also how class plays a part when analyzing media and representations of African American women when they did appear in film through the 1990s. When examining animation, it is important to consider that people of color and women rarely contributed to their own representation through content as the domination of white male animators informed all behaviors and traits of characters, including those outside of their own experience. Hooks recognizes that individual and group experience can strongly shape interpretation, but producers still consciously and unconsciously include ideological messages that aim to maintain white supremacist capitalist patriarchy and those messages need to continue to be challenged so they are not reinforced in those unable to resist. Class expectations are also constantly present in television, as the medium and industry developed during the growth of consumerism and the promotion of the ideal related to the middle class white suburban lifestyle.[95]

In his work, Todd Boyd recognizes this systemic racism and his historical analyses also reveal the impact representation, particularly among African Americans, has in both popular cultural content and in the production of culture within a society. In his three-volume *African Americans and Popular Culture*, Boyd argues that the consumption of popular culture is one of the few places whites have consistently faced representations of, and sometimes even productions by, non-whites throughout American history. Relying on a large range of sources and scholars, the first volume focuses on theater, film, and television, with Boyd contextualizing the texts and representations he analyzes by situating both within larger U.S. history. Boyd also exemplifies multi-faceted research that does not examine any aspect of production or dissemination of culture in a vacuum, recognizing the complexity of a society that maintains institutional racism, but also contains a cultural system that offers opportunities for both positive and negative visibility revealing how those opportunities have been presented in the past and in contemporary media. Although he only discusses animation in passing, this comprehensive work and his other research examines the same industries and companies that animation operates and originates, providing alternative cultural histories beyond the white male dominated interpretations that are so prevalent in education and our understanding of media and cultural progress.[96]

Christopher Lehman's *The Colored Cartoon* helps supplement Boyd's interventions into the media, by examining the origin and development of African American representations in animation through the 20th century. Lehman's analysis supports the claim that these representations have cultural and psychological impact while revealing the complex reasons behind the enduring stereotypical and misinformed visualizations of non-white people in media, specifically animation. Rather than looking at particular films or a specific studio, Lehman takes a more holistic approach and is able to provide evidence of the roots of these often racist interpretations and why the derogatory representations have been so hard to completely remove from the industry, including the fact that the white audience, the only one considered throughout much of media history, actually enjoyed these images since it helped reinforce their superior position in society.[97] Lehman's analyses are especially strong when examining the 1960s and 1970s, Hanna-Barbera's peak, in his other book, *American Animated Cartoons in the Vietnam Era: A Study of Social Commentary in Television and Film 1961–1973*. Lehman surveys animated content produced in this era while also considering contemporaneous issues of the era like Civil Rights and war.[98] Similarly Karl Cohen's *Forbidden Animation: Censored Cartoons and Blacklisted Animators in America* provides analyses about why certain content has been blocked or changed, both before release and over time as sensibilities and perspectives progressed, highlighting insensitive or derogatory portrayals of marginalized groups throughout animation history. Companies often quietly remove certain scenes or films from their libraries as they downplay the offensive nature of the older content.[99]

This recognition that revenue is often prioritized over respect for marginalized populations is present in most critical analyses of media and animation; however, the research of Lee Artz explores capitalist and American neoliberal ideology in animation. Considering the majority of animation consumed around the world is produced by American studios, Artz examines the production of popular animation from the studios responsible for the most profitable characters, franchises, and content for messages that support continued political economic and psychological domination by America and the West. In "Animating Hierarchy: Disney and the Globalization of Capitalism," he argues that the marketing of 1990s Disney feature films and their narratives within these films aim to maintain the status quo and reinforce racial, gender, and class hierarchies that place (typically) white males at the top as the savior of all other people and groups. Even when the hero can be identified as non-white, like in *Aladdin*, American neoliberal ideology is still present, celebrating wealth and individualism while casting women as damsels and those from lower socioeconomic levels as failures within the meritocracy. This Western elitism and American exceptionalism is also present in the visual representations as characters, regardless of their identity or their ethnic background are still are drawn according to Western European facial and body aesthetics.[100]

In 2015, Artz published a follow-up article, "Animating Transnational Capitalism," which addressed how the globalizing animation market was presenting opportunities to support international capitalist relations through themes that promote individualism, deference to authority, and adherence to conspicuous consumption and consumerism. The transnational cooperation motivated by this globalization enables producers to better mold the messages to the expectations of various nations and cultures as they maintain the central themes, introducing or reinforcing capitalist ideologies throughout the world. In short, the executives and producers working within the animation and media industries want to maintain the ideological structures that create a market where a company like Disney can earn yearly revenues equal to the GDP of Panama. We are simultaneously distracted and indoctrinated into this ideology through consumption of the content, which is flexible in its presentation around the world and is the source of their profits.[101]

Entertainment has been a distraction to this control for centuries, and the fact that animation enables producers to blur the line between fantasy and reality helps to mask the ideological messages. One consistent strategy has been the utilization of anthropomorphic characters to mask the reinforcement of racial, gender, class, and sexual expectations within media content. J. Halberstam's "Animating Revolt/Revolting Animation: Penguin Love, Doll Sex, and the Spectacle of the Queer Nonhuman" examines the use of anthropomorphism in animated media to reinforce white Christian patriarchal ideals related to family, romance, and love. The animated animal kingdom is seemingly governed by the same expectations of monogamy, heterosexual relationships, and family that have been promoted in Western society for centuries. This is especially powerful when considering that this content is typically produced with children in mind, if not marketed exclusively to younger audiences, presenting these ideological themes in a format that is easily digestible and can influence minds that are still learning what is appropriate and inappropriate within a society.[102] The initial identification of the character as an animal creates a perceptual obstacle for the audience to consciously recognize the humanity or identity being represented, which can be used to communicate ideologies associated with white male supremacy invoking concepts like the Fanonian mask or Duboisian veil.[103] Images are powerful, especially repetitive images of white supremacy that are consumed by a vulnerable audience whose veil is darkened by the assumed harmlessness and comedic nature of animated images and sounds.[104]

Methodology

When challenging any history or understanding, one of the integral steps is reviewing current narratives, knowledges, and texts with a critical eye and the understanding that only a small segment of the population has written these histories and those outside of that Western white maleness are often misrepresented, marginalized and forgotten. Much of the information to conduct this rewriting of history is available, albeit sometimes in disparate places; scholars are responsible for collecting it, organizing it, and analyzing it before offering new perspectives on traditional views of the past. Since this project will not focus on any particular piece of content, text, or piece of media it is a more general document analysis, gathering information from various sources and analyzing them to describe how they reinforce or challenge our current perspectives of the past. For this specific project, the analysis will reveal how political economic conditions and the development and evolution of the animation industry influence Hanna-Barbera, its producers, and the content they disseminated in America. This background information may also reveal whether they knowingly created content that either reinforced, or even challenged, the status quo connected to white male capitalistic supremacist ideology. This method also allows for the historic contextualization of the events and content discussed in the project as societal and other influences are also recognized during this reconstruction of the historical narrative surrounding the subject.[105]

Reorganization and critical examination of the information collected from these documents can help rewrite a history that has been hidden or overlooked. Document analysis is often used in conjunction with other qualitative research approaches; however, for critical political economic historical research, document analysis can be the main method, and considering the wide range of documents and texts from which information can be drawn, it is naturally a mixed method approach since information is collected from past studies and research that have employed a variety of research methods. Content or textual analyses, interviews, and secondary participant observation have all been employed by scholars and writers in the research/documents being reviewed and organized for the purpose of better understanding the motivations and decisions behind the productions containing various representations and ideologies. The also enables the use of information from popular or mainstream publications, production notes, and autobiographies to supplement information gathered from research that is considered formally or correctly gathered by the academy. For the sake of this project, programs and series will be considered documents and will be analyzed to supplement or support claims concerning the effects of various decisions and outside influences on trends related to ideological messages and representations consumed by the public. Individual episodes will not be coded for the sake of this study; however, other reputable deep analyses of content completed by other scholars are included as evidence supplementing production notes, news articles, and personal revelations by those involved in these productions. A document analysis takes elements from both qualitative textual and thematic analyses, deconstructing the documents to reveal patterns of behavior related to ideological messages. Lastly, since most of this content reached the height of popularity decades ago, only audience studies conducted at the time of airing have significant value in this analysis.[106]

According to Glenn Bowen, analyzing documents can serve five purposes: contextualization of phenomena, creating new questions or areas of inquiry, providing supplementary data, tracking changes or development within an entity or phenomenon, and to verify or corroborate evidence. This project hopes to achieve all five goals, but contextualizing, creating new areas of inquiry, and tracking changes are of particular interest as information is gathered and analyzed from various documents. There is less risk of outside influence that is often present in an experiment, and it allows researchers to examine long periods of time analyzing documents for information, both contemporary and from the time of production, relating to context and trends; gathering and verifying as many reputable sources as possible is key in this approach, since the project and conclusions can easily be misled by an incomplete or discreditable document.[107]

When writing about the shows, the term cartoons and animated are used interchangeably in many instances, but in this piece the term cartoon is reserved for shorts and programming not aimed at adults while animation is used as a broader term to describe the genre represented by drawn or generated moving pictures. Also, because many of these programs "package" multiple shorts to create a longer program, the larger program will be referred to as the "program" or "series" while the episodes within these programs will be known as segments to help avoid confusion.

Research Questions

The criticality of the analysis is clearly informed by human-focused theoretical fields like Critical Race, Feminist, and Queer theories, and focuses on two questions:

Have popular Hanna-Barbera productions contributed to the reinforcement of white male heteronormative capitalist ideology?

What role have the political economic influences inside and outside the studio played on these representations?

Clearly the first question needs to be answered before moving onto the second question, and examining studio notes related to content and marketing, along with industry histories and the animation itself will provide enough evidence of whether themes that support white male heterosexual capitalist supremacy are present in the plots, settings, and the traits of the various characters in the films or television programs. Considering the history of the industry, racist, sexist, homophobic, or pro-capitalistic messages in Hanna-Barbera productions are undoubtedly present, but since their productions have been so overlooked as a subject of this critical analysis, the extent of these representations cannot be assumed. When it is present, the documents are then analyzed to attempt to reveal why these themes or representations exist in various content, and what factors inside and outside of the studio influenced the films and programs consumed, often repeatedly, by the animation audience.

Considering William Hanna and Joseph Barbera are responsible for over a dozen feature films, 114 short films, 150 television programs, and 1000 episodes representing hundreds of hours of content, there is no way one single project can deeply analyze all the animation the duo produced over their sixty years working together. It is a collaborative effort, which begins with critical surveys of the history of their work to find trends and disrupt the common imperialist interpretation that communicates the past as a progressive march of white achievement to the present. Uncovering the creation of franchises and production of content that reinforces white male capitalist supremacy not only reveals how and why these messages are disseminated, but whether they are intentional and how they can be prevented in the future, hopefully creating a more sensitive, representative, and inclusive media environment.

Chapter Breakdown

Each chapter examines the production history of Joseph Barbera and William Hanna chronologically. The first chapter focuses on the duo's time at MGM through the 1950s, paying special attention to their most successful and enduring series at the film studio, *Tom and Jerry*. The second chapter describes their transition into television as they established their own animation studio and developed techniques for the lower budgets and shifting expectations presented by the emerging medium. Chapters 3 and 4 describe their studio's growth into the top television animator as they helped establish weekend mornings as havens for children's content. During this time, Heteropatriarchal capitalist perspectives and representations continued to dominate animated content, ideologies that have been present in the duo's content since their time at MGM. Chapter 5 discusses the studio's attempts at representing women and people of color in the wake of the Civil Rights movements and the rise of advocacy groups in the 1960s as the duo searched for their next star after the creation of several popular characters the previous decade.

Chapters 6 and 7 analyze the studio's transition as the faced numerous changes in the media industry, motivated by increased accessibility of media technologies, like cable and home video, inside the home along with the deregulation of American media market. Decreased oversight and reduced ownership limits changed the way studios, distributors, and exhibitors/broadcasters conducted business. This led to more syndication, experimentation, and opportunities for animators as available channels for distribution increased. Chapter 8 describes Hanna-Barbera's revitalization in the 1980s behind the popularity of *The Smurfs* and other properties as the continuing evolution of the media environment led to major shifts in the animation industry. Chapters 9 and 10 examine the studio's last major transition as ownership changes and consolidation led to major changes on the screen and behind the pen. Chapter 11 discusses Hanna-Barbera's role in establishing Cartoon Network as the animation duo's influence faded in their namesake studio. Chapter 12 analyzes the continued rise of Cartoon Network and its sister station, Adult Swim, as the duo's creations continue to maintain a profitability and presence in the public consciousness through recent and planned productions starring Hanna and Barbera's many characters.

1

1940–1957:
The MGM Years

Theatrical Beginnings at the "Other" Animation Studio

In the mid- to late 1920s Metro-Goldwyn-Mayer emerged as one of the major movie studios in Hollywood behind box office hits like *Ben-Hur* (1925) and *The Broadway Melody*, winner of the Academy Award for Best Picture in 1929. Recognizing the popularity of Disney and Warner Bros. cartoons, particularly the success of Mickey Mouse, MGM entered the animation market by signing a distribution deal with Celebrity Pictures, which hired Ub Iwerks after compensation disputes with his friend Walt Disney. Iwerks' Flip the Frog and Willie Whopper series could not compete with Disney's Mickey, Minnie, and Goofy and Warner Bros.' Bosko. The relationship yielded no successful films or popular characters, and by the end of 1933 Iwerks and Celebrity Pictures' Pat Powers began distributing their own ComiColor films. MGM hired Hugh Harman and Rudy Ising from Warner Bros. after the duo's budget disputes with Warner producer Leon Schlesinger. Harman-Ising productions owned the rights to Bosko, which was originally trademarked as "Negro Boy" and helped establish Warner as Disney's main competitor throughout the early years of the Golden Age of Animation.[1]

Harman-Ising Productions never replicated the success they had at Warner, and MGM opened its own cartoon studio hiring the larger studio's former head of short features, Fred Quimby, to lead the studio in 1937. Maintaining the practice of hiring animators with Disney roots, Quimby raided other animation studios, hiring Friz Freleng from Leon Schlesinger Productions and a number of animators from Terrytoons in addition to rehiring both Harman and Ising after they spent time as freelancers, which included work on Disney's *Snow White and the Seven Dwarfs*. MGM animation began to establish itself by the late 1930s even as characters like Donald Duck and Porky Pig helped Disney and Warner maintain their spots at the top of the animation industry. In 1939, Harman's anti-war film *Peace on Earth* was nominated for the Oscar for best Cartoon Short Subject, helping MGM develop a style separate from the Big Two cartoon studios at the time, whereas much of their earlier work merely tried to replicate the style and success of the Disney and Warner animators.[2]

During the production of *Peace on Earth*, William Hanna, who originally came over with Harman and Ising in 1934, and Joseph Barbera, who worked for Terrytoons before Quimby hired him over to MGM, were partnered under Ising to produce one-shot cartoons as Ising focused on films featuring the cartoon studio's first star, Barney bear. In a relationship that would cross eight decades, storywriter Barbera and director Hanna's first film together was *Puss Gets the Boot* starring a cat named Jinx and a mouse named Jasper. With Harman and Ising's productions attracting most of the attention within the cartoon studio, *Puss Gets the Boot* was largely ignored, and Quimby asked Hanna and Barbera to create new characters for their next short, since few at the studio found the film funny and Quimby saw little potential for the cat and mouse duo. However, both audiences and critics loved the cartoon, which became a financial success and earned a nomination for Best Cartoon Short, losing to Ising's *The Milky Way*, the first non–Disney film to win the award.[3]

Jasper and Jinx Put the Duo on the Map

The lack of confidence in the cat and mouse pair, renamed Tom and Jerry, during the series' first few years of production is supported by the fact that the duo continued to be assigned one-shot films through 1943. This may have been partly due to the overall failure of the adaptation of the *Katzenjammer Kids* comic strip, *Captain and the Kids*, which both Freleng and Hanna worked on and whose lack of success convinced Freleng to go back to Warner Bros. Six months after *Puss Gets the Boot* was released, Hanna and Barbera produced *Gallopin' Gals*, about racing fillies. Maggie is the shy horse at the track who is left out of the gossip between the other horses, whose vainness catches up with them when they are distracted while posing for the photo finish while Maggie is able to pass them for the victory. Partially due to the success of *Tom and Jerry*, *Gallopin' Gals* was their last short to star a female character for over 25 years. *Officer Pooch* was released in September of 1941 following a dog police officer as he is chased by packs of dogs as he attempts to save a litter of kittens, in a Keystone Cop–inspired plot.[4] These films were quickly forgotten as MGM turned their attention to Tom and Jerry, along with Droopy who debuted in 1943, utilizing their stars to compete with Disney and Warner Bros.

Although the story of Hanna and Barbara's meeting is often communicated as serendipitous if not fateful, considering how insular the industry was, as evidenced by the hiring and rehiring of Harman and Ising, it may have only been a matter of time until they met. Barbera early work was as a story writer and drawer where Hanna gravitated toward directing over his decade in the industry before meeting Barbera. What was amazing about their partnership was the fact that such a simple formula would result in one of the most popular cartoon franchises in history, eventually earning the duo seven Academy Awards and fourteen nominations over eighteen years. The simplicity may have been the draw considering the Great Depression and impending war lead people to seek a distraction and enjoyed the storylines based on the banalities of everyday life, in this case, the rivalry between mice, cats, and dogs.[5]

Within this simplicity, are complex ideas related to American ideology that frequently appear and reinforce ideas for an audience living in a society going through major political and economic upheaval. Most of the strategies employed within the *Tom and Jerry* series to reinforce ideologies can be identified in other animation or media content; however, Tom and Jerry were able to separate themselves from other characters and films being released by studios like Warner and Disney through Hanna and Barbera's unique approach to the 114 *Tom and Jerry* short films, the most films an animation duo has produced together starring the same characters. Most of the films may have had the basic framework of "cat chases mouse"; however, they still contained messages commenting on the changing geography and demographics of America, white heteronormative capitalist supremacy, and America's acceptance of violence and moral superiority domestically and internationally by those controlling and working to maintain the hegemonic structure within the United States. Hanna and Barbera worked in animation and children's television for over sixty years; however, it cannot be forgotten they are also white males with middle class backgrounds, who, through their work at MGM, not only established their animation and character development styles for the rest of the careers together, but they, and the most of the other writers, producers, and animators they worked with, also enjoyed white male privilege, which affected the way they represented certain people and ideas within these films, particularly as it related to the quickly transforming mid–20th-century American society. These films also represent the origins of many of the stylistic and ideological characteristics that would define not only productions overseen by Hanna and Barbera, but animation throughout the 20th century, especially on television.[6]

Of Mice and Meaning: Anthropomorphic Rodents (and Their Enemies) in American Myth

There is little doubt that American ideology celebrates the idea of the underdog. Traditional American history communicates an appreciation for those seen as overmatched beating a dominant force, especially when that victory is connected to a virtue and an overall narrative of progress. United States culture and history building has typically supported this idea from the earliest stories that form the foundation of American myth from the idea that an explorer just happened upon the continent and helped introduce Western Civilization to half of the world. According to this myth, Christopher Columbus fought financing issues to achieve his dream to find a shorter trade route to India only to end up in what would become the Americas and prove the world was not flat. As historical research has shown, the myth of the world being flat was dispelled long before Columbus, and the explorer was really an opportunistic businessman who was directly responsible for tens of thousands of deaths and the start of the transatlantic slave trade leading to the death of millions of indigenous, African, and other non–European peoples, starting an era of white Western supremacy that continues today.[7]

This progress continues through the American Revolution where oppressed struggling "colonists" fought against unfair taxation and a lack of representation in the British government with an underfunded and understaffed military single handedly beating the most powerful military in the world rather than rich white landowners, upset over being controlled by rich white landowners thousands of miles away, winning a war of attrition on home soil with the help of two other very powerful nations, Spain and France. This "progress" continues through the idea of Manifest Destiny, where the belief that American expansion was inevitable with the wilderness and the presence of other populations in this space as merely obstacles to be overcome for the sake of progress. This "progress" occurs through hard work, perseverance, and courage masking the violence and destruction caused by the refusal of Americans to be deterred from this fate. For many, this was a moral and religious mission, and the expansion of the country represented American Exceptionalism whose roots are in the "City on the Hill" ideal that imagined the establishment of the United States as the next step in the linear progress of civilization. Stories of heroism in the frontier and the taming of the people and nature that occupied the "Wild Wild West" only supported these actions.[8]

Individually, Horatio Alger brought stories of rags to riches into the public consciousness, continuing to reinforce the idea that, within a capitalist society there is no excuse for an individual not to success as long as they (or he) work hard and live a moral life, an idea explored by Max Weber in "The Protestant Ethic and the Spirit of Capitalism," which was released six years after Alger's death and the end of the Gilded Age. Even as American imperialism and expansion continued into the 20th century, helping the nation emerge as a true "world power," the country had to continue to overcome larger forces of evil represented by Nazism and ideological challenges to capitalism and "democracy" like Soviet Socialism. The fondness for the underdog can also be seen in American politics where candidates rely on presenting themselves as arising from a marginalized position to achieve success by pulling themselves up by their bootstraps and have decided to serve others looking to do the same.[9.]

The First American Performative Popular Culture

The title of true American was only really extended to white (mostly male) figures, who continue to use laws and practices to maintain their superiority. This ideology that works to marginalize the majority of the population is also communicated in media and culture, and at the end of the 19th century one of the most popular forms of entertainment was vaudeville shows, with blackface performances and minstrel acts as these shows' biggest draws. As film replaced vaudeville performances, these themes of overcoming adversity, American exceptionalism, and displaying white male superiority by representing other populations negatively made their way into movies and in animation, which also had foundations in vaudeville. Due to a combination of familiarity and technical limitations, blackface characters like Felix the Cat were among the earliest animation stars.[10.] About ten years after Felix's peak during the silent era another blackface-inspired character would eventually come to represent the underdog common man, Mickey Mouse. The early Mickey films portrayed the rodent as carefree, lazy, and irresponsible, but as his popularity grew his color and design reflected more Caucasian aesthetic ideals while his actions were much less mischievous as his role shifted from star to role model and icon for a multinational media corporation.[11.] His diminutive nature and "aw, shucks" Midwestern personality perfectly represented the myth of the American Underdog, which masks his role as the icon for what would become one of the largest and most scrutinized corporations in the world as a supporter of white heteropatriarchal capitalism. This position of "American Underdog" is typically occupied by humble characters representing the ideals of white bootstrap individualism, and other characters, like Jerry, who are more mischievous, confident, and disruptive are unable to be a true American Underdog figures and, at best, can occupy the position of antihero against authority and the authority's/predator's/state's monopolization of power and violence.[12.]

Character design evolved past the simple blackface-inspired characters of the silent era, but anthropomorphic characters continued to be used frequently to mask behavior and stereotypes based on constructions of race, gender, and sexuality. Diminutive, docile animals like birds, pigs, and dogs were transformed into anthropomorphic stars for Disney and Warner. These stars continue to embody misrepresentations of marginalized groups, but it became more subtle, whereas the more obvious derogatory portrayals were mostly left to ancillary characters. As some of them became stars, their designs and personality were often changed to represent the American underdog and rugged bootstrap individualism that President Herbert Hoover promoted throughout his presidency after the stock market crashed and America entered the Great Depression. Similar to the way popular historical rhetoric continues to view America as an exceptional underdog with moral superiority, the outlandish behavior of characters like Donald Duck and Bugs Bunny was excused by their perceived status lower on the food chain until they became large enough stars that their actions had to be toned down becoming more appropriate fare, if not role models, for the younger (white) audience. Hanna wanted to ensure that Tom and Jerry never entered that stage where they become more of an icon than a character, so the duo maintained the same disruptive and rebellious characteristics for Jerry throughout the series, never entering the transition period experienced by Mickey, Bugs, and Donald after their star turns.[13.]

Cartoon Violence

One of these behaviors, which also became one of the identifying features of the Golden Age of Animation cartoons and the *Tom and Jerry* series more specifically, was the rampant, exaggerated violence perpetrated throughout the films and programs. Live-action representation of gratuitous violence has long been criticized in media content, especially as it related to younger audiences; however, cartoon violence often avoided the same scrutiny since it was considered fantasy. Examining the entire body of films, the violence is complicated when look at it from each of the stars' perspectives. Jerry is often the more violent of the two and some would argue that Tom was right in his actions, defending his home from an intruder, regardless of who occupied the space/land first. Accentuating Jerry's violence is the fact that his actions are successful more often and are much more destructive than Tom's, resulting in the consistent dismemberment of the cat. Jerry's diminutive nature, and position as the underdog, makes his actions humorous to the audience. This creates conflict where the audience celebrates the mouse's rebellion even as very few deny the cat's position of authority. It is just assumed Tom and his family deserve to be in the space and own the home and land in which they live, and Tom's position of authority and designation as an enforcer is not questioned because it seems natural. The only films that do not involve Tom chasing Jerry find the two rivals team up when their interests converge; however, this fragile alliance is typically short lived when one, often Tom, ends the friendship when it is no longer advantageous for him. For example, in *Dog Trouble* they team up to defeat and expel Spike, portraying the "natural" enemy of the cat, a dog, who has made both of their lives difficult. After Tom and Jerry are successful in having the dog ejected from the home they resume their contentious relationship when Tom's tail accidently gets caught in a mouse trap towards the end of the film, which Tom uses as a reason to chase Jerry again.[14.]

Jerry and his attempts to destroy Tom may not be completely excused by the cat's position of authority; however, Tom's power that is merely derived from being born a cat also needs to be questioned or challenged in the same way people who find themselves in positions of authority because the privilege afforded to them by socioeconomic, racial, gender, or sexual factors need to be questioned and challenged. Jerry's violence is portrayed as humorous and disruptive whereas Tom's violence is often reactionary and is rarely questioned, since he occupies the authoritative predatory position, highlighting the hierarchical positions of the small mouse and the cat. Jerry's initiation of the violence and his intentions are occasionally less benign, including attempts at getting Tom thrown out of the house or his consistent teasing; however, Jerry's main focus is food and shelter within the home Tom protects. Tom often goes beyond his responsibilities as house protector to torment the mouse, an activity he clearly enjoys, smiling as Jerry tries to run while the cat holds his tail or traps him in a bowl. Tom is bestowed the authority to police the home in any way he wants with minimal oversight from the owners of the home and his handler, and although the extent of Jerry's disruptions can definitely be questioned, there is also very little direction in how Tom should police, leaving the cat significant discretion about how to best deal with Jerry.[15]

In spite of his size, Jerry, the brown mouse, is clearly smarter and luckier than the light grey furred cat, but Tom still operates in a position of privilege. This predator privilege is consistent in these rivalries, especially in later Golden Age films and pairings, like Sylvester (free house cat) versus Tweety (caged canary), Wile E. Coyote (unlimited resources) versus the Roadrunner and later designs of Mickey versus the black Pete the cat. Although Jerry often initiates violence, Tom is also protecting the middle-class privilege that is represented in the home he lives and is charged to protect. Jerry's position as the underdog antihero places him in a position where the audience often roots for his victory; however, the acceptance of Tom's position in preventing Jerry from getting food and resources, and the fact he chases the mouse at all, is rarely questioned or challenged, and even continues in adaptations of the series today.

Minstrelsy and Blackface in Tom and Jerry

Hanna-Barbera's *Tom and Jerry* films also contained more blatant racist images beyond the color binary that helped reinforce white male supremacy within the content, helping blackface and stereotypical minstrel representations remain in animation through the 1950s. These images were not new, but the style, simple plot, and humor development within *Tom and Jerry* led to many of the same jokes to be repeated. The fact that the main human character in the series is a derogatory caricature of a Black woman highlighted Hanna-Barbera, MGM, and the animation industry's reliance on these images for humor well past World War II, reinforcing superiority among white audiences

Tom and Jerry in their most famous pose (Sangmesh Desai Sarkar/Shutterstock.com).

and inferiority among Black audiences. As MGM struggled financially in the 1950s, they also frequently reissued earlier film, keeping older films of the series, which in turn maintained images and stereotypes from vaudeville and earlier cartoons from which Hanna, Barbera, and other animators drew inspiration.[16]

Any child (or adult) who watched these short films from their debut in the 1940s and 1950s through the 1980s, when these cartoons continued to be seen in their original form on broadcast and cable television, is familiar with the gag. A car backfires, a fire ignites, or a bomb explodes in a character's face and the flare-up leaves a black residue. The character then opens its mouth and looks at the camera, with large white eyes and oversized lips peeking through the soot. Most of the time the joke, and the blackface, would only be momentary, but Hanna and Barbera did pause on the character's face to ensure the audience saw the blackface transformation and recognized the joke. This quick-change joke also targeted Asian populations when characters crash through a piano or a record collection, and when the dust settles, they take on a stereotypical large-toothed look complete with conical hat. Although many of these films were originally made for general audiences and adults, when children did view them in the theater or on television they learned to find humor in this appropriation, becoming conditioned to see this racial caricature as acceptable, along with reinforcing this humor among older audiences.[17]

Viewers were consistently exposed to the brief blackface and minstrel imagery in these jokes, but in a few films the use of blackface and African caricaturizing was a major plot device. These films have since been removed from contemporary *Tom and Jerry* films available to the public, but they continued to appear on television through the mid–1990s before they were banned from inclusion in DVD collections starring the cat and mouse. They are also included in digital collections, often including a disclaimer in recognition of these derogatory images, warning viewers they are a "product of their time" of production.[18]

In *Mouse Cleaning* (1948), Tom's face is blackened by coal and to complete the minstrel stereotype he talks in a manner similar to Stepin Fetchit to trick another character and avoid trouble for making a mess by speaking in a way to which Tom's African American handler can relate or is even attracted.[19] Two 1951 films, *Casanova Cat* and *His Mouse Friday*, also relied on extended blackface jokes and visual stereotypes as a part of the story. In *Casanova Cat*, Tom blackens Jerry's face with cigar smoke and actually forces him to dance to entertain him and his date. Jerry's performance touches upon issues of the forced performance and labor of African Americans and displays of dominance and power by those in positions of superiority.[20] *His Mouse Friday* moves the stereotypes to an international locale when Tom and Jerry are shipwrecked at the beginning of the film in a parody of *Robinson Crusoe*. Like the novel that celebrates white supremacist imperialism, Tom and Jerry must face "natives" or "savages" on the island. The people populating the area try to eat Tom and Jerry, and even though they are a cat and mouse, their anthropomorphism helps portray the inhabitants as cannibals, like the characters Crusoe encountered in the book. Reinforcing the racism, the inhabitants also have dark skin and big lips, communicating the inferiority of international populations of color, particularly ones in areas seen as "exotic" about which Western white population remain willfully ignorant. The entire situation was put into motion when Jerry uses blackface and deep stereotypical vocalizations to trick Tom into thinking the mouse is one of the "native" inhabitants to avoid his own demise. They later face the actual inhabitants, who confirm the accuracy of Jerry's portrayal and violently chase the duo, licking their enlarged lips at the thought of eating the two. The film actually ends without resolution as the "cannibals" continue to chase Tom and Jerry as the film fades to the credits.[21]

In many ways the anthropomorphism can mask these subtle but significant characteristics or portrayals. Because there is so little dialogue, unlike their Warner brethren, it is hard to judge possible racialization of animal characters the same way Bosko's Southern African American vernacular or Bugs Bunny's white Brooklynite accent reveals how the producers identified their anthropomorphic stars.[22] The use of anthropomorphic animals to veil representations of stereotypical racial and gender characteristics that will be seen more in later creations by Hanna and Barbera for television and segments like the one mentioned above where Tom emulates Stepin Fetchit's voice foreshadows this masking and the reliance on imitative voices as the duo prepared to switch visual media in the 1950s. The vast majority of characters in the productions of Hanna and Barbera are male, which is not surprising considering the demographic history of both animated content and production; however, in the times a female character is seen, her anthropomorphism often hides the stereotypes and generalization placed upon her by the white male producers.[23]

Tom Cat

Living up to his name, Tom Cat, the co-star of the series, has several love interests throughout the run of the short films, including two iterations of a cat named Toots. In *Puss n' Toots*, the female cat is small and fluffy with multiple bows to avoid any gender confusion and is portrayed as superficial, only finding interest in Tom when showered with gifts. Jerry interrupts the courting and Tom chases Jerry resulting in a battle that eventually knocks Tom unconscious. Jerry then kisses Toots, seemingly without her consent, and then struts in celebration of his victory. Toots reappears as a bobby soxer in *Zoot Suit Cat* two years later but has somehow developed the ability to speak. In the

Poster for *His Mouse Friday*, released July 7, 1951. Jerry is in blackface while the stereotypically drawn island inhabitant looks on (Everett Collection, Inc./Alamy Stock Photo).

beginning of the film Toots dismisses Tom's gifts and advances, but does so through Harlem jive, a type of African American Vernacular English, associated with jazz culture that was popular in the 1930s and 1940s. Much like Tom mimicking Stepin Fetchit's voice, the fact that Toots is a cat helps mask the appropriation that has historically occurred with African American culture like jazz or practices like language. Tom is finally able to impress Toots by dressing in a zoot suit and dancing with her, but Jerry interrupts his attempts at courting through violence and even cutting in to dance with Toots. Much like in *Puss n' Toots*, Jerry seems to pursue Toots just to annoy Tom, positioning Toots as a sort of trophy to be won, and in Jerry's case, lord over his feline counterpart.[24]

This whole scene is complicated even further by the presence of the zoot suit, which Jerry claims in the end after it is shrunk, as a symbol of hipness or being cool. The film was released eight months after the start of the Zoot Suit Riots in Los Angeles and across the country with white servicemen and civilians stripping and assaulting suit wearing youths under the guise of patriotism, it was reported that this was due to the suits being decadent and taking up too much material at wartime. In actuality, non-white youths were targeted due to rising racial tensions in the area related to Japanese internment and the Sleepy Lagoon Trial, in which 17 young Chicanx men were arrested for the murder of Jose Diaz in Commerce, California. Both the defendants and the victims were identified as gang members leading to 600 Latinx being targeted and arrested by police as zoot suits became synonymous with criminal activity by non-white populations. This eventually led to white mobs to take it upon themselves to cleanse the streets of zoot suiters, almost all of which just happened to be Mexican-, Filipino-, or African American in a number of cities including Los Angeles, Philadelphia, and Chicago.[25]

The only love interest of Tom's that appears in multiple films is Toodles Galore,

Poster for *The Zoot Cat*, released February 26, 1944. Tom's fur appears darker in the poster than his typical grey (Everett Collection, Inc./Alamy Stock Photo).

who stars in five Hanna and Barbera–directed films between 1946 and 1952. She is a long slender cat with white fur, long eyelashes, lipstick, and seemingly permanent eye shadow, making her look more human than the other characters. Much like Toots, she is portrayed as a materialistic woman who requires gifts to decide on a mate; however, she never speaks and barely moves, ensuring Toodles lacks any true personality beyond what she superficially presents to Tom and the other characters courting her, including Jerry, who, as with his courtship of Toots, is partially motivated to romance Toodles because it frustrates Tom. Also, further complicating Toodles' presence is the fact that she seems to be wealthy, or at least lives in a wealthy home. The film *Casanova Cat* starts with Tom walking to Toodles' residence reading an article describing how Toodles has inherited millions of dollars. The celebration of superficial expectations for women, materialism, and class in embodied in Toodles, as no dialogue or conversation is needed for Tom and Jerry to desire or fall in love with her.[26]

Mammy Two Shoes

These images, jokes, and individual films represent clear evidence of how these cultural and ideological stereotypes endure through media; however, the most enduring racist and sexist feature of the Tom and Jerry series is the presence of Mammy Two Shoes. As so subtly suggested by the character's name, Two Shoes is modeled after the fictional mammy stereotype that arose in American culture in the 19th century and continued to be consumed by the public in film, television, and advertising through most of the 20th century. The character was created to desexualize African American women working within the home, and around their white master or employer, while also masculinizing these women within their own home as they stereotypically took on the more dominant role in their own family, feminizing their own husbands and partners. The caricature occupies intersections of oppression as a woman and an African American living in a country that heavily marginalizes both groups, embodying many of the gender and race issues in the series as described above. Two Shoes was specifically modeled after Hattie McDaniel's Mammy character in *Gone with the Wind*, speaking with the same exaggerated Southern African American Vernacular, distinguishing her from the few other characters that spoke throughout the series, which seemingly takes place in the suburbs of New York City. The voice actor responsible for Two Shoes' voice, Lillian Randolph, was not credited in the original films, highlighting the issues of diversity and recognition in production that would also arise in Hanna and Barbera's later productions.[27]

Any questions about original meanings and intentions surrounding Mammy Two Shoes were confirmed by later editing and redubbing of the character's voice.[28] In most films, the audience could only see Two Shoes' legs as she violently admonished the cat after Jerry frames Tom for a mess or not following her orders. Those associated with Hanna-Barbera and Warner, under which the duo's studio later became a subsidiary, would argue that Two Shoes owned the home Tom and Jerry occupied while editing scenes of her working as a maid or housekeeper, in the few films featuring her that were kept in regular rotation. They later changed the character's voice, and later, skin tone in the few films starring Two Shoes that continued to appear on television and in video collections, with an accent that sounds slightly Irish and legs that have a lighter skin.[29]

These images and representations seem obvious or blatant today, but many audiences overlooked them or thought they were normal subjects for comedic fodder. When

Amazon placed disclaimers on the sale pages for digital copies of older *Tom and Jerry* films sold on their website, fans of the original series were taken aback, communicating their disbelief that the content of the series would be deemed insensitive or even racist, accusing Amazon of being a victim of pressure from "politically correct" individuals and groups.[30] However, even if an older audience did somehow recognize these issues in original consumption of these cartoons or is able to contextualize what it watches, what has to be remembered is that a younger or less aware audience, who may have been introduced to the series in its current adaptations, could come upon these older films without the historical or discursive knowledge to understand the context in which these cartoons were produced, leading them to consume outdated, offensive, derogatory content that could inform their views of society and the people that live within it.

Even Mice Have Privilege:
Tom and Jerry as Post-War Propaganda

Like the other major animation studios, the MGM Cartoon Studio produced propaganda films throughout World War II to support the rise of patriotism during the war while profiting off of the emotional response to the war occurring in Europe and Asia. Aside from jokes and commentary supporting America and featuring derogatory content about the enemies, particularly the Japanese within the films during this period, Hanna and Barbera also directed and contributed to several World War II propaganda films including the 1943 film *Yankee Doodle Mouse*, their first to win the Academy Award. In the film, Tom and Jerry have a World War II–inspired battle featuring technology, transportation, and weapons from the period. A reference to ration stamps was cut when the film was reissued in 1950. A few months later, MGM released *War Dogs*, which found a collection of canines, including Spike, preparing to go to battle. Due to the violence and the racial representations in many of these propaganda films, they have been heavily censored or excluded from collections, although as an Oscar winner, *Yankee Doodle Mouse* is included in edited form in most content packages sold to networks and through ancillary markets. However, the support for the ideals that would drive America's post-war growth was clear in films that were released toward the end, and after, the war.[31]

As discussed, *Tom and Jerry* operated as a stylistic and ideological proving ground for Hanna and Barbera over the 18 years they were responsible for directing the series. Even though the duo premiered in 1940, they would represent a white middle-class suburban ideal that would become synonymous with the baby boom and the postwar deurbanization that led to the aesthetically and racially homogeneous 1950s suburbia, particularly outside America's biggest cities. Suburbanization, and the ideology behind "white flight," began to spread at the end of the 19th century as more African Americans and immigrants arrived in urban areas, especially in the Northeast, but movement was slow through the 1920s until it was nearly stopped by the Great Depression. The series may have premiered toward the end of the Depression, but the films communicated these ideals that had been present in the (white male) American psyche for decades. Although the majority of the series takes place inside, stories and settings within films provide evidence about MGM, and other cartoon studios' perspectives on acceptable living situations and socioeconomic expectations of the target audience, white adults and families, who represented the majority of people moving to the suburbs and would recognize the settings from their own lives and experiences.[32]

The first sign of the suburban location represented in the series is the home that Tom occupies and Jerry "intrudes." Jerry's designation or identity is as a cute country house mouse, rather than a rat or another pest that is more likely to be found in an urban home. The home itself, a large, detached house with a porch and multiple yards, is an example of middle-class sensibilities and style, with decorative home decor like pictures, vases, and multiple radios representing conspicuous consumption. These items were used as weapons and destroyed in the battles between the cat and mouse; however, their presence and their value, which is represented in the punishment Tom receives for the destruction, clearly point to these items being status symbols for the lifestyle of whomever owns the house, oversees Tom, and employs Two Shoes.[33]

The exterior of the house confirms its location outside of the city. Although exterior animation of the home occasionally switch from a country, rural home to a suburban home in a neighborhood, it is clearly not an urban dwelling. In some episodes, like *Fine Feathered Friend* (1942), the property seems to be a farm complete with chickens, while other episodes like *Sleepy-Time Tom* see the cat interact with other felines in a neighborhood complete with trash collection in the alley, judging from where the strays live in the neighborhood. Later episodes in the series would inexplicably take Tom and Jerry to locations around the world to provide new settings and situations for the redundant chase plots; however, even when the series prepared to end in 1958, Hanna and Barbera continued to return the cat and mouse to their suburban/country home after visiting these other locales.[34]

Geographically the home is most likely located outside of New York City, one of the metropolises that experienced the most significant suburbanization after World War II. This promotion of the suburban lifestyle went beyond the setting of the series, with episodes like *Mouse in Manhattan* warning against the dangers and temptations of the urban. In this 1945 film, Jerry gets stuck in gum, used as a shoe polisher, and is almost run or crushed on several occasions as he tries to keep up with the frantic pace and many distractions of city life. He even encounters urban alley cats, who are clearly more violent and sharp-toothed than Tom and the other cats he encounters, while these felines live in a more concentrated area. At the end Jerry is shot at by police when they think he is a burglar after accidentally finding himself in a jewelry store running from the cats. The mouse eventually runs all the way home to the house outside the city, even kissing Tom as he returns home to his country safe haven.[35]

This suburban setting is integral for *Tom and Jerry* and future Hanna and Barbera productions. The banality of life outside of the city allows the audience, and producers, to recognize humor in everyday occurrences and situations instead of the "distractions" of a hectic urban lifestyle, possibly filled with temptation and dangers. This has been true for both live-action and animated comedy, especially after World War II as white Americans fled to the suburbs. Episodic and situation comedies during the decades after World War II, largely took place in suburban and rural settings to better relate to this target audience and avoid real life issues like drugs, violence, and poverty. Even when these films and programs set in the suburbs did move to include these issues and the experience of the urban it was often a "very special episode" where the dangerous element, typically drugs, is seen as unusual and an intrusion on this space brought to the location by an outside element often originating or living in the urban. There were a few shows, like *The Honeymooners*, that took place in cities, however, these shows still presented the city as a place for working (or lower) class childless individuals and couples.[36] Even the earliest family sitcoms, like *Leave It to Beaver*, presented storylines that highlight the danger of the urban through their own experience in the city or the presence of city-dweller characters bringing a dangerous or immoral element, like alcohol or drugs, into the safe suburban space.[37]

Hanna and Barbera embraced this trend in many of their later series, but like many of the other characteristics that defined Hanna-Barbera cartoons it originated with *Tom and Jerry*. In the 1951 film *Jerry's Cousin*, Jerry reaches out to his cousin Muscles to come to help him deal with Tom, who, at the time of Muscles' arrival into the suburbs, is throwing sticks of dynamite at the mouse. As Muscles walks up the block to the home, all the other predatory animals in the neighborhood hide. Muscle's living location is revealed at the beginning of the film through a Hogan's Alley sign, a reference to the comic strip that took place in a rough urban neighborhood, removing any doubt that he lives in the city. The film, which had the working title *City Cousin*, sees the edgier Muscles beat Tom and the other neighborhood cats into submission leaving Tom kissing Jerry's feet through Muscles' intimidation. Muscles' actions are clearly a victory for Jerry, but also create a binary between the dangerous urban and safe suburban, recognizing that the violence of the city is something to be avoided, and when it comes in contact with the (white) suburban world the urban element creates disruption in the secure, quiet suburban world.[38]

In 1953, MGM shut down their cartoon unit for a year, transitioning funds from that department to the development of 3D films, a film technology that was not fully developed for wide use for another fifty years. In 1954 they reopened the animation studio, with Hanna and Barbera leading the unit, putting *Tom and Jerry* back into production. The films had the same basic chase plot, but two (and a half) new characters increased the suburban Baby Boom sensibilities celebrated in the series. George and Joan, a white couple living in a middle-class suburban home, were introduced as the new handlers of Tom and Butch after Mammy Two Shoes was retired partially due to the death of Hattie McDaniel in 1952. In several films only Joan is present, suggesting George commutes to work while Joan is left to do domestic work at home, and eventually, take care of the baby they have in the series. The couple appears in eight shorts between 1954 and 1958 before MGM permanently shut down the cartoon studio after realizing reissued shorts were earning the same amount at the box office as the new films Hanna and Barbera released throughout this late period at MGM. Fortunately for the animation duo, the earlier shutdown of MGM led them to a new medium that they would help revolutionize throughout the next three decades: television.[39]

Exiting the Golden Age

Similar to Hanna and Barbera's later creations, which will be explored in the following chapters, *Tom and Jerry* is often placed behind their counterparts at Disney and Warner in the annals of animation history. Every one of the 114 films released by MGM between 1940 and 1958 was directed by the two animators, winning seven Academy Awards in the category of Animated Short Film, a number only matched by Disney's *Silly Symphony* series, which featured 75 one-shot films with several different directors and very little character continuity throughout the series.[40] By the time *Tom and Jerry* debuted, Mickey Mouse had basically been retired from film, becoming an icon for Disney, which, at the time, was the only animation studio not associated with a larger film studio. MGM's cartoon unit was often overlooked or seen as nonessential, and was frequently threatened with closure and budget cuts, which occurred several times throughout the late 1940s and 1950s, leading to the unit's permanent closure in early 1957. As

Hanna discusses in his autobiography, this hands-off approach may have created budget anxiety, but also allowed the duo to focus on the films and characters, rather than transitioning the duo into role models and marketable company icons like Mickey, or to a lesser extent, Bugs Bunny, for Warner Bros. cartoons. This focus on the development and maintenance of characters would help define Hanna and Barbera's approach to animation and marketing as they moved away from film throughout the 1950s. However, this focus may also explain why Hanna and Barbera are also overlooked, because many of their characters may be loved and remembered, but not necessarily considered iconic.[41]

After rumors of a complete shutdown spread in 1957, both Hanna and Barbera began work on side projects for television, creating animated commercials and title sequences for shows like *I Love Lucy* and films *Invitation to Dance* and *Dangerous When Wet*. Hanna also started a television animation production company, Shield Productions, with Jay Ward, who was partly responsible for *Crusader Rabbit*, the first animated show produced exclusively for television, and later *Rocky and Bullwinkle*. Hanna left Shield after the rights of *Crusader Rabbit* came under dispute, and quickly re-partnered with Barbera forming H-B Enterprises in 1957 with the help of director George Sidney, which they met working on the dance sequence with Jerry and Gene Kelly in *Anchors Aweigh*. By December of the same year their first original program debuted on NBC, sixth months before MGM stopped distributing new *Tom and Jerry* films. Screen Gems handled distribution and marketing while Harry Cohn, president of Columbia Pictures, the parent company of Screen Gems, provided working capital in exchange for 18 percent ownership of the studio. They also hired a number of animators and voice actors from MGM, which enabled the studio to become operational less than two months after MGM shut down their cartoon studio.[42]

For the animation duo, and the larger industry, *Tom and Jerry* represented a bridge between film and television animation. The series was basically a theatrical situational comedy, a format that was created on radio and became one of the most enduring genres on television. As the animation industry shifted its attention to television, distributors realized that animated shorts, which were traditionally six to eight minutes, could easily be repackaged into television shows. Shorts featuring popular characters like Bugs Bunny and Popeye found the most success, with quality becoming less of a concern than it was for shorts produced for the theater due to television's technological limitations. This made the transition easier for Hanna and Barbera and Warner Bros. animation, while Disney used television to also explore live-action production. By the end of the decade Hanna-Barbera had several regularly scheduled programs in production, winning their first Emmy in 1959. The early years of H-B Enterprises, which became Hanna-Barbera Productions in 1959, featured some of their most unique and creative work, with the trial and errors of this period informing the duo's approach and leading to the company's peak from the mid–1960s to the early 1980s.[43]

Unfortunately the attributes Hanna and Barbera carried over from the Golden Age and their time at MGM that helped made them successful also carried negative characteristics and ideologies. As white males, working with mostly other white males trying to appeal to a white audience, the representations of non-white, non-male characters are uninformed and misrepresent marginalized groups. This was also supported by the witch hunt of progressive voices pushed by Joe McCarthy and the Red Scare, which blacklisted a number of entertainers on both sides of the camera, supporting a more conservative approach to media production and storytelling for over at least a decade.[44] Their consistent celebration of conspicuous consumption, capitalism, and the white suburbia also continued into television, as more humanistic characters positively represent the boot-strap individualism and status-driven capitalism in more direct ways within their television series. Although the strategies would shift depending on societal awareness and pressures, these issues would persist throughout the 45 years the duo was active in their company, while new ones arose as human rights movements and continued international conflict influenced and challenged the content.

2

1958–1962:
Transitioning to Television

Smarter Than the Average Studio: Timing and Capitalism
in Early Television

Hanna and Barbera's last few years at MGM prepared them for the transition to television, giving them an advantage over other major animation studios, which continued to focus primarily on theatrical production through the early 1960s. When MGM reopened the studio in 1954, both animators continued to accept television projects as a way to supplement their pay at MGM. Fred Quimby, the head of the unit, retired in 1955 and Hanna and Barbera were promoted to the position. They oversaw two Academy Award–nominated projects, even while the studio faced consistent budget cuts, and continued to direct new Tom and Jerry films. By the late 1950s the market for theatrical animation started to decline; the 1948 *U.S. v. Paramount* decision eliminated the exclusive theater agreements that allowed for block booking that included cartoon shorts. The decline in theatrical animation was also facilitated by the fact that nearly 75 percent of homes had a television and studios recognizing that reissued films could earn as much as new films at a much lower cost. Many studios ended up selling their back-catalogues to other companies.[1]

MGM also faced significant internal turmoil, particularly between executives in New York and the studio heads in California. Louis B. Mayer was fired in 1951 when profits declined significantly after the war, and the studio went through several presidents in the next few years resulting in a power struggle between Joseph Vogel and Mayer, which ended after the latter's death in 1957. That same year, the loss from the box office bomb *Raintree County* led to the first unprofitable year in the studio's history, and MGM decided to shut down the cartoon studio to reduce costs as they continued to profit off of older animated films they rereleased.[2]

This ten-year period when they became the heads of MGM animation, created a television studio, and established themselves as leaders in animation on the emerging medium served as a testing ground as the duo figured out how to operate within the different challenges presented by the economics and expectations of the television industry and post-war America. This included a more fragmented audience, a growing recognition of the child audience, increased licensing and merchandising, and the distribution structure of television. These and other factors led to some growing pains for H-B Enterprises, which became Hanna-Barbera Productions in 1959, as they learned to navigate the unique obstacles of a medium that was available for use in families' homes 24 hours a day, but their early entry into television also helped the television animation studio reach its peak throughout the 1970s. This transitional period from film to animation was also integral in the development of the ideologies that they continued to present throughout the next 40 years of their career. Although the messages they presented in the series may have progressed over time, their approach and formulas often helped maintain conservative or even outdated ideologies promoting white Christian patriarchy, neoliberalism, American exceptionalism and imperialism. The presence of these concepts and ideas is not unique for television or animation; however, the ubiquity of Hanna-Barbera creations by the late 1960s and the eventual targeting of younger audiences meant they potentially influenced the viewpoints concerning these topics for generations of viewers.[3]

From the Big Screen to the Small Screen

By the time Hanna and Barbera took over as head of the MGM Cartoon studio, the entire output involved characters from *Tom and Jerry*, including Spike, who began to appear in his own films, and Droopy, who was created by animation legend Tex Avery in 1943.[4] As Quimby transitioned into retirement the three collaborated on a remake of Hugh Harman's *Peace on Earth* titled *Goodwill to Men*, which added post–World War II imagery to the cautionary tale about the destructive nature of war. The first film featured animals telling the story of how war led to the extinction of humanity, in spite of the presence of a "book of rules," a not-so-veiled reference to the Bible. In *Peace on Earth*, released in 1939, a wise owl reads through the Ten Commandments and Old Testament verses within a damaged church before the animals rebuild civilization calling it Peaceville. The film earned an Oscar nomination and was reportedly nominated for a Nobel Peace Prize as the war escalated in Europe. The pacifist message in *Peace on Earth* could also be considered an argument for isolationist policy in the United States, as the country ignored the atrocities at the hand of the Nazis. Much like today, arguments based in economics and selective non-violence were often used to hide possible racial or ethnic reasons for political decisions, in this case to hide possible Anti-Semitic arguments to stay out of the war occurring in Europe.[5]

The remake in 1955, which, like the first, was released in December for the Christmas season, was even more overtly religious, with a Deacon mouse replacing a grandfatherly chipmunk as the storyteller whose sermon is said in a destroyed church rather than told to young chipmunks in a small cottage. The remake predicted the destruction of humanity and featured contemporary weapons like fighter jets and bazookas that were developed during or after World War II. It also included more Biblical verses from the "book of rules" including several from the New Testament. *Goodwill to Men* ends with a congregation of forest animals gathering for Christmas mass and singing a version of "Hark! The Herald Angels Sing." This overt Christian message was not surprising coming from the Irish-Catholic Hanna and Italian-Catholic Barbera, whose faith and reverence for Christianity is seen throughout their careers both indirectly and directly as Christian themes found their way into their entertainment series. Barbera also pushed for approval to develop a series of animated films based on Bible stories, which were later produced.[6]

They continued to oversee the production of new films through 1957; however, most of the shorts were merely remakes of older films with changed settings and themes. For example, the Oscar-nominated *One Droopy Knight* was actually a remake of *Señor Droopy* where the eponymous dog and his rival, Butch, take on a dragon instead of a bull.[7] Although the updated film did not contain the racial and cultural stereotypes of

Mexicans, the plot and jokes in *One Droopy Knight* were nearly the same as the 1949 film.[8] Although the success of remakes like this may have influenced MGM's decision to move on from new production and rely on reissued films, it would also inform Hanna and Barbera's approach to program development as successful formulas, plots, animation, and even the characteristics of the stars of their productions were replicated or reused consistently throughout the studio's peak. Knowledge of how to work around budgetary restrictions was integral as they began negotiating with George Sidney, Screen Gems/Columbia, and NBC concerning the development and dissemination of their first series for television.[9]

Skepticism Creates Obstacles

Crusader Rabbit may have achieved what some consider success with 195 episodes produced for television syndication from 1950 to 1952, but networks were still wary of regularly scheduling animated programs produced for television. The big networks, NBC and CBS, and the "third network" ABC were open to broadcasting theatrical animation, especially series and characters that had track records of success.[10] Unfortunately for NBC, the theatrical animation studio they signed a deal with, Columbia, did not have any characters that neared the success or popularity of Mighty Mouse, Woody Woodpecker, Heckle and Jeckle, or Popeye, which all (re)captured an audience when their films were repackaged for television. At the time, Hanna and Barbera, who had partnered with Sidney to form H-B Enterprises, were developing their first original television series and were looking for a distributor and network for the series. Sidney connected the animation duo with Columbia president Harry Cohn, who agreed to work with them in exchange for an 18 percent stake in the newly formed studio. John Mitchell, the president of Screen Gems, the TV distribution subsidiary of Columbia, pitched *The Ruff and Reddy Show* to NBC, who balked at committing to full half hour animated episodes for Saturday morning.[11] NBC and Screen Gems compromised by broadcasting the new animation as wraparounds to help support the package of color Columbia cartoons they bought. The series also featured live-action sequences produced by Roger Muir of *Howdy Doody* fame and starring Jimmy Blaine and several puppets operated by *Howdy Doody* veteran Rufus Rose. Blaine was replaced by Robert Cottle in later (re)broadcasts of the show in the early 1960s, when the program achieved its largest audiences, competing with *Captain Kangaroo* for highest ratings in their Saturday morning time slot.[12]

For each episode, Hanna and Barbera were responsible for producing about seven minutes of animation, the same length as a traditional *Tom and Jerry* film. When producing their famous series for theaters, MGM provided them with up to $50,000 per film, whereas each episode of their new series had to be produced for under $3,000. As a result, the duo had to rely heavily on limited animation techniques to create the cartoons for NBC. All studios utilized some of these techniques, like repeated or static backgrounds, reduced character movement, reused scenes, and simpler drawings, to a certain extent.[13] Animators from United Production Associates experimented with this style through films like *Gerald McBoing-Boing* (1950), which garnered praise from both critics and audiences, and helped legitimize the expressed use of the technique throughout the 1950s. *Gerald McBoing-Boing* prioritized dialogue, sounds, and jokes over detailed visuals, and created a framework for the use of limited animation in both theatrical shorts, but more importantly, television animation, famously replicated by Hanna-Barbera and Warner Bros.[14]

The animators fully utilized all of these limited animation strategies, while even creating their own techniques to cut down on the drawings required to develop an episode. This included giving characters collars so they only needed to animate from the neck up in many scenes, only moving their mouths when they spoke, pausing for audience reactions or laughter and creating longer opening theme songs to reduce the animation necessary to fill each episode. This also required them to rely more on dialogue and vocal characterizations to entertain the audience.[15] This was made slightly easier by the fact that the show was aimed at a younger audience, who either appreciated or did not notice the repeated scenes, rhyming character names, and overused simplistic catchphrases which were uttered by two voice artists and impressionists who would become synonymous with Hanna-Barbera productions, Don Messick and Daws Butler. The only character to speak extensively in *Tom and Jerry* was Mammy Two Shoes; otherwise, the stars would speak sparingly aside from the pain screams that would come from being the victim of the frequent violence.[16] Those in the industry derided their approach with Chuck Jones, one of the innovators of limited animation, calling it animated radio, and Disney admitting they did not consider the new studio competition.[17]

Ruff and Reddy premiered in December of 1957, five months after Hanna and Barbera were officially let go from MGM. The marketing leading up to the premiere of the show made clear the connection between the animation duo's involvement and their popular creation, *Tom and Jerry*. Like the film series, *Ruff and Reddy* featured a traditionally adversarial pairing, a cat and a dog, but unlike in the Oscar-winning series, the co-stars were friends who cooperated throughout the adventures presented in each episode. The premiere episode attempted to be topically relevant, with the cat and dog traveling to MuniMula, a metal covered planet, two months after the USSR launched the Sputnik satellite. The series struggled to find an audience the first few months on air even though it followed the legendary *Howdy Doody*, with many markets opting for local programming over the new show. However, by the summer of 1958, *Ruff and Reddy* was regularly seen in most major markets and Hanna-Barbera had their first successful series, leading to the development of their first fully animated series for television, which premiered in syndication later that year.[18]

Remnants of MGM

In 1953, Tex Avery resigned from MGM leaving behind the rights to his *Droopy* series, which had debuted a new character, Southern Wolf, just before Avery stopped worked on the series. Hanna and Barbera took over the series as executive producers, featuring the wolf in two more Droopy films *Blackboard Jumble* (1957) and *Sheep Wrecked* (1958). The wolf was well-intentioned but slow witted and featured a Southeastern accent and whistled the Civil War song "The Year of Jubilo" or "Kingdom Coming" as he strolled away from a predicament or injury, like being caught in a bear trap. In *Blackboard Jumble*, he works as a teacher overseeing a classroom attended by young Droopy lookalikes. At one point in the film he dons a Confederate hat and has the schoolpups paint the Confederate flag, revealing Southern Wolf to be a sympathizer for the Confederacy.[19]

As Hanna and Barbera developed new programs to pitch to sponsors, they used Southern Wolf as a model for their newest star, a Bluetick Coonhound, increasing his emotional responses and awareness. *The Huckleberry Hound Show* picked up Kellogg's as a sponsor with an over the phone pitch. The cereal producer, whose ads were handled by the Leo Burnett agency, was looking to partner with more animated programs as a strategy to reach the growing number of children and family television viewers after their sponsorship of *The Woody Woodpecker Show* proved successful.[20] After *Huckleberry Hound* secured Kellogg's as a sponsor, Barbera went to Leo Barnett to pitch two more series, which were also approved by the agency and joined the canine on their first series to exclusively feature their animation.[21]

The Huckleberry Hound Show followed the same formula as the programs that packaged theatrical shorts together, featuring three shorts and general wraparound programming that connected the three segments. Huckleberry Hound starred in one of the shorts during each episode and served as "host," making it one of the first shows since *Crusader Rabbit* composed completely of animation produced for television. Named after the Mark Twain character, Huckleberry Hound was voiced by Daws Butler in an accent previously used for Southern Wolf and Ruff the dog which was suspiciously similar to the North Carolina accent of Andy Griffith, whose popularity as a comedian and actor was growing at the time.[22] The second segment on the program, *Pixie and Dixie, and Mr. Jinks* featured two mice and a cat with an adversarial relationship, a concept the animation producers knew a little about from their experience at MGM. The segment was not nearly as violent as *Tom and Jerry*, instead relying on actual dialogue, unlike their MGM counterparts, and basic slapstick for the humor. As his name suggests, Dixie, who was voiced by Butler, had a southern accent that resembled a higher version of the voice used for Huckleberry Hound while Pixie merely had a high-sounding northern accent provided by Messick. Mr. Jinks, whose voice was also provided by Butler, was clearly modeled after Marlon Brando and often muttered to himself, "I hate those meeces to pieces!" and the twin mice outwitted the cat.[23]

Although Huckleberry became Hanna and Barbera's first true television star, the third segment on the program had arguably the longest-lasting legacy. Yogi Bear, constantly flanked by his loyal sidekick Boo Boo, continues to be one of the most recognizable stars created by the two animators. Like with Huckleberry, Dixie, and Mr. Jinks, Butler provided the voice of Yogi, named for the baseball player, Yogi Berra, clearly imitating popular comedian Art Carney, who co-starred with Jackie Gleason in *The Honeymooners* sketches and series while Boo Boo was voiced by Messick. ABC, the network that aired *The Woody Woodpecker Show*, was considered for *The Huckleberry Hound Show*, but both Kellogg's and Screen Gems felt they could reach more markets in syndication. By 1959, *Huckleberry Hound* could be viewed by audiences in 192 of the 263 markets available at the time, more than double the markets that had ABC affiliates. It was also the duo's first international television hit, reaching an audience of 16,000,000 around the world by the end of the program's run in 1960.[24] The series was the first completely animated series to win the Emmy Award for Outstanding Achievement in Children's Television and reached the top ten in ratings in most major markets, which was especially impressive considering television producers and executives continued to be skeptical of programs marketed toward children.[25]

The Huckleberry Hound Show may have been considered a "children's show," but there was significant evidence of the program's crossover appeal with older audiences. Along with the ratings, Huckleberry began to appear in adult films like the Dean Martin comedy *Who Was That Lady?*, directed by Sydney, and *Breakfast at Tiffany's* when Audrey Hepburn infamously puts on a Huckleberry mask. The show was scheduled in most markets in the late afternoon or even early primetime, time periods with more 19- to 34-year-olds tuning into the show after they got home from work.[26] The show was also different from anything on television at the time. Popular sitcoms like *I Love Lucy* and *The Honeymooners*, both of which debuted with young childless couples, had ended by 1957, replaced by family sitcoms like *Leave It to Beaver* which featured banal general humor appropriate for parents to watch in the same room with their children. Westerns, Adventure, and Detective programs were also filling the television schedules by this time. Theatrical shorts, which made up the majority of animation on television at the time, may have originally been aimed at a general or even adult audiences, but many of the films were no longer as topical and many of the more mature or offensive films were edited or completely removed from rotation. This left fewer films that relied on the racial or discriminatory humor adopted from vaudevillian performances. The shorts that remained viable for television carried over the slapstick and music, which appealed to children who, unlike the adults, were viewing these films for the first time. Adding to the childish appeal of these shows aimed at young audiences was the presence of a live-action host, who typically adopted a professional or familial persona like "captain" or uncle, keeping the young audience entertained between shorts. *Huckleberry Hound* may have seemed like a children's show to many due to the animation, but the themes and humor appealed to many adults just as much as children.[27]

The animation style of *The Huckleberry Hound Show* was in no way revolutionary, utilizing the same limited animation techniques as seen in *Ruff and Reddy*, although it was clear that Kellogg's involvement in the later show had led to better financing with more intricate character designs and higher quality background animation. Audiences became more comfortable with the fact that television animation was never going to match the visual quality of its theatrical counterparts, and they began to appreciate, or at least tolerate, the unique characteristics of television animation, including the increased reliance on dialogue and puns.[28] Hanna and Barbera also oversaw the utilization of gags popularized in Warner and their own MGM films, including the use of the chase as a comedic device and Huckleberry's frequent breaking of the fourth wall as he paused to look at the audience milking the joke or describing his plan, similar to Bugs Bunny's interactions with viewers as he battled Daffy and Elmer Fudd. This is not surprising considering Michael Maltese, who began his career at Warner in 1941 and joined Hanna-Barbera in 1958, was the lead writer for many of the early series for the studio.[29]

Maltese was also the head writer on H-B Enterprises' only venture into theatrical shorts, *Loopy de Loop*, a French-Canadian wolf who attempts to change the

Fisher-Price Huckleberry Hound Toy from 1961 (Vintage-pix/Shutterstock.com).

perception of lupins as he assists people and communities in each film.[30] The series debuted in November of 1959, a month after Maltese's last Wile E. Coyote/Road Runner film premiered for Warner Bros., which was clearly inspired by Hanna and Barbera's *Tom and Jerry* and was one of the most successful cartoon film series of the 1950s. Loopy's efforts are often misunderstood or the reputation of wolves precedes him as he is typically run out of town or the location he is visiting by the occupants by the end of the films. Columbia distributed the series as they tried to compete with Warner, who still produced profitable theatrical shorts into the 1960s. Columbia still sought the international film star they never created during the Golden Age of Animation. Hanna-Barbera produced 48 *Loopy* films between 1959 and 1965 with limited fanfare, ending the series as both the animation studio and film distributor decided to focus on other projects, including Maltese's work on another series with a French-accented anthropomorphic animal, Pepe Le Pew.[31] The series was adapted into a syndicated television series in 1969 and sold to individual media markets as a children's program.

Huckleberry Hound was a huge success for both Hanna-Barbera and Kellogg's, leading the animation studio and cereal maker to partner again and develop a second animated program for syndication. By the time *The Quick Draw McGraw Show* entered development, both companies were aware of the presence of the teenagers and young adults among the animation audience. *Quick Draw* clearly had a more satirical edge that was meant to appeal more to older audiences than *Huckleberry Hound*. Like the eponymous dog, Quick Draw only appeared in one short and in wraparound segments that connected the three segments of each episode. The anthropomorphic horse, who only walked on his hind legs, was accompanied by his sidekick, a Mexican burro, complete with sombrero, named Baba Looey with Daws Butler lending his voice to both characters. Quick Draw had a voice similar to Disney's Goofy while Baba Looey had a stereotypical Mexican accent. Although Looey was Mexican his personality was inspired by the Cuban Desi Arnaz, even taking his name from one of Arnaz's songs.[32]

This type of misinformed portrayal of Mexicans increased during World War II as animation studios, particularly Disney, included the white male animators' perspectives of what Latin American culture looked like as they tried to increase sales to Latin American markets. In 1955, Warner Bros. introduced a character that continues to be the most popular character of Chicanx descent in animation history, Speedy Gonzalez. Hanna-Barbera followed suit, introducing their first non-white star since Mammy Two Shoes of *Tom and Jerry* infamy. Unsurprisingly original broadcasts featuring Baba Looey were less than culturally sensitive or aware; however, in international versions dubbed for sale in Mexico and Latin America, Looey became the star. Audiences in these countries ignored or disidentified with the less sensitive portions of the portrayal of Looey to focus on the fact that there was actually a Chicanx character in an animated series. In Spanish versions, Quick Draw also maintains his American accent, making the eponymous star seem like the alien of the series, which was edited to push Baba Looey to the forefront.[33]

The Western parody contained many of the same issues contained in the shows and films it attempted to satirize. The portrayal of the Old West as a land or territory that needed to be conquered to continue the progress of Western civilization was present in Quick Draw like it was in most Westerns. Baba Looey's role as the sidekick of color continues a tradition, which had most recently been represented by the character Tonto in the popular Lone Ranger series. Quick Draw also frequently embodied the alter ego, "El KaBong," a Zorro-like character who would injure his enemies by hitting them with a guitar. Any references to Zorro, a Californio character developed earlier in the century, was completely white washed when Quick Draw became El KaBong.[34]

The second segment within the larger show, *Snooper and Blabber* featured a cat and mouse detective team both voiced by Daws Butler. Blabber Mouse spoke with a lisp while Butler imitated Ed Gardner for the voice of Super Snooper. The third segment, like the first two, satirized a popular genre, the family comedy, starring a father-son pair of dogs. The *Augie Doggie and Daddy Doggie* segment was very similar to the *Spike and Tyke* series the duo produced for MGM, merely replacing the American bulldog duo with two dachshunds. The new series was a parody of shows like *Leave It to Beaver*, which had not premiered when *Spike and Tyke* films were originally released in the 1940s and early 1950s.[35] The series was also the first to not star either Don Messick or Daws Butler, with Doug Young providing his Jimmy Durante impression for the voice of Daddy Doggie. Although *Quick Draw McGraw* was not as critically revered as *Huckleberry Hound*, it provided further evidence that animated fare aimed at general audiences and adults could be successful, much as it was in theaters during the Golden Age. Mitchell suggested Hanna-Barbera develop a show that fully targeted the adult audience with human characters in a format that consistently draws the young adult audience, the half-hour situational comedy. As production continued on *Ruff and Reddy*, *Huckleberry Hound*, and *Quick Draw McGraw*, Hanna and Barbera developed a new series to premiere in the fall of 1960.[36]

Hanna and Barbera were not subtle about their willingness to rely on successful formulas and imitate already popular voices and plot structures. In their first three television programs voice actors imitated Andy Griffith, Art Carney, and Jimmy Durante and at MGM infrequent dialogue featured Tom and Jerry sounding similar to celebrities like Stepin Fetchit and Hattie McDaniel, complete with the racist ideologies contained in stereotypical mimicry by whites of non-white vernacular and accents. The use of imitation and reliance on past formulas also helped maintain outdated ideologies since the older source material used as inspiration also represents sensibilities from the time the original content was disseminated. This reliance on formula was not unique for animation, as *Gunsmoke* spawned numerous imitators like *Bonanza*, the *Rifleman* and even *Quick Draw*, maintaining the white imperialist frontier ideologies celebrated in Westerns that romanticized the invasion of these lands by people of European descent.[37] The satire may have made fun of genres, and imitated already popular voices and formulas.[38]

The Modern Stone Age Family: Television, Capitalism, and Hanna-Barbera's Whitewashing of America's Past, Present, and Future

Economically, this reliance on imitation, parody, and satire reduced risk, since producers had evidence that a particular show structure or type of humor was already profitable before starting production on a show. Even though television animation was less expensive than its theatrical counterpart, it was still at least as expensive as most live-action programs, and at this point, many executives still felt that animation had limited appeal among older audiences, so Hanna-Barbera utilized already successful live-action formulas when pitching their shows to networks and sponsors. When developing their new series for adults, they decided to emulate what continues to be one of the most replicated sitcoms in television history, *The Honeymooners*. Hanna and Barbera knew they wanted to focus the series on a blue-collar worker, his wife, and their neighbors/best friends. They originally considered featuring a family, but Mitchell felt a child might turn off some adults as they might assume it was a family or children's program. The animation duo had to then decide on a theme, wanting to utilize an unusual or unfamiliar setting to increase the availability of sight gags and puns.[39] They considered several historical settings including Ancient Rome, Colonial America, and even the Old West again, pitching programs starring both Cowboys and Native Americans. They actually considered several Native American groups, including Eskimos, as the inspiration for characters, but eventually settled on a vague fictionalization of prehistoric times, to avoid pressures from ethnic groups over possible insensitive or inaccurate portrayals. Unfortunately, most of these groups were later represented in Hanna-Barbera programs aimed at children.[40]

The Neanderthal motif in visual comedy had also proven successful with the debut of the popular comic strip *B.C.* in 1958. Also, while leading MGM, Hanna and Barbera oversaw a Tex Avery cartoon called *The First Bad Man* (1955) in which a robber in prehistoric Dallas tries to steal from a bank. Many of the visual jokes and designs from the film made it into *The Flintstones*, and Ed Benedict, who also worked on the Avery film, helped Hanna and Barbera with the early layouts and character designs for the show so the similarities are not surprising, especially considering the relatively short time frame they had to develop the series.[41] Lastly, the lack of public knowledge about the vast time period considered "prehistory" allowed the writers and producers to take an anachronistic approach to the program's comedy, with fewer questions about the accuracy of the settings, practices, and representations.[42]

Since Hanna and Barbera were creating a new subgenre of television, they produced a sample cartoon to include in the presentations they made to the major networks, as the duo and Mitchell felt a syndicated show, which could air at 7:30 p.m. at the latest, would not reach the entire 19–34 demographic that they sought. In this short pilot, the family was given the name Flagstones, with Gladstones also considered, but the names were too close to names already associated with other entities, Flagstons were the last name of Hi and Lois while Gladstone was a recommended telephone exchange name for Los Angeles at the time.[43] They settled on the name the Flintstones and moved the Rubbles in next door before pitching the series to the "big two" networks, NBC and CBS. Executives from both networks declined, struggling to see how a cartoon could fit within their schedule or be marketed toward adults. ABC, on the other hand, continued to be the third network as it tried to play catch-up with the two more established broadcast institutions and was more open to taking risks on unproven formulas or formats. Previously, ABC was the first network to air Westerns while their deal with Disney helped to establish the television network's entertainment division and set a precedent for future deals between networks and film studios as the animation and media giant provided content for the growing network. ABC also discovered through *The Woody Woodpecker Show* what Hanna-Barbera realized through the cross-demographic appeal of Huckleberry Hound: there is an older audience that wanted to consume new animated content.[44]

By late 1959, even with the support of ABC and Screen Gems, *The Flintstones* still needed sponsorship and Hanna-Barbera was responsible for finding the right partner for the program. This was made harder by the fact that they still only had the two-minute sample film and some sketches to present to potential advertisers. The typical soft drink and cereal companies offered their names, and money, mostly based on the success of

Huckleberry Hound and *Quick Draw McGraw*, but all the parties involved knew that even a sponsor associated with a younger demographic could undermine attempts to draw in teenagers and adults to the program. Miles Laboratory picked up the show, being drawn in by the cross-demographic appeal of the program for their One-a-Day Vitamins, and remained as sponsor of the show throughout its original run on ABC.[45] The second sponsor, Reynolds Tobacco, hoped to avoid accusations of advertising to children, so they wanted to make sure the show was clearly adult; however, they undoubtedly liked the idea of selling their product to younger audiences, and creating possible brand recognition for their popular Winston brand of cigarettes with children and especially teenagers, who could smoke in many states.[46]

When *The Flintstones* finally went into production, Hanna-Barbera was given a budget of $65,000 per episode, well above average for a new show at the time. Also, because of the production schedule of the show, which took over six months, they needed a full season commitment from both the sponsors and the network, which only increased the risk taken by all parties. *The Flintstones* debuted on September 30, 1960, at 8:30 p.m., the first full-length regularly scheduled animated sitcom produced for a television network.[47] The time slot suggested to the audience that it was aimed at adults, but ABC also hedged its bets by placing the show on Friday night, the least viewed weeknight on the television schedule. This decision would unknowingly affect the direction of the program throughout its first run on television. Although there may possibly have been fewer single adults and young couples at home on Friday, there were more families, young teenagers, and children watching prime time television than other nights when they may have been forced to go to bed earlier, or the adults of the family dominated program choice. Research has also shown that children often like to "watch up" and consume media intended for older audiences as they fulfill desires to be seen as more mature, exposing them to jokes and messages intended for teenagers or adults.[48]

The Yabba-Dabba Debut

The show was not an immediate critical success with many reviewers dismissing animation as a children's medium and lamenting that the show was merely a copy of *The Honeymooners*, which was still widely available in syndication. Neither the scheduling nor the mixed reviews prevented the show from becoming a hit as it ended the season in 18th place in the ratings. Considering the younger portion of the audience did not register in the ratings, this initial success represented significant adult audience for the animated series. Although many of the jokes and gags were fairly standard for broad situational comedy at the time, the ability of the writers and animators to utilize the Stone Age and animation to satirize 1960s popular culture is what set *The Flintstones* apart from many other sitcoms at the time, which still largely featured families and broader, child-appropriate humor.[49] The series' iconic theme song did not premiere until the third season, but each episode was previewed with a short scene that appeared later in the episode before the theme played, which was an instrumental called "Rise and Shine" the first two seasons. The theme and the preview of the later scene cut down on the animation needed for each episode. The original song very closely resembled "The Bugs Bunny Overture," the theme from *The Bugs Bunny Show*, which may have helped motivate the switch to "Meet the Flintstones" in the third season, which was accompanied by several other changes that season which will be discussed further in the next chapter.[50]

The Flintstones' ability to present cultural commentary on a wide range of topics, from rock and roll to the space race, attracted a wide range of audiences who operated within a limited television schedule inundated with a mixture of family-friendly fare, dramas, and westerns.[51] It should also be noted that midway through the airing of the first season, and production of the second, Mel Blanc, the voice of Barney Rubble along with many of the top Warner characters including Bugs Bunny, was in a near fatal-car accident with Daws Butler filling in for five episodes before Blanc requested a recording studio to be set up around his bed so he could continue working.[52]

About a month after the first season ended, and well into the production of the second season, a speech by Newton Minow changed perspectives about the television landscape through the 1960s. Three months after being appointed by the Chairman of the Federal Communications Commission, Minow made his first speech to the National Association of Broadcasters where he called television a vast wasteland, criticizing the amount of violence and mindless content was available on the medium. Aside from commenting on the "murder … mayhem … blood and thunder" he targeted several genres of television, specifically westerns, police shows, and cartoons.[53] With a significant portion of the upcoming season already in production, Hanna-Barbera, ABC, and Screen Gems moved forward with the same format and sponsors. Even with the negative attention cartoons garnered from Minow's speech, *The Flintstones* drew the second highest viewership for Friday night, falling just outside the top 20 in the ratings for the entire 1961–1962 season, their second on ABC. As all of these parties looked ahead to the third season, economic realities and pressure from advocates led the producers to adjust the structure of the program moving forward.[54]

What About the Animals?

During *The Flintstones'* first season, Hanna-Barbera's first spin-off series, *The Yogi Bear Show*, premiered in January of 1961. Similar to *Huckleberry Hound* and *Quick Draw McGraw*, Yogi and Boo Boo only starred in one portion of the package series, which also introduced *Snagglepuss* and *Yakky Doodle* to the Hanna-Barbera cartoon stable. The show only brightened Yogi's star as he continued to be the most popular animal character for Hanna-Barbera, becoming the studio's first true icon in the early 1960s. His popularity was especially noticeable among children, an audience with growing economic importance, especially as the company started to license its characters to more companies. Snagglepuss, whose voice was an imitation of Bert Lahr, the Cowardly Lion in *The Wizard of Oz*, achieved moderate popularity and appeared in several other series produced by the studio, arguably achieving his most success as a supporting character in the 1970s. The Donald Duck-sounding Yakky had a few cameos after appearing on *The Yogi Bear Show* but did not appear regularly in any series after Yogi's first series ended production in 1962.[55]

Hanna and Barbera's experience with the sudden shutdown at MGM was clearly influencing their approach to production, as they continued to develop shows with five programs already on the air, still concerned any of their agreements or shows could suddenly be cancelled. After a very successful first season of *The Flintstones*, ABC, Columbia, and Hanna-Barbera had even higher expectations for the second regularly scheduled series, *Top Cat*. In the 1950s and 1960s two of the most popular non-family sitcom formats featured young childless couples, like *The Honeymooners*, and those that had a "rebellious" white male who constantly schemes to avoid authority figures and earn easy money. *The Phil Silvers Show* was one of the earliest and most popular programs from this second format, and as it had done with *The Honeymooners*, Hanna-Barbera directly imitated the format and style of the popular sitcom, which ran from 1955 to 1959, replacing the Army and soldiers in Silvers' show with an alley and cats. The show takes place in Hoagy's Alley, a play on words inspired by Hogan's Alley.

They tested the format with the *Hokey Wolf* series, which replaced Yogi on *Huckleberry Hound* when the bear received his own series, and Hanna-Barbera decided to develop a more mature version of the series with new characters that ran a full half hour. Arnold Stang supplied the voice, replacing Butler after the pilot as Butler's commitment on other programs and films took priority over the new series. Stang closely imitated Silvers' Sgt. Bilko's voice and speech pattern, leaving very little doubt where Hanna-Barbera found its inspiration for the show. All the entities involved assumed that the faster pace and higher quality animation of *Top Cat* would make it an even bigger hit than *The Flintstones*, which aired at 8:30 on Friday nights. ABC offered *Top Cat* the same time slot on Wednesday nights, hoping the new show would help bring audiences over from NBC's popular *Perry Como Show*. Unfortunately for ABC and Hanna-Barbera, *Wagon Train* led NBC's primetime lineup and was the top-rated show of the season. CBS had also premiered *The Alvin Show* that season featuring the singing chipmunk trio, appearing earlier in primetime the same night as *Top Cat*, possibly diluting the novelty of mid-week animation.[56]

The sponsors of *Top Cat* may have influenced perceptions about the show. Unlike *The Flintstones*, which cemented its status as an adult show by partnering with R.J. Reynolds Tobacco, *Top Cat*'s top sponsors were Kellogg's and Bristol-Myers's Bufferin, an aspirin brand that released a children's version of its buffered medicine in 1962. Another factor that influenced public perception was the use of anthropomorphic cats rather than the human characters in *The Flintstones*. *Top Cat* and the other alley cats did interact seamlessly with the "human world," specifically Officer Dibble, who was the authority figure replacing Colonel Hall from *The Phil Silvers Show*, but the presence of cats as the main cast may have helped create a decidedly younger reputation for the series, which was only reinforced by early marketing and reviews of the show. The advertisements leading up to the premiere typically featured the vested star alone or with his cast of co-starring felines, without any assurance to adults that the show was written for them.[57]

Along with the scheduling, marketing, and sponsorship, another unexpected issue that plagued the ratings was the change from the military locale of *The Phil Silvers Show* to the neighborhood setting featured in *Top Cat*. A large audience of military personnel and veterans appreciated the former program's satire and jokes based on life as a soldier, not necessarily the rebellious scheming portion of the show replicated in *Top Cat*. Hanna-Barbera also may have felt handcuffed by the growing criticism that inspired Minow's speech a few months before the show's premiere and eliminated some of the more adult themes and plots. Originally, the show was to be called *Tomcat* with Hanna saying publicly that they changed the name to avoid confusion, or trademark issues, involving *Tom and Jerry*; however, there is evidence, including the title itself and the visual portrayal of the cats as hipsters, more stories involving the star's romantic pursuits were considered in development before these concerns led the writers to focus almost exclusively on Top Cat's various plans to make money quickly.[58]

The end of the 1961–1962 season marked a turning point for television and Hanna-Barbera on several fronts. After *Top Cat* was officially ruled a disappointment for the cartoon studio, Columbia, and ABC decided to adjust their focus. All of the networks and production companies had a year to react to the fallout from Minow's speech and increasing pressure from advocacy groups and began to move away from the genres and characteristics described by the FCC chairman in his speech. There were fewer Westerns, police programs, and adult sitcoms as NBC, CBS, and ABC also began to recognize the growing family audience and the influence the presence of younger viewers had on the programming choices of these families.[59] Past issues like the higher cost of animation also created hesitancy from Screen Gems and ABC to fully invest in primetime animation, especially as the licensing and merchandising side of the business grew, with the majority of products inspired by animation marketed to

Top Cat and Officer Dibble in one of their many interactions (Moviestore Collection Ltd./Alamy Stock Photo).

children, reducing incentive to produce another animated series targeting adults. *The Flintstones* had firmly established itself as a true success after two top-25 seasons in the Nielsen ratings, but even with this established audience Hanna-Barbera agreed with ABC and Screen Gems to take the show, and ultimately the animation studio, in a different direction.

During this time, the *Tom and Jerry* series was revived by MGM, since they held the rights to the duo after Hanna and Barbera left the studio. Gene Deitch, who had previously worked for United Productions of America before establishing his own studio in Czechoslovakia, was already producing *Popeye* cartoons for King Features before MGM contacted him to direct the reboot of the cat and mouse series in 1961. The new shorts, with a smaller budget and a more surreal quality, with settings outside the home, were a commercial success, dethroning *Looney Tunes* as the top series after 16 years but failed to garner any Oscar nominations. The 13 shorts are considered by many as the worst of the *Tom and Jerry* theatrical shorts. Before production began Deitch only saw a few of the Hanna-Barbera produced shorts, contributing to a different visual style and comedic approach from the original films. After Joe Vogel, the head of production who hired Deitch, left MGM the studio did not renew the animator's contract.[60]

It's a White Male Television Cartoon World

In the first five years Hanna-Barbera Productions was in operation they produced an average of 55 half hour episodes a season plus 23 *Loopy de Loop* films. They also created over a dozen popular characters, most of which had one thing very obviously in common. Most of them were, or portrayed, white heteronormative males, and the ones who could have been seen falling outside this constructed intersection were a result of problematic plots, portrayals, and storylines. This identification of characters, even anthropomorphic ones, is supported by the fact that so many of the characters imitated popular white male actors. They were also constantly displaying their masculinity, whether it was through stereotypical activities or jobs in individual episodes like Huckleberry's hunting or Quick Draw's job as a cowboy or the consistent assurance of the characters' heteronormativity through the presence of a wife, love interest, or son. Women were mostly invisible in these anthropomorphic worlds, until they are needed to reinforce the fact that the male characters have no real attraction to each other, since duos like Yogi/Boo Boo and Fred/Barney spend more time with their male counterparts than their romantic partners.[61]

Though these characters did spend an inordinate time with their best friends, *The Yogi Show* and *The Flintstones* included the first two recurring supporting female characters for Hanna-Barbera Productions: Cindy Bear was Yogi's love interest throughout the series, while Wilma and Betty, Fred and Barney's wives, respectively, were major supporting characters in the prehistoric comedy. Cindy in the early series and movie plays a damsel complete with a southern accent and parasol. She stars in three episodes of the original spin-off, either relying on Yogi to save her or being courted by the star as he competes for her affections.[62] Wilma and Betty played the Alice Kramden and Trixie Norton roles on *The Flintstones*, particularly throughout the first two seasons as many of the plots revolve around Fred and Barney avoiding their wives' wrath as they try to hang out at the lodge or enter into get rich quick schemes, both of which continue to be common plot devices in situational comedies. Like his live-action counterpart, Ralph, Fred often yells at Wilma, although the threats of domestic violence are much rarer in the cartoon, whereas Wilma is often depicted hitting Fred with frying pans and vases. Both Wilma and Betty are housewives, who, aside from a few episodes, are typically secondary characters to their male counterparts, often seen completing stereotypical housewife duties, which are made easier by the various appliances represented by animals forced to complete these tasks, like a small mastodon being used as a vacuum cleaner. The few episodes in which they are featured, which did not occur until the middle of the second season, followed them in stereotypically female plots taken from other sitcoms, like the episode in which they enter a baking contest. There is one episode in which Betty does get a part-time job, but that is to surprise Barney with a rocking chair, not because of any true financial difficulties ever discussed on the show.[63]

The first two seasons may have been inspired by *The Honeymooners*, but unlike the Kramdens, the Flintstones were an up-and-coming middle class couple with Fred's union salary at the quarry paying him enough to buy the many appliances that fill their home while also allowing them to take regular vacations. As with *Tom and Jerry*, most of these series take place in suburban or rural settings, mirroring the mass suburbanization predicted by the animation duo's MGM films. In one episode of *The Yogi Show*, the star accidentally gets lost in the city, experiencing the same overwhelming experience Jerry Mouse had in *Mouse in Manhattan*.[64] The few times the Flintstones end up in an urban area they experience trouble resulting from the negative perception of the prehistoric urban parodies like Indianarockolis or Frantic City and their many temptations.[65]

The only series that bucked this trend of setting shows in the tranquil country or suburbs was *Top Cat*, which takes place in Hoagy's Alley, Manhattan. As described above, the series is set in an alley where the star and his cast of friends are involved in the common sitcom plots involving various money-making schemes and romantic pursuits while constantly dealing with Officer Dibble's interference and constant attempts to evict them from the alley. This storyline where anthropomorphic animal characters are in constant conflict with the rules imposed by white male authority figures is featured in many Hanna-Barbera series produced at the same time or after *Top Cat*, including Yogi Bear's experience in Jellystone.[66]

Although it was mainly unintended by the original producers, the conflict between *Top Cat* and the police was seen by some audiences as representing the experience of disenfranchised and marginalized groups who are constantly looking for ways to escape poverty, even sometimes utilizing extra-legal means to do so, leading to constant negative interactions with law enforcement who seem to target them. The fear of being expelled from their alley home with nowhere else to go is always threatening their existence. The group is actually referred to as a gang in the series, placing a level of criminality on the cats, and may have been part of the reason (white) American audiences did not appreciate the show as much as its live-action counterpart, *The Phil Silvers Show*, which starred soldiers rather than criminalized alley cats. It is important to note that *Top Cat* continues to be one of the most iconic cartoon characters in Latin America, particularly in Mexico where Don Gato is still seen in reruns and feature films battling with Oficial Matute. The show also achieved moderate success in Europe and both Matute and Dibble are still used as derogatory words for police in certain parts of the world.[67]

Loopy de Loop also contained these "othering" themes, as the French-Canadian wolf was unable to break the stereotypes that surrounded his species no matter how helpful or upstanding he is to the community he encounters, although he continues to use nonviolent tactics to earn the trust of those he lives among. Unlike *Top Cat*, whose reputation is based on the situation in which he finds himself due to poverty, leading him and the other alley cats to live in the alley and rely on extralegal means for money and resources to survive, Loopy seems to be hated solely based on the stereotypes connected to his species regardless of how he tries to assimilate. This was the experience of millions of Americans belonging to marginalized groups who, regardless of how hard they worked or how selflessly they gave back to society, are constantly rejected by those in power. The series also ran during a period in which organization and awareness surrounding movements like Civil Rights and women's liberation were growing exponentially. The intention behind these themes that may be seen by some as socially progressive is questionable, especially considering the series' reliance on jokes and stereotypes related to accents, language, and cultural difference. *Loopy* and *Top Cat* do present evidence that television animation, and the audience consumption of it, could offer opportunities to challenge the status quo and resist ideologies, particularly through satire, while viewers utilized their agency to create meaning that the producers had no intention of presenting.[68]

Avoidance Is Not Tolerance

Another character in which audiences may have created meanings or identities not intended by the creators was Snagglepuss, who officially debuted on *The Yogi Bear Show*, with earlier versions of the character briefly seen on *The Quick Draw McGraw Show*. The mountain lion's color, way of speaking, and absence of a female love interest convinced a portion of the cartoon's audience that he was gay. His pink coloring, the presence of a lisp, his way of dress, neat lifestyle, and theatrical catchphrases fulfilled a number of stereotypes connected to gay men at the time. Butler's imitation of Bert Lahr's cowardly lion also created a connection with *The Wizard of Oz*, which quickly became popular among populations that identified as gay, with the books and film being interpreted as representing their experience throughout the early 20th century. The books, particularly *The Road to Oz*, had a number of characters and themes that supported LGBTQ ideas and experiences. The film's popularity exposed a huge audience to some of these ideas and interpretations, with Dorothy's friends representing possibly gay outcasts. The lion in particular is described as "dandy" and is seen as living a lie as a lion who is too scared (or has no desire) to hunt and fulfill his role as "King of the Beasts." He is clearly not a coward throughout the book and film, as he assists Dorothy in her journey, but his unwillingness to adhere to the violent expectations connected to his identity as a lion also welcomes conversations about the conflation of gender and sexuality especially as it relates to displays of masculinity.[69] In future Hanna-Barbera productions these characteristics, like the imitation of certain voices and voice actors, lack of romantic or sexual interest, and style of dress are often characteristics utilized by the audience to disidentify with the content and the character to produce queer identities for characters who do not explicitly communicate their sexuality.[70]

The importance of this alternative meaning making by the audience is increased when considering the invisibility of non-white populations in animation at the time. As Golden Age short films were packaged for syndication and sale to the networks, many of the films had to be edited, if not censored completely, due to growing pressure from advocacy groups fighting against the decades of stereotypical and derogatory representations in the media. In early television and other post–World War II animation non-white groups were mainly ignored as producers worked to avoid criticism and misrepresentations by largely eliminating the presence of these populations in popular media, particularly African Americans. Aside from a few exceptions, most notably Speedy Gonzales, this also occurred in Hanna-Barbera productions, which continued to almost exclusively feature white male stars in their content through the 1960s. The animation studio was more concerned about the new direction of the company as it continued to learn from the successes, and failures, and adjust to the different structures and expectations inherent in television as the medium's presence in households surpassed 90 percent, although the development of *The Flintstones* showed that they knew the way they represented characters mattered to the audience.[71]

Throughout the late 1950s and early 1960s, although they faced some obstacles, Hanna-Barbera established itself as the top studio for direct-to-television animation, leading the industry as it transitioned from its distribution model that relied exclusively on theaters with television serving merely as a secondary market. Even with this success, they still proceeded cautiously, understanding that awards and enthusiastic fans were not always enough when profits are involved, as the abrupt closure of the MGM Cartoon Studio exemplified. This motivated their continued high output as the television animation market was still organizing itself and network executives were still trying to figure out how to best market potentially lucrative animation. The next few years would help cement Hanna-Barbera's legacy in animation and American television even as shifts in the studio's ownership structure led to some initial uncertainty. But along with eventual corporate stability, the establishment of time slots for animation and the support of powerful media figures led to nearly twenty years of consistent success for the animation studio as its characters became household names throughout the country and even the world.

3

1962–1964:
A Page Right Out
of (Television) History

Fine Tuning the Cartoon Factory

Hanna and Barbera's experience at MGM made them acutely aware of finances and the need to secure multiple revenue sources and maintain the rights over their creations, which they had lost with *Tom and Jerry* when they left the film studio. After the disappointing first and only season of *Top Cat*, ABC became more hesitant about broadcasting animation in prime time while Screen Gems continued expanding their business, focusing more on live-action television and broadcast ownership, buying several television and radio stations in America and Puerto Rico. Screen Gems President John Mitchell also received increasing scrutiny from other executives about the large financial commitment the company was making in producing and distributing Hanna-Barbera cartoons.[1] If *Tom and Jerry* was the proving ground for the duo's style and humor, and 1957–1962 represented the transition to television, the next few seasons allowed the duo and studio to perfect their production and business approach, providing a framework for television animation in the following decades. The ideologies, messages, and representations contained in their content evolved but continued to support similar stereotypes and roles communicated in earlier films and programs, although the content, production, and marketing moved to target families and then children almost exclusively.

As Hanna-Barbera Productions approached their sixth television season, the animation studio had turned into a factory, with up to five or six shows in production at any one time. They also continued to accept side projects like television commercials and title sequences, most famously for *Bewitched*, which premiered in 1964. They moved into their own lot, which further legitimized the production company, but also put more pressure on Hanna-Barbera to be profitable as they now owned the studio and real estate they occupied, including the mortgage and cost of improvements to the facility.[2] The studio was also adjusting to programming changes as *The Quick Draw McGraw Show*, *The Yogi Bear Show*, and *Top Cat* all ended their original productions runs, replaced by two series, a package series introducing three new anthropomorphic characters to the studio's stable of stars, and another show representing the animation producer and ABC's last attempt at a regularly scheduled full length animated sitcom in primetime until the 1990s.[3]

High Output, Low Risk Animation and the Representations It Inspires

The Hanna-Barbera New Cartoon Series premiered in syndication in the fall of 1963. Although they had produced other package series like *Yogi Bear*, *Quick Draw McGraw*, and *Huckleberry Hound* this was the first series that placed the studio's reputation before any specific characters or stars. The series featured three cartoon segments, *Wally Gator*, *Touche Turtle and Dum Dum*, and *Lippy the Lion and Hardy Har Har*. Lippy and Hardy were an optimistic lion and humorless hyena, respectively, and followed similar "get rich quick" plotlines as featured in *Top Cat*, merely adding the odd coupling to the show's presentation. Touche was a musketeer modeled turtle who, with his dog sidekick Dum Dum, comically attempt to save damsels and assist royalty following similar plots, albeit in a different locale and time period, as *Quick Draw McGraw*. Station affiliates, however, wanted to build off of the popularity of Yogi Bear and the other funny animal characters created by Hanna-Barbera, so in their marketing many referred to the show as *Wally Gator and Friends* to capitalize on the most popular character. Wally Gator's look, characteristics, and situation were remarkably similar to Yogi Bear's. Butler did imitate comedian Ed Wynn, rather than Art Carney, for Wally's voice.[4]

Having a Kid Changes Everything

As the studio prepared for the third season of *The Flintstones*, ABC, Screen Gems, and Hanna-Barbera met to discuss the future of their relationship. Even though *The Flintstones* ended a second season in the top 25 of the ratings, financial concerns related to high production costs and the disappointing season of *Top Cat* convinced all three entities to look to increase income from ancillary revenue sources. As characters like Huckleberry Hound and Yogi Bear grew in popularity, they began to appear more in more advertising and were featured in merchandise like dolls, toys, and even comedy records.[5] Children in particular were drawn to these products, as they were able to bring representations and images of their favorite characters into the home. Hanna and Barbera had very few issues with licensing their characters to pretty much anyone to help increase profitability and visibility of the growing number of cartoon stars employed by the studio; however, ABC and especially Screen Gems, who was investing heavily to expand their business holdings, were concerned that much of the programming coming from the studio did not directly target merchandise-buying children or families. They understood that younger audiences would still watch animation directed toward adults, but they really wanted shows that attracted both children and parents, not only to increase the shows' potential audience, but also they wanted parents to approve of the cartoon so they would buy products connected to the show and its characters, especially after Minow's speech the previous year.[6] These considerations led to huge changes in the popular animated sitcom, and contributed to a transition that led Hanna-Barbera to eventually move away from producing programs primarily targeting the adult audience.[7]

Hanna-Barbera brainstormed about how to make the show more family friendly, and quickly agreed to give the Flintstones a child. The original concept art for the series featured a son, Fred Jr., and early marketing material including a Little Golden Book visualized a family for the franchise, so the idea was not new to the producers. Also, considering the country was seeing the full effects of the Baby Boom, it did not seem unnatural to introduce a baby to the show, following the formula set by *I Love Lucy*.[8] The introduction of a third Flintstone also brought a number of changes to the format and structure of the program. Since the show was now outwardly inviting children to watch, they decided to end the partnership with Winston cigarettes, making One-a-Day and Miles Laboratory the primary sponsor and adding Welch's Juice to support the more family-friendly show. The studio already had 18 episodes produced for the third season before ultimately deciding to introduce a child, so the studio and ABC used the time to market the familial expansion throughout the season.[9]

Considering the art and story rooms were filled with men, and the original series had a son as a part of the family, it would be expected that the eponymous couple would have a boy, but early in the process the head of marketing for the studio came to Hanna and Barbera and told them that Ideal Toys communicated that a female doll would sell better than a male doll and they would make a deal if the Flintstones had a daughter. Producers switched course and began to plan on a baby girl to be born in the middle of the season. Writers had to also decide how to introduce the baby to the program, which was mainly composed of standalone episodes with little story connection throughout the series.

It was clear in the first season that producers were still figuring out what characters would be featured on the program. Dino, who did not appear on the actual program until the fourth episode, was seen in the opening and closing credits with blue coloring rather than his famous purple. A sabretooth cat was the star of the closing credits in early seasons, but the pet, Baby Puss, was seen sparingly in series episodes. Unlike pets, who were utilized mostly for gags, producers felt that a baby could not be introduced without some type of lead-up to the child's arrival since they would represent a significant portion of the Flintstones' lives. Writers constructed a six-episode story arc as the Flintstones prepared for the baby's arrival throughout Wilma's six-week pregnancy, which the audience

Fred Flintstone float at the 2017 Chicago Thanksgiving Parade (Ganeshkumar Durai/ Shutterstock).

is led to believe was not necessarily planned by the couple. The introduction of this arc officially began the transition from episodic adult or general audience sitcom to a serial family comedy, which slowed the pace of the stories in episodes and relied on simpler humor for the sake of children drawn into the living room by the arrival of Pebbles and the family focused promotion of the third season.[10]

Hanna-Barbera premiered its third prime time sitcom on ABC in the fall of 1962, relying on the time displacement formula that made *The Flintstones* an instant hit. Instead of the Stone Age, the new sitcom took place in the future and starred a whole family, hoping to capitalize on the same licensing and merchandising revenue that *The Flintstones* pursued through the introduction of Pebbles. The Jetsons were a traditional nuclear family, with George the male breadwinner, Jane the "housewife," their teeny bopper daughter Janet, and Elroy, the curious pre-pubescent son. The show was sponsored by 3M and its Scotch Tape, which fit well with the family audience and made sense since it was the first Hanna-Barbera sitcom to prominently feature a white-collar office setting. Scotch Tape's newest product, the permanently transparent Magic Tape, was introduced in 1961 and utilized the futuristic setting in the sponsored advertising with the program.[11]

Like its prehistoric counterpart, *The Jetsons* relied on semantic humor based on anachronistic space puns and the visualization of what the future could look like in 100 years if we maintained the same sensibilities.[12] In 1961, Warner Bros. Cartoon Studio closed and a few of their animators were hired at Hanna-Barbera, which contributed to the style and quality of *The Jetsons* and other Hanna-Barbera productions. The animators' ability to represent a far off but imaginable future continues to be utilized fifty-five years later to visualize a time where Space Age styles, technologies, and infrastructure have altered human life and societal operations and expectations.[13]

The reception for *The Jetsons* was arguably more disappointing than *Top Cat*. The show had tested higher with focus groups than any of the studio's previous productions, and Barbera thought the space theme would be an even bigger draw than its Stone Age counterpart as the Space Race increased in intensity throughout the late 1950s and 1960s.[14] Similar to *Top Cat*, ABC scheduled *The Jetsons* against more established live-action shows chasing the same demographic, families. *The Jetsons* aired on Sundays at 7:30, led in by repeats of *Father Knows Best* and opposite *Dennis the Menace* on CBS and *Disney's Wonderful World of Color* on NBC. *Dennis the Menace* was a top 20 show the previous three seasons and was led in by the top 20 *Lassie* while Disney's anthology series was one of the most popular with families, placing in the top 25 in the ratings throughout the 1960s. The animated sitcom could not compete with the larger networks' offerings, ending the season outside the top 30 and without a renewal offer from ABC.[15]

While *The Jetsons* struggled in early prime time on Sunday, *The Flintstones* continued its successful run on Friday nights, placing in the top 30 for the third straight season. ABC was also the last network to introduce color in September 1962, so even though all the episodes of *The Flintstones* were produced in color, the show was broadcast in black and white throughout the first two seasons.[16] Audiences did decline throughout the season; many teenagers and younger adults originally tuned into the show throughout the first two and a half seasons because of the unique comedic opportunities presented through animation, but they slowly left the show as the humor became more family-oriented. This was offset by the growing merchandising revenue and increased child audience that was tuning into the show with their parents. Products featuring Pebbles, Dino, and the rest of *The Flintstones* cast flooded stores from cereals and candies, to dolls and playsets. The continued solid ratings and merchandising bonanza provided by *The Flintstones* kept Hanna-Barbera in regularly scheduled prime time for at least another season.[17]

Anthropomorphic Stars Signal a New Direction

The telefilm *Magilla Gorilla: Here Comes a Star* was a pilot for Hanna-Barbera's new series, *The Magilla Gorilla Show*, returning to the strategy of naming each franchise after a "star" character after many affiliates had a hard time marketing *The Hanna Barbera New Cartoon Show*. Magilla was joined by *Punkin Puss & Mushmouse*, a "hillbilly" cat and mouse pair who often fought, similar to the Hatfields and McCoys, trying to capitalize on the increase of rural-focused comedies on television like *The Beverly Hillbillies*. The third segment, *Ricochet Rabbit and Droop-a-Long*, was a parody of *Gunsmoke* that revived many of its gags and puns from *Quick Draw McGraw*. The series premiered in January 1963 soon after the film and was an instant hit, reaching the top spot in the syndication ratings in most markets, premiering in the afternoon in many major metropolitan areas like New York. This was partly due to the heavy marketing campaign spearheaded by the show's sponsor, Ideal Toys, which signed on to sponsor two Hanna-Barbera shows in 1964–1965 after producing many of the popular *Flintstones* toys and dolls the previous year. As one of the first shows targeting children to receive direct sponsorship from a toy company, the partnership blurred the line between commercial and program. This merging of program and advertising came under widespread scrutiny from organizations like Action for Children's Television throughout the 1960s.[18]

The eponymous star was the most enduring character of the series, although as a whole the overall plot, storylines, and humor were redundant for fans of past shows *Huckleberry Hound* and *Yogi Bear*, both of which were sold into syndication and still aired regularly in most markets. In the new series, Magilla lives in a pet store, owned by Mr. Peebles, who is desperate to sell the gorilla, slashing the price for the animal in the opening theme and throughout the series. Most of the episodes in the initial series feature Magilla finding a home only to be returned to the store after either an unprepared owner is overwhelmed by taking care of the gorilla or, more often, the people who obtain Magilla only need his services for a short time, like thieves or football coaches, hoping to exploit his strength.[19]

The Push to Saturday Morning

The next season, Hanna-Barbera only had two shows in production as the studio adjusted to shifts in the television animation landscape. It was becoming evident that adult animation in prime time might not be the most profitable platform for their productions. As more animation was produced and adapted from film to television it was clear that there was more content than time slots made available for cartoons by the networks. More syndicated animation was broadcast on weekday afternoons, but the popularity of game shows and soap operas, and the higher sponsorship fees they commanded, limited the time slots local network affiliates were willing to dedicate to cartoons. Weekend mornings were a haven for children's programming on radio even before World War II, which continued as television evolved throughout the 1950s. Syndicated animation began to occupy Saturday and Sunday mornings as networks and distributors realized that children will rewatch the same animated program repeatedly, a fact that aided in

MGM's decision to rely on reissued cartoons after 1958. The Baby Boom also provided large young audiences and would continue to produce new audiences for animation and children's programming through the 1980s as children of the Boom, and later their children, continued to grow up with cartoons, often being introduced to the programs by older siblings and parents.[20]

By 1963, most of the shows and characters no longer in production had found a second home on weekend mornings even though shows like *Top Cat* and even *Quick Draw McGraw* were originally produced for more mature audiences. Children still loved the anthropomorphic characters, puns, and slapstick humor, leading to long runs in syndication even for programs that did not do well in the original runs. This was especially true for *The Jetsons*, as reruns from the sitcom's only season premiered on Saturday morning the fall after their broadcast on ABC and were an instant hit with younger viewers who appreciated the space puns and writers' take on the future, which they may have missed while watching the other programming available in prime time the previous season.[21]

The Jetsons' success on Saturday morning actually created a number of conventions that informed Hanna-Barbera's style and approach to producing cartoons specifically for Saturday morning.[22] The show's catchy theme song, which lasted over a minute when including sponsors, became one of the most recognizable in the history of television while also serving an important practical role in the show's production that was consistently replicated in future animated programs. Hoyt Curtin, who joined Hanna-Barbera as the musical director through *The Ruff and Reddy Show* composed the song and was responsible for most of the memorable themes and scores for the studio's many series between 1957 and his retirement in 1986, although Ted Nichols filled the role 1965–1972. Curtin's theme also helped the studio stay culturally relevant, with the music often reflecting the popular musical styles at the time.

Creating lengthy opening and closing themes actually cut down on the required animation for each show, with the opening and closing credits filling close to 10 percent of the show's running time. *The Flintstones* had an instrumental theme before the well-known, longer opening "Meet the Flintstones" was introduced during the third season, several weeks after *The Jetsons* and its theme song premiered.[23]

In the human-dominated world occupied by *The Jetsons*, the most popular character with this young audience was actually the dog, Astro. The Great Dane, with his overwhelming love and affection for the family, his pacifist demeanor, and his ability to talk, albeit replacing all first letters with R's, was the main draw for many young fans watching the show on Saturday morning and was prominently featured in much of the merchandising connected to the now-syndicated series. Don Messick provided the voice of Astro, developing the model for many of the talking dog characters that became an identifying feature of Hanna-Barbera's animated output. Considering the expense of animation, *The Jetsons* also served as evidence of the value of animated programs, both original and reruns, in syndication, which motivated studios and distributors to continue to produce and disseminate animation, since struggles in initial broadcasts or exhibition could be offset by numerous rebroadcasts, merchandising, and sales to local affiliates.[24]

Coincidentally, as *The Jetsons* found a second life in syndication, *The Flintstones* continued to drop in the ratings. ABC moved the show to Thursdays at 7:30 p.m., hoping the earlier start time could draw in younger children who may have been put to bed by 8:30 p.m. Fridays and possibly force their parents to also watch the program. The program also changed its animation style, featuring softer lines, more color, and smoother animation that became synonymous with their children's programming. From a ratings standpoint, this strategy failed as the show fell out of the top 30 for the first time at the 7:30 p.m. time slot with lead-ins from less popular local programming also contributing to the declining ratings.[25] Hanna-Barbera continued to expand the program's merchandising empire as producers introduced Bamm-Bamm to the Rubble family. The adoption was aimed at boys who would not play with the stereotypically feminine Pebble toys and dolls. Later research on toys and play showed that girls were willing to play with toys marketed toward boys but not vice versa.[26] Other studies also showed non-white children actually preferred white dolls over dolls that were a closer representation of their own aesthetics or skin tones.[27] Both of these studies supported the continued reliance on white male animated characters, adding an economical dimension to why animation has been dominated by white male characters, since they could be sold to all gender and racial demographics, unlike characters representing other identities.

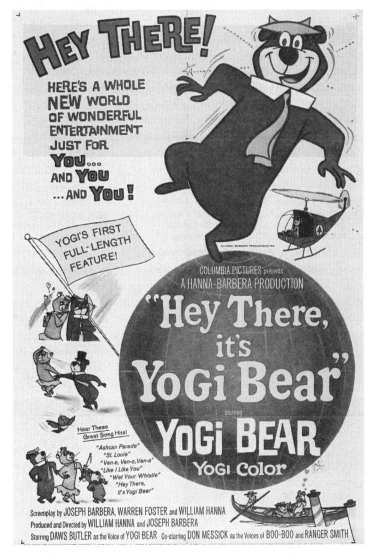

Poster for *Hey There, It's Yogi Bear*. The first full-length theatrical film from Hanna-Barbera was released June 3, 1964 (PictureLux/The Hollywood Archive/Alamy Stock Photo).

Hanna-Barbera released its first feature length film, *Hey There, It's Yogi Bear* in the summer of 1964, where Yogi and Boo Boo save Cindy after she is sent to the zoo. The following fall the studio added two more shows as *The Flintstones* and *Magilla Gorilla* continued their runs on ABC and syndication, respectively.[28] *The Jetsons* marked the studio's last attempt at developing a family sitcom in conjunction with a network, instead focusing on different genres within animation as Hanna-Barbera continued to introduce a consistent stream of new characters to children's television and syndication.[29]

Animating Ideology in the Traditional Family Sitcom

The Flintstones and *The Jetsons* are two of the most popular and successful properties for Hanna-Barbera, forming a legacy on both the novelty of being the only two animated human-based sitcoms on prime time television through the 1980s and their long runs as Saturday morning mainstays. The animation may have seemed novel, but they were modeled after traditional sitcoms and family comedies seen throughout the 1950s and 1960s which contained, and reinforced, expected gender roles and family structures. Even the first two seasons of *The Flintstones*, which only featured the two couples, had Fred and Barney working in the quarry while Wilma and Betty were expected to maintain the household as housewives, and later, mothers. Their work is extremely important but is often overlooked because it does not earn an official salary like digging holes while riding on the back of a dinosaur. Reinforcing these gender expectations were the episodes in which Fred or Barney is expected to care for the baby without the mother, the stereotypical childcare expert of the pair. In the first episode after Pebbles was introduced, Fred is expected to care for his daughter with the help of the mother-in-law but asks her to leave after their contentious relationship boils over, introducing a second gender-based plotline popular in family sitcoms, the critical mother-in-law. Fred, unsurprisingly, is unable to care for his daughter without the help of a woman, reinforcing his role as a breadwinner and Wilma's (and her mother's) role as caretaker.[30]

The traditional and sexist stereotypes connected to housewives or those whose primary work occurs in the home were even more rampant in *The Jetsons* where the marketing material for the futuristic sitcom described the female lead Jane as "typical housewife, who spends more than she earns."[31] This is supported in the opening theme where she takes George's wallet to go shopping after he offers her a single bill. The fact that all of Jane's work is seemingly automatic, and she apparently watches soap operas throughout the day, further undermines the domestic work of all parents, but especially mothers. Jane's supposed laziness is featured more than the fact that George makes six figures to work less than ten hours a week, even lamenting that he cannot buy enough on his salary.[32]

Janet, the daughter, is portrayed as a teeny bopper with few interests outside following celebrities and listening to music, while her younger brother is busy with schoolwork and various technical toys, including the children in the gender stereotypes perpetuated by the show. *The Flintstones* also contained stereotypes through the portrayal of the children that were added in the third and fourth seasons. Pebbles was naturally born of *The Flintstones*, and although she had her precocious moments, she was a fairly typical sitcom daughter. Bamm-Bamm, on the other hand, was adopted by the Rubbles after a prolonged custody battle with a wealthier couple who was prepared to adopt the boy until they became pregnant and gave the child to the Rubbles. Bamm-Bamm has super strength and is often seen destroying objects to the dismay of the Rubbles. This portrayal of adopted children inherently having issues or destructive tendencies is often overlooked, and since the stereotype is partly backed by the reality that adopted children do have a more difficult time related to their behavior and experiences, it is a stigma about which many children who go through the adoption process are very aware.[33]

Similar to the rest of television, particularly sitcoms, people of color remained mainly invisible; however, while most other sitcoms were set in contemporary times when neighborhoods and many aspects of daily life continued to be segregated, they did not portray an all-white past and future that *The Flintstones* and *The Jetsons* projected throughout their runs. *The Flintstones* only featured one character of color who never spoke, merely displaying darker skin, and was seen in the background of an episode where Fred leads a Cave Scout organization to an international conference.[34] This communicates that white people created civilization and, considering they lived in prehistoric America, that people of European descent actually develop the first societies in America without the presence of any indigenous groups or people, reinforcing white ownership of the land and supporting rhetoric that they are solely responsible for human progress.[35]

This white-led progress is further reinforced by *The Jetsons*, which portrays a nearly exclusively white future where those occupying Orbit City live in raised housing and rely on flying vehicles for transports. Along with the aesthetics and style of the show, which were made to look futuristic by modeling the homes after the Space Needle, the series also highlights the advances in aviation and expectations for how future civilizations will live. It was not until the show was reincarnated in the 1980s that it was explained that the houses were built above a world polluted by humanity. Considering only white people are occupying the high-rise homes, where are the other populations on Earth? It can only be assumed that they are either left to languish on the surface of earth that has been inundated with pollutants or have been expelled from Orbit City somehow. It is also important to note that most of the working class occupations have been automated with robots doing everything from housekeeping to manufacturing, which is increasingly becoming a reality for many working class individuals throughout the 21st century.[36] These shows also premiered during a period of significant "white flight" in American history as what was perceived as urban decay helped support continued white suburbanization in the country along with the segregation of neighborhoods. *The Jetsons* in particular exemplified this desire of white people to "escape" these conditions into homogeneous neighborhoods where decay, or more importantly non-whiteness, was not seen.[37] Today, as more cities gentrify, they are dealing with the racial and economic complications related to largely white, young, middle class individuals and families moving into neighborhoods formerly occupied by populations that are non-white and/or living at lower socioeconomic levels than the new invading population. Building above these communities, with new more expensive "modern" housing replacing single-family homes, can be linked to similar construction currently going on in urban areas that are resulting in higher rents and costs of living that displace the populations that have maintained these areas and survived for decades as the invading populations lived in the suburbs.[38] The two series bookend white progress from its apparent origins where white humans have dominated so heavily that even the animals submit and serve them as appliances to a future where technology and apparently unlimited resources made available to a select few have created a white futuristic utopia. These issues with representation only increase with the inclusion of more human characters in later series since race could not be visually veiled by the characters' non-human identity.

Another ideology that is bookended by the past and future portrayals of civilization is capitalist ideology supported by the status achieved through conspicuous consumption by the characters on the show. *The Flintstones* may live in prehistoric times, but they adhere to 20th century trends and practices as the growing consumer market and suburbanization are represented by the animal-powered appliances, automobiles, and the stone cookie cutter homes. They are constantly looking for the next new technological advancement, whether it be a garbage disposal or record player, to make their lives easier and keep up with the possessions of others in Bedrock, never questioning the consumer market created by the need to constantly update appliances and other technologies. Fred's constant desire for newer or bigger items like cars and televisions can also be considered a display of masculinity as he looks for ways to distinguish himself from other men, particularly neighbors and coworkers, with similar statuses and salaries.[39] *The Jetsons* supported these same ideologies by portraying a future where lives are made exponentially easier by the complete inundation of technology on the family and the rest of society. *The Jetsons* and the denizens of Orbit City are unable to live without these technologies, and unlike the appliances in *The Flintstones*, the presence of the robotic aids feels natural and does not communicate the same level of satire as its prehistoric counterpart. This also limited *The Jetsons* to the same sitcom tropes and humor that had been seen on television for more than a decade and may have contributed to its low ratings during its original broadcast during primetime on ABC.[40]

In some interpretations, other Hanna-Barbera shows featuring anthropomorphic animals also reinforced racist ideologies and supported segregation. Similar to Yogi Bear and Top Cat, Wally Gator has to live in the world in which various restrictions and expectations are placed upon him by the humans who oversee the world in which he lives. However, rather than dealing with a park ranger in a large national park, Wally lives in captivity in a zoo and often escapes just for the opportunity to see the outside world. At times, he is captured and sent back to enclosure, but Wally often returns to his captive life voluntarily, seeming to find comfort in the routine and predictability of life at the zoo. Whether it is the identification of Jellystone Park as the home for Yogi, or the constant reinforcement of the idea that Top Cat and his friends do not belong in the alley through constant reminders and expulsion from Officer Dibble, Wally represents a line of Hanna-Barbera programs where an animal character must realize where he belongs in a human-dominated world, which is some type of captivity where their actions can be monitored, controlled, and adjusted as needed.[41]

Magilla takes this animal living in a human-controlled world theme to another level when the gorilla's condition is considered. Rather than being constricted by an institution like a zoo or a national park, Magilla is actually for sale in a pet store with a white owner desperate to sell the giant primate. In each episode Magilla is sold to another person often looking to utilize his strength or abilities for profit, exploiting the primate before returning him to the store. Unfortunately, the connections with the enslavement of Africans are only strengthened by the use of a gorilla to portray Magilla considering the racist artwork and media that imagined African Americans as subhuman primates.[42] Later content featuring Magilla no longer had him confined to the pet store, most likely due to the limited plotlines that could be cultivated from him living in a pet store rather than possibly insensitive connections to the character's condition.[43]

Many of these issues and misrepresentations continued to persist in Hanna-Barbera content the rest of the decade. In fact, even more groups would become subjects of the studio's white male European interpretation of history and society as Hanna-Barbera explored different genres, themes, and plotlines in an attempt to move away from the sitcom format and maintain a presence in primetime. This growth produced the first animated dramas by the studio and series set outside the United States, leading to new problems for the studio related to misrepresentation and unquestioned support of capitalism and American/Western exceptionalism.

4

1964–1969:
Equal Representation,
Where Are You?

A New Time Slot, a Younger Audience, but the Same Representational Issues

The 1964–1965 season was on the horizon, and Hanna-Barbera only had two shows in production returning from the previous season. The primetime disappointments of *Top Cat* and *The Jetsons* and lukewarm reception of *The New Hanna-Barbera Cartoon Show* motivated the studio to consider other genres for their cartoon shows while expanding their offerings for Saturday morning, which was increasing its position as a haven for children's cartoons. The studio increased its production output to four to six shows a year, focusing again on character creation across multiple shows rather than supporting larger, more complex series or franchises, like *The Flintstones*. Even with mediocre first runs of some of its sitcoms, Hanna-Barbera's success and the licensing opportunities presented by its partners had quickly established the studio as the most reliable producer of television animation in the industry, an expansion that led to structural and operational changes for the studio, the effects of which trickled down to the content.

Animating Adventure

Hanna-Barbera continued to work with ABC, developing a prime time and a weekend show for the network, selling ABC, and other broadcasters, programming specifically produced for Saturday morning broadcasts. The prime time program was the studio's first drama, while the cartoons aimed at younger audiences continued to utilize funny anthropomorphic animal characters. The productions included more adventure themes than the earlier shows, marking the beginning of Hanna-Barbera's shift away from creating sitcom parodies, as writers and animators looked toward different media and genres for inspiration beyond the family comedy, which was becoming stale.[1] The drama marked an expansion of styles as it attracted more artists from other animation companies and even comics, leading to more media entities to request their services as the studio's reputation moved beyond comedy.[2]

Hanna-Barbera started development on an adaptation of the popular radio series *Jack Armstrong, All American Boy* about a globe-trotting teenager who follows his uncle, an industrial capitalist, around the world taking on adventures while his uncle conducts business. Animators began drawing the series, utilizing limited animation but creating more realistic backgrounds and character designs than in their previous series. Comic book artist Doug Wildey approached Joseph Barbera after several years of freelance work, which included several Western-themed comics and work on the animated series *Space Angel*. Barbera appreciated Wildey's designs and asked him to create some initial artwork for the *Jack Armstrong* adaptation. General Mills, who created Armstrong and still owned the rights to the series and character, refused to allow Hanna-Barbera to use the character without compensation, so the studio asked Wildey to create a series that had similar plotlines and themes, but different enough that General Mills could not claim infringement.[3]

The design and approach to the animation were not dramatically different from what other artists had utilized, but *Jonny Quest* was truly visually unique for the time. Anthropomorphic animals and unrealistic or "cartoonish" animation dominated television, and more realistic animation was seen almost exclusively in film due to the cost and different expectations of each audience. Hanna-Barbera was able to transfer limited animation to an action-adventure show, which often has more movement and complex scenes than a common sitcom. Animators still limited character movement, but to increase the dramatic feel, they used a more dynamic score than previous shows. Music was clearly a victim of the lower budgets the duo faced when they moved from MGM to television, but it was important for this series to communicate the serious and dramatic tone of the show. They also developed new strategies to show action, like having characters slide into frame after running to show movement without using different cels. Wildey also brought in comic artist Alex Toth to help with the animation for *Jonny Quest*, who went on to do the artwork for several of the studio's action series throughout the 1960s.[4]

The show's eponymous character was an eleven-year-old boy who follows his father, Dr. Benton Quest, a scientist and government contractor, on adventures as he researches, and often protects, American mineral and technological interests around the world.[5] They are accompanied by Dr. Quest's bodyguard, Race Bannon, who also acts as Jonny's protector and tutor. Bannon is a special agent working for the show's equivalent of the CIA, Intelligence, not only protecting the Quests but also to ensuring they are not captured for the purpose of assisting the enemy. Jonny's brother Hadji was a Kolkatan orphan before being adopted by Dr. Quest when the boy saves the doctor's life after a lecture. Hadji was trained in judo by an American Marine and seems to have mystic powers which he uses to assist his father and brother in their missions. They are all joined by Bandit, the Quests' French bulldog and one of the few non-anthropomorphic dogs created by Hanna-Barbera. Wildey actually wanted a more exotic pet, like a parrot or monkey, but Barbera specifically requested the Quest family have a dog, since it would be easier to market as a toy. The series was set in the near future, where hydrofoils, hovercrafts, jetpacks, and lasers are commonplace in international diplomacy, peacekeeping, and battles.[6]

Jonny Quest premiered in September 1964 on Friday night at 7:30 p.m. as ABC continued to experiment with the time slot, which lacked the consistent national evening news lead-in NBC and CBS had in their schedules. Both networks had expanded their evening newscast to thirty minutes by this time, while ABC's news program languished in third as affiliates broadcast the national news program at different times before and after prime time programming. *Jonny Quest* was an instant hit for ABC and Hanna-Barbera, with many children and teenagers drawn to the futuristic animated action series, a first for a regularly scheduled show on a network. Barbera had requested the show have a

James Bond feel, specifically citing *Dr. No* as an inspiration for the program. Adults and critics also appreciated science fiction storylines two years before *Star Trek* premiered. Halfway through the season, the series was moved to Thursday to take advantage of the growing popularity of *Jonny Quest*, switching days with *The Flintstones*, whose ratings continued to decline.[7]

The Unstable Business of Animation

The other premiere of the fall of 1964, *The Peter Potamus Show*, was a package show that continued the studio's reliance on anthropomorphic animals due to their marketability. In all the series on the program, the stars replace humans in various occupations or adaptations of earlier works. Peter Potamus, whose voice is an imitation of comedian Joe E. Brown provided by Butler, is accompanied by So-So the monkey on their world adventures in their hot air balloon, which can also travel through time. Butler used a similar imitation for Lippy the Lion. Although *Peter Potamus* increased the suspension of reality from previous shows by featuring a time-traveling, globe-hopping hippopotamus, the program represented a transition away from the "captive animal in a human controlled world" trope. The second segment of the program, *Breezly and Sneezly*, was a replica of *Yogi Bear* featuring a polar bear and seal who plan schemes to break into a local army camp, which helped to maintain some connection with the captivity trope as the two animals must deal with the intrusion of the camp and the fact they are unwelcome in the area claimed by (white) humans. The third segment, *Yippee, Yappee, and Yahooey*, was a parody of the Three Musketeers starring the eponymous sheepdogs in the role of the swashbuckling heroes. Butler provided the voice of Yahooey, imitating the voice of Jerry Lewis, another famous actor on the decline at the time. *Peter Potamus* was also the second show sponsored by Ideal Toys, which led to heavy marketing of the characters and toys as Hanna-Barbera prepared to premiere the series. Like *Magilla Gorilla*, they even include a reference to the toy company in the show's theme song, exemplifying Hanna-Barbera's continued cooperation with sponsors. In 1966, *Peter Potamus* and *Magilla Gorilla* were sold into syndication together, furthering the trend in which segments were frequently switched and rerun as new package programs.[8]

Hanna and Barbera had firmly establish themselves as the top television animators in the United States, as Disney continued to concentrate on theatrical film and Warner had closed down its cartoon studio, contracting its animation production to DePatie-Freleng in 1964, a production company founded by two former Warner employees who had just won an Oscar for the first film of their series, *The Pink Panther*.[9] In a relatively short period the studio had created a number of popular characters and series, proving the profitability of television animation and highlighting the unique opportunities presented by the genre, especially among younger audiences, like repeated exposure to content and the ability to advertise products connected to the characters during the program. By 1965, Hanna and Barbera had offers from several larger studios, including Universal, expressing interest in buying the television animation production company. Universal was located next door to Hanna-Barbera's offices, occupying the 400 acres adjacent to the animation studio's six. As they waited for offers from Universal and other companies, Hanna-Barbera developed two new shows for the 1965–1966 season. They also received news from ABC that *Jonny Quest* was going to be cancelled, while *The Flintstones* was being renewed for one last season. The network felt the complaints about the violence on *Jonny Quest* were not worth the investment especially after the show's ratings dropped when ABC moved the action series to Thursdays opposite *The Munsters*. The switch did help *The Flintstones* increase its ratings slightly and earn its sixth season, which also helped to increase the quantity of episodes that were later sold into syndication.[10]

An official offer never came from Universal as a financial downturn changed its economic priorities, but Taft Broadcasting, a growing media conglomerate, stepped in with an offer of $12,000,000 for the studio with the ability for Hanna and Barbera to maintain creative control of their studio. Screen Gems also made an offer, but it included less money and loss of oversight for the founders of the studio. Taft also sweetened the deal by offering to hire its agent, Sy Fisher, away from Screen Gems. Unlike Universal, which was still distributing Walter Lantz cartoons at the time, Taft had no experience overseeing animation or even television production. This led to very little interference from the company, which owned several radio and television stations at the time of the acquisition. The deal was officially delayed a year as Harry Cohn's family, who still held a stake in the studio from his time at Columbia, sued over what they felt was an undervaluation of the company. The studio had to scramble to find distributors for many of its cartoons through 1968 as the lawsuit was settled and they were fully integrated into the corporate structure at Taft, which also shared distribution responsibilities with Screen Gems, Warner Bros., and various other co-producers.[11]

During this era of transition, Hanna-Barbera began working closer with NBC producing its first Saturday morning series for the network, the hour-long *Atom Ant/Secret Squirrel Show*, which was in essence two shows of three segments each packaged together debuting in the fall of 1965 through a telefilm pilot. Atom Ant was a superhero ant who derived his powers from atomized glasses, as Hanna Barbera began to capitalize on the superhero craze that was growing throughout the 1960s. The general plot involving an understaffed police force needing help from a superhero, and many of the episode storylines, were borrowed from Batman.[12] Hal Seeger's *The Milton the Monster* show, which premiered on ABC a few weeks later, contained a series *Fearless Fly*, starring an insect who also obtains his powers from special glasses, crowding the super powered insect marketplace.[13] The other title character parodied the numerous secret agent shows and films of the time, like the *James Bond* series, earning the designation of Agent 000 on the show. *Secret Squirrel* actually debuted six days before Mel Brooks' *Get Smart* premiered, a show it is often compared.[14] The *Atom Ant* half of the show also included *Precious Pupp*, the first of many series to feature a mischievous, snickering dog. The pup was joined by Granny Sweet, who was typically oblivious to her companion's actions, similar to Granny in the *Sylvester and Tweety* series of cartoons. The third segment, *Hillbilly Bears*, starred the Ruggs; Paw, Maw, Floral, and Shag in a direct parody of *The Beverly Hillbillies*, drawing from the stereotypical and even derogatory idea of a gun-toting hillbilly, complete with occasionally incomprehensible Appalachian accents, banjos, and constant feuds with the neighbors. The *Secret Squirrel* side also included *Squiddly Diddly*, a show very much like Wally Gator, where a squid is constantly trying to escape his human-forced captivity to see the outside world before being forced back into his tank at the aquarium. The third series, *Winsome Witch*, was the first from the studio to star a woman in the title role, both on screen and in terms of voice talent, which was provided by Jean Vander Pyl, the voice of Wilma Flintstone. Winnie is an inept witch, who often tries to help but her confusion leads to mistakes and humorous situations that are ultimately resolved at the end, similar to *Bewitched* (1964) and *I Dream of Jeannie* (1965). Many of the storylines in this segment had Winsome helping fairy tale characters, but its position between a

Joseph Barbera (left) and William Hanna with Atom Ant and Secret Squirrel in a 1965 promotional photograph for NBC (AF Archive/Alamy Stock Photo).

superhero and spy parody made the female-led sitcom spoof feel out of place. This was the last show distributed by Screen Gems, which was forced out of the partnership with Hanna-Barbera due to the purchase of the studio by Taft.[15]

For the Kids? Action, Adventure, and Nostalgia on Saturday Morning

The other series credited to Hanna-Barbera productions that premiered in 1965 was *Sinbad Jr. and His Magic Belt*, the first co-production for the animation studio. The series consisted of three five-minute shorts and was originally created by Sam Singer for American International Television, but Hanna-Barbera was asked to come in and improve the quality during production. As the title suggests, the eponymous star is the son of the famous sailor who finds a magic belt that gives him superpowers. Hanna-Barbera's influence was seen most in Salty, his sarcastic parrot companion, continuing the tradition of funny talking animals in their productions, both as stars and companions to human characters.[16] Along with *Yippee, Yappee, and Yahooey* the season before, *Sinbad Jr.* is an example of the studio's increased production of classic literature adaptations, rather than relying completely on inspiration from contemporary media, a strategy Disney had been profiting from for decades.[17]

The 1965–1966 season also marked the last for *The Flintstones*, which found a home on Saturday morning the next fall after the premiere of Hanna-Barbera's second feature-length film, *The Man Called Flintstone*, which served as an unofficial series finale. One character who did not appear in the film is The Great Gazoo, who was introduced midway through the season and is seen as a desperate attempt to attract viewers to the declining series. To further establish the marketing of *The Flintstones* reruns as a children's show, Miles Laboratory started producing the famous Flintstones Chewable Vitamins in 1968.[18]

In the spring of 1966 ABC also broadcast the Hanna-Barbera produced *Alice in Wonderland or What's a Nice Kid Doing in a Place Like This* featuring songs written by *Bye Bye Birdie*'s Charles Strouse and Lee Adams. The animation industry has long relied on classic literature for inspiration particularly Disney, who released its own *Alice in Wonderland* in 1951. Hanna-Barbera may have been testing its ability to produce suc-

cessful full-length films not connected with its television franchises, although they did not completely leave out its television stars featuring cameos by Fred Flintstone and Barney Rubble in the role of the Caterpillar. The animated film featured a number of voice cameos including Sammy Davis, Jr., and Zsa Zsa Gabor. Sponsored by Rexall and Coca-Cola, the film was a modern take on the classic story, with Alice following her dog into the television introducing her to all the characters of Wonderland. The film and music were largely overlooked, which may have been a result of the inability to include the stars of the film in the soundtrack due to contractual and budget restrictions, including Sammy Davis, Jr., who played a beatnik Cheshire Cat but was replaced by Scatman Crothers on the recordings.[19]

During the 1966–1967 season, Hanna-Barbera had four new shows on the air. The first, another co-production, was produced with Larry Harmon, who was better known as Bozo the Clown. *The Laurel and Hardy Show* was one of a collection of attempts trying to capitalize off of the growing nostalgia trend for entertainment from the 1930s and 1940s. Both Stan

The popular children's vitamin that Miles Laboratories (bought by Bayer in 1979) debuted in 1968 (Roman Tiraspolsky/Shutterstock.com).

Laurel and Oliver Hardy had passed at the time, so Harmon and Jim MacGeorge provided the voices for the animated adaptation of their act and films. The show had been in the conceptual stages for six years after Harmon had purchased their likenesses for merchandise, but the series was not produced until Hanna-Barbera and documentary film director David L. Wolper became involved, with the show premiering a year after Hardy's death. The series featured the duo finding themselves in precarious situations similar to their older shorts or the Three Stooges, who starred in their own animated series the previous season.[20]

Frankenstein Jr. and the Impossibles premiered on CBS the same fall as *Laurel and Hardy* debuted in syndication. Both segments were parodies of superhero shows at the time, with the first borrowing very lightly from the Mary Shelley novel. Frankenstein Jr. was a younger version of the monster, not the scientist, who fights villains with various more modern components like laser eyes and rocket boots, similar to the improvements made to the Six Million Dollar Man which premiered eight years later. He also had access to an arsenal of futuristic weapons and had the help of his handler, Buzz Conway. In the second segment, The Impossibles was a Beatles-like band used as a cover for three superheroes, Fluid Man, Coil-Man, and Multi-Man, who battled bad guys like the Fiendish Fiddler, and other parodies of villains from comics and the recently premiered *Batman* series. The segment quickly found itself under the scrutiny of children's advocacy groups due to the violence. These groups had a growing influence on what was considered acceptable content, targeting shows with violent and other content seen as inappropriate.[21]

The two other new shows to premiere this season were also adventure shows, the first of which was less comedic than *Frankenstein Jr. and the Impossibles*. *Space Ghost and Dino Boy* was created for CBS featuring two segments, *Space Ghost* and *Dino Boy in the Lost Valley*. *Space Ghost* was a fairly standard superhero series, but it was the first completely original superhero created by Hanna-Barbera. As the name suggests, it also tried to capitalize on the continued interest in space travel as Space Ghost battled aliens and creatures from other planets throughout the series. Although it was largely overlooked at the time it is still recognized by animation fans due to the artwork of Alex Toth on the series.[22] Dino Boy, a young child who parachutes out of a crashing plane into a prehistoric South American valley while his parents remained on board, was another series that tried to put an unsupervised adolescent in the role of hero, like *Jonny Quest* or *Sinbad Jr.*[23]

The second series, the *Space Kidettes*, was created for NBC and featured children as astronauts who went on various space adventures. The marketing material for the show promoted the show as *The Little Rascals* set in outer space, trying to draw the younger four- to eight-year-old demographic NBC sought to bring to their Saturday morning programming. The show was more accurately inspired by Peter Pan, with the Kidettes following a treasure map as they battled Captain Skyhook and his companion, Static.[24]

The last project that debuted for Hanna-Barbera in 1966–1967 was by far the most ambitious, a live-action/animation hybrid adaptation of *Jack and the Beanstalk*. The film starred Gene Kelly, whom they worked with while at MGM for the dance sequence featuring the actor-dancer and the animated Jerry Mouse in the 1945 film *Anchors Aweigh*. Kelly helped secure $400,000 from NBC for the one-hour film, which was about a quarter of the amount per minute compared to the *Anchors Aweigh* scene more than twenty years earlier. The studio struggled to finish the film under budget, and Kelly threatened to block the film from release in anger over the quality. NBC, for which Hanna-Barbera had produced several series previously, disagreed and released the film, winning an Emmy for best children's program. The film quickly became dated visually, but it was one of the first hybrid films produced exclusively for television.[25]

Quantity Dominates Quality

The next season was by far the most prolific for Hanna-Barbera. After the Taft deal was finalized the duo was able to concentrate on production, leading to seven new shows premiering in the 1967–1968 season. *The Abbott and Costello Cartoon Show* was the only comedy series of the seven and had a similar nostalgic concept as the *Laurel and Hardy Show*, although it did have Bud Abbott voicing his own character, providing work for the struggling comedian. *Samson and Goliath* was a series loosely based on Samson of biblical fame starring a young boy and his dog who travel across the country helping people. Young Samson, which is also the alternative title for the series, is able to gain super strength when he touches his gold bracelets together. Like *Space Kidettes* it was distributed by General Mills' ad agency Dancer Fitzgerald Sample, and sponsored by the consumer food conglomerate. It was later renamed *Young Samson*, to avoid confusion with the Christian stop-motion series *Davey and Goliath*, which premiered in 1961.[26]

Moby Dick and Mighty Mightor also premiered that season with the first segment, *Moby Dick*, featuring two teenage boys who, after being saved by the whale, fight undersea danger with Moby Dick and their pet seal Scooby.[27] *Mighty Mightor*, in spite of getting second billing, was featured twice in each episode of the series. The segment stars a teenage caveman who receives a magical club that gives him superpowers which he uses to protect his village. The premise has some similarities to the Norse mythological figure Thor and his hammer Mjölnir, which premiered in Marvel Comics in 1962.[28]

The characters in *Moby Dick and Mighty Mightor* were designed by Toth. That same season he also helped create the *Herculoids* about a group of humans charged with protecting the primitive planet of Quasar and all of its citizens, a series that continued to add complexity to space science fiction with societal commentary later popularized by *Star Trek* and *Star Wars*. *The Herculoids* was a huge hit and led CBS to cancel another one of his creations, *Space Ghost*, to put more money toward the new space series.

Toth also designed the characters for the adaptation of the comic book series, *Fantastic Four*, which premiered on ABC, the only series Hanna-Barbera produced for the network that year, and was scheduled opposite of *The Herculoids*. The adaptation was largely overlooked but it is notable that it is one of the few productions featuring Marvel characters not currently owned by Disney. On CBS, *Birdman and the Galaxy Trio* was another Toth superhero creation and was scheduled against *Moby Dick and the Mighty Mightor*. Birdman, the alter ego of Ray Randall, fights crime with the power of flight and the ability to use solar energy as a weapon with shield powers endowed upon him by the Sun god Ra. *The Galaxy Trio* segment features Vapor Man, Meteor Man, and Gravity Girl as they use their superpowers to fight extraterrestrial crime as a part of the Galactic Patrol, starring one of the studio's first female superheroes. Lastly, Toth designed the characters for *Shazzan*, an action series starring Nancy and Chuck, siblings who find two halves of a ring that transports them to a mystical Arabian world where they go on adventures with their flying camel Kaboobie and their genie, Shazzan.[29]

Venturing into New Programming

The production of the hybrid *Jack and the Beanstalk* in 1967 lead to more live-action shows debuting in the fall of 1968 for the studio, joining two more animated series that season. The most ambitious non-animated program was *The Banana Splits Adventure Hour*, a packaged show sponsored by Kellogg's with segments following the adventures of a large costumed live-action rock band wrapped around short segments. The show's format was very loosely based on *Rowan and Martin's Laugh-In* and *The Monkees*, featuring the extravagant costumes of Sid and Marty Krofft who would go on to create *H.R. Pufnstuf*, later crediting Hanna-Barbera for their start. Each week comedy skits and song performances were interspersed throughout the episodes around the various live-action and animated shorts that were featured on the show. During the second season the performances took place at Coney Island amusement park in Cincinnati, which Taft Broadcasting purchased in 1969. The other series included in the hour were two adaptations, *Arabian Knights* and *The Three Musketeers*, along with *Micro Ventures*, an educational segment about a father and his kids' adventures with a shrink ray, which teaches them about the world around them from the perspective of an insect. The fourth series, *Danger Island*, was meant to be a live-action adaptation of *Jonny Quest* featuring Professor Irwin Hayden, his assistant Link, and daughter Leslie, who explore an unnamed tropical

The Banana Splits (from left, Bingo, Drooper, Snorky and Fleagle) ready for their next performance (Pictorial Press Ltd./Alamy Stock Photo).

island group. The serial was moderately successful, breaking a three-hour story into 36 segments, unique compared to the studio's typically episodic approach. The segment was directed by Richard Donner who later directed *The Goonies* and *Lethal Weapon*. Due to Donner's participation, Hanna and Barbera accepted executive producer, rather than directorial, credits.[30]

Relying heavily on adaptations in 1968, Hanna-Barbera developed *The Adventures of Gulliver* which finds Gary Gulliver and his dog being assisted by the Lilliputians as they look for his father and a treasure after being shipwrecked.[31] The series would join *The Banana Splits Adventure Hour* (renamed *The Banana Splits Friends Hour* in syndication) as one of the segments during the live-action program's second season. The other adaptation, *The New Adventures of Huckleberry Finn*, was the studio's first hybrid series, which was produced for NBC after the success of *Jack and the Beanstalk*. Huckleberry Finn featured three young actors as Huck, Becky Thatcher, and Tom Sawyer surrounded by animated characters, similar to Disney's infamous *Song of the South*. The show was initially popular, earning the stars teen idol status for a short time, and achieved ratings higher than most Saturday morning shows airing in early prime time in most markets. This approach and desire to capture the family audience, by airing the show Sundays at 7:00 p.m., hurt the series in many markets since it faced off against a more established family series, *Lassie*. This led NBC to cancel the season after the original 20 episodes aired, replacing Huck with *Mutual of Omaha's Wild Kingdom* midseason.[32]

Wacky Races was arguably the most enduring series premiering in 1968, representing the growing partnership between Hanna-Barbera and CBS's Fred Silverman, who started working with the studio as head of daytime programming, originally buying *Space Ghost* from the animators. The series was inspired by the popular 1965 comedy *The Great Race*, in which a collection of very different drivers compete in a long-distance race with humorous results. It was originally supposed to be part of a larger game show where contestants bet on certain cars to win, the show was co-produced with Heatter-Quigley Productions, who most famously created *Hollywood Squares*.[33]

For the series, producers created 23 new characters who raced individually and as teams in eleven very unique vehicles. Each episode represented a segment of the race, but the interaction between the characters, not the results, were the focus of the show. The writers relied on broad stereotypes, many of which they had utilized in earlier shows, to fill out the race field. This included mobsters, hillbillies, lumberjacks, servicemen, along with parodies of the Addams Family and the Red Baron. Each vehicle had special features and technologies, and the characteristics of the driver matched the theme of the car. It was the first of the endless race programs that became synonymous with the studio throughout the 1970s, and in the mind of both the studio and Silverman, it acted like a season long backdoor pilot to introduce numerous characters as they aimed to launch future series. Silverman later became (in)famous for this strategy, spinning off *The Jeffersons* and *Maude* from *All in the Family*, using an episode of the more established show as a pilot for a new program. With *Wacky Races*, Silverman wanted to see which characters tested well with audiences before giving the stars their own series.[34]

Spin-Offs and Talking Dogs

Those spin-offs came the next season in the fall of 1969 when the two most popular characters from the series received their own shows. Penelope Pitstop, Dick Dastardly, and his dog Muttley were originally supposed to star in a show together, but the latter two were dropped in preproduction and given their own show. In *Dastardly and Muttley in their Flying Machines*, the title characters, flying a World War I–era fighter and drawing from the Red Baron motif, consistently fail to stop a carrier pigeon, subtly named Yankee Doodle Pigeon, from delivering messages across battle lines. The theme song, "Stop the Pigeon," was written to the tune of the "Tiger Rag." As Dastardly and the other villains of the Vulture Squadron crash and explode, Muttley is often seen laughing raspily at his handler's failures. The series was inspired by *Peanuts'* Snoopy's regular battles with the mythical fighter pilot and another 1965 comedy film, *Those Magnificent Men in Their Flying Machines*, in which a number of competitors compete in a race between London and Paris in 1910 during the early days of flight.[35]

The Perils of Penelope Pitstop was inspired by the 1914 serial *The Perils of Pauline*, in which the eponymous character constantly faces some type of danger before either being rescued or escaping the situation. Many of the storylines, and even the score, were a satirical take on silent era damsel drama stereotypes, including the narrator and cliffhanger endings. *Penelope Pitstop* added a twist by often having the title character rescue her rescuers, the Ant Hill Mob, who acted as her less than capable protectors in *Wacky Races* as well. In each episode she is pursued by Sylvester Sneekly, a lawyer for an estate in which Pitstop is set to inherit. If Pitstop dies he receives the fortune, so he takes on the role of The Hooded Claw to try to murder the heiress, a costume only Pitstop is unable to see through. Sneekly and The Hooded Claw are both voiced by Paul Lynde in his first role for the studio; however, he was uncredited. This was Hanna-Barbera's first half hour series to star a woman in the title role, with each episode written by Warner veterans Michael Maltese, Joe Ruby, and Ken Spears.[36]

Dick Dastardly and Muttley chasing Yankee Doodle Pigeon in one of their Flying Machines (Pictorial Press Ltd./Alamy Stock Photo).

Ruby and Spears had teamed up as writers after meeting in the editing department at Hanna-Barbera and were put to work on a new show at the request of Silverman, who was worried that the superhero cartoon craze was fading while also noticing the popularity of Filmation's teenager-led *The Archie Show* on his network. Silverman wanted to differentiate the series from the comic book adaptation by including a mystery element in the mold of Abbott and Costello's monster films along with elements from *The Many Loves of Dobie Gillis*, a sitcom that aired earlier in the decade that featured a good-looking lead, two opposite female counterparts (one smart and plain, one shallow but stereotypically attractive), and dim-witted scraggly, beatnik inspired comic relief. The developing series was also inspired by Enid Blyton's *Famous Five* book series where four children and their dog solve mysteries during their summer holiday from boarding school.[37] Originally, the group of five teenagers was supposed to be in a band, solving mysteries between gigs, but this plotline, and the original title *Mysteries Five*, was abandoned along with one of the members who was replaced with Scooby-Doo, the eponymous dog.[38]

Ruby and Spears created Freddy, Velma, Daphne, and Shaggy, a collection of teenagers who drive around in their "Mystery Machine" solving crimes as amateur detectives. They are joined by a talking dog reminiscent of Astro, who was originally a secondary character for the Silverman vehicle before his popularity led the studio to feature the brown Great Dane more in the series and marketing. *Scooby-Doo, Where Are You!* became arguably the most enduring Saturday morning property for the studio, leading to several series throughout the next decade that attempted to replicate the format and success of *Scooby-Doo*. The Warner influence was clear in the first season, particularly when Scooby produced costumes and other props to confuse the villain leading to long chase scenes, much like Bugs Bunny cartoons, but writers found this distracted from the mystery and Scooby was made cowardly in later episodes of the series.[39]

The lesser known *Cattanooga Cats* premiered the same day as *Scooby-Doo* and was produced by the studio for ABC. The series was produced out of the *Banana Splits* mold with a band of animated cats serving as the wraparound content for several cartoons that appeared through each hour-long episode. The show found moderate success on Saturday morning, but maintains a cult following due to the psychedelic inspired animation used during the music segments. The program also included the serial *Around the World in 79 Days* where the great-grandson of Phineas Fogg competes for a million-dollar prize to beat his ancestors' journey around the Earth. Two *Tom and Jerry* inspired series, *It's the Wolf!* and *Motormouse and Autocat*, were also featured. *It's a Wolf!* featured Mildew Wolf chasing a lamb, Lambsy, who is protected by a dog, Bristle Hound, leading to violent expulsion of the wolf from the pasture. *Motormouse and Autocat* featured a mouse and cat racing each other as they set up traps and other obstacles for each other. Paul Lynde received his first voice credit from Hanna-Barbera for the series playing Mildew along with Casey Kasem, who voiced the drummer Groove of the Cattanooga Cats and also provided the voice of Shaggy on *Scooby-Doo*.[40]

Representation in the Age of Mass Production

The 1960s ended very differently than it began for Hanna and Barbera, when they were still trying to establish themselves as an animation studio, relying on 1950s styles, tropes, and formulas when they entered the decade. By the end, they had firmly established their own style, becoming the most prolific producers of animation for television, creating dozens of memorable characters, hundreds of episodes, and also selling their studio for millions of dollars, which injected important resources and support into the still-growing studio and allowed the production company's namesakes to concentrate on what they do best, overseeing the production of popular animation that appealed to broad audiences.[41]

Disney deserves credit for being one of the first animation creators to understand the ancillary value of a popular character, but Hanna-Barbera was far less discriminating about the companies to which it licensed its characters, helping to build the children's merchandising market we see today. We are now used to seeing cartoon characters not only in toy stores, but on every box of cereal, throughout clothing stores, and pretty much anywhere that sells to children (and often adults). The studio appreciated not only the extra revenue coming in from licensing, but the increased visibility of having a character like Yogi Bear on everything from candy to socks to campgrounds. However, between marketing considerations and continued reliance on past shows and works for inspiration the misrepresentational struggles were still clearly present for the studio, who, after the cancellation of *The Flintstones* and sale to Taft Broadcasting, became a cartoon factory targeting mostly children with varying levels of quality and originality between shows. The closing of Warner Animation Studio, the debut o*f Sesame Street*, Hanna-Barbera's focusing primarily on children's television, and the formation of advocacy groups like Action for Children's Television in the late 1960s had lasting effects on the animation industry that developed throughout the 1970s and will be discussed further in upcoming chapters.[42]

Sexist Representations in the White Male World of Animation Production

As the production of *The Perils of Penelope Pitstop* highlighted, there were very few women in leading or starring roles throughout the decade and the vast majority of the female character that were in co-starring or supporting roles were romantically connected to a male who got higher billing, like Wilma on *The Flintstones* or Cindy bear's relationship with Yogi. They also fulfilled stereotypical roles, like housewife, "eye candy," or damsel in distress. Although it contained many of the same stereotypes about the fragility and naiveté of women that have been present in media content for centuries, Penelope Pitstop at least represented some attempt to feature a female lead with agency and some identity outside of traditional marriage or being an object of desire; however, Penelope still embodies a number of stereotypical features of femininity, including a pink and purple form fitting driving suit and a car that contained an automated lipstick applier. Even as representations of women expanded after the success of *Penelope Pitstop*, they still often filled a limited number of specific roles, like the attractive, but naive, blonde or the sensible and more plain-looking brunette, while males filled a much larger range of roles and occupations in series.[43]

Drawing Stereotypes: Race and Ethnicity in 1960s Cartoons

Hanna-Barbera seemingly made no attempt to equally represent any non-white groups or ethnicities; in fact, as the studio produced more adventure shows and began to set shows in international locations, it often relied on stereotypes about the people and culture inhabiting the location while simultaneously whitewashing literature and history. A few of the shows even supported post–World War II imperialism connected to American exceptionalism and Western neoliberalism, as white characters from the United States and Europe often served as saviors for the local population who are portrayed as naive natives if not cannibalistic savages. Aside from a few of the voice actors, most of the talent, writers, and animators were white males, which continued to be reflected in the characters they created, who were mostly male and, aside from a few interpretive cases, were anthropomorphic characters that were presented as "raceless" which would point to whiteness since their experience and identity is normalized and not discussed. This whiteness is also supported by the fact that many of the inspirations for the voices of anthropomorphic characters were white male celebrities. Human characters were visually white to the extent non-whiteness is rendered invisible, and even when characters were inspired by non-white or non–Anglo characters like Samson or Sinbad.[44]

The first show to truly go international was *Jonny Quest*. The Quests did have a home in Florida, but most of the series takes place in various locations around the world, where Dr. Quest, his sons, and Race Bannon often encounter violent locals who disrupt the government research and operations on which Dr. Quest consults. He is said to be "one of the top three scientists in the world," but does not seem to have a specialty, bouncing from archaeology, to marine biology, to geology between and within episodes, as an apparent expert in all sciences. His adopted son was an Indian orphan before being adopted, but he is able to save Dr. Quest's life because of the judo he learned from an American Marine who was stationed in Kolkata. Hadji is the "seventh son of a seventh son" and either embodies mystical powers or is a master of illusion as he performs different "tricks," like levitation and snake charming, to assist the various missions as needed. He wears a bejeweled turban and Nehru jacket, fully highlighting his difference from the rest of the crew.[45]

Hadji's value is derived from his usefulness for not only the Quest family, but the United States government. At the time of *Jonny Quest*'s release, the United States had just significantly increased its military presence in Vietnam and was training local troops to assist in its ground and ideological war with the Viet Cong and USSR. Hadji's value and skills represent a positive view of this imperialistic strategy where colonizing nations train local troops to fight wars on their behalf, an approach employed by America for centuries. Hadji can act as a liaison between America and the occupied India, while the government also exploits his skills for its own profit and gain.[46]

To fully communicate the fear and misrepresentation of Asians, the only recurring villain in *Jonny Quest* is Dr. Zin, a Yellow Peril stereotype which was popular at the time due to the Cold War and conflicts in Asia. He is a criminal mastermind, representing what could happen to citizens of non–Western countries without American or European influence or intervention, acting as a counterpart to Hadji's apparent support, if not reverence, for the United States. When not facing Dr. Zin's interference they often clash with locals who want to either interfere with the research or industrial work being conducted on the behalf of the U.S. government or need to be saved by the Quests. In separate episodes, they have to eliminate terrorists' threats in Nepal and Hong Kong. European treasure hunters and villains are interspersed among the "hostile natives" and naive local populations the "research" group faces in each episode. This reinforcement of Western white superiority was even in the test scenes, when the then-unnamed family escapes what looks to be African warriors in a hovercraft, and in the opening theme as they escape stereotypical Amazonian warriors. In the third episode, an archaeologist friend in Egypt has become an Arab revolutionary framing Dr. Quest for stealing an artifact that has awakened a mummy. This storyline was featured just a decade after Gamal Abdel Nasser became president of the same country after the 1952 Revolution. They also have to escape angry, savage locals in both the Amazon and Africa while freeing the enslaved populations in both locations, seemingly connecting these locations with the institution of slavery which the United States engaged in less than a century before the premiere of the series. Aside from the identification of the Pygmy ethnic group, which was one of the few groups that the mostly white, American audience knew by name and would identify with from Africa even though they live throughout the world, the populations were generally lumped together as "Amazonian" or "African" without factual recognition of the specific group, further dehumanizing the many groups occupying those regions.[47]

Hadji, and really *Jonny Quest* as a series, promotes the idea of American, white exceptionalism by portraying the Quests, who represent the U.S. government, as saviors. Both evil and "noble" Westerners are constantly represented as being intellectual superiors and more advanced technologically than non-Western populations. The Quests with the support of the U.S. government are seen saving local populations that are being exploited and defeating violent "natives," but there are never questions about why Americans are there in the first place, or if they have any hand in the exploitation. This does not prevent the show from commenting on other countries' colonizing actions, as many of the enemies seen exploiting and enslaving local populations are from Western Europe, particularly Britain. There are never questions about the research Quest is doing on behalf on the U.S. government, even in the several episodes where local populations sabotage the work of the United States, who apparently have a right to their land and minerals. The show was taken off the air in the early 1970s and edited before being rebroadcast; however, most of the deletions were of violence, while many of the ethnic stereotypes remained.[48]

Danger Island contained many of the same stereotypes, particularly in relation to the villains. The professor, his daughter and assistant are in the area looking for his brother who went missing searching for an archeological site. They are in constant conflict with Captain Mu-Tain, a Dr. Zin replica, who oversees a band of pirates hoping to find the same site due to the rumors of a treasure. The "researchers" also have to avoid three different groups of cannibalistic locals in what looks like a South Pacific island chain. Clearly the assumption in all of this is that the group and whoever they represent are peaceful people who only want to respectfully visit the land, find a relative, and possibly uncover a lost civilization for the sake of knowledge. The lack of cultural respect and awareness in these real-life situations is represented by museums' continued insistence in maintaining ownership of cultural items that have been excavated from sites without the permission from the groups who have an actual connection with the items. They are joined by a teenage boy, Chongo, who lives on the island and can only communicate through noises and bird calls, reinforcing the portrayal of the savage. The group often has to help Chongo out of dangerous situations as the mischievous "boy," who was played by a 38-year-old Hawaiian man.[49] He is the sidekick of Elihu Morgan, a shipwrecked merchant marine. Morgan is the first African American character, animated or real life, to have a recurring speaking role on a Hanna-Barbera series.

Amalgamating Arabia

In 1965, Hanna-Barbera continued to misrepresent people and culture from South Asia and the Middle East, co-producing the first of several series that drew from the collection of stories *One Thousand and One Nights*, which date back as far back as the 9th century, but were not translated into English until the 18th century. Although stories featuring Sinbad the Sailor were not added until several centuries after the original manuscript was published in the 14th century, he became one of the most well-known characters from the collection of stories. *Sinbad Jr. and His Magic Belt* was actually the first series produced by William Hanna and Joseph Barbera not to feature original characters. Even though the duo came in later in the production process, they still had some control over the design of the characters, which clearly whitewashed the background of the sailor.[50] He is purportedly the son of an Arabic sailor from South Asian and Middle Eastern fiction; somehow he appears to be Caucasian with very little mention of his background throughout the series. He does have brunette hair, upsetting the trend of blondening non-white historical figures as a part of their whitewashing, but the presence of a parrot, a stereotype derived from Western literatures, further removes Sinbad Jr. from his Eastern origins.[51]

Several decolonial writers from Du Bois to Fanon, Cabral, and Rodney recognize this whitewashing and erasure of history as one of the primary strategies of imperialist nations. By eliminating the culture of the group while appropriating the positive and integral parts of its history, the colonizers are able to build an association between all progress and the superiority of the West and reaffirm the inferiority of the colonized and oppressed by communicating that they have no history and they have not contributed to human progress, although characters like Hadji communicate that they *could* be a part of this progress if they just support the mission of colonizers and neocolonizers to achieve the largest profits and spread capitalist ideologies.[52] Another interesting characteristic is that each half-hour episode of *Sinbad Jr.* included three five minute shorts, leaving 15 minutes of time for the purchasing network to fill. Some combined each episode with a short from another series, most notably *The Alvin Show*, although other markets just filled the rest of the time with commercials and other interstitial consumer content as some networks utilized the time to sell more commercials and allow advertisers to reach kids, marketing merchandise featuring the characters they watched that same morning.[53]

This historic and literary whitewashing continued later in the 1960s as Hanna-Barbera produced two more series that took non-white history and characters and westernized them to fit within the Eurocentric perspective on the past. As the big three networks continued to broadcast reruns of *Jonny Quest* and *Sinbad Jr. and his Magic Belt* on Saturday and Sunday mornings, the studio debuted both *Shazzan!* and *Samson and Goliath* in 1967. Like *Sinbad Jr.*, *Shazzan!* was clearly an adaptation on the Western understanding of *One Thousand and One Nights* featuring two blonde white children who find two rings with a divided center stone that transports them to 16th-century "Arabia," or at least the white male animators' vision of the Middle East during this period. When they combine their rings they summon Shazzan, a genie who grants any wish they choose, except the ability to transport them back to their suburban home in New England. To return, the siblings need to bring the rings to the rightful owner with the help of Shazzan, their flying camel, Kaboobie, and various magical items like a cloak that renders them invisible, and a magic rope.

Shazzan! not only Westernizes the *One Thousand and One Nights* stories but implants white children as the protagonists in these stories that originally featured those inhabiting the Middle Eastern and Southern portions of Asia. This separation of portions of Arabic and Persian mythology like genies from their source material and the blending of these tropes with Western literature had been occurring far before Hanna-Barbera, but much of that literature was aimed at adults and was typically read once or twice. Children were repeatedly exposed to these whitewashed "historical" and literary adaptations in a form that has been proven to be easily digestible for them. When they think of these stories, places, and peoples they may associate them with the cartoons they watched that first exposed them to representations of these groups that their nation has colonized, but with which they otherwise have very little connection and may never interact with throughout their entire lives. Also, considering the Eurocentric focus of Western education, the likelihood that they are exposed to the source material or even historical context for these stories is very low. As a result, these cartoons and other media become their only exposure to any type of representation featuring this group, greatly warping their understanding of non–Western culture, peoples, and experiences.[54]

The same day *Shazzan!* debuted on CBS, *Samson and Goliath* debuted on NBC. Again, rather than portraying Samson as having some connection with the biblical Israelite figure from the Southern Levant he is instead presented as a superhero who is able to summon the mythical strength of the ancient Samson by hitting his wrists together, transforming him to a muscle-bound hero and his dog Goliath into a lion that is able to shoot lasers from his eyes. Through the series, Hanna-Barbera is not only misrepresenting the biblical story of both Samson and Goliath by invoking both their names with very little association beyond the strength of both figures, but also misrepresenting the actual history of the period as well. Although they may have been contemporaries in biblical history they were actually opposing figures, considering Samson was an Israelite and Goliath a Philistine.[55]

Like Sinbad, Samson is portrayed as white with darker hair, but with very little resemblance to any type of Semitic race from the Near or Middle East. This biblical whitewashing has been a persistent theme in Western art as European conceptions and interpretations of the bible, Jesus, and Judeo-Christianity appropriated the ideas and representations through many of the Western based denominations originating from these religious that were largely established in the Near and Middle East.[56] This Eurocentric interpretation not only informs the way Western audiences understand history, but all the audiences in which this content is exported. As Fanon notes, Western culture is created by white producers for the consumption of white audiences, affirming the supremacy of the West and the inferiority of those outside the West that have been exploited for centuries. Although it is more likely that the non–Western population will be exposed to the historical and cultural context of this content, unfortunately the fact that the cultural imperialism of various Western countries, particularly the United States, floods the media market and confuses the true origins and context of these stories, helps support the continued attempts from the West to appropriate the pieces of non-white culture they see as valuable while adjusting the stories to make the colonizers seem like the center of all history and culture.[57]

Hanna-Barbera's last visit to the Middle East and Asia in the 1960s was a show called *Arabian Knights*, which was broadcast as a segment for the live-action *Banana Splits Adventure Hour.* As the title suggests, the series was adapted from *One Thousand and One Nights* but was much closer to the spirit of the original text than *Sinbad Jr.* or *Shazzan!* Even with this seemingly progressing cultural awareness, the studio continued to adjust the stories for their own benefit and the promotion of a Eurocentric perspective on history.[58] The protagonist is the Persian Prince Turhan, who is still visually represented as a Caucasian with dark hair and, like most of the non-white characters, with the exception of Hadji, is voiced by a white actor. His love interest, the Princess Nida, is also visually presented as white, and is voiced by Shari Lewis of *Lamb Chop* fame. Even when staying closer to the source material, animators like Hanna-Barbera cannot help but let representations of the West seep into their content, continuing the reinforcement of white patriarchal capitalist ideologies in animation and other Western media. The stories in *Arabian Knights* are closer to the source material, but similar to issues related to the dissemination of the Bible and its stories, the replacement of the non–Western character with one that represents Aryan, Anglo, or even Germanic cultures visually and aurally promotes Eurocentric perspective that the West has dominated human progress and culture.[59]

Baby Steps from a Giant Talking Dog

Scooby-Doo, Where Are You! very much represented a new era for the production company, as it marked an increased focus on children's television, while also exemplifying the changing styles and sensibilities for the studio at the time. The show was one of the first to feature "regular" contemporary teenagers, who, unlike Jonny Quest, reflected contemporary fashion and trends. After *Penelope Pitstop*, it was the first full length series to have female co-stars, although, in all these series, except for the largely forgotten *Winsome Witch*, male stars still outnumbered the females. Not surprisingly, they were led by one of the males, Fred Jones, wearing a white shirt, blue jeans, and an orange ascot, signaling a middle class, preppy upbringing. Fred is actually named after Fred Silverman, who helped develop the show after the success of another CBS program featuring contemporary teenagers, *The Archie Show*. Daphne Blake, Fred's assumed love interest, is modeled after gold-digger Thalia from *The Many Loves of Dobie Gillis*, often filling the role as the damsel in distress as her curiosity and intuition gets her into dangerous situations, hence the descriptor "danger-prone." Much like Fred, she dresses in contemporary clothes including a micro-dress and scarf and is known for her fashion sense. It is noted within the series that she comes from a wealthy family.[60]

Velma Dinkley, the other female character, does not embody the same stereotypically attractive feminine qualities as Daphne, wearing an oversized sweater, long skirt, and glasses modeled after the plain Zelda in *Dobie Gillis*, who had an unrequited love for the title character. She is by far the smartest of the group; with a science background and wide-ranging intelligence, Velma represents the stereotype that smart women are less traditionally attractive if not homely. Due to this portrayal as a bookworm with little interest in romance, Velma quickly became an icon for lesbians searching for characters with which they could identify, or disidentify.[61] This deconstruction, leading to the shifting of the intended meaning or representation of starring characters, would occur frequently throughout the 1970s and 1980s with shows like *Laverne and Shirley* and *Cagney and Lacey*.[62] Clearly sexuality was never discussed during the 1969 children's series; however, the use of animation and romantic ambiguity allowed audiences to place their own meaning upon Velma. In the original series, the audience is given very little information about the personal lives of Velma and the rest of Mystery Inc., creating opportunities for otherwise marginalized viewers to find some connection with characters in a television environment that was/is constantly promoting heteronormativity by creating fanfiction or a backstory that more accurately represents their own experiences.[63]

The eponymous star of the show, Scooby-Doo, was modeled after Astro and got his name from a line in the Frank Sinatra song "Strangers in the Night." Like Astro, he had some anthropomorphic elements; for example he could stand on his hind legs, hold things even without opposable thumbs, and most distinctively, talk, albeit replacing all the first letters of words with R's. Inspired by Bob Hope in his comedic mysteries, Scooby, in spite of his size, is a coward who only temporarily becomes brave when the group absolutely needs it. His best friend, Norville "Shaggy" Rogers, is modeled after the beatnik character Maynard in *Dobie Gillis,* wearing a long t-shirt and jeans, lacking the posture or aesthetics of Fred. He is portrayed as less intelligent and more cowardly than the others, using filler words in his speech while frequently getting distracted by food or his own laziness. He and Scooby are typically the first to face the villain, which they usually do while scavenging for food. Shaggy is Scooby's handler, adopting the Great Dane as a puppy, but he is never seen disciplining or training the dog. Shaggy's constant hunger, confusion, and identification as a beatnik or hippy attracted accusations that he was a marijuana smoker, an activity often associated with both groups. Due to Warner's desire to keep the property wholesome, and Ruby and Spears reportedly being offended by the marijuana references in the 2002 film, references to Shaggy as a stoner and allusions to Velma identifying as queer were edited out of the final version of the movie.[64]

As mentioned above, the female members of the team are clearly integral to its success as a detective agency; however, Fred is usually the one to solve the crime, or at least the one to announce the resolution, even if he had very little to do with actually exposing the villain and his plans. Velma and Daphne still play stereotypical female characters, with the smarter character being represented as unattractive and the more stereotypically feminine character being vapid, shallow, and prone to making mistakes that place her in dangerous situations. It is also important to note that the stars of *Scooby-Doo,* like all of Hanna-Barbera's human stars, were white with very little evidence of an ethnic

The iconic Mystery Machine is a popular attraction at conventions and auto shows (Khairil Azhar Junos/Shutterstock).

background outside of Western Europe, including their last names. When it premiered, *Scooby-Doo* went head to head with another mystery show, *The Hardy Boys*, based on the novel series. The Filmation series, which premiered a week before *Scooby-Doo*, was the first to feature a recurring African American character in a Saturday morning cartoon. *The Hardy Boys* helped to further highlight the lack of diverse representation in *Scooby-Doo* and other animated programs, but the Great Dane and Mystery Inc. still went on to become one of the most successful Saturday morning series of all-time.[65]

At the end of the 1960s, Hanna and Barbera surpassed thirty years working together, developing numerous styles and formulas that defined their studio. By this time they created enough program frameworks that they could rely less on parodies of shows and characters from other producers and more on building franchises and lucrative properties that could be sold to networks and whose rights they controlled. The new generation of programs were almost exclusively kids' shows that were broadcast repeatedly on weekend mornings, leading to broader themes and plotlines. The new shows inspired by the popular Hanna-Barbera productions of the past could allow for more diverse representations in shows that did not rely on imitating certain characters or frameworks, most of which were originally derived from white American ideals. These opportunities to present a more realistic and racially aware television animation were not always taken, and when they were, there was often hesitancy on the part of producers as older animators, many from the Golden Age, who controlled the studios continued to influence the representations and ideologies in the content.

5

1970–1975:
Success Breeds Complacency

New Decade, Old Habits

In only a few years, Hanna-Barbera's focus shifted from adults and general audiences to younger viewers, profiting off the growth Saturday morning and the merchandise empire being built upon popular characters and cheaply made plastic toys. Their reputation as a cartoon factory continued to expand as their footprint on children's television grew, especially through the work of Fred Silverman, whose partnership with the studio led to weekend mornings on CBS being a showcase for Hanna-Barbera cartoons throughout the early 1970s. They continued to develop popular characters, but the tropes and programs became redundant as quantity fully overtook quality, targeting an audience considered less discerning, if not appreciative of repeated viewings of similar content, which was also supported by the continued popularity of older programs like *Yogi Bear* and *The Flintstones*.[1] *Scooby-Doo, Where Are You!* may have signaled a different direction for their half-hour programs, but they also shuffled their shorts to create "new" series and maintain older series' marketability, maximizing the profit from every single property as they continued their reign over Saturday morning.[2]

The children's media environment had also changed dramatically in a little more than a decade. Audiences and time slots that were afterthoughts became highly profitable, as advertisers further recognized the buying power of young Baby Boomers. Programmers also realized that, even though children's programming, specifically animation, may have had higher budgets than some live-action productions, the repeatability of the programs and popularity of properties like *Scooby-Doo* made animation a mostly profitable risk, if not investment, since the right series could be rerun for decades. CBS dominated weekend mornings as the 1970s approached, utilized as part of a larger strategy to attract a younger audience, as Baby Boomers, and their children, continued to grow as an economic force.[3] Changes in strategy and leadership helped the other networks catch up to CBS throughout the 1970s, with Hanna-Barbera leading the way as its characters and series consistently outlasted executives' expectations on all three national commercial networks. Other animation producers also joined the market as broadcasters scrambled to fill the expanding time slots represented by weekend mornings and weekday afternoons. Networks were scheduling over twelve hours of children's programming a week, not including local syndication, opening time slots for newly emerging television animation production companies that diversified the market some, but did not truly challenge Hanna-Barbera's domination through the 1970s. The studio had become a well-oiled animation assembly line, but unlike the manufacturing of Model T's, their productions contained representations that were often at the mercy of business decisions and a lack of diversity behind the pen. This led to issues related to both visibility and misrepresentation even as American ideologies were being challenged by various social movements and increasing recognition of the diverse demographics of the American public. Similar to other media at the time, the animation studio was willing to profit off of the marketability of this progress without actually engaging with the issues being raised by those risking everything to resist the supremacy of white patriarchal heteronormativity.[4]

One Year of Recognition Is Enough:
African American Representation in 1970

By 1970, at least one-sixth of the people living in the United States identified as non-white, the highest number since the Civil War, according to the census.[5] Hanna-Barbera was able to go thirteen seasons and produce over three dozen series and films without prominently featuring an African American character in a starring role. Part of this continued lack of representation may have been a result of backlash from the Mammy Two Shoes character, who was ultimately removed, edited, or re-voiced for syndication throughout the 1960s. Instead of representing a group or culture they knew nothing about and risk criticism, they, like many animators and media producers, decided to ignore the entire race, which represented over 11 percent of the United States population. Other non-white races, identified with peoples from Hispanic, Arabic, and Asian countries, were the focus of the bulk of derogatory representations after World War II while African Americans were barely seen, particularly in cartoons. This whitewashing of animation finally came to a head in 1970s, as the emergence of public media offered a different media structure than the other networks, with public financing and private underwriting presenting opportunities to broadcast content that connected more directly with the experiences of non-white and working class populations without the oversight of white male executives whose primary concerns are ratings, advertisers, or even merchandising purely for profit, leading to an aversion to risk, change, or anything that challenges that status quo.[6]

Although PBS broadcast television for all ages and tastes, one of the areas they most impacted was children's television. As discussed earlier, *Sesame Street* entered a children's media environment that not only had been whitewashed, but was also classist, often targeting children from middle or upper socioeconomic levels since they, or their parents, were the ones with disposable income to spend on various toys, cereals, and licensed products. *Sesame Street* and other PBS programs like *The Electric Company*, which debuted in 1971, could not only afford to be truly educational, since advertising revenue was not a concern, but they could also target an audience largely ignored by advertisers, children in lower income areas, particularly children of color, who lived in urban areas and often did not have the same access to early childhood education as those in the suburbs.[7] *Sesame Street*'s clever writing, which entertained both children and adults, promoted co-viewing within families, hoping guardians would assist children with the lessons, helping the program become an instant success. The producers made it a priority to hire non-male and non-white cast and crew members, offering a large portion of the child population the ability to see representations of themselves and their experiences on television for the first time.[8]

The research throughout the development of the series was key in better understanding how children consume and learn from television content. *Sesame Street* was not only integral in placing value on a child audience outside of the white middle-class, but also producing important research about the effects of media exposure on children to better reach them with the educational messages. Some of this research also helped for-profit children's television better market their content and characters to children. This included merchandising, which *Sesame Street* utilized to help children connect with the characters on the show, selling plush dolls that closely replicated the Muppets on the program. This approach supported Hanna-Barbera's marketing strategy of heavily merchandising programs while prioritizing animal characters, which are often easier to market in licensed merchandise. The tangible toy adds another element or sensory experience to the child's consumption of the content, which can increase the ability for the child to relate to their favorite character.[9]

Popular Culture and Sports Support Progress in Other Areas

Coincidentally, as Hanna-Barbera prepared for the 1970–1971 television season, CBS signed a deal with a popular basketball team, which, after reaching its competitive peak in the 1950s, changed its style, becoming one of the most popular traveling entertainment acts of the 1960s and 1970s. The Harlem Globetrotters were established as a barnstorming basketball team in the late 1920s as segregation limited professional opportunities for Black players. The team was established in Chicago but adopted the New York neighborhood as home since it was seen as the center of African American culture at the time due to the Harlem Renaissance. After the NBA desegregated in the 1950s, they utilized their superior basketball skills to add tricks, humor, and fan interaction to their exhibitions, which often included making an all-white Washington Generals team look foolish in the "games." Throughout the 1960s the team continued to expand their visibility with appearances in films and shows like *Ed Sullivan* and *What's My Line?* They also increased licensing and exposure for the team's stars like Curly Neal and Meadowlark Lemon through merchandising and sponsorships.[10]

Considering the comedy and outlandish feats featured in their performances, Fred Silverman saw the perfect subjects for the first Saturday morning series to feature a predominantly African American cast. Silverman met with the animation duo about the series, and they agreed to use the hit program *Scooby-Doo* as a loose framework for the series, but instead of solving mysteries they used their basketball skills to remedy local conflicts around the world. The show still featured a talking dog and for some reason a white grandmother figure who acts as the bus driver and manager for the team. It was one of the first productions from the studio to also employ multiple African American voice actors including Scatman Crothers and Eddie "Rochester" Williams.[11] The series was the first co-production between Hanna-Barbera and a network, providing the animators with more resources than their typical series. These resources were most evident in the soundtrack for the series which included several popular covers including "Duke of Earl" with Jimmy Radcliffe providing vocals and "Rainy Day bells" sung by former Cadillac J.R. Bailey.

Scores have always been an integral part of animation production, but the success of The Archies' "Sugar, Sugar," which premiered on Filmation's *The Archie Show* in 1969 and held the top spot on the US Billboard Hot 100 charts for four weeks increased awareness concerning the ancillary music market for animation. This market began with *Snow White and the Seven Dwarfs*, the film with the first commercially issued soundtrack,

helping songs like "Heigh-Ho"
become mainstream hits.[12] The
Beatles' animated series brought
this marketing strategy to Saturday morning, initiating a trend
of rock n' roll focused cartoons.
Originally, *Scooby-Doo, Where
Are You!* was supposed to feature a mystery solving rock band
before the musical concept was
abandoned.[13] Although ancillary media like comics, books,
and vocal recordings of programs
were included in Hanna-Barbera's
business strategy from the beginning, they expanded their strategy
to shows that could include music
like "Sugar, Sugar," now regarded
as one of the biggest hits of the
time period.[14]

Archie Comics and music
intersected for Hanna-Barbera in
the other Saturday morning series
from the studio to premiere that
season, *Josie and the Pussycats.*
The Archie Show continued to be
a hit for CBS through 1970, and
Fred Silverman conceptualized a
similar series featuring Josie and
her band, the Pussycats, which

Fred "Curly" Neal and Hubert "Geese" Ausbie in a
Wonder Bread Promotional Card released in 1974,
four years after the debut of their eponymous animated show (Mark Anderson/Flickr).

debuted as a comic in December 1969 as a preview of the animated program's debut the
next fall.[15] Silverman approached Archie Comics executives John and Richard Goldwater
and Josie creator Dan DeCarlo about the animated program. DeCarlo agreed to reboot
the comic into a music-based series, including the addition of Valerie, an African American bass player, who replaced the Caucasian Pepper in the comic and the development of
the television show.

As production began on both the cartoon and the soundtrack, William Hanna
reportedly requested that animators feature Pepper, rather than Valerie, in the Saturday
morning series. La La Productions' Danny Janssen, who had put together the live-action
group that mirrored the animated characters and was already recording the songs to be
featured on the show, refused to change his band, which featured African American and
Hispanic singer Patrice Holloway, younger sister of former Motown artist Brenda.[16] Holloway had performed the background vocals on the Joe Cocker and the Grease hit cover
"With a Little Help from My Friends" and helped produce the pop R&B sound producers
needed for the fictional band.[17] Janssen won the argument, and earlier the same morning
The Harlem Globetrotters premiered, *Josie and the Pussycats* debuted with the first African American female star in animated television and arguably the first positive portrayal
of this intersection of gender and race in popular animation history.[18]

The presence of an African American character and the all-female band were the only characteristics that made *Josie and the Pussycats* truly unique. As discussed above, the series was already a comic adaptation that CBS hoped could replicate the success of another adaptation of the comic series from which *Josie* was spun-off. Ostensibly, *Josie* was an amalgam of their hit from the previous season, *Scooby-Doo*, and *The Monkees*, a Screen Gems live-action production that had entered Saturday morning syndication the year before and become a huge hit among children after a mediocre primetime run. Each episode of *Josie and the Pussycats* featured a mystery, which was solved by the group and their friends after traveling to various exotic locations to perform. The cast included their manager Alexander Cabot III, his jealous sister Alexandra, both of whom were brought over from the comic series, and roadie Alan, a Fred Jones doppelganger who debuted in the rebooted series and played Josie's love interest. Since it was a Hanna-Barbera series, it also starred an anthropomorphic animal, Sebastian the Cat, who mirrored Alexandra's attempts to undermine the band while also helping the group escape during their capers. The show was not only the first Hanna-Barbera series to star multiple women in

The cast of *Josie and the Pussycat* (clockwise from top, Sebastian, Alexander Cabot III, Alan Mayberry, Alexandra Cabot, Melody Valentine, Valerie Brown and Josie McCoy). Valerie was the first Black female star of a Saturday morning cartoon (AA Film Archive/Alamy Stock Photo).

the title role, none of which played the damsel role, but also featured a musical and detective group led by a woman.[19]

Hanna-Barbera's relationship with Silverman motivated CBS to consider the first regularly scheduled prime time series since the cancellation of *The Flintstones* in 1966, but the network wanted a test run for the series before fully committing to an expensive genre that had historically struggled in prime time. CBS offered a summertime slot for the series to see if it could gain an audience before the series would be regularly scheduled in January of the next year.

Unfortunately, aside from a change in occupation from quarry worker to football player, *Where's Huddles?* was basically a remake of *The Flintstones*, which was still popular in weekend syndication, even lifting plots directly from the Stone Age sitcom. Quarterback Ed Huddles replaced Fred and his offensive lineman Bubba McCoy took over for Barney as teammates on the fictional Rhinos football team. There was very little football on the show since it focused on the duo's attempts to supplement their apparently low football salaries. Despite legendary broadcaster Dick Enberg providing the voice of the Rhinos' announcer and the presence of the African American Freight Train, a possible homage to Dick "Night Train" Lane, there was very little to note about the series. CBS declined to pick up after the initial ten-episode run in the summer of 1970, even discontinuing reruns of the unpopular series by the next summer.[20]

The Studio Hits a Rut

The legacy of the productions from the 1971–1972 season is at best limited. One notable new practice was the use of Hanna-Barbera's own laugh track, which became the subject of frequent ridicule over the years. Historically, many sitcoms and most cartoons used the laugh tracks created by CBS sound engineer Charley Douglass. Douglass used a keyboard-like machine that could eventually cue 320 different laughs on 32 loops. The Hanna-Barbera machine, which was a McKenzie repeater, had five total laughs that were played repetitively in their programs throughout the decade, increasing the scrutiny around laugh tracks and forced laughter, especially when considering, as with the rest of the content, mostly white males are deciding what is comedic. This infamously inferior laugh track, along with limited animation utilized by Hanna-Barbera and other animation studios, only contributed to the reputation of Saturday morning as a repository for low-quality, if not annoying, programs and cartoons for children.[21]

A collection of programs premiered on Saturday morning in 1971 with very few notable characteristics as Hanna-Barbera mined past successes to produce "new" series, using reruns of older series that continued to attract new young audiences each season. This was especially true for *The Flintstones*, which included 166 episodes from its original six season prime time run, over ten times the average animated series run at that time. The popularity of the Stone Age family led to a spin-off series featuring the youngest members of the Flintstone and Rubble clans, Pebbles and Bamm-Bamm, reimagined as teenagers. Hanna-Barbera continued to try to tap into the popularity of *Scooby-Doo* and *Josie and the Pussycats* by portraying the high school-aged stars as members of an up-and-coming band and featuring popular music in each episode, much like *The Archie Show*. The plots for the episodes were fairly realistic, even when considering they took place in the "Stone Age," focusing on the trials and tribulations of high schoolers before a musical performance led to finding solutions for common teenage problems, like crushes and popularity. The show found moderate success in its first season as younger audiences continued to be drawn in by older teenage characters and seemed to appreciate the realistic storylines. *The Pebbles and Bamm-Bamm Show* was also supported by a strong voice cast which included Sally Struthers, who went on to star in *All in the Family*, and Jay North, who played Dennis the Menace in the popular live-action series. Critics, however, hated the show and the bastardization of *The Flintstones* brand, leading to only one season in production. It did help to keep the property relevant, leading to several other series and films over the next two decades.[22]

Continuing to rely on past formulas, *Help! … It's the Hair Bear Bunch* premiered on CBS between *The Harlem Globetrotters* and *The Pebbles and Bamm-Bamm Show* in most markets, starring three bears trying to escape the zoo. Combining elements of *Yogi Bear*, *Top Cat*, and *Magilla Gorilla*, the bears escape their human-produced captivity, trying to find freedom while at the same time attempting to get rich quick as they avoid zookeeper Eustace Peevely's attempts to keep them captive. Aside from their updated 1970s clothes and hairstyles there was very little difference between the *Hair Bear Bunch* and the storylines featured in reruns of the past shows from which it was molded. Hair Bear, with his yellow Afro, was the leader of the group, providing the comforts of home in "Cave Block 9" while leading the escape attempts and schemes. Square Bear is the muscle, wearing a fishing cap that covers his eyes and shaggy haircut, and Bubi Bear is a double-speaking bear who often acts as a decoy and distracts Peevely or other humans to help the group escape. Many episodes actually end with Hair Bear providing excuses for Peevely and his failures, helping their adversary keep his job. The animators also renewed use of familiar voices with William Callaway imitating Phil Harris to provide the voice of Square Bear and John Stephenson imitating Joe Flynn from *McHale's Navy* as the zookeeper Peevely after the studio passed on Flynn to voice the character.[23]

The third series, *The Funky Phantom*, helped reinitiate the animation studio's relationship with ABC and led Hanna-Barbera to launch a subsidiary in Australia after co-producing the series with Australian production company Air Programs International. The morbid premise featured three teenagers and their dog finding the ghost of a Revolutionary era soldier and his cat inside a clock after they locked themselves and died inside while hiding from the British. The ghosts, Jonathan Wellington "Mudsy" Muddlemore, with a voice similar to Snagglepuss, and Boo the cat, help Skip, April, Augie, and their dog Elmo solve various mysteries they encounter in the Looney Duney, basically adding a metaphysical group member to the *Scooby-Doo* formula. The show was not only unpopular with children, but advocacy groups also complained that the program portrayed an inaccurate history of the American Revolution to young children. The show was notable for being the first animated voice credit for former Monkee Micky Dolenz.[24]

If It Ain't Broke, Copy It as Much as Possible

The lackluster 1971–1972 season may have been a result of Hanna-Barbera's huge production schedule at this time that led to seven new series, nine animated specials, a live-action television movie, The Flintstones on Ice special, and two theatrical feature films, one animated, one live action, in the 1972–1973 season. This output can be partially credited to the support of a young executive at CBS named Michael Eisner who continued to work with the animators, seeing the value in children's media as Silverman began to focus more on the prime time schedule after becoming head of programming in 1970.[25] Fifteen years after the debut of their first television series, Hanna-Barbera was reaching the peak of its popularity as Saturday morning saw its full potential realized in the eyes of programmers and marketers of children's television. However, with any peak comes a decline, which would occur in the succeeding decade as the children's television and animation industries shifted as a result of changes in policy, audience taste, and increased attention by advocacy groups. This increasing focus by organizations like Action for Children's Television, which started as a local group in Boston concerned about advertising in children's television programs like *Romper Room*, was partially due to the oversaturation of moderate-to low-quality animation with what was perceived as very little educational and social value for the young audience. The popularity of PBS series like *Sesame Street*, also served as proof for many that children's television can be both entertaining and generally beneficial for the social development of children.[26]

Three of the new series were either spin-offs or continuations of previous series, with two of the series, *The Flintstone Comedy Hour* and *The New Scooby-Doo Movies*, having a running time of a full hour. The *Flintstones* spin-off combined shorts from *The Pebbles and Bamm-Bamm Show* with new adventures featuring Fred and his friend Barney. The new episodes were basically more condensed versions of later episodes of the original series, with the duo's outlandish misadventures being the sole focus of the segments (within the larger show) with interstitial materials featuring the Bedrock Rockers who were inspired by The Archies. *The New Scooby-Doo Movies* was one of many reimagined series starring the Great Dane and team of teenage detectives that followed the original series. This one was notable because each week another celebrity guest starred and provided the voice for their animated counterpart. Hanna-Barbera had previously utilized imitations of celebrities to connect with the audience's familiarity with popular comedians and past stars like Scatman Crothers who provided voices for the company, but this was the first series to regularly feature celebrity cameos, a tactic often used in live-action sitcoms to entice audiences and became a popular device in later animated series. On occasion, casts from other series, like *The Three Stooges* and *The Addams Family,* actually played their characters, not only drawing in children with the presence of other popular characters and celebrities, but adults as well. The third spin-off, *Josie and the Pussycats in Space*, merely took the original series and gave it an intergalactic setting after the group is locked in a capsule and launched into space. The series did add the alien character Bleep and gave Hanna-Barbera an additional sixteen *Josie and the Pussycats* episodes to sell into syndication.

Two more family comedies also hit the airwaves in the form of *The Roman Holidays* and *Wait Till Your Father Gets Home*. Both shows were derivative of *The Flintstones* and *The Jetsons*, which continued their successful runs in syndication even as Hanna-Barbera produced new programs to replace them. Ancient Rome was actually one of the settings originally considered for *The Flintstones*, but concerns about criticism over historical inaccuracies, like they faced with *The Funky Phantom*, pulled creators even further back into history to the Stone Age. Thinking kids were less intelligent and knowledgeable, they moved forward with this concept, but years of watching films like *Ben-Hur* and *Spartacus* gave young audiences a cursory knowledge of Ancient Rome, which was enough to see through all the anachronisms and misrepresented civilizations in the series to go along with the redundant storylines. *Roman Holidays* starred Gus Holiday, his wife Laurie, children Percocia and Happius, and pet lion Brutus. Holiday works as an engineer for Mr. Tycoonius hoping to avoid getting kicked out of his apartment at the Venus de Milo Arms. If the mind-numbing Latin inspired names were not enough to turn off kids, and co-watching adults, then the constant and blatant inaccuracies and redundant storylines did, like the fact Venus de Milo is Greek or the plots were lifted directly from *The Flintstones*.[27]

Wait Till Your Father Gets Home was Hanna-Barbera's last true attempt at producing a prime time sitcom, as the studio tried to take advantage of a new FCC rule that gave the 7:30 p.m. time slot back to local affiliates, limiting national prime time to three hours and forcing local stations to scramble to fill the half hour with programming that would attract viewers and keep them watching between early evening and prime time.[28] In future decades, the time slot was quickly filled by game shows and human interest programs like tabloids and news magazines, but for the first few years producers and distributors like Filmways and Viacom produced a number of scripted series hoping to reach a national audience through syndication. A few series like *Sha Na Na* and *The Wild Wild World of Animals* found niche audiences, while one, *The Muppet Show*, became a huge hit leading to the popular franchise of characters created by Jim Henson, who designed the characters on *Sesame Street* as well.

Hanna-Barbera's attempt was a sitcom in the style of *All in the Family*, which debuted as a hit the season before.[29] Tom Bosley, who went to star in *Happy Days*, provides the voice for Harry Boyle, the underpaid working class suburban dad struggling to understand a changing world. Harry's two teenage children, Alice and Chet, support the leftist politics represented by the women's liberation, civil rights, and hippie movements, but often have to come to terms with reality related to economics and gender roles. The youngest son, Jamie, follows his father's more conservative beliefs, often defending Harry in arguments with the older siblings. Harry's wife Irma typically remains neutral, trying to calm the contention between the different generations within the same household. Their neighbor, Ralph, puts Harry's conservatism into perspective as a John Birchian right-wing conspiracy theorist determined to win the Cold War by himself, at least rhetorically. This generation gap was often the source of storylines for the program, which writers hoped would appease the cross-demographic audience that included teenagers who were meant to identify with Alice and Chet and older audiences that appreciated Harry's point of view. Like *Roman Holidays*, *Wait Till Your Father Gets Home* was seen on NBC in most markets, lasting three seasons and standing as the last animated series produced for prime time to last more than one season until the 1990s.[30]

The same season DePatie-Freleng also debuted *The Barkleys,* created and written by former Hanna-Barbera employees Joe Ruby and Ken Spears. As another show inspired by *All in the Family*, the program had almost the exact same format as *Wait Till Your Father Gets Home*, with anthropomorphic dogs replacing the human Boyles. The show had even less of an impact than its Hanna-Barbera counterpart; the failure of the canine-led show helped convince Ruby and Spears to take Fred Silverman's offer to oversee CBS's Saturday morning programming, adding two more familiar faces in the meetings between the network and the animation production company.[31]

Action, and Misrepresentation, Returns for H-B

The other two series produced for the fall of 1972 were action shows that would have been largely forgotten if not for the representations they contained. *Sealab 2020*, as the title suggests, is set in a futuristic undersea biodome and stars Dr. Paul Williams, a Native American from the Chinook nation, as a part of a clunky attempt at diversity which included very few cultural identifiers beyond the description of his background and his slightly darker skin tone. Each week the lab is terrorized by a sea creature or the scientists must react to some oceanic or environment disaster. *Sealab 2020* was largely inspired by *Star Trek*, with Dr. Williams' assistants even being referred to as oceanauts throughout the series. One of these oceanauts, Ed, was portrayed as African American, mirroring the presence of Lieutenant Uhura on Gene Roddenberry's legendary series. The program only featured one female co-star, as the studio targeted boys with the underwater action-adventure series, which, in true Hanna-Barbera fashion, included an anthropomorphic dolphin for comic relief.[32]

The second show, *The Amazing Chan and the Chan Clan*, was a detective-comedy series adapted from the *Charlie Chan* novels written by Earl Derr Biggers. The Honolulu–based Chinese detective appeared in nearly 50 films through the 1940s but attempts to revitalize the series after this era largely failed, partially due to the racial stereotypes embodied in the character. This did not stop Hanna-Barbera from producing a series starring Chan and his "children" solving crimes with the help of their dog Chu Chu. To eliminate any doubt this was a Hanna-Barbera series, the older children comprised a band named the Chan Clan that performed toward the end of each episode, often during a chase scene, similar to *Josie and the Pussycats*. To add to the problems presented by the nonsensical premise was the portrayal of the individuals of Chinese descent, particularly among the children. In fact, the imitated Chinese accents made dialogue so indistinguishable that they had to immediately redub the series for future broadcasts. One of the children to provide the redubbed voice was Jodie Foster, who was only eight at the time and went on to earn her first Oscar nomination for *Taxi Driver* four years later. Ironically, this was the first time Charlie Chan was actually played by an actor of Chinese descent—Keye Luke, who played Charlie Chan's "Number One Son" in the original films and provided the voice of Brak in the original Space Ghost series.[33]

Animating Telefilms

As the market for children's television cartoons entered its peak, ABC decided to start a special series that was modeled after the popular "Movie of the Week" but for kids, where their favorite cartoon characters starred in a different hour-long film each Saturday morning throughout the season. The *ABC Saturday Superstar Movie* featured films from all the major television animation studios at the time, including Hanna-Barbera, Warner, Rankin-Bass, Filmation, and DePatie-Freleng.[34] The high budgets and ABC's involvement and marketing led to unique crossovers and several films being utilized as pilots for future series. Hanna-Barbera produced seven films for the series, all but one premiering in the fall of 1972. The first Hanna-Barbera contribution, and the second episode of the series, starred Yogi Bear and many of their other popular characters from the 1950s and early 1960s in an attempt to revitalize the franchises, exposing a new generation to Huckleberry Hound, Quick Draw McGraw, and others. In the film, Yogi is forced to gather all the animals as an environmental disaster threatens Jellystone Park. With the help of Jellystone staff member Noah, they build a flying ark to find a clean place to live, but realize pollution is everywhere and that it is up to them (and the children watching) to be more ecologically minded and help clean up the environment. *Yogi's Ark Lark* acted as a pilot for *Yogi's Gang*, a prosocial series that had the characters fight off villains that represent various environment and social vices like waste and greed.[35]

None of the other films produced by Hanna-Barbera for the series had the lasting power of *Yogi's Gang*, which only ran half a season the next fall. The studio produced a two-part adaptation of *Oliver Twist*, *Oliver the Artful Dodger*, and adapted *Gidget*, from the popular beach films, in *Gidget Makes the Wrong Connection*, and Tabitha from *Bewitched* in *Tabitha and Adam and the Clown Family*. Another film, *The Banana Splits in*

Hocus Pocus Park, brought back the costumed group in an animated/live-action hybrid film. The last adaptation, *The Adventures of Robin Hoodnik*, was an all-animal adaptation of the classic tale which premiered a year before Disney's popular feature film version. Although a few of the films were meant to be one-shot movies, most of the movies acted as test pilots for new series and franchises, with only two, the aforementioned *Yogi's Gang* and Filmation's *The Brady Kids*, being brought to series by ABC.[36]

Hanna-Barbera continued to rekindle its relationship with ABC, as Silverman focused on a collection of new trendy programs occupying his prime time schedule on CBS after the rural purge the season before. In another attempt to placate critics, Hanna-Barbera produced an animated adaptation of *Last of the Curlews* as the first Afterschool Special for the network. Like *Yogi's Ark*, it had a pro-environment message as it followed the life of the bird species nearing extinction, even humanizing the birds in the program. Although the original book was published in 1954, the adaptation came on the heels of a number of policy changes by the U.S. government as a result of pressure from environmental groups including the establishment of the Environmental Protection Agency in 1970. The film earned Hanna-Barbera an Emmy for Outstanding Achievement in the Field of Children's Programming, their first since *The Huckleberry Hound Show* 14 years earlier.[37]

The studio also tried its hand at holiday specials with *The Thanksgiving That Almost Wasn't* and *A Christmas Story*. Both films star talking animals helping children "save" holidays for their families and acquaintances. *The Thanksgiving That Almost Wasn't* was a retelling of the traditional narrative surrounding the origins of Thanksgiving, in which a squirrel helps find a pair of boys, a Native American and Pilgrim, who get lost in the woods ahead of the mythical meal between the two groups. The Christmas special found Goober the dog and Gumdrop the mouse trying to deliver a Christmas letter to Santa on behalf of a young boy. After attempts to connect with Santa throughout the film fail, they fall asleep only to find Santa read the letter when he visited their home, delivering what was requested in the letter, a room full of presents for Timmy and his family. Both films were largely forgotten, the latter film in particular due to sharing a title with the live-action film released ten years later. The movies were distributed by Avco Broadcasting, which also limited the marketing resources available for the films.[38]

Five years earlier, when Taft acquired Hanna-Barbera, the broadcasting conglomerate considered eliminating the animation unit and concentrating on producing other programming.[39] Joe Barbera took this as an opportunity to produce live-action content to better secure the studio's position within the larger company, especially as Taft discussed cutbacks. The result of these attempts included *The Banana Splits*, *The Adventures of Huckleberry Finn*, and the 1972 film *Hardcase*, a Western produced for the anthology series ABC Movie of the Week. The film starred Clint Walker as Jack Rutherford, a veteran of the Spanish-American War who returns to his Texas ranch to learn his wife Rozaline, played by Stefanie Powers, married a Mexican "revolutionary leader," Simon Fuegus, who has sold Jack's land and assets to buy weapons and other resources for his "band" of soldiers. Jack kidnaps the leader to get his money back, offering him both to Fuegus' allies and the Mexican government, who consider him a fugitive from justice. The film was a ratings surprise, ranking in the top 10 in the week, leading to several other live-action television productions by Barbera and the studio.[40]

One of the most enduring productions in the studio's history was Hanna-Barbera's first theatrical film with completely original animation, the first of three feature films not to star one of Hanna-Barbera's original characters.[41] *Charlotte's Web* was released in March of 1973, an adaptation of the classic E.B. White children's novel co-produced with Sagittarius Productions and distributed by Paramount Pictures. Hanna-Barbera was again taking a page from Disney, which had built an empire on adaptations of children's literature, but had been unable to acquire the rights to adapt the novel from White.[42] Throughout the production and release, White conferred with legendary animator Gene Deitch, who had started a partnership with Weston Woods Studios producing adaptations of children's picture books. Coincidentally, Deitch had directed thirteen *Tom and Jerry* shorts for Rembrandt Films in the early 1960s, before moving to less commercial recognized productions including *Munro*, the first foreign film to win the Academy Award for Best Animated Short in 1961, and the first adaptation of a J.R.R. Tolkien novel, *The Hobbit*, in 1966. Neither Weston Woods nor Deitch had the budget to produce a novel adaptation of that scale and depth, which allowed Hanna-Barbera to obtain the rights. White lamented that he wished Deitch were directing the film, rather than new directors Charles A. Nichols and Iwao Takamoto, especially after seeing the songs and score Hanna-Barbera included in the film. They moved forward with a score produced by the Sherman Brothers, rather than Mozart as White suggested. The brothers, who wrote more film scores than any other duo in history, famously produced popular scores for Disney movies like *Mary Poppins* and *The Jungle Book*, two other literature adaptations, the former winning them two Academy Awards.[43]

Considering the film stars a farm of talking animals, it was the perfect vehicle for the studio's first feature film not connected to a show or character created by Hanna-Barbera. For the voices, Hanna-Barbera attracted a number of stars to work alongside the studio's typical talent like Don Messick and John Stephenson. Henry Gibson (Wilbur), Paul Lynde (Templeton), Agnes Moorehead (Goose), Danny Bonaduce (Avery Arable), and Dave Madden (Ram) had all been on *Bewitched*, for which the studio produced the title sequence. Popular actress Debbie Reynolds provided the voice of Charlotte, reportedly offering to take on the role for free because of her fondness for the novel.[44] Musical numbers aside, the film itself was a fairly close adaptation, even including the tragic existential questions that made the book a classic piece of coming-of-age literature for adolescents, unlike Disney who adjusted fairy tales to ensure that each of their adaptations had clear cut happy endings. Most critics agreed that the film was faithful to the original text but lamented the music and the quality of animation that paled in comparison to its Mouse-led counterpart. The film found moderate success in its original release but became a home video hit as one of the top selling VHS tapes of the mid–1990s and was nominated as one of the top 10 animated films of all time by the American Film Institute. A few days after *Charlotte's Web* premiered, *Baxter!* debuted in New York based on the book *The Boy Who Could Make Himself Disappear* about a young boy with a speech impediment trying to navigate his relationship with his parents. The live-action film was co-produced by the studio with British producer Anglo-EMI and Westinghouse Broadcasting.[45]

Recycling Is Not Just for Trash

Hanna and Barbera, capitalizing on their good relationships with all the major networks, continued their high output across the next two seasons debuting 15 new shows, eight in 1973 and seven in 1974, along with the continued production of *The Flintstones Comedy Hour*, which was cancelled in 1973, *Wait Till Your Father Gets Home*, and *The New Scooby-Doo Movies*, with the latter two shows remaining in production

Poster for *Charlotte's Web,* released March 1, 1973 (Everett Collection, Inc./Alamy Stock Photo).

through 1974. During this time they also worked with NBC executive Donald Carswell to develop Peter Puck, a character used to explain rules and strategy to hockey viewers during NBC's Hockey Game of the Week and CBC's Hockey Night in Canada, a strategy employed by other networks, including FOX's Cleatus the robot in 2005, to engage young fans.[46] The studio also released three *ABC Afterschool Specials*, another *Saturday Superstar Movie* (then known as *The New Saturday Superstar Movie*), and *Movie of the Week*. As with the high output the previous season, the quantity of content resulted in very few memorable series and films, but both the successful and unsuccessful attempts to launch new franchises and create popular characters informed the development of later content as Hanna-Barbera, and television animation as a whole, continued its slow decline in the second half of the 1970s and the early 1980s. The spring of 1975 also marked a huge transition in the leadership of networks along with several technical advancements that changed the power balance among what was now the "Big Three" broadcast networks.[47]

Of the eight series premiering in the fall of 1973 no fewer than six were mystery or adventure shows modeled after previous programs, particularly *Scooby-Doo, Where Are You!* and *Josie and the Pussycats*. Arguably the most forgettable series of this collection was *Butch Cassidy and the Sundance Kids*. The show followed a band, Butch on lead vocals, blonde Marilee on tambourine, brunette Steffy on bass, and Wally on drums. The show was a direct copy of *Josie and the Pussycats*, even using the same storylines and dialogue from the original series. The characters also fit very broad stereotypes popularized by *Josie* and *Scooby-Doo* with the good-looking lead singer, the sensible brunette, the attractive but occasionally ditzy blonde, and the male drummer who is less attractive than the lead and acts as comic relief. The group, which like Josie's band, lives a double life as a pop band and detectives, are joined by Wally's anthropomorphic dog, Elvis. Part of the unpopularity of the show may have been due to confusion over the title, which many children surely thought the series was an adaptation of the popular 1968 film or at least a Western, rather than another carbon copy of a past success, leading them to quickly change stations. One notable feature was the casting of Micky Dolenz as the voice of Wally, who continued to receive more voice work only a few years after working as the drummer and one of the lead vocalists for The Monkees.[48]

Two more shows that reworked scripts from *Josie* and *Scooby-Doo* were *Speed Buggy* and *Goober and the Ghost Chasers*. Speed Buggy featured three teenagers, Mark, Debbie, and Tinker, and their anthropomorphic dune buggy which can be summoned by a remote walkie-talkie. Partially inspired by the "Chugga-Boom" vehicle in *The Perils of Penelope Pitstop* and emulating both the popular Japanese-import *Speed Racer* and Disney's *The Love Bug*, *Speed Buggy* basically played the role of Scooby-Doo in the series, helping the teenagers defeat the villain or criminal on their adventures while adding comic relief to the proceedings. Mercifully, though, the teenagers were not in a band. Although the storylines were redundant and the show lasted only one season, *Speed Buggy* became one of the more popular creations to originate from this era, partially due to the fact the series was broadcast on all three networks between 1973 and 1978, appearing in syndication on NBC and ABC after its original run on CBS. The *Speed Buggy* cast also appeared in a crossover episode with Scooby-Doo, increasing the visibility of the vehicle.[49]

For audience members who wanted a mediocre copy of *Scooby-Doo, Goober and the Ghost Chasers* featured Goober the dog and his teenage companions Ted, Tina, and Gillie solving supernatural mysteries, often with the help of guest stars, similar to *The New Scooby-Doo Movies*. Unlike in *Scooby-Doo*, some of the ghosts they find are real and not merely a villain in a costume, and when it is someone acting as a ghost it is often not for malevolent reasons. The group uses various tools and substances to determine whether the ghost is real and to defeat the possible specter. Goober, unlike Scooby, has the ability to become invisible when scared and does not speak with the same impediment. The series had very little success in its original run as ABC's counterprogramming to CBS's popular *Star Trek: The Animated Series* but was notable due to the presence of the Partridge Kids in eight of the first eleven episodes before they disappeared for the last portion of the season, possibly due to the development of their own animated series. Other guest stars included Wilt Chamberlain and Michael Gray. The series may have been produced to appease advocates who complained of the superficiality of many cartoons from Hanna-Barbera and other studios since many of the storylines featured the gang battling a ghost from classic literature like MacBeth or Captain Ahab, although the plot was only loosely connected to the original work through very broad summaries. As earlier shows would suggest, the studio had no qualms about representing literature from other cultures, again drawing misappropriated inspiration from *One Thousand and One Nights* in one episode while misrepresenting indigenous Incan culture in another.[50]

The last original star and series to debut in the fall of 1973 was *Inch High, Private Eye*. As the title of the NBC series so subtly suggests, the show follows the adventures of a diminutive detective, his inquisitive blond haired, blue eyed niece, their friend Gator who acted as the dimwitted muscle for the group, and trusty St. Bernard, Braveheart, who plays the role of the funny animal of the series while carrying all of Inch High's gadgets.[51] There was not much notable about the series aside from a very similar mummy storyline as *Goober* and an entire cast inspired by popular characters and celebrities, a trope more frequently utilized in Hanna-Barbera's earlier shows. Inch High was a combination of Jack Benny and Maxwell from *Get Smart*, one of the series that inspired the animated program. Lori, his niece, was a carbon copy of Laurie Partridge, leading to misspellings in many articles about the show, and Gator was an amalgam of Jethro from *Beverly Hillbillies* and Gomer Pyle. A.J. Finkerton, the head of the detective agency, included another Joe Flynn imitation while his design mirrored Mr. Drysdale of the *Beverly Hillbillies*, with Mrs. Finkerton sounding very similar to Jane Hathaway, Drysdale's secretary on *The Beverly Hillbillies* which was cancelled in 1971 during the rural purge but was still popular among children through afternoon syndication.[52]

As discussed above, *Yogi's Gang* was the rare combined crossover spinoff introduced by the pilot, the telefilm *Yogi's Ark Lark*. The concept around the series made sense: gather the older characters waning in popularity, put them all together, and add a prosocial and pro-environment message to appease advocates and critics while the nostalgia and novelty of the characters interacting hopefully leads to solid ratings, renewed interest, merchandising opportunities, and good press similar to other educational shows like *Sesame Street*. Unfortunately, the execution was not there for what was a fairly straightforward series. The first issue was related to the overall storylines: the dialogue was fairly standard schtick from Hanna-Barbera, perfect for fans of slightly older programs like *Wally Gator* and *Snagglepuss*, but not necessarily an attraction for younger audiences. The group is forced to defeat unoriginal villains like Lotta Litter while flying around on the Ark, leading to extremely predictable storylines that at times became preachy. From an aesthetic and aural standpoint, the program was very low quality even for Saturday morning animation. The mostly static backgrounds and transitions suffered from poorly planned animation, leading to even more pronounced issues associated with limited animation. The laugh track was also inferior to other Hanna-Barbera shows even compared to the series in which the characters originally starred. Even the most diehard Yogi fan could not overlook these imperfections, especially since earlier Yogi series did not include a laugh track, leading to the show's demise before the calendar even reached 1974.[53]

Making Cartoons Out of Real People

In spite of similar issues with quality and the laugh track, another spin-off series had a little more lasting power than *Yogi's Ark*. The Addams Family first appeared as guest stars in *The New Scooby-Doo Movies* the previous year before Hanna-Barbera moved forward with an animated series after the audience response from the episode starring the macabre family. The Addamses first appeared on television in a live-action series that ran for 64 episodes between 1964 and 1966, but their appearance in *The New Scooby-Doo Movies* was the first animated appearance for the characters that originated in a satirical print cartoon in *The New Yorker*.[54] Hanna-Barbera designed the animated characters from Charles Addams' drawings, and most of the cast, including John Astin (Gomez) and Carolyn Jones (Morticia) reprised their roles as voices in "Scooby-Doo Meets the Addams Family."[55] Although the adaptation of the family, which featured the teenage detectives of Mystery Inc. house sitting for the Addamses when Gomez and Morticia take a trip, was adjusted some to ensure appropriateness for children, it was not a far departure from the original cartoon's style and the characters' personalities in the comics. The series, on the other hand, was another redundant retread in the mold of the original *Scooby-Doo* where the family traveled in an RV modeled after their Victorian home as they face various mysteries and misadventures. One of the running gags of the animated program that was transferred from the one-panel comic and live-action series was the family's lack of awareness about how they are seen by the rest of society, who are put-off, if not fearful, of the family. Both Astin and Jones had to be replaced for the series, but Jackie Coogan and Ted Cassidy reprised their roles as Uncle Fester and Lurch, respectively. Jodie Foster, who had made her debut redubbing voices for the *Amazing Chan,* actually provided the voice of Pugsley. The family was joined by a number of funny animals to further establish the Hanna-Barbera influence including Ocho the Octopus, Mr. V the Vulture, Ali the Alligator, and Kitty-Cat the Lion. The series, which was created for NBC, was actually scheduled against *The New Scooby-Doo Movies,* the show from which it was spun-off, creating an uphill ratings battle for the family. It did help the series when it was moved to an earlier time slot, lasting on NBC for three years even after only one season in production.[56]

A second adaptation of a 1960s live-action sitcom, *Jeannie,* premiered in the fall of 1973 right before *Speed Buggy* on CBS. The series follows the eponymous character from the popular *I Dream of Jeannie,* which like *The Addams Family* had become popular among adolescents in syndication, as she helps the star teenager Corey through the trials and tribulations of high school while they also navigate their romantic attraction. The presence of a female Jeannie was the only true similarity between the animated and live-action series. In the cartoon, Jeannie was a teenager with a red ponytail and her "master" is a surfer not an astronaut. Corey is joined by his friend Henry and many of the storylines involved Corey and Henry competing with their rival, portrayed as a stuck-up rich student, S. Melvin Farthinghill.[57] Jeannie had an apprentice genie, Babu, who often made mistakes granting wishes that Jeannie was forced to constantly fix. The involvement of Fred Silverman and Hanna-Barbera's old partners, Screen Gems, led to casting choices beyond Hanna-Barbera's typical voice actors, including Bob Hastings as Henry and a pre–*Star Wars* Mark Hamill as Corey. The association with the original series and a change from the *Scooby-Doo* imitations should have provided the series with a foundation for a successful run, especially when considering the marketing around the series including a crossover on *The New Scooby-Doo Movies,* which was broadcast earlier in the morning, a week after the premiere of *Jeannie.* Unfortunately, the show was clearly inspired by *The Pebbles and Bamm-Bamm Show,* with derivative and silly storylines that were described as insulting the intelligence of the young audience by groups like the National Association for Better Broadcasting—which, interestingly, praised *The Addams Family,* in which, as described above, the characters drove around in a Victorian house on wheels with an anthropomorphic land octopus.[58]

Adaptations and Advocates

The New Scooby-Doo Movies and ABC's *Saturday Superstar Movies* yielded uneven results in the 1973–1974 season. ABC and Hanna-Barbera had decreased production on the *Scooby-Doo* series and only produced one *New Saturday Superstar Movie* for 1973 as production of both of these guest-star led series and movies proved arduous and none of the episodes, telefilms, or series originating from the backdoor pilots proved to be especially memorable or successful. Their last *Saturday Superstar Movie, Lost in Space*, inspired by the live-action science-fiction series, was not picked up as a series and *The New Scooby-Doo Movies* production was cut in half as Hanna-Barbera looked to move on to different characters and concepts, gradually scaling their overall production schedule back to focus on television series for the rest of the decade. Their Australian division produced three film adaptations of classic novels that aired in the fall of 1973 on CBS's *Famous Classic Tales* sponsored by Kenner, *The Count of Monte Cristo, 20,000 Leagues Under the Sea,* and *The Three Musketeers.* The Australian division was being used more frequently, particularly in the production of adaptations and content not involving their most popular characters while Hanna-Barbera continued to use literature as a way to stave off criticism about the lack of educational or social value in their popular properties, producing seven more *Famous Classic Tales* between 1975 and 1981.[59]

In a similar attempt to appease children's television advocates in the winter of 1974, Hanna-Barbera and ABC premiered another adaptation that was a modern animated take on Edmond Rostand's *Cyrano de Bergerac.* Starring Jose Ferrer as Cyrano, after he won the Oscar for playing the same role in 1950, and Joan Van Ark as Roxanne, the film was meant to familiarize a new generation with the classic play. Cyrano was one of three *Afterschool Specials* Hanna-Barbera produced for ABC that premiered between January and April 1974. The second, the live-action *The Runaways,* focused on two teenagers trying to survive in the dangerous city, and the hybrid special *The Crazy Comedy Concert* was a film hosted by Tim Conway and Ruth Buzzi in the mold of Disney's *Silly Symphonies* that was produced to teach children about classical music. None of the *Afterschool Specials* were particularly memorable, although *Runaways* did earn Hanna and Barbera their first Daytime Emmy despite continuing the studio's negative perception of urban life. In January of 1974, they also premiered *Shootout in a One Dog Town* as an *ABC Movie of the Week,* a live-action telefilm closely inspired by the 1952 classic *High Noon.* The specials helped the studio's reputation by connecting with more critically acclaimed content for both children and adults.[60]

The last series premiering in the 1973–1974 season was also an adaptation, as the studio attempted to find success with its first true comic-inspired superhero series since the *Fantastic Four* in 1967. *Super Friends,* a toned-down version of National Publications' *Justice League of America,* was produced for ABC to compete against Hanna-Barbera's own *The Addams Family* and *The New Scooby-Doo Movies.* Silverman's rise through the executive ranks at CBS was aided by *The Adventures of Superman* in 1966, which, with *Space Ghost,* helped CBS's Saturday morning grow during the superhero trend in cartoons between 1966 and 1967. That series, produced by Filmation, along with *Scooby-Doo* and other Hanna-Barbera productions, helped establish CBS as a leader on Saturday morning in the 1960s. The episodes were repackaged as *The Superman/Aquaman Hour of Adventure* while Batman and Robin also made a late 1960s animated television appearance in their own series, which was repackaged into an hour-long series with episodes of *Tarzan* before everything was shuffled again to pair Batman and Superman. Other National Publications characters guest starred on all these series, including the most popular members of the Justice League.[61]

Superheroes to the Rescue

Television animation trended away from comic superheroes before ABC and Hanna-Barbera decided to re-enter the animated superhero market in 1973. ABC, which had obtained the rights to the Justice League of America for adaptation, wanted a series devoid of realistic violence and other content that could be seen as offensive by parents and advocacy groups who worried that the series would replicate violence in the comics. Hanna-Barbera also wanted to avoid associations with the military as the Vietnam Conflict continued to drag on, so they went with the name *Super Friends* to cut off any accusations of extreme patriotism as potential younger viewers looked negatively upon American involvement in Southeast Asia. The "friendlier" superheroes focused their energies on teamwork and presenting prosocial messages rather than defeating enemies with brute strength and violent use of their powers.[62] The Super Friends included Batman and Robin, voiced by Olan Soule and Casey Kasem, who provided the same characters' voices on the Filmation series joining Ted Knight (narrator) as holdovers, along with Superman, Aquaman and, for the first time as a regular on an animated series, Wonder Woman. The female superhero, who debuted in comics in 1941, first appeared in animation on Filmation's *The Brady Kids*, but concerns over adult themes related to bondage and the character's gender and sexuality helped limit her appearances in the first thirty years of her existence. Wonder Woman was included to decrease criticism about the lack of self-reliant women in leading roles in cartoons, and coincidentally helped extend the franchise's run when interest in the character increased after the hit live-action show premiered in 1975. The group was joined by new characters and superheroes in training Wendy and Marvin, and of course, as a Hanna-Barbera series they had a talking animal, Wonder Dog.[63]

The producers hired a child psychologist to assist with the show, an approach utilized successfully by shows like *Sesame Street* and *Fat Albert and the Cosby Kids*, to ensure the show was not only appropriate but also provided young audiences with positive, prosocial messages. Most of the episodes involved a villain or misguided individuals creating an ecological or conservational disaster that the heroes are forced to fix. Each episode they are joined by other National superheroes like Green Arrow and Plastic Man, exposing a new generation to the characters and later introducing new elements to the series like the Hall of Justice, which found their way to the *Super Friends* and *Justice League* comic series. Alex Toth, who had overseen past superhero shows *Space Ghost* and *Birdman*, was supervising the studio's Australian division and provided creative input for the series. When the pilot came back to Barbera, he made drastic edits to increase the cuts, explosions, and sound effects to reduce long, "interminable" scenes that could repel the younger audience that Silverman desired when he requested a toned down version of the Justice League.[64] Although the series had a successful first run and inspired several reboots in the succeeding decade, many current fans of the characters see the *Super Friends* franchise as too childish or cartoonish compared with comic versions of the characters.[65]

Changes in the Industry Force Adjustments

For Hanna-Barbera and its partners, the 1974–1975 season was an unexpected transitional year. Feeling comfortable with the relationship it had with the networks and co-producers, the studio experimented with different genres and formats, but these attempts were short lived as the animation duo faced structural changes throughout the television industry. They still produced a few programs based on previous formulas, including the creation of one of their most enduring characters. Possibly inspired by the success of *Super Friends*, Hanna-Barbera created an original "superhero" comedy series. *Hong Kong Phooey* starred Penrod "Penry" Pooch, a completely anthropomorphized dog working in a human world as a janitor at a police station. Convinced of being a master of martial arts after taking a correspondence course and reading the "The Hong Kong Kung Fu Book of Tricks," when Penry overhears a crime being committed over dispatch he changes into Hong Kong Phooey and attempts to thwart the criminal himself. Penry also rides in the Phooey mobile, a pagoda-styled car with a collection of gadgets and the ability to change into different vehicles like a boat or plane. Spot the cat, who lacks the anthropomorphic qualities of Penry, assists the superhero as the true problem-solver of the pair with Penry's overconfidence often creating precarious situations for the canine. Joe E. Ross, who played Officer Toddy on *Car 54, Where Are You?*, and previously voiced Peevely's assistant Botch on *Help! It's the Hair Bear Bunch*, provided the voice of Sergeant Flint reviving his catchphrase "Ooh, Ooh!" from the police series.[66]

The dispatcher, Rosemary, takes the call, relaying the information to Sgt. Flint while it is overheard by Penry as he cleans. Rosemary has a crush on Hong Kong Phooey, presenting an interspecies romantic interest in the children's series. The misinformed representations of Chinese and Asian culture did not prevent the series from a long run in syndication after ABC and Hanna-Barbera ended production at the end of 1974. Interestingly, even with all the attempted connections with Hong Kong and China, Scatman Crothers voiced Hong Kong Phooey. The first African American to voice one of Hanna-Barbera's numerous animal stars, Crothers should be credited with most, if not all, of the success of the series by giving the animated star a trademark voice and personality within the imitative television animation environment.[67]

Scatman Crothers voiced Hong Kong Phooey, who appears here in his Pagoda Car with his cat Spot (AF Archive/ Alamy Stock Photo).

One of the strangest of all of Hanna-Barbera's live-action-to-animation adaptations starred the Partridge Family, who appeared in eight episodes of *Goober and the Ghost Chasers* the previous season before disappearing from the series without explanation on the show. Behind the scenes, Hanna-Barbera had started producing a reboot of *The Jetsons* focusing on older versions of Judy and Elroy, since the original series still maintained a presence in syndication a decade after its only season. This development was altered when Fred Silverman saw an opportunity in the impending cancellation of *The Partridge Family*, the popular live-action Screen Gems series starring the musical traveling family. The live-action ABC series was perfect for a second life in syndication and was actually growing in popularity internationally, as the episodes, and music, were marketed in the United Kingdom and other countries outside the United States.[68] This premise was ideal for Hanna-Barbera, which had created and adapted several series in a similar format where the stars are in a band and play a song (or two) as a part of the larger storyline. The studio decided to replace *The Jetsons* with the Partridges and *Partridge Family 2200 A.D.* was born. The sitcom still featured the family traveling and playing gigs but inexplicably they did so in intergalactic locations rather than in their garage or on the road throughout the United States. The family traded their multicolor bus for a flying car as they continued to play and deal with issues among the group with the help of Veenie the Venetian, Marion the Martian, and Orbit, a robotic dog. Danny Bonaduce (Danny Partridge), Brian Forster (Chris), and Suzanne Crough (Tracy) reprised their roles from the live-action series. Susan Dey did play Laurie for the first two episodes before being replaced by Sherry Alberoni, a former Mouseketeer who had begun her work with the studio as Alexandra in *Josie and the Pussycats*. David Cassidy and Shirley Jones, the highest billed stars from the original series, did not reprise their roles as Keith and Shirley respectively. Cassidy was dealing with personal issues, while Jones said later she did not remember the series or being asked to be involved, which, if true, may suggest the studio assumed it could not afford her or Cassidy. Limited budgets were also displayed in the quality of the animation and stories, which were below the two series after which *Partridge Family 2200 A.D.* was modeled, *The Jetsons* and *Josie and the Pussycats*, with the latter group already starring in their own outer space spin-off in 1972. The decline of family or teen based bubblegum pop bands and counterprogramming in the form of another animated adaptation of a popular syndicated series, Filmation's *The New Adventures of Gilligan*, which did feature the whole cast voicing their animated counterparts, made it easy for young audiences to ignore. The family that inexplicably survived a two-century jump into the future could not make it into 1975 before being cancelled.[69]

The only other comedy produced by Hanna-Barbera for the 1974–1975 season did not feature any unique storylines or tropes, but it was the first show from the studio that did not include any organic characters, animal or human. Starring a Volkswagen Beetle racecar taking on a gang of motorcycles with the help of a 4x4 Sheriff and motorcycle officer, *Wheelie and the Chopper Bunch* was not the first Hanna-Barbera series to be inspired by Disney's *The Love Bug* movies, the second of which was released in the summer of 1974. That distinction belonged to the previous season's *Speed Buggy*, which also starred a vehicle that communicated in horns and other car noises. In *Wheelie*, the "Chopper Bunch," the officers, and Wheelie's love interest, Rota Ree, could all speak, making Wheelie's communication approach that much stranger. The series followed similar plot patterns as "B" motorcycle movies of the 1960s where the "gang" comes into a town and initiates chaos before the hero can either overcome the obstacles created by the villain, in this case during Wheelie's races, or defeat the villains outright to help other innocent vehicles. Like *Hot Wheels*, which was one of the first toy-inspired series on Saturday morning, Wheelie and the officers are helped each week by different vehicles like trucks and helicopters that Hanna-Barbera and its licensors hoped to sell.[70] With unimaginative plots and storylines, *Wheelie* was the first half-hour show in five years to be split into three segments. The six-minute episodes left nearly twelve minutes of commercial time, and in a true sign of cross-promotion, Wheelie used his horn occasionally to play the chime of NBC, the network the show appeared on throughout the season. Facing reruns of its own studio's *Scooby-Doo* and Warner's *The Bugs Bunny Show*, the program was not able to compete and was largely forgotten.[71]

Drawing Drama

In one of the few true attempts at innovation during the 1970s, Hanna-Barbera created two animated dramas to try to add variety to the schedule, which, aside from two series by the Krofft brothers, was completely occupied by animated comedies the previous season. The first series, which was inspired by the popularity of daredevils like Evel Knievel and the series *Speed Racer*, followed a family of performers as they traveled with a circus that they also managed. The series was originally named Wild Wheels and starred a character named Dare Devlin, but the series was ultimately titled *Devlin* and his first name Dare was switched to Ernie on the insistence of ABC to tone down any connections with danger in the marketing material. ABC also required safety tips in each episode to help mitigate complaints of having a negative influence on the viewers.[72] Ernie is joined by his orphaned teenage sister Sandy and brother Tod as they try to sustain the circus. Even with the action, it is not surprising that children were not drawn to a drama that dealt with serious themes like family dynamics and financial struggles. *Devlin* also had to compete with two adventure shows, the studio's own *Valley of the Dinosaurs* and *Land of the Lost*, which reduced the uniqueness of the dramatic series.[73]

In *These Are the Days*, Hanna-Barbera attempted to capitalize on the nostalgia trend that helped *The Waltons* and *Little House on the Prairie* become two of the top ten shows on television. The realistic animation for the period drama was clearly more detailed and complex than the drawings used for their comedy and most of their action series, with the exception of *Jonny Quest*. Like Shirley Partridge, Kathy Day, the matriarch, is a widow raising her children with the help of her father Homer. Although the show takes place during the first decade of the 20th century, it featured storylines that dealt with issues familiar to the young audience, like school relationships and sibling rivalries. Critics and advocates celebrated the series due to its prosocial message and lack of silly, unrealistic storylines, but children were not nearly as enamored by the series, especially considering they were often already forced to watch *The Waltons* and *Little House on the Prairie* as a part of shared family television time. The series was off the schedule after a second season of reruns aired on ABC in 1975.[74]

The studio's other two premieres of the season were adventure series set even further back in time. New findings and theories related to dinosaurs led to a renewed interest in the extinct creatures throughout the late 1960s and early 1970s, which trickled into popular culture and Saturday morning by the middle of the decade. Hanna-Barbera produced two series that premiered in 1974 that tried to capitalize on the public's fascination with prehistory. Hoping to also placate critics, Hanna-Barbera consulted with the American and Los Angeles County Museums of Natural History to ensure (some level of) accuracy in the development of a live-action series that was ultimately titled *Korg: 70,000 B.C.* The series was intended to be an educational series following a family of Neanderthals during the Ice Age, but the main aspects of the family's life, including hunting, death, and sex, are left out or watered down to make sure the content was appropriate for, and did not scare, the young audience. The series, which was produced in a faux documentary style, featured Burgess Meredith as narrator who would go on later that year to star in the first of two consecutive films that earned him Academy Award nominations for Best Supporting Actor, *The Day of the Locust* (1975) and *Rocky* (1976). Hanna-Barbera, ABC, and their partners clearly had high hopes for the series with a number of related products, including a Milton-Bradley board game, being released concurrently with the series. The action and prehistoric appeal were not enough to overcome the educational focus and the weak lead-in represented by *Devlin*.[75]

Conceptually, the animated *Valley of the Dinosaurs* should have been successful, starring a science teacher, John Butler, and his family who experience an accident during a rafting trip on the Amazon and are transported to an anachronistic prehistoric world. Unfortunately, that same season NBC and the Krofft Brothers premiered *Land of the Lost*, a large-scale live-action series with nearly the exact same premise, except the lead is a widower and the path to the prehistoric world is somewhere in the Grand Canyon on the Colorado River. *Valley of the Dinosaurs* was also scheduled directly opposite of *Land of the Lost* and *Devlin*, the latter of which aired right before *Korg*, leading to the hit series on NBC overshadowing or directly defeating three Hanna-Barbera series. In the largely forgotten series, John is joined by his wife Katie, children Kim and Greg and dog Digger as they try to survive in the strange world. They meet a Neanderthal-like "cave" family, husband Gorok, wife Gara, children Tana and Lok, and pet stegosaurus, Glump. Gorok's family help the Butlers settle, as the modern family introduce technologies like the wheel and sailboats to the hidden world. The building of these tools held an educational lesson about the science and machinery behind these discoveries, similar to the way *Land of the Lost* was meant to explore linguistics and communications through the creation of a language specifically for the Krofft production.[76] One of the consistent plotlines of the series found John's condescending attitude getting in the way of cooperation and respect, before the wives and children step in and humble John as they work to survive and escape the prehistoric world. In spite of stereotypical "cave-dweller" broken English dialogue, the presence of multiple "funny animals," and a few too many puns from the children, the storylines and animation in *Valley of the Dinosaurs* were well above the typical Saturday morning or Hanna-Barbera fare, but from a marketing standpoint, the series was a victim of timing and scheduling as series was "Lost" among similar programming.[77]

Struggling in a New Era of Animation, Television, and Representation

When taking a bird's eye view of Hanna-Barbera's production output between 1970 and 1975, it is hard not to notice the sheer amount of content from the studio that inundated American television, particularly on Saturday morning. Hanna-Barbera was responsible for over three-quarters of children's television on the schedule by the 1970s, producing and releasing all of this content while many of their older shows, like *The Jetsons*, continued to capture the quickly changing children's audience each season with younger viewers becoming fans of past series as they got older. Looking closely at the series and films produced throughout this half decade, it is clear Hanna-Barbera recognized the continued success of older and adapted characters and series, as a large portion of their content was either created out of the mold of older series (e.g., *Goober* from *Scooby*), were spin-offs (*Yogi's Ark*) or were direct adaptations of literature (*Oliver the*

Artful Dodger), film (*The Amazing Chan*), television (*The Addams Family*), or comics (*Super Friends*). As a result, many of these series, and their stars, got lost in the stream of similar shows, and even when Hanna-Barbera was truly innovative or produced content outside of its typical mold, the success was often limited due to circumstances beyond its control. *Charlotte's Web* could have been a true turning point for the studio, in the same way *Snow White and the Seven Dwarfs* helped Disney transition from a small animation studio to an influential media company, but bad press related to E.B. White's displeasure with the adaptation hurt public relations around the classic film. This caused some fans of the book to reject the film, though evidence of its original potential is contained in ancillary sales of the film decades later.[78] Some bad luck, like the Krofft Brothers and NBC premiering *Land of the Lost* the same day and time as *Valley of the Dinosaurs*, also contributed to several of their productions not reaching the levels of success that the studio and their partners hoped.[79]

Even with these moments of innovation, Hanna-Barbera still relied on redundant formulas, plots, and character designs that maintained many of the same issues with representation of race, ethnicity, gender, and culture that had been present in productions by Hanna and Barbera for over thirty years. The studio, and the animation industry, clearly lagged behind Hollywood as a whole as African American representation increased exponentially throughout 1960s and 1970s with Sidney Poitier's Best Actor Oscar win for *Lilies in the Field* in 1964, *I Spy*, the first original scripted television series to star an African American, and *Julia*, the first to star an African American woman, serving as a few of the many milestones throughout this period. This in no way represented equal visibility, but it was still an improvement over animation's underrepresentation. Unlike early shows, like *Amos and Andy*, the representations were positive even if the engagement with African American culture was limited. A combination of luck and the talent of Patrice Holloway led to one season in which Hanna-Barbera actually featured original characters that did not derogatorily represent non-white populations. Considering it was still white writers, these representations were far from perfect, but for children of color, particularly African American children who had to endure over seven decades of either being ignored or portrayed negatively in animation, it should have been a step in the right direction. Unfortunately, Hanna-Barbera went right back to the representations and formulas it was familiar with to maintain its bottom line and to continue to attract the familiar audience, white males, not creating a new non-white star or co-star until 1978, which further highlighted the studio's disconnect in representing and reaching non-white audiences that will be discussed further in the next chapter.[80]

African Americans and Animation

The shows and characters that debuted in 1970 were a step over the very low bar set by the studio and the animation duo over their nearly four decades in the industry, but *The Harlem Globetrotters* still contained questionable content and representations, some of which existed before development of the series. After their transition from purely basketball players to entertainers, some in the African American community questioned whether their position as the jesters of the hardwood was the best portrayal of African Americans, especially when considering the team, like other media, were the only interaction with non-white populations many suburban families experienced. Seeing the players joking around during the game was considered by some to be "Uncle Tomming" as the players entertained the majority white crowd in arenas and on screen, and by some as disrespecting the game and making themselves look foolish. Considering the team continues to perform around the world, these concerns have not slowed their success, but there is always risk of misrepresentation or exacerbating the issues above when you do not have the voices of those being portrayed and business and content decisions are being made by studio and network executive with little connection to these experiences. Also, *The Harlem Globetrotters* animated series lacked any true engagement with African American culture, even though the team originated from a milestone of African American culture, the Harlem Renaissance, and whose existence was necessitated by segregation in professional basketball.[81]

This lack of engagement with African American culture was even clearer in *Josie and the Pussycats* where Valerie shared the marquee with her two band mates and the Cabots. As discussed above, Hanna did not even want Valerie on the show, hoping that Archie Comics and CBS would move forward with Pepper as the third bandmate in the series. Fortunately, La La Productions, who oversaw the music, refused to entertain the notion, but the writers still had to write for a female African American character, an intersection they had no experience in representing with cultural awareness. As with *The Harlem Globetrotters*, the writers presented this character through the lens of white male supremacy, so even though visually and aurally she displayed many of the characteristics that are associated with African American women, her actions and personality still fit within white male expectations and practices, especially when Valerie is seen as less attractive or lovable than the white Josie because of her intelligence.[82] It is also important to note that these barriers were finally broken in television animation through programs inspired by sports and music, two areas of culture where, according to representational scholar Todd Boyd, a "sense of Blackness could be articulated and even turned into a profitable commodity." Although popular culture can be a site where non-white and non-male voices can be heard, it is typically with the promise of profit for those in the industry that have traditionally identified as white males.[83]

Josie and the Pussycats also magnified Hanna-Barbera's continued issues with gender and representing female or non-male characters. The program was the only series to star multiple female characters and to have a cast that was not majority male characters. Clearly the writers were creating characters based on their own experience while their continued reliance on past plots and tropes led to the recycling of very similar white, mostly male characters. *Jeannie* also recycled many of the issues that faced the live-action series concerning a female genie serving a male master who often wants to control her powers.[84] Fortunately the massive success of *Scooby-Doo* created a mixed-gender formula for their later series, signaling some progress, but males still led the groups in the series and occupied the majority of starring and supporting roles. This is especially true for the plethora of funny animal stars, which, aside from the romantic interests, were almost exclusively male and, with the exception of *Hong Kong Phooey*, were voiced by white male talent. In many ways the small step for progress for Hanna-Barbera and other animators around 1970 merely highlighted how far television animation needed to go to equally and responsibly represent non-white populations, an issue that is still plaguing the industry today.[85]

Even with the presence of Scatman Crothers, *Hong Kong Phooey*, along with *The Amazing Chan and the Chan Clan*, further exemplified the company's issues representing other races and cultures. Because of a renewed "yellow panic" motivated by the Korean War and Vietnam War, and increased sensitivity concerning the criminalization of African Americans and Latinx populations in film, ethnicities originating from Asia became an easy source of villainy and derogatory representations in the late 1960s and 1970s. Clearly *Hong Kong Phooey*, both the show and character, appropriates Chinese culture throughout the series, lumping together practices and traditions from several cultures and groups originating from Asia.[86] Even with a voice actor of Chinese descent, the *Amazing Clan* had similar issues regarding white writers and animators failing to knowledgeably represent non-white people. The original voices for the "Chan Clan" alone were enough to nearly get the series kicked off the air, since the dialogue was so racist and broken it was unintelligible to the audience. As discussed above, Hanna-Barbera stopped producing original content starring African American characters after 1970, and by 1972, after the *Amazing Chan Clan* they did the same with those from China, Chinese-Americans and other ethnicities originating from Asia.[87] They did make one more attempt in 1977 to create several original non-white supporting characters, superficial portrayals which will be discussed further in the next chapter.

Classist Cartoons

Even when examining the white characters, both human and animal, the diversity of backgrounds and representations is extremely limited. Not all characters had last names but when they did many of the surnames corresponded with their species like Bear and Cat. The characters that did have last names, with obvious exceptions like Charlie Chan, had Anglo-Saxon or Germanic surnames, supporting arguments that most of their characters were not only white, but originating from Western Europe. Families like the Boyles (*Wait Till Your Father Gets Home*) and Butlers (*Valley of the Dinosaurs*) exemplified the middle class heteronormative American "dream" of, at the very least, economic comfort, if not the ability to display disposable income.[88] The Butlers are on a family rafting trip on the Amazon before they are swallowed into another dimension, continuing the ideologies represented in earlier family shows like *The Jetsons* and *The Flintstones* portraying the ideal white upper middle class family in two different time periods, while also assuming vacations were a shared experience for all Americans. In the case of the *Valley of the Dinosaurs*, it juxtaposed contemporary expectations with the communicating of history as a white-led progress through time. This whitewashing of history also occurs in *Korg: 70,000 B.C.* and especially *These Are the Days*, which presented the same rose-colored nostalgic view of history as shows like *The Waltons*.[89] Even when entire families are not shown on a regular basis, for example in *Scooby-Doo* or *Josie and the Pussycats*, the studio still displays white middle class sensibilities through their characters. Daphne Blake, Velma Dinkley, and Fred Jones clearly display the style of those coming from white suburban households while Shaggy seems to be a hippie by choice, especially since it is revealed that his father is a police officer. They also live in what looks to be a middle to upper class shore town most likely on the Pacific Coast. Crystal Cove, Mystery Inc.'s home, seems to be located in Orange County around the Laguna Beach area. Franchises like *The Flintstones*, *Scooby-Doo*, and *Yogi Bear* in combination with the constant reliance on formulas and syndicated reruns ensure that these ideologies were not just disseminated but broadcast repetitively through a time block that had become one of the most consistently profitable for the broadcast networks.[90]

For decades, Hanna-Barbera was considered the newcomer or a niche company, as it constantly had to reaffirm the possibilities represented first by television animation, then the market for animation aimed at adults, and lastly, as a children's media producer. *Scooby-Doo* was very much their breakthrough series in their effort to establish themselves on Saturday morning, and the productions of the next decade could be seen as evidence of a certain level of complacency even as they disseminated more content than ever before. They relied on formulas, particularly their own as the studio became a sort of cartoon factory. Very few series originated from outside of this assembly line, where minor changes to aesthetics and storylines were meant to mask the redundancy of many of their cartoons, particularly the series aimed at children on weekend mornings. Although it did not win over critics, the strategy created opportunities for Hanna-Barbera to dominate the children's media as the audience continued to consume this repeated content, and if they ever did get bored, a new generation was ready for consumption the next season.

Hanna-Barbera and the broadcast networks had no qualms about taking advantage of children's appreciation for repetitiveness as this strategy produced a sense of familiarity for children constantly dealing with new experiences and information.[91] Some of the content, like *Charlotte's Web*, really was innovative for the animation studio, but for the most part the profitability of redundant series and limited animation took precedence over creating quality animated content. In many ways this studio that helped influence both the animation and television industries had transitioned from rebellious innovator to another giant in the media, and competitors, some of which were directly influenced by Hanna-Barbera, emerged as they attempted to attract audiences who wanted something different than another show out of the *Scooby-Doo* mold. The relationships the studio built over their first three decades would help them continue their dominance, but challenges from other studios, changes in the industry, and deregulation would influence the direction of the company as they continued to squeeze maximum profit from the franchises and formulas on which they relied.

6

1976–1978:
Profits, Policy, and Popeye

American Neoliberalism Grows

Entering the second half of the 1970s, Hanna-Barbera was producing the most television animation of *any* American studio. After several years of high output, they scaled back production for the 1975–1976 and 1976–1977 seasons, riding the popularity and profitability of the dozens of programs that already filled the schedule from previous seasons. This reserve of content and contracts covering the next several seasons also placed Hanna-Barbera in an advantageous position. While major shifts in leadership at all three major networks led to disruption and change for other genres and production companies, the animation studio's long track record of success often led executives to call on their collection of programs and characters to ensure stability to their weekend mornings. This reliability was a double-edged sword, since it also limited opportunities to create or innovate beyond their typical characters, styles, and formulas, contributing to the decline that started earlier in the decade and would continue through the early 1990s.[1]

Industry changes spurred by continued growth and new technologies led to the restructuring of the major networks and animation producers over the next few years. This restructuring combined with pressure from advocates along with policy and economic shifts in the American media system helped create the foundations for a new era in both the animation and television industries that took hold throughout the second half of the 1970s, although American media did not fully enter into this era until neoliberal American ideology was fully realized under Reagan. Many of the necessary structures and institutions were built not only through these industry shifts but also through ideological messaging in various media. As discussed in earlier chapters, Hanna-Barbera was fully complicit in supporting ideals that were associated with American capitalism and neoliberalism, both in their business practices and their content, but over the course of a few years new producers entered the industry and started competing with the animation duo at their own game.[2]

One Risk Too Many:
Filmation Challenges Hanna-Barbera

Only one new show was produced by the studio for the fall of 1975. Hanna-Barbera had invested significant resources and time into the large output of the previous two seasons, hoping that at least a few of the shows would catch on with young audiences. Only *Speed Buggy* and *Valley of the Dinosaurs* remained from the influx of shows from the two preceding seasons, a possible signal that Hanna-Barbera was losing touch with Saturday morning viewers, especially with respect to creating popular franchises and characters. Along with these two shows and their new production for CBS, the rest of the Hanna-Barbera representation came in the form of older shows like *Scooby-Doo, Where Are You!* and *The Jetsons*, which were reaching new viewers as their original audiences had moved on from Saturday morning as they got older. Only a few years after dominating three-fourths of the weekend morning schedule, their impact was down about 30 percent as networks looked to diversify their lineups with shows from different production companies like Filmation, which had become Hanna-Barbera's biggest competitor with hits like *The Archie Show* and *Fat Albert and the Cosby Kids*. More live-action fare was also featured on weekend mornings, most notably from the aforementioned Filmation and the Krofft Brothers. After their own unsuccessful attempts at live action with shows like *Korg: 70,000 B.C.* Hanna-Barbera stopped producing live-action dramas for children while Taft began distribution of programs from its subsidiary Solow Productions, including *A Man from Atlantis*. Solow was spun off of the animation studio's live-action unit, eliminating most of Hanna-Barbera's live-action budget.[3]

Some of this decline could be linked to the leadership changes at the networks as Fred Silverman, who continued to be Hanna-Barbera's closest network partner, was hired away from his position at CBS by ABC becoming the President of Entertainment for the "third" network.[4] This reshuffling presented opportunities to children's television producers outside of Hanna-Barbera to take risks as they attempted to develop the next hit show or idolized character. Four Sid and Marty Krofft live-action productions were scheduled across all three major networks in the fall of 1975, successful series like *H.R. Pufnstuf* and *Land of the Lost,* leading to the proliferation of Krofft series and motivating other production companies to attempt to develop live-action series, with very limited success.[5] By 1975, Hanna-Barbera had mostly given up on live-action series, but Filmation had moderate success with the live-action superhero series *Shazam!*, co-produced with DC and adapted from the publisher's comic series of the same name. Hanna-Barbera continued to produce live-action specials, like *The Phantom Rebel* about two adolescents that help an American Revolutionary guerrilla soldier escape from British pursuit. The special aired as a part of *NBC's Special Treat*, a series of specials developed as a response to *ABC's Afterschool Specials* targeting adolescent viewers.[6]

In the fall on 1975, Filmation debuted *Isis*, which featured the first live-action female superhero in a weekly television series, and combined it with *Shazam!* to create hour-long packaged episodes for NBC.[7] Another live-action Filmation production, *Uncle Croc's Bloc,* debuted on ABC during the same hour time slot as *Shazam!/Isis* starring Charles Nelson Reilly as Uncle Croc, an outwardly dissatisfied, possibly inebriated host of a local children's television show. Young audiences completely missed the satire contained in the series, and it was a ratings and marketing disaster for ABC and Filmation as critics and advocacy groups expressed concern over the mature themes and jokes, which were punctuated by an adult laugh track. The show was taken completely off the air by 1976, replaced by *Super Friends*, which was public confirmation that Silverman was again going to rely on Hanna-Barbera to rebuild its Saturday morning while also moving away from Filmation. This also cemented Filmation's position behind Hanna-Barbera in the Saturday morning food chain, especially with Silverman and ABC. Filmation did have co-productions with DC and Archie Comics, helping the company remain profitable even as producers attempted to create original characters with the same cultural impact as Yogi Bear or Fred Flintstone.[8]

Avoiding Violence with Animals and Comedy

The one new show starred old friends that had helped the animation duo get their start in the industry. *The New Tom and Jerry Show*, produced in association with MGM, starred the cat and mouse duo in their first cartoons produced exclusively for television. Reissued and edited *Tom and Jerry* short films were popular in syndication for nearly two decades with Gene Deitch and Chuck Jones directing 47 new *Tom and Jerry* films throughout the 1960s in the original chase format adding to Hanna and Barbera's 114 total shorts sold to networks and affiliates. The 1975 series reimagined the cat and mouse as buddies in the mold of Yogi Bear and Boo Boo. Although there are times when the two compete, attempts to hurt or maim the other are completely removed from the relationship, to the disappointment to many ABC executives who lamented the growing influence of standards and practices and pressure from advocates, particularly on children's television and cartoons. Unfortunately, the continued presence of the older theatrical films undermined the new series, as audiences who appreciated the high animation quantity and violent comedy were disappointed to see another retread of past Hanna-Barbera formulas and storylines.[9] Furthermore, Tom and Jerry did not talk, so all the dialogue came from supporting characters, which contributed to confusion. The 48 new shorts were added to the *Tom and Jerry* syndication package sold to networks; however, the older films remained more popular than the new series as networks pressured animation studios producing new shows to limit, if not completely eliminate, violence.[10]

Hoping to use the popularity of *Tom and Jerry* to buoy a new character, Hanna-Barbera combined *The New Tom and Jerry* with *The Great Grape Ape Show*, starring another funny animal character, to create an hour long show to compete with two more veterans of the Golden Age of Animation, Bugs Bunny and Road Runner. The Warner Bros. duo teamed up for their own hour-long program on CBS after Silverman reacquired both shows from ABC before he was hired away from the network in May of 1975. Most of the content in *The Bugs Bunny/Roadrunner Show* consisted of repackaged theatrical shorts produced by Warner and then after 1965, DePatie-Freleng, with the new producers also animating interstitial content connecting the cartoons. The new series helped introduce a new generation to the Warner stars, leading to several other similar series that also brought characters like Daffy Duck, Sylvester Cat, and Porky Pig back into mainstream consciousness. Like the older *Tom and Jerry* films, the reissued Warner shorts featured violence and adult content that was produced in a different time, an excuse that could not be utilized for the production of new animation. We often see this rationale used for the continued reverence for racist, sexist, and bigoted texts and individuals of the past, which allows these figures, and their messages, to maintain a place in the public consciousness. The fact that animation has a much longer shelf life than the majority of live-action content with its broad themes and humor and the aesthetic qualities that could more easily be remastered or reformatted for different media and continued distribution presents opportunities for certain animation, characters, and messages to remain popular across generations.[11]

In *The Great Grape Ape Show*, the eponymous star was a 40-foot-tall purple ape who rode around on top of a van with his friend Beegle Beagle. Grape Ape has the mind of a human toddler, with his clumsiness and misinterpretations causing problems for those around him, which he often is able to fix with his size. He often responds to Beagle's presence by repeating his name over and over and jumping around in excitement.[12] The gorilla's color was most likely a way to aid with marketing and further separate their giant ape from merely being seen as a comedic King Kong, which might have actually helped the series since it is considered among the least innovative for Hanna-Barbera, a studio with a long history of imitation. The studio and network did not give up on the oversized simian over the next few seasons, partnering the show with other segments and series, hoping it would still catch on with children.[13]

The first of these attempts occurred in the fall of 1976 when Mumbly joined the hour-long *The Tom and Jerry/Grape Ape/Mumbly Show* as ABC and Hanna-Barbera pushed Tom and Jerry and Grape Ape on a less-than-receptive audience for a second season. The producers still hoped that *The Tom and Jerry Show* could capitalize on the renewed interest in reissued theatrical animation from the Golden Age. New episodes of *The Mumbly Show* joined reruns of the former two programs, kicking off ABC's Saturday morning against *Sylvester and Tweety* and *The Woody Woodpecker Show*. Mumbly was a mixed breed dog, possibly conceived as the twin to Muttley since they share the same look and mannerisms, including communicating through a series of snickers, looks, and, yes, mumbles. The format and the character were also inspired by Peter Falk's Columbo and his superior, the credit-stealing Captain Schnooker, was modeled after another popular television detective, Terry Savalas' Kojak. The creation of this "new" character may have been due to the fact that Heatter-Quigley Productions partially owned the rights to both Muttley and Dick Dastardly as the co-producer of *Wacky Races*, and to avoid sharing profits or credit, the studio created Mumbly. The packaging of the series did not work and the show was shortened to a half an hour before being completely cancelled at the end of the season. Grape Ape, Beegle Beagle, and Mumbly were seen in other Hanna-Barbera properties while the animation duo had to wait another fifteen years to again work with the cat and mouse they created.[14]

The Great Dane to the Rescue

Clearly Saturday morning, like the larger television industry, was going through a transitional period with the schedule pieced together with a mix of old and new live-action and animated fare. Each network also had longer packaged shows that sometimes mixed content from different eras, creating awkward programs like *The Tom and Jerry/Grape Ape/Mumbly Show* and opening opportunities for other producers like the 90-minute *The Krofft Supershow*. Fred Silverman immediately went to work on ABC's portion of the schedule, severing ties with Filmation and calling on Hanna-Barbera over the next few seasons to help stabilize the number three network's children's programming. Silverman had also brought Ruby and Spears over to ABC to oversee Saturday morning after they helped Silverman grow CBS into arguably the top network weekend mornings, so it is no surprise that they would call on the talking Great Dane that brought them all the most success. Ruby and Spears created *Scooby-Doo* seven seasons earlier, and Silverman made sure he obtained the rights to the franchise when CBS allowed the contracts to rerun *Scooby-Doo, Where Are You!* and the *New Scooby-Doo Movies* to end after the 1975–1976 season as it looked to revamp its lineup after Silverman's departure.[15] Returning to the half hour format of the original series, *The Scooby-Doo Show* continued to follow Mystery Inc. as they again attempted to solve various mysteries and capture villains disguised as ghosts and monsters. They did add a new Scooby country cousin, Scooby-Dum, modeled after Edgar Bergen's Mortimer Snerd, who had a recurring, but not regular, role on the series.[16]

Hoping to find success with the strategy that ultimately failed with *The Tom and Jerry/Grape Ape/Mumbly Show*, they partnered Scooby-Doo with another Great Dane who was a superhero with a voice similar to Red Skelton's Gertrude and Heathcliff, which had also served as one of the inspirations for Magilla Gorilla. *Dynomutt, the Dog Wonder* inexplicably had mechanical limbs that could extend, but the star often struggled to control his power as his partner, Blue Falcon (alter-ego of art dealer Radley Crown), was forced to deal with his canine sidekick's mishaps while also defeating the enemy.[17] The show was notable for increasing the separation between the straightly drawn human characters, like Blue Falcon, and the more cartoony animals as originally seen in shows like *Scooby-Doo* and *Josie and the Pussycats*. This highlighted the fantasy of anthropomorphic animals, like Dynomutt, who can easily communicate, interact, and even assist humans. Unlike the human characters in the former series, Blue Falcon, voiced by Gary Owens of *Rowan and Martin's Laugh-In*, presented almost no humor in his portrayal as Hanna-Barbera felt this helped create contrast and better accentuate Dynomutt's comedy. *Dynomutt* was also notable for the portrayal of the Mayor of Big City as one of the first African American public officials in Saturday morning animation, voiced by Los Angeles reporter Larry McCormick. The partnership in the larger series seemed to work, with several crossover episodes featuring both canines on *Dynomutt* helping to boost the popularity of the superhero as Tom and Jerry could not do for Grape Ape and Mumbly. By mid-season, the series was extended to ninety minutes to accommodate the inclusion of reruns of *Scooby-Doo, Where Are You!* This created a cornerstone in Silverman's rebuild of ABC's weekend morning schedule along with introducing another notable character to add to Hanna-Barbera's stable.[18]

Hanna-Barbera's other production also featured a character that may have not been an overwhelming success but still garnered some popularity among the Saturday morning audience. The hit movie *Jaws* debuted in 1975, convincing beachgoers to stay out of the ocean for several summers while inspiring a fascination with sharks that influenced popular culture and children's media, similar to the way new information on dinosaurs inspired an influx of prehistoric media earlier in the decade.[19] The animation studio that rarely missed an opportunity to capitalize on a trend created *Jabberjaw*, an anthropomorphic Great White Shark living 100 years in the future among humans in an underwater civilization. Feeling the concept was too realistic, Hanna-Barbera portrayed Jabberjaw as a drummer for The Neptunes, a band that travels between cities as it prevents the destruction of the underwater world by various villains between its weekly gigs. Drawing on successful gags and formulas from many of their most popular shows, like *Scooby-Doo* and *Josie and the Pussycats*, Hanna-Barbera gave *Jabberjaw* the same cast structure of these shows. Half of the band were women, but the leader, Biff, was still a white male in the mold of Fred Jones, and the women still filled the stereotypical roles of the dark haired, plain, and sensible one (Shelly) and the attractive ditzy blonde (Bubbles). Further reducing originality was Jabberjaw's personality, modeled after the Three Stooges' Curly Howard, borrowing the catchphrase, "I don't get no respect" from Rodney Dangerfield.[20] Jabberjaw found a niche in the public consciousness in subsequent programs after only sixteen episodes were produced during the original series' run on ABC. The Ruby and Spears creation was not quite the hit that the duo hoped to produce for ABC and Hanna-Barbera, partially due to competition from

Misterjaw, another shark-inspired series appearing during the *It's the All-New Pink Panther Laugh-and-a-Half Hour-and-a-Half Show Introducing Misterjaw* on NBC at the same time; however, *Jabberjaw* and *Dynomutt* did signal the studio's continued viability on Saturday morning after uncertainty the previous season.[21]

The last series produced for 1976–1977, *Clue Club*, was another series of the *Scooby-Doo* mold starring four teenagers and their two dogs solving crimes. The slight twist was that the two dogs, Woofer and Wimper, could only communicate with each other and the audience while helping the humans who operated the private detective agency, Larry, Pepper, D.D., and Dottie, solve crimes. Both Southern Bloodhounds wore deerstalker caps with the white-furred Woofer providing the comic relief for the series and Wimper playing the oft-sleeping straight man (or dog). The show was one of the first of many children's programs through the present to feature a young computer "whiz" that assists the group through his knowledge of technology. Also, unlike the other mystery shows in which the young detectives often were dissuaded from local authorities from assisting with the investigation, the Sheriff in *Clue Club* often requested help from the teenagers. Even with this mini-comeback by Hanna-Barbera, questions still remained concerning the long-term profitability of Hanna-Barbera properties as the studio's reputation for lower quality animation continued to haunt the animation duo.[22]

After Two Decades, What Now?

This reputation fully caught up with the studio in 1977–1978, a season in which Hanna-Barbera attempted to again increase its output to the levels from earlier in the decade, but upon examination it is clear the programs broadcast on all three networks and syndication throughout the season lacked the same writing or character development of their earlier series. In fact, of the five programs to debut in the fall of 1977, two were repackaged collections of old series with added segments and one was a spin-off of a co-produced adaptation. The two original programs were hour-long package shows, a format that sometimes repelled young audiences with short attention spans. Local affiliates who filled their schedule in half an hour segments were also put off by this format, and the studio was forced to restructure these shows after their original run for sale into second-run syndication, which represented a significant portion of the studio's business as it entered its 20th season as an animation studio.[23]

The first "package show" was actually more of a program block produced by Hanna-Barbera featuring five different series from the studio across a two-hour running time. *The Scooby-Doo All-Star Laff-A-Lympics* continued Silverman's love affair with the Great Dane he helped create as producers hoped the presence of Scooby and a number of other past stars could help boost the visibility of the new segments that were included in the block. Three of the shows were already part of *The Scooby-Doo/Dynomutt Show* while the two new series, *Laff-A-Lympics* and *Captain Caveman and the Teen Angels*, premiered as a part of the larger block in the fall of 1977. In the latter series, a parody of *Charlie's Angels*, the Mel Blanc-voiced Captain Caveman was found by three teenage women in a block of ice before being thawed revealing a prehistoric man with the ability to pull objects from his hair while also using his super-powered club to fly. Hanna-Barbera had previously used the idea of a magic club in the action series *The Mighty Mightor* in more dramatic fashion. In a true hat tip to the late 1970s, the club's powers often failed at the worst time, sputtering before he drops from the sky, leading to jokes about the energy crisis. "Cavey" spoke in "neanderthal" where he left out articles and switched pronouns, e.g., "Me think car is there." Although they still filled stereotypical roles, the ditzy blonde (Taffy), the rational, albeit frightened brunette (Brenda), and the smart one (Dee Dee), in an attempt at diversity Dee Dee was actually African American, embodying the persona of Velma from *Scooby-Doo* with a look similar to Valerie from *Josie and the Pussycats*. Dee Dee was also voiced by an African American, with Vernee Watson providing the talent for the character. Creators Ruby-Spears, Hanna-Barbera, and Silverman clearly had high hopes for the characters, even including them in the other new series during the block before the segment officially premiered.[24]

Maintaining Visibility: Packaging Old Characters and the Syndication Market

The other segment, *Laff-A-Lympics*, combined elements from *Yogi's Gang* and *Wacky Races* in a parody of *Battle of the Network Stars*. Bringing back most of the studio's popular stars throughout its twenty years in existence, *Laff-A-Lympics* aimed to draw the audience that had been fans of various Hanna-Barbera properties over the years, by including 45 different characters broken up into three different competing teams. *Yogi's Yahoos* attracted fans of early Hanna-Barbera shows featuring the studio's characters created before 1968, and *Scooby's Doobies* was comprised of the stars from later programs.[25] Characters not included in the competition like Fred Flintstone and Jabberjaw guest starred,

Captain Caveman and the Teen Angels (from left, Brenda Chance, Dee Dee Sykes, and Taffy Dare) (AF Archive/Alamy Stock Photo).

placing the original Hanna-Barbera characters featured throughout the series well over fifty. *Josie and the Pussycats* could not be included due to the rights to the characters being owned by Archie Comics, which may have partially explained the inclusion of Captain Caveman and the Teen Angels to fill Scooby's team. The third team, the Really Rottens, were villains from across the entire history of the studio joined by a number of new characters including the Creepley family. Not surprisingly, they often cheated as the other two teams cooperated and competed fairly. As with *Wacky Races*, the scripted competition was secondary to the Olympic parodies and competition jokes featured throughout the series. The entire block was a big hit, helping ABC garner so much positive attention it pushed CBS to shuffle the schedule two more times throughout the season. CBS even purchased and broadcast episodes of *Scooby-Doo, Where Are You!* to compete against a block containing the same show. Like *Yogi's Gang*, the show was a way to keep many of these characters in the public consciousness while also introducing younger viewers to the franchises. Hanna-Barbera hoped the programs, even the older ones, could maintain syndication value if audiences remained familiar across generations of viewers.[26]

For their other show featuring repackaged segments, Hanna-Barbera and Columbia Pictures partnered to construct the first series that the studio attempted to sell through barter syndication. The television environment was expanding rapidly, with the first superstation, WTBS, launched by Ted Turner in 1976, while cable proliferation and available channels, particularly independent stations, were increasing. This had two effects on the animation and children's media industry: first of all, it put more value on syndication since local or city stations were becoming regional if not national in the cases of WTBS and WGN-TV, through consolidation, stronger antennas and cable, increasing the audience for each station or market in which they sell the program.[27] Cable and independent stations also created more airtime, with most stations filling their weekly morning and afternoon schedules with children's television and cartoons. This expanded the market, while giving second life to older or less popular shows that would have been left off a more constricted schedule, representing the perfect low-cost content for smaller networks. Barter syndication involves a distribution company, in this case Columbia, trading the ability to air the program for access to airtime, either splitting the advertising revenue with the broadcaster or allowing the distributor to use the platform for future sales of the program.[28] To test this market, Hanna-Barbera repackaged six of its shows from earlier in the decade, *The Flintstone Comedy Hour*, *Goober and the Ghost Chasers*, *Jeannie*, *Partridge Family 2200 A.D.*, *The Pebbles and Bamm-Bamm Show*, and *Yogi's Gang*, into *Fred Flintstones and Friends*. The segments were connected through wraparound content featuring Fred introducing the different cartoons voiced for the first time by Henry Corden after Alan Reed passed away earlier that year.[29] The shows were re-edited into multi-part serial stories, with a collection of segments of each show making up the half hour program. The program was supposed to be broadcast daily, and the serialization was meant to draw viewers in throughout the week as audience members theoretically would want to tune in daily to see the conclusion of the storylines. With so little original content the show was no more memorable than any of the individual series within the program; however, it helped familiarize the studio with a program selling strategy that continued to grow in significance through the late 1970s, becoming a main channel for the broadcasting of children's animation throughout much of the 1980s. In fact, Claster Television, renamed from Romper Room Inc. who had previously created, produced, and distributed *Romper Room* before selling to the toy company Hasbro, distributed the program along with other popular children's series like *Transformers* and *The Muppet Babies*

Fred Flintstone welcomes guests to Bedrock City in Coconino County, Arizona, which opened in 1972 after the success of the original in Custer, South Dakota, which opened in 1966. A third opened in British Columbia in 1975. By 2019, all three had been closed or redesigned (Carol Highsmith/Library of Congress).

throughout the 1980s as various media companies took advantage of the growing syndication market.[30]

Along with the two previously mentioned series, Hanna-Barbera returned to their package roots in two of their new programs as well, premiering 10 different segments across two programs produced for NBC and CBS. The first series, *CB Bears*, premiered. on NBC in the fall of 1977 with the eponymous characters and five other segments filling the 60-minute program. The first series, like *Captain Caveman*, was a parody of *Charlie's Angels* starring three bears who drive a trash truck solving mysteries with the help of Charlie, their female guide that assists them through the citizen band radio in their truck. With names inspired by disco dances, Hustle, Boogie, and Bump were modeled after the *Hair Bear Bunch*, with Hustle even sharing Hair Bear's Phil Silver-esque voice. The storylines were fairly standard Hanna-Barbera mystery plots previously seen in numerous series. Whereas *CB Bears* derived most of the comedy from jokes and puns, the second series of the program was the first since *Tom and Jerry* to feature little to no dialogue, although the format was closer to Road Runner and Wile E. Coyote rather than the duo's cat and mouse creation. The eponymous bird of *Blast-Off Buzzard* chased Crazylegs the snake throughout the series as the reptile delighted in the buzzard's failures.[31]

The next segment in the cavalcade of mediocrity that was the *CB Bears*, *Heyyy, It's the King,* was inspired by the popular *Happy Days* with a lion named King fulfilling the role of Fonzie. He is joined by high school classmates and best friend Skids (alligator), Big H (hippopotamus), Clyde (monkey), Sheena (lioness), Yukayuka (hyena), and Zelda (ostrich), as the group finds themselves in various humorous scenarios in an idealized 1950s America. *Heyyy, It's the King* may have been missing an elephant, but pachyderm fans were appeased with *Undercover Elephant* who, with Loudmouse, solved mysteries as employees of Central Control in the spoof of spy properties like *Mission: Impossible*. Unlike the previous four segments, the last two did not feature animals, opting for humans and specters instead. *Posse Impossible*, a Western spoof whose characters first appeared in similar form in *Hong Kong Phooey*, starred the Sheriff of Saddlesore who must rustle up criminals in spite of his hapless posse Stick, Blubber, and Big Duke, the last of which was voiced by Daws Butler imitating John Wayne. The last series was possibly the most innovative concept, starring three ghosts, the eponymous *Shake, Rattle, and Roll* who run a hotel for other supernatural creatures while trying to keep humans out, including Sydney Merciless, a ghost chaser who wants to exterminate all ghosts.[32]

The second package series was scheduled opposite of *CB Bears* in November after premiering on CBS in a different time slot, originally competing directly with *Scooby's Laff-A-Lympics*. *The Skatebirds* was a hybrid series in the mold of *The Banana Splits* composed of live-action sketches featuring costumed actors which acted as wraparounds for four other series. The Skatebirds, Knock-Knock, Satchel, and Scooter, were often chased by Scat Cat in their segments, but unlike the Banana Splits they did not perform songs, only increasing the show's reputation as a cheap knockoff of the Kroffts' creations. Joining *The Skatebirds* were *Woofer and Wimper, Dog Detectives*, a segment that was merely edited *Clue Club* episodes that premiered the previous season, with a different title that highlighted the most likable characters from the series.[33]

Also premiering on *The Skatebirds* was *Wonder Wheels*, a segment in the mold of *Speed Buggy*, with the car replaced with a motorcycle driven by Willie Wheeler, voiced by Micky Dolenz, who was assisted by his girlfriend Dooley Lawrence. A third segment, *The Robonic Stooges*, reimagined the Three Stooges as mechanical superheroes, similar to Dynomutt, who solve mysteries for their boss Agent 000 at the Superhero Employment agency. On the surface the concept seems contrived; the original Stooges had all passed by 1975, and parents still loathed the slapstick comedians. However, CBS did notice a jump in interest during this segment when measuring viewer response, leading to its own series the next season. Following the model of *The Banana Splits*, *The Skatebirds* had a live-action segment, *Mystery Island*, a near copy of the former series' *Danger Island*. The most notable different in the general plot was the crashing of the crew's plane on Mystery Island rather than a shipwreck onto Danger Island. On *Mystery Island* three young scientists, Chuck Kelly and siblings Sue and Sandy Corwin, are forced to crash by Dr. Strange as the villain tries to gain control of their onboard computer, P.O.P.S, which he believes will help him conquer the world. As a possible attempt to address criticism about the gender imbalance and portrayal of women, Sue is a computer engineer, giving the program two different segments featuring female computer whizzes, with *Clue Club*'s Dottie representing the other. The series was off the air by January, debuting again the next season as a half hour program featuring *Mystery Island* and *Wonder Wheels* with *The Robonic Stooges* bringing Woofer and Wimper to their own spun-off half hour series.[34]

The last series of the season was Hanna-Barbera's only full-length new show, although it was a spin-off featuring characters familiar to both the studio and Silverman. After the success of the *Wonder Woman* live-action series, interest in the DC superheroes was renewed so ABC and Hanna-Barbera decided to revive the *Super Friends* in *The All-New Super Friends Hour*. Although the episodes were broken into four segments, ABC and Hanna-Barbera wanted the audience to know that none of the new episodes would feature old segments of the original series. In each episode, the first and last segment paired two superheroes in an adventure, with the last segment often pairing a regular cast member with a guest star, several of which were created for the animated series and became regulars in a higher budget series the next season. The second segment starred the newly created Wonder Twins, Zan, Jayna, and their space monkey Gleek in prosocial plots where the siblings teach teenagers positive lessons about the dangers of actions like vandalism or bullying. The third segment was the longest and included the entire group, including the Wonder Twins, defeating different villains each week. The show was the lead-in for *Scooby's Laff-A-Lympics* and became a huge success, helping ABC challenge the other two networks in Saturday morning while prompting the production of another *Super Friends* series the next season.[35]

Surviving the Changes, but Barely

ABC may have caught up with CBS and NBC on the backs of the *Super Friends* and *Scooby-Doo*, but Fred Silverman was still disappointed at the overall quality and creativity displayed in the television animation produced. He refused to work with Filmation after the disaster that was the *Uncle Croc Bloc*, relying on the Krofft brothers and Hanna-Barbera to fill the schedule, but the latter's offerings for the season beyond *The All-New Superfriends Hour* and *Scooby's All-Star Laff-A-Lympics* were disappointing. Recognizing that most of their successful series the last decade, including *Scooby-Doo, Where Are You!* and every segment of *Laff-A-Lympics*, were created by Joe Ruby and Ken Spears, Silverman helped them establish their own animation studio in 1977, agreeing to broadcast their first production, establishing a partnership between the new studio and the growing network that led to Ruby-Spears Productions' first nine series appearing on ABC. The network's president of entertainment hoped that the new studio could push Hanna-Barbera to invest the necessary time, money, and attention to improve the quality of its content. Due to the increasing demand for children's television and animation, Hanna-Barbera was able to remain successful throughout the 1970s even while repetitively recycling the same storylines, tropes, and characters. Considering that Ruby and Spears created *Scooby-Doo*, Hanna and Barbera had not created a hit show with original characters since *Wacky Races* a decade earlier, but the establishment of the new studio did spread many of the aesthetics and styles that had become synonymous with Hanna-Barbera throughout the previous twenty years.[36]

Celebrating (Certain) Holidays and Milestones

Two decades on air, and forty years as partners, were celebrated on Thanksgiving in 1977 through the special *Yabba Dabba Doo! The Happy World of Hanna-Barbera*. Hosted by Gene Kelly, who starred with Jerry Mouse in *Anchors Aweigh* (1945) along with the studio's live-action *Jack and the Beanstalk* (1967), the special looked at the duo's many productions while sharing how their cartoons are produced. Continuing the celebration, CBS also broadcast *Hanna-Barbera's All-Star Comedy Ice Revue* in January of 1978. In a roast of Fred Flintstone for his 48th birthday, Fred and Barney mix up the days, forcing the ice performers to stall until the guest of honor arrives.[37]

To celebrate the start of baseball later that year, NBC broadcast the baseball-themed *The Flintstones: Little Big League*. Hilarity ensues when Fred and Barney begin coaching their children's opposing teams. NBC was the third network to broadcast a Flintstones special that season after ABC broadcast *A Flintstones Christmas* in December of the previous year, the first time since 1966 new *Flintstones* animation appeared on the network. The special was an extended version of the fifth season episode "Christmas Flintstones," and truly highlighted the anachronism of the program, and the Christian bias of the studio, when considering that the Flintstones, as a prehistoric family, would have no knowledge of Christmas or the birth of Christ. The bias is clear when considering the fact they had not created any specials for non–Christian holidays up to that point.[38]

A few days before *A Flintstones Christmas* another Christmas themed movie, *The Gathering*, appeared on ABC. A departure from the animation and children's fare associated with the studio, *The Gathering* is a live-action prime time telefilm that follows the terminally ill Adam Thornton, played by Ed Asner, as he invites his estranged family to get together for one more Christmas before his death. Aside from his wife Kate, played by Maureen Stapleton, he does not want anyone to know about his illness, hoping to reconcile with his family without the pity or trauma of his impending death. The film was written by James Poe, who won the Academy Award for Adapted Screenplay in 1956 for *Around the World in 80 Days*, and directed by Randal Kleiser, who directed *Grease* the following year. The film earned five Emmy nominations in 1978, winning for Outstanding Special.[39]

Barbera often admitted he wished he produced more live-action content, and he executive produced *Mother, Juggs, and Speed* starring Bill Cosby, Raquel Welch, and Harvey Keitel in 1976. The film reportedly made over five times its budget at the box office, but Barbera would be limited in the live-action films he could produce due to contractual obligations to Taft. He did continue to advocate for the studio to produce more live-action content, creating a live-action sitcom pilot, *The Beach Girls*, for the 1977 season that was not picked up, and in the Spring of 1978 the studio premiered two live-action telefilms, the Afterschool Special *It Isn't Easy Being a Teenage Millionaire*, about a teenage girl who learns that she cannot buy happiness after winning the lottery, and a thriller, and *The Beasts Are in the Streets* about a truck crashing through the fence of an exotic wildlife preserve, releasing the animals into a community in Texas.[40]

That fall, also on NBC, the studio premiered *KISS Meets the Phantom of the Park*, a musical-mystery film featuring the band using its "superpowers" to save an amusement park. Debuting at the height of their popularity, the script was closer to a *Scooby-Doo* episode than a fantasy film, and the band felt it made them seem like a joke and buffoonish, which was accentuated by the band members' bad acting, limiting the marketing and promotion the studio and network could create for the special.[41]

The studio continued to pursue regular scheduling in prime time with *The Hanna-Barbera Happy Hour* that ran for five weeks toward the end of the season in April and May of 1978. The variety show starred two life-sized puppets, Honey and Sis, who sang, danced, and performed in sketches that parodied popular programs of the time, like *Laverne and Shirley* and *Three's Company*, a comedic strategy with which Hanna-Barbera was clearly familiar. The show was not renewed after the original run, which included a number of guest stars like Tony Randall and Betty White and featured wardrobes by Bob Mackie. At the same time, *The Hanna-Barbera Happy Hour* was in production, the hybrid variety series *The Funny World of Fred and Bunni*, starring impressionist Fred Travalena, was in development. In the pilot, Travalena was the live-action character while the animated, aesthetically attractive Bunni played the role of his conscience. The series, which like *Happy Hour* and *The Gathering* were produced for a prime time adult audience, was not picked up, possibly because of the continued hesitancy of putting regularly scheduled animated adult programming on network television along with the sexualization of an animated character.[42]

Unfortunately for ABC, *The Gathering* and *The Flintstones* special would be the last new Hanna-Barbera programs with Silverman at the network. The producer accepted an offer to become CEO and President at NBC, announcing the move in January of 1978, several months before the first Ruby-Spears series broadcast on ABC. He immediately made his presence felt through NBC's Saturday morning lineup, removing all shows, including *CB Bears*, but ironically leaving Filmation's *Space Sentinels*. He called upon Hanna-Barbera to fill the two and half hours between 8 a.m. and 10:30 a.m. with reruns of *Hong Kong Phooey* and a new package series *Go Go Globetrotters* that combined reruns of Alex Toth's *Herculoids* and *Space Ghost* with *The Harlem Globetrotters* and *C.B. Bears*, which was the only segment spared from package series of the same name. Aside from revitalizing their Saturday morning programming, Silverman had helped ABC move away from the "third network" status through a wide range of programming including the sexist "jiggle tv" programs represented by *Three's Company* and *Charlie's Angels* while also broadcasting *Roots*, one of the most influential and successful mini-series of all time, exposing much of white America to the long, violent, and tragic history of African Americans in the United States. NBC hoped that hiring Silverman away from their rival would help revive their own fortunes, having fallen behind the other networks, only registering three scripted series in the top 20 in the ratings the previous three years.[43]

When You Are on Top Everyone Aims for You: Adjusting to a Changing Industry

Hanna-Barbera continued to be the top television animator in the industry through the late 1970s, but the divide had clearly closed as a collection of other studios like Filmation, DePatie-Freleng, Sid and Marty Krofft, Rankin/Bass, and the spun-off Ruby-Spears helped break up the near-monopoly Hanna-Barbera had built earlier in the decade. By this time, both animators had entered their late 60s, and may have been showing some signs of disconnect between themselves, the audience, and the society in which they lived. The studio continued to find success, but they were mostly riding past hits and the relationships they built with networks and executives, particularly in television. In particular, their relationship with Silverman helped them maintain significant visibility in children's television and was also fruitful for Ruby and Spears, two writers whose eye for characters led them to become Silverman's right-hand people for Saturday morning, strengthening the bridge between the executive, Hanna, and Barbera, before supporting Ruby and Spears' creation of their own production company while still maintaining his relationship with the older studio.[44]

Advocacy groups like Action for Children's Television (ACT) and the success of PBS shows like *Sesame Street* continued to alter expectations for children's television. Except for some villain tossing and building explosions, pressure from groups had convinced animation studios to avoid most types of replicable violence, whether it be clashes in action-adventure series or brutal slapstick synonymous with *Tom and Jerry* and Golden Age Warner Bros. films. Although Warner package series like *The Bugs Bunny/Road Runner Show* became institutions on weekend mornings, the actual animation studio had shut down in 1969, a year after ACT was formed in Boston. Bugs Bunny, his co-stars, and Warner's library of over 1,000 shorts not only helped the characters stay in the public consciousness through Saturday morning, but provided more than enough content to satisfy children before they became too old for children's cartoons and a new generation of viewers adopted the show.[45] Unfortunately, Hanna-Barbera lacked the archive of content that

Warner had built over three decades in film and television. Unlike the Golden Age animated film studio, Hanna-Barbera did not have access to their film archive, which was owned by MGN. All the content that was available for them to offer to networks produced after they established their own studio in 1957. It is not a coincidence that their most popular characters were created before 1970; clearly their early series showed more originality than their later content built from formulas and molds of their earlier shows, but these programs, like the Warner cartoons, also contained much more violence, slapstick, and adult humor before criticism from parents and advocacy groups motivated the industry to do everything it could to avoid bad press and negative interactions with networks' standards and practices departments.

Rerunning Ideology

In the late 1970s, the average household owned 1.5 televisions, with over half of those televisions being color.[46] With many homes still owning only one color television, parents had most of the control over when and what children could watch, and although many took a passive approach, networks and producers still wanted to avoid becoming banned in homes by parents receiving information about appropriateness from critics and fellow parents. Although it is recommended *Sesame Street* be co-viewed between adults and children, parents still felt comfortable sitting children in front of Big Bird and public television for hours, whereas some parents cringed at the idea of their children spending five hours watching explosions and fighting. As Hanna-Barbera, and the industry, diluted their new content to avoid scrutiny, the earlier shows and films, with most of their violence intact, maintained their popularity in syndication and on the Saturday morning schedule.[47]

Many of these shows and reissued films were also originally produced for general audiences, targeting adults in between feature films in a double feature or in prime time television. The more mature content not only appeased children's desire to "watch up" and consume content aimed at older audiences, but it also extended the young audience's interest in the content, since the earlier programs and films contained humor and storylines they could grow into while still being able to enjoy the slapstick and animated characters when younger.[48] New characters created by Hanna-Barbera throughout the 1970s did not attract audiences nearly as wide as their 1960s characters, a fact unfortunately displayed by *Scooby's Laff-A-Lympics*. The spin-off series featuring these characters, like *Yogi's Gang*, only highlighted the contrast between the older content and their new productions, with networks and local stations preferring to air the 1960s series, even when offered the spin-offs and newer series in syndication packages. This fact was recognized by the studios themselves as they created two-hour package series, combining popular older series and characters with newer series, hoping to attract audiences to new characters through the established popularity of their classic shows. Unfortunately, children are slightly more discerning than given credit for, and a significant number of these shows ended production and even their first run only a few months after their premiere, often getting replaced by older shows and franchises.[49]

As a New Decade Comes, Politics and Progress Increase

As the 1980s approached, the animation industry faced a restructuring that left many animators behind, as new producers with more resources and less oversight entered the market. This included cable, with one of the first children's networks, Pinwheel, launching as the C-3 network in the Columbus, Ohio, area as a part of the QUBE cable system. The next year Warner purchased Sat-1 from Jim and Tammy Faye Bakker, making several of their networks available nationally to other urban areas with cable systems. *Pinwheel* became a programming block after Warner rebranded the children's network for national sale, agreeing to name the new venture "Nickelodeon." Nickelodeon did not truly take off in popularity until the mid–1980s as more homes got cable and the network, alongside its sister company MTV, came under the ownership of Viacom.[50]

Political shifts were also beginning to create unforeseen obstacles for the aging animators. They had largely avoided any real political associations or positions throughout their careers, ignoring most trends, like the hippie or beatnik trend, until they were accepted into the mainstream and their inclusion were seen as mere recognition of their existence rather than taking any real stance.[51] Even their jokes about the energy crisis in *Captain Caveman* avoided any real scrutiny due to the fact that it had become a part of daily life for most Americans by that time. They did partner with the Georgetown Center for Strategic and International Studies to produce *ENERGY: A National Crisis*, which featured *The Flintstones* characters taking viewers through the "history" of energy before promoting a message of conservation.[52]

Joseph Barbera and William Hanna spending time with some of their most popular stars (from left, Yogi Bear, Barbera, Scooby-Doo, Fred Flintstone, Bamm-Bamm Rubble, Hanna holding Pebbles Flintstone, Huckleberry Hound and George Jetson) (RGR Collection/Alamy Stock Photo).

The film was made available to schools and through syndication, but it also made light of an ideological issue related to very real tensions involving the United States (and the West) and nations of the Middle East, especially after America's support of Israel during the Yom Kippur War. In shows like *Jonny Quest*, several of the villains even parodied these Middle Eastern leaders. These tensions also inspired the revolution in Iran throughout the late 1970s, helping to create a second energy crisis. The Saur Revolution in Afghanistan in 1978 pushed the U.S.S.R. to consider military action in the country, an action the United States opposed, which, along with the Camp David Accords, helped end the detente between the Cold War powers. The Carter Administration's handling of these issues, along with other divisive decisions ranging from the creation of the Department of Education to the later boycott of the Olympics, led to a post–Nixon, neoliberal-led revitalization of conservative ideology leading up to the 1980 election.[53] This wave led to sweeping policy change that trickled down to television, children's media, and animation. Hanna-Barbera continued its normal practices for a couple more years, but the next decade forced the studio to react and again change how it operated, including facing the reality that their ages might be becoming an impediment to connecting with an audience, and that at some point they would have to relinquish their total control over the studio and its productions.

Hanna-Barbera's legacy, library, and relationships with established figures in the industry helped slow the decline, but signs their influence was waning appeared as the value of their content dropped over time and their business networks weakened in the midst of drastic changes in the television and animation industries. The next decade, but in particular the next few years, continued their attempts to stay in the public consciousness as they were currently constructed. A few worked to extend their relevance as it became more evident their animation style, humor, and representations were becoming outdated, while other productions companies started mimicked what Hanna-Barbera did stylistically and promotionally as well as or better than the studio as they entered their third decade.

7

1978–1981:
Holding On to the Past
as the Future Approaches

No Longer Smarter Than the Average Animator:
New Decade, Same Approach

As the industry entered the last full season of the decade, it was business as usual for Hanna-Barbera. They continued their high output, averaging over six shows a season between 1978 and 1981. Their approach was shifting, as they continued their usual production of adaptations and formulaic comedies, but beginning in 1978, there was a noticeable increase in the number of co-productions the studio entered into involving already established properties. Two of these series debuted in the fall, and much like their series that featured reissued episodes and spin-offs, the production of these series helped reduce risk and sell shows to the networks who were facing an economic downturn that would lead to a recession in the early 1980s. The networks were also becoming increasingly skeptical of the long-term viability of the current economic structure of children's television and animation while also facing increased competition from cable.[1] As a result commercial broadcast networks were less likely to take chances on properties that did not have some evidence of success. In fact, only one show premiered that fall without some association with a past franchise: Ruby-Spears Productions' first series *Fangface*, which, in spite of the creation of the new character, was a fairly obvious copy of *Scooby-Doo*, as Ruby and Spears hoped to capitalize on their most famous creation.[2]

Representation continued to be a huge problem for television animators, as their reliance on past characters and established franchises along with the continued dominance by white animators supported the same highly whitewashed animation environment that had been present back through the Golden Age of Animation and the industry's origins at the beginning of the century. Similar to the way *Sesame Street* proved that educational, prosocial television could be successful and entertaining, pushing many other children's media producers to do the same, the public television series also became evidence that children's television and animation could be more diverse and represent the experiences of various races, groups, and even classes.[3] A team of producers, educators, and child psychologists developed the show to supplement the lack of early childhood education available particularly to populations of color in urban areas, basically the exact opposite audience most media producers tried to attract with their content. Groups like the NAACP consistently criticized this commercial environment, and pressure from both

Civil Rights and parents' groups pushed several studios to attempt to represent diversity, but without increased inclusivity behind the camera or pen, these attempts appeared uninformed, superficial, and even offensive. The tokenism during 1978 was especially evident as generic and stereotypical non-white characters were awkwardly added to series and franchises without much true knowledge of the group or race being represented.[4]

Tokenizing Franchises

Hanna-Barbera opened the 1978–1979 season with one of these legacy franchises, premiering the series and the star of their newest co-production with the print syndicator King Features, a subsidiary of Hearst, the owner to the rights to the most famous animated sailor of all time, Popeye. *The All-New Popeye Hour* premiered on Saturday morning in September of 1978, with CBS hoping that the sailor's first appearance in a made-for-television cartoon since the largely forgotten *Popeye the Sailor* series nearly 20 years earlier would prove successful.[5] The network even had an hour special the Wednesday after the initial premiere to promote the return of new Popeye cartoons to television, the first of two prime time *Popeye* specials that season. The animation and comedy writing were more complex than was expected from the studio, possibly to justify CBS's investment, which included obtaining original *Popeye* animator and voice artist Jack Mercer, while also hoping the comedy could make up for the near complete avoidance of violence.[6] Over the course of the program's production run, the series featured several segments starring the eponymous sailor, Olive Oyl, Bluto, Swee'Pea and several other characters from the comic.

The first segment, *Popeye*, featured comedic storylines from the E.C. Segar-created strip while *The Adventures of Popeye*, as the title suggests, is more of an action series. *Popeye's Sports Parade*, which pitted Bluto and Popeye against each other in Wimpy-judged athletic events, was meant to promote fitness while also adding in a *Wacky Races* inspired never-ending competition approach. This was also seen in the fourth segment to appear in the original series, *Popeye's Treasure Hunt*, where Popeye and Olive Oyl, owners of Popeye and Olive Treasure Seekers Ltd., race Bluto to treasures around the world. As in many of their other globetrotting series like *Jonny Quest,* the representations of other nations and cultures were superficial at best and discriminatory at worst. To add to the prosocial message while observing an FCC mandate encouraging more positive lessons in children's television, the program included "Popeye's Safety Tips." Starring Popeye and his nephews Peepeye, Pupeye, and Pipeye, the short clips featured the sailor teaching the youngsters, and through them the audience, basic home safety lessons, for example how to avoid injuring oneself on "eletrikal appliankes." The contrast between the Public Service Announcements and the rest of the show was clear and became the subject of mockery by some in the audience.[7] Even Popeye's pipe could not escape standards and practices, becoming a musical instrument rather than a smoking device. In 1981, the series was cut to a half an hour and renamed *The Popeye and Olive Oyl Comedy Show* with two new segments, "Private Olive Oyl," inspired by the film *Private Benjamin* starring Goldie Hawn that found comedy in portraying women as out-of-place in the military. The second segment, "Prehistoric Popeye," brought a Flintstonian approach to the franchise, transporting the 20th-century sailor into the Stone Age.

As an attempt to help change their reputation as a purveyor of only shallow entertainment, Hanna-Barbera's Australia Unit, in which they owned a 50 percent stake, produced ten *Famous Classic Tales* specials based on Western Literature and American myth for CBS, including *Black Beauty* in the fall of 1978 along with the segment that appeared during *The All New Popeye Hour*, to break up the program and introduce a new character they owned and could market. *Dinky Dog* appeared as the middle segment during the 60-minute program, the first segment, then in the series, produced by the unit to appear on regularly scheduled American television.[8] The program, clearly inspired by the comic strip *Marmaduke* and the children's book series *Clifford the Big Red Dog*, starred Dinky as a sheepdog who, after being brought home as a puppy, grows to be the size of a horse. His size and clumsiness often cause problems for his family, Sandy, a ditzy blonde, Monica, the sensible brunette, and their uncle Dudley, who is constantly looking for reasons to get rid of his niece's dog. In the end, Dinky always fixes his mistakes through his kindness, earning a reprieve from the grumpy uncle. The segment quickly disappeared from American television after the original run of *The All-New Popeye Hour*, but it did maintain life in syndication as its own series while the giant canine developed a fan base in Canada.[9]

The *Popeye* series was able to find some success in spite of the removal of violence that had become synonymous with the franchise, but a character that struggled against the pushback from Standards and Practice was Godzilla, the eponymous star of *The Godzilla Power Hour*, another 60-minute co-produced package series from Hanna-Barbera. The inability to use violence forced Hanna-Barbera to turn Godzilla into a monster who assisted the team of researchers that included Captain Carl Major, Dr. Quinn Darian, her nephew Pete, and research assistant Brock calling the monster when the team needs assistance. They are also joined by Godzilla's "nephew" Godzooky, a clumsy, awkward relative of the giant lizard who tries to fly and spit fire but often fails, providing the comic relief in the series. Barbera admitted that input from censors forced them to remove many of the characteristics historically associated with Godzilla. The network blocked any content involving the giant reptile destroying buildings or spitting gamma rays; instead, he was given heat vision like Superman.[10] Continuity was also a constant issue, especially in regard to the size and look of the monster between episodes or even scenes. The animation was substandard, even for Hanna-Barbera, which was only made more obvious by their other premiering series that fall, including a segment during *The Godzilla Power Hour* drawn by comic veteran Doug Wildey, who had earned accolades for his artistic contributions to *Jonny Quest*. Toho, the Japanese film company that held Godzilla's intellectual property rights, may have predicted issues with the series during development since they blocked Hanna-Barbera from using the monster's trademark roar, even after licensing the series to the American studio.[11]

Each episode of *Godzilla* was split into two parts with the first ending in a cliffhanger and the Doug Wildey animated series *Jana of the Jungle* separating the first and second halves of the narrative. The *Tarzan*-inspired series starred Jana, a young blonde woman who was thought to have been killed in a boating accident but survived in her father's wildlife preserve. She wears a very short animal skin and a chakram-like necklace that she uses as a throwing weapon as she defends the jungle against poachers while searching for her lost father with the help of researcher Dr. Ben Cooper, Montaro, an indigenous descendant of a warrior who possesses the Staff of Power that can send cause earthquakes through the earth, and a collection of animals that includes the white tiger Tico. As mentioned above, the comic-inspired animation was lauded, exposing a new generation of viewers to Wildey's designs and characters 15 years after *Jonny Quest* first aired. In fact, the initial acclaim for Jana's animation led Hanna-Barbera and NBC to extend the 60-minute show to 90 minutes to accommodate the addition of reruns of *The Adventures of Jonny*

Quest after interest in Wildey grew following *The Godzilla Power Hour*'s premiere. Interestingly, CBS also had a Tarzan series, *Tarzan and the Super 7*, packaging several Filmation action series into a 90-minute show as one of Filmation's many attempts to follow Hanna-Barbera's approach of including several different shows or segments in longer programs. *Tarzan and the Super 7* was retitled from the previous season's *The Tarzan/Batman Adventure Hour*. Along with the new title the program was expanded to 90 minutes after adding *Jason of Star Command*, one of the animation industry's many attempts to capitalize on the massive success of the *Star Wars* series of films, the first of which had premiered in the spring of 1977 and been a huge box office, and merchandising, hit.[12]

Late Start to the Animated Space Race

Hanna-Barbera could never overlook a trend, and they premiered their own *Star Wars*-inspired series, *Yogi's Space Race*, on NBC right before *The Godzilla Power Hour*. The studio had produced several series that tried to capitalize on past public infatuations with space, including the mid–1960s series *Space Kidettes* and *Josie and the Pussycats in Outer Space* in 1973.[13] The new Yogi-led series made clear its associations with the popular franchise, even using a similar font for its title card.[14] The series featured four new segments, introducing several new characters along with a number of its past stars, including Huckleberry Hound and Jabberjaw. The first segment, "Yogi's Space Race," was very similar to *Wacky Races*, with a team "winning each week" while racing throughout the galaxy. The segment teamed one established Hanna-Barbera star with a newcomer from the series, hoping to help popularize them through the association with a veteran character. Unlike *Wacky Races* there were only six teams, two of which were actually good and bad versions of the same character. The other racers only see the good versions, Captain Good and Klean Kat, while their alter egos Phantom Phink and Sinister Sludge, which only the audience can see as they attempt to cheat, disrupt the race like Dick Dastardly and Muttley did on the series that inspired *Yogi's Space Race*. The show's namesake appeared with new character Scare Bear, with Boo Boo not appearing on the new series. Huckleberry Hound was paired with Quack-Up, a debuting duck who wears aviator goggles and an old flying helmet with a propeller on the top. Jabberjaw and Buford the dog joined forces while the completely new team of Nugget Nose, Wendy, and Rita rounded out the field. Like *Laff-A-Lympics* or *Wacky Races* the show is presented like a sportscast with the narrator often interacting with the audience. El Fabuloso, a Spanglish-speaking computer who keeps track of the racers, helped to accentuate the series' association with both science fiction and the public's increased interest in computers.[15]

The second segment, *Galaxy Goof-Ups*, was another space series, this time teaming Yogi, Jabberjaw, Scare Bear, and Quack-up as space patrol officers who struggle at their job while spending most of their time hanging out in a disco club. They were led by Captain Snerdley, who often is blamed for the other four's mistakes by General Bullhorn. As a product of the late 1970s, most episodes included psychedelic dance scenes at a galactic disco.[16]

The other two segments in the one-hour program had no associations with outer space as Hanna-Barbera relied on older formulas to produce new segments and introduce new characters. *The Buford Files* starred the previously mentioned dog who helped siblings Cindy Mae and Woody solve mysteries. The bloodhound had an impeccable sense of smell and ears that often turned into satellite dishes as they picked up sounds from long-distances. He had a weakness for howling at the moon, which often revealed the location of the three when hiding while a pesky raccoon typically distracted Buford in each episode. This was Hanna-Barbera's first attempt at a show in the mold of *Scooby-Doo* after Ruby-Spears formed their own studio the previous year.[17]

The second segment, *The Galloping Ghost*, starred Nugget Nose, a prospector ghost who acts as a guardian for two employees of the Fuddy Dude Ranch, Wendy and Rita, owned by grumpy rancher Fenwick Fuddy. Throughout the series, Fuddy threatens to fire his two employees until Nugget Nose intervenes after a gold nugget on Wendy's necklace summons him. The Galloping Ghost was the first segment completely animated in Europe, with Filman, a studio run by Carlos Alfonso and Juan Pita in Madrid, Spain, producing the cartoon. In the 1980s Hanna-Barbera and other animation studios would more frequently outsource some animation work for budgetary reasons, but the practice had been utilized for decades.[18] Unsurprisingly, *Buford and the Galloping Ghost* was split from the two space series, premiering as a thirty-minute program in the spring of 1979.[19]

Super Additions: Creating New Members of the Justice League

After the success of *The All-New Superfriends Hour*, Hanna-Barbera started development on *Challenge of the Superfriends*, which was more ambitious than the previous series associated with the property and was composed of two connected half-hour segments. In the original character designs, Alex Toth originally included Captain Marvel, but Filmation had previously produced *Shazam!* starring the character along with *The Adventures of Batman*, which, like *Shazam!* also prevented the use of a number of DC characters, particularly certain villains.[20] Thirteen villains were chosen for the Legion of Doom, each leading an attack on the Justice League of America throughout the season.

The series introduced the Halls of Doom and Justice, and the first of two segments in the series welcomed several newly created guest stars as full-time members of the Super Friends: Black Vulcan, Samurai, and Apache Chief. As the subtle names suggest, the characters were clear attempts at increasing representational diversity in children's television and animation. All three characters were created by Hanna-Barbera. Although DC did have a few African American characters, including the John Stewart Green Lantern and Black Lightning, Hanna-Barbera created Black Vulcan after Black Lightning's creator, Tony Isabella, refused to permit his creation to appear in the cartoon. The new character embodied many of the same powers as Black Lightning.[21] The Japanese Toshio Eto, or Samurai, is the only superhero of Asian descent in the series, replicating the powers of the comic publisher's Red Tornado, an android character with the ability to conjure high powered winds who actually originated as a female character in 1968.[22] Apache Chief, who uses the phrase "E-nuk-chuck" to grow ten times his size while also possessing the ability to speak with animals, was the first Native American star of a Hanna-Barbera series. The second segment focused on adventures featuring the core Justice League members, Superman, Batman, Robin, Wonder Woman, and Aquaman, alongside the Wonder Twins who were introduced the previous season.

In January of 1979, Hanna-Barbera and DC partnered to create two live-action prime time specials under the name, *Legends of the Superheroes*, starring a number of DC superheroes and villains, including Adam West and Burt Ward reprising their roles as Batman and Robin. The first special featured the heroes celebrating the retirement of Scarlett Cyclone, an older superhero created for the special who is easily confused and acts as a stereotypical elderly person, before the Legion of Doom interrupts the ceremony revealing they have hidden a bomb somewhere in the city. The heroes are tricked into drinking a potion that takes away their powers but they still find the bomb and defeat the villains, showing they do not need their powers to succeed. The second special of the special was a roast of the superheroes featuring several other one-off heroes created for the series performing in the special making fun of the DC characters with several satirical interviews and hero profiles taking place throughout the second hour. One of the new heroes was the African American Ghetto Man, who performs a stand-up routine during the roast.[23]

Four days after the second special aired, the pilot for *Sergeant T.K. Yu* debuted. The series followed a Korean police detective who moonlights as a stand-up comedian while adjusting to working in America while studying the law enforcement methods of the L.A.P.D. The crime drama was not picked up as Barbera continued to attempt to cross over into more live-action production.[24]

More Specials, Crossovers, and Reboots

One successful collection of specials involved *The Flintstones*, who appeared in two separate prime time programs the previous season on two networks, a Christmas special on NBC and the baseball special a few months earlier on ABC. The success of the first special led NBC to ask Hanna-Barbera to revive the series for the next spring featuring the family with Pebbles and Bamm-Bamm again appearing as toddlers for the first time since the original series. Like the first two seasons of *The Flintstones*, *The New Fred and Barney Show* mostly focused on the exploits of the title characters. Most of the episodes followed plots from the original series, while the others made light of fads of the late 1970s or added a supernatural element with the inclusion of genies and witches. Similar to issues faced by *The New Tom and Jerry Show*, *The New Fred and Barney Show* largely paled in comparison to the animation and humor featured in the original series, even with *The Flintstones* nearing the 20th anniversary of its premiere. Since the original show, particularly the first two seasons, was written for adults, the humor in the earlier series was more mature and complex while the larger budget of the primetime series highlighted the inadequate animation featured in the 1979 spin-off.[25] Regardless, the popularity of the characters carried the revival for two short seasons, the first airing for ten episodes in the spring of 1979 and the second for seven episodes the following fall as a part of the package series *Fred and Barney Meet the Thing*. The studio also produced several specials as a part of this revival including the retrospective, *The Hanna-Barbera Hall of Fame: Yabba Dabba Doo II*, a sequel to the original special hosted by Bill Bixby. *The Flintstones Meet Rockula and Frankenstone* premiered two weeks after the retrospective just before Halloween in 1979, ten days after the broadcast of the last new episode of *The New Fred and Barney Show*. The telefilm featured both lead couples running from prehistoric versions of monsters from 19th-century Western literature.[26]

Fred and Barney Meet the Thing, an hour-long program, combined episodes of *The New Fred and Barney Show* and *The Thing*, a new series very loosely based on the Marvel superhero most famous for his membership in the Fantastic Four. A series featuring the group produced by DePatie-Freleng premiered the previous season, but Hanna-Barbera's relationship with Marvel, which owned the comic book rights to several of the studio's characters including Scooby-Doo, led the comic publisher to co-produce this adaptation of the Thing.[27] Fred, Barney, and the Thing only interacted during the opening title and some of the interstitial bumps as they were two completely separate segments, one action, one comedy, packaged together. In the series, the Thing is the alter-ego of teenager Benjy Grimm who can turn into the super-strong superhero by tapping two rings together and saying, "Thing ring, do your thing!" He is joined by the attractive brunette love interest Betty, her blonde tomboy sister Kelly, Betty's boyfriend, the wealthy Ronald Radford, and teacher Ms. Twilly. Only Kelly and her father Dr. Harkless know that Benjy is also the Thing, who uses his strength to help his friends while the group assists the community by solving mysteries with storylines inspired by *Scooby-Doo*.[28] There was no connection with the Fantastic Four storylines, with Hanna-Barbera writers creating all the plots. WarnerMedia held the rights to the segment while Disney, through its purchase of Marvel, held the rights to the Thing.[29]

In 1979, the series expanded to 90 minutes with Hanna-Barbera adding *The New Shmoo* to the series in the spring, changing the title to *Fred and Barney Meet the New Shmoo*. As in the other series, there was no actual "meeting" going on, with the only appearances together occurring in titles, bumpers, and promotional materials. The Shmoo had originally appeared as a recurring character/species in the *Lil' Abner* comic strip over a four-month period in 1948. The character caused a small stir after assumptions about the Shmoo's satirical intent led both capitalists and communists to accuse Capp of supporting the other. In the storyline, the Shmoo is found by Abner, who recognized that the strange, armless, bowling pin shaped creature could produce already packaged eggs and milk, while also reproducing asexually.[30] They actually desire to be eaten by humans, and when looked at hungrily, the Shmoo would kill itself for the sake of the humans. Although it is an answer to all food problems, including morality issues associated with killing animals without consent, they are destroyed because western economies fail due to the massive price drop in food. Creator Al Capp maintained he was not making any social commentary through the storyline, and even with the criticism, the Shmoo became a merchandising hit, appearing in a wide range of products through the 1950s. Hanna-Barbera hoped the series would renew interest in the character and licensed products connected to the alien. *The New Shmoo* was another program out of the *Scooby-Doo* mold as the creature helped Mickey, Nita, and Billy Joe solve mysteries while employed by Mighty Mystery Comics. Before joining Fred, Barney, and the Thing in December, the *New Shmoo* animated series premiered in late September 1979, only six weeks before Capp's death.[31]

Tapping into comics, superheroes, and past franchises once again, Hanna-Barbera extended the *Super Friends*' catalog the next season with *The World's Greatest Super Friends*. Scaling back the group, including the removal of the new characters from the previous season while retaining the Wonder Twins, the new series borrowed stories from myth and classic literature, including an episode inspired by *The Lord of the Rings*. As with previous iterations of the franchise, Hanna-Barbera attempted to avoid violence, instead celebrating the teamwork fostered through the heroes' use of their superpowers. This was not enough to appease advocacy groups like the National Association of Better Broadcasting, which criticized the vigilante justice in the series. A panel constructed by *TV Guide* in 1980 targeted the *Super Friends* specifically, with experts saying that the new show continued to celebrate the same violence as earlier series, which may have been evidence that some advocates and experts were not even watching the series they were so willing to condemn.[32] The series was also notable for including a satirized version of the Ayatollah Khomeini, who led the 1979 Iranian Revolution, in the premiere episode that appropriated *One Thousand and One Nights*, "Rub Three Times for Disaster."

Hoping to find success with the adaption another classic franchise, Hanna-Barbera obtained the right to produce a *Casper the Friendly Ghost* television series based on the Harvey Comics character. Originally appearing in Famous Studio shorts during the Golden Age, he made his Saturday morning debut in 1963 in *The New Casper Cartoon Show* that featured older shorts and new episodes produced by Paramount. In yet another attempt to capitalize on *Charlie's Angels, Casper and the Angels* features Casper as he acts as the guardian angel for two female motorcycle cops, the ditzy Mini and the more intelligent, but less patient, African American Maxi, who patrol outer space two hundred years into the future. The show was also incorporates characteristics from the popular show *CHiPs*, a crime drama that followed two motorcycle officers on the California Highway Patrol. Mini was modeled after Penny Marshall from *Laverne and Shirley*, with two bumbling cops, Nerdly and Fungo, imitating Lenny and Squiggy. They are joined by the new ghost Hairy Scary, who supported Casper while scaring enemies to assist the officers. Casper also appeared in two holiday specials, the first of which, *Casper's Halloween Special*, found Casper wanting to trick-or-treat before joining young orphans who help him defeat other ghosts trying to ruin Halloween. The Casper special aired the same night as *The Flintstones* Halloween telefilm on the eve of the holiday. The other special, *Casper's First Christmas*, co-starred Yogi, Huckleberry Hound, and several other Hanna-Barbera stars in the only program where properties from both companies appeared together in the same cartoon.[33]

Continuing the parade of adapted franchises and spin-offs, *Scooby-Doo* returned with new mysteries, a different focus, and an infamous family member. Fred, Velma, and Daphne were reduced to secondary characters, as the experiences of Shaggy, Scooby, and Scooby's nephew Scrappy-Doo were centralized in the plot. ABC began threatening cancellation of *Scooby-Doo* in 1978 as the formula became worn, a fact parodied in the prime time special, *Scooby Goes Hollywood*, which premiered in December 1979. In the telefilm, Scooby becomes too big for his more humble small screen Saturday morning roots and goes to Hollywood to become a movie star before the love of his original fans brings him back to television. The new series, *Scooby-Doo and Scrappy-Doo*, turned off some of the fans of the older series, as the new character proved annoying to some, but overall the formula tweak helped revitalize the franchise with the irrational confidence of the tiny Scrappy counteracting the cowardice of Scooby and Shaggy, creating a comedy team that appealed to younger children.[34] This also

As usual, despite his diminutive stature Scrappy-Doo is ready to fight as Shaggy and Scooby cower in fear (PictureLux/The Hollywood Archive/Alamy Stock Photo)

renewed ABC's confidence in the franchise, leading to several more iterations featuring the Great Dane. Pat Stevens, the voice of Velma since replacing the original actor Nicole Jaffe in 1973 after the latter's retirement, left the franchise midseason, replaced by Marla Frumkin.[35]

Silverman's influence at NBC and relationship with Hanna-Barbera were clear in the 1979–1980 season, with 80 percent of the schedule filled by series from the studio, including *The Jetsons*, which, in spite of the fact it ran only one season over sixteen years earlier, continued to be popular and regularly scheduled on Saturday morning. Silverman brought back one of his earlier successes, *The Harlem Globetrotters*, reimagining the basketball team as crime fighting superheroes in *The Super Globetrotters*. It was also the first Globetrotters series that Hanna-Barbera did not co-produce with a third party, instead partnering directly with Saperstein Productions, the media and marketing arm of the company established by the team's founder. The original series was produced with CBS, which retained the rights to the reruns as well. As in the original series, the team defeats its enemies and resolves conflicts through basketball, but whereas in the old series they would happen upon conflicts as a part of their touring, in the later series they learn about trouble with the help of the Crime Globe, utilizing superpowers in the second half of each episode to defeat the enemy. Portrayals of the real Globetrotters were featured in the show, with African American actors providing the voices, including the first African American game show host, Adam Wade, playing Sweet Lou Dunbar.[36] Several of the superpowers including liquid (fluid) man, spaghetti (coil) man, and Multi-Man were taken directly from the 1966 Hanna-Barbera series *The Impossibles*. In the spring, the show was packaged with *Godzilla* creating the awkwardly marketed *Godzilla/Globetrotters Adventure Hour* as an attempt to milk more profit from two licensed franchises.[37]

Importing Ideas from the (Global) South

For the 1979–1980 season, as an attempt to further capture the international market while continuing to address criticisms from children's media advocates concerning their lack of educational productions, Hanna-Barbera partnered with the Mexican media company Televisa to animate new episodes starring Cantinflas, an animated version of the character/pseudonym created by Mario Moreno. The original 1972 series appeared on Televisa, and Hanna-Barbera produced 52 new shorts that found Cantinflas continuing his adventures through various stories inspired by history, myth, and literature to educate children. In the original English dubbed syndication package produced by the American studio Cantinflas was renamed Amigo, as children in the United States were unfamiliar with Cantinflas and Amigo was one of the few Spanish words American children, and animators, knew. *Amigo and Friends* had a short run in syndication in America before Televisa and Hanna-Barbera packaged all 104 episodes from both iterations of the series for international syndication, profiting from Cantinflas' popularity outside of the U.S. Hanna-Barbera also continued to contribute artwork to educational filmstrips produced by RADMAR, Inc., an arrangement that started in 1978, resulting in 26 filmstrips over a two-year period featuring characters from the studio's most popular series that addressed a wide range of topics from safety to the senses.[38] Yogi Bear also starred as spokesbear for both California Earthquake Preparedness month and, in the 1980s, the D.A.R.E. (Drug and Alcohol Resistance Education) program starring in promotional materials for both organizations. Walt Disney famously utilized this approach using popular cartoon characters to educate children, and increase visibility of the character, by producing propaganda for the U.S. government during World War II. Young soldiers connected with the films starring Mickey and his friends, lending a familiar face to informational films about topics like safety and sexually transmitted diseases.[39]

The huge output of the 1979–1980 season was capped off by several live-action productions, including two full-length films that premiered the same week in December. The first, a telefilm, was the sequel to the award winning *The Gathering* occurring two years after Adam's death as Kate starts dating someone new. Maureen Stapleton's character was the primary focus of the film. A few days later, the theatrical feature film *C.H.O.M.P.S.*, about a robot dog programmed as a home protection system, premiered four days before Christmas. The inventor, Brian Foster, constantly argues with his boss, Ralph Norton, while developing a friendship with his daughter, Casey, as they protect C.H.O.M.P.S. from a rival security company attempting to steal the now sentient technology. The movie, starring Conrad Bain (*Maude, Diff'rent Strokes*) and Valerie Bertinelli (*Eight Is Enough*), originally was developed as an action film but the son of Barbera's partner, Samuel Arkoff of American International Pictures, suggested using a friendlier dog breed similar to Benji over a Doberman pinscher, leading to a family comedy rather than an action movie. The film did not do well with critics or the box office, a failure Barbera blamed on Arkoff, ultimately ending their relationship only one film into their nine-film agreement.[40] Barbera also produced the live-action *Belle Starr*, a telefilm about the female outlaw which was largely forgotten after its release the following spring.[41]

Golden Age Studios Come Back in Force

As discussed in the last chapter, the 1980s were a decade of upheaval for Hanna-Barbera along with the television and animation industries as a whole. That change began to accelerate in 1980 as political economic shifts changed approaches to financing production and airing content. As these shifts were initiated, several of the true veterans of animation reentered the market with the support and resources of larger companies, some of which grew into conglomerates by the end of the decade. Warner Bros.' reopening of its animation studio in 1980 after a decade of outsourcing its animation was driven by renewed interest in its characters, particularly after the success of the Chuck Jones produced *The Bugs Bunny/Road Runner Movie* in 1979. The film increased requests from older fans for new content after viewing the same reissued shorts from previous decades on television for more than twenty years. Early productions for the resurrected studio were new wraparounds for compilation films and series and by the next year Friz Freleng rejoined the studio after DePatie-Freleng was absorbed into Marvel Productions. In 1979, they also renewed the production of shorts, the first time content similar to their classic films was produced exclusively for television resulting in several prime specials starring Bugs Bunny, Daffy Duck, and the other popular characters. The increased visibility also led to several feature films, increased licensing, and even partnerships with theme parks that brought the Looney Tunes their most attention since the Golden Age.[42]

Not to be outdone, Disney was also reenergizing after more than a decade of malaise, changing its practices and recognizing the shifts in the American and international media markets. Disney entered into a joint venture with Paramount Pictures, adapting two films for release in 1980 and 1981. It was the first time in the 56-year history of the company that Disney agreed to co-produce a film. Walt, who died in 1966, was acutely aware of the value of owning the rights to characters and properties. He did not see the need to collaborate with other media companies, especially after his experience with Universal Pictures, which maintained the rights to the *Oswald the Lucky Rabbit* series Walt created for distribution by the larger company after he left the studio.[43] After Roy O. Disney's death in 1971, the studio struggled to equal its past success and the company changed course. Walt's son-in-law, Ron Miller, hoped to recapture of the European market behind Paramount's success internationally after taking over as president of the company from Donn Tatum, the first president from outside the Disney family. Miller also secured distribution outside of the United States through its Buena Vista division as well.

The first film produced was *Popeye*, which Paramount owned the theatrical rights to after distributing the series of cartoons starring the sailor between 1932 and 1957. When Paramount lost bidding for the film rights to *Annie*, Robert Evans asked what comic strips the studio did own the rights to, hoping to produce a musical to compete with the comic and Broadway adaptation of *Annie* that was coming from Columbia Pictures. They settled on *Popeye*, hoping to cast Dustin Hoffman as the title character before hiring Robin Williams, with Lily Tomlin playing Olive Oyl. *Popeye* was largely considered a flop even though it did make money, since Disney and Paramount had such high projections for the film. Coincidentally, the soundtrack and musical performances were well received. Due to Hanna-Barbera's ownership of the animation rights, the opening sequences were produced by the television studio, rather than Disney.[44]

Popeye was Disney's second film to receive a PG rating, the first being *The Black Hole*, which was another flop that premiered in late 1979. The third, *Dragonslayer*, also struggled at the box office in spite of involvement from Industrial Light and Magic and several Oscar nominations; however, it found a second life in the home video market, which was expanding rapidly after the introduction of Betamax and VHS in 1975 and 1976, respectively. Through Walt's planning, Disney was always cognizant of ancillary markets, even mentioning television rights in distribution contracts as far back as the early 1930s, and in 1980 they launched Disney Home Video to oversee the production and distribution of cassettes featuring their films and shows, helping to expand the new medium which included the establishment of the video rental business. Disney also dipped its toes into the syndication market with *The Mouse Factory*, a Ward Kimball–produced series that had guest stars introducing shorts and clips from famous films. Disney had long maintained a place in prime time through *The Wonderful World of Disney* anthology series, but they never established a place on Saturday morning like Warner, possibly due to the perception that the low quality of the animation airing on weekends could hurt Disney's reputation.

This caution that deprived children of Disney content in time slots aimed at them may have also contributed to the initial success of the Disney Channel, a premium cable network that launched in 1983. The project was initiated in 1977 but delayed due to the construction of EPCOT before being renewed in 1982. Nickelodeon had launched a few years earlier, but a cable network with Disney's support and catalog helped legitimize the viability of a children's cable network while providing evidence that niche networks could be profitable as cable expanded. The Disney Channel reached profitability in just over a year, which, unbeknownst to many in the children's media and animation industries, would contribute to sweeping changes concerning how they operated and interacted.[45]

If Hanna-Barbera was aware of these impending changes, they did not react publicly or shift their operations in any way with the 1980–1981 season featuring their usual menu of spin-offs, reissued shorts, adaptations, and formula-inspired series. They even attempted another live-action series in 1980, *the B.B. Beagle Show*, which was a prime-time puppet program in the mold of *The Muppet Show*. The program was not picked up, but six new series and several specials did air on all the networks and syndication as the industry continued shuffling in the background. Also at the end of the season, the long partnership between Fred Silverman and the animation duo would end, but not without one last success between the longtime associates.[46]

Bringing Old Characters into the New Decade

In preparation for the 1980–1981 season, Silverman was banking on the continued revived interest in *The Flintstones* and contracted another series starring the Stone Age cast of characters along with several others from more recent series all convening in Bedrock. *The Flintstones Comedy Show* contained six new segments, with several different formulas or tropes set in the prehistoric city. The first segment, *Flintstones Family Adventures*, was a family sitcom with storylines similar to the original series updated to reflect new cultural trends and common experiences, like the energy crisis and the popularity of recreational vehicles. The second segment, *Captain Caveman*, acted as an origin story for the superhero showing him work at the *Granite Gazette* alongside Wilma and Betty. Like Clark Kent, Captain Caveman dresses in glasses and a tie in his alter ego as Chester, the office assistant for the newspaper. The third segment, *Bedrock Cops*, was a police procedural parody that found Fred and Barney working as part time officers, with most of their work involving capturing Rockjaw, the pet of the Frankenstones, who starred in the fourth segment. The family is introduced as the Flintstones' neighbors, and as the name suggests, they are a family of monsters like *The Addams Family* or *The Munsters*. Another formulaic segment, *Pebbles, Bamm-Bamm, and Dino*, was created out of the Scooby-Doo mold featuring teenage versions of the two children and Pebbles' pet dinosaur solving mysteries around Bedrock. Dino also starred in the last segment, *Dino and Cavemouse*, a segment clearly inspired by *Tom and Jerry* as the pet dinosaur chases the prehistoric rodent throughout the Flintstones' home. The segment was also directed by Tex Avery, the famous animator whom Hanna and Barbera worked with at MGM and brought out of his semi-retirement to write for the studio. Coincidentally, the newest *Tom and Jerry* series, which was produced by competitor Filmation and renewed the original formula created by the animation duo, aired just before *The Flintstones Comedy Show* on CBS. The Flintstones also appeared in two of four *The Flintstone Primetime Specials* that fall, both of which aired before the series premiered on Saturday morning in November. The specials of this series appeared the following fall. The first special, *The Flintstones' New Neighbors*, introduced the new Frankenstones, while the second, *The Flintstones: Fred's Final Fling* aired two weeks before the package series' premiere in November and found Fred living out his last 24 hours after receiving a misdiagnosis that he will die the next day.[47]

ABC was also hoping to continue capitalizing on Hanna-Barbera franchises with a production of yet another *Super Friends* series. In this latest incarnation, titled *Super Friends* (1979), the core five members, Superman, Batman, Robin, Wonder Woman, and Aquaman, along with the Wonder Twins, star in seven-minute adventures, a departure from the previous two *Super Friends* series which featured half hour adventures. The shorter episodes were easier to write, shift around, and repackage for syndication. Responding to familiar criticism about a lack of diversity on the series, writers added El Dorado in the second season, whose origin story and explanation of his background was never fully detailed due to the 1981 writers' strike. He is of Mexican descent and obtained his powers through some association with pre–Columbian civilization. Unlike Black Vulcan, Apache

Chief, or Samurai, El Dorado never appeared in a comic or as an action figure during the show's run, but he was voiced by a Mexican actor, Fernando Escandon.[48]

The "third" network also continued its broadcasting of the *Scooby-Doo* franchise, partnering the Great Dane and his nephew with another Harvey Comics property it obtained the rights to, *Richie Rich*. *The Richie Rich/Scooby-Doo Show* combined *The Richie Rich Show* and *Scooby-Doo and Scrappy-Doo*, which was actually a new series of seven-minute shorts that shared its name with the half hour series that appeared the previous season. This sixty-minute program included six shorts, three from each series. Richie Rich found himself in a wide range of adventures from dealing with various threats to his family to battling aliens, while the Scooby-Doo shorts only featured the dog, his nephew, and Shaggy solving more condensed mysteries. The series was notable for its marketing and title, which placed Hanna-Barbera's own star dog second on the marquee without Scrappy while being the first appearance of Richie Rich in animated content, 27 years after he premiered in Harvey Comics.[49] The same fall Hanna-Barbera's last *ABC Afterschool Special*, *The Gymnast*, premiered in October about a teenager who experiences problems after moving to a training facility to become a top gymnast.

After his move to ABC in 1975, Fred Silverman was tasked with saving *Happy Days* after scheduling *Good Times* against the new sitcom, almost leading to the cancellation of the series set in the 1950s. After Silverman's intervention, *Happy Days* ran for nine more seasons and inspired several spin-offs and adaptations including *Laverne and Shirley* and Hanna-Barbera's *Fonz and the Happy Days Gang* that reimagined the most popular character from the series and his friends as cartoons, with Henry Winkler, Ron Howard, and Donny Most all reprising their roles from the live-action series. The Saturday morning cartoon found the three friends, and Fonzie's dog Mr. Cool, who mimicked many of his handler's catchphrases and traits, traveling to different time periods after being given a time machine by the alien Cupcake. This fit with the supernatural elements of the original series, which included the introduction of Mork the alien. *Mork and Mindy* helped launch the career of Robin Williams, debuting as a backdoor pilot through *Happy Days* in 1978 and 1979.

In each episode, the group attempts to return to 1957 Milwaukee but mishaps place them in the wrong year where they must assist mostly mythical historical figures like Medusa and King Arthur. This enabled ABC to promote the series as educational, garnering positive reviews from critics and parents, who may have also appreciated their favorite sitcom characters appearing in animated form. The show was reportedly supposed to be a *Dr. Who* cartoon, but that rumor has been debunked. Unfortunately, a short production schedule and mediocre artwork undermined much of the positive attention the show received.[50]

The most forgettable effort from the studio was the *Drak Pack*, a show animated by their Australian unit that starred Drak, Frankie, and Howler as descendants of classic monsters fighting crime to make up for the negative actions of their fathers. The writing was clearly from Hanna-Barbera with an overwhelming amount of puns and wordplay even for the studio. The characters work out of the Dredquarters and ride around in a Dredigible. The animation coming from their international branch was of especially low quality, even for Saturday morning. By the late fall Drak and his friends were losing out to older shows like *Jonny Quest* and *The Jetsons*, dooming the young monsters to a single season run. The series was the first where Jayne Barbera, Joseph's daughter, was the executive in charge of production, moving up at the studio her father co-chaired after starting as a production assistant on *Wheelie and the Chopper Bunch* in 1973.[51]

Tapping into the Growing Syndication Market

One of the industry shifts Hanna-Barbera was prepared for was the increased focus on syndication, especially as independent stations and cable networks searched for content to fill their schedule. They had packaged several of their cartoon sitcoms together in the 1977 syndicated series *Fred Flintstone and Friends* in an attempt to capture some of this growing market, and the studio did the same with six of the action shows to construct the anthology series, *Hanna-Barbera's World of Super Adventure* for first-run syndication. It included episodes of *Space Ghost and Dino Boy*, *Birdman and the Galaxy Trio*, *Fantastic Four*, *Shazzan!*, *The Herculoids* and *Moby Dick and the Mighty Mightor* and help revitalize several of their adventure franchises.[52] Hanna-Barbera also continued to produce specials to improve their reputation with advocacy groups with CBS airing the adaptation of *The Great Gilly Hopkins* in January of 1981 as a part of their *Afternoon Playhouse* series.[53]

This lack of programming for the growing number of independent and unaffiliated stations caught the attention of Al Masini, who at the time worked for TeleRep, which handled advertising for several of these stations. Masini gathered representatives from independent stations in a number of the major markets, including WGN-TV (Chicago) and WPIX (New York), to figure out a way to encourage the production of programming, which was nearly monopolized by the major networks. The meeting resulted in Operation Prime Time, forming a consortium which allowed the independent stations to negotiate with producers and advertisers as a collective unit. This resulted in a collection of programs, telemovies, and miniseries, the most famous being *Entertainment Tonight* and *Lifestyles of the Rich and Famous*. Hanna-Barbera contributed to this effort through *Yogi's First Christmas*, which found Yogi and Boo Boo awakened from their hibernation by several other early Hanna-Barbera characters who have come to Jellystone Lodge on holiday vacation. Yogi goes to work as both Herman, a hermit who lives on the mountain, and the owner's nephew Snively try to sabotage Yogi as he attempts to complete his responsibilities at the park before the villains are forgiven in time for Christmas celebrations. Boo Boo sings the song "Hope," which was previously heard in *A Christmas Story* and *The Flintstones Christmas*. In many markets the film was shown in four half-hour parts and was the only Hanna-Barbera production for Operation Prime Time.[54]

Another sign of the changing times was Silverman's experience at NBC. After massively successful runs at both CBS and ABC, his work at NBC was more volatile, as he had several high-profile failures including the sitcom *Hello, Larry*, the drama *Supertrain*, and the near collapse of *Saturday Night Live*.[55] He helped Hanna-Barbera maintain their success on Saturday morning, filling the NBC schedule with productions from the television animators. As Silverman prepared to leave NBC to form what would become a massively successful production company, he approved two specials to air during the same week. The first, *The Funtastic World of Hanna-Barbera Arena Show*, was a live-action special filmed in Perth, Australia, and hosted by Michael Landon featuring roller skaters dressed as Hanna-Barbera characters performing routines in the vein of Ice Capades, possibly testing the market for a traveling show two years after the *Hanna Barbera All-Star Ice Revue* aired on CBS.[56] The owner of Ringling Bros. and Barnum & Bailey Circus, Irvin & Kenneth Feld Productions, which at the time was a subsidiary of Mattel, had purchased Ice Follies and Holiday on Ice in 1979 before approaching Disney about licensing their characters for an ice show, which still runs as *Disney on Ice* today. *The Funtastic*

Yogi Bear and Boo Boo welcome families to the Jellystone Park in Fredericksburg, Texas. They still serve as the mascots for the chain of RV parks more than 50 years after the first park opened in 1969 (Jacqueline F Cooper/Shutterstock.com).

World special may have doubled as sales material for another organization to do the same with the studio's own stable of stars.[57]

The second special, which aired on Friday, was also the pilot for NBC's newest Saturday morning series. Silverman was on vacation in Aspen when he saw his daughter Melissa playing with a strange blue doll in the gift shop, which he thought might make a good subject for a cartoon series. The *Les Schtroumpfs* were created in a 1958 comic by Peyo, a Belgian artist, about a community of small blue humanoid creatures living together in a forest village. After seeing the comic, Stuart R. Ross bought the North American merchandising rights in 1975, which quickly turned into a popular toy line. The NBC special *Here Comes the Smurfs* premiered in primetime on June 25, 1981, a few months after Silverman left the network.

This was not the first animated film to feature the characters, with Peyo assisting the production of the 1965 black and white collection of shorts *Les Aventures des Schtroumpfs*, released in Belgium. Peyo also oversaw the production of the full-length color feature, *The Smurfs and the Magic Flute*, which debuted in Belgium in 1976; however, the film was not released in the U.S. until 1983 after the Hanna-Barbera series became popular. The U.S. series that grew from the NBC special premiered the next fall and helped the

Promotional poster for *The Smurfs and the Magic Flute*, **released in the United States on November 25, 1983 (Everett Collection/Alamy Stock Photo).**

studio stay relevant as numerous changes the next few years led to significant changes for Hanna-Barbera and its owner Taft Broadcasting.

Race, Representation, and the Start of the 1980s

Representing race was clearly a problem for Hanna and Barbera, dating back to portrayal of African Americans in *Tom and Jerry* cartoons at MGM, but this period in the late 1970s and early 1980s exemplified the disconnect between the almost exclusively white males and society. Among the animators at the studio, African American artist Floyd

Norman and especially character designer and director Iwao Takamoto were some of the very few examples of diversity behind the scenes while a small collection of non-white and female voice actors also contributed their talents. Their presence either had very little influence on how race and gender were represented, or more worrisome, these representations were the outcome *after* intervention from some of these parties.[58] One reason why the former was true could have been fear related to past experience. Takamoto, who was interned as a teenager during World War II even though he was born in California, was acutely aware of the stereotypes and rhetoric still surrounding those of Japanese descent after the war as he looked for employment as an artist. He was originally hired at Disney, partly due to their relatively more liberal hiring practices toward non-white races, but he did note that very few people who identified as Jewish worked for Disney during his tenure. Even after moving to Hanna-Barbera in 1961, he was typically tasked to work on funny animal shows, creating characters like Astro and Scooby-Doo after receiving scripts and storylines, leaving him very few opportunities to interject his influence beyond tweaking some visual elements.[59] The studio did not hesitate to utilize their successful, and less criticized, series that featured non-white characters to put up the facade they were more diverse than they actually were. For every *Harlem Globetrotters* or *Josie and the Pussycats* there were dozens of shows starring white teenagers or a funny animal character whose voice is an imitation of an established white actor. It became harder for them to ignore advocates of equal representation, but their attempts, especially with respect to the *Super Friends*, were clear examples of the dangers of superficial representations without the necessary background knowledge or experience related to portraying groups outside their own experience. These superficial attempts typically resulted in stereotypical and even offensive representations of the non-white ethnicities and races they included in their content.

Comic book producers have historically struggled with diversity as, much as in animation, white male artists created content featuring white male heroes for consumption by white male audiences. *Super Friends* was an adaptation of the *Justice League of America*, with Hanna-Barbera taking several of National/D.C.'s most popular characters for the first series in 1973 and adding their own flair by including original characters, two white teenagers and a talking dog. The five core characters included five white heroes, four men and Wonder Woman, with other members of the D.C. universe, all of which were white males. Considering they had already taken liberties with the comic by adding characters, there was clearly room for interpretation when it came to the characters and art. In fact, D.C. had introduced an African American Green Lantern, John Stewart, in 1971, signaling there may have been some room for flexibility about how the superheroes were represented, especially since they did not really explore characters' alter egos, aside from mentions of Clark Kent and Bruce Wayne, who, as the two most popular superheroes in the series, Superman and Batman, respectively, would have been the least likely to be adjusted anyway. Green Lantern did not appear in a franchise cartoon until 1978, even though, considering the consistent stream of DC superheroes guest starring on the series, they could easily have animated one as non-white. For a variety of possible reasons, including concerns about angering fans of the comics, they decided to avoid this route. In addition, as *Josie and the Pussycats* have proven, there very well could have been toy and merchandising reasons for Hanna-Barbera avoiding changing the races of any of the characters for the cartoon or introducing non-white characters.[60]

This second strategy was utilized in *The All New Super Friends Hour* in 1977, which introduced Black Vulcan, Apache Chief, and Samurai as guest stars. They became full-time cast members in *The Challenge of the Super Friends* the next season, but between the production of the two series DC had introduced Black Lightning, created by Tony Isabella. The creator refused to license the character, likely over concerns about how Hanna-Barbera would represent the first original African American character for the company. Black Vulcan maintained many of the same powers and a similar costume design, but never received any type of origin story, background, or alter ego, removing many of the characteristics or connections to his purported race. Apache Chief did have an origin story, which in spite of his identification with a specific people or tribe, amalgamated indigenous practices through a stereotypically white lens. As a teenager, he goes on a walk with his tribe's chief when they are attacked by a bear. The chief gives the adolescent some type of magical powder that exponentially increases his physical and mental abilities, including the power to grow several times his height using the phrase "eh-neek-chock." He also occasionally displayed the power to speak to animals while speaking broken English and misappropriating Native American philosophy. This type of patronizing view of "the other" with non–Western cultural and spiritual beliefs was seen previously with Hadji, where the "exotic" nature of their cultural practices and non–Judeo-Christian beliefs is highlighted and portrayed as mystical. It completely overlooks the complexity of Indigenous practices and the variety of Native groups, tribes, communities, and customs, equating them with magic or sorcery. Superheroes like Superman and Aquaman did not derive their powers from their whiteness or any cultural background rooted in reality, with Superman coming from another planet while Aquaman was originally from the mythical Atlantis. As a hero without any actual "powers," Bruce Wayne's inherited wealth was probably the closest thing to white privilege being an actual superpower. Samurai's powers were similarly patronizing, as he is able utilize his knowledge of "ancient" practices to manipulate the elements, using jumbled Japanese phrases to do so.[61] Of the three non-white characters included in *The Challenge of the Super Friends* only Black Vulcan was voiced by an actor that matched the character's race.

El Dorado, introduced in the second season of *Super Friends* in 1981, was not fully developed, in part because of the writers' strike in 1981, and held ambiguous powers that included teleportation. He spoke with a Mexican accent and was apparently found in the woods near Aztec ruins, again patronizing an entire nation's cultural heritage labeling it exotic and magic. His powers may just be random but his vague, yet extensive, knowledge of Pre-Columbian history and his ability to help the *Super Friends* the few times they venture into Latin America points to the idea that some type of Aztec mysticism is responsible for his powers while playing the role of liaison for the colonizers that Hadji played in *Jonny Quest*.[62]

These issues were on full display during *Legends of the Superheroes*, a two-part special which included a roast of the superheroes. Skits that found the superheroes in "real life" situations or humorous relationships, like The Flash attending counseling or the very small Atom and Giganta getting married. Aunt Minerva, an obscure gun-toting DC character from Shazam who came to the roast looking for a sixth husband, would have only been recognized by the most ardent comic fan, who may have already been turned off by the low-budget nature of the special. The fact that the special appealed to very few was seen in the ratings, with both parts finishing second to last in their respective weeks. One of the most infamous portions of the series was a standup routine by African American comedian Brad Sanders, who performed his roast as the "superhero" Ghetto Man, who protects and serves "minority areas" according to emcee Ed McMahon. He is dressed in patched up clothes and begins his routine discussing the lack of diversity among the superheroes before making several stereotypical jokes about frying Hawkman like chicken and saving people trapped in a broken elevator in a housing project.[63] Considering the audience and the lack of diversity, there is also the argument they were laughing at him and the condition of poor non-whites rather than laughing at the satirical nature of the jokes.

The White Savior in Animation

Another issue associated with the popular *Super Friends* franchise, which had been a problem for the comic industry since superheroes were introduced and for Hanna-Barbera as far back as *Jonny Quest*, is the presentation of the stars and characters as white saviors. Episodes in the first season featured the core heroes defeating villains with a few of National/DC's other popular white male characters. These enemies are portrayed as either evil villains who are stealing minerals for their own benefit, or scientists causing havoc due to misguided attempts to make the world a better place, like the two teenagers destroying all the gold because they think it is the root of all evil. The show was marketed as a prosocial program focused on the environment. Instead of focusing on the industrialization and other real causes of pollutions, most of which originate from the West, they create singular fictional villains to represent these larger problems like global warming and water destruction, producing a disconnect between the root causes and the fantasy presented in the series.

The next two series found the Super Friends, and their newly created non-white teammates, fighting enemies and protecting populations on earth and in outer space. In episodes from *The All-New Super Friends Hour* and *The Challenge of the Super Friends*, the superheroes travel to places like India and nameless South Pacific countries to provide necessary medical care and defeat dictators. This was far from unusual for the studio, who had Scooby-Doo and other mystery solvers like Josie and the Pussycats help local populations, like in the fictional Cinqo, Mexico, while on vacation or on their regular travels as a musical act. In the case of the longer mystery shows, the producers could show the (often teenage) detectives interacting with the local population, forming enough of a bond to want to help them when the community is overwhelmed by a variety of dangers including the ghost of a Spanish King or a quiver of attacking cobras. Scatman Crothers, who voiced Hong Kong Phooey, contributed to several series as the most prolific African American voice actor for the studio, although the range of characters he was asked to voice was limited, even playing completely different beatnik characters named Scat Cat in two separate films by two separate studios. Crothers' experience was also a sign that the industry as a whole had limited perspectives about acceptable roles, and portrayals, for African Americans actors and characters in animation.[64]

Female Characters Support, but Rarely Lead

The composition of these groups or casts also signaled the continued issues with representing gender equally in their cartoons. Hanna-Barbera did expand its character molds with the success of *Scooby-Doo, Where Are You!* in 1969, regularly including female characters, particularly when a team was featured or a larger cast was needed for the program. After the *Josie and the Pussycats* series ended there were no female-led shows aside from a few live-action sitcom adaptations like *Jeannie* that had the genie serving a male master. In several of the shows starring funny animals, like *CB Bears* or series starring

Yogi or Scooby that brought back old characters, the casts were almost exclusively male, and as discussed earlier, aside from *Hong Kong Phooey* and a few other exceptions most of those voices were imitations of white male actors.[65]

When female characters were included, there was a hierarchy in which archetype was utilized in the series with the attractive, typically blonde supporting character coming first and the sensible or smart brunette coming next. Sometimes they would adjust the hair color, but the general character design was the same. In the rare circumstance where a third female character was needed like in *Josie* or *Captain Caveman and the Teen Angels,* a red haired or African American woman was included. In *Captain Caveman,* Dee Dee Sykes was the de facto leader of the Teen Angels with a design similar to Valerie and personality similar to Velma from *Scooby-Doo,* exemplifying the overall lack of character designs, especially related to women and people of color, from the studio.[66] One exception to this was *Casper and the Angels* where the second police officer, Maxi, is an African American woman; however, she is portrayed as having a short temper. It may have been unintentional, but the stereotype of the angry African American woman had long been present in animation, and Hanna-Barbera's lack of diversity only highlighted character flaws and stereotypes embodied by non-male and non-white characters that represent the intersection of marginalized groups like Maxi.[67]

Interestingly, as the studio moved away from family sitcoms in the 1960s, portrayals of blatantly heterosexual characters and relationships declined as the focus on younger audiences removed any real displays of romance between characters. There was no real reason to have any type of romance or relationship storylines with the stable of mostly asexual teenagers, funny characters, and adaptations of live-action sitcoms, since children did not seem interested. Producers did not want to turn the young audience off with romance and, unlike with violence, there was no real reward to the possible risk of alerting advocates by introducing anything that could be conceived as sexual tension in shows for children. Occasionally, like with Fred and Daphne from *Scooby-Doo,* there were subtle hints of interest that led older fans to assume romance, but anything beyond hints of a crush were rarely portrayed, especially when the studio eliminated the production of adult animated series by the mid–1970s.[68]

The blatant visualization of heterosexuality and heterosexual romance may have been reduced, but the constant portrayals of an upper middle-class lifestyle were not, as characters, many of which were teenagers, rarely dealt with issues related to money or other problems faced by those living in lower socioeconomic conditions. In fact, many of the characters had open access to vehicles and other gadgets, traveling and living without restrictions. Richie Rich only served to highlight this disparity, especially with diverse shows like *Sesame Street* and Filmation's *Fat Albert and the Cosby Kids* among the few animated and children's shows that represented people living outside white, suburban, middle class comfort.[69]

Operations at Hanna-Barbera continued as usual as the studio entered its fourth decade in the industry. Shows featuring the styles, characters, and formulas that had become synonymous with the animation duo continued to appear throughout weekend mornings and in syndication as old competitors folded and new ones emerged. This included Ruby-Spears, which became a sister company to Hanna-Barbera after Taft acquired the studio in 1981 only four years after it was established by the animators with the help of Fred Silverman. Ruby-Spears was among a spate of acquisitions by the media conglomerate that included numerous radio and television stations, film studios, and theme parks. Hanna-Barbera was no longer a primary focus, and in 1981 Taft split into two divisions, Taft Entertainment, including Hanna-Barbera and their other production companies, and the Taft Television and Radio Company, which oversaw all of their media outlets.

This growth was a sign of the overall consolidation of the industry that would only increase under Ronald Reagan, who defeated Jimmy Carter in the 1980 election. Reagan, and Mark Fowler, whom he nominated to chair the FCC in 1981, quickly worked to deregulate the television industry, removing rules that restricted conglomeration, cross-media ownership, and reduced overall oversight on content. The studio did everything it could to survive, continuing to produce multiple series a year, even creating one of the iconic series of the era, but these changes, and the evolving economics and structure of the American media system, forced the aging duo to make significant adjustments about how they operated including how they handled control over their iconic characters.

8

1981–1985:
Trickle Down Animation

Reaganomics Hits Cartoons

Ronald Reagan came into office behind promises of economic stimulation and sweeping deregulation of numerous industries including airlines, finance, and telecommunications. Preparations for the 1981–1982 season were well underway when Mark Fowler was appointed chair of the FCC in May 1981, so children's animation for the season was produced under the regulatory structure they had faced throughout the 1970s, but these restrictions began to be challenged by the middle of that decade. When cable grew beyond a television delivery system for rural communities, FCC leadership, particularly Richard Wiley, cleared some of the ownership and programming regulations that helped media conglomerates like Taft expand their holdings with less scrutiny, making it easier for production companies to share their content among the growing number of stations and networks. However this growth shifted dramatically in 1980 after the end of the syndication exclusivity (syndex) rules were eliminated.[1] The rules, originally enacted in 1972, granted local networks exclusive rights to syndicated programming to prevent emerging cable networks, particularly regional superstations and cable networks, from devaluing the local stations' investment in programming by airing the same content.[2] Before the rule was eliminated, networks like TBS and WGN were blacked out in smaller markets airing the same shows. The change not only empowered these superstations, but also allowed stations from larger urban markets to enter smaller markets through cable, creating competition for local stations with fewer resources than their regional counterparts. This led to a more consolidated selling market, with regional and national cable programming reaching millions of people through a single contract with a single entity. Although networks regularly scheduled children's programming and animation on weekend mornings, selling reruns into syndication has long served as an integral revenue source for television while an increasing number of shows were being sold directly into syndication, as demand for programming grew with the number of available stations and networks in each market. Audience expectations for television were quickly expanding beyond the three or four stations that had long represented the only programming choices.[3]

Hanna-Barbera was familiar with syndication, utilizing the market throughout its history, first as a way to get adult animation on air and then increasingly for the programming targeting younger viewers throughout the 1970s as new networks and stations looked to fill some of their schedule and supply children's programming. *Fred Flintstone and Friends* represented the studio's entrance into barter syndication, which became an important source of content for new stations that did not have the upfront capital to pay for the programming, instead relying on shared advertising revenue or free airtime to obtain programming from distributors. Already established franchises and popular series were in high demand, but for new shows it placed all the risk on the studio and distributors, since they had no guarantee that they would be able to recoup their costs. Co-producing these series spread this risk among multiple entities, while inviting new actors into animation production hoping to capitalize on the popular genre and reach children with their content and products. This included toy manufacturers and other companies looking to sell to children, a practice that had largely been squashed in the 1970s after the scrutiny placed on Ideal Toys' sponsorship of *Magilla Gorilla* and *Peter Potamus* and the production of *Hot Wheels*, inspired by the popular Mattel toy car line.[4] Advocacy by ACT and oversight by the FCC worked to reduce subtle advertising in children's television, since young audiences struggle to distinguish between the actual show and commercials. However, since the Standards and Practices departments of the big three networks did not extend to the programming of local affiliates and independent stations, oversight on syndicated programs was almost non-existent.[5] The FCC also did not have jurisdiction over content on cable, making the producers of the programs and the cable networks the only true censors. Avoiding public scrutiny and the possible loss of advertising revenue, rather than regulatory supervision, was the only true motivation for censorship.[6] However, in 1981, the length of operation licenses increased to five years from three, which reduced some of the pressure to prove they were fulfilling the obligations of their license including serving the public good. Decisions about license renewal would be determined by an FCC led by Fowler, who described television as a toaster with a screen. The chair considered the medium a mere appliance that needed little government regulation in a larger free market.[7]

Parents or Government: Who Oversees Children's Consumption of Cartoons?

Oversight of children's television and animation, particularly on cable and in syndication, was made more difficult by the fact that rules concerning content in shows aimed at children were so vague.[8] Direct advertising during programs, too much time dedicated to commercials, and replicable violence were all considered banned, but there were no clear guidelines about what qualified as excessive or imitable. Complicating these attempts at oversight were the debates in Congress about whether the FCC should be more concerned about (de)regulating ownership restrictions or spending their time and resources ensuring content and coverage was appropriate and fair.[9] The Democrat–led Congress attempted to pass bills, including one by California Representative Lionel Van Deerlin, the head of the Communication Subcommittee, which gave FCC more control over ownership while focusing less attention on censorship. The bill did not pass, and pushback from Republicans began to be felt both through Fowler's appointment and the party winning a majority in Congress during the 1980 election.[10] Democratic work to create a regulated market that supported more variety in ownership and viewpoints was defeated by the desire for an unregulated free market by Reagan-led moderates and conservatives. By early 1982, long-held regulations like the Financial Syndication (fin-syn) rule, which prevented broadcast networks from owning the programs they broadcast or having a financial stake in the show they syndicated, and the Fairness Doctrine, which forced stations to air competing views concerning local politics and controversial issues, were being challenged and ultimately eliminated.[11] Although Hanna-Barbera was prepared to operate in this new environment, by the end of the decade, after a short period of revitalization, other influences beyond their control would force the studio to adjust their structure and the aging animators to consider giving up some control over their iconic studio.

In this shifting animation environment, styles and approaches to production did not change much, but the subject of the programs was clearly shifting as children were offered more and more products and technologies to occupy their attention. The toy industry went through a transitional period in the mid–1970s as companies like Hasbro and Mattel reconfigured their operations. Electronic entertainment devices, corporate restructuring, and the entrance of more international companies, particularly from Japan, forced once-dominant toy companies to re-strategize what, and how, to sell to children. While Hasbro streamlined its operations as it considered their next move, Mattel entered the emerging video game market first with handheld electronic games, then with the creation of its second-generation console, Intellivision, in 1980.[12]

This transition reintroduced a marketing strategy targeting children that companies attempted in the late 1960s, which had prompted the formation of ACT in 1968 and increased oversight on advertising in children's television, including restrictions on series adapted from licensed products.[13] *Romper Room* was a national children's television program created in 1953 that was unique in that the series was also franchised to local affiliates in larger markets that wanted to produce the program specifically for their local audience. In 1969, ACT criticized the Boston version of the series for selling *Romper Room*-branded products during the program. The same year another show received national attention for their in-program marketing.[14]

Toying with Animation

Mattel had utilized animated series to advertise the toy company and market its products since the 1950s through sponsorship of *Matty's Funday Funnies*, an afternoon package series that starred corporate mascot Matty Mattel introducing reissued theatrical films from Famous Studios.[15] This synergy between production and toy companies increased, and Ideal Toys agreed to sponsor two Hanna-Barbera series premiering consecutive seasons in 1963 and 1964, *The Magilla Gorilla Show* and *The Peter Potamus Show*. The partnership allowed Ideal and Hanna-Barbera to coordinate their marketing and production so the merchandise for both series, which was of higher quality than most licensed toys at the time, could be advertised along with the show in preparation for each series' premiere. Since both programs debuted in syndication, planning was difficult, given that the studio could not ensure episodes of the show would air every week in every market. Both shows found new life on ABC in 1966 without Ideal's sponsorship; however, this marketing strategy and partnership between Ideal and Hanna-Barbera proved more profitable through another ABC series, *The Flintstones*. The introduction of Pebbles in 1963 and then Bamm-Bamm in 1964 came through a cooperative effort with the toy company, helping the dolls and other merchandise featuring the characters become instant hits the same years *Magilla Gorilla* and *Peter Potamus* premiered. Clearly the legendary prehistoric sitcom's popularity contributed to the success of merchandise connected to the series; however, the fact that *The Flintstones* was seen nationally the same day and time slot each week on ABC made it easier to plan the marketing of the products around content in the show. In the case of Bamm-Bamm, the order of the episodes was actually shifted to accommodate the release of toys connected to the character. The studio planned to intro-duce Bamm-Bamm in the 100th episode, but "Little Bamm-Bamm Rubble" was the 90th episode to air, leaving nine episodes where the newest Rubble disappeared before return-ing in the 101st episode, which was possible through the largely episodic nature of the program. Licensing and merchandising had long been an important revenue source for animation, but the economic structure of television forced studios to push these con-siderations to the forefront as lower budgets and higher financial risk created a need to increase revenue streams from other areas often seen as an afterthought to other types of content. Animation quality and content took a backseat to creating easily merchan-disable franchises and characters, as studios like Hanna-Barbera made creative compro-mises in the production of their cartoons to get them on air.[16]

As a network desperate for quality content as they struggled to catch up to CBS and NBC, ABC was the most receptive to taking chances on unconventional shows, including children's programs sponsored by toy companies, and in the case of *Hot Wheels*, inspired by a licensed product. ABC had picked up *Magilla Gorilla* and *Peter Potamus* in spite of the scrutiny placed on the programs concerning their sponsorship by Ideal, which included a mention in the program theme songs. The network had a previously estab-lished relationship with Mattel when it became one of the first networks with a regu-larly scheduled animated series, *Matty's Funday Funnies*, debuting on Sunday afternoon in 1959.[17] Ten years later, Mattel sponsored the Kenneth Snyder Properties' production *Hot Wheels*, loosely based on one of the toy company's most popular lines. Immediately the FCC began receiving comments; some expectedly came from parents and advocacy groups, but a significant portion of the complaints were from other toy companies clearly jealous of Mattel's marketing strategy.[18] By the second season, the FCC required ABC affiliates to log the entire show as advertising time, leading to the cancellation of the pro-gram in 1971.[19]

Money May Be Green, But Success Can Be Blue

The flood of toy-inspired series would not begin to rise again in earnest until the 1982–1983 season; however, Hanna-Barbera had already proven adept at partnering with toy companies and adapting franchises from other media throughout their history. They had created dozens of programs based on comics, live-action series and films, and even a basketball team, so when Fred Silverman told the studio they would not get a Saturday morning commitment without the American rights to create a series on a fran-chise only known to most American children through toys, they were as prepared as any animator. *The Smurfs* proved to be the perfect transitional series as television anima-tion entered a new era where broadcast networks and their owners turned their atten-tion away from investment in children's television. Competition from cable motivated the broadcast networks to invest less in children's television production as the expanding syndication market presented networks with programming they could air with very lit-tle financial risk.[20] This also removed oversight from the networks, leading to an eventual decline in educational and prosocial messages in children's programming, for which net-works already had fairly low requirements. *The Smurfs* debuted under the old regulations and system, but the facts that it was technically adapted from a comic and the storylines featuring the small anthropomorphous blue beings were banal and prosocial helped them avoid the scrutiny normally reserved for series based on licensed properties, partic-ularly toys. The show was an instant hit, earning several nominations including an Emmy win for Outstanding Children's Program in its second season while becoming the longest produced show for Hanna-Barbera, eventually airing the most episodes of any series in American animation history to the point and inspiring numerous specials and films. This was also the last series Silverman commissioned for NBC before leaving the network to form his own production company.[21]

The Smurfs was a very simple concept, but the artist Peyo had built such an intricate world for the colony that it offered infinite possibilities for an animated program.[22] *Les Schtroumpfs* was introduced in 1958 in the Johan et Pirlouit (Johan and Peewit) comic series, and by the next year the blue creatures were spun-off into their own series in the Franco-Belgian comic magazine *Spirou*. They became an international merchandising hit, building a licensing empire around products featuring the many characters from the comic. Plastic figurines were particularly popular and a huge revenue source for Dupuis, SEPP's parent company, and then the toy company Schleich in the 1970s as the toys traveled across the Atlantic. There were a few general molds for the figurines and then they were painted to represent different Smurfs, each of which was named and dressed according to their personality or job. In the comic, Papa Smurf, the leader of the village, has 99 children, so there was a consistent stream of new characters, but the cartoon centered on a few Smurfs, like Brainy, Hefty, and Grouchy. In 1964, Smurfette was introduced when the main antagonist, Gargamel, created her as a way to defeat the Smurfs, whom he wants to eat and use for potions. After infiltrating the group, Papa Smurf turns her into a "real Smurf" before she leaves the village at the end of her storyline. This basically serves as the storyline for the first episode of the cartoon series, as Smurfette is reintroduced as a permanent character in the Hanna-Barbera production. A few argued that this was to create an object of heterosexual desire, but like the introduction of Pebbles and Bamm-Bamm in 1963–1964, it was to ensure there were characters available to create merchandise that would appeal to both genders. With an international toy empire already established all the parties involved, which included Hanna-Barbera, Peyo, and the Belgian media company SEPP, were prepared to fully profit from the show's crossover success. The program was also significant because it was one of the only times since their tenure at MGM where Hanna and Barbera did not own the rights over one of their productions.[23]

Hanna-Barbera may have shifted its creative process to accommodate the production of *The Smurfs*, but the studio as a whole continued to operate the same way they had the previous twenty-four seasons on television, finding inspiration through formulas, characters, and plotlines that had already proven successful. The second series to debut in 1981–1982 was actually an imitation of *The Smurfs*, a series that had not even premiered while *Trollkins* was in production. They may have wanted to hedge their bets regarding *The Smurfs*, hoping the slight change in formula would result in two series with infinite ancillary possibilities, or, most likely, they wanted a similar series in which they controlled the rights to the characters. The Trollkins live in a hollowed tree in a community lead by Mayor Lumpkin, a short-fused politician whose son, Blitz, finds himself involved in various adventures around Trolltown with his friend Pixlee, an attractive female who happens to be the only human looking character, and her dog Flooky. Pixlee's father is Sheriff Trollsome who is charged with protecting the town with Deputroll Flake, frequently facing Choppers, imitations of *Chopper and the Wheelie Bunch* in the form of Trolls. Along with *The Smurfs*, the show was also clearly inspired by the *Dukes of Hazzard* with the Southern accents and country movement strengthening the connection between the two franchises. Unfortunately, the *Trollkins* did not achieve a fraction of the success as *The Smurfs*, as a lack of any familiarity with the characters and a still developing licensing market for the tree-dwellers doomed the Trollkins to be lost among Smurfmania. Increasing the struggles for the Trollkins was the fact that their show was scheduled directly against *The Smurfs*, and the massive unpopularity of the Trollkins at the time helped *The Smurfs* win the time slot before the citizens of Trolltown disappeared from CBS's schedule by 1982.[24]

The Smurfs was clearly the studio's, and NBC's, Saturday morning jewel in 1981; however, Hanna-Barbera also had high hopes for *The Kwicky Koala Show*, which featured three segments all written by Tex Avery in a style reminiscent of theatrical shorts he produced that were revered, and often imitated, in the industry. Avery had started working for Hanna-Barbera after depression and other issues pushed him in and out of the industry throughout the 1960s and 1970s. He found work animating commercials, including famous Raid commercials from the era, but Hanna and Barbera were able to convince their old MGM colleague to come work for them. The title character, who was developed from the Droopy mold, was a mild-mannered Koala who, instead of gaining strength after cleverly avoiding his enemies throughout the cartoon like Droopy, could use his supersonic speed to avoid enemies like Willard Wolf, similar to Speedy Gonzales. Even though the series was produced in Australia, and koalas are only native to the continent, Kwicky had an American accent in the version that aired in the United States. The second segment starred *Crazy Claws*, a wildcat with the voice of Groucho Marx who uses his wit and quick moving claws to avoid the hunter Clyde and his dog Bristletooth. The pair acted similarly to Dick Dastardly and Muttley, as Ranger Rangerfield in turn pursued them for hunting in a national park. The last segment, *Dirty Dawg*, featured the title character and his friend Ratso, a clear hat tip to *Midnight Cowboy,* a movie with which the child audience hopefully would not be familiar, as they tried to find food and shelter. They were pursued by Officer Bullhorn, a caricature of the hippie-bashing cops that were seen during the 1968 Democratic Convention.

Tying the segments together were wraparounds starring the *Bungle Brothers*, two beagles named George and Joey trying to find success through their vaudeville act. The writing on the show seemed to have a quicker pace and more energy than past shows from the studio; however, Tex Avery's death during production and the budgetary restraints that led to compromises in the animation prevented the show from fully realizing its potential and possibly revitalizing this style of animation. One feature that did help *Kwicky Koala* stand out some from the pack was the fact that it was filmed in a higher resolution than the American Hanna-Barbera productions.[25]

More Space for Space

Following the release of the *Star Wars* sequel *The Empire Strikes Back*, children's television producers continued to set series in space. Hanna-Barbera's *Space Stars* was a less-than-inspired effort to try to capitalize not only on the continued fascination with space but broader science fiction as well. The segments of the package series were clear attempts to continue to milk as much as possible from the formulas popularized by two of their most popular shows, *Scooby-Doo* and *Super Friends*. Although the program was broken into six segments, half of them featured new episodes of past series, two segments of *Space Ghost* and one featuring *The Herculoids*, the latter of which transitioned into a science fiction adventure series in its new incarnation. The third segment, *Teen Force*, was technically new but clearly followed a formula popularized by *Super Friends*. Episodes of Filmation's *Teen Titans* and *Fantastic Four* were also still airing and were clearly more popular than the *Teen Force* episodes being produced by Hanna-Barbera. Kid Comet, Moleculad, and Elektra traveled the universe defeating villains and helping individuals out of precarious situations. The only truly notable aspect of the series was the presence of *Police Academy's* Mike Winslow as aliens Glax and Plutem, providing the comic relief for the segment. The fourth series, *Astro and the Space Mutts*, starred the Jetsons' Great Dane Astro accompanied by Cosmo and Dipper, two other dogs who assist their human leader Space Ace as he polices the universe. The fifth segment, *Space Stars Finale*, teamed the stars from all the previously mentioned segments as they encounter adventures in this crossover. The NBC-packaged program struggled against other Hanna-Barbera programming including old episodes of *Scooby-Doo* on CBS.[26]

Another series against which the 60-minute *Space Stars* was scheduled was *Laverne and Shirley in the Army*. As the title so subtly suggests, the series starred the pair of friends from the live-action sitcom enlisting into the Army as toned-down antics from the sitcom were transferred from Milwaukee (and later Southern California) and the Shotz Brewery to a military base. In 1979, during the live-action series' fifth season—the two women actually joined the Army in a two-part episode after continued disrespect at their factory jobs, helping to inspire the animated series alongside the 1980 Goldie Hawn film, *Private Benjamin*.

The premise of the episodes and the film involved women that were physically and mentally unprepared for military life before doing just enough to earn the respect of their fellow soldiers. Hanna-Barbera had produced *Fonz and the Happy Days Gang* for Paramount and CBS to some success, so the network and co-producing studios moved forward with creating an animated adaptation of one of *Happy Days'* spin-off series, which Fred Silverman had helped develop in 1976. Penny Marshall and Cindy Williams, Laverne and Shirley, respectively, in the live-action series, voiced their cartoon alter egos. In the cartoon their direct superior was Sergeant Squealy, a pig who often threatens to report the duo to Sergeant Turnbuckle as they clumsily attempt to fit into military life.[27]

Hanna-Barbera bookended the 1981–1982 season with a few specials featuring both old and new characters. ABC aired the third and fourth primetime *Flintstones* specials in October of 1981. The first, *Wind-Up Wilma*, featured the eponymous character becoming a star pitcher for the Bedrock Dodgers after she thwarts a pair of criminals by throwing a cantaloupe at them as they try to rob a grocery store. Fred is angered by her newfound fame as Wilma's career forces Fred to increase his work at home, overshadowed by his partner in what is seen as a masculine pursuit. The second special, which aired a week later, featured Fred trying out an activity becoming more popular at the time, running. *Jogging Fever*, which was animated at Filman studio in Spain, was the last special that aired as a part of this prime time revival of the prehistoric franchise. In the special, Fred signs up for the Rockstone Marathon to prove to his boss that he is not out of shape after a failed physical, becoming a celebrity as the first resident of Bedrock to enter the race. The *Smurfs* season also ended on a special after the cartoon was introduced to the audience in the same way the previous summer. Airing in primetime on NBC in April of 1982, *The Smurfs' Springtime Special* saw all the blue denizens of the forest come together to save Mother Nature, who is anthropomorphized as a type of fairy and is the only other entity other than Gargamel that knows of the Smurfs' existence. He puts a spell on Mother Nature which leads to a premature winter. *The Smurfs*, with the help of forest animals, defeat Gargamel and are able to save Mother Nature and their forest home.[28]

The Smurfs not only helped revitalize Hanna-Barbera, but also the children's media and television animation industries, as the massive popularity of the series and already established merchandise empire provided a new framework for shows to enter a continually deregulating television market. The first *Strawberry Shortcake* special released in 1980, based on the American Greetings character created by Barbi Sargent and the popular Kenner toy line, is considered by many as the first show to take an idea from the toy fair to the television screen. However, as a regularly scheduled award-winning program with an international following, *The Smurfs* was truly a phenomenon whereas *Strawberry Shortcake* was merely a fad whose original peak was over within five years.[29] At the same time, Fowler began working to open up the "free market" for television and telecommunications as a whole. Along with extending the time between license renewals, the FCC also increased the number of stations a single company could own from seven to twelve by 1985, encouraging further consolidation of media ownership. As other animation producers transitioned into this new market, the next season Hanna-Barbera tapped a new medium to produce one of first regularly scheduled series since *Hot Wheels* inspired by a licensed product.[30]

Animating Pixels

Video games had exploded into popular culture through the 1970s and 1980s as arcades dotted suburban malls and consoles turned televisions into game centers. Throughout the 1970s companies like Atari and SEGA created increasingly intricate games, even licensing franchises like *Happy Days*, hoping to add interest in games that were extremely similar across companies.[31] Improved technologies led to deeper games with more levels, better graphics, and a larger spectrum of colors and shapes. Compared to today's games, the flood of titles in the 1970s and early 1980s looks extremely rudimentary, but lessons learned from what is considered the second generation of video game consoles led to the current market today, and the few survivors from the era continue to compete in the industry. At the time, quick game production in the ever-changing video game market was the focus, so very few memorable characters were developed. In the late 1970s, an employee for Namco created a game where a white (then yellow) circle went around a maze eating smaller circles, or pellets, while avoiding ghosts who guard the mazes throughout the game. The employee was paid $3500 and the game was released in May 1980 in Japan with Midway handling the distribution in the United States the following fall. The game went on to be the most popular title of the early 1980s, inspiring several sequels, and more importantly for Hanna-Barbera, introduced the first true video game star.[32]

The seemingly infinite levels and colorful arcade cabinet featuring the game's characters helped *Pac-Man* explode in America after a mediocre showing in Japan. Namco was not expecting the game to become a hit across the Pacific, assuming the (male) North American video game player would prefer their *Rally-X* racing game. The crossover appeal among players of both genders and ease of initial play helped the series surpass 30 million users and one billion dollars in both game and merchandise sales within 18 months. The yellow circle even inspired a top 10 Billboard hit, *Pac-Man Fever*, and a sequel, *Ms. Pac-Man*, as Namco attempted to capitalize even further on the largely ignored female video game demographic by adding a bow to the yellow circle.[33]

The game was family friendly, as it was one of the first popular games where players largely avoided the enemy, rather than being the aggressor. It was one of the first games where the enemy actually reacted to the movements of the main character. It was also one of the first arcade games to feature simple cut scenes between levels with animation where Pac-Man chases the ghosts. Blinky, Pinky, Inky, and Clyde (Sue in *Ms. Pac-Man* and the TV series as an attempt at gender diversity among ghosts) each have their own personality and movements within the game.[34]

The popularity of the characters, and the merchandise, made Pac-Man the perfect franchise to be the first video game character featured in a regularly scheduled children's program. It also served as the perfect transition show as animators like Hanna-Barbera and Filmation began to further explore the possibility of turning toy lines and merchandising franchises into television shows, after the success of *The Smurfs*. The popularity among the female audience also made the franchise appealing for a cartoon. There were clear advantages of producing content that featured characters that had already proven popular with kids in the form of merchandise. As marketing from the era has shown, video game and console producers were not sure whether to advertise their products as toys, media, computer, or something completely different. This confusion along with the deregulating media environment may have helped *Pac-Man* avoid the same scrutiny faced by past toy inspired shows as animators tested the waters concerning partnerships between children's media producers and companies selling various products to children. Although there were Pac-Man dolls, t-shirts, and even cereal, the main product was a game that, at the time, was mostly played in video arcades, so parents typically did not come in direct contact with the main product, reducing scrutiny, and when they did, they were frequently playing the game themselves.[35]

Even with the well-known characters, Hanna-Barbera had to basically start from scratch when developing the series since there was no real plot in the game. There was no reason why Pac-Man was trying to gather/eat all of these pellets in increasingly difficult levels or why these ghosts were protecting the maze. Fortunately, the animation

The Happy Pac Couple in their natural habitat, the arcade, in Los Angeles, California (Martina Badini/Shutterstock.com).

duo were more than familiar with "never-ending chase" series, which was the perfect format to maintain the limited elements that fans actually saw as synonymous with the video game franchise. *Pac-Man* lived in Pacland, a town completely made up of anthropomorphic circles, with his wife/partner (Ms.) Pepper Pac-Man, Baby Pac, and their pets, Chomp-Chomp and Sour Puss.[36] Pac-Man is the Chief of Security for Power Forest which contains power pellets that are used as both a source of food and energy, or Pac Power, for the Pac population. The ghosts were turned into "Ghost Monsters," which was their original designation in the Japanese release, and serve as henchpeople for Mezmaron, a Darth Vader copy from the video game who selfishly wants the pellets for himself, acting in a manner similar to Gargamel.[37] Hanna-Barbera avoided advocate criticism concerning violence by only having *Pac-Man* "eat" the organic Monsters if it was absolutely necessary to protect the forest or his family, but like the game, they reconstituted back at Mezmaron's headquarters.

Riding the coattails of "Pac-Man Fever," the series was a hit after its premiere on ABC in late September 1982, leading other networks to partner with animation studios to produce series based on recent video game hits. The most famous of these resulted from a partnership between CBS and Hanna-Barbera's sister company Ruby-Spears to develop *Saturday Supercade* for the next season featuring several popular characters from other game franchises.[38] Pac-Man's initial popularity as a cartoon did not last, as the repetitive story lines turned some off; however, the character did carry the series through several iterations across two seasons with 42 thirty-minute episodes produced, more than twice the typical Hanna-Barbera series up until that point. This was partially due to the immense interest, and money, from sponsors, which led to over eight minutes of advertising per episode during the first season This was reduced to five when interest in the series, and *Pac-Man*, declined and scrutiny concerning the advertising increased by mid–1983. Hanna-Barbera also produced holiday prime time episodes, *Pac-Man Halloween Special* and *Christmas Comes to Pac-Land*. In the latter short film, like many other Hanna-Barbera characters in holiday specials, the circular being is responsible for saving Santa and Christmas. Although the show itself could hardly be labeled a classic, its early success helped motivate other animators to pursue not just video game properties, but toy and merchandising franchises for inspiration, while Hanna-Barbera's designs for the characters became the model for Pac-Man's future appearances in other media.[39]

Another Hanna-Barbera production in the early stages of this trend was *Shirt Tales*, which was adapted from a collection of characters created by Janet Elizabeth Manco that were featured on cards and other products produced by the Hallmark company starting in 1980. The characters were young-looking anthropomorphic animals who wore shirts with phrases that reflected their thoughts and emotions. The series was a huge hit for the card company, and as with *The Smurfs*, Hanna-Barbera saw infinite merchandising possibilities featuring an ever-expanding roster of animals; unfortunately, it ended similarly to the *Trollkins*. The series starred five banal animals, Tyg Tiger, Rich Raccoon, Pammy Panda, Digger Mole, and the Bogart imitation Bogey Orangutan living in the trunk of a tree in a public park. They are alerted when danger threatens the park and others through messages on their shirts, communicating on their missions through a holographic wristwatch straight out a science fiction movie. They are helped, and kept in line, by the parental-like superintendent of the park, Dinkle. The low-quality animation and the basic if not illogical storylines that often found the characters wandering into precarious situations with no one although they lived in a populated community hurt the series. *Shirt Tales* was also scheduled against *Pac-Man* and Warner Brothers shorts. The series was largely ignored during its surprising two-season run on NBC.[40]

Adding true insult to the injury that was the failure of the *Shirt Tales* cartoon series was the fact that *The Care Bears*, a series created by the "Those Characters from Cleveland" division of American Greetings, starred in their first special in the Spring of 1983 in conjunction with a highly successful plush toy line produced by Kenner. The specials created by Atkinson Film-Arts, a Canadian film company, led to a successful theatrical film and then series, which first entered the American market in syndication before ABC picked it up for its Saturday morning lineup. French-American animator Diffusion Information Communications (DiC) originally produced the series before the Canadian Nelvana took over in the second season a year after DiC took over the production of *Inspector Gadget* from Nelvana. The success of these series marked the entry of new companies that not only could compete with Hanna-Barbera and other veteran television cartoon studios in their own arena, especially with the support of merchandising companies, but also these series, particularly *The Care Bears*, attracted young females, an afterthought for many animators. These companies also distributed the work of international animators who increased their presence in the American market as networks and stations broadened their search for affordable content as the need for broadcast and cable television content quickly expanded.[41]

Hanna-Barbera tried to tap into this international market with the series *Jokebook*, which actually aired on Fridays in the early evenings on NBC, hoping to capture a more mature animation audience with a collection of international, award winning animation. Marty Murphy, who previously designed characters for *Wait Till Your Father Gets Home*, supervised the Hanna-Barbera contribution to the series, wraparounds featuring recurring characters like Eve and Adam and a barbershop quartet parody called the *Mount Rushmores*.[42] The shorts were reissued theatrical animation, which often copied the plot structure and joke sensibilities of the Golden Age of Animation that was already seen on television for decades, particularly through the Warner Bros. cartoons. The shorts also lacked any title cards or identifying information, giving the perception that these cartoons were produced for television, rather than years earlier for foreign theaters. Seven episodes of *Jokebook* were produced for the spring of 1982 as a test for a longer run during the 1982–1983 season, but only three episodes aired due to low ratings. Hanna-Barbera had long worked internationally, establishing an Australian unit and working with artists from Europe, Asia, and Latin America, but companies originating from these markets were now establishing a presence in North America, further challenging animation dominance of companies located in the United States. Hanna-Barbera helped produce a French series, *Lucky Luke*, based on the popular Franco-Belgian comic series of the same name about an American cowboy, but it had little success producing content directly for international markets, partially due to lack of cultural understanding, although some of its dubbed cartoons become popular throughout the world, including Italy where Barbera's Italian surname attracted fans from the European nation.[43]

Drawing a Line from Primetime Sitcoms to Saturday Morning

The remaining Hanna-Barbera output consisted of typical adaptations and retreads of successful series of the past, like *The Flintstones* and *Scooby-Doo*, as they attempted to maintain their most popular characters' visibility and value. They even brought many of their 1960s funny animal stars back for *Yogi Bear's All-Star Comedy Christmas Caper* where the eponymous bear escapes Jellystone to work as a department store Santa. There he meets Judy, the owner J. Wellington Jones' daughter, who is sad because her billionaire dad has to work during Christmas. Yogi explains some parents have to work before he and Boo Boo escort her to find her father. The bears are accused of kidnapping her before Judy explains the situation and they all learn the meaning of Christmas and sing around a fire.[44]

The studio also produced several adaptations inspired by live-action series and even a telefilm starring Gary Coleman. The comedy *The Kid with a Broken Halo* stars Coleman as an angel in training, whose casual, sarcastic attitude forces his teacher to constantly correct his actions as a guardian. The NBC series spun-off from the special had the same basic premise, featuring angel Andy LeBeau, voiced by Coleman, dispatched by his superior, Angelica, each week to help a different person, while the villain Hornswoggle tried to disrupt his efforts. The cartoon series, which premiered four months after the film, seemed like more of a promotional vehicle for Coleman, who was still staring in *Diff'rent Strokes*, than a real series.[45]

In a similar vein, *The Dukes*, an adaptation of *The Dukes of Hazzard*, premiered on CBS opposite of *The Gary Coleman Show* as a midseason replacement in the spring of 1983 with the live-action show still running on the same network. The live-action series was so outlandish many thought it might lend itself well to an animated adaptation, but production shortcuts and even less mature storylines written for children undermined any possibility of success. The fact the series focused on cousins Coy and Vance Luke, played/voiced by Byron Cherry and Christopher Meyer, also undermined the series. The cousins, who replaced Bo and Luke when the actors, John Schneider and Tom Wopat, refused to show up to the set in 1982 as they pushed for higher pay, turned off young audiences who were more familiar with the original Dukes from reruns on weekday afternoons and weekends. All the other live-action main characters voiced their animated alter egos, but the plotline was tweaked, which had the Dukes, with the help of Daisy, competing against Boss Hogg and his dog Flash in a different race each week. Uncle Jesse introduced and ended each episode as he read about the adventure on a postcard with his pet raccoon, Smokey. One controversial aspect was the presence of the Confederate flag throughout each episode, including in the title sequence each week.[46]

Laverne and Shirley returned in the 1982–1983 season, but this time in a retitled series also starring the Fonz and his dog, Mr. Cool. *Laverne and Shirley with the Fonz* had the four running a mechanic's shop at the army base. Cindy Williams had quit the live-action show in August of 1982, and the remaining episodes of the Laverne and Shirley segments were voiced by her close friend Lynne Marie Stewart, who played Miss Yvonne in Pee-wee Herman's HBO special, and later, children's series. Only eight episodes were produced partially due to Williams' unexpected departure, and reruns filled the rest of the series as Hanna-Barbera fulfilled their obligations with ABC and Ruby-Spears, who produced the other segment within the series that featured stars from another *Happy Days* spinoff, *Mork & Mindy*.[47]

In the fall of 1982, Hanna-Barbera released its second full length animated feature film that did not feature any of the studio's trademark characters, *Heidi's Song*. The film took the Johanna Spyri novel and turned it into a contemporary musical, with 15 songs filling the soundtrack. As with to *Charlotte's Web*, Hanna-Barbera Productions placed high hopes on the adaptation of Western literature, hoping to compete with Disney, as the legendary animated film studio struggled throughout this period. However, the film was an overall letdown, disappointing those who were used to high quality Disney feature films of the past like *Snow White* and *Cinderella*, which were occasionally reissued and found massive success in the home video market as proof of their enduring quality. *Heidi's Song* was a box office bomb as audiences, especially children, were turned off by the clunky storytelling, long musical numbers, and lower quality animation, which may have been a step up for Hanna and Barbera but was still of noticeably lower quality than their Disney counterparts. The film was distributed by Paramount, which had been disappointed by its partnership with Disney that resulted in *Dragonslayer* and *Popeye* in 1979 and 1980, respectively, and may have wanted to help Hanna-Barbera eat into the Mouse's business.[48]

In another series co-created with their sister company, Hanna-Barbera helped produce a program starring arguably Ruby and Spears' most popular creation, *Scooby-Doo*, in the package series *The Scooby & Scrappy-Doo/Puppy Hour*. In another sign that Hanna and Barbera might be preparing to relinquish more control over their studio and productions, they actually co-produced two of the three segments for the 60-minute show, with Ruby-Spears producing the third segment without the studio that gave them their start in television animation. The first segment was the third season of *Scooby-Doo and Scrappy-Doo*. The episodes were written and laid out by Hanna-Barbera but animated and edited by Ruby-Spears Enterprises. This was the same strategy utilized for the new segment, *Scrappy and Yabba-Doo*, in which Scooby's young nephew joins his uncle Yabba-Doo, Scooby's younger brother, and Deputy Dusty as they face adventures in the Wild West. *The Puppy's New Adventures* segment was produced solely by Ruby-Spears as an extension of four specials adapted from Jane Thayer's children's book series they produced for *ABC Weekend Special* from 1978 to 1981.[49] The last series of the season, *The Flintstone Funnies*, was a half-hour version of another package series, *The Flintstones Comedy Hour*, which aired on NBC featuring rerun segments.

Comedy vs. Cybertronians: Competing Against Hyper-Violent Masculinity

For the 1983–1984 season, the studio scaled back production while also riding the popularity of the now two-time Emmy Award winning *Smurfs*, including the 1983 special, *My Smurfy Valentine*, but it did put out a few new shows as the animation industry still adjusted to what amounted to seismic shifts in the way it operated. Hanna-Barbera had adapted several licensed properties the last two seasons, but the merchandising focus was increased in a new collection of shows led by the premiere of *He-Man and the Masters of the Universe*. Mattel and Filmation partnered to develop the toy line and series together, with Mattel releasing the first toys in 1982 and Filmation creating the franchise's backstory. They pitched the show to ABC, who turned it down in fear of criticism about not only the toy tie-in but the violence and physical appearance of the characters. The toy-maker and studio decided to sell the show directly into syndication, the first toy-based show to be distributed in this manner. As discussed above, the lack of involvement from the networks' Standards and Practices departments removed many of the obstacles for Mattel and Filmation to include violence; a shirtless, muscular hero; and limited prosocial messages. The masculine energy on the series was so strong, and the female audience and toy sales so low, they had to introduce He-Man's sister, She-Ra, to the series, who later received her own syndicated spin-off.

After over a decade of learning strategies to avoid the ire of advocates and censors, Hanna-Barbera and other animators had to compete with Mattel and Filmation who had taken advantage of the changing television market and found a way to circumvent regulatory safeguards to deliver to children content that had been essentially banned since the late 1960s. The series helped to accelerate the controversial trend of prioritizing marketing partnerships, the blending of advertising and entertainment, and shallow, violent plots. Other toy-based shows, like Sunbow (a subsidiary of Griffin-Bacal Advertising), Marvel, and Hasbro's *G.I. Joe: A Real American Hero*, which premiered as a five-part mini-series a week after *He-Man*, featured Public Service Announcements at the end of the episodes to try to counteract the lack of prosocial content in the actual show.[50]

As these shows became huge successes as TV series, toy lines, and even comics, Hanna-Barbera continued to focus most of their energy on Saturday morning. Compared to the ultra-violent and masculine *He-Man* and *G.I. Joe*, much of the Saturday morning schedule truly looked like kiddie fare as censorship and public opinion forced animators to focus on comedy and positive messaging while avoiding any type of displays of violence. For the 1983–1984 season, Hanna-Barbera only created one completely original animated series, while contributing new segments or episodes to programs that premiered in previous seasons. This one show, the *Robin Hood* inspired *Biskitts*, attempted to capitalize on the format pioneered by the massively successful *Smurfs*, starring a large cast of over a dozen puppies placed in charge of a treasure after the king of their home, Biskitt Island, dies. His brother and ruler of neighboring Lower Suburbia, King Max, tries to steal the treasure with the help of dogs Fang and Snarl and the jester Shecky, named after Shecky Greene, a comedian who made the late-night rounds in the 1960s, clearly outside the young audience's knowledge base. To add to the small dogs' problems was a wildcat named Scratch that also tried to eat the Biskitts throughout the series. The convoluted plot, at least for a children's series, lack of established characters or merchandise, and scheduling against two Hanna-Barbera legends, the Flintstones and Scooby-Doo, doomed the series from the start. It was moved by CBS to Saturday afternoon in the spring, leading into Hanna-Barbera's live-action entry for the season, *Benji, Zax, and the Alien Prince*, which was also moved to a later time slot after low ratings.[51]

Benji, Zax, and the Alien Prince followed Yubi after he is sent to earth to protect a young royal from the tyrant Zanu who kills Yubi's father, the king, and imprisons the queen. He is protected by his droid Zax and joined on earth by Benji, a stray dog who befriends the alien and his robot. This was the only series featuring the same Benji that was created by Joe Camp and starred in a series of four films. Yubi is able to survive on earth with the help of a bracelet, called a cipher, which enables Antarians to survive in Earth's atmosphere. Even with the *Benji* connection and a plotline that clearly combined elements of both *Superman* and *Star Wars,* the series was largely overlooked, surviving for a few years in reruns in North America and a few other countries after the original thirteen-episode production run ended in 1983.[52]

Hanna-Barbera's remaining Saturday morning output aired on ABC, with three new or altered series premiering in the fall. The first new series, *The New Scooby and Scrappy Doo Show*, was technically a spin-off of both *Scooby-Doo, Where Are You!* and the *Scooby-Doo and Scrappy Doo Show* featuring Scrappy helping Shaggy and Scooby solve crimes as they act as teen reporters. Daphne was reintroduced to the property in the first season while Fred and Velma came back in the second season under the title *The New Scooby-Doo Mysteries* with a new *Thriller*-inspired title sequence. The series did not bring much innovation to the franchise, but it did extend the number of episodes available to

Hanna-Barbera to sell into syndication. Margaret Loesch, who also worked at Marvel Productions, one of the companies responsible for competitors *Transformers* and *G.I. Joe*, served as supervising executive for the series while working for Marvel, helping to reestablish a partnership between Hanna-Barbera and the comic producers, which had acquired animation studio DePatie-Freleng in 1981.[53]

It is important to note that Hanna-Barbera did partner with Ruby-Spears, pairing *Pac-Man* with the sister studio's new series in hopes that the spherical eater could help buoy their new production featuring one of the most unlikely toys to receive its own series, the Rubik's Cube. In *The Pac-Man/Rubik, the Amazing Cube Hour*, when the color tiles on the cube line up it becomes Rubik, a super-powered gremlin-looking character with superpowers like flight, which disappear when he becomes scrambled. The Ruby-Spears series was significant because it was one of the very few shows on Saturday morning to feature a Hispanic family along with a theme song by the Puerto Rican boy band Menudo. The presence of the Rodriguez family in the series highlighted the severe lack of representation of the Hispanic population even though animation had a huge Latinx and Chicanx following in the United States and internationally.[54]

The other "new" series merely added a new segment to existing property in hopes of renewing interest in the older series while helping the new series grow by connecting it with an established brand. This series was Hanna-Barbera's second attempt to create a series inspired by a physical toy line, after the premiere of *Shirt Tales* the previous season. The Monchichis were stuffed toy monkeys created by the Japanese Sekiguchi Corporation in the mid–1970s and licensed to Mattel for distribution in America. They starred in a Japanese anime series in 1980 before Hanna-Barbera created a program starring the animals in a Smurf-like plot where the Monchichis and their leader Wizzar must defend themselves against the evil Horrg and the Grumplins that help him. *The Monchichis* took over the slot vacated by *Pac-Man* to create *The Monchichis/Little Rascals/Richie Rich Show* featuring mostly reruns of the third series, with only four new *Richie Rich* episodes produced for the fall of 1983.[55] *The Little Rascals*, a co-production between Hanna-Barbera and King World Production, had premiered the season before, placing animated versions of *Our Gang* in a more contemporary environment where the Rascals face various adventures and situations. In the series, Buckwheat is portrayed as a computer whiz creating instruments for the group to assist them in completing tasks. The entire series faced low ratings after the removal of *Pac-Man* and was split into separate half hour series by ABC. Also, as a possible response to the presence of the Rodriguezes in *Rubik, The Amazing Cube*, *The Little Rascals* introduced a Latina character in 1983, but by that time they were facing a lawsuit from former cast members from the *Our Gang* shorts after King World Syndicates did not obtain their permission to use their likenesses for the Hanna-Barbera cartoon.[56]

There Is Money to Be Made: Deregulating Children's Television

As the 1984–1985 season approached, more deregulatory actions were proposed and passed, accelerating changes in the animation industry to which Hanna-Barbera was clearly attempting to react. They had already placed greater focus on product-based shows, as they tried to replicate the success of not only *The Smurfs*, but the flood of more successful toy-based programs that appealed especially to boys. Programs like *He-Man*, *G.I. Joe*, and *Transformers*, which debuted in 1984, were barely more than twenty-minute infomercials for the toys and other products portraying the characters, but both the shows and toy lines were successful as they were used to support the other, offering infinite character and merchandising possibilities.

By 1985, requirements for non-entertainment programming and restrictions on advertising were both eliminated as the FCC's definition of "public good" was clearly being broadened, removing much of the government oversight concerning children's television, an effort strengthened by the overwhelming reelection of Reagan in 1984. General audience cable networks, like Turner's TBS and TNT and Paramount's USA Network, which were completely outside the FCC's oversight, launched children's programming blocks while Nickelodeon and Disney Channel were quickly developing into formidable children's media companies. USA Network in particularly was leading the cable charge in broadcasting popular children's animation on cable, first airing many of Hanna-Barbera's 1970s hits before acquiring reruns of *He-Man*, *G.I. Joe*, and many of the other toy-based shows from the decade. To keep up with the tastes of the audience and changing economics of the animation industry, Hanna-Barbera shifted its focus to try to capitalize on the trends and shifting expectations for how shows should be developed to maximize profits.[57]

One of these trends involved creating shows that could introduce an infinite number of characters, partially to add variety into the program but more importantly to sell more products as the young consumers attempted to collect entire lines of action figures, playsets, or figurines. Several of these toy lines and franchises were imported, with the country in which the property originated serving as a sort of test market for the merchandise, while others were developed or reintroduced with the toy company and producer cooperating to ensure plot and marketing continuity. *The Smurfs* had already proven popular as a comic and in merchandising before Hanna-Barbera and Peyo began production on the series, a negotiation overseen by Freddy Monnickendam, who at the time was the head of SEPP International. After a dispute between Peyo and Monnickendam concerning the direction of the American series, which Peyo wanted to keep faithful to the comic while Monnickendam wanted a more "mainstream" storylines to sell to the North American audience, they settled out of court and Monnickendam was forced out of the program's production.

Embittered by Peyo's actions, Monnickendam looked for a new series to develop to compete with, and eventually overtake, *The Smurfs*. Nic Broca had created the "Diskies," who appeared in the Franco-Belgian *Spirou et Fantasio* in 1981 before Broca renamed the characters for their own series. *The Snorks* live underwater in Snorkland, breathing out of tubes, or snorkels, coming out of their heads. There were seven main Snorks, and one pet Octopus, which were the focus of the series along with an infinite number of support Snorks and sea creatures with stars and love interests Allstar Seaworthy and Casey Kelp playing the main protagonists. As explained in the first episode, which debuted on NBC in the fall of 1984, the Snorks learned about human civilization in the 17th century when a Spanish Armada ship sank and they saved the captain from drowning. Their underwater culture then developed alongside human civilization on land, resulting in Snorkland resembling a bustling suburban municipality. The Snorks do interact with people in a couple episodes, but for the most part, they are thought of as myth or legend by humans.[58]

From a licensing standpoint, *The Snorks* attracted a fraction of the attention or revenue of their blue counterparts living in the forest. When the show debuted, they did not have the international merchandise or toy empire in place that *The Smurfs* had built over the decades after their debut in 1958. *The Snorks* had only existed for two years when they were adapted into an American television series, so even Europeans were still learning about Snorkland when they were brought to life through animation, whereas Smurfs figurines and toys were available for more than a decade when that series premiered a few years earlier. In terms of writing and artwork, *The Snorks* was considered on par with or even better than *The Smurfs*, as the presence of actual female Snorks created more possibilities in terms of storylines, allowing for plots that focused on multiple female Snorks. Smurfette was prominently featured on her show, but the lack of other female Smurfs until the fifth season, through the pre-pubescent Sassette, and the fact that technically there were no naturally occurring female Smurfs, created a strange dynamic in the Smurf Village. The writers never explain how Papa Smurf sired 98 kids without a Mama Smurf, who is never mentioned in the series. The jokes and gags in both series were very similar, with "Snork" replacing "Smurf" as the versatile word of choice and a number of slapstick gags and puns transferred from *The Smurfs*, but the presence of more contemporary interactions and storylines in the underwater series better connected with older audiences who may have grown past the slightly more juvenile *Smurfs*. Unfortunately, those older audiences typically do not buy toys or similar merchandise.

Possibly taking a cue from *Johnny Quest* and other Alex Toth series, the backgrounds and humans feature animation that is more realistic while the Snorks were designed to be more cartoonish, highlighting the fantasy or myth connected to their existence. An underwater smear and transitions helped accentuate the deep-sea location of the series much better than Hanna-Barbera's earlier underwater series like *Moby Dick and the Mighty Mightor*.[59]

Old Heroes in a New Television World

Holding on to the hope that the *Super Friends* franchise still had some life in the increasingly violent animation environment, Hanna-Barbera produced *Super Friends: The Legendary Super Powers Show* for ABC, bringing back most of the characters from past series, including Black Vulcan, Samurai, Apache Chief, and El Dorado, and adding the teenage Firestorm, with DC stalwarts Aquaman and The Flash only appearing in the opening sequence. Although the franchise was over a decade old, *The Legendary Super Powers Show* represented Hanna-Barbera's commitment to adjusting the multimedia economic environment in animation. Like many of the studio series, the animated version of the Super Friends appeared in DC comics series, but the storylines did not always match up, and most of the action figures manufactured that portrayed the characters on the show were modeled from the comic version, limiting tie-ins with the actual series. When developing *The Legendary Super Powers Show* Hanna-Barbera worked with both Kenner, who manufactured the first *Super Friends* line of figures, and D.C. to ensure the toys, comics, and animated series all lined-up with each other, creating multimedia synergy between all properties. All three companies were now playing catch-up after the success of shows like *He-Man* and *G.I. Joe* helped the rivals of all three partners take advantage of the reduced oversight of animation and children's television. Unlike those shows, the new *Super Friends* series was regularly broadcast on what was becoming a very different Saturday morning schedule, with more shows imitating popular syndicated series along with a collection of video game-inspired series taking over time slots occupied by holdovers from the previous era.[60]

Another characteristic *The Legendary Super Powers Show* and many new shows on Saturday morning shared with their syndicated cousins was the decreasing running time, leaving more time for commercials and advertisements. Many new shows left upwards of 10 minutes, or one-third of the running time, for advertising within each half-hour show, over twice what was determined appropriate by the FCC less than a decade later.[61] In spite of the shorter running time, which featured two ten-minute short adventures, the quality of animation was considered the best of any of the iterations of the *Super Friends,* possibly due to pressure of Kenner and D.C. to ensure the cartoon's artwork and production values would not hurt the overall success of the series or merchandise, which had been an issue in the past for the studio. Linda Carter was unable to reprise her role as Wonder Woman due to other obligations, but it was the first time the character was seen in the costume featuring the overlaying W logo.[62]

The new *Super Friends* series may have embraced the economic and marketing structure of the toy-based shows, while their entry into the syndication market this season displayed the studio's commitment to not only the changing industry's financial structure but also the search for properties to adapt into successful series and merchandise lines, with the help of toy companies. Popy (later Bandai) released a collection of robots as a part of the *Machine Robo* line in 1982 to compete with the *Diaclone* and *Micro-Change* spin-off figure lines that Hasbro bought the rights to and renamed *Transformers* in 1983. The same year Tonka started to import the *Machine Robo* figures as a part of two different series, the *Rock Lords,* which were rock-like creatures that turn into weapons, and the *GoBots,* who like the *Transformers* were robots that could change into different vehicles. Tonka's American release of the *GoBot* toyline occurred several months before Hasbro was able to get the Transformers into toy stores in the United States. This helped Tonka's toy line get a head start on the Transformers, ensuring the GoBots were available in time for the 1983 holiday shopping season. Unfortunately for Tonka, it was early in the popularity of robots and they had competition. As they prepared an animated show with Hanna-Barbera to promote the line, Hasbro and Sunbow started development on *The Transformers* after the success of their *G.I. Joe: A Real American Hero* mini-series. Although two children's books were produced by Golden Books for the *GoBot* program, unlike series such as *Transformers* and *He-Man,* no comic was created to promote the series or the toyline.[63]

Even though *The Challenge of the GoBots* technically debuted a week before *The Transformers* was first broadcast in syndication, the inferior toys, marketing, and lack of familiarity with the storyline for much of the audience due to the absence of a comic doomed the *GoBots* from the start. It was largely lost in the fandom around *Transformers,* which was supported by the three co-producers that had more experience in this type of programming and cross-promotion through *G.I. Joe.* Like *The Transformers,* the *GoBots* plot focuses on the battle between two warring factions of robots, the evil Renegades and the Guardians, after the former nearly eliminates all humans before "The Last Engineer" changes into a robot, or technically a cyborg, replacing his body parts with robotic ones. Interestingly, these human origins of the robots actually allow them to have genders, unlike *The Transformers* who are a masculine race of robots that seem to have no gender. *The Transformers* do finally introduce a feminine character that also plays the love interest to Optimus Prime late into the second season.

Although cartoon violence was for the most part overlooked in children's television, guns and realistic injuries to humans were still cause for criticism, so the *GoBots,* like the soldiers on *G.I. Joe,* shot lasers rather than bullets. As in *Transformers,* the *GoBots'* identification as robots avoided scrutiny since any damage was considered destruction of property, not injury or death, even though they were sentient and technically understood

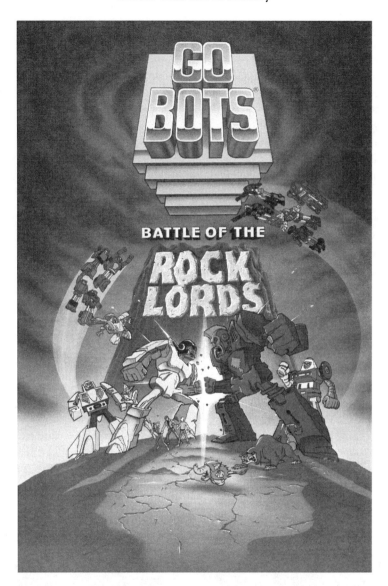

Movie poster for *GoBots: Battle of the Rock Lords*, released in the United States on March 21, 1986 (Everett Collection/Alamy Stock Photo).

what was happening. Although the *GoBots* never made the impact *The Transformers* did, and the series was acquired by their parent company, Hasbro, in 1991, it does hold the distinction of being one of the first series for Hanna-Barbera to debut direct to cable syndicated episodes the next year.[64]

Hoping to introduce a new generation to the *Pink Panther* franchise, Friz Freleng and David DePatie, whose studio only existed in name as a part of Marvel, partnered with Hanna-Barbera and Mirsch-Geoffrey, who produced the original *Pink Panther*, to create a new series starring the sons of the eponymous cartoon character. In the series the father continues to remain silent while the children have learned to speak. As with the *Biskitts* and *Shirt Tales*, Hanna-Barbera hoped to reach a younger crowd through both the series and licensing with a collection of cute animal characters who experience (mostly) prosocial adventures as they are faced with different problems and disputes. Pre-pubescent Pinky and his younger brother Panky are a part of the Rainbow Panthers, a group of differently colored panthers who learn about friendship and life together. Many of their conflicts involve a group of lions named the Howl Angels, who are technically the Panthers' rivals, but maintain a love/hate relationship with their panther counterparts as they often learn to cooperate with each person. Those expecting a continuation of the clever humor of *The Pink Panther Show* were highly disappointed as the new series had very little connection to the earlier cartoons and resembled the collection of "cutesy" shows with infinite plush-worthy characters more popularly represented by *The Care Bears*. *The Pink Panther and Sons* aired between *The Snorks* and *The Smurfs* on NBC, but the show could not take advantage of its time slot, getting lost among the more popular shows.[65]

Producing in a Quickly Transitioning Market

The Smurfs' continued success, which included an Olympic-themed special, *The Smurfic Games,* that aired in the spring during the buildup to the Los Angeles Summer Games in 1984, allowed Hanna-Barbera to experiment in developing the fourth program from the studio that aired on NBC in the fall of 1984, a live-action series starring a superhero orangutan.[66] In *Going Bananas*, Roxanna Banana escapes from the zoo and is adopted by the Cole family before she is hit by a beam from a spaceship, giving her super powers. This puts the Coles in precarious situations as the primate struggles to control her powers as the family is pursued by criminals, one of which is played by James Avery, who want to use her for some type of "evil" activity. The series also featured music videos with scenes of animals overlaying popular songs, hoping to capitalize on the trend that helped MTV grow into one of the most popular networks among young viewers, and satirical commercials with animals parodying popular films, shows, and products. Haim Saban, who co-produced the theme song to this and several other series, including *He-Man*, went on to create his own production company, which was responsible for creating the *Power Rangers* franchise when he imported and re-edited a live-action show from Japan.[67]

To finish up the season, Hanna-Barbera released a number of specials based on novels for both *ABC Weekend Special* and *CBS Storybreak*, the second series premiering in the spring of 1985 to offset criticism connected to the flood of toy and video game-inspired series. Both series of specials were animated with adaptations of *The Velveteen Rabbit* and *How to Eat Fried Worms* being among the most popular books to be turned into cartoons. *Scary Scooby Funnies* debuted in October, bringing back the *Scooby-Doo and Scrappy Doo* shorts as a replacement for *Wolf Rock TV* starring Wolfman Jack in an animated role. They also debuted a new Smurfs Valentine's Day Special in February, *Smurfily Ever After*, where wood elves and recurring characters Laconia and Woody get married. The mute Laconia, one of the first Hanna-Barbera characters with a sensory impairment, debuted in the third season episode "Smurfing in Sign Language," teaching the Smurfs the basics of American Sign Language after Gargamel steals their voices, allowing them to communicate and ultimately get their voices back. The marriage also forces Smurfette to think about her own marriage prospects as the only female Smurf, without the series actually addressing reproduction or the sexual preferences of the group.[68]

The studio was able to maintain a place toward the top of the television animation hierarchy by continuing to ride the success of its popular franchises, which now included *The Smurfs*, while still producing solid, if unspectacular, series like *GoBots* and *The*

Snorks, which may have been overshadowed by the other similar series but improved upon past animation and still found enough of an audience to warrant multiple seasons in production and long lives in rerun syndication. During this period, the studio notice-ably increased the episodes produced for each individual show, as 65 episodes, the equiv-alent of five Saturday morning seasons, became the industry standard for syndication of animation. For some programs, including *GoBots*, the minimum 65 episodes were pro-duced for the first "season" and broadcast daily so they could quickly resell the program into second-run syndication the next season, increasing visibility for the franchises and the connected products.

As the studio worked to keep up with the changing industry, they were about to face changes at the corporate level from which Taft could no longer protect its most endur-ing subsidiary as the media industry as a whole reorganized. This was a result of the constant deregulation, consolidation, and challenges from new companies, particularly those from outside of the United States. This media environment also contributed to the reemergence of past issues related to race and gender for an industry already struggling with equal representation as reduced oversight and increasing merchandising concerns led to a regression related to diversity in animation.[69]

Toying with Race, Gender, and Socioeconomics

Traditional ideology about children and appropriate toys led to increased gendering of programs during this period. Programs and franchises like *He-Man* and *G.I. Joe* fea-tured hyper-masculine characters and violent storylines geared toward boys. Alternate series like *The Care Bears* and *She-Ra: Princess of Power* were aimed at young girls, with the latter series created as a female-led spin-off and alternate to *He-Man*. However, ani-mated shows specifically targeting the young female audience were less likely to be pro-duced since it was thought that girls were more willing to watch shows targeting boys than boys were to watch shows oriented toward girls. Parents feed into these ideas, since traditional gender ideology leads parents to feel more uncomfortable buying their sons toys that are considered more feminine.[70] In addition, it is assumed that boys watch more animation than girls, but this may be a result of most animation at this time, particularly television cartoons, being produced by males.

Toy and merchandising considerations helped to further the continued whitewash-ing of animation. Many shows continued to feature anthropomorphic animal charac-ters voiced by white actors, and when human characters were featured they were almost exclusively white, aside from some tokenism in older franchises like *Super Friends* and new series like *G.I. Joe*.[71] Due to conditioning, children of color have historically been more likely to buy toys featuring white characters than vice versa, giving the producers an excuse to limit diversity. *Rubik, the Amazing Cube* did feature a Hispanic family, but, partially due to the fact the program was unpopular, the Rodriguez family's inclusion in merchandise was very limited.[72]

Similar to gender and race, the 1980s animation environment continued to overlook the experience of audiences outside of middle-class suburbia. One of the few shows that featured characters of color living in a lower income environment, Filmation's *Fat Albert and the Cosby Kids*, ended its production run in 1985, and the remaining programs, including the vast majority of Hanna-Barbera shows produced during the first half of the 1980s, were set in suburban environments. One show, *The Biskitts*, even featured a locale named Lower Suburbia and another, *The Snorks*, had characters living in what looked like an underwater suburb. Complicating this issue were the relatively expensive toys and merchandise marketed by these shows. The most expensive G.I. Joe playset retailed for $129.99 in 1987, or more than $300 in 2021 when adjusted for inflation. Entire socioeconomic classes faced a lack of representation on screen, and exclusion in play off-screen. As Reagan entered his second term the presence of these issues was reinforced as entire populations were ignored or left out of children's media and animation.[73]

9

1985–1990:
Toys and Technology

Whitewashing Through American Capitalism

It is hard to overstate how quickly the animation and children's media industries were changing as a result of deregulation, syndication, and cable. By the beginning of the 1985–1986 season, there were three times as many shows featuring licensed characters as in the two seasons earlier, with over 40 programs based on toys and other products airing during the season.[1] The changing economic realities of the industry led new companies, and some veterans of animation, to increase their production for television as children's media became a collection of infomercials aimed at young audiences, with a few less superficial shows thrown in to add variety and to deflect criticism. This also led to a significant regression in the diversity of representations in animation as merchandising considerations overtook creative ones, and the gendered, racist manufacturing and marketing of toys contributed to a regression in what was already an industry struggling to equally represent its audience as white males continued to dominate behind the scenes.

Animation had always faced significant issues with representation, but the need to promote toy lines that often only courted one gender created a divided animation environment where boy and girl viewers were not only separated, but young viewers who identified as female were presented with very few options in content produced with them in mind. This content was produced by men clearly making assumptions about what young girls like, since many of the sepia-filtered girls' shows were inundated with pastel colors and superficial storylines that were often diluted versions of plots seen in their male-focused counterparts, with a higher reliance on magic over weaponry.[2] The female viewer was at least being recognized (albeit extremely superficially), unlike in early television animation, with a few shows like *Sesame Street* putting in the effort to represent marginalized populations, although even this monumental program has promoted traditional ideologies related to gender roles.[3]

The ideological pressure that pushed all children and parents, regardless of race or ethnicity, to prefer white dolls and figures led to a whitewashing of shows that featured human or humanoid characters. The remaining programs continued to feature "funny animal characters," often with toy lines as in *The Care Bears*, where producers avoided direct references to race but still communicated that the franchises promoted equality due to the variety of different individuals, animals, or personalities that lived in one place. This strategy fell far short of true representation of racial and ethnic diversity that recognized different backgrounds and experiences even within groups. This portrayal of diversity was also most likely lost on young viewers, who might not be able to make the connection between different colored bears and the construction of race or ethnicity.[4] Many animators traded creative control and even risked huge losses to acquire the rights to these series, as the toy companies pushed to feature as many characters as possible on screen at all times. The need to include new products in the programs drove up costs and frustrated writers and animators who were forced to listen to creative input from executives representing Hasbro and Mattel.

Hanna-Barbera had quickly shifted its operations, committing to product-inspired series early in the 1980s, while still creating content that featured its most popular characters and the studio's now-infamous approach to show development and style of animation. *The Smurfs* in particular showed the studio was still a force in animation, even as its share of the market and schedule declined as local stations and the growing cable networks battled to acquire content. Weekday afternoons had always featured some children's television, but that content was mostly reruns or local versions of shows like *Romper Room*. The syndication market, and the large initial output for many of these shows, allowed for new episodes to air weekly, if not daily, and cable presented opportunities for children's television to be seen in the evenings or early morning before school. After decades of game shows, news programs, soap operas, and other adult programming airing during these time slots on the broadcast networks, cartoons could now be consumed throughout the day.[5]

Despite this smaller share of the market, Hanna-Barbera maintained their typically high output of shows even as the episode count per season on many of the productions increased fivefold to satisfy syndication demands. However, as the studio was successfully adjusting to the new animation and children's media market, Taft began to struggle, attempting to keep up with larger media companies in a consolidating media environment. Taft's struggles began to affect Hanna-Barbera by this season, and the high output and cut budgets forced the studio to make concessions. This included outsourcing more of its animation, relying on third parties and contractors, particularly from South Korea, and co-producing more shows. This led to a continued relinquishing of control, and more content inspired by outside properties and licensed products to reduce financial risk. After 20 years of ownership stability, the studio would pass through several hands by the end of the decade and faced the possibility of dissolution even as one of the most popular and successful cartoons of the 1980s continued to air on Saturday morning, a time slot Hanna-Barbera had helped establish. However, even Saturday morning faced an uncertain future as children's television expanded to seven days a week through cable and syndication.

Free Market Cartoons

This uncertain future facilitated a transitional period for Hanna-Barbera, leading to only three new original series from the studio debuting on Saturday morning. Of these, two were spin-offs of series that aired the previous season, extending popular franchises as audiences unknowingly watched some of their favorite characters in new episodes for the last time. The first of these series, *The Super Powers Team: Galactic Guardians,* was really just a continuation of *Super Friends: The Legendary Super Powers Show* that put a greater emphasis on adventures in space, following two *Star Wars* inspired series, *Ewoks* and *Droids,* produced by Nelvana on ABC's schedule. The superhero franchise returned to 30-minute episodes featuring a single adventure with storylines more dramatic and tense than past series and artwork that more closely resembled the comic book character designs from D.C. and Jack Kirby. The Wonder Twins, Black Vulcan, Apache Chief, and El Dorado were all removed as regular characters, replaced by two other teenagers from the comic pages, Firestorm, who debuted in the previous television series, and the African American Cyborg, hoping to attract a slightly older audience for the newest incarnation of the *Super Friends*. Unfortunately for fans of the Super Friends, NBC had extended its *The Smurfs* block to 90 minutes after the first season, beating all competitors scheduled against it, including a number of Hanna-Barbera productions.[6] This was the last *Super Friends* series to feature new episodes after 12 seasons in production as a part of ABC's Saturday morning schedule.[7]

The other spin-off aired immediately after *Galactic Guardians* in most markets, featuring Scooby-Doo and his nephew Scrappy in the last animated series in which the latter has appeared.[8] Scrappy had long been a polarizing character in the franchise, with many finding his presence annoying and redundant, since he was more of a plot device to increase conflict than a fully developed character. He is often cited as an example of a series "jumping the shark" through the addition of a character.[9] In another sign producers were struggling with new storylines to feature the Great Dane, they added several new characters while Fred and Velma were again removed from the cast. Joining Daphne, Shaggy, Scooby, and Scrappy were Vincent Van Ghoul, an imitation of Vincent Price voiced by the actor, and Flim-Flam, a young Tibetan con artist. In the series, two ghosts, Weerd and Bogel, followed the group. *The 13 Ghosts of Scooby-Doo* begins when the four somehow crash in the Himalayas when trying to fly to Hawaii for vacation. While in a small town, they release the thirteen most dangerous ghosts, along with Weerd and Bogel who are hired by the more powerful ghosts as henchmen to stop the detectives. They meet Flim-Flam after he is kicked out of town for trying to sell a potion and he brings them to Van Ghoul, who locates their plane and warns them of the incoming townspeople who think the group knows they are all werewolves. Flim-Flam helps them escape and joins them on their mission to recapture the ghosts, and Van Ghoul becomes a consultant for the group, assisting them with his crystal ball. In a possible attempt to revive support for Scrappy, in this series he fulfilled more the role of Fred, who is apparently off at summer camp, while Flim-Flam becomes the overconfident "troublemaker" of the group. Although the overall plots were redundant, the artwork and the comedy within the episodes were considered some of the best since the series premiered in 1969, partially due to the presence of writer Tom Ruegger, who went on to help revitalize Warner through shows like *Tiny Toons Adventures* and *Animaniacs*.[10] Immediately after *Thirteen Ghosts*, *Scooby's Mystery Funhouse* aired featuring segments from the previous three Scooby and Scrappy-Doo series. Both were off the ABC schedule by the spring, replaced by reruns of *Laff-A-Lympics* and Warner Bros.' *The Bugs Bunny Show*.[11]

Young Children and the Home Video Market

As a possible attempt to court younger children and satisfy critics of the increasing focus on superficial toy-based cartoons, Hanna-Barbera agreed to produce a series based on the *Berenstain Bears* book series written and illustrated by Stan and Jan Berenstain since 1962. The series became popular because the relationships between family members and the lessons taught were not patronizing as they promoted messages of responsibility and respect. The family had appeared in several Buzz Potamkin-produced holiday specials throughout the first half of the decade before the series was picked up by Hanna-Barbera and CBS. The series, co-produced with Southern Star and animated in Australia, was one of the few shows from the studio up until this point that did not credit Hanna or Barbera as executive producers. Along with the subject matter, the book series and show were unique because they took place in a rural setting rather than the suburban or occasionally urban locations of most children's media, where sales were unsurprisingly the highest. The series followed many of the books' stories, although it featured Raffish Ralph and Weasel McGreed more than the literary series, as writers relied on sitcom-inspired storylines for some of the episodes. It earned a Daytime Emmy nomination in 1987 for Outstanding Children's Programming and won the Humanitas Award in 1988, another sign of Hanna-Barbera's 1980s renaissance. Along with the popularity of the books, the series of specials produced for NBC by the Cate Brothers Company earlier in the 1980s was released on VHS tapes just as the home video market was developing, making the video adaptations a popular early addition to home and school libraries.[12]

Film and television studios, particularly those responsible for children's media, quickly realized that the videotape market could represent a valuable ancillary market but were concerned about the potential downside of giving consumers, and retailers, so much control over content. In 1984, Universal and Sony faced off in the United States Supreme Court arguing over whether recording content off the television through a recorder, in this case a Betamax with the ruling covering VHS as well, constituted fair use. Sony, as the manufacturer of Betamax recorders, was sued by Universal who ultimately lost the case when it was ruled that video recording by consumers was covered under fair use in the Copyright Act of 1976. This gave consumers even more reason to purchase the already-popular devices, quickening the television's transition into a full entertainment center with the help of video games and the cable box.[13] This was especially important for the child audience since they appreciate the comfort and familiarity of repeatedly viewing the same content, like cartoons, instantly creating a market for young audiences' favorite content.[14]

The other concern for media producers related to video tapes was the rental market, which was mostly unregulated through the mid–1980s as many video rentals were coming from convenience stores and even photo developers renting video tapes they bought from local stores, prompting several distributors to refuse to do business with companies like Fotomat. Disney was the first company to create tapes specifically for rent, setting up a program with "authorized dealers" to prevent unlicensed rental of their videos. The establishment and growth of chains like Blockbuster made it easier for distributors to oversee the rental market, as most of the studios followed Disney's lead and authorized dealers to rent their videos as a more organized rental industry replaced rack jobbing at variety stores, setting up displays for products not normally sold in a location. Worldvision started distributing VHS editions of Hanna-Barbera programs and films in 1983, with some content and films, like *Charlotte's Web*, finding a second life in the ancillary video market.[15] The studio's first direct-to-video effort was much different than its Saturday morning cartoons, adapting stories from the Bible into half-hour episodes. The studio had made its Christian viewpoints clear in the several adventure series and series episodes they adapted from the Bible along with the numerous specials celebrating Christian holidays. The films provided a contemporary viewpoint on the stories from both the Old and New Testament hoping to connect younger audiences with Bible lessons that might not resonate with children in the 1980s. *Greatest Adventures: Stories from the Bible* starred three teenagers, Margo, Moki and Derek, as they travel throughout time witnessing Bible tales. Barbera had been pushing the project since the 1960s, but the ability to sell the product directly to homes, schools, and churches through Worldvision Enterprises, which Taft acquired in 1979, pushed the studio and distributor to finally move forward with the project.[16]

The Influence of the Networks Continues to Decline

Continuing to pursue markets beyond regularly scheduled network television, Hanna-Barbera developed a program block to sell directly into syndication. Earlier they sold individual or similarly constructed package shows directly into syndication, but the block, which debuted at 90 minutes and was extended to two hours the next season, united several old and new shows. This was similar to past packaged shows they developed, making it easier to sell more content to local stations and networks while giving them control over the block's branding. *The Funtastic World of Hanna-Barbera* also allowed the studio to sell a rotating collection of programs to avoid the cost and responsibility of producing 20 episodes or more for each show's season to create enough value for individual syndication. The block aired on Sundays, weekday afternoons on cable, and on local affiliates in most markets, with all Taft stations carrying the program. Reruns of *Challenge the GoBots* joined three new shows and a reboot of Hanna-Barbera's most popular franchise. *The GoBots* starred in a theatrical feature where they battle the *Rock Lords*, another subseries from Bandai's *Machine Robo* line, before the Rock Lords let go of their skepticism to join the Guardians GoBots, forming an alliance to defeat the Renegades. The film introduced Tonka's Rock Lords toyline to the American market, but otherwise was a failure, partially due to the shortened production schedule. They rushed the production of the film to undercut the more successful *Transformers: The Movie*, which premiered five months later; however, *Transformers* was produced over two years. Margot Kidder, Terry Savalas, and Roddy McDowall all contributed their voices to the new characters for *GoBots: Battle of the Rock Lords*, which barely surpassed a million dollars in the domestic box office.[17]

In a possible sign Hanna-Barbera was not quite ready to move on from old formulas, *Yogi's Treasure Hunt*, originally named *Funtastic Treasure Hunt*, gathered many of the popular 1960s characters as they traveled in the SS *Jelly Roger* receiving orders from Top Cat to find a different treasure that had been lost or stolen, returning it to the rightful owners. They are challenged by the SS *Dirty Tricks* driven by Dick Dastardly and Muttley who want the treasure for themselves, creating a never-ending competition format that crossed elements of the *Indiana Jones* film series with shows like *Wacky Races*. Hanna-Barbera's methods continued to improve, and *Yogi's Treasure Hunt* boasted arguably the highest quality animation since the original series, but the recycled storylines and more child-friendly bear led to limited attention from the audience across the program's two seasons in production. Yogi had also lost his edge as his days of stealing pic-a-nic baskets were far behind him. The block included wraparounds hosted by some of the most popular characters that also appeared in *Treasure Hunt* including Yogi, Snagglepuss, Quick Draw McGraw, and Huckleberry Hound. They also introduced "HBTV," a copy of Disney Channel's DTV, which itself was inspired by the popularity of MTV, where popular songs are backed by recycled animation from the studio, creating music videos appropriate for the young audience.[18]

In a more well-received continuation of an older franchise, Hanna-Barbera reincarnated the popular *The Jetsons* after reruns had aired on weekend mornings for over twenty years, one of the few animated shows to be regularly scheduled on all three networks. The new series, which are considered the second and third seasons of the program, added a few new characters including Orbitty, the Jetsons' pet alien, Orwell, Mr. Spacely's nephew, and R.U.D.I., a sentient computer that appeared in one episode in the first season. The two new seasons added 51 episodes, with 41 produced for the second season, creating a total of 75 episodes, enough to also sell into second-run syndication after the new seasons' run on the *Funtastic World* block. The show mostly followed the structure of the 1963 season, but along with the new characters, writers and animators added some appliances and new music to better represent contemporary technologies and styles. To new audiences the idea of the future presented in the original set of episodes was becoming quaint as society caught up to Hanna-Barbera's perspective of what the future would look like back in 1962. It also focused more on the influence of computers, rather than robotics, to reflect American trends which had moved beyond fascination with the Space Race.[19]

The other two shows that filled segments in the first season of the *Funtastic World* both reflected Hanna-Barbera's continued commitment in producing shows with obvious product tie-in possibilities. *Galtar and the Golden Lance* was a clear attempt to capitalize on the popularity of *He-Man*, as the studio hoped it could attract a toy maker to produce figures based on the characters. In the series, Galtar is a warrior who uses his powerful golden lance to challenge Tormack, who has usurped the throne, killing most of the royal family and their court. Princess Goleeta and her brother Zorn, who is able to control thoughts, are the only surviving royals and join Galtar on his adventures. Both Galtar and Goleeta take on a collection of monsters and aliens as they look to avenge their parents' murders. The series was another sign Hanna-Barbera had moved on from relying on limited animation, with increased details in the animation of the human characters and backgrounds. For the series, Hanna-Barbera relied more heavily on animation contractors from countries like Taiwan to do much of the animating for much cheaper, allowing for more time spent by animators on design and detail. Unfortunately, *Galtar* was lost among a collection of similar franchises, including *He-Man* and *Conan the Barbarian*, never equaling the merchandising and multimedia success of those properties.[20]

The last series to debut in 1985 hoped to cash in on the popularity of series like *The Care Bears* and the studio's own *Smurfs* as a series aimed at younger views featuring a group of cute creatures that could be licensed and collected by young consumers. The *Paw Paws* were a community of Native American bear cubs who must travel through the forest while being pursued by the Meanos, led by another cub, Dark Paw, and his bumbling henchmen. Like the Smurfs and Care Bears, each Paw Paw has a name that matches its personality or defining characteristic like Brave Paw and Princess Paw, the main antagonist among the tiny bears. Even though Hanna-Barbera decided to identify the bears as Native American, there was little cultural relevance or accuracy in their attire or actions, including the occasional tendency to practice a "traditional dance" or cite "tribal customs" as a reason for their actions. They are protected by a Totem of three animals, an eagle, bear, and turtle, that come to life to help and defeat Dark Paw when the cubs are threatened by the Meanos. The series was accompanied by a short-running toyline by Applause that included two-inch figurines of the show's many characters and a plush of the Paw Paws' tiny dog PuPooch.[21]

Fred and Jonny Join The Jetsons

Before Hanna-Barbera looked to the future and the 1986–1987 season, they stopped to remember their past in CBS' *The Flintstones 25th Anniversary Special* hosted by Tim Conway, Harvey Korman, and Vanna White. Featuring new animation and a long list of live-action and animated guest stars, the prehistoric family was honored for its contribution to television with a mix of old clips and new animation. Robert Guenette, director of Hanna-Barbera *Hall of Fame: Yabba Dabba Doo II*, returned to lead the retrospective examining the seminal series and the many spin-offs it inspired, including a preview of a new entry to the *Flintstones* property that premiered the next fall.[22]

The Flintstone Kids debuted in the fall of 1986 as an attempt to capitalize on the trend most popularly exemplified by the *Muppet Babies* that infantilized older characters to revitalize the property and attract younger viewers, familiarizing them with the property and developing loyal fans. Barbera and Squire Rushnell, the ABC head of programming at the time, had previously contacted Coleco and Cabbage Patch Dolls creator Xavier Roberts about creating a show starring the dolls. They were unable to get the rights, so they went ahead with a show starring younger versions of *The Flintstones* characters. On a larger scale this strategy was utilized on cable through the relationship between Nickelodeon and its sister network, MTV, where Viacom hoped early exposure to Nickelodeon would foster loyalty. When the young viewer got older there would be an easy transition to the content on MTV aimed at older viewers.[23]

Like *The Muppet Babies*, *The Flintstones Kids* reimagined the franchise's stars, Fred, Wilma (Slaghoople, pre-marriage), Betty (Bricker in the series, but McBricker in canon), Barney, and Dino as kids growing up in Bedrock. In the original series, the franchise had established in the fourth season episode, "Bachelor Daze," that Fred and Barney met their respective wives in their early twenties, but the apocryphal *The Flintstones Kids* broke continuity from previous series with producers hoping that the target audience would not notice the changes. Continuing a trend that started earlier in the decade, the animation for *The Flintstone Kids* was clearly improved from other *Flintstones* spinoffs, particularly those from the 1970s, with producers relying more on computers to produce animated content, which also shortened production times and allowed the studio to outsource more work. Individual artists, especially those responsible for overlooked portions of the animation process like inking and drawing backgrounds, were needed less with software and international animators replacing work by hand by American artists. ABC, which like the *Muppets* was later purchased by Disney, did not hide its intention to overtake the animated versions of the popular puppets, scheduling back-to-back episodes of *The Flintstones Kids* directly against *The Muppet Babies* following *The Care*

Toys featuring Freddy Flintstone and Wilma Slaghoople, stars of *The Flintstone Kids* (Nicescene/Shutterstock.com).

Bears. The latter also represented the most significant challenge to *The Smurfs* during its time on NBC, with CBS scheduling the show against Hanna-Barbera's long running series in 1984, a time slot held by *The Muppet Babies* throughout the rest of the decade.[24]

The Flintstone Kids featured four segments, partially due to the assumption that the younger audience's attention span could not carry them through a full program.[25] Three of the segments starred the prepubescent stars and one featured Captain Caveman and his son, which, like the other segments, breaks continuity with past series by introducing a storyline and character not recognized in previous series starring the superhero. "The Flintstone Kids" segment was the main story each week that featured the young stars, which also included Nate Slate, Fred's future boss, bully Ronald Ratrock, the wealthy Dreamchip Gemstone, and aspiring detective Philo Quartz, the first regular African American cast member in the history of the franchise. The second segment, which was dropped after the first season, was *The Flintstone Funnies*, where the four main cast members are placed in fantasy sequences where they imagine themselves in different stories or myths, like *Frankenstein* or *Indiana Jones*. The third segment, *Dino's Dilemmas*, featured different adventures and situations presented from the pet dinosaur's point of view. The fourth segment, *Captain Caveman and Son,* featured the aforementioned superhero and his offspring, Cavey Jr., as a superhero team. The segment is presented like a meta Saturday morning show watched by the cast of *The Flintstones Kids* with Captain Caveman often breaking the fourth wall by speaking to the young animated audience. The episode "Rocky's Rocky Road" in the second season won the Humanitas Award for its discussion of bullying.[26]

The Flintstones was not the only franchise that was renewed for the season. With the success of *The Funtastic World*, which was extended to over four hours in some markets in 1986, Hanna-Barbera was looking for past shows that could be rerun and possibly rebooted through syndication, especially after the success of the new *The Jetsons* episodes that premiered the previous season. By this time, episodes of *The Adventures of Jonny Quest*, which still maintained a solid following, were still being sold into syndication but many episodes had significant portions cut due to edits related to both running time and content. The re-edited episodes focused more on Bandit to replace some of the violent scenes and more mature themes that were present in the series that originally debuted in prime time aimed at general audiences over 20 years earlier. As Hanna-Barbera prepared to add *Jonny Quest* reruns to the *Funtastic World*, they also decided to produce new, more child-appropriate episodes featuring the young adventurer. Added to the cast of *The New Adventures of Jonny Quest*, which some actually consider the second season of the original series, was Hardrock, a petrified warrior Dr. Quest finds underground within the ruins of an ancient city. Hardrock, who was voiced by Jeffrey Tambor, was introduced in "The Monolith Man" in the seventh episode of the first and what was ultimately the only season, as writers most likely assumed the show would last past the first thirteen episodes. Unfortunately, the new episodes did not add much to the franchise; the reboot contained less mature, watered down storylines lacking the drama, excitement, and even violence that attracted fans to the original series, which were airing alongside the new episodes. Also hurting the new episodes was the animation since the original animation from artists like Doug Wildey and Alex Toth for the 1960s series is still considered some of the best in the history of the company. Hadji's character was also not updated, with producers giving the Kolkatan character even more powers to help the Quests out of perilous situations. This increased the mysticism and exoticism that surrounded him, which was already problematic in the 1960s, let alone nearly a quarter century later.[27]

The New Adventures of Jonny Quest was the only show to debut exclusively in syndication that season, as Hanna-Barbera tried to maintain some presence on Saturday morning, even as that timeslot's influence on the industry was in the midst of a slow decline. Collaborating again with SEPP and Freddy Monnickendam after the moderate success of *The Snorks*, Hanna-Barbera produced *Foofur* based on characters created by Black artist Phil Mendez. The series' eponymous star is a lanky blue Phil Harris-inspired dog who lives in the mansion of his late handler, and with the help of his niece, Rocky, turns the home into a refuge for homeless and rejected animals. Amelia Escrow, the realtor in charge of selling the estate, does not know the animals live there and scare potential buyers away from the home, but her Chihuahua Pepe does and tries in vain to alert his handler of the freeloaders costing her the sale. Several of the other dogs were also modeled after famous actors including Jackie Gleason (Louis the Bulldog) who joined the ambiguously accented Fritz-Carlos, the spoiled Annabell, and a "jive-talking" street cat, Fencer, who may have been included to add some vocal diversity to "the good guys." Along with Ms. Escrow and Pepe, three Rat Brothers antagonized the squatting animals but joined the group to save the house when threatened by Escrow or other outsiders. The same season *Kissyfur*, a series about a father-son circus bear duo, debuted as a regular series featuring characters also created by Phil Mendez after several specials aired in prime time the previous season. Both series were broadcast on NBC and were largely overlooked, and as a result they are often confused even though the two series were very different and *Kissyfur* was actually produced by DiC.[28]

The female audience had long been overlooked by Hanna-Barbera, who had improved in terms of representation since the 1960s, but it could be argued they never created a show that specifically courted non-males. This could have been based on the assumption that girls may venture into gendered content, and merchandise, aimed at boys, but boys were highly unlikely to watch more feminine programming due to possible ridicule from peers and fear from parents. Hanna-Barbera felt that shows that included female characters and had an audience across genders, like *Scooby-Doo* or *The Smurfs*, were enough of a commitment to a demographic that made up over half the population and potential audience. With the success of *She-Ra*, Hanna-Barbera finally attempted to create a show specifically for women, *Wildfire*, about a young girl, Sara, living in the American West who finds out she is a princess in another dimension. In a Superman-like twist, Sara was sent to Montana by a magic horse, Wildfire, to protect her from enemies on Dar-Shan. She is summoned back through a protective amulet that a sorceress, Lady Diabolyn, wants to use to take over Dar-Shan after her step-sister, Queen Sarana, who is also Sara's mother, dies. Sara is helped in Dar-Shan by sorcerer Alvinar, Dorin, a young boy, and Dorin's horse Brutus. On Earth, her adopted father, John, and her Native American friend Ellen assist Sara. The series was one of many during this period, including *Snorks* and later seasons of *The Smurfs*, for which Cuckoo's Nest Studios in Taipei assisted with the artwork.[29] Critics commented that the storylines were shallow and somewhat patronizing toward young girls, and the series was ending production after thirteen episodes before any licensed toys were produced.[30] Between *She-Ra* and *My Little Pony*, *Wildfire* was lost among better produced, and marketed, shows with both series featuring connected toy lines by Mattel and Hasbro respectively. Unlike her twin brother *He-Man*, She-Ra never received her own comic series, most likely due to DC debuting a very similar character, *Amethyst, Princess of the Gemstones*, in 1983.[31]

One Hanna-Barbera program from the fall of 1986 that did have a very successful toy line was *Pound Puppies*. The animated adaptation of the collection of plush toys had debuted the previous fall in a syndicated telefilm package alongside another Tonka property, *Star Fairies*, which was not picked up as a full series. The films were also produced for sale exclusively on VHS, the first wide-release not to also appear on Betamax, and the *Pound Puppies* film became one of the most popular children's film rentals that year.[32] In the telefilm a dog from a wealthy family, Violet Vanderfeller, is captured by Dabney Nabbitt while trying to escape dognappers. She is taken to the pound where she meets the Fonz-inspired Cooler; a cheerleader dressed dog named Bright Eyes; Nose, a nasally New Yorker; and Howler, an inventor who can only communicate in howls. Cooler and his friends help Violet eventually escape and find her family. All the characters but Violet and Nabbitt returned for the series on ABC, with the former unmentioned in the series and a dog named Whopper being added, so named because he constantly lies. Nose is replaced by Nose Marie, a "southern belle," to add more gender diversity to a show that acted as an advertisement for a toy line that was marketed toward both boys and girls.

Inspired by *Hogan's Heroes*, the animals run the "pound" in which they live, working to find themselves homes. In the new series Katrina Stonehart is the grandniece of Millicent Trueblood, a millionaire who established the pound after the puppies' home in Wagga-Wagga was destroyed by Captain Slaughter. Katrina inherits the property and wants to tear down the home with the help of her daughter Brittina and the feline Catgut. Katrina's niece Holly lives with the Stoneharts and has the same ability to speak to the puppies as Millicent, helping the puppies protect their home. In the second season the show was completely revamped with zero continuity, basically forming a new show, the *All New Pound Puppies*. Rather than one longer episode, the producers split the second season episodes into two segments. In this version, Katrina Stonehart has no desire to destroy the pound; rather she plays the role of warden, treating the shelter like a prison as the pound puppies avoid her, meeting at their headquarters. Through the work of Ruegger the series continued the trend of higher quality animation from Hanna-Barbera. The series also helped launch the career of Nancy Cartwright, who still plays the role of Bart Simpson.[33]

Competing against the anthropomorphized puppies was an animated adaptation of a popular 1985 film featuring a young man transforming into a canine. *Teen Wolf* transported the Howard family from Beacontown in the film to Wolverton as teenager Scott and the rest of his family faced difficulties trying to fit in as werewolves. Co-produced by the company's Australian unit and Southern Star Productions, it aired for 21 episodes across two seasons on CBS. The animated series never approached the popularity of the original film, but it did feature storylines that addressed such issues as disability and bullying. Only James Hampton, who played Scott's father Howard, reprised his role from the live-action film.[34]

Keeping One Foot in Film

Six years earlier Hanna-Barbera started production on a feature film, *Rock Odyssey*. The film takes pop idol Laura through the history of rock and roll music as she searches for love. Taft and their distributors, concerned over the violent Vietnam War imagery in the animated film, shelved the project, which was pushed back further by the box office failure of *Heidi's Song*. During a congressional address in March 1983, ABC's VP of children's programming mentioned the project, but production of the film was not renewed for several more years. To help connect the time divide between the beginning and the end of production they added the pop song "Wake Me Up Before You Go-Go" by Wham set to older clips of Hanna-Barbera cartoons, similar to the approach to "HBTV." The movie was supposed to be a more family-friendly *Heavy Metal* or a more modern *Fantasia*, but it failed to garner the positive attention of either film. The movie debuted in July 1987 at the Los Angeles Animation Celebration and is currently contained in the Library of Congress, but it never aired on ABC or got released on home video.[35]

Another film that was shelved for several years was *P.K. and the Kid* about an aspiring professional arm wrestler who meets an abused 14-year-old girl and takes her to the arm wrestling championships as her stepfather angrily pursues them. The film was produced by Sunn Classic Pictures, a division of Taft, and written by Neal Barbera, Joe's son, in 1983 but was not released until January 1987 after the actress who plays the teenage girl, Molly Ringwald, had become a star in *Sixteen Candles* (1984) and *Pretty in Pink* (1986). Even with Ringwald's name attached, it was largely overlooked, partially due to *Over the Top*, a film also about arm wrestling written by and starring Sylvester Stallone. *Over the Top* came out the next month and also flopped at the box office, reaffirming the lack of public interest in arm wrestling films.[36]

The family telefilm *The Stone Fox* debuted on NBC in late March 1987 as counter programming to the Academy Awards. In the adaptation of the book, which was co-produced between Taft, the Canadian Allarcom Limited, and Hanna-Barbera, the twelve-year-old Willy must enter a dog race to win $500 and save his grandfather's farm.[37] Although most of their animation was aimed at children, Taft and Hanna-Barbera still used live-action specials to target teenagers and family audiences. This strategy led to limited success due to low budgets, a lack of promotion, and inconsistent production schedules.

A movie they did release widely in October 1987 was their first anime inspired production. *Ultraman: The Adventure Begins,* co-produced with the Japanese studio Tsuburaya Productions, starred a trio of stunt pilots for the "Flying Angels," Scott Masterson, Chuck Gavin, and Beth O'Brien, who are caught in a flashing light and become the host bodies for warriors from Altara. The warriors have come to Earth to defeat monsters from planet Sorkin, assisted by three robots, Andy, Samson, and Ulysses. They fly highly technical aircraft, and when the situations become especially dangerous one or more of the heroes become the supersized Ultraman, which they use to defeat the equally large King Maira. The film, which was released in both North America and Japan, was also supposed to be a pilot for a series to air in both countries, but neither the film nor the character attracted the attention of young audiences in America. A home video version of the film was not released until 1993 as a response to growing popularity of English-dubbed Ultraman media, which had been popular in Japan since the 1960s.[38]

New Owner, New Problems

As Hanna-Barbera prepared for the 1987–1988 season, their planned output, which only included two new shows, one for Saturday morning, and several telefilms and specials, was much lower than usual, a possible reaction to Taft Broadcasting's instability and eventual sale to TFBA Partners for $1.4 billion in April 1987. Taft had begun selling off its assets earlier in the year as a result of overextending itself financially by acquiring properties throughout the late 1970s and 1980s. By the late summer Carl J. Lindner, the founder of Great American Insurance, which like Taft was headquartered in

Cincinnati, Ohio, was in the process of a hostile takeover of Taft, which was completed in late September, right before the release of *Ultraman*. Linder changed the media corporation's name to Great American Broadcasting and began looking toward restructuring the company. Over the next few years many of Taft's former properties were sold, merged, or eliminated as Lindner worked to make the conglomerate profitable after years of losses under Taft's board. The corporate chaos created instability for the production companies, distributors, and studios acquired by Great American in the takeover as the new ownership, which had very little media experience, did not offer nearly the same level of support as Taft.[39] This chaos was felt all over the industry, particularly after Mark Fowler and the FCC removed the three-year waiting period before a new owner could resell a station during Reagan's first term. As a result, a number of stations in most major markets changed hands, and even affiliates, some several times, interrupting two decades of relative stability on the corporate level.[40]

One series to debut during this upheaval was co-produced with Toei Animation and Kenner, featuring the toy company's newest line, *Sky Commanders,* a collection of soldiers and mountain climbers who are fighting General Plague and his "Raiders" as they try to obtain an energy source, Phaeta Seven, that could be used to take over the world. The radioactive material was hidden deep inside the earth before it emerged when a seismic disturbance revealed a hidden continent. Complicating the soldiers' mission are the unpredictable weather and geological activity on the land mass, which is only navigable through flight, "laser cables" or ziplines that allow them to travel above the mutant-occupied terrain. The convoluted plot and lack of companion comic to help audiences, particularly young boys, connect with the supposedly multicultural characters prevented both the television and toy series from gaining any traction. The fact that the series was inspired by both *Star Wars* and *He-Man* also contributed to its being mostly ignored by audiences. The designs of the toys, which looked like cheaper versions of the G.I. Joe line, were only notable because some of the characters included ziplines, which the few children who actually bought the toys could use to replicate the scenes on the show. The showed aired the summer of 1987 before it was cancelled before the start of the 1987–1988 season.[41]

A series that did premiere that fall was another attempt to capitalize from the infantilization fad, *Popeye and Son*, which premiered on CBS in the fall of 1987 just as Taft prepared to change hands again. In the series, Popeye and Olive Oyl have married in a different timeline, producing an offspring, Popeye Junior. Junior replaced Swee'Pea, who had appeared in the comic strip, shorts, and previous Hanna-Barbera series with some question about his relationship with Popeye and Olive Oyl. Popeye's son has the same super strength as his spinach-powered father but hates the leafy greens that give them their strength. The storylines were similar to those seen in the Popeye segment of the previous iterations of the franchise, *The All New Popeye Hour and The Popeye and Olive Comedy Show*, merely adding conflict between Junior and Bluto's son, Tank.

At the time, Saturday morning as a whole was struggling as production delays and conflicts between producers and networks caused scheduling and promotional issues in preparation for the season, which Hanna-Barbera's situation at Taft only exacerbated. Some studios were overwhelmed producing content for both the broadcast networks and expanding syndication market. Due to the lack of oversight in syndication, producers felt like they had more freedom to produce fare that included violence and other content parents might find objectionable, circumventing the networks as they targeted adolescents. Saturday morning had taken a noticeably juvenile turn by the 1987 season with most shows aimed at children under 10 featuring cute animals, toy-inspired programs, and several pre-pubescent humans in the starring roles. By this time broadcast networks were considering abandoning the adolescent audience completely, focusing almost exclusively on the younger demographic.[42]

The Hanna-Barbera Superstars 10

Hoping to maintain some presence for their older properties, Hanna-Barbera continued to release specials and telefilms. The last *Smurfs* prime time special, *Tis the Season to Be Smurfy*, premiered on NBC during the holiday season with the Smurfs learning about Christmas and bringing cheer to an elderly couple. Between 1987 and 1988, Hanna-Barbera released a series of ten films with the first four debuting in consecutive weeks in syndication starting in September 1987 as *The Hanna-Barbera Superstars 10*, hoping to capitalize further on the ancillary market, particularly home video. They felt the series of films could capture both the children's market and the nostalgia market with each film produced like an extended version of an episode from the original show that inspired it. The first film, *Yogi's Great Escape*, found the eponymous bear, his sidekick Boo Boo, and three bear cubs left at their doorstep running away from Jellystone and Ranger Smith after budget cuts threaten the park. The bears experience a variety of misadventures, even getting help from Snagglepuss. After finally getting caught in New York City, Yogi receives a call from the president who has halted the closing of Jellystone. Yogi Bear also starred in the fourth film in the series, *Yogi Bear and the Magical Flight of the Spruce Goose,* in which he, Boo Boo, Augie Doggie, Daddy Doggie, Snagglepuss, Quick Draw, and Huckleberry accidentally launch Howard Hughes' famous plane and use it to save animals in perilous situations around the world. At one point, they land on a volcanic island inhabited by a civilization who confuse the villain Dread Baron for some type of deity, Malagula, and give him gold to appease him. The group is captured before a volcanic eruption allows them to escape the island and a pair of aliens they had been crossing paths with throughout the film.[43]

The second film of the series was by far the most popular: *The Jetsons Meet the Flintstones*, in which a time traveling accident by Elroy forces Hanna-Barbera's two most famous families to finally cross paths. Both families travel back and forth to each other's time with side stories featuring Fred and Barney ending their friendship after losing their jobs at the quarry and Judy falling for a Stone Age rock star. The film was the top-rated syndicated program that fall and became one of the top rented children's videos, leading to a mild resurgence of both franchises. It is also frequently referenced as one of the few animated crossover films or programs to actually work.

The fourth film, *Scooby-Doo Meets the Boo Brothers*, was a film-length version of *Scooby-Doo and Scrappy-Doo* that found the two dogs joining Shaggy on a trip to his uncle's country estate, which he inherits and which contains a treasure, finding clues left behind by his deceased relative. The three are helped by the Boo Brothers, a trio of bumbling ghosts who work to exterminate other ghosts since they are without a home, as they face off against the Skull Ghost, who is also aware of the treasure and races with Shaggy, Scooby, and Scrappy. They also have to deal with an ape who escaped a derailed circus train. The Great Dane and his friends find the treasure first but are held hostage at gunpoint by the villain. They eventually escape and then catch him, unmasking the "ghost" and revealing he is the Sheriff that pretended to help them earlier in the film. Shaggy gives the mansion to the Boo Brothers so they can have a home.[44]

The remaining six films premiered throughout 1988 with the first of these airing four months after *Scooby-Doo Meets the Boo Brothers* in March. The fifth film of the series, *Top Cat and the Beverly Hills Cats,* starred the eponymous feline and his gang in a feature-length film that adapted two episodes from the original series, relocating Hoagie's Alley to Southern California. Gertrude Vandergelt delivers a fake letter to Benny saying she has died and left her fortune to the cat after he saved her life as a part of a larger plot reveal that her butler Snerdly was untrustworthy. He tries to murder Benny several times before dressing him as a dog at a costume party and having him thrown in the pound. The cats find the rightful heir, Vandergelt's niece Amy, who Snerdly has forced to work at a car wash. However, they arrive after the deadline, but as Snerdly prepares to inherit the fortune, it is revealed Vandergelt actually faked her death and disguised herself as Sid Buckman so she can catch Snerdly's unethical behavior.[45]

The sixth telefilm starred Huckleberry Hound in a parody of Westerns including *High Noon*, *A Man with No Name*, and *High Plains Drifter*. In *The Good, the Bad, and the Huckleberry Hound* the Dalton Gang terrorizes Two-Bit, California, before Huck is made sheriff and is able to trick the Daltons, who mistakenly run into a prison thinking it is a hideout. The film was the last time Daws Butler voiced the popular character, dying three days after the cartoon debuted in May 1988.[46]

In *Rockin' with Judy Jetson*, the seventh film, the eponymous daughter of George writes a song for Sky Rocker and attends the musician's concert to her father's disapproval. Sky is captured by Felonia Funk who wants to destroy music, before Judy and the Zoomies, a race of music loving aliens, rescue Sky, while Elroy, accompanied by Astro and George, pursues the missing Judy. Felonia tries to use a device called the Mental Flosser to control the universe, but she is thwarted through the power of music.[47]

The eighth film, *Scooby-Doo and the Ghoul School*, lead Shaggy, Scooby, and Scrappy to a school for ghouls, occupied by parodies of old movie monsters, after they accept a job as gym teachers at what they thought was a school for human girls. The three prepare the female monsters for a volleyball match against the Calloway Military Academy, which they win in spite of the cadets from the academy trying to cheat. During a visit, the fathers warn the three that they will be in trouble if any harm comes to their daughters. The witch Revolta tries to poison the students and make them her minions, but the trio, with the help of the cadets, arrives just before midnight to save girls. The film debuted two weeks before Halloween.[48]

The ninth film, *Scooby-Doo and the Reluctant Werewolf*, featured a Monster Road Rally starring many of the popular movie monsters that were seen in young female form in the previous Scooby-Doo movie. As Dracula prepares the rally he receives a letter that Wolfman will not be coming, so he decides to create another werewolf. They must expose a human to the moonlight in the following three nights and the next human on the list happens to be Shaggy, who just won a road rally. While on a date with his girlfriend Googie he is turned into a Werewolf but refuses to race unless Dracula agrees to change him back if he wins. Shaggy wins the race but Dracula still refuses before his wife reveals the spell to turn him back is in the vampire's books. The group escapes Transylvania with the book before Googie uses the spell to turn her boyfriend back into a human.[49]

The last film, *Yogi and the Invasion of the Space Bears*, premiered one week after *Scooby-Doo and the Reluctant Werewolf* in November 1988 and brought back Yogi, who is now being threatened with expulsion to Siberia before he and Boo Boo are abducted by aliens and cloned. The robot clones attempt to take over Jellystone before the real Yogi and Boo Boo return to help Rangers Smith and Roubideaux destroy the robots and save the park. The last two films were produced with digital ink and paint, rather than traditional cels. Also, unlike the previous nine films, which were released for home video soon after their television debuts, *Yogi and the Invasion of the Space Bears* did not come to VHS until 1991. This was also Daws Butler's last project.[50]

Just Say Yes to Positive P.R. Opportunities

By 1988, not even Hanna-Barbera and *The Flintstones* could ignore the War on Drugs started by Nixon and accelerated by Reagan, whose wife, Nancy, led the charge behind the "Just Say No" anti-drug campaign aimed at kids. The studio produced a number of educational films and public service announcements throughout the late 1970s and 1980s for distribution to schools and churches. *The Flintstone Kids' "Just Say No" Special*, which avoided any subtlety in its title, was a prime time special featuring the pre-pubescent stars learning the importance of saying no. In the first part, Wilma is tempted to hang out with a new group of kids who do drugs, including Stoney the pothead, pressuring her to partake before she refuses. In the second vignette, Fred and his friends are trying to earn money to attend a Michael Jackstone concert. They enter a road race in which they beat Stoney and his friends aided by their clear-headed, sober thinking. At the end of the cartoon Nancy Reagan discusses the importance of drug abstinence, again using popular television to try to reach children, a strategy implemented throughout the Reagan two-term administration.[51] LaToya Jackson contributed an original song cleverly named "Just Say No" and an anti-drug version of "Beat It" that is played during the race and performed by Kipp Lennon due to Jackson's contractual obligations. Lennon more famously supplied Jackson's singing voice in the 1991 *The Simpsons* episode "Stark Raving Dad," in which Michael Jackson supplied the speaking voice talent under a pseudonym. In only 25 years, *The Flintstones* had gone from promoting cigarettes to starring in anti-drug propaganda. Yogi also started in an anti-drug film sponsored by Drug Abuse Resistance Education (D.A.R.E.), the school-centered program run by police departments that taught middle schoolers about drug abstinence. The film, *D.A.R.E. Bear Yogi*, was shown in schools as a part of the larger program while he served as the mascot before being replaced by Darren the Lion during the 1990s.[52]

Hanna-Barbera rarely ignored a trend, and when a number of game shows starring children, including *Double Dare* and *Finder Keepers*, became popular on cable the studio decided to create their own for *The Funtastic World of Hanna-Barbera*. Game shows, if developed correctly, are relatively cheap to produce especially with sponsorship, have short production schedules, and can be rerun a number of times. Looking back, simple rules and physically demanding obstacle courses seemed to be the common characteristics among the successful children's games shows of the era. *Skedaddle* had neither of those things, running only six weeks before the show's complicated premise and lack of athletic challenges led to cancellation. In the game, two teams of four adolescents are given an object by one of three dinosaurs, Slam, Dunk, and Seymour, that they pass like a hot potato between team members trying to reach a predetermined number of right answers to score points. In the bonus round, they are given multiple choice questions, sitting on a stool that corresponds with their answer at which time a bucket is turned over. If they were correct, it would be empty; if wrong, green slime would cover them. At that point the ambiguous substance that was green slime had become synonymous with Nickelodeon, where it was first featured on one of the first popular shows they broadcast, the Canadian *You Can't Do That on Television*.[53] The game show and presence of "slime" was a sign Hanna-Barbera was clearly paying attention to the children's media trends originating from cable, including the fast rise of the Viacom-led Nickelodeon, which also broadcast *Double Dare* and *Finders Keepers*, both of which were originally filmed at a public media studio in Philadelphia.[54]

The Yogi telefilms helped renew interest in the original shorts starring the picnic basket-tempted bear, leading to 45 new shorts premiering throughout the fall of 1988. These were often combined with the 33 original episodes for the syndication package to sell to networks and stations. This was the first Yogi property not to feature Daws Butler, who had voiced the character for thirty years before passing away in 1988. Yogi was still less interested in stealing food than in the first series, with *The New Yogi Bear Show* relying more on old sitcom storylines and a heightened level of self-awareness displayed in the humor. The crossover "all-star" characters like Snagglepuss and Quick Draw were also gone with series originals Yogi, Boo Boo, Cindy Bear, and Ranger Smith joined in Jellystone Park by Smith's assistant Ranger Roubideux, who debuted in *Yogi and the Invasion of the Space Bears*; Ninja Raccoon and his mother; and Blubber Bear from Arkansas who had previously appeared almost 20 years earlier in *Wacky Races* as the pet of the driver of the "hillbilly" car, Lazy Luke. This was the last series in which Yogi appeared in his original form (and age), thereafter making only cameos in shorts and programs starring other characters until he appeared in the 2010 live-action film *Yogi Bear*.[55]

Conceiving Fantastic Max

The other syndicated series to debut that season during the *Funtastic World* block represented another attempt by Hanna-Barbera to reach out internationally for content, as Nickelodeon was doing successfully as it imported animation from Canada, Europe, and Asia. A series originally titled *Super Baby* was developed by Welsh media company Siriol Productions about a toddler who is visited by an alien, giving him superpowers including advanced mental capacity and the ability to travel through outer space. The show was modeled after another Siriol show, *SuperTed*, about a super powered plush bear, which also found its way across the Atlantic the next season. Mike Young, who left Siriol the next year, helped adapt *Super Baby* into a series for Hanna-Barbera, premiering under the title *Fantastic Max* in the United States in 1988, a full year before it officially debuted in Britain. Max was joined by the nervous butler alien A.B., clearly inspired by *Star Wars'* C3PO, and FX, the alien who originally bestowed powers on the young superhero. In most episodes, Max is on some type of adventure before a problem arises, which Max has to overcome with his powers. To fully welcome Max to the Hanna-Barbera family three other space-related characters, George Jetson, Space Ghost, and *The Flintstones'* The Great Gazoo, appear in the third episode in non-speaking cameos.[56]

Fantastic Max did well enough in the American market to motivate Hanna-Barbera to continue the production of the franchise that inspired Fantastic Max, *SuperTed*. The plush superhero was originally brought to life in a collection of children's books by Mike Young to help his son overcome his fear of the dark. Warner approached Young about the film rights, but he wanted the character to remain culturally Welsh and bring jobs to his nation, so he partnered with Welsh public service channel S4C and Siriol to create the series. In the story, *SuperTed* is a defective Teddy bear who is thrown away before receiving superpowers from a magic cloud. He travels with Spottyman, from planet Spot, helping people around the world defeating villains like Texas Pete, Skeleton, and Bulk. The series, which premiered in 1983 and ran for three seasons, contained the same dry wit as one of the most popular British animation series of all time, *Danger Mouse*, which was among the earliest popular cartoons on Nickelodeon. Reruns of the Welch version of *SuperTed* were airing on the Disney Channel when *The Further Adventures of SuperTed* began production. The new series, which is set in California rather than Cardiff, featured many of the same characters, but the Hanna-Barbera influence was definitely present as the now more muscular, deep voiced bear starred in storylines that parodied American pop culture, moving away from the satirical adventures seen in the original cartoon. The series debuted in January of 1989 on the *Funtastic World of Hanna-Barbera*, and although the animation, which was outsourced, was much better than the original, the financial issues and personnel changes at the studio prevented the series from rising above recycled jokes and parodies, and it was cancelled after a season, airing in the United Kingdom the next season.[57]

Hanna-Barbera continued to keep a toe in the Saturday morning waters, partnering with SEPP International to create a series based on Martin Short's popular sketch comedy character Ed Grimley. Short created the character in 1982 while a cast member on the popular Canadian sketch comedy show *SCTV*, produced by Toronto's Second City comedy troupe, which at the time was also airing on NBC. Short moved to *Saturday Night Live* in 1984, bringing with him the popular character, who also appeared in a Showtime special in 1985. Hanna-Barbera and SEPP developed *The Completely Mental Misadventures of Ed Grimley*, based on the fidgety, immature "nerd," premiering the series in fall 1988. The show was a fairly ambitious effort, particularly for a studio facing ownership uncertainty as producers hired several popular past and present members from Second City and the improvisational world. Catherine O'Hara, Jonathan Winters, Christopher Guest and Dave Thomas provided regular and guest voices, even playing some of their past characters in the hopes to attract a new generation of viewers to sketch comedy. The writing was wittier and of a higher pace than many other shows of the time, which may have worked against the series as the Saturday morning audience continued to get younger, with many of the references going over the young viewers' heads. A recurring segment featuring *SCTV* cast member Joe Flaherty playing a character from the live-action show, Count Floyd, a host of a campy 1950s horror show, was one of the most obvious examples of the divide between some of the comedy and the audience, a significant number of which were born several decades after the content being satirized aired. Although it gained a cult following with adults, gaining a second life in cable animation aimed at more mature audiences, it was cancelled after 13 episodes, failing to connect with young children, leading Hanna-Barbera to also abandon the development of another series starring an Academy Award winner, Whoopi Goldberg.[58] Coincidentally, NBC replaced Ed Grimley with *Camp Candy*, co-produced by DiC and Saban Entertainment, starring another Second City alum, John Candy.[59]

Infantilization Invites Irrelevance

Hoping to continue to capitalize on the infantilization trend still occurring in animation, Ruegger and Hanna-Barbera decided to dip the cast of *Scooby-Doo* into the fountain of youth in 1988 and reimagine Mystery Inc. as pre-teen mystery solvers with more confidence than knowledge. Both the younger versions of Scooby and Shaggy are fairly similar to earlier incarnations of the characters with both the dog and his friend easily scared and motivated by food. The adolescent Daphne and Fred are both more impulsive caricatures of their original characters. The younger Daphne is represented more cynically, and as a satirical take on her wealth, she often relies on her butler Jenkins to help her with even the simplest tasks, like showing emotion. Fred is more extroverted than his older counterpart, using his vast imagination to come up with a (typically wrong) conclusion about the perpetrator, often accusing a classmate that is literally named Red Herring. Velma, who like Fred had not appeared in a Scooby-Doo series since the 1970s, continued to be the true crime solver of the group, although she now carried a mobile computer that served as a crime laboratory. The show is backed by a rock and doo-wop score that was a step above the normal studio soundtrack. Ruegger, who had helped develop the previous two *Scooby-Doo* series, also for ABC, expanded on the irreverent humor he experimented with in those two series along with *The Snorks*. Recognizing the personality traits and behavior patterns from the other seven series and several specials, a "meta" approach was utilized that was a wink to the loyal audience that could recall the older episodes and appreciated the good-humored mocking. Considering its reliance on formulas, adaptations, and the public's overall familiarity with the characters, Hanna-Barbera was the perfect subject for this type of self-reflexive humor. Led by Ruegger's script writing and direction, *A Pup Named Scooby-Doo* exemplified possible strategies for Hanna-Barbera and other animation studios looking to maintain visibility for their iconic characters without relying on the same designs and formulas that had become old and redundant after decades of reruns.[60] At the end of the season *The Smurfs* also ended their production run with Hanna-Barbera, and since Peyo held on to the rights to his characters, the studio would not produce any new content featuring them even as new films were released 20 years later.[61]

Unfortunately, another media company was looking to re-establish its animation studio and revitalize its cast of stars, Warner Brothers. Bugs Bunny and friends had held a consistent presence on Saturday morning since the 1950s, but some of their characters, and their cartoons, had surpassed 50 years of age, and younger children were not connecting with the *Looney Tunes* like they once did. In 1988, Great American Broadcasting sold Worldvision Enterprises, who continued to own the syndication rights to content from Hanna-Barbera. Worldvison was purchased by Aaron Spelling Productions along with most of the former Taft properties, except for Hanna-Barbera and Ruby-Spears. This created a separation between the company responsible for distribution and the studio producing the content, which contributed to the relatively low output the previous two seasons. Budget cuts and uncertainty created instability within the company, with Hanna and Barbera unable to promise their staff job security more than one season at a time. Jean MacCurdy had gotten her start at Warner before moving to Hanna-Barbera to produce shows like the *Shirt Tales*, *The Smurfs*, and several *Scooby-Doo* series with Tom Ruegger. In 1989, seeing the instability as an opportunity, Warner hired MacCurdy who brought Ruegger and a number of other animators and writers from Hanna-Barbera with her, many of whom worked on the first season of *A Pup Named Scooby-Doo*. In 1990, *Tiny Toon Adventures* premiered as the first in a line of popular cartoons with cross-demographic appeal revitalizing Warner Animation. The humor, which was similar to but more outlandish than *A Pup Named Scooby-Doo*, helped to re-establish the presence of general audience and more mature animation, a market also supported by *The Simpsons*, which premiered in December 1989. Steven Spielberg executive produced several of these early 1990s Warner series, which also included *Animaniacs*, helping the reincarnated animation studio establish itself and legitimizing the series, especially among adults.[62]

Steven Spielberg had previously produced *A Land Before Time* and *An American Tail*, the latter of which was written by David Kirschner and became the highest grossing non–Disney animated feature up until that point. In 1989, Kirschner, who had also created the Chucky character for the *Child's Play* horror series, was appointed president of the studio by Great American Broadcasting head Charles Mechem, and the new executive immediately went to work re-strategizing Hanna-Barbera's approach. He hoped to emulate the way Disney operated as he looked to expand Hanna-Barbera's presence in areas outside of television, a medium he saw as having increasingly limited profit potential with an increasingly fragmenting audience turning to cable and the home video market. Disney had built its empire on feature films and theme parks and Kirschner looked to do the same with Hanna-Barbera, pushing the studio to test both markets by the end of 1990. The new president learned quickly, however, that these strategies can only go so far without the content to back it up, and the studio was losing significant talent to rival studios.[63]

Even as Hanna and Barbera dealt with all of these changes, they were able to stop and celebrate more than half a century as partners in *A Yabba Dabba Doo Celebration: 50 Years of Hanna-Barbera*. The special, hosted by Tony Danza and Annie Potts, looked back at the long careers of the animation duo, featuring newly produced animated and live-action wraparounds mentioning their many accomplishments and connecting clips and other retrospectives from their time at MGM and *Tom and Jerry* to upcoming projects, including a theatrical feature film. The special aired on TNT, which was owned by Turner Broadcasting, to which Hanna-Barbera regularly sold programming, further establishing a relationship that continued to grow throughout the next decade.

Saturday Morning Continues to Shift

One only had to look at the Saturday morning schedule in the fall of 1989 to recognize the changes at Hanna-Barbera and in the animation industry as a whole. Not only was the audience drawn to cable and syndication, but *Saved by the Bell* also premiered on Saturday morning, the popularity of which led NBC to dedicate most of its Saturday mornings to live-action teen comedies throughout the 1990s under the TNBC banner, looking again to attract the adolescent audience.[64] Along with a CBS prime time special, *Hagar the Horrible: Hagar Knows Best*, that adapted early storylines from the popular comic, only two programs, which were scheduled against each other in the same time slot, were produced by the studio for Saturday morning. The second season of *A Pup Named Scooby-Doo*, without Ruegger and most of the original production staff from the first season, competed against *Dink: The Little Dinosaur*, another cute animal series. *Dink,* which like *Hagar* aired on CBS, was also co-produced by Ruby-Spears and was a clear imitation of Spielberg's *The Land Before Time* with the eponymous brontosaurus and his friends even resembling the star of the popular film that was released 11 months before the Hanna-Barbera, Ruby-Spears series premiered in the fall of 1989. In each episode, the group learns some type of prosocial message after making a mistake or finding themselves in precarious positions. Most overlooked *Dink*, as kids wanting to watch a cartoon about dinosaurs could just pull a copy of the higher quality *The Land Before Time* rather than the slow moving, educationally focused, and patronizing television series. The need for programming on Saturday morning did allow the juvenile dinosaurs to last two seasons on CBS.[65]

The second, and final, new Hanna-Barbera series to premiere in the fall of 1989 was based on another property from the United Kingdom whose popularity traveled across the Atlantic. *Paddington Bear*, a Peruvian bear who is adopted by a British family, starred in a series of children's books written by Michael Bond before starring in a series of shorts in 1975. The series was syndicated in the United States, appearing first on PBS before becoming early programming for Nickelodeon and the Disney Channel. Hanna-Barbera partnered with British Central Independent Television to create the new series, which debuted on *The Funtastic World* in December 1989. The Browns returned, but added to the cast was an American cousin, David, and a villain, Mr. Curry, voiced by British actor Tim Curry. The new series separated itself from the book and earlier series by featuring many sitcom-inspired storylines with constant mix-ups and confusion fueling the plots. This seemed to work against them as fans of the rain-protected bear stayed loyal to the original storylines and animated series, which still aired through cable and public media.[66]

Hanna-Barbera stayed active in the syndication world and even contributed to the infamous *Cartoon All-Stars to the Rescue* on April 21, 1990, which was promoted as a big cartoon crossover featuring the Smurfs, Garfield, Bugs Bunny, and ALF, among others. It was actually an anti-drug public service announcement overseen by Roy E. Disney and produced by Buzz Potamkin. It was simulcast on all four national networks and several independent and cable networks featuring an introduction from President George H.W. Bush and First Lady Barbara Bush who inherited the "War on Drugs" and "Just Say No" campaign from their predecessors. The special, produced by Southern Star Productions, was completed only days before broadcast and continues to be an example of low quality 1980s anti-drug propaganda directed at kids, similar to Hanna-Barbera's production of *D.A.R.E. Bear Yogi* the previous year.[67]

New Leadership, Big Risks

Kirschner's influence was immediately felt in the summer of 1990, as Hanna-Barbera prepared for a return to its mid–1980s output, and the family of the future finally made its way to the silver screen in an environmentally focused feature film aptly titled *Jetsons: The Movie*. In the film, Spacely has found a new material on an asteroid that can reduce product costs on Earth by 90 percent, but the mining operation experiences issues, including several vice presidents overseeing the project suddenly quitting. George Jetson is hired to supervise the mine when one night he meets the alien Squeep who is a member of the Grungee species that is responsible for sabotaging the mine's construction because it digs directly into his colony's civilization. The Jetsons help the Grungees convince Spacely to stop drilling and turn the mine into a plant to recycle used Sprockets, which the aliens operate for Spacely, stopping destruction of their home. It is never explained what the Grungees gain from working for Spacely other than avoiding the destruction of their home. The movie was beset with problems throughout filming including the deaths of Daws Butler (Elroy) before production started and of both Mel Blanc, who voiced Spacely, and George O'Hanlon (George Jetson) during production, with Jeff Bergmann finishing dialogue for both characters. The pop star Tiffany took over the role of Judy Jetson after Judy's original voice, Janet Waldo, recorded all her lines, prompting voice director Andrea Romano to ask that her name be taken off the credits.[68] Producers, including Barbera, thought Tiffany might help attract a younger audience and he felt that adding a popular singer could also help with sales of the soundtrack. The box office gross was disappointing, while Kirschner and

William Hanna (left) and Joseph Barbera with the family of the future, George and Jane Jetson, kids Elroy and Judy, dog Astro, housekeeper Rosie the Robot and an angry Mr. Spacely, in a promotional photo for *Jetsons: The Movie* (RGR Collection/Alamy Stock Photo).

Hanna-Barbera had hoped the film could create some cash flow while drawing interest in other features starring their many characters.[69]

Kirschner continued to solicit business partners, working with Hallmark as Hanna-Barbera continued to pursue toy-based properties to adapt into shows and capitalize on the continued growth of the children's media and consumer market. *The Yum Yums* were a plush toy series created by Hallmark and Kenner whose stomach and ears are covered in different sweets, like candy and cookies. Like *The Care Bears*, created by American Greetings, the *Yum Yums* were released as a set to entice children to collect the multi-colored stuffed animals who smelled like candy. In *The Yum Yums: The Day Things Went Sour*, which aired on CBS as a possible pilot for a series, the group builds a theme park, which is destroyed by the Sour Pusses before the Yum Yums overcome the troublemakers and build the park again for all to enjoy.

The pilot was not picked up, but Hanna-Barbera continued to work with Hallmark, animating the *Timeless Tales* series with the card company, which took classic fairy tales and added an environmental message to the story. The series of eight cassettes was introduced by Olivia Newton-John and also included a booklet about how the viewers can help the environment. Hanna-Barbera and other children's media producers recognized that individually focused environmental messages that discussed daily actions, rather than trying to address large scale pollution, were an easy way to create educational, prosocial content while avoiding most claims that they are being political, particularly in the promotion of liberal ideas, in their content, which may have turned off segments of the audience.[70]

In another sign of changes, Kirschner and Hanna-Barbera partnered with Universal Studios, who distributed *Jetsons: The Movie,* replacing Paramount and the smaller distributors that disseminated earlier films including *Charlotte's Web* and *Heidi's Song.* Universal had distributed Kirschner's *An American Tail* and was interested in featuring a ride starring the ever-growing cast of Hanna-Barbera characters with feature film-quality animation for their theme park in Orlando. On the ride, Elroy is kidnapped by Dick Dastardly and Muttley as the other characters give chase. Kurtz and Friends, who worked on *Jetsons: The Movie*, started work on the animation but quit due to creative differences. Sullivan Bluth Studio, who worked with both Universal and Kirschner on *An American*

The Funtastic World of Hanna-Barbera opened on June 7, 1990, at Universal Studios Florida and Busch Gardens Williamsburg, closing in 2002 and 2004, respectively (Dave/Wikipedia).

Tail, picked up the remaining production for *The Funtastic World of Hanna-Barbera* ride, which debuted a day after the release of *Jetsons: The Movie*. The motion simulator was the first ride film with primarily computer-animated imagery, taking place in a film auditorium with moving chairs at Universal Studios theme park, in Orlando, which also housed Nickelodeon Studios at the time, and Busch Gardens Williamsburg.[71]

Less than a year into Kirschner's tenure at Hanna-Barbera things were clearly transitioning after several years of relative stagnancy. The situation was far from stable, as Hanna-Barbera started to rack up debt after disappointing box office returns from *Jetsons: The Movie* and the increased production schedule led to the studio entering the red. This debt grew after years of moderate profits because of their strategy of minimizing risk through the development of budget-conscious productions. Kirschner took a few chances that did not work out as planned, which in previous years Hanna-Barbera could make up over time, but Great American Broadcasting was facing an increasingly dire financial situation that was forcing it to consider selling its animation studios, the conglomerate's most valuable properties. Only a year after the takeover, Great American sold Worldvision to Aaron Spelling Broadcasting to try to recoup some of the costs, although the distributor continued to oversee dissemination of the studio's content. Hanna-Barbera maintained its output for the 1990–1991 season even as it faced the deficit. Kirschner and the animation duo hoped they were one hit away from turning around the declining financial situation at the studio. This dedication by Hanna and Barbera would lead to several big changes would extend the duo's career into the next century.

The Whiteness of Unregulated Capitalism

Throughout its first quarter century, Hanna-Barbera slowly evolved with the rest of the industry, although all of animation had a long way to go before they were going to approach anything that resembled equal representation in children's television and cartoons. Throughout the 1970s and 1980s pockets of diversity arose on Saturday morning and independent television, but the wave of deregulation that was accelerated by the neoliberal rise of Reagan and his FCC appointee, Fowler, who reduced or eliminated many rules regarding ownership and content oversight, turned television into a largely unregulated free market medium. Television has struggled for a long time to balance its responsibilities to the public good and the economic desires of stakeholders, quickly turning children's television, which was arguably the most regulated area of the industry, into a money grab. Without regulators, advocates had no entity to help pressure producers to maintain some level of positive messaging. The FCC has never had jurisdiction over representation of race or gender, but now the removal of oversight through deregulation, the rise of channels of dissemination outside the purview of the commission, and the inclusion of more third party producers like toy companies and international studios, with their marketing concerns and lack of familiarity with the demographics of the United States, both whitewashed animation and divided the audience by gender, mirroring the marketing approach used for so long to sell toys.[72] Products representing white characters flooded the shelves and the airwaves, backed by white heteropatriarchial ideology that had built a market where toys featuring white male characters were acceptable for everyone while white boys rarely bought toys featuring women or non-white characters. Rather than challenge the status quo, both toy companies and animators decided to cash in, filling out the parts of the schedule that did not feature human characters with a rainbow menagerie of cute animals. The very rare times they did try to be more inclusive, the attempts were so superficial and uninformed that when they were not examples of appropriation, they displayed cultural, racial, and even gender ignorance. Hanna-Barbera was never at the forefront of representational equality in animation, but the new economic structure of the industry had stalled even the little progress they had made since the 1960s.[73]

The studio's reliance on adapting merchandisable properties, which started with *The Smurfs* and *Pac-Man* in 1981 and 1982, respectively, removed much of the character design and representational control from the studio, placing it in the hands of outside producers, some of which were unfamiliar with American culture and populations. As exemplified by these two shows, this led to an increase in anthropomorphic animals, creatures, and even objects that had no race placed on them by ideological constructions and could easily be sold as toys. Considering Hanna-Barbera productions were originating from a staff of mostly white males there was always a level of tokenism when they did include non-white representations, like in *Captain Caveman and the Teen Angels*. In an animation industry that continued to feature vaudevillian blackface minstrelsy through the 1960s these token representations unfortunately were baby steps toward progress, especially when considering non-white audiences were consistently required to create their own meaning through the mere presence of a non-white character just so they could consume the animation broadcast to them.[74] The race or ethnicity of stars no longer had to be explained since the stars were now yellow circles and Rubik's Cubes, and although there was an occasional attempt at including more racially or ethnically diverse secondary characters, it was clear that the combined lack of diversity behind the scenes and the influence of merchandising was leading to severe regression related to representational equality in commercial animation.[75]

One issue that arose, especially on Saturday morning, was the increase of entertainment-focused shows aimed at viewers under eight. Before syndication and cable divided the market, networks produced shows that may have been appropriate for elementary school viewers but were aimed mostly at adolescents, so the most popular shows were able to attract multiple age groups, an environment reinforced by a lack of choice. With little to no oversight of syndication and cable, shows aimed specifically at older children, mostly boys although a few shows like *She-Ra* attempted to attract young girls, grew to be hits as violence and superficial entertainment became easy ways to draw in toy-hungry children. Meanwhile, the equally merchandise-driven shows on the networks, who were subject to FCC oversight, relied on cutesy animals and colonies of creatures. Although they may have briefly included what was thought of as age appropriate, prosocial messages like sharing and respect for others, their characters could be sold as collectable sets of toys and plush animals. Between the simplicity of the Saturday morning messages and lack of pro-social content in the syndicated cartoons for older children, aside from clumsily added PSAs, there was a huge gap in societally aware, prosocial content for older children that could approach complex issues of racial acceptance and gender equality, both through representations and storylines. As much as producers wanted to believe that the multicolored Biskitts or Snorks represented equality, young children most likely were not making the connection. In syndicated shows like *Galtar*, *Super Friends*, or reboots of *Scooby-Doo* the need to have lead characters that would attract the largest audience of possible consumers reduced diversity efforts by the mid–1980s. The maintenance of characters from the 1960s, 1950s, or even 1940s also supported this wave of whitewashing that completely eroded the very small island of non-white male representations that was built over several decades in the animation industry.

Gendering Animation

Representations of non-male characters took a huge turn as well, as the audience, similar to the different age groups, became separated as a result of marketing considerations, especially as children got older and were increasingly expected to fulfill gender roles. *He-Man* and his twin sister *She-Ra* were the clearest example of this attempt to separate the audience. She-Ra, in her Wonder Woman-esque outfit, may have seemed like a feminine counterpart to the muscular hero, and her presence represented one of the very few female superheroes in animation up until this point, but her reliance on magic rather than skill or brawn like her brother created a clear gendered separation. Exacerbating this issue was her merchandise, which featured a Barbie-esque line of outfits and bright colors compared to *He-Man* whose earth toned armor and allies was more geared to stereotypical expectations for how boys should play. These separations would have appeared in *Giltar* and *Wildfire* as well, if the Hanna-Barbera series resonated at all with audiences and led to more merchandise related to both series. At least *She-Ra* was still an action series, whereas toy companies had historically created completely different toy lines, and expectations, for young girls. For every *G.I. Joe* there was *My Little Pony*, and for every Barbie there were Hot Wheels. This approach had bled into animation. With young boys watching and playing with Transformers or GoBots, girls may have been in a different room or reserved time for *Jem* or hoped for reruns of *Josie and the Pussycats*.[76]

This gender separation was less pronounced in shows for younger viewers, which were increasingly occupying the Saturday morning schedule. Some shows or toys gained a reputation for being more feminine, but the characters in shows like *The Care Bears* or the less successful *Biskitts* were less beholden to gender expectations as they tried to attract all children. The genders of the characters were even less obvious in plush form where they were known by their descriptive name without pronouns or human gender norms displayed in the shows. The characters on *The Care Bears* program did represent both genders, although it has long been assumed that Care Bears were "girl toys" due to their pastel colors and popularity among young females.[77]

The attempts to remove gender were aided by the fact that these shows were located in communities or colonies where humans either do not exist or live on the periphery. Hanna-Barbera's *Snorks* and especially *Smurfs* capitalized on this strategy, in spite of the strange gender dynamic in the comic and cartoon that also influenced the toy line. There were a few times where these shows for younger viewers did try to expand their racial and cultural messaging, but whether it was due to the lack of voices reflecting the experiences of the actual groups being represented or attempts to simplify these cultures for the younger audience, these portrayals were clearly appropriative. The most obvious examples of this were the *Paw Paws*, a community of animals who, for some reason, have adopted stereotypical Native American clothes and customs based on Western ideas about how these are actually supposed to look or be performed.[78] Also, shows like *Scooby-Doo* and *Super Friends* continued to travel to other countries and locations in new episodes and reruns, continuing the promotion of content that supported American exceptionalism celebrated through the inferiority of other countries and the ability to be a white savior for other cultures.[79]

In a famous 1991 *New York Times* article Katha Pollitt coined the term "Smurfette

Principle" to describe the phenomenon in many shows when there is only one female character among a group or community of men. In this scenario, the woman becomes the outlier that exists only to highlight the normalcy of male domination, where her presence reflects what is not masculine and in turn different and lesser.[80] This happens in the majority of shows where women are not the target audience, assuming that women will watch disproportionately male shows, but men will be turned off by shows that even approach some level of equality in the casting, a strategy employed by toy companies for decades. For Smurfette, and many of these lone female characters, their entire identity revolves around her gender; she is not Grumpy, or Brain, or Farmer Smurf, she is just Smurf with a feminine suffix. Smurfette, who also embodies the aesthetic requirements of human beauty, was created artificially in both the comic and cartoon series to disrupt and destroy the utopian male world while also serving as possible evidence of the Smurfs' heterosexuality for parents concerned about what messages an all-male village might be sending their kids.[81] When Papa Smurf "saves" her from her evil ways, her black hair turns blonde, her dress shortens and gains lace, and her eyelashes extend, a look accented by high heels. *The Smurfs* were far from the only ones practicing this strategy. Several iterations of *Scooby-Doo* only featured Daphne, and *The Muppets*, with Jim Henson beginning a partnership with Disney in 1989, also fell into this trap through Miss Piggy, a franchise seen on Saturday morning through the *Muppet Babies*. Most of the Hanna-Barbera shows created after *Scooby-Doo* were male dominated; however, it was not quite as pronounced with *The Snorks*, *Biskitts*, and other ensemble shows featuring multiple female characters. Women still represented the statistical minority in these worlds and were typically seen as secondary characters or love interests.

The influence of capitalism and neoliberalism was in full force by the beginning of the 1990s, with profits and merchandising dominating all other concerns. This was motivated by the removal of most of the safeguards and oversight through the gradual deregulation of the FCC, which in turn reduced the effectiveness of advocacy groups, who could no longer rely on the commission to confront networks and enforce rules that were now no longer in place. Hanna-Barbera was at the forefront of this change in the early 1980s, as *Pac-Man* represented one of the earliest examples of toy-based shows and the overall transition of animation into neoliberalism. The next decade found the studio in a position to help make lasting changes in the animation, children's media, and television industries. The situation may have been unintentional and a product of the increasingly changing media environment, but the result helped Hanna-Barbera remain one of the true pioneers of television and animation as they helped lead the industry into a new era alongside Disney, Warner, and Viacom's Nickelodeon.

10

1990–1993:
Corporate Changes
and New Strategies

You Cannot Out-Disney the Mouse

Changes came quickly for Hanna-Barbera as it prepared to change hands yet another time. The buying frenzy led some companies, like Great American Broadcasting, to over-extend as they tried to obtain as many assets as possible in the deregulated market. The elimination of rules preventing quick resale of television channels along with the increasing number of cable networks had reduced the value of stations acquired only a few years earlier. The media company hired David Kirshner to help Hanna-Barbera expand beyond its modest television success to compete with animation giants like Disney, who had built an entire media empire from an early foundation in animation. The animation duo and studio chairs were also nearing their 80s, riding their success through characters created over thirty years earlier. The studio maintained profitability through the 1980s with successful shows like *The Smurfs*, but as a result of the increased reliance on co-productions and adaptations, they did not own the long-term rights to these properties, preventing the studio from profiting off of these franchises' long term value. In less than a year, the historically profitable studio was facing rising debt, as Kirshner and Hanna-Barbera pursued risks, including feature films and theme park attractions, that did not attract the attention they had hoped for the animators who had been much more budget conscious in the past to avoid these situations.[1]

Even with syndication packages involving *The Flintstones* and *Scooby-Doo* acting as consistent revenue streams, high profile failures forced Great American to seek suitors for Hanna-Barbera and Ruby-Spears as the parties involved soon realized the investment required to compete with Warner and Disney. Both of these legendary studios had much wealthier corporations overseeing the operation of their animation departments and were fully investing in the television animation market after years of avoidance as they relied on reissued film content to maintain a presence on television. Both studios entered the first-run syndication market in 1990, with Disney focusing on a time slot that had previously been home to reruns, soap operas, and news programs: weekday afternoons. Uncertainty reigned throughout the season as these new challenges arose as they released a full collection of programs clearly influenced by deals facilitated by the studio's new head. Viacom's Nickelodeon was also becoming a legitimate competitor and in 1990, Disney Channel was joining Nickelodeon as a basic cable station in many markets after

The Smurfs, seen here flying a Brussels Airline plane, are loved around the world, but especially in their native Belgium (Markus Mainka/ Shutterstock).

launching as a premium network in 1983.[2] In fact, for the first season ever, all of the series created for the season were co-produced with companies outside of the Hanna-Barbera/ Taft/Great American corporate structure.

The 1990–1991 season was devoid of the release of any specials or films as the studio recovered from the financial setback of *Jetsons: The Movie* and awaited its fate while potential corporate buyers kicked the tires on the animation studio.[3] As Hanna-Barbera dealt with economic and political changes affecting their parent company and the industry, the studio still managed to produce six shows for syndication and Saturday morning, although Hanna and Barbera only received executive producer credits on three of them, with Kirschner getting credit for two of the shows and the three producers sharing it for the sixth show.

Kirschner Deepens the Hole

Kirschner was credited as creator for *Wake, Rattle & Roll*, which debuted in syndication co-produced by Four Point and Hanna-Barbera Productions for daily broadcast in the early morning. In an attempt to capitalize on the popularity of educational or "edutainment" television, the program was a mix of educational lessons taught in the live-action segments starring Sam Baxter and his video-playing robot D.E.C.K.S.[4] Throughout the program the duo plays a mixture of Hanna-Barbera cartoons and other clips while a time machine brings visitors from the past, both real and fictional, to teach lessons related to science, history, and geography. The first of two cartoon segments was a spin-off of *Wacky Races* and attempted to revitalize the many all-star series the studio had produced.

Fender Bender 500 featured a number of their most popular stars created in the 1950s and 1960s battling in another never-ending race format. This time competing in monster trucks, teams featuring Yogi and Boo Boo and Huckleberry and Snagglepuss

Sam Baxter (R.J. Williams) and his robot D.E.C.K.S promoting *Wake, Rattle & Roll* in 1990 (United Archives GmbH/Alamy Stock Photo).

battled in vehicles designed around the characters, like the bears' giant picnic basket truck. The show basically recycled storylines from *Wacky Races* and other competition series, but the lone female racer, *Winsome Witch*, truly exemplified the dearth of female characters they had created in their history. It was understandable that they did not want to bring back *Penelope Pitstop*, since her car and "gimmick" was actually racing. This removed the visual humor related to the themed cars along with the fact that Penelope had also already appeared on two race series, so most of the jokes related to her were already made, although that never stopped the studio in the past. They could not use *Josie and the Pussycats* or *Jeannie* because Archie and Columbia, respectively, owned the properties. Daphne and Velma from *Scooby-Doo* were probably their most popular female characters from the 1960s not blatantly associated with a male character or husband, but they were currently appearing in *A Pup Named Scooby-Doo*. Aside from her mostly forgotten series, this was Winnie's only other appearance.[5] The other segment, *Monster Tails*, starred the pets of popular movie horror monsters living in a castle and finding themselves in situations and misadventures related to their horror-inspired lifestyles. For example, in separate episodes Catula must protect his tomato juice from leeches while Dr. Heckell the dog accidentally drinks a potion and becomes an evil version of himself, adapting the classic Stevenson novel.[6]

Wake, Rattle & Roll faced several problems, the first of which being the expectation it would be syndicated in the morning by local affiliates. Both Nickelodeon and Disney Channel launched morning programming blocks to compete with PBS' children's shows, but the morning programming was aimed at preschoolers who were not required to go to school in the morning.[7] Although some school-aged children are "morning people" most were either not watching television on weekday mornings or were fine with watching reruns before eating their sugary cereal and running out the door to catch the bus. Also, not all markets had morning blocks open for syndicated children's television, while networks like Nick, Disney, and PBS could control their national schedules. These national networks could also limit or direct the amount and type of advertising that was broadcast particularly for their morning preschool blocks to avoid scrutiny about advertising to very young children, a luxury a syndicated show or block was not always given. This also increased the need to have strong merchandising for preschool shows to earn a profit, and the retreaded characters in the *Wake, Rattle & Roll* segments did not have the draw of Mickey, Big Bird, or Eureeka on their competitors' networks.[8] The show premiered the same year as another edutainment show, *Captain Planet and the Planeteers*, which debuted on TBS two days before *Wake, Rattle & Roll*. In a true sign of the changing market, *Wake, Rattle & Roll* was sold to Disney Channel and showed exclusively on the network in the afternoons under the name *Jump, Rattle &Roll* as the formerly premium station transitioned to basic cable to directly compete with Nickelodeon.

Kirschner, hoping to use Hanna-Barbera's experience in adapting live-action properties and comedians into cartoons, agreed to co-produce two series to capitalize on franchises already popular with children and teenagers. The first series, *Bill & Ted's Excellent Adventure*, is based on the 1989 film by the same name starring Keanu Reeves, Alex Winter, and George Carlin, all of whom reprised their roles in the animated series. The program was co-produced with Orion Television and Nelson Entertainment who were responsible for the film. The producers removed much of the irreverent humor that made the film popular and took a more "edutainment" approach. The show featured stories from standard American history books that typically celebrated white Western progress, which was not unusual for the studio and was previously seen in several series like the *Super Friends* or the video series *The Greatest Adventure: Stories from the Bible*.

CBS did not pick up the series for a second season, but FOX, which was emerging as the fourth broadcast network, adopted the concept as it was producing its own live-action series based on the franchise, with a sequel to the first film premiering in the summer of 1991. The new series was produced by DiC and replaced the voices from the film with actors who played Bill and Ted in the live-action series. FOX aired only eight episodes of the DiC reboot through its FOX Kids programming block, but the series did outlast its live-action replacement, which was off the air after seven episodes.[9] The FOX Kids block was produced in response to the creation of the Disney Afternoon, which was being developed as a syndicated programming block when Michael Eisner and Disney bought Los Angeles station KHJ, renamed KCAL, and moved the popular *Ducktales* over from the local FOX affiliate KTTV after several FOX affiliates had been airing the show for a year. Barry Diller, the chairman of FOX who had worked with Eisner through Paramount, asked the other affiliates to remove the show, which they eventually did, leading to Diller developing a similar block to compete with Disney's, which aired *DuckTales* when it launched two days after FOX Kids. Margaret Loesch, who had worked at Hanna-Barbera and then helped facilitate deals with the studio as the head of Marvel Productions, was hired as the head of FOX Kids programming.[10]

Rick Moranis starred in two hit movies in 1989 popular with young potential animated audience members, *Ghostbusters II* and *Honey, I Shrunk the Kids*. Utilizing his nerdy, overwhelmed persona seen in those films and others, like *The Little Shop of Horrors*, as motivation for the animated version of his character, Moranis plays a teacher who accidentally takes a job at a school for monsters, the second horror-themed comedy cartoon of the season. A very similar premise was used in the 1988 telefilm *Scooby-Doo and the Ghoul School*. Moranis played Max Schneider, who teaches a disruptive class of movie monster offspring at Gravedale High, in a plotline inspired by *Welcome Back, Kotter*. The main cast of students was clearly inspired by other sitcom tropes: Vinnie Stoker, the Fonz-like son of Dracula, the Richie Cunningham-modeled werewolf Reggie Moonshroud, and Frankentyke, a Bart Simpson/Frankenstein cross. Joining Moranis behind the mic were Shari Belafonte, Harry's daughter, who played the zombie Southern belle, Blanche, and Ricki Lake, who played the obese, often body shamed, Cleofatra in an attempt to capitalize on her role in the film version of *Hairspray*. The series, whose full name, *Rick Moranis in Gravedale High*, did everything it could to capitalize on the actor's popularity at the time, was nonetheless cancelled after a season, as was *The Completely Mental Misadventures of Ed Grimley*, which starred Moranis' Second City counterpart Martin Short. New episodes were preempted in several major markets by reruns of other series on co-producer NBC's Saturday morning schedule.[11]

Disney had built much of its animation empire on the international, particularly European, market, and Hanna-Barbera continued to pursue opportunities internationally, collaborating with production companies outside of the United States to produce shows that aired in both American and foreign markets. The studio partnered with Italian public broadcaster RAI to create *The Adventures of Don Coyote and Sancho Panda* loosely based on the writings of Miguel de Cervantes. The two animal characters, like Don Quixote and Sancho Panza, travel throughout the countryside helping people as Coyote experiences heroic visions like the novel's lead character Don Quixote. Rosinante and Dapple, their trusty horse and burro respectively, who speak but are still ridden by the two star animal characters that are fully anthropomorphic, assist Coyote and Panda. Agency of non-anthropomorphic animals has long been an issue animators like Disney have failed to address, most famously in regards to Pluto and Goofy. The show, which aired the previous season in Europe, ran during *The Funtastic World of Hanna-Barbera* syndicated programming block.[12]

The second series, which was co-produced with the British studio Sleepy Kids Communications, focused on a dog and four humans who patrol the dreams of kids to protect them from nightmares. *Midnight Patrol: Adventures in the Dream Zone* was adapted from stories written by Martin and Vivien Schrager-Powell about their rescue dog Potsworth, which they agreed to let Hanna-Barbera turn into a series splitting revenue 50–50. Along with Potsworth, who is given a know-it-all attitude reminiscent of Mr. Belvedere, are a multicultural group of adolescents, African American boy Carter, the white sister-brother pair Rosie and Nick, and Asian-American girl Kaiko, who agree to join each other to fight off the Nightmare Prince in the Dream Zone after they fall asleep. The program replaced two other British co-productions on *The Funtastic World*, *Paddington Bear* and *SuperTed*, as those involved in *Midnight Patrol* hoped that the moderate success of the merchandising surrounding Potsworth would lead to a toy empire in America. Kids in the United States just did not connect with the characters; however, the show was a success in England under the title of *Potsdam and Co.* due to the BBC's concerns about suggesting that children should stay up after midnight. The show attracted five million viewers in the United Kingdom, becoming the second highest rated children's program in England that year. Ultimately, though, the show, and Potsworth, never truly reached the level of success on television or in merchandise that Hanna-Barbera and the Powells had hoped.[13]

50 Years Later: *Tom and Jerry* Establishes a New Partnership

Unbeknownst to Hanna-Barbera and Kirschner, the last series that debuted in 1990 ended up representing the transition Hanna-Barbera would face toward the end of the season. In 1986, Turner bought the cartoon library from MGM, including the rights to Hanna and Barbera's most popular theatrical creation, *Tom and Jerry.* The studio partnered with Turner Entertainment and put the cat and mouse through the infantilization machine to create a new show with Tom as a kitten and Jerry as a mouseling continuing to fight as they had for over half a century. Along with the segment of *Tom and Jerry Kids* based on the classic shorts, two other segments involved two father-son dog duos, Spike and his son Tyke and Droopy and Dripple. Both segments featured the father teaching his son life lessons, Spike within the neighborhood and Droopy at the occupations he was given each week as he competes with McWolf for the attention of the human Miss Vavoom, named Red in the original Avery shorts. A now-speaking Blast-Off Buzzard joined the series in the fourth season as he leads a wake of vultures as they chase Crazylegs. The series was the first Hanna-Barbera cartoon produced for FOX and became one of the earliest hits for the new network's Saturday morning lineup. More significantly, it further strengthened the relationship between Turner and Hanna-Barbera established through the broadcaster's syndication of the animation studio's content.[14]

Turner's interest in Hanna-Barbera went beyond the occasional co-production or adaptation with the animation studio after the success of the studio's animation blocks throughout the late 1970s and 1980s on Turner Broadcasting System (TBS) and Turner Network Television (TNT). WTBS was originally established as local independent station WRJR in 1967 with Ted Turner purchasing the station in 1970, changing the call letters to WTCG. In the station's early years, Turner worked around a limited budget by broadcasting reruns and live sports, including professional wrestling and Atlanta baseball. The station also rebroadcast dubbed Japanese cartoons, including *Speed Racer*, which cost less than their American-produced counterparts, to attract young viewers before the purchase of *The Flintstones* reruns led to consistent broadcasting of the Hanna-Barbera library through Turner properties.

In 1976, the same year Ted Turner purchased the Atlanta Braves baseball franchise to prevent them from moving and eliminating the station's most consistent programming, Turner uplinked the WTCG feed to the Satcom-1 satellite, making the station available to cable systems in several cities. In many smaller markets that accessed television through coaxial lines, the network, which changed its call letters a last time to WTBS in 1979, was the only independent network offering unaffiliated programming. In 1986, Turner bought MGM from Kirk Kerkorian before selling back the studio a few months later while retaining the library. Turner also retained the studio's large animation library, including *Tom and Jerry*, *Popeye*, and pre–1948 Looney Tunes and Merrie Melodies cartoons. The Pop-eye and early Warner cartoons were acquired by MGM from United Artists in 1981. Combined with Three Stooges shorts, the cartoon films became part of a *Tom & Jerry and Friends* programming block airing in the early mornings and afternoons every day as the network focused more on rebroadcasting theatrical films. TNT was launched in 1988 to air the older content from the extensive MGM library Turner had acquired less than two years earlier. As Great American Broadcasting faced rising debt, Turner again saw an opportunity to reshape the television landscape.[15]

Just Another Season Until…

Hanna and Barbera's role at the studio was clearly shifting entering the season. Low output resulted in only one program executive produced by the duo out of the three released by their namesake studio for the 1991–1992 season. Somewhat symbolically, it is also the last series under this ownership to star Yogi Bear (albeit in a new form) and a number of other characters the duo created for television in the 1950s and 1960s that formed the foundation upon which they built the now 34-year-old animation studio. *Yo Yogi!* continued the studio's use of infantilized characters, starring Yogi, Snagglepuss, Huckleberry, and a number of other characters living in Jellystone Town working as detectives, helping now-Officer Smith solve mysteries and deter criminal activity. The show, created from the *Scooby-Doo* mold, also featured new character Roxie Bear who joined Dick Dastardly and Muttley as Yogi and Cindy bear's rival. In a true sign of the times, the group hangs out at the Jellystone Mall as the studio tried to update its humor and style as an attempt to remain culturally relevant. The premise was further complicated by the presence of other Hanna-Barbera characters like Hokey Wolf and Quick Draw McGraw appearing as adults while their same-era counterparts were teenagers. The low-rated series is most known for its blatant advertising tie-ins with Kellogg's which included 3-D glasses in several of its cereals to allow viewers to watch certain scenes that attempted to utilize the technology. The disappointment and expense of *Yo Yogi!* and other animated series led NBC to significantly decrease the animation it broadcast as *The Today Show* and cheaper live-action fare filled the Saturday morning schedule. This was also the last "legacy" series to be produced by the studio for the broadcast networks, ending an era in which the stable of Hanna-Barbera stars regularly appeared in new and rebooted series on weekend mornings since the late 1950s.[16]

Yo Yogi! was joined on Saturday morning by *The Pirates of Dark Water*, which premiered as a series on ABC in the fall of 1991 after the success of a mini-series titled *Dark Water*, which aired in the FOX Kids programming block on the emerging "fourth" broadcast network. The series was created by David Kirschner to attract older children with more complex writing and animation than was typically associated with Hanna-Barbera. In fact, most of the animation work was done by Fils Cartoons in the Philippines, truly separating the series from the studio's other content that contained simpler animation without the detailed facial expressions and vast worlds created by Fils. The series starred Ren, the prince of Octopon, and his "monkey-bird" Nidler, who must protect his kingdom on the planet Mer against Dark Water, a liquid entity looking to inundate Octopon with water leading to the destruction of the entire planet. Ren must find the 14 treasures of Gor to save his kingdom and planet from its flooded fate. Unlike most other animated series, the episodes in *Dark Water* were connected, creating a narrative throughout the season as each episode started where the previous episode ended. The series, in spite of the realistic animation and talented writing, was a victim of the changing market as Saturday morning had become, almost exclusively, a destination for younger children. *Dark Water* was appreciated by the few older children who still tuned in to Saturday morning programming, but the attention required from the audience went way beyond what could be expected from a viewer under 10, especially considering that many children may not tune into the same show each week. In this pre-streaming age, children would get lost in the narrative if they did not watch the series from the beginning, leading to a quick change back to CBS and familiar reruns of the *Teenage Mutant Ninja Turtles*. Hoping that they could attract this older audience on cable, the show was syndicated in its second season on *The Funtastic World of Hanna-Barbera* but as many producers continue to find out, serial programs have a difficult time finding success in syndication since viewers may not tune in to the same syndicated show at the same time every day. The show may also not air on the same days and times in every market, and may be preempted for other programming, making it hard to market less popular syndicated shows nationally. This is why episodic sitcoms and dramas often command the most money in syndication, since the audience can drop into the series at any time and be entertained with minimal knowledge of the storylines.[17]

In 1989, Hanna-Barbera consultant Mark Young helped Canadian media producer Cinar create *Young Robin Hood*, which aired in Europe before making its way to Canada in 1990. The success of the Kevin Costner film *Robin Hood: Prince of Thieves*, which went on to become the second highest grossing movie of 1991 after premiering in July, led Hanna-Barbera to import the program for its *Funtastic World* programming block, the only show to debut on the block that fall. Fitting with the studio's infantilization trend, the series acts as an origin story for the fictional character who is joined by "Brother" Tuck, Little John, and Maid Marian as he battles a young Prince John who is running Nottingham as Sheriff while Richard the Lionheart is fighting in the first Crusade. In addition to the characters from the original story, Mathilda, Marian's nurse and chaperone; Hagalah, a sorceress and surrogate mother for the young orphaned Robin Hood; Gilbert, Prince John's assistant and Robin's rival for Marian; and Gilbert's jealous sister, Gertrude, joined the cast. Like *Dark Water*, *Young Robin Hood*'s animation and stories seemed to be more realistic and detailed compared to most other animation appearing on television; however, like *Dark Water* this higher quality animation still contained some of the Hanna-Barbera trademarks, specifically funny animals with Robin's falcon Arrow, Gilbert's dog Bruno, and Hagalah's cat Miranda all adding levity to the action series. Both seasons aired on *The Funtastic World* and the series has been cited as an example of shifts in the television animation industry that recognized audiences', particularly older viewers', desire for higher quality animated content. This was part of a larger transition that was on the horizon, and Hanna-Barbera would be one of the most influential actors in this shift throughout the 1990s.[18]

Well If a 24-Hour News Network Can Work, What About Cartoons?

In 1991 Ted Turner and his Turner Broadcasting, after close to a decade working with Hanna-Barbera Productions, purchased the studio with Apollo Investment Fund from the struggling Great American Broadcasting for $320 million. The deal included the studio, the entire Hanna-Barbera library excluding a few co-productions like the *Harlem*

Globetrotters, and the Ruby-Spear library, which added more modern cartoons to Turner's extensive cartoon library. TNT was launched in 1988 to broadcast Turner's MGM acquisitions and in February 1992, Turner announced he would be launching a new network completely dedicated to animation in the fall.[19] The Ohio-born businessman had built his media business throughout the southeast before purchasing the station that would become the first superstation, TBS. In 1980, Turner changed cable again when he launched the Cable News Network against the advice of other broadcasters who said a 24-hour news station could not work. He faced similar criticism after his February 1992 announcement as broadcasters derided his idea for a 24-hour cartoon destination, pointing out that there were two children's networks, Disney Channel and Nickelodeon, playing animation. Both networks switched to exclusively live-action adult programming in the evening, with the latter switching to a completely different channel, Nick at Nite, in prime time since children went to bed.[20] Turner felt, however, that his Cartoon Network could attract an audience overlooked by media producers and broadcasters in regard to animation: older viewers like adolescents, and, particularly, adults. Nielsen revealed in 1992 over one-third of the Disney Channel's audience were childless adults, and with his ownership of over 8,500 hours of animation at the time of launch, Turner felt the low startup costs and familiar characters could draw not only children, but this adult animation audience that was further revealing itself through the popularity of *The Simpsons*. The Springfield–based family began to shift its focus to feature more satire, parody, and mature content that appealed to adults and were trademarks of a significant portion of the cartoons in the Turner library, including *Looney Tunes*, *Tom and Jerry*, and prime time Hanna-Barbera cartoons. The Cartoon Network, which dropped "The" in 1995, launched on October 1, 1992, premiering on over 200 cable systems including in New York, Philadelphia, and Washington, D.C.[21]

Hanna-Barbera was fully absorbed into Turner and Cartoon Network, producing all but one program for the network after the launch. Fred Seibert, the former head of MTV networks, was hired by Turner to oversee Hanna-Barbera and early Cartoon Network programming. Seibert helped both MTV and Nickelodeon become the top networks among children, teenagers, and young adults, creating cross-demographic brands that appealed to both genders and multiple age groups. The Nickelodeon brand was often the entry point for children's media consumption, leading them to MTV and other Viacom properties as they became older. Seibert had pulled the children's network from the brink of bankruptcy, turning it into the top network among child and adolescent viewers while also helping MTV become a cultural phenomenon.[22] His presence helped the Cartoon Network grow in the ratings as the reemergence of animation that had largely been pushed off the networks and the low-budget irreverent interstitial material, which included sock puppets, attracted an audience that was tired of the sterilized presentation of most animation available that was largely directed at children.[23] Just before Seibert was hired at Hanna-Barbera, Nickelodeon launched the first three Nicktoons including *Ren and Stimpy*, which was so popular with adults it also aired on MTV in primetime.[24]

Nicktoons marked the biggest investment in programming in Viacom's history up until that point and welcomed outside animation studios like Klasky-Csupo to the network headed by Gabor Csupo and Arlene Klasky, one of the few female producers of television animation. Klasky-Csupo also animated *The Simpsons*, with the creative team of the hit FOX series often speaking condescendingly about what would become Nickelodeon's biggest success, *Rugrats*. Throughout the 1980s and early 1990s, Nickelodeon largely relied on imported animation while Disney Channel did the same to supplement the relatively limited amount of non-film animation it owned at the time. Nicktoons, in particular, showed the subscriber base and young cable audience had grown large enough to justify producing quality animated programming produced exclusively for individual cable networks. Even though the network only launched in two million homes, compared to the 58.7 million subscribers for Nickelodeon and 7.1 million paid customers for the Disney Channel, which was in the process of transition to basic cable, the Cartoon Network was entering a quickly expanding cable television market that was serving more and more viewers.[25]

Turner Broadcasting System Inc., which also oversaw the operation of TBS and TNT, heavily promoted the Cartoon Network, helping it quickly expand its reach. Early programming blocks were simulcast on the animation station and its sister networks, increasing demand from subscribers of TNT and TBS, both of which were available to nearly 60 million viewers by 1992. Turner also packaged the Cartoon Network with his two more widely known networks, forcing cable systems looking to obtain or renew their subscription to the other two networks to broadcast the Cartoon Network. Lastly, word of mouth quickly spread from the northeast throughout the country about this new animation network that not only played cartoons 24 hours a day, but also played uncensored, or at least less heavily censored, versions of their favorite cartoons that had not aired on television in decades.[26] In just over two years, the Cartoon Network would become one of the top-10 cable networks in the country as the cross-demographic appeal resulted in high demand for the new network.[27]

The Home Video Market Continues to Grow

The impending sale did not deter the studio from continuing to release content on television and video tape. The documentary *The Flintstones: A Page Right Out of History* was released direct-to-video in the spring of 1991, celebrating one of the studio's most successful franchises. The end of 1991 also featured the first Hanna-Barbera content disseminated by Turner, as they took over distribution responsibilities from Worldvision. Turner Home Entertainment distributed both *Timeless Tales* and *Greatest Adventure* for the rest of the two video series' runs. The day before the sale to Turner was announced publicly, Hanna-Barbera's first CGI special, *The Last Halloween,* aired on October 28, 1991, on CBS. Overseen by David Kirschner, the special followed four Martians who come to earth to collect coobi (candy) that is rare on the red planet. They find two children who help them gather candy from the town factory, defeating Mrs. Gizbourne who is draining Crystal Lake, which the factory relies on to produce candy, to conduct her experiments. The special effects, supplied by George Lucas' Industrial Light & Magic, won the Primetime Emmy for Best Visual Effects in 1992.[28]

The next year they produced another Halloween special, *Monster in My Pocket: The Big Scream*, adding an animated special to the toy franchise's canon. The special was largely overlooked as it did not follow the same continuity line as the comic books and toy line and was not carried on the ABC affiliates in every market. It was quickly released on video with special edition toys to attract buyers and recoup some of the costs. The half hour film also did not include several of the more controversial characters from the toy series, including several based on Hindu deities, but it did include the Jamaican "Wolf-Man" and several inaccurate depictions of characters of ancient myth.[29]

The studio also debuted three new series throughout 1992, including two midseason replacement series. Hanna-Barbera had built the foundation of its small empire on prime time animation, and after the success of *The Simpsons*, two members of the big three networks tapped the television animators to try to emulate the success of the family Matt Groening's series, who were clearly inspired by Hanna-Barbera's Stone Age counterparts. The first primetime series to debut did so in January on ABC, the same network that aired *The Flintstones* three decades earlier. *Capitol Critters*, which was co-produced with 20th Century FOX and Steven Bochco, creator of *Hill Street Blues* and *Doogie Howser, M.D.*, starred Max, voiced by Neil Patrick Harris, a country mouse who watches his entire family get exterminated after going out to get some food. As she dies, his mother tells him he has a cousin in Washington, D.C., and Max travels there, meeting a number of other pests living at the White House, including two cats who act as the foil to the rodents and bugs. The series dealt with serious issues like drugs and segregation, but the intended adult audience may have been confused since some of the marketing, including toys given away by Burger King, targeted children. The series struggled in the ratings and was cancelled after six episodes, with the remaining seven episodes airing the following summer. *Capitol Critters* actually lasted longer than the studio's other prime time series, *Fish Police*, adapted from the comic of the same name that premiered on CBS a month after the ABC series. With known actors, comedians, and rising stars like John Ritter, Hector Elizondo, Buddy Hackett, Robert Guillaume, Tim Curry, Ed Asner, and Megan Mullally, both CBS and Hanna-Barbera had high hopes for the series. Unfortunately, the dark film noir style of the comic was exchanged for silly animation and fish puns, as adults were again turned off by the sophomoric humor. The studio and the producers involved in both series displayed continued difficulty in producing more mature animation that appealed to adults while avoiding blatantly inappropriate material for younger audiences, who may be attracted to the animation.[30]

The last series to premiere in 1992 was both the first series targeting children that debuted with Hanna-Barbera operating as a subsidiary of Turner Broadcasting and one of the last Hanna-Barbera series to air on the broadcast networks. After the success of the 1991 film *The Addams Family*, Hanna-Barbera adapted an animated series based on the reimagined versions of the Addamses as seen in the comedy. Hanna-Barbera had originally produced an identically named series in 1973, but that was adapted from the 1960s television series in the Scooby-Doo mold. In the new series based on the film, the family must deal with its neighbors, the Normanmeyers, who want the Addamses to move from idyllic Happydale Heights. Fans of the film and the Addams Family franchise were not enamored by the cartoon as the bright hues and comedy did not reflect the morbid dark humor of the property's other content. Trying to replicate shows like *Tiny Toons Adventures* with constant gags and puns while still holding to the formulaic plot structure seen in most other Hanna-Barbera cartoons, the show was confusing to older audiences and critics. It was popular among children who helped make it the top Saturday morning series for ABC that season.[31]

Two more specials also premiered in the spring of 1993, possibly as a preview of future programming and series that would appear on Turner properties, including Cartoon Network, which was scheduled to debut that fall. *I Yabba Dabba Do*, which aired a week before Valentine's Day on ABC in 1993, moves the franchise forward a few more years past *The Pebbles and Bamm-Bamm Show,* reimagining the young pair as professionals, Pebbles working at an ad agency and Bamm-Bamm as a mechanic, as they continue their relationship. After they agree to marry, it is revealed Fred lost their entire savings betting on the Bedrock Broncos and is fired when he loses his temper at Mr. Slate while asking for a raise. He asks Barney for help, but they are both conned by a real estate business associate and are left without any money for their children's wedding. Pebbles and Bamm-Bamm go to Rock Vegas to marry while Fred is thrown out of the house for lying about gambling to Wilma. Betty and Barney help Fred get to Vegas where Barney wins enough money to pay for the wedding and send the children to live in Hollyrock after escaping several other misadventures.[32]

Another two-hour special (90 minutes without commercials), *Jonny's Golden Quest* attempted to fill in some of the backstory not addressed in the original series, acting as a follow-up to *The New Adventures of Jonny Quest*, with the same voice actors reprising their roles from the 1986 series. In the telefilm, Race's ex-wife Jade and Dr. Rachel Quest, who makes her franchise debut, join the Quests. They find Dr. Zin trying to clone himself as he prepares for his own death, leading to toxic runoff from his hideout and mutated reptilian clones, which he employs as his henchmen. The group, including Hadji, are captured when Dr. Rachel Quest is killed along with Dr. Zin while they were struggling. As this is all happening they meet Jade's daughter Jessie after she comes to the group looking for her scientist "father" Vincent Devlon, a lie that was orchestrated by Dr. Zin, who is shown to be alive after the audiences find out it was actually his clone that was killed alongside Benton's wife. Jessie and Jonny develop feelings for each other, as Jonny also deals with his anger towards his father, whom he blames for his mother's death. It is revealed that Race is actually Jessie's father before Zin is killed and the heroes save the world. It was originally supposed to air as a part of *Hanna-Barbera Superstars 10* to help move the 1980s series forward, but production delays and the sale to Turner pushed the release back to 1993 when it premiered on the USA Network. It was the first telefilm to premiere on cable after over a decade of Hanna-Barbera programming appearing on the USA Cartoon Express Block. Both films were immediately released onto home video and all the series, and films, from both properties were soon seen on the premiering Cartoon Network a few months later.[33]

In less than five years, Hanna-Barbera had been sold twice, creating a half decade of instability and uncertainty that the studio survived but not without enduring some major shifts, including a name change to H-B Productions Inc. They lost a number of their most talented animators to other studios, particularly through the Tom Ruegger-led exodus to Warner, forcing the studio to cut back production for the few years leading up to its sale to Turner. However, many of the longest tenured animators and writers like Hanna, Barbera, and Iwao Takamoto, who had risen to become Vice President of Creative Design after drawing many of the studio's most famous characters and overseeing their successful merchandising lines, were still with the company serving as executives and advisors for the restructured company. They continued to develop and produce films including *Tom and Jerry: The Movie*, released in Europe in October 1992. As a part of the film's development, Barbera met with Michael Jackson to explore working on the film and creating other content featuring the pop star, but corporate restructuring and Jackson's personal issues prevented any projects between the animator and musician from coming to fruition. The sale gave new life to the animators, their studio, and their characters as Cartoon Network offered a growing, and stable, outlet for their properties and creations. The animation duo was in their 80s, and it was clear their influence on their namesake studio was waning as the industry continued to shift around them. This was evidenced by the multiple sales and their shift to becoming not just a television animator, but more specifically a cable television animator, representing a new model for the distribution of cartoons moving forward. The influence on the animation industry of what was now becoming the "Big Four" networks was waning as broadcast television was no longer the primary destination for fans looking to watch cartoons at home, as home video and cable quickly mitigated the monopoly that the broadcast networks held for close to thirty years.[34]

1990s Network, 1940s Sensibilities

It should be noted that, as discussed above, during the period in which Turner was establishing Cartoon Network as one of the most popular cable networks in the country it relied heavily on not just Hanna-Barbera's earlier television output like *The Flintstones* and *Scooby-Doo* but also pre–World War II theatrical shorts. In 1955 and 1956, the syndication rights to black-and-white and pre–1948 Looney Tunes/Merrie Melodies were sold to Sunset Production and Associated Artists Production, respectively, so all of the Warner shorts seen on television through programs like *The Bugs Bunny Show* were originally released after August 1948. The television rights for the early cartoons were eventually bought by MGM and then Turner and were broadcast as a part of the animation network's early programming. Cartoon Network's reliance on these cartoons along with the older MGM series like *Tom and Jerry* reintroduced sixty-year-old jokes and ideologies that the industry, and society, still struggled to eliminate. There were a collection of cartoons that were either completely banned, heavily edited, or even redubbed in the case of Mammy Two Shoes in old *Tom and Jerry* shorts; however, many of the jokes that objectified women, misrepresented or derogatorily portrayed various races, ethnicities, and groups remained.

The adult viewers may have been able to contextualize these cartoons but the children watching typically do not have this ability. The fact that it was a "cartoon" network created a sense of security among parents as they let their children watch the content unsupervised even though a significant portion of this early programming was originally produced for general and adult audiences. This content did ultimately act as place holders as Cartoon Network developed and acquired its own content, but many of the same issues about representation and portrayal of marginalized groups arose again with the broadcasting of these older cartoons, and the influence they had on the new generation of animators in the industry. As the network's evolution from rebroadcaster to producer occurred, Hanna-Barbera helped the industry transition again, overseeing production at Cartoon Network, including a collection of innovative shows that helped separate Cartoon Network from the other children's media producers in the industry. Although their legacies were becoming more influential than their actual presence, Turner's purchase renewed interest in Hanna, Barbera, and their properties while helping the studio, as H-B Productions, maintain a strong presence in the changing television and animation industries.[35]

11

1993–1996:
Cable Connects Kids
of All Ages to Cartoons

The Cartoon Network Spreads

The availability may have been limited, but through word of mouth and Turner's knowledge of the television landscape, leveraging the Cartoon Network with his established TBS and TNT networks, the new network grew quickly. When it was launched, Turner owned well over a year's worth of animated content, keeping operating costs fairly low during the first 18 months of exponential growth. Their main competitors, Disney and Nickelodeon, were both producing relatively expensive original programming as both networks worked to maintain their audience as they both surpassed a decade on-air. Betty Cohen, who was named executive vice president of the developing network before a promotion to president of the Cartoon Network, focused on marketing rather than creating or obtaining programming the first year, hoping that the volume and novelty of the cartoons could carry the network while it expanded its reach and audience through cable systems across the country.[1] Cohen oversaw the creation of the checkerboard logo and a promotional campaign that overloaded the senses of potential consumers with images and sounds. This gave the audience a preview of the cartoon antics they could expect from the animation network, with the 24-hour availability repeated throughout advertisements and other promotional materials.[2] It was over a year until the network introduced any new content beyond interstitial material, the first show being the mostly forgotten *The Moxy Show* debuting in December 1993, starring a computer animated dog and flea introducing the network's library of classic cartoons.[3]

Seibert Takes Over

Fred Seibert was now overseeing H-B Productions, which again changed its name, to Hanna-Barbera Cartoons, Inc., in 1993. The studio's namesakes continued to be active in the company they founded, producing new programs while consulting with Seibert and the new collection of animators whom the former head of MTV and Nickelodeon welcomed to the studio. Unlike David Kirschner and even Hanna and Barbera, Seibert avoided interfering with the creativity of the new, younger talent, letting them experiment, developing innovative cartoons that helped separate the cartoon channel from the other children's networks to which it was compared. Seibert hired a number of animators from California Institute of the Arts (CalArts), which has long been a talent pipeline for Disney, including Craig McCracken, Donovan Cook, Genndy Tartakovsky, and Butch Hartman. He also hired Seth MacFarlane from Rhode Island School of Design and Buzz Potamkin who had helped develop the "I Want My MTV" campaign for Seibert as head of Buzzco Production. Potamkin was the first head of the animation company Southern Star Productions, established in 1984, which was owned by Taft and oversaw Hanna-Barbera's Australian productions before he was hired as production head for the animation studio. Also, after creative differences led to the firing of several of the creators and writers of the popular, and controversial, *Ren & Stimpy Show*, including John Kricfalusi and Mike Reiss, both were hired by Seibert, bringing an edge and irreverence to their content, a characteristic that is still associated with the network. By 1993, the new group was releasing content, but Turner first broadcast these original cartoons on TBS and TNT as part of their children's programming since the more established networks were available in almost 30 times more homes. These blocks indirectly promoted the Cartoon Network, since all of these shows quickly made their way to the new venture while TNT even simulcast Cartoon Network programming in an effort to expose audiences who did not have access to the 24-hour animation network through their cable system. This put pressure on markets across the country to pick up the network before an original show ever premiered. As new audiences tuned into the Cartoon Network they were (re)introduced to Hanna-Barbera's vast library of cartoons. This was the most recent content available on the new network and, along with Hanna and Barbera's *Tom and Jerry* MGM shorts, represented the vast majority of color cartoons on Cartoon Network along with most of the limited early live-action fare as the *Banana Splits* also found their way to the network.[4] Familiarity and fondness for animation produced by the duo also created low-cost opportunities for young producers to deconstruct and satirize cartoon formulas that were developed over the history of the industry and art form. H-B Productions still had to fulfill its obligations for the 1993–1994 season, but as the studio transitioned, it scaled back production for the short term before providing the foundation that built the Cartoon Network into one of the top entertainment channels on cable among several demographics.[5]

The Slow Shift from Broadcast to Cable

One of these obligations to the broadcast networks was a show that marked the return of Droopy to television, starring in his own show for the first time in the character's history. Dripple, Droopy's son, appeared on *Tom and Jerry Kids,* bringing the basset hound back into the animation spotlight. Hanna and Barbera actually took over the *Droopy* series of films from Tex Avery while at MGM, earning an Oscar nomination for *One Droopy Knight* in 1957. A spin-off series, *Droopy, Master Detective*, produced for FOX, was a parody of detective and police procedurals that have appeared on television since the 1950s. Hanna-Barbera and Turner Entertainment produced 23 new *Droopy* shorts for the 13-episode season. Joining Droopy was another Avery creation, *Screwball Squirrel*, who was a clear imitation of the Bugs Bunny's early design and personality for which Avery was responsible, only appearing in five cartoons in the 1940s before being resurrected in a segment for the new *Droopy* series. Turner, which had secured the rights to Droopy in the acquisition of the MGM library, was examining the value of some of its older properties it now owned. Several shorts featuring *Wild Mouse* and *Lightning the Super Squirrel* also appeared on the series, though lacking the creativity and manic energy of the original Tex Avery shorts. Droopy in particular was consistently miscast in post–MGM cartoons as later animators tried to make him a star rather than the joke or punchline he represented in his original shorts. The lack of personality limited available storylines for Droopy, as the visual humor that made the MGM cartoons so popular was replaced by redundant jokes and puns. The same can be said about *Screwball Squirrel*, but writers had slightly more room to alter the squirrel to fit with the verbal humor of these cartoons due to the audience's lack of familiarity with the character. In spite of this, the gags also became redundant as animators and writers tried to both recapture the energy and visual chaos of the original MGM films and replicate the clever dialogue that helped make *Tiny Toon Adventures* and *Animaniacs* hits. Both of these series appeared on the FOX Kids weekday afternoon programming block by 1993 and were huge hits for Warner, who, along with Disney and Nickelodeon, represented the biggest competition for Hanna-Barbera and Turner at the time, even as the Cartoon Network played older Warner cartoons.[6]

Another animal-focused justice series took a very different approach, borrowing from a number of popular characters and tropes of the past and present to create a darker series that reflected the more mature tastes of older animation fans. *SWAT Kats: The Radical Squadron* took place in Megakat City, a metropolis occupied by anthropomorphic cats fighting against a collection of paranormal enemies and extraterrestrial activity in their city. The Enforcers, led by Ulysses Feral, are given the task to protect the city, but their egos often get in the way, forcing mechanics Chance "T-Bone" Furlong and Jake "Razor" Clawson to turn into the Swat Kats after they are kicked out of the Enforcers for disobeying Commander Feral while pursuing the series villain, Dark Kat. Seibert, who admitted the show was inspired by the new *Batman* animated series, hired self-taught Yvon and Christian Tremblay while trying to rebuild the talent working at the studio. Buzz Potamkin was also hired to help oversee development and production of the series. *Swat Kats* also borrowed supernatural elements from *X-Men: The Animated Series*, the idea of a world taken over by a species of animals from *DuckTales* and Disney comics' Duckburg, and the presence of anthropomorphic vigilantes from *Teenage Mutant Ninja Turtles*. Even though several shows from the season like Marvel's *Biker Mice from Mars* contained similar tropes with human-like animals occupying a post-apocalyptic inspired world, the animation, adventure writing, and even the sound, which was in high-quality stereo rather than the lower quality sound and music long associated with early television animation, helped *Swat Kats* become the top syndicated children's show in 1994, airing in *The Funtastic World of Hanna Barbera* and TBS throughout its two seasons on air and later on Cartoon Network in second-run syndication. *Swat Kats* most likely would have continued beyond the second season, but merchandising delays led to budget issues for the expensive program, and Ted Turner's objection to the levels of violence led to the show's cancellation with six episodes from the original run remaining unproduced.[7]

Prosocial with a Punch

During a congressional hearing in 1995, Turner mentioned the cancellation of *Swat Kats* as an example of his company being proactive in providing positive programming for children while celebrating another program that became one of the most enduring of the early 1990s while acting as a serial Public Service Announcement co-produced with Proctor and Gamble. *Captain Planet and the Planeteers* originally ran from 1990 to 1992, created by Barbara Pyle, Robert Larkin III, and Turner himself, hoping to increase the educational content on TBS and other networks.

The first three seasons were fairly heavy handed in their environmental messaging, taking on villains like Duke Nukem and Hoggish Greedley as these caricatures tried to destroy the planet for their own profit. Many of these villains were voiced by celebrities who worked for a discounted rate to contribute to the "edutainment" series motivated by strategies employed by *Sesame Street* to keep the co-watching adult in the room via the presence of familiar culture or celebrities. Whoopi Goldberg, who played the original Gaia, the spirit of Earth; Sting; and Martin Sheen all lent their voices to the series that featured the diverse group of five Planeteers, who represented different physical or conceptual characteristics of nature or "Mother Earth," using their super-powered rings to call Captain Planet when the situation became especially dangerous. Wheeler, the Anglo-American, represented Fire; Ma-Ti, a Native American, was Heart; Gi from an unnamed Asian nation represented Water; Linka from Eastern Europe had the power of Wind; and the African Kwame was Earth or soil. Sushi the monkey was the comic relief of the show, providing occasional assistance to the group. As with *Sesame Street*, Turner hired a team of educational and scientific experts to provide guidance, but that could not overshadow the mediocre animation and repetitive dialogue that continues to haunt a generation of children. Interestingly, the environmental focus distracted advocates from noticing the frequent violence and destruction featured on the show, particularly the punishment doled out by Captain Planet. When Turner completed the purchase of Hanna-Barbera, production of the fourth season was transferred from DiC with the updated title, *The New Adventures of Captain Planet*.

The series became more practical in its lessons, teaching children about their environmental impact and ways around the home to help reduce pollution, rather than advocating large movements like the boycott of meat. The new version also focused on teaching misguided people rather than fighting villains. This reflected the neoliberal push, moving from large scale corporate environmentalism to placing the responsibilities on individuals to "save the planet.[8] The Hanna-Barbera production was only slightly better in quality, but the frequent broadcast of the program, up to three times a day in some markets, combined with the message and parental approval helped *Captain Planet* become one of the enduring cartoons of this transitional period for the industry. Along with the 1992 Don Bluth film *FernGully: The Last Rainforest*, it marked another period of environmental awareness in animation after a collection of specials and series in the 1970s, including several from Hanna-Barbera, particularly *Yogi's Ark Lark* and the series it inspired, *Yogi's Gang*.[9]

In fact, Hanna-Barbera released its own nature/forest-based film, *Once Upon a Forest*, in the summer of 1993, which they co-produced with the Welsh HTV. The film starred four "Furlings," Abigail the woodmouse, Edgar the Mole, Russell the hedgehog, and Michelle the badger, who go on a field trip with their badger teacher Cornelius, encountering a road for the first time where the group is almost run over and hit by a bottle a driver throws out the window. Upon returning from the trip they see their forest home of Dapplewood engulfed in a poisonous gas from an overturned tanker. Trying to save her family, Michelle runs in before succumbing to the gas herself. When Abigail pulls her out and she revives, they realize all their family and friends have seemingly been killed in the accident. They are told they need to find herbs to save Michelle and the group sets out to find the necessary medicine before returning to Dapplewood. As they get back they see humans approaching. While running, Edgar is caught in a trap before he is released and a group trying to clean up the accident destroys the trap, helping the animals realize some good humans exist. When Michelle is cured, much of the village returns, although it is confirmed her parents were killed, and Cornelius agrees to take care of the young badger. The heavy-handed environmental film was a huge disappointment, losing $6.4 million on a $13 million budget compared to *FernGully* which earned a profit of $8 million on a $24 million budget a year before.[10]

2 Stupid Dogs, *One New Direction*

The last show premiering in 1993 exemplified the new direction of the studio and the future of Cartoon Network, representing the innovative vision a new generation of animators had for Hanna-Barbera Cartoons. The establishment of cable networks dedicated to airing, and eventually creating, animated content presented tremendous opportunities for young animators looking to get into the business. Donovan Cook, who was part of the hiring push supported by Turner and Seibert, got his start with the Disney Channel assisting with various animated projects including the short *The Prince and the Pauper*. After its release, Cook began pitching a show starring two chronically unintelligent dogs, a smaller canine with a Napoleon complex and a large, slow moving sheepdog, to several companies including Steven Spielberg's Amblin Entertainment, which produced *Tiny Toon Adventure*s but balked at the idea after production issues with its own prime-time sitcom *The Family Dog*. Hanna-Barbera stepped in and not only greenlit *2 Stupid Dogs* but gave the 25-year-old Cook creative control over development of his creation. The 22-year-old Craig McCracken and 23-year-old Genndy Tartakovsky were hired as art directors for the series, and Buzz Potamkin was executive producer, with neither Hanna nor Barbera being listed in the credits. Also providing support was animation director Vincent Waller and John Kricfalusi, both of whom previously worked on *Ren & Stimpy* before they left the show after 18 episodes over creative differences with Nickelodeon. Early in his career Kricfalusi had actually worked on *Super Friends*, calling his work for Hanna-Barbera and Filmation the worst animation of all time before working on the reboot of *The Jetsons* in 1987, inserting more outlandish animation and humor than its 1960s predecessor.[11]

Many of the creative differences between Nickelodeon and Kricfalusi were partially based on the gross, graphic humor featured throughout the episodes of *Ren & Stimpy*, some of which found its way into *2 Stupid Dogs*. The two series also shared the presence of two animals whose unintelligent, if not moronic, behavior and loud yelling and fighting is the fodder for much of the humor. The young animators were willing to take chances, like long, drawn-out jokes that could alienate the young audience but drew in older viewers, many of whom would become a significant portion of Cartoon Network's audience. For example, in the first episode, the smaller dog, who like his larger friend is not named in the series—each is credited as Little Dog and Big Dog—spends five minutes of a seven-minute segment trying to understand how an automatic door at a supermarket functions. Cook, who was a huge fan of Hanna-Barbera cartoons growing up, recreated the flat two-dimensional style made famous by the studio's early cartoons with more contemporary, mature humor, an approach that would be imitated numerous times during the budget-conscious early years under Turner and Cartoon Network.

The program featured a second segment of shorts sandwiched between the *2 Stupid Dog* segments, which, upon Seibert's request, was a reboot of an older Hanna-Barbera series. Cook was allowed to pick any of the less popular early characters and decided to resurrect Secret Squirrel into *Super Secret Secret Squirrel*, a contemporary version of the spy parody cartoon. Although it was seen as a clone of *Ren & Stimpy*, it was well received and introduced animation fans to the style and humor of a new generation of animators who were clearly inspired by and consulted with Hanna and Barbera, earning a nomination for a Daytime Emmy, but losing to Nickelodeon's *Rugrats*. The second season faced several issues beyond the control of Cook and the other animators: several of the voice actors from *Secret Squirrel*, Jess Harnell, who played Secret Squirrel, Tress MacNeill and Rob Paulson, who voiced several recurring characters, left to concentrate on *Animaniacs* full time. *Animaniacs* was in production at the same time as *2 Stupid Dogs* and became another huge hit for Spielberg and Warner. When *Super Secret Secret Squirrel* production stopped, many audience members assumed the entire series was cancelled since, during the second season, only one of the three segments contained new episodes. All of the animators went on to create other shows for Hanna-Barbera and Cartoon Network with the Emmy-nominated *2 Stupid Dogs* acting as the signal that the studio, which was nearing its 40th anniversary, was ready to compete with the new generation of animators at Nickelodeon, Disney, and Warner.[12]

Meet the (Live-Action) Flintstones

The 1993–1994 season also featured the release of six different specials and telefilms along with the studio's first live-action feature film since *C.H.O.M.P.S.* in 1979, an area of production that Barbera long wanted to explore. The first telefilm they released that year was a special based on a holiday with which the studio was very familiar, Halloween. *The Halloween Tree*, based on the Ray Bradbury novel of the same name, premiered on TBS in October, the third special to premiere on cable and the first on a Turner network. The telefilm, which was also broadcast on the Cartoon Network and released on home video, followed four friends, Jenny, Ralph, Wally, and Tom, as they chased Carapace Clavicle Moundshroud trying to retrieve the spirit of their friend, Pip. They follow Moundshroud throughout history as they learn about the historical origins of the holiday and their costumes. Ralph is dressed as a mummy, so they travel to ancient Egypt before going to Stonehenge and learning about the Dark Age Celtic stories involving witches, which Jenny is imitating. Wally, who is dressed as a monster, is responsible for the trip to the Notre Dame Cathedral while Tom's skeleton costume is explained through the Mexican holiday of Dia de los Muertos. They eventually catch Moundshroud but he says it is too late to save their friend's spirit. They agree to trade a year of their lives to save their friend, which Moundshroud agrees to before disappearing. The special, which was nominated for two Daytime Emmys, winning one for Outstanding Writing in an Animated Program, was narrated by Bradbury and featured the voice of Leonard Nimoy as the villain. Interestingly, the group of teenagers seemingly failed to include any non-white friends. This was odd since at the time most programs, exemplified by shows like *Captain Planet*, tried to at least seem more diverse, although it would frequently result in a certain level of tokenism.[13] The special continues to be played on Cartoon Network and its sister properties around Halloween.

David Kirschner, along with Buzz Potamkin, produced *The Halloween Tree* and the second holiday special of the season, *The Town Santa Forgot*. Based on the poem "Jeremy Creek" by Charmaine Severson, the special premiered on NBC in early December. In the telefilm, a spoiled boy name Jeremy Creek sends his list to Santa Claus, who thinks the long list of toys is actually for several children. Santa realizes that he has overlooked a town also named Jeremy Creek in the past, so he accidentally delivers the toys to the economically depressed town. Jeremy learns the new meaning of Christmas and begins to accompany Santa each Christmas Eve to deliver gifts before outgrowing the job as a teenager, opening the seat to another child like himself who learns the importance of selflessness. The story is told to a group of children by an older man, and it is insinuated that the man is Jeremy. The special, like *The Halloween Tree*, continues to be played by several networks around the holidays.[14]

Another Christmas special premiered a little over two weeks later on ABC, produced by Hanna and Barbera and starring their famous Stone Age family in a half hour misadventure moving the series several years into the future after Pebbles and Bamm-Bamm's wedding. In *A Flintstones Family Christmas*, while preparing for their children and grandchildren's visit, Fred and Barney are robbed by a young boy dressed as Santa who is identified by Police as Stony, a young orphan who had been in and out of foster care due to his penchant for theft. Feeling empathy for the young boy's situation, Wilma offers to adopt the child in spite of Fred's apprehension. While waiting for the younger members of the family, who are delayed by a blizzard, Wilma, Betty, Fred, and Barney go Christmas tree shopping. When the couples discover they can only afford a small tree, Stony tries to help by gambling, but after a man is angered by losing to the boy, he chases Stony, who hides behind Fred. When Stony truthfully defends himself against the man's accusations of cheating, Fred supports the boy which results in the man hitting Fred with a tree. At the hospital, Fred finds out from his boss that he can no longer participate in the Christmas parade after the incident. Stony then kidnaps the boss to try to allow Fred to again be a part of the festivities. Discovering the plan, Fred lets his boss out of the bathroom Stony has locked him in and is taken to jail with the young boy where they bond while waiting for their release. The special earned a prime-time Emmy nomination for Outstanding Animated Program, an accomplishment the original series never achieved.[15]

Earlier that month, two days after the premiere of *The Town Santa Forgot*, the sequel to *I Yabba-Dabba Do* also aired on ABC, *Hollyrock-a Bye Baby*. Following up with Pebbles and Bamm-Bamm after their move to Hollyrock, the Flintstones visit their children where it is revealed that they are having a baby and Bamm-Bamm is working toward becoming a screenwriter. As the two sets of parents worry about the future of their children and grandchildren, Fred and Barney experience a series of misadventures as they attempt to sell Bamm-Bamm's script, including getting mixed-up in a robbery, accidentally thinking a stolen pearl is a bowling ball, leading to two criminals, Rocky and Slick, chasing the two future grandfathers. Eventually they all make it to the hospital where the criminals are arrested and Pebbles has twins, a boy and a girl, the former receiving the name Chip due to having a loud mouth like his grandfather, a chip off the old block, and the daughter receiving the name Roxy due to the strength she inherits from her dad. The special still airs as a part of special Mother's Day programming. The two *Flintstones* specials in December of 1993 were the last to feature the families living in this future timeline, as Turner and Hanna-Barbera returned the franchise to its original timeline, starting with a film the next year.[16]

That next spring the studio continued the trend of holiday specials, producing an Easter special starring the infamous basket stealer and his sidekick Boo Boo. *Yogi the Easter Bear* found Yogi in another precarious situation with Ranger Smith again threatening to expel Yogi from Jellystone, this time to the Siberian Circus, after Yogi dresses as the Easter Bunny and tricks the blind watchperson Mortimer into letting him access the park's supply of candy for the celebrations. Boo Boo agrees to find the Easter Bunny to save the celebration and Yogi's place in Jellystone, which Smith accepts even with his bad childhood memories of Easter when he did not receive the chocolate egg he wanted. Yogi and Boo Boo seek the guidance of the Grand Grizzly who gives the pair directions to find the bunny, but when they arrive at his home on a mountain summit, they find out he was kidnapped by a businessman named Paulie who wants to replace all candy eggs with plastic ones he produces. After they all find out that the eggs are actually laid by a magical chicken named Millicent, they all rush to her henhouse to retrieve the mystic animal. Meanwhile Ranger Smith is struggling to stall the children at the Easter jamboree before Yogi and his friends all crash the celebration, leading to Smith's promotion by the visiting Supreme Commissioner, saving Yogi's home in Jellystone. Smith also receives the raspberry-chocolate egg he always wanted as a child.[17] The film was the last time Don Messick performed as Ranger Smith and Boo Boo before passing away in 1997. A month later, a documentary *The Flintstones: The Best of Bedrock* premiered on FOX chronicling the franchise's long history in preparation for the biggest production to star the Stone Age family.[18]

The Flintstones live-action film was released on May 27, 1994, for Memorial Day weekend and the start of the summer movie season. It was produced by Hanna-Barbera and Spielberg's Amblin Entertainment with distribution by Universal Pictures. The film returned to the period immediately before the Rubbles adopt Bamm-Bamm, who again is portrayed as a problem child. It is revealed that Fred, portrayed by John Goodman, loans the Rubbles money much to the chagrin of Wilma's (Elizabeth Perkins) mother Pearl, played by Elizabeth Taylor in her last film role. During the adoption it is also revealed that Cliff Vandercave, the executive vice president of Slate and Company, played by *Twin Peaks* star Kyle MacLachlan, and his assistant Sharon Stone, played by Halle Berry, are planning to steal money from the company. The employees take an aptitude test to decide a new vice president as Vandercave attempts to find a scapegoat for his scheme, with Barney (Rick Moranis) switching his test with Fred's to help his friend who he knows will fail. Barney achieves the highest score, but Fred receives the promotion after the switch and is forced to fire Barney due to Fred's score, which is the lowest in the company. Fred becomes spoiled by the success, even dismissing all the other employees, leading to Wilma and Pebbles leaving to live with Pearl. Fred learns of the plan when he returns to the quarry to make up for his mistake, but the workers try to hang Fred and Barney, who have reconciled, before the pair escape. The former employees are told that Vandercave is responsible after Wilma and Betty (Rosie O'Donnell) find the Dictabird from his office, who reveals the whole plan. Vandercave kidnaps Pebbles and Bamm-Bamm and ties them to a machine before Fred destroys it and Barney saves the toddlers. The destruction of the machine inadvertently leads to the creation of concrete, for which Fred receives credit but refuses a promotion, instead asking Mr. Slate to rehire the workers as the Stone Age ends and both Barney and Fred return to their families.

In spite of the film's largely negative reviews, and Barbera's disappointment over the story, it still managed to make $342 million worldwide on a $46 million budget, making it the fifth highest grossing film domestically and sixth internationally in 1994.[19] Much of the criticism was based on the mature content in what many assumed would be a film purely for children and families. The adult content did help the franchise return to its general audience roots, and like the specials, renewed interest in the property, which was now airing regularly on the Cartoon Network.[20]

Poster for the live-action *The Flintstones* film, released May 23, 1994, starring John Goodman and Elizabeth Perkins as Fred and Wilma Flintstone, Rick Moranis and Rosie O'Donnell as Barney and Betty Rubble, Elaine and Melanie Silver as Pebbles and Hilynur and Marinó Sigurðsson as Bamm-Bamm (AF Archive/Alamy Stock Photo).

The Night Owls Get Their Own Cartoon

The spring of 1994 also marked a big milestone for the Cartoon Network with the premiere of the first show fully produced by the studio specifically for the network. *The Moxy Show* was produced by Colossal Pictures, while *2 Stupid Dogs* debuted on TBS before re-airing on the Cartoon Network. Turner wanted late night programming, aside from older theatrical cartoons, that appealed to adults through contemporary humor to compete with the nighttime programming on Disney Channel and Nickelodeon/Nick at Nite. Although Hanna, Barbera, or their studio were not technically involved beyond their association with the network, the series' creator, Mike Lazzo, decided to deconstruct and repurpose animation from a past Hanna-Barbera series to work around the low budget and lack of resources at his newly formed studio, Ghost Planet Industries. *Space Ghost Coast to Coast* was a parody of late-night talk shows with Space Ghost as the host and former villains Brak, a giant mantis, acting as a bandleader and the lava-man Moltar working as producer as a punishment for their crimes after being captured by the superhero/host.

In each episode, Space Ghost "interviewed" celebrities who appeared via video in live-action form. The interviews were often awkward due to misunderstandings between the host and celebrity, who was actually interviewed at a different time with the questions often changed later. The irreverent series became popular with adult audiences who appreciated the unique use of animation that moved away from the sitcom parodies, while also using the interview format to make celebrities and public figures look foolish, which would become one of the main sources of humor for later shows like *The Daily Show*. Similar to the way *2 Stupid Dogs* represented the future of animation for Hanna-Barbera/Cartoon Network, *Space Ghost Coast to Coast* did the same for the irreverent, ironic, and mature adult programming that would become a staple of the network in the future. The series also contributed to increasing demand for the network, which ended the year among the top five cable networks in spite of the fact that its first successful original show had just premiered in April 1994.[21]

Droopy, Master Detective was the only series that year not to make it past the 1993–1994 season. The renewal of their other series benefited Hanna-Barbera and Turner since the 1994–1995 was their first without any new series from the studio since it was established by the animation duo in 1957. The studio was adjusting to revitalization supported by Turner along with the success of the Cartoon Network and *The Flintstones* feature film. They did release several specials featuring many of their stars past and present, including *Jonny Quest versus The Cyber Insects*, along with an adaptation of an unpublished Dr. Seuss children's book.

The first special, *Scooby-Doo! In Arabian Nights*, premiered on TBS in September 1994 starring Scooby and Shaggy who travel to "Arabia" to become food tasters for the Caliph but are pursued after eating all the food. The pair dress as women but the Caliph falls in love with them, so they tell him two stories to make him fall asleep so they can escape. The first, "Aliyah-Din and the Magic Lamp," is based on *Aladdin* but switches the gender roles so the Prince is the one required to find a mate and Aliyah-Din is a female street urchin. The film follows the general story where the protagonist finds a lamp and a genie provides her three wishes to get the royal heir to fall in love with her by wishing to become royalty, as seen in the Disney film released two years earlier. The genie is played by Yogi with his apprentice portrayed as Boo Boo. After defeating the Sultan's vizier Haman, who is using Aliyah-Din and his collections of potions, to try to subsume the throne, they eventually find out Aliyah-Din actually does descend from royalty and she marries the prince, receiving a big wedding as her third gift. The second story stars Magilla Gorilla as Sinbad the Sailor who mistakes a cruise ship for his pirate ship, leading to a series of misunderstandings and misadventures for everyone on board. The film is the last time Don Messick (Yogi and Boo Boo) and Allan Melvin (Magilla Gorilla) would voice their legendary characters.[22]

The last special of the year, *A Flintstones Christmas Carol*, was released around

Thanksgiving 1994 for syndication and home video. The film features the entire town of Bedrock in a production of *A Christmas Carol* where Fred learns humility after letting the starring role go to his head, making amends with his family, particularly Wilma, for being selfish and acting like a Scrooge.[23]

The first special of 1995 was actually a clip show featuring scenes from the first two seasons of *SWAT Kats* airing on TBS during the first week of January. The special premiered two weeks after the last episode of the second season ultimately marking the end of the series. The next month *Daisy-Head Mayzie* aired on TNT, adapted from the unpublished book written by Dr. Seuss, who passed away in 1991. The animated special is narrated by the Cat in the Hat starring Mayzie, a young girl who sprouts a daisy from her head much to the surprise of her family, friends, and town. An agent helps Mayzie become rich and famous before the Cat in the Hat convinces Mayzie to return home after she learns of the agent's greed and that love and family is more important than wealth and fame. As a tie-in, the book was released a month before the cartoon, the first book published after his death. *Daisy-Head Mayzie* followed the author's first number one best-selling book *Oh, the Places You'll Go*.[24]

Finding Their Niche

As the 1995–1996 season began Hanna-Barbera and Cartoon Network were just figuring out their new direction. The success of the all-animation network, the renewed interest in Hanna-Barbera properties, and the popularity of *The Flintstones* movie helped Turner determine that properties owned and inspired by Hanna-Barbera had value beyond reruns. The emergence of *Space Ghost Coast to Coast* opened the network to animation audiences who may have been too old for the fare on Nickelodeon and Disney Channel but found the new animation on other cable networks like Comedy Central, which was now airing adult animation like *Dr. Katz: Professional Therapist* and premiered *South Park* two years later, too mature.[25] Many fans were seeing their favorite characters portrayed in new ways, with the young up-and-coming animators bringing an ironic, contemporary perspective to stars like *Space Ghost*. The self-awareness and lack of pretension in the network's programming and marketing aided in the creation of the irreverent personality for the network, particularly in the content aimed at teenagers and adults, rebelling against the industry conventions represented by Disney and even Nickelodeon. As Cartoon Network was establishing itself through the legacy of Hanna and Barbera, the studio and network were not spared in the quickly consolidating American media environment, with several more deals causing a seismic shift in the animation industry, particularly on television.[26]

Mergers and outright purchases of numerous smaller studios and media companies exemplified the deregulation that occurred in the 1980s and rippled into the 1990s. In 1986 alone, Turner purchased MGM, General Electric acquired RCA and NBC, and National Amusements purchased Viacom, which had acquired MTV Networks, including Nickelodeon, from Warner-Amex the previous year.[27] In the spring of 1995, South Dakota Senator Larry Pressler introduced Bill § 652, better known as the Telecommunications Act of 1996. News of the bill, which was passed by the Senate in June and then the House in October, created a buying frenzy among media companies looking to take advantage. The bill expanded ownership deregulation, as larger conglomerates bought up smaller media entities they felt had value or were vulnerable financially. Many of these smaller entities did the same thing on a smaller scale in the 1980s and early 1990s, but many were overextended, creating opportunity for companies like Disney and Time Warner, which was created when Time and Warner Bros. merged into one company in 1990.[28]

During this period just before the bill's official passage in 1996, a number of companies were purchased or merged. These deals affected the television industry most significantly, motivated by deregulation along with the emergence of FOX and cable as legitimate competitors to the "Big Three" networks. In 1993, the Financial Interest and Syndication Rules, which were put in place in 1970 to prevent broadcast networks from monopolizing the television content by banning the broadcast of televised content by the same media company that produced it, were completely eliminated after over a decade of relaxation.[29] This allowed parent companies to air their own content on the networks, something cable networks had been able to do from the rules' inception, since they were not under the supervision of the FCC. Also contributing to the television realignment was FOX obtaining the media rights to broadcast National Football Conference games, which pushed the still-growing network to pursue more affiliates to reach most major markets, as a number of stations shifted affiliation to ensure they could broadcast lucrative National Football League games. Along with FOX, who purchased a number of stations from New World Communication in larger markets like San Diego and Boston, Westinghouse also helped accelerate the acquisition frenzy by acquiring CBS in 1995. By 1996, 70 stations in over 30 markets switched affiliations, as both NBC and ABC also adjusted to their own acquisitions.[30]

Consolidation and Cartoons

As mentioned above, General Electric bought NBC through RCA in 1986 a year after Capital Cities acquired ABC, a company more than four times its worth. Warren Buffett's Berkshire Hathaway also acquired 25 percent of ABC as the financier of the deal. At the time, the $3.5 billion purchase of the network by the media company, which at the time only owned several mid-size market stations, was the largest non-oil merger in history. The purchase made Capital Cities/ABC the largest owner of stations even after they were forced to sell some in several markets due to ownership and geographical restrictions related to licensing by the FCC.[31]

In spite of the sell-off, Capital Cities/ABC continued to expand its holdings in the more loosely regulated media environment, starting a TV production company with the talent agency Brillstein-Grey Entertainment and purchasing a majority stake in the animation studio DiC Entertainment in 1993. In the summer of 1995, it was announced Disney was planning to purchase Capital Cities/ABC, which also included ESPN and several other cable networks, expanding the media conglomerate's holdings particularly on television. Disney started as a small animation studio over 70 years earlier and was now finalizing a $19 billion deal.[32] This, combined with the deal between Westinghouse and CBS, led President Bill Clinton to threaten to veto the bill over the rapid consolidation of the media industry over only a few months. Disney's deal in particular exemplified the future of the media industry as it gained control over what were considered the four most powerful forms of mass communication at the time, film, cable, broadcast, and telecommunications, integrating its company vertically as deregulation created opportunities from conglomeration.[33] Although the Act did push broadcasters to submit ratings so parents could use a V-Chip, which was required through the Act to be built into televisions to block content, the conglomeration affected the industry much more heavily than a small safeguard could ever overcome.[34]

Animation producers and broadcasters like DiC and Nickelodeon changed hands multiple times during this decade of mergers and acquisitions from the mid–1980s to mid–1990s, and Hanna-Barbera was no different. The studio was revitalized by the Turner purchase in 1990 after Taft and Great American Broadcasting's financial struggles. Before the acquisition, constant questions about the viability of its parent company created volatile uncertainty at the studio, leading to a talent drain from Hanna-Barbera with many of the animators going to Warner. This helped the legendary animator grow into a force in television several years later with shows like *Tiny Toon Adventures* and *Animaniacs* nearly a decade after the studio was reopened in 1980 following an 11-year closure.[35] Coincidentally, the struggles and closing of Warner Bros. in the 1960s had helped Hanna-Barbera grow when a number of its own animators, including Chuck Jones, joined the television animation studio after they lost their own jobs. These two studios that frequently crossed paths in the insular animation industry became sister companies when Time Warner agreed to merge with Turner in a $7.5 billion deal on October 10, 1996. The deal put Warner Bros. studios and Hanna-Barbera under the same corporate umbrella while further expanding the cartoons and franchises upon which Cartoon Network could capitalize. The popular post–1948 Warner cartoons were immediately added to the animation network's library and content properties overseen by Time Warner, including DC Comics and Looney Tunes. The content featuring these franchises not only could now be aired on the network but also offered a new stable of characters and franchises for future productions.[36]

Although the merger eventually brought further consolidation within Time Warner, Hanna-Barbera Cartoons continued to operate as usual in 1995. The FCC was officially reviewing the merger and the details were finalized over the next year. The studio premiered its first new show produced directly for Cartoon Network along with the last Hanna-Barbera show that would premiere on Saturday morning.[37] The influence of Saturday morning was clearly waning as cable and home video fragmented the animation audience, and producers looked toward these other avenues that offered more frequent exposure to content. This last show in the legendary time slot was a co-production with New Line Cinema adapting the popular comedy film *Dumb and Dumber* into an animated show for ABC right before the network was officially acquired by Disney. None of the stars, including Jeff Daniels and Jim Carrey, reprised their roles, but the film's co-writer Bennett Yellin did help develop the series. Bill Fagerbakke, who played Dauber Dybinski on *Coach*, lent his voice as Harry Dunne (the Jeff Daniels role in the film), and Matt Frewer, who voiced the computer-generated TV host Max Headroom, picked up Carrey's movie role of Lloyd Christmas. In many ways, the series was a throwback to older Hanna-Barbera series with misadventures, flat, stylized animation, and even a talking animal, a beaver named Kitty. For fans of the film, the show was a disappointment as the series did not follow the plot points or inherit the more mature, irreverent humor of the original film. The program also premiered around the same time as the animated version of another Jim Carrey vehicle, *Ace Ventura, Pet Detective*, which aired on CBS. This, along with ABC's new ownership and middling ratings, pushed *Dumb and Dumber: The Animated Series* into cancellation. The series was syndicated on Cartoon Network after it ended its run on ABC, while the studio turned its full attention to producing content for the animation network.[38]

What a Cartoon! What an Encore

As 1995 approached, Fred Seibert had visions for the network and the studio beyond the *Dumb and Dumber* adaptation that would premiere in the fall. Even with thousands of hours of cartoons, some cable providers were still wary about picking up the new network due to the lack of new and original programming. Some cable companies felt there was more value in carrying Nickelodeon and Disney Channel while newer, more popular cartoons could also be found during children's programming blocks on other broadcast and cable networks. Fred Seibert recognized this and was interested in producing the network's first completely original series, with the help of Hanna-Barbera Cartoons. At the time, the vast majority of animated content available to the network were shorts created for both theaters and television. Series like *Looney Tunes* and *Tom and Jerry* were composed of numerous short films, which were combined into loosely themed programming blocks, much as they were in the early days of television. Aside from *The Flintstones* and a few other series produced for prime time, the Hanna-Barbera cartoons also followed this format, giving the studio flexibility in rearranging the shows, which was especially effective with the young audience, whose attention span and higher generational turnover made it easier to present the programs as new. Seibert wanted new programming that fit this mold, but he soon realized that shorts actually cost more per minute to produce than full-length shows, and the cost to produce shorts for the new series was prohibitive for the still emerging network.[39]

Understanding the economic and production obstacles in front of the studio, Seibert pitched an anthology series where 48 shorts would be produced as "succeed or fail" pilots. This allowed emerging and independent animators the opportunity to pitch their show, to be produced through Hanna-Barbera Cartoons and broadcast nationally on Cartoon Network.[40] Between 1993, after the series was originally announced, and 1995 over 5,000 pitches were collected and reviewed for the 48 spots. Along with Hanna and Barbera, Friz Freleng was recruited by Seibert to be a consultant for the series as the executive was a big fan of the *Looney Tunes* series to which Freleng contributed. Former *Ren & Stimpy* director John Kricfalusi became Seibert's connection to young, fresh animators who may have been overlooked by the traditional American animation companies, helping to spread the word. The call also led international animators to the network, which was almost exclusively American-produced cartoons at the time. Seibert hoped that the increased variety on the network could lead to drawing larger, more diverse audiences beyond the white males that had long been the main target of most animators.[41] Seibert also challenged customs of the industry by offering the animators royalties for their production while allowing them to maintain the rights to their creations if the series was picked up by the network.[42] This way, the studio did not have to pay for the production of storyboards, while animators were still motivated by the opportunity to have their shorts broadcast, and possibly even picked up as series, without losing control of their creations. Seibert and other executives would have no creative input, ignoring the supervisory approach Nickelodeon and Disney utilized to establish a reputation and format for Cartoon Network programming that remains with the broadcaster to this day.

It was clear Hanna and Barbera's influence in the company was further diminishing as the lines between their namesake studio and the network were blurred. After *Dumb and Dumber* premiered that fall the studio exclusively produced animation for Turner, and as Seibert and the network worked together to further expand viewership for the network, which included most of the Hanna-Barbera productions, it was clear that the separation between "Hanna-Barbera" and "Cartoon Network" was merely a formality that was dissipating. The development of the *World Premiere Cartoons* show further defined the animation duo's role as consultants, advisors, and public figures representing the studio and Cartoon Network, as the duo were only credited in four of the 48 shorts.

However, the new show did help repair Hanna-Barbera's reputation among animators, as it had long been thought of as a commercial animator full of artists who had "sold out" to produce cheap, low-quality cartoons. As names like Ralph Bakshi and Bruno Bozzetto began to surface as possible collaborators for the series, animators whose standards may have precluded them from working with the studio or producing for American television in previous years were now pitching ideas to have their short produced with the help of Hanna-Barbera Cartoons and Cartoon Network.[43]

As evidenced by the open call for pitches, Seibert and Turner were ready to test new strategies to help get the series, and the network, more attention. Along with Bakshi and Bozzetto, the entire Hanna-Barbera staff, including the crew that helped develop *2 Stupid Dogs*, Hanna-Barbera's first hit for Turner as a subsidiary of the media company, contributed work to the series. The contributors also varied in age from Friz Freleng, who was in his late 80s at the time and passed right after the series premiere, and Jerry Eisenberg, who had helped develop a number of hits for Hanna-Barbera in the 1960s and 1970s, to Seth MacFarlane, an animator in his early 20s whose contribution to the series served as a rough pilot for the popular series *Family Guy*.[44]

A number of the animators, including MacFarlane, stayed with Hanna-Barbera after the series' first run as the massive open call also served as an audition for many rising animators looking for an opportunity to get their work seen by the public.[45] Kricfalusi was supposed to direct shorts for the series, but Seibert commissioned them as separate projects. This was done to possibly avoid overloading the series with parodies of Hanna-Barbera cartoons (both of Kricfalusi's shorts were satires of Yogi Bear) or to avoid further scrutiny and conflicts with animators. A censorship controversy also arose, leading to Bakshi removing his name from the credits of his shorts, which were edited after being deemed inappropriate for general audiences. This contributed to Seibert delaying Kricfalusi's contribution after the animator dealt with similar issues related to *Ren & Stimpy* and Nickelodeon.[46]

The low promotional budget also forced Turner, Hanna-Barbera, and the studio's "Creative Corps" to find creative ways to promote the series and the network. This included preview trailers for the network on home videos of Hanna-Barbera and Turner animated content. They even sent out "Taste of Cartoon Network" VHS tapes to influential members of the animation industry and certain potential customers to help promote the network. They wanted to push cable customers, possibly motivated by their children's pleas, to pressure their service providers to include Cartoon Network. As *World Premiere Cartoons* progressed further in its development, a few of the early cartoons were included on the tapes over a year before they officially premiered on the network. These early versions of the shorts worked as children wanted to see not only the thousands of hours of older animation available, but also these new, irreverent cartoons, which at that point were rarely seen on cable animation outside of the first two seasons of *The Ren & Stimpy Show*. The Creative Corps also sent out limited edition fluorescent posters that introduced the shorts and their characters to the audience ahead of the debut in February 1995. Cartoon Network and its related channels were one of the first cable networks to utilize guerrilla-marketing techniques, and they continue to embrace this type of promotional approach, which became more popular as more marketers recognized unconventional and viral strategies through the development and growth of the Internet and social media.[47]

The massive open call also welcomed voices, perspectives, and characters whose representation was previously limited in the animation industry. Unfortunately, all the credited directors of the shorts selected were male; however, more animators of color were brought into public consciousness. This includes animators Van Partible and Achiu So from the Philippines, a nation Hanna-Barbera relied on heavily for animation, and Cuban-American Robert Alvarez, who had started working for Hanna-Barbera fifteen years earlier on *The Super Globetrotters* after getting his big break as an assistant on *The Yellow Submarine*. Although the staff behind the scenes did not necessarily reflect awareness of the historic sexism and racism, the first show to premiere as a part of *World Premiere Cartoons* starred three young females in the title roles. In fact, several of the most popular shorts from the series included female protagonists or antagonists as major, if not starring, characters. Linda Simensky, who was head of original animation at the time after working at Nickelodeon, was especially aware of the continued oversight related to the female animation audience and pushed for more animation that appealed to girls. Simensky wanted to attract both genders rather than just young boys, which had been the focus audience for animators for so long.[48]

Unlike many shows, particularly animated, directed at adolescent children, the creators of the *World Premiere Cartoon* shorts did not underestimate or patronize the intelligence of the audience, which included adults. The new generation of animators understood that children had been watching cartoons, some from Hanna-Barbera, with repeated formulas and jokes for years, so animators were able to move beyond the typical tropes, even satirizing them, while offering more different, irreverent, and even mature content in their shorts, and eventually series, on Cartoon Network. Animators even included older pop culture references to keep co-watching parents and older animation fans interested, while still appealing to children with the animation, storylines, and humor. This strategy to make content that is (mostly) appropriate for children while also being entertaining for older audiences was long employed by other "children's shows," most notably *Sesame Street*, which used contemporary pop culture and figures to draw parents and educators to the show, encouraging them to co-watch with their children. The strategy employed by Hanna-Barbera and Cartoon Network was not nearly as altruistic, as they were merely looking to draw in the largest audience possible, while the presence of parents was often more a detriment than a benefit for some of the more controversial shorts.[49] This strategy also separated Cartoon Network from Disney Channel, which targets families, and Nickelodeon, the "first network for kids.[50]

As 1995 approached, Seibert and Cartoon Network prepared for a big rollout of the series, picking President's Day for the event that would be known as the World Premiere Toon-In and simulcast on TNT and TBS. The event followed over a month of heavy promotion on the Turner networks and advertisements on other networks.[51] In addition, they planned a "Dive-In" for that summer where Turner and Cartoon Network worked with water parks and swimming pools across the country to exhibit the shorts. Along with the "Dive-Ins" they planned other events before the shorts aired on the network, which helped draw viewers by offering prizes and activities that helped promote the shorts and characters. These promotional events targeted fans who either did not have access to the network in their market or were not fully aware that the network was moving away from being a mere forum for reruns of old cartoons into a force in the animation and television industries. Space Ghost was also included in the activities, serving as the host of the Toon-In, conducting interviews with several creators, playing clips from future shows, and debuting the first *World Premiere Cartoon*, *The Powerpuff Girls*.

The production became known as the "President's Day Nightmare" by Ghost Planet Industries (later Williams Street Productions) partially due to the work required to

Statues of the Powerpuff Girls, Bubbles, Blossom, and Buttercup, welcoming guests to Children's Day 2016 in Bangkok (Thailand enchanted_fairy/Shutterstock.com).

prepare the animation for the Toon-In. Many of the shorts were still in production when the *Space Ghost Coast to Coast* staff was trying to construct the introductory, interstitial, and interview portions for the event.[52] For the next two years, new shorts premiered on Sundays, and after enough shorts premiered, they were packaged into a half hour program that included a premiering short surround by cartoons that debuted earlier in the series' run. By the end of 1995, 18 new shorts premiered on Cartoon Network as both the animation and television industries took notice of the new network and the content it was producing, which was different than most of the other content broadcast by competitors Nickelodeon and Disney Channel. The series also directly challenged its future sister company, Warner Bros., which was experiencing a renaissance through the popularity of its own irreverent, satirical series like *Animaniacs*.[53]

Aging Out of Relevance

Hanna-Barbera Cartoons Inc. was responsible for overseeing the production of all of the *World Premiere Cartoons*. The next summer the series was retitled as *What a Cartoon!*, which was the original working title. As the calendar changed, the studio's future within Turner was further confirmed when Cartoon Network Studios' first *What a Cartoon!* premiered in the second week of January 1996. The studio was established in 1994 as a subsidiary within Hanna-Barbera Cartoons Inc. with the first short credited to the studio, *Podunk Possum*, acting as the broadcast debut for the new studio. As the Time Warner/Turner merger was being reviewed by the Federal Communications Commission, it was clear that the reputation of Hanna-Barbera did not hold the same weight it once did, especially when it was not connected to one of their legacy franchises like *The Flintstones* or *Yogi Bear*. The impending addition of a more popular animation brand, Warner Bros., would also accelerate this transition as Hanna and Barbera faced the end of their careers as they surpassed six decades in the business. Production of the series had ostensibly switched to Cartoon Network Studios about halfway through, with the full shift in the credits occurring the day before the merger between the media giants was approved by both companies' boards of directors.[54] In fact, of the last 19 shorts to premiere on *World Premiere Cartoons*, only four were produced or directed by Hanna or Barbera, one of which was the 1997 short *Dino: The Great Egg-Scape*, the second of the series to star Dino and the last short to be directed by Barbera. A year earlier, Hanna also directed his final short, *Wind-Up Wolf*, as he prepared for his impending retirement by releasing his memoir in 1996, two years after Barbera did the same. The biographies were evidence that both animators saw the writing on the wall; even if their characters and creations remained popular, they knew it was time to step aside and let the new generation of animators take over their studio and properties. The industry as a whole was transitioning into a new era of animation, arguably the most fruitful and highly regarded since the end of the Golden Age in the 1950s.[55]

After the first *What a Cartoon!* shorts debuted between February and August 1995, Cartoon Network held a vote to determine the most popular of these 16 shorts. *Dexter's Laboratory*, which was the second full short to premiere, won the vote, leading Seibert to ask Genndy Tartakovsky to create two more Dexter pilots for Hanna-Barbera and Cartoon Network, one appearing on *What a Cartoon!* and the other as a standalone short. The pilots achieved high ratings and garnered critical attention for the growing network, leading to a full series featuring the young scientist and his antagonizing sister. Cartoon Network continued their approach of packaging shorts into longer shows as Hanna-Barbera had done since the 1950s. *Dexter's Laboratory* shorts were combined with two other segments, *Dial M for Monkey* and *The Justice Friends*. The first segment starred Dexter's pet monkey who lived a double life as a superhero, unbeknownst to his handler. The second segment was a sitcom parody of *Super Friends* starring three superheroes living as roommates modeled after some of the superheroes from Marvel Comics that helped Tartakovsky to learn English after moving to the U.S. from Russia at age 7 to avoid rising anti–Semitism.

Neither of these segments came close to achieving the popularity and success of the title segment, which revolved around its star and his secret laboratory. The young inventor is given an ambiguous accent because, according to the creator, all scientists in popular culture seem to have non–American accents, in spite of the fact his parents and sister are clearly American. As he works in his laboratory, competing with his rival Susan "Mandark" Astronomonov as Mandark develops schemes to destroy Dexter's Laboratory and his inventions, Dexter must also deal with Dee Dee, his sister, who is the only other family member who knows about the laboratory. Dee Dee is able to avoid the numerous security measures to infiltrate the secret lab and haphazardly play with his research and equipment. The animation style was inspired by the Warner Bros. series *Merrie Melodies*, particularly the work of Chuck Jones in *The Dover Boys of Pimento University,* and premiered only a few months before Warner became sister subsidiary to Hanna-Barbera/Cartoon Network. The program actually premiered on TNT on April 27, 1996, before airing on Cartoon Network the next night, as Turner continued to promote the animation network through its other, more widely available networks. After bouncing around projects within *What a Cartoon!*, Seth MacFarlane also directed several episodes of the series in 1998 after his own cartoon, *Larry & Steve*, which served as the inspiration for *Family Guy*, debuted in 1997.[56]

Venturing into the Uncertain World
of Preschool Programming

Cartoon Network was clearly growing as a network aimed at both children and general audiences, but much of its content was comedies not suitable for younger children. As an attempt to broaden its programming as Time Warner prepared to take over Turner, the network debuted a preschool programming block with new episodes premiering on Sunday mornings. Cable networks did not have the same educational oversight from the FCC, oversight that was supposed to be strengthened by the 1990 Children's Television Act and the Telecommunications Act of 1996. Cartoon Network executives understood that older children leave to go to school or might not be up as early. Wanting to receive positive attention from advocates, Nickelodeon and Disney Channel both took a cue from PBS and built their own younger programming block. Both eventually launched full networks dedicated to preschool programming, Disney Junior and Noggin, the latter a joint venture between Viacom and Children's Television Workshop (CTW), which eventually became Nick Jr. Also working with CTW, Cartoon Network launched two new shows that took elements from *Sesame Street* as it tried to appeal to the youngest of viewers.[57]

Big Bag was a live-action show that featured animated segments aimed at preschoolers. As with its sister show, *Sesame Street*, which was also overseen by CTW, Jim Henson Productions created Muppets for the program while localized international versions were produced for other countries including France and Britain. One animated segment from *Big Bag*, *Troubles the Cat*, was the first completely original cartoon to feature Latinx characters on United States television.[58]

The second show, *Small World*, introduced young children to cartoons from around the world, which were much cheaper to broadcast than new animation, particularly from America. This was a similar strategy to that invoked by Pinwheel/Nickelodeon as the network established itself in the 1970s and 1980s in spite of small budgets. Much like *Big Bag*, international versions of *Small World* were produced featuring a number of cartoons from North America including several popular series from PBS including *Arthur* and *Caillou*.[59]

Joining these two programs was Hanna-Barbera Cartoons' first series aimed specifically at preschoolers featuring characters from a popular franchise.[60] *Cave Kids* debuted in the fall of 1996 starring the young versions of Pebbles and Bamm-Bamm with Dino acting as the babysitter for the young characters learning life lessons mostly focused around prosocial behavior. *Cave Kids* only lasted eight episodes, partially due to the low quality animation imported from longtime Hanna-Barbera Filipino production partners Fil-Cartoons, while *Big Bag* and *Small World* ran for two and five seasons, respectively. *Cave Kids* even aired on public media in a majority of the country, but airing on broadcast stations did not help the show avoid cancellation after the short run.[61] The network continues to struggle to draw in younger children, eventually dedicating early morning programming to its most popular children's programs. Their last true attempt at preschool programming was the Tickle-U block in 2007, which did include several shows that found success on other networks, including *Peppa Pig*.[62]

Along with *Small World*, the programming block *Toonami* also became a forum for Cartoon Network to broadcast international animation but aimed at older children and adults, much of it anime from Japan. When *Toonami* launched in March of 1997, *Jonny Quest* was one of the few contemporary action franchises owned by Hanna-Barbera or

Warner. Older action series like the *Superman* cartoons of the 1940s along with the collection of action series from Hanna-Barbera from the mid- to late 1960s including *Herculoids* and *Super Friends* and other series created by Alex Toth did air but felt dated compared to contemporary action animation. Cartoon Network also added popular toy-based action shows from the 1980s including *Thundercats*, which was produced by Rankin-Bass but owned by Warner after it purchased Larimer-Telepictures in 1989. They also acquired *Voltron: Defenders of the Universe*, whose rights were still held by Toei animation. Inclusion of the *Voltron* series helped establish a strong relationship between Cartoon Network and one of the top anime producers in Japan. The next season several other Japanese-produced series including *Sailor Moon* and *Dragonball Z* premiered on *Toonami*, establishing it as one of the few places outside of specialty video stores where cartoon fans could watch series that were already classics in the minds of many anime fans.[63]

Mike Lazzo, the head of Toonami, wanted a more mature action block, and he, Sean Adkins and Jason DeMarco created *Toonami*, which replaced the programming block Power Zone, which was renamed from Afternoon Adventures and featured older adventure shows like *Speed Racer* and *Fantastic Four*. The block was an instant hit, even running for a short time on the broadcast network The WB. The series was also a boost for Lazzo, Adkins, and DeMarco, who continued to attract audiences, particularly older audiences, with blocks and programs like *Toonami* and *Space Ghost: Coast to Coast*. Their involvement would also lead to the creation of Cartoon Network's programming block and later sister network, Adult Swim, in 2001, which also became one of the top networks on television among its target demographic, adults 18–49.[64]

As things settled at Time Warner's newest subsidiary, the presence, or lack thereof, of both Hanna and Barbera continued to become more noticeable. They were still advising Cartoon Network and Turner/Time Warner, particularly concerning the many properties that they helped create and whose public visibility was being maintained both on the television and movie screens, including the successful *The Flintstones* film. Both continued to receive producer and creator credits on projects featuring their characters, but the *What a Cartoon!* show represented the last cartoons the two would direct as they became less involved in the daily production at the network and their namesake studio. Their influence was still strongly felt at Cartoon Network and the industry as a whole as their creations continued to receive exposure throughout the media and merchandising landscape through every purchase of Pebbles cereal or every time a television personality compares the future with *The Jetsons*.[65] Their style also clearly influenced the new generation of animators working for the studio and within the industry. Although their voices were waning, they continued to be a part of the next step for the network and studio as Cartoon Network fully established its identity as the new millennium approached.

Going Beyond Visual Representations

As discussed in relation to *The Powerpuff Girls* and the new generation of animators, representation on the network, and in turn animation, was clearly improving. Representation of gender featured the most noticeable improvement with the influence of Warner Animation's Jean MacCurdy and Cartoon Network executive Linda Simensky pushing their respective companies to feature more representations of women and young girls. This was seen in characters like Babs Bunny on *Tiny Toon Adventures*; Dot Warner on *Animaniacs*; the numerous female co-stars on *Rugrats*, on which *Cave Kids* was modeled;

and *The Powerpuff Girls*. However, even with this increased equality related to representation within the gender binary, non-white characters and non-white, non-male animators were still relatively rare aside from a few outliers like *Troubles the Cat*.

Even with the presence of MacCurdy and Simensky, many animators continued to draw and represent female characters the same way that artists did throughout the Golden Age of Animation. This created issues related to gender roles and body image even as the gap between the numbers of male and female characters was reduced. As with the vast majority of animation for children, race was rarely openly discussed in episodes aside from the occasional "very special" episode, so most of these judgments are based on visual and vocal characteristics. The characters' look, speech patterns, and most of the vocal actors continued to be white, providing evidence of a continued lack of diversity that has plagued animation for over a century. Aside from the anime on *Toonami*, most of the animation imported, particularly for *Small World*, was imported from Western Europe and Canada. The United States' northern neighbor ironically did not have Cartoon Network programming available to them until Teletoon launched in 1997, a full year after animation deriving from the country began appearing on *Small World*. Even in the case of *Toonami*, the English dubbing often removed many of the Japanese cultural features and contexts, which had long been a problem all the way back to shows like *Speed Racer*, leaving only the visual content to present any semblance of Japanese art and culture.[66]

Even as the sensibilities of the young generation of animators helped the industry progress and introduce a wider range of experiential representation and parodies, including adopted characters (*Cow and Chicken*), or even the satirization of masculinity (*Johnny Bravo*), the lack of diversity behind the camera, or the pen, could still be felt on screen. Even though Cartoon Network would be at times at the forefront of this progress within mainstream animation, the industry was starting from a place of such inequity in representation that it continues to struggle to catch up to where some other media forms have progressed, which is not nearly far enough. This process is made more difficult by the fact that, although the divide has been greatly reduced since the debut of *The Simpsons*, most animation is still produced for children and general audiences. This makes it harder to broach these subjects while continuing to rely on long held popular tropes or formulas that make it harder for entities or the industry as a whole to progress without possibly risking alienating the audience and reducing their bottom line through more innovative, and financially riskier, content.

Even with these struggles, the younger executives and programmers for the networks were more open minded than the previous generation to not only diversifying representation but also giving artists and producers of color opportunities on the network that they may not have had on television in previous years. This open mindedness combined with its mostly irreverent approach to animation helped Cartoon Network separate itself from its competitors and challenge not only the other networks to which it was connected but all of cable as one of the most popular networks in the United States.

12

1996 and Beyond:
Digitization and Consolidation

The Present and Future Overtake the Past

From its inception in 1992 through the rest of the decade, Cartoon Network seemed to be operating with one foot in the past and one foot in the future, continuing to rely heavily on its huge catalogue of classic cartoons. Along with *Space Ghost: Coast to Coast*, the introduction of *What a Cartoon!* and the shorts that were featured throughout the series, some of which became early hit series, represented the first steps in constructing a more modern brand. The executives at the network were looking to establish a unique identity for the network, hoping to fill the niche between the more mature animation on mostly live-action networks like Comedy Central and the children's fare seen on Nickelodeon and Disney.[1] As the next millennium approached, Cartoon Network would find its own place in the media landscape, while at the same time those entities associated with past eras of animation, including the classic characters and the influential figures, found their own home separate from the network, maintaining visibility. They did have to leave something in the past, Hanna and Barbera. As the foundation for Cartoon Network became more secure, their guidance became obsolete.

This next generation of animators and programmers for Cartoon Network also recognized the opportunity in modernizing the presentation of animation, and television as a whole, continuing to expand their irreverent approach to their content, promotion, and marketing. The network introduced itself in many markets through the distribution of unique posters and promotional videos. The network also marketed itself through unique events, like the "Dive-In," to attract attention with relatively minimal costs. After the Time Warner merger, the network had more support and resources than ever, but it still maintained a gritty edge to its marketing informed by its low budget beginnings, reflecting a more grassroots strategy in opposition to the carefully curated and over-produced promotions seen on Nickelodeon and Disney. Their early interstitial material often satirized the content and storylines from classic cartoons while drawing in potential viewers, particularly children, with intense commercials featuring frequent cuts and a fast-speaking narrator, promoting the network as the fast-paced option for animation and children's content.

As the network became more firmly established in the television landscape it moved away from promos featuring classic characters underscored by Raymond Scott's "Powerhouse," which Warner had frequently used in their *Looney Tunes* and *Merrie Melodies* cartoons. It also utilized bumpers, short pieces of content that provided a buffer between commercials and the program, as a creative and marketing outlet.[2] Bumpers were historically used to help children distinguish between advertising and entertainment content; as a cable network not under the supervision of the FCC, Cartoon Network was not legally obligated to broadcast bumpers. With the network's historic connections to broadcast network animation, it made sense for programmers to modernize the use of bumpers to better promote the network, satirize the past structure of cartoon broadcasting, and display its artists' creativity as the original programming was still fairly limited.[3] The network's original programming was garnering attention, including an Academy Award Nomination for "The Chicken from Outer Space," which was the pilot episode for *Courage the Cowardly Dog*. However, creation and development of series were still almost exclusively completed through *What a Cartoon!*, a structure that remained through the 1990s even after Seibert left to create his own studio in 1997. Mike Register, vice president of the network, took over the anthology series overseeing the production of the shorts/pilots after the productions were renamed *Cartoon Cartoon* in July 1997. Register also helped oversee the launch of CartoonNetwork.com in 2000.[4]

For nearly five years, from the original open call for submissions to the end of the series' run in 2003, the vast majority of the original programming, except for *Space Ghost: Coast to Coast*, came from the anthology series or its followup program *The Cartoon Cartoon Show*. This approach limited the ability to seek content from outside this structure, making promos, interstitial content, and bumpers one of the few places newcomers to the network and studio could communicate their creativity outside of supporting the production of these other series. However, as the network was figuring out its next step, particularly regarding original programming, the studio responsible for the popular *Space Ghost: Coast to Coast* expanded the network's late night adult offerings while constructing an identity for the time slot. Those responsible for the content featured the rest of the day worked to further establish Cartoon Network's identity as they looked toward the next wave of original content.[5]

Music and Animation: The Soul of Animation Evolves

The young animators and programmers also brought a more contemporary sensibility about how the content and promotional material were presented. One of the most noticeable perspectives was the soundtracks and scores to their programs and interstitial material, especially for their late-night adult programming and original shows and blocks like *Toonami*. Animation had long relied on classical and instrumental music within films, with show tune–influenced songs helping Disney separate themselves as a producer of high-quality animated content, especially after *Snow White*, which was the first commercially released soundtrack. Going back to animation's vaudeville origins, music had always been an important element to convey emotion and tone, even as dialogue became a more integral part of animation production after the premiere of *Steamboat Willie*. In the short films that represented the vast majority of animation through the Golden Age, producers had to build an entire narrative in a seven-minute film, and music was used to move the story along. Some series, like Hanna and Barbera's *Tom and Jerry*, had almost no dialogue and relied heavily on the music to convey emotion and drama. *Silly Symphonies* and *Merrie Melodies* both built animation around the music, with the latter utilized as music videos to promote the Warner Bros. catalogue.

Music continued to play a vital role in television animation, used to supplement or distract from the limited animation. Intricate theme songs also became synonymous with television animation, particular Hanna-Barbera, who utilized longer theme and closing songs to cut down on the animation needed for each episode with theme songs like "Meet the Flintstones" becoming well known among generations of children who watched the series, and heard the theme song, every week.[6] The popularity of "Sugar, Sugar," which was written for Filmation's *The Archie Show*, prompted a number of shows with a more blatant musical element, like *Josie and the Pussycats*. The creation of bands and original music produced for animated television programs represented another revenue source through tours and record sales as studios and networks continued to look for more ancillary markets for their content. It also helped the programs connect with contemporary culture with scores and catchy theme songs that reflected popular music at the time.[7] Music became less of a consideration in the toy-based programs as the scores for the programs took a backseat to the promotion of the product. A generation of children can still sing the themes to *Transformers* and *Teenage Mutant Ninja Turtles*, just as previous generations still know the words to the themes for *The Flintstones* or *Scooby-Doo*, evidence that music was not overlooked in these series.[8]

Early on, Cartoon Network utilized music from the animation it acquired along with music from the public domain to save money, but as its programming expanded so did the music featured on the network. After *Toonami* proved to be a hit, DeMarco wanted to move away from the Golden Age-inspired approach to scoring animation and invite musicians and artists with a more contemporary sound to help supplement the content they were broadcasting. By 2000, *Toonami* began to feature hip-hop inspired theme songs and scores, and by the middle of the first decade of the 2000s, DeMarco was working with artists like MF Doom and Killer Mike to produce albums under a new label. This commitment to what is truly a non-white art form would also be reflected in some of the animated programs they broadcast, especially as they expanded their adult programming block throughout the early years of the 2000s. Most of their animators, producers, programmers, and executives continued to be white and male; however, they were at least more aware of the possibilities created by diversifying the content included on the network and were making attempts at presenting a wider-range of voices and perspectives in animation.[9] It cannot be overlooked, however, that the majority of hip-hop consumers are white males from the suburbs, so even though these artists were receiving exposure, it did not alienate the traditional animation audience, a concern for producers when featuring non-white or non-male visual representations and perspectives in animation, comic books, and video games.[10]

Young Animators Bring Fresh Perspectives

The need for Hanna and Barbera's assistance in developing Cartoon Network, its studio, and animation was decreasing quickly, as greater competition and younger contributors helped the animation to progress further. The revitalization of the industry was supported by Disney's theatrical renaissance; the growth of cable, particularly niche networks targeting children and fans of particular media content, like animation, and the growth of several companies with interests in animation, like Warner and Viacom, fueled by deregulation and consolidation. With so many options, animators were motivated to create more unique content, but due to the new generation of animators' knowledge of past eras, they were also able to help the craft and content progress while maintaining a connection with past animation and characters. This strategy also helped Cartoon

Network create a unique brand while maintaining a connected with its preceding/parent studios, Hanna-Barbera and Warner Bros. The network's programmers took more chances while also shifting the long-held formulas utilized by legendary animators. By still utilizing some of these formulas and approaches they limited risks associated the characters and storylines presented to the audience, while the influence of the younger animators also helped the industry evolve.[11]

Developing an Identity for Cartoon Network

Although its approach focused on producing animation that was entertaining for general audiences but appropriate for children, Cartoon Network still had to work to find its identity with certain content challenging its identity while also helping the network more firmly define how it presents, or brands, itself to the audience. Two of the shorts that forced the network to better define its future were produced by John Kricfalusi, who had been let go from *The Ren & Stimpy Show* on Nickelodeon after consistently butting heads with executives concerning the appropriateness of the humor on the show. Kricfalusi credits legendary animator Ralph Bakshi for "saving" him from Saturday morning, helping the young animator develop his irreverent and graphic style of animation.[12] Kricfalusi was instrumental in the development of the *What a Cartoon!* series and developed two satirical shorts starring Boo Boo and Ranger Smith that were supposed to be included in the anthology series, but it was determined the style and mature humor of the shorts did not fit the style of program. Both *A Day in the Life of Ranger Smith* and *Boo Boo Runs Wild* were released on the network independent of the anthology series in 1999. The first short starred Ranger Smith, portrayed as hating his job, going through all his depressing responsibilities at Jellystone, while the second starred Boo Boo, who enters a feral state after the frustration over all the rules for animals at the park pushes him over the edge. Along with the graphic, gross-out humor that became synonymous with Kricfalusi's work, it also included explicit sexual humor and imitable violent behavior. The shorts were rarely seen on Cartoon Network after their premiere but did find new life as the network expanded its late night offerings. For the daytime network that was largely promoted to children in spite of the general audience approach, Cartoon Network airing the shorts on a limited basis created a clear line of what content would be accepted by the network as appropriate for its younger audience watching during the day and early evening.[13]

Cartoon Network entered the next century fully prepared to make the transition from broadcaster of old cartoons into a unique network led by original, mostly animated, programming produced in house, separating it from the other animation under the Time Warner conglomerate. The network only premiered one new show in 2000, but like *2 Stupid Dogs* and *Dexter's Laboratory*, the series very much represented the future of the network and its programming. *Sheep in the Big City* debuted as a pilot on *The Cartoon Cartoon Show* as a part of the "Cartoon Cartoon Summer" in 2000. During this period, the network released several shorts similar to its predecessor, *What a Cartoon!*, to increase the diversity of content available to audiences and test out pilots that could be picked up as series. Like Nicktoons, *Cartoon Cartoon* also became the umbrella term for all Cartoon Network produced and distributed series and shorts between 1997 and 2003. *Sheep in the Big City* is often overshadowed by earlier shows like *Dexter's Laboratory* in relation to their influence on the larger network, but the series, which was picked up and officially debuted in November, only three months after the broadcast of the pilot, very much represented the new generation of animators' approach to animation that often ignored and even satirized conventions and formulas in animation. The 32-year-old Mo Willems was the creator of the series. Willems had gotten his start as a writer for *Sesame Street* before working for Nickelodeon on *KaBlam!*, an animated sketch comedy show where he created *The Off-Beats* for *Sheep in the Big City*.[14]

The Cartoon Network series was produced in conjunction with Curious Pictures, whose most famous productions had been animation for the first season of *Pee-wee's Playhouse* and *Elmo's World*. Jay Ward's *Rocky & Bullwinkle* inspired the comedy in the series by featuring frequent interaction/involvement with the narrator, who often speaks to the characters on screen as they break the fourth wall. As in Ward's series, characters in *Sheep in the Big City* often comment about their presence on a television show by discussing the production and broadcast processes within the show, satirizing the larger industry. The literal humor that often mocked conventional approaches to animation and television storytelling also presented more intellectually mature humor without relying heavily on graphic visuals or controversial jokes. As with the Kricfulasi Ranger Smith shorts, the producers of their original programs were still learning what would be accepted by standards and practices and what would be edited, if not banned outright. A 1997 episode of *Dexter's Laboratory*, "Rude Removal," was banned from broadcast due to profanity and inappropriate language. In the story, Dexter invents a machine that splits the personalities of the young scientist and Dee Dee into rude and polite. The rude versions went on profanity-laced tirades, and although the language was bleeped the combination of assumed language and graphic humor, including a mooning, was enough for Linda Simensky and standards to deem the episode inappropriate. Simensky commented that she enjoyed the episode, but it was not appropriate for the target audience of the program.[15] The episode did run at several film festivals before finally airing in late night on the network 16 years later. As the young animators continued to learn on the job, *Sheep in the Big City*, which was the highest premiering series for the network at the time, exemplified the clever writing and humor that could draw in their target audience, adolescent children, while still being appealing to adults. The producers also avoided the scrutiny that several shows like *Ren & Stimpy*, *Tiny Toon Adventures*, and Nickelodeon's *Rocko's Modern Life* faced over its controversial content. Leaders of the contemporary television animation industry, like Nickelodeon, Disney, and Cartoon Network, emerged behind young producers who were still testing the boundaries as employees or contractors for these animation giants.[16]

The Digital Tier and Deconstructing Old Cartoons

During the 1990s, digital television's technology improved and cable systems began adopting multi-channel systems that would allow them to expand the number of channels they were operating through digital compression.[17] As when television expanded through cable in the late 1970s and 1980s, the networks in the digital tier were niche networks, presenting programming with a specific theme or audience. This included numerous regional television networks that became available in markets outside their place of origin like MSG Network, or they were offshoots of already popular networks like ESPN, which launched ESPN Classic and ESPNews as digital stations in 1995 and 1996, respectively.

Taking advantage of the lower subscription and broadcasting rates offered by digital cable, Cartoon Network launched Boomerang as a repository of all the old cartoons that were losing time to the popular original and acquired programs, many of the latter coming from Warner Bros. productions, like *Tiny Toons*, finding their way onto Cartoon Network. Boomerang was originally a programming block that debuted on the network during its first year as it tried to draw in baby boomers who still held fond memories for past animation particularly from Hanna-Barbera and Warner. Starting in 1997, TBS broadcast *Disaster Area*, which played the same older series as the Boomerang block on its sister network, and the popularity of both led Turner to launch Boomerang as a standalone network on April 1, 2000. As with Cartoon Network, Hanna-Barbera's library, along with *Tom and Jerry* and theatrical Warner and MGM series like *Looney Tunes*, became the main source of programming for the new digital network, particularly in its early years. With a destination created for fans of older animation, many of whom were adults who could conceivably purchase the cable package that included Boomerang, the basic cable network could concentrate on contemporary animation that appealed to their target demographic, attracting larger audiences with newer content and characters.[18]

In late December of 2000, another programming block that strongly influenced the direction of the network ostensibly debuted, although it would not launch with an official name until September of the next year. Mike Lazzo, who had created *Space Ghost: Coast to Coast* and established its studio Ghost Planet Industries, adopting its current name, Williams Street Productions, in 1999, wanted to improve the late-night offerings of Cartoon Network. Lazzo looked to compete against the more adult late night programming on both Disney Channel and Nickelodeon with the latter network creating Nick at Nite, whose dramatically different demographic led Nielsen to track it as a separate network.[19] The production head saw an opportunity to create late night shows to replace the blocks of older cartoons that had historically filled the late night Cartoon Network schedule, like *Toonheads*, which supplied audiences with facts and trivia during interstitial times to try to draw in older cartoon fanatics to rewatch cartoons from Warner, Hanna-Barbera, and MGM. Another show, *Late Night Black and White*, also targeted this audience by playing even older pre-color shorts from the 1930s through the 1950s. The animated content in these blocks quickly filled the schedule on Boomerang, creating opportunities in the late-night schedule.

By this time, *The Simpsons* had been on the air for over a decade, becoming one of the most successful comedy series of all time, leading to a flood of adult animated series including *King of the Hill, Beavis and Butthead, South Park*, and in 1999 Seth MacFarlane's *Family Guy*. This motivated Lazzo to push for the production of their own animated series that targeted adults as the primary demographic.[20] Just before dawn on the East Coast on December 21 and December 30, Cartoon Network broadcast four "stealth pilots" without any promotion or notice listed as special programming on television scheduling grids. With two "original" series and two *Space Ghost: Coast to Coast* spin-offs, Mike Lazzo officially launched a new era for Cartoon Network. These programs recognized the humor and sensibilities of older animation and comedy fans, who made up over a third of the network's audience, while keeping the content separate from the child-appropriate content and branding featured on the larger network.[21]

The two "original" series were actually satirical deconstructions of Hanna-Barbera characters and content. Similar to *Space Ghost*, Lazzo found this approach was not only cheaper to produce, but the parodies of popular Hanna-Barbera characters featured on the programs also created instant familiarity between the audience and the shows, featuring characters and animation that the now adults had grown up watching on Saturday morning. The first show, *Sealab 2021*, deconstructed and redubbed animation from Hanna-Barbera's 1972 series *Sealab 2020*, rewriting the storylines and dialogue of the show creating a completely different program that satirized not just older action cartoons but all science fiction and dramatic programming. As with *Space Ghost*, Hanna and Barbera were a little hesitant to greenlight the deconstruction of the environmentally focused series, but eventually signed off on the new take on the old animation.[22]

Harvey Birdman, Attorney at Law did not rely as heavily on stock footage, but still reimagined the 1960s superhero Birdman as a lawyer helping Hanna-Barbera characters with various legal issues. *Harvey Birdman* satirized storylines or characters from the legendary television animators, particularly programs from the 1960s and 1970s. For example, the plot of the first episode revolves around a custody battle between Dr. Benton Quest and Race Bannon over Jonny Quest who Bannon claims is actually his progeny. *Harvey Birdman* not only placed these stars of children's cartoons into adult situations, but both series proved that adults cared less about animation quality or uniqueness and were more concerned with cartoons that contained mature humor and content. As a cable network, Cartoon Network also had the advantage of being outside the purview of the FCC, which provided the network's late-night programmers and producers more flexibility in terms of mature content. Broadcast networks airing adult animation, particularly FOX, were under more scrutiny from the Commission.[23]

The cast of *Sealab 2021* (from left, Dr. Quentin Quinn, Debbie Dupree, Captain Hank Murphy, Marco Rodrigo Marquez, Derek "Stormy" Waters (AF Archive/Alamy Stock Photo).

Along with *Harvey Birdman* and *Sealab 2021*, two *Space Ghost* spin-offs premiered in the early morning hours in late December. *The Brak Show* starred the eponymous "space cat" super villain from the 1966 series who had become a dopey side character in *Space Ghost: Coast to Coast* and *Cartoon Planet*, a programming block he hosted that ran on TBS and Cartoon Network through 1998. *The Brak Show* was a parody of the *Leave It to Beaver*–type family sitcoms of the 1950s and 1960s. Two variety specials titled *Brak Presents The Brak Show Starring Brak* did not garner the attention the staff at Williams Street had hoped, and they retooled the show to portray Brak as a pre-teen living in suburbia with his Mom (Marsha Crenshaw/Joanna Daniel), who shares his large teeth and mask-like face, and his Hispanic-accented undocumented human father (George Lowe). Zorak, another villain who appeared on *Space Ghost* and *Cartoon Planet*, played Brak's best friend in true Eddie Haskell form while their neighbor Thundercleese, an aggressive killbot who is also their lawn-obsessed neighbor, was voiced by African American voice actor Carey Means. The series was not as popular as the other shows that premiered, but the unconventional approach, placing these characters formerly known as cartoon villains or superheroes into deconstructed television tropes that have been present on television since the 1950s, proved to be a successful strategy. Older audiences continued to be attracted to the nostalgia and satire while unfamiliar audiences appreciated the non-traditional approach to animation and humor.[24]

Means also voiced a character on the last stealth pilot, *Aqua Teen Hunger Force*. From the first episode, the unorthodox animation and content of *Aqua Teen Hunger Force* was introduced by its hip-hop theme song, a genre of music that was rare in animation, aside from *Toonami* and some clumsy attempts to feature unoriginal rap songs in children's animation to make it seem cool or edgy. *Aqua Teen* instead commissioned Schoolly D, a Philadelphia rapper that many consider one of the originators of gangsta rap, to write and produce the show's theme song, along with providing occasional narration and commentary throughout the episodes.[25]

Aqua Teen Hunger Force was Williams Street's first show that completely broke away from the direct influence of Hanna-Barbera, although the characters were first seen in *Space Ghost: Coast to Coast*. It featured three anthropomorphic food products, a milkshake (Master Shake), a box of fries (Frylock), a meatball (Meatwad), and their human neighbor, Carl Brutananadilewski. The original premise had the pathological liar Master Shake, the dimwitted Meatwad, and the rational Frylock solving mysteries, à la *Scooby-Doo*, but they quickly moved away from that trope. The mystery approach of early episodes was used to get the show approved after producers had a hard time understanding the value of an episodic show featuring food in random situations. The program fully embraced its surreal and subversive elements as it moved forward, utilizing animation to present situations and gags that were not only impossible in live-action content, but not seen before in animation, like the willingness to completely disregard a linear narrative mid-episode.[26] The program was not only episodic, but the irreverent storylines often did not connect or contain continuity as the three anthropomorphic fast-food items lived their lives in New Jersey. The stars, who originally appeared as promotional characters for a restaurant in *Space Ghost*, were tormented by the rude, obnoxious Mooninites who regularly came to earth to disrupt the lives of the trio. *Aqua Teen Hunger Force* was also one of the only adult animated shows at the time to prominently feature African American voice talent, with Means providing the voice of Frylock on the program in an animated world where animators continued to rely on mostly white voice talent to portray African American and other characters of color. The presence of Schoolly D as the theme composer, performer, and narrator also represented a move to better recognize non-white artists and culture, even if this was really a baby step forward in an animation industry that continued to be almost completely whitewashed both behind and in front of the pen.[27]

The stealth pilots were a preview for a new programming block aimed at adults that Cartoon Network planned to launch the next fall. Lazzo, who has been involved in Turner animation since the 1980s, was named programmer for the block. As the block, and the shows, prepared for their official debuts the network continued its unorthodox marketing techniques. At the San Diego Comic Con in July 2001 along with previews of the shows that would fill the programming block in the fall they gave away CDs with the theme songs from the new shows and t-shirts that looked like a roll of bandages a lifeguard might carry.

Adult Swim (stylized [adult swim]) debuted on September 2, 2001, with *Home Movies*, a show cancelled by UPN two years earlier that Lazzo picked up for the block. Cancelled and syndicated adult animation, particularly from networks outside of the big three, became a significant early resource for the block. The executives at Williams Street, who are responsible for the programming on Adult Swim along with much of the block's original programming, wanted to formally separate themselves from the more child-oriented Cartoon Network to let teenagers and adults know that the programming would be directed to them while informing parents about the change in intended audience. It also helped keep younger viewers loyal to the network as they got older and aged out of the younger programming on Cartoon Network, a strategy utilized by Nickelodeon by establishing a younger Nick Jr. audience that could grow up with the Nickelodeon/MTV brands.[28] Although there are legitimate criticisms concerning the saturation of media into children's lives, and the conditioning of children to be consumers of certain

Aqua Teen Hunger Force's Meatwad welcomes guests to San Diego Comic-Con in 2015 in the form of a tent (whysteriastar/Shutterstock.com).

content, it has been a marketing and content strategy that has been financially beneficial for both networks.[29]

The establishment of a block explicitly aimed at adults not only pushed the network to produce more mature animated content, but also allowed them to present material and perspectives that did not solely rely on formulas and stereotypes that had been seen in animation throughout the history of the industry, sometimes even satirizing them in their content. This includes the broad, white middle class male inspired content that has dominated television and film animation in previous decades. Even their interstitial material was different than other networks, and the bumpers they used to separate their shows and advertisements often broke the fourth wall, addressing the audience through simple white text on a black background.[30]

Number One in the Hood G:
Hip-Hop Continues to Help the Network Grow

As discussed above, hip-hop seemed to be one of the avenues that Cartoon Network/Adult Swim utilized to help infuse non-white culture into the network. Hip-hop and rap has been consistently appropriated, even in animation, exemplified by shows like *HammerTime* that broke the genre down into the most stereotypical form possible. Adult Swim at least offered a forum for the music while also providing evidence that more modern music, particularly hip-hop, could complement contemporary animation of all types, from comedies to drama to adventure. Historically, hip-hop and rap has been utilized to challenge societal norms, including systemic racism. The generation of adult animation initiated by *The Simpsons* took on many societal issues head-on, although the continued white domination of animation through the 1990s and 2000s limited deeper level examination of racial issues. In spite of the limited racial interventions, the willingness to question the status quo and the popularity of hip-hop among younger demographics created a natural connection between Adult Swim and hip-hop.[31] In addition, although their representation within animation has been very limited, Blacks have long been consumers of animation and anime, strengthening the connection between the genres.[32]

Adult Swim and Williams Street dove even deeper into their connection with hip-hop a few years after Adult Swim launched as a programming block in 2001. DeMarco bought a record produced by hip-hop artist Pelican City, whose off-stage name was Brian Burton and who now performs as Danger Mouse. The executive wanted to include music from the album in the *Toonami* block he helped create. He called Burton who gave him a list of hip-hop artists who might also be interested in having their music on the network. Danger Mouse suggested that MF DOOM, whom he was collaborating with as Danger Doom, might be interested as an animation fan in contributing.

Their first album together, *The Mouse and the Mask*, on which DeMarco was credited as executive producer, sampled sounds from Adult Swim shows and reached number two on *Billboard's* U.S. Independent Albums chart. In 2007, DeMarco started Williams Street Records and Adult Swim, which was designated as its own network similar to Nick at Nite in 2005, started accepting submissions, including from Los Angeles DJ Flying Lotus. DeMarco started the Singles Program in 2009, which made the music of independent artists, from hip-hop, electronic, rock, and other genres, available free through the Adult Swim website, promoting the artists and songs on both the network and its website. Two years later, DeMarco introduced Killer Mike and El-P who formed Run the Jewels, a highly regarded independent hip-hop act that have produced four albums while maintaining a close connection to the network.[33]

Independent musicians, especially in hip-hop, often have a difficult time getting their work disseminated, particularly after the Telecommunications Act of 1996 removed ownership limits for radio station owners, leading Clear Channel (now iHeartMedia) and other conglomerates to rush to purchase stations throughout the country. This consolidation of the industry and elimination of independent local stations in many major markets led to a reduction of alternative and hip-hop stations. With fewer outlets to get independent music heard, the network continues to be a national platform for independent artists.[34]

Swimming into the Future

Adult Swim's official launch in 2001 was in many ways a final sign that Cartoon Network was ready to move on to a new era, hoping to evolve past its reputation as a broadcaster of (very) old cartoons into a leader in the animation industry, particularly on television, a legacy carried over from Hanna-Barbera. The launch of Boomerang the previous year was truly the start of this transition, and within the next year Hanna-Barbera was fully absorbed into Cartoon Network Studios, which had actually been established as a subsidiary of the legendary television animation studio. The decision was made after William Hanna passed away from throat cancer on March 22, 2001; the last production from Hanna-Barbera was fittingly a *Tom and Jerry* short, *The Mansion Cat*. In a true sign of the new era, the short premiered on Boomerang, the only Hanna-Barbera *Tom and Jerry* short to do so in the history of the studio and the network. Barbera continued to contribute to Cartoon Network and Turner, consulting on *Scooby-Doo* (2002), a feature-length live-action film that Hanna had also consulted on before his death, seeing the talking Great Dane brought to life with CGI. Throughout the rest of his life, Barbera was most involved in series and films featuring the popular characters from the studio he presided over, including two animated series starring the Mystery Inc. crew and a *Tom and Jerry* series. The last film Barbera wrote and directed, *The Karate Guard*, in which he constructed the storyboard with longtime colleague Iwao Takamoto, had a limited release in theaters and premiered on broadcast television through Kids WB in October 2005 before its debut on Cartoon Network in early 2006. *The Tom and Jerry Tales* premiered in September 2006 also on Kids WB, three months before Barbera's death, representing the last projected he was credited on while alive. Takamoto passed away three weeks after Barbera, officially ending the Hanna-Barbera era at the network although the characters live on in reruns and reboots.[35]

By the time Barbera and Takamoto passed away, the Hanna-Barbera name had existed only in archives for over five years, with new content featuring the former animated television studio's cast of characters distributed under the Warner or Cartoon Network brand. This increased the separation between the two men most responsible for the Hanna-Barbera catalogue and the media company that now oversaw their properties. Recognizing the legacy of the studio that distributed more television animation than any other American media company across their four decades in operation helps in piecing together the true history of American communication, not just the narrative produced by the mostly white men in power. This reveals both the positive and negative aspects of their influence not only in animation, but also in television and media. The narrative of media history, like the histories of many other industries, is presented as a smooth, linear progression with constant advancements by white men. However, the development of media and television, like American history as a whole, has been bumpy with consistent setbacks, exclusions, and even exploitation as representations and ideas have typically supported those in power. Media content, like television, is a powerful communication tool that ideally should be used to inform and represent. Often it has been utilized to exclude by only presenting the narratives and perspectives of a dominant class. Viewers are exposed to these ideologies from a very young age as perceptions concerning appropriate content are built around avoiding certain language and mature content and not necessarily representing a more equal or fair world.[36]

No media entity operates in a vacuum, and Hanna-Barbera's place and influence in the annals of film, television, and media history cannot be overlooked just because some may feel their content was low quality or that children's programming and/or cartoons do not deserve the attention. This programming that influenced generations of children, and adults, needs to be analyzed if we want to construct a complete history, which includes the negative aspects of their productions. Past content influenced the perspectives of those currently in power while contemporary content will influence the same in future generations. We are finally seeing some impact from this analysis and criticism as popular shows respond to their use of white actors to voice non-white characters and the lack of representation on their shows and behind the scenes.[37]

The vast amount of programming Hanna and Barbera disseminated continues to have an immeasurable impact on generations of children, and to ignore that influence on the lives of millions while shaping the television, animation, and children's media industries would be irresponsible for any historian or researcher whose work even touches

Yogi Bear, Justin Timberlake, and Boo Boo at the premiere of the live-action/computer-animated film *Yogi Bear* on December 11, 2010. Timberlake voiced Boo-Boo for the film (DFree/Shutterstock.com).

upon any of these areas. *The Jetsons*, a show that aired for one season over fifty years ago, continues to represent many baby boomers' vision for the future, while reboots of franchises like *Scooby-Doo* also keep older productions in the public consciousness.[38] Hopefully, this research not only increases research on Hanna-Barbera but all the other entities that have been ignored or overlooked as a location for truly critical historical media work due to their perceived quality or age. Organizations or actors from earlier periods of media both in America and around the world before media studies, television studies, and other disciplines were established are being overlooked as attention is turned toward quickly emerging digital technologies and media. Revealing and critically engaging with media practices and policies from the past can help us better navigate the various issues we continue to face in our current media environment.

Conclusion:
Growth Does Not Mean Progress

Billion Dollar Animation and Representation

Disney and Warner are often thought of as the legacy studios in animation, leading the industry from the beginning of the Golden Age, but this revisionist history erases not only each company's periods of struggle, including the strike and near bankruptcy of Disney in the 1940s and Warner's shutdown in the 1960s, but also the contributions of other animators who helped shape and maintain the industry. Beginning less than a decade after the premiere of *Steamboat Willie* ushered in this Golden Age of animation, William Hanna and Joseph Barbera's careers spanned over eight decades beginning near the peak of the Golden Age, helping the era extend into the 1950s while working for MGM. As visionaries, they saw the future of animation in television, and although some look down at this era of the industry due to the decline of theatrical animation, Hanna-Barbera created some of the most iconic characters and cartoons between the 1950s and 1980s. They helped establish both primetime animation and Saturday morning, becoming synonymous with the latter, which was the main forum for dissemination of cartoons for generations of children and animation fans. As they neared the end of their careers, they further established another market for animation, cable television, becoming the foundation for the first 24-hour animation network.[1] Their experience in television animation contributed to the expansion of the industry as Cartoon Network, with the involvement of Hanna-Barbera, joined Nickelodeon and Disney in producing animation for their networks. Along with the work of Fred Seibert and young animators, they helped Cartoon Network and Adult Swim become top ten networks in the Nielsen ratings.[2]

As the industry continues to experience an era of financial success including franchises surpassing a billion dollars annually, it is important to have a complete understanding of the art form and industry, positive and negative, beyond the narrative of progress often presented by undetailed or biased histories.[3] These histories are often written by industry insiders whose perspective frequently lacks a critical eye. Building a complete history of any entity, medium, or phenomenon includes recognizing both the advancements and the policies and circumstances that supported these advancements. This includes the creation and maintenance of certain ideologies and representations that rely on the promotion of white male heteropatriarchal capitalism. Reasons for this beyond the maintenance of privilege include a lack of diversity behind the scenes and the reliance on outdated tropes or formulas due to the cartoon producers' use of parody and satire and the need to have an audience that is familiar with the source material for the humor.[4] This has created a whitewashed and discriminatory environment for animation, even compared to other media. Even the smallest progression in the representation of non-whites, non-males, and even those socioeconomically living below what is considered middle or upper class is celebrated in an industry that continues to limit the diversity of representations in its content. Analyzing all the content from all animators, not just the successful properties from the biggest studios still in operation, would be a big step in fully understanding both the animation industry and media as a whole.

Inclusivity in the Exclusive Business of Animation

Even when examining a media producer and disseminator that is thought of as progressive in the industry, like Williams Street or Adult Swim, corporate interests and profits often override the desire to include more voices, which is an especially restrictive situation for animation, whose high production and distribution costs often limit the creation of animated content to large corporations that have the resources to support these costs. Not wanting to upset the status quo or repulse the current audience, corporate considerations have frequently blocked attempts to distribute content that represents the experience of a wider group of voices, especially if it contrasts with messages currently being promoted by the larger company.

For example, *The Boondocks*, based on the popular if controversial comic strip of the same name created by Aaron McGruder, premiered on Adult Swim in 2005, and in 2007 two episodes from the second season were removed from broadcast without official comment from the network, Turner, or Time Warner. It was revealed later that Viacom, owner of BET, which was heavily criticized in both episodes for their portrayal of African Americans on their network, especially after it was sold to the conglomerate, threatened distributor Sony Pictures with a lawsuit if the episodes ran on the network. The final straw for McGruder came during the third season when he again was threatened with censorship after Tyler Perry, who had several shows airing on Turner networks, complained about a parody of him in a 2010 episode of the series. McGruder left the show, leading to a fourth and last season for the show without the creator and artist who gave voice to Huey, Riley, and Grandad Freeman.[5]

The Boondocks had a theme song produced by hip-hop artist Asharu that supported a score grounded in the musical genre. Hip-hop continues to be one of few sources of non-white voices in animation. Although the music has maintained a constant presence on the network, there was a clear dearth of animation created by and representing African Americans over the last few years, particularly after the cancellation of *The Boondocks* in 2014. It was announced in the spring of 2017 that Adult Swim had picked up rapper Tyler, the Creator's new series *The Jellies!* which follows an African American lead character who learns he was adopted by a family of jellyfish, going on a journey of self-discovery.[6] Tyler, who is Black and composes music for the series, was actually asked why the lead character was Black at San Diego Comic Con and discussed the popularity of animation among children of color even though they are extremely underrepresented within the genre.[7] Although the involvement of more companies and the need for content to fill the schedules of these networks has created some progression in terms of both inclusion behind the pen along with representation on the screen, the status quo continues to influence not only the content media companies are willing to support but the perspective of the audience about what is accepted or tolerated in animated content. This perspective often leads to shows whose stars and casts are primarily white or represent whiteness. Interactions like Tyler experienced at Comic Con are not new or unique for animation but are evidence about the amount of work it will take to shift how producers operate, especially considering the fact that the audience, whom they need to buy or consume their product, often expect to see characters representing whiteness. Many of the characters have existed for generations, and long held perspective, formulas, and tropes from the past continue to inform animation today, and fans often react negatively when the race of a treasured character is questioned or changed.[8]

The blackface-inspired Mickey Mouse continues to be one of the most recognizable icons in the world. As a result, the question remains: Can animation ever remove itself from its minstrel origins, and if so, how long will it take? Companies continue to profit from characters that celebrated Jim Crow and segregation and were developed in a media environment with even less awareness and inclusivity than we experience in American media today.

We have some outlying examples of this representation progress from *Fat Albert* to *Dora the Explorer* and *Doc McStuffins*, but moving forward, the industry will have to figure out if they want to continue to profit from the influence of art and humor presented in animation of the past. It is unlikely they will abandon any content that produces revenue, so then will they provide the appropriate contextual understanding of the societal conditions under which it was produced? Can animators move beyond the traditional representations, tropes, and talent-scouting structure that continue to create an animation environment dominated by white males?

Cartoon Network has made noticeable progress in the representation of gender, sexuality, and family as a number of current shows portray non-heterosexual relationships and non-traditional family structures. *Ben 10*, the network's longest running original series, features Ben Tennyson and his cousin who are on a road trip throughout the several iterations of the franchise and both are primarily cared for by their grandfather. *The Amazing World of Gumball* features a cross-species relationship between a pink rabbit father, Richard, and the blue cat mother, Nicole, who have three children including an adopted fish son. Another example is *Clarence*, which ended production in 2018 after three seasons, that portrays Clarence as a child of a single mother whose best friend Jeff has lesbian mothers, both of which are voiced by actors who identify as lesbians. Much like in the non-animated world, however, intersectional characters are hard to find since "alternative" lifestyles, or those that do not fulfill heteropatriarchal expectations, are more accepted among white communities. Also, attraction and relationships between younger cartoon characters are, until recently, almost exclusively heteronormative in animation aimed at audience members represented by the characters.

A Century Later: Non-Male Animators Are Recognized

This problem is also prevalent when it comes to gender, as the male perspective continues to dominate animation on screen and behind the pen. Brenda Chapman was the first female to direct a major animated feature film when Dreamworks' *The Prince of Egypt* was released in 1998, later becoming the first female to direct the Academy Award Winner for Best Animated Feature, *Brave*. Although Pixar, the production company behind *Brave*, and others have made small steps to try to address both the lack of representation on the screen and lack of gender diversity behind the scenes, they still struggle to represent gender equally. This is partially due to the preconceived notions of media companies about women consuming animation. When media companies do support female animators, fans may lash out at networks and media producers for presenting a female view or address the misogyny in the content.[9]

Adult Swim, as a leader in animation outside of the mainstream, is expected by some to facilitate progress in these areas, but most shows continue to star male characters backed by male producers. Dan Harmon, co-creator of one of Adult Swim's top shows, *Rick and Morty*, made an effort to hire more female writers and feature more female-led storylines for the show's third season. Similar to the harassment faced by women in the wake of the Gamergate scandal, several of the new writers were threatened, slandered, and even doxxed through social media as anonymous "fans" of the shows used the internet to assault these writers and animators. The animation industry is not solely responsible for supporting feminism in its content, but considering how it has so long been a male space, like comics and video games, animation producers and broadcasters like Adult Swim are in a unique place. They can push back against this misogynistic discrimination and influence millions who have been indoctrinated in, and seek to protect, white male heteropatriarchial values.[10]

Challenges to these values have occurred in recent years, including instances on Cartoon Network and Adult Swim along with several streaming services. Cartoon Network's *Steven Universe* has been celebrated for its inclusive storylines and characters. On the series Steven works with three humanoid aliens called Gems to protect the world. In a nod to classical mythology, Steven is half Gem but unlike the original myths, all the Gems identify as female. Rebecca Sugar, who identifies as a bisexual non-binary woman, originally worked on another critically acclaimed Cartoon Network series, *Adventure Time*, and was the first female to solely create a series for the network. The series has been nominated for numerous awards and was the first animated series to win the GLAAD award for Outstanding Kids & Family Program. It is also celebrated for featuring female superheroes in starring roles with all three Gems voiced by women of color. In 2018, the series was the first animated children's program to feature a same-sex marriage proposal.[11]

Even over a decade after the death of Joseph Barbera, these issues continue to hold relevance for Hanna-Barbera properties as their creations are considered for future projects and reboots. In 2017, Boomerang launched as an over-the-top streaming service offering on-demand viewing of Hanna-Barbera and Warner cartoons, many of which premiered between the 1960s and 1980s, allowing the network, which is marketed to children, to help older cartoon characters like Yogi Bear and Tom and Jerry remain in the public consciousness through the growing streaming market. Warner recently began creating new and rebooted series for the service, including new episodes of *Wacky Races*. Warner Bros. Animation also regularly produces direct-to-video films starring *The Flintstones* and other characters while Cartoon Network and Adult Swim still produce and rerun more contemporary programs featuring members of Hanna-Barbera's stable of stars like *Scooby-Doo* and *Space Ghost*. These films and series also appear on the network, along with rebooted series starring *Tom and Jerry* and other Hanna-Barbera creations, with these programs continuing to help Cartoon Network remain one of the top viewed daytime networks in America. Similarly, Adult Swim, whose foundation was built on deconstructed Hanna-Barbera series and characters, is now among the top networks among the 18–34 and 18–49 groups, leading the ratings among these valuable demographics for several seasons.[12]

What Is Next for the Hanna-Barbera Stars

As Warner and Cartoon Network look forward, there are more changes on the horizon. A merger between Time Warner and AT&T, which already oversees DirecTV, created an even larger media conglomerate with a footprint in wireless communication as the media prepared for another round of consolidation under the Trump Administration. The newly created WarnerMedia also launched the streaming service HBO Max in May 2020, featuring thousands of hours of content from their many subsidiaries and properties, including series from Cartoon Network, Adult Swim, and series produced by Hanna-Barbera like *The Flintstones*.[13]

Also maintaining an international presence, another early Hanna-Barbera creation, *Top Cat*, regularly appears in direct-to-video releases of variable quality. After the successful theatrical release of *Top Cat* in 2011 produced by the Mexican studio Anima Estudios and Argentinian Illusion Studios the feline maintains his popularity outside of the U.S., especially in Latin America.[14] In fact, several Hanna-Barbera and Warner properties continue to maintain high levels of popularity in Latin American countries and Europe, including *Speedy Gonzales* in Mexico. The company even rebranded Boomerang around the world in 2014, a year before doing the same in the United States, reinforcing the importance of the international market for animation.[15]

The Boomerang network, as previously discussed, has a big international following and has launched several new shows, including *The Tom and Jerry Show*, through the streaming service.[16] Outside of Boomerang direct-to-video, specials were the most likely place audiences would see new content featuring characters created by Hanna-Barbera. Scooby-Doo starred in several of these specials, teaming up with

HBO Max: The streaming service, launched May 27, 2020, is serving as another platform for Hanna-Barbera's various properties (Daniel Constante/Shutterstock.com).

brands like Lego and World Wrestling Entertainment as an attempt to create crossover appeal.

The Jetsons also may make their return to network television in a Robert Zemeckis live-action multi-camera sitcom whose pilot was in production as of 2019.[17] It has also been reported that Elizabeth Banks and Brownstone entertainment were working on a reboot of *The Flintstones* aimed at an adult audience.[18] Yogi Bear and most of the cast from *Yogi's Gang* will also make his return in the series *Jellystone!* which started production in 2020. Streaming has seemed to open opportunities to revitalized the Hanna-Barbera properties with both *The Flintstones* and *Jellystone!* likely airing on HBO Max. Comics have also reemerged as a platform with a number of Hanna-Barbera characters receiving their own series. DC Entertainment, also owned by WarnerMedia, has adapted several series starring characters like Scooby-Doo and the Wacky Racers, reimagining the casts in more realistic and graphic situations.[19]

Warner Bros. Animation is also hoping one of Hanna-Barbera's most popular characters of all time, Scooby-Doo, can initiate the theatrical future. The Great Dane starred in an animated feature in 2020, which Warner is hoping will revitalize interest in a number of Hanna-Barbera characters on the silver screen.[20] Through *Scoob!* Warner hopes to launch a Warner/Hanna-Barbera theatrical universe that connects a number of properties through feature films, creating a comedic animated version of the Marvel superhero universe spearheaded by the comic/entertainment company and its parent company, Disney.[21] Due to the COVID-19 pandemic, *Scoob!* premiered on video on demand featuring all members of Mystery Inc. while also reintroducing audiences to other Hanna-Barbera characters like Captain Caveman, Dick Dasterdly, Dynomutt and the Blue Falcon. Although it received mixed critical reviews, the development of a sequel was announced in 2021.[22]

The immortality of these properties and the ability to update content featuring the characters allows them to never fully disappear, even when they are occasionally forgotten. The consistent presence of many of these characters over time only

Promotional poster for *Scoob!*, released for digital download May 15, 2020 (BFA/Alamy Stock Photo)

increases the importance of understanding the motivations and inspirations for animation even after the original content ceases production or their creators leave the industry. The pursuit of profit creates constant opportunity for the rebirth of these characters, often bringing back past content, representations, and ideologies. The latest Tom and Jerry series may have eliminated many of the negative portrayals from the original theatrical shorts, but the presentation of these older shorts continues, buoyed by the presence of the cat and mouse on Cartoon Network, Boomerang, and HBO Max. These films still contain some of these negative representations, prompting warnings from Amazon and others, which were met with criticism about political correctness from fans wanting to see the uncensored violence and racism in the films.[23]

The ability to dub and tweak animation for different markets, cultures, and languages also helps it continue to remain in the public's consciousness around the world. Live-action content does not transition internationally as well as animation due to the awkwardness of voice dubbing, and the increased difficulty in editing the content for a particular culture or non–American nation, which is why action films with minimal dialogue are among the best performers in the international box office.[24]

Fandom and affection for past portrayals of the character also increases the difficulty for even new producers to shift the direction or representations in the property. For example, if *The Flintstones* were rebooted, would Bedrock, let alone the family, represent more inclusivity and diversity? Or, would the canon created by the original six-season series and the several spin-offs be too much to overcome if a producer wanted a legendary character like Fred or Yogi to not be white and better represent America as it truly is, not how certain populations, particularly white males, see it? Several other genres and industries, including comic books and media inspired by comic characters, are dealing with similar issues as producers and conglomerates, like Marvel/Disney, try to adjust characters who were created in even less inclusive artistic and social environments so they fit within contemporary sensibilities. For example, multiple producers who have worked on iterations of the Scooby-Doo franchise have discussed attempts to present Velma as gay, including James Gunn who wrote the Scooby-Doo live-action film in 2002 and its sequel in 2004. Gunn confirmed he wrote Velma to be explicitly gay before the studio blocked it. Tony Cervone, who developed the 2010 series *Scooby-Doo! Mystery Incorporated* and has worked on a number of Scooby-Doo productions with frequent writing partner Spike Brandt including the 2020 movie, also confirmed Velma was gay in a response to a fan who said Velma's identification as LGBTQ+ was against the franchise's canon.[25]

The producers and media companies want to appear more aware about the impact of representation but are often held back by many fans who are turned off by any changes that deviate too far from the source material or content. Although it is easy to point to animation and hope it becomes more inclusive, it is part of a complex system that ultimately tries to maximize revenues from mainstream commodities supported by the profit structure politically and economically supported by the capitalist system. The mainstream has historically been represented through whiteness, and others are either targeted through niche media or expected to adapt to this environment.[26]

As studios, properties, and brands like Hanna-Barbera are obscured or lost in the complex organization created by the mass consolidation of the media that has led to a few corporations controlling the vast majority of content, particularly in America, we must also recognize how we got here and reveal influential entities. Many of these names are disappearing from public consciousness as these properties become absorbed into the new company. In the last 30 years alone, Hanna-Barbera has been bought by Turner, which merged with Time-Warner in 1996 created by a merger three years earlier. Time-Warner was bought by AOL in 2000 before AOL was spun off from the company in 2009 and then Warner did the same to Time Publishing five years later. Finally, AT&T merged with Warner in 2017, creating WarnerMedia, consolidating Warner and its subsidiaries under the telecommunication giant.

Even as the studio is buried under this avalanche of conglomeration, the huge impact on not only how animation, but media as a whole, is created, marketed, and distributed cannot be ignored. Hanna-Barbera worked through limited resources, uncertain executives, and audience perceptions to make the studio one of the most influential production studios in the history of television. As television and visual media as a whole shift as a result of new delivery paths created by the digitization of content, we must understand the past mistakes and successes in these industries to avoid creating the same shortcomings and limitations, especially as they relate to how society is represented and culture is communicated.

Chapter Notes

Introduction

1. Michael Barrier, *Hollywood Cartoons: American Animation in Its Golden Age* (New York: Oxford University Press, 1999), 190.

2. Dan Webster, "Hanna Time Bill Hanna Partnered with Joe Barbera, Has Earned the Love of Children of All Ages with His Animated Characters," *The Spokesman-Review,* July 15, 1996, http://www.spokesman.com/stories/1996/jul/15/hanna-time-bill-hanna-partnered-with-joe-barbera/. As a result of media consolidation during the 1990s Hanna-Barbera was eventually acquired by Warner Bros.

3. Jerry Beck, *The Hanna Barbera Treasury: Rare Art and Mementos from Your Favorite Cartoon Classics* (New York, Insight Editions, 2007), 5–6.

4. Heather E. Harris, "Queen Phiona and Princess Shuri—Alternative Africana 'Royalty' in Disney's Royal Realm: An Intersectional Analysis," *Social Sciences* 7, 10, 206, https://doi.org/10.3390/socsci7100206.

5. Christopher P. Lehman, *American Cartoons of the Vietnam Era: A Study of Social Commentary in Film and Television 1961–1975* (Jefferson, NC: McFarland, 2007), 90.

6. Bryan Cairns, "Scoob! Writer Explains the Maybe-Origins of the Hanna-Barbera Cinematic Universe," *SyFy,* May 20, 2020, https://www.syfy.com/syfywire/scoob-scooby-doo-franchise-screenwriter-free-guy-interview.

7. Megh Wright, "Brett Gelman Explains His Decision to Cut Ties with Adult Swim," *Vulture,* November 14, 2016, https://www.vulture.com/2016/11/brett-gelman-explains-his-decision-to-cut-ties-with-adult-swim.html.

8. Claire Suddath, "A Brief History of Mickey Mouse," *Time,* November 18, 2008, http://content.time.com/time/arts/article/0,8599,1859935,00.html.

9. Barrier, *Hollywood Cartoons,* 547.

10. Karl F. Cohen, *Forbidden Animation: Censored Cartoons and Blacklisted Animators in America* (Jefferson, NC: McFarland, 1997), 22–23.

11. Richard M. Breaux, "It's a Cartoon! The Jackson 5ive as Commodified Black Power and Civil Rights Ideologies," *The Journal of Pan-African Studies* 3 (2010), 84.

12. Donald Crafton, *Shadow of a Mouse: Performance, Belief, and World-Making in Animation* (Berkeley: University of California Press, 2012), 27.

13. *Internet Movie Database*, "Episode Cast for 'The Tom and Jerry Show,'" http://www.imdb.com/title/tt3559124/epcast. Warner continues to use old recordings of Hanna's voice for Tom and Jerry in recent series.

14. Richard J. Leskosky, "The Reforming Fantasy: Recurrent Theme and Structure in American Studio Cartoons," *The Velvet Light Trap* 24 (Fall 1989), https://search.proquest.com/docview/1306639612/citation/6DC307A463004878PQ/1?accountid=14503.

15. Susan Ohmer, *George Gallup in Hollywood* (New York: Columbia University Press, 2006) 207.

16. Nicole Laport, "Disney And Pixar Fight to Rule The Mouse House," *Fast Company,* June 20, 2016, https://www.fastcompany.com/3060475/disney-andpixar-fight-to-be-the-mouse-house-animation-alpha-pluto.

17. Lisa Belkin, "Why Kids Watch Movies Again and Again," *The New York Times,* November 12, 2009, https://parenting.blogs.nytimes.com/2009/11/12/kids-and-movies/.

18. Ted Sennett, *The Art of Hanna-Barbera: Fifty Years of Creativity* (New York: Viking Studio Books, 1991), 79.

19. Jerry Beck, *The Flintstones: The Official Guide to the Cartoon Series* (New York: Running Press, 2011), 11.

20. Jessica Gelt, "200 Years of Authenticity (or lack thereof) in Casting," *Los Angeles Times* July 13, 2017, http://www.latimes.com/entertainment/arts/la-ca-cm-authenticity-casting-timeline-20170713-htmlstory.html.

21. Leonard Maltin, *Of Mice and Magic: A History of American Animated Cartoons* (New York: Penguin, 1987), 5.

22. Thomas Lamarre, "The Biopolitics of Companion Species: Wartime Animation and Multi-Ethnic Nationalism," from *The Politics of Culture: Around the Work of Naoki Sakai,* edited by Richard Calichman and John Namjun Kim (New York: Routledge, 2010), 81.

23. C. Richard King, Carmen R. Lugo-Lugo, Mary K. Bloodsworth-Lugo, *Animating Difference: Race, Gender, and Sexuality in Contemporary Films for Children* (Lanham, MD: Rowland & Littlefield, 2010), 18.

24. Maltin, *Of Mice and Magic,* 3.

25. Motion Picture Association of America,

"Theatrical Market Statistics: 2016," http://www.mpaa.org/wp-content/uploads/2017/03/MPAA-Theatrical-Market-Statistics-2016_Final.pdf; Amid Amidi, "47 Animated Feature Films to Look For in 2017," *Cartoon Brew,* December, 28, 2015, http://www.cartoonbrew.com/feature-film/47-animated-feature-films-in-2016-preview-126197.html. Comcast now owns Dreamworks along with NBC/Universal.

26. Souad Belkhyr, "Disney Animation: Global Diffusion and Local Appropriation of Culture," *Etudes Caribeenes* 22 (August 2012), https://etudescaribeennes.revues.org/5863?lang=en.

27. Chyng Feng Sun and Erica Scharrer, "Staying True to Disney: College Students' Resistance to Criticism of the Little Mermaid," *Communication Review 7,* no. 1 (2010), http://www.tandfonline.com/doi/abs/10.1080/10714420490280189.

28. Jayne Pilling, "Intro," *Reader in Animation Studies,* edited by Jayne Pilling (London: John Libbey, 1997), ix–xi.

29. David Perlmutter, *America Toons In: A History of Television Animation* (Jefferson, NC: McFarland, 2014), 3–5.

30. *Ibid.,* xi–xiii.

31. Evelyn Arizpe and Moag Styles, "Children Reading at Home: A Historical Overview," *Handbook of Research on Children's and Young Adult Literature,* edited by Shelby Wolf, Karen Coats, Patricia A. Enciso, and Christine Jenkins (New York: Taylor & Francis, 2011), 4–5.

32. Ellen Wartella and Byron Reeves, "Historical Trends in Research on Children and the Media: 1900–1960," *Journal of Communication* 35, no. 2 (1985), 120–125.

33. Jonathan Gray and Amanda Lotz, *Television Studies* (Malden, MA: Polity, 2012), 9–10.

34. Paul Lazarsfeld and Robert Merton, "Mass Communication, Popular Taste and Organized Social Action," *The Process and Effects of Mass Communication,* revised edition, edited by Wilbur Schramm and Donald F. Roberts (Urbana: University of Illinois Press, 1971), 554–578.

35. Julia da Silvia, "Children and Electronic Media: How Much Is Too Much?" American Psychological Association, June 2015, https://www.apa.org/pi/about/newsletter/2015/06/electronic-media.

36. Audra Wolfe, "Project Troy: How Scientists Helped Refine Cold War Psychological Warfare," *The Atlantic,* December 1, 2018, https://www.theatlantic.com/science/archive/2018/12/project-troy-science-cold-war-psychological-warfare/576847/.

37. Scott Stossel, "The Man Who Counts the Killing," *The Atlantic,* May 1997, https://www.theatlantic.com/magazine/archive/1997/05/the-man-who-counts-the-killings/376850/.

38. James W. Carey, "Some Personal Notes on U.S. Journalism Education," *Journalism* 1, no. 1 (2000), http://journals.sagepub.com/doi/abs/10.1177/146488490000100103.

39. David L. Altheide, "Media Hegemony: A "Failure of Perspective," *Public Opinion Quarterly* 48, no. 2 (January 1984), https://doi.org/10.1086/268844.

40. Sut Jhally, "George Gerbner on Media and Culture," *The Electronic Storyteller: Television & The Cultivation of Values,* Media Education Foundation, 2009, http://www.mediaed.org/transcripts/The-Electronic-Storyteller-Transcript.pdf.

41. Michael Curtin, "Beyond the Vast Wasteland: The Policy Discourse of Global Television and the Politics of American Empire," *Journal of Broadcasting and Electric Media* 37, no. 2 (1993), https://doi.org/10.1080/08838159309364211.

42. Renee Hobbs and Amy Jensen, "The Past, Present, and Future of Media Literacy Education," *The Journal of Media Literacy Education* 1, no. 1 (2009), https://digitalcommons.uri.edu/jmle/vol1/iss1/1/.

43. John Fiske, *Television Culture* (New York: Routledge, 2011), 88.

44. Stuart Hall, "Encoding and Decoding," *The Cultural Studies Reader,* edited by Simon During (New York: Routledge, 2007), 480.

45. Tanja Thomas and Merle-Marie Kruse, "Cultural Studies," *The International Encyclopedia of Political Communication,* January 2016, http://onlinelibrary.wiley.com/doi/10.1002/9781118541555.wbiepc166/full.

46. Theodor Adorno and Max Horkheimer, "The Culture Industry: Enlightenment as Mass Deception," *The Cultural Studies Reader,* edited by Simon During (New York: Routledge, 2007), 407.

47. Horace Newcomb, "Television and the Present Climate of Criticism," *Television: The Critical View* (New York: Oxford University Press, 2000), 1–13.

48. Joe L. Kincheloe, "Says Who? Who Decides What is Art?" *Art, Culture, and Education: Artful Teaching in a Fractured Landscape,* edited by Karel Rose and Joe L. Kincheloe (New York: Peter Lang, 2004).

49. Bonnie J. Dow *Prime-Time Feminism* (Philadelphia: University of Pennsylvania Press, 1996), xv–xvi.

50. Thomas Doherty, "The Wonderful World of Disney Studies," *The Chronicle of Higher Education,* July 21, 2006, http://www.chronicle.com/article/The-Wonderful-World-of-Disney/9806.

51. Society of Animation Studies, https://www.animationstudies.org/v3/.

52. Paul Jones, "The Technology Is Not the Cultural Form? Raymond Williams Sociological Critique of Raymond Williams," *Canadian Journal of Communication* 23, no. 4 (1998), http://cjc-online.ca/index.php/journal/article/view/1058/964.

53. Ellen Seiter, "Different Children, Different Dreams: Racial Representation in Advertising 1," *Journal of Communication Inquiry* 14, no. 1 (1990): 31–47. E

54. Jonathan Starck and Adrian Hilton, "Surface Capture for Performance Based Animation" *IEEE Computer Graphics and Application* 27, no. 3 (2007), http://ieeexplore.ieee.org/abstract/document/4178157/?reload=true.

55. Crafton, *Shadow of a Mouse,* 4–6.

56. W.E.B. Du Bois, *Black Reconstruction in America, 1860–1880* (New York: Free Press, 1995), pp. 700–701.

57. Phil Chidester, "'Respect My Authori-tah':

South Park and the Fragmentation/Reification of Whiteness," *Critical Studies in Media Communication* 29, no. 5 (2012), 403–420, http://nca.tandfonline.com/doi/abs/10.1080/15295036.2012.676192.

58. Judith Butler, *Gender Trouble: Feminism and the Subversion of Identity* (New York: Routledge, 1990), 33–35.

59. Teri Silvio, "Animation: The New Performance?" *Journal of Linguistic Anthropology* 20, no. 2 (2010): 422–438.

60. Patricia J. Williams, "Metro Broadcasting, Inc vs. FCC: Regrouping in Singular Times," 191–204, *Critical Race Theory: The Key Writings That Formed a Movement*, edited by Kimberle Crenshaw, Neil Gotanda, Gary Peller, Kendall Thomas (New York: The New Press, 1995), Introduction, xiii–xxxii.

61. Inés Galiano Torres, "Audience's Perception of Cultural/Ethnic Stereotypes in TV Shows," *European Scientific Journal* 11, no. 10 (2015).

62. Monica Biernat and Diane Kobrynowicz, "Gender- and Race Based Standards of Competence: Lower Minimum Standards but Higher Ability Standards for Devalued Groups," *Journal of Personality and Social Psychology* 72, no. 3 (1997): 544–557, http://dx.doi.org/10.1037/0022-3514.72.3.544.

63. Michaela D. E. Meyer, "Representing Bisexuality on Television: The Case for Intersectional Hybrids," *Journal of Bisexuality* 10, no. 4 (2010), 366–387, http://www.tandfonline.com/doi/abs/10.1080/15299716.2010.521040.

64. Walter Mignolo, *The Darker Side of Western Modernity: Global Futures, Decolonial Options* (Durham: Duke University Press, 2011), 2–3.

65. Frantz Fanon, *Black Skin, White Masks* (New York: Grove, 2008), 124–126.

66. Edward Said, *Orientalism* (New York: Random House, 1994), 26.

67. Chandra Talpade Mohanty, "'Under Western Eyes' Revisited: Feminist Solidarity through Anticapitalist Struggles," *Signs* 28, no. 2 (2003), 499–535.

68. Reiland Rabaka, *Against Academic Apartheid* (Plymouth, UK: Lexington Books, 2010), 35–28.

69. Sarah Begley, "Now There's a Class on the Philosophy of *The Simpsons*," *Time*, November 16, 2016, http://time.com/4573080/simpsons-philosophy-university-class/.

70. Nicholas Sammond, *Birth of an Industry: Blackface Minstrelsy and the Rise of Animation* (Durham: Duke University Press, 2015).

71. Nicholas Sammond, *Babes in Tomorrowland: Walt Disney and the Making of the American Childhood, 1930–1960* (Durham: Duke University Press, 2005).

72. Nicholas Sammond, "*Dumbo*, Disney, and Difference: Walt Disney Productions and Film as Children's Literature," *The Oxford Handbook of Children's Literature*, edited by Lynne Vallone and Julia Mickenberg (New York: Oxford University Press, 2011), https://www.oxfordhandbooks.com/view/10.1093/oxfordhb/9780195379785.001.0001/oxfordhb-9780195379785-e-8.

73. Nicholas Sammond, "Who Dat Say Who Dat? Racial Masquerade, Humor, and the Rise of American Animation," *Funny Pictures: Animation and Comedy in Studio-Era Animation*, edited by Daniel Ira Goldmark and Charles Kell (Berkeley: University of California Press, 2011), 129–152.

74. Jason Mittell, "The Great Saturday Morning Exile: Scheduling Cartoons on Television's Periphery in the 1960s," *Prime Time Animation: Television Animation and American Culture*, edited by Carol A. Stabile and Mark Harrison (New York: Routledge, 2003), 33–54.

75. Jason Mittell, *Genre and Television: From Cop Shows to Cartoons in American Culture* (New York: Routledge, 2004).

76. Jason Mittell, *Television and American Culture* (New York: Oxford University Press, 2010).

77. Robert McChesney, *The Problem of the Media: U.S. Communication Politics in the Twenty-First Century* (New York: Monthly Review, 2004).

78. Kevin Sandler, *Reading the Rabbit*, edited by Kevin Sandler (New Brunswick: Rutgers University Press, 1998).

79. Steve Goldstein, "ASU Scooby-Doo Scholar Unmasks 51 Years of Mysteries," *KJZZ*, June 5, 2020, https://kjzz.org/content/1589347/asu-scooby-doo-scholar-unmasks-51-years-mysteries. Due to the COVID-19 epidemic the film was released to streaming and on-demand platforms.

80. Maltin, *Of Mice and Magic*.

81. Barrier, *Hollywood Cartoons*.

82. Beck, *The Flintstones*, Beck, *The Hanna-Barbera Treasury*.

83. Hal Erickson, *Television Cartoon Shows: An Illustrated Encyclopedia 1949–2003* (Jefferson, NC: McFarland, 2005).

84. Hal Erickson, *Syndicated Television: The First Forty Years 1947–1987* (Jefferson, NC: McFarland, 2001).

85. Jeff Lenburg, *Encyclopedia of Animated Cartoons* (New York: Facts on File, 2008); David Perlmutter, *America Toons In: A History of Television Animation* (Jefferson, NC: McFarland, 2014); David Mansour, *From Abba to Zoom: A Pop Culture Encyclopedia of the Late 20th Centuries* (Kansas City: Andrews McMeel, 2005); Jeff Lenburg, *William Hanna and Joseph Barbera: The Sultans of Saturday Morning* (New York: Chelsea House, 2011).

86. Daniel Wickberg. "Heterosexual White Male: Some Recent Inversions in American Cultural History," *The Journal of American History* 92, no. 1 (2005): 136–157.

87. Collier Meyerson, "Fighting White Supremacy Means Owning Up to American History," *The Nation*, August 14, 2017, https://www.thenation.com/article/fighting-white-supremacy-means-owning-up-to-american-history/.

88. Joseph Barbera, *My Life in 'toons: From Flatbush to Bedrock in Under a Century* (Nashville: Turner, 1994); Bill Hanna and Tom Ito, *A Cast of Friends* (Dallas: Taylor, 1996), Iwao Takamoto and Michael Mallory, *Iwao Takamoto: My Life with a Thousand Characters* (Jackson: University of Mississippi, 2009).

89. Dhavan V. Shah, Douglas M. McLeod, Melissa R. Gotlieb, and Nam-Jin Lee, "Framing and Agenda Setting," *The Sage Handbook of Media Processes and Effects* (2009), 83–98.

90. Sasha Torres, *Black, White, and in Color: Television and Black Civil Rights* (Princeton: Princeton University Press, 2003).

91. "Public Broadcasting Act of 1967," Corporation for Public Broadcasting, https://www.cpb.org/aboutpb/act/.

92. Aniko Bodroghkozy, *Equal Time: Television and the Civil Rights Movement* (Urbana: University of Illinois Press, 2012).

93. Jennifer Barker, "Hollywood, Black Animation, and the Problem of Representation in 'Lil Ol' Bosko' and 'The Princess and the Frog,'" *Journal of African American Studies* 14, no. 4 (2010): 482–498; Jose Esteban Munoz, *Disidentifications: Queers of Color and the Performance of Politics* (Minneapolis: University of Minnesota Press, 1999).

94. Kevin Young, "Schomburg Center for Research in Black Culture Receives James Baldwin Letters," interview with Audie Cornish, NPR, April 13, 2017, http://www.npr.org/2017/04/13/523804448/schomburg-center-for-research-in-black-culture-receives-james-baldwin-letters.

95. bell hooks, *Reel to Real: Race, Sex, and Class at the Movies* (New York: Routledge, 2009), 3.

96. Todd Boyd, *African Americans and Popular Culture* (Westport, CT: Praeger, 2008).

97. Christopher P. Lehman, *The Colored Cartoon: Black Presentation in American Animated Shorts* (Amherst: University of Massachusetts Press, 2007).

98. Lehman, *American Cartoons of the Vietnam Era: A Study of Social Commentary in Film and Television 1961–1975* J(efferson, NC: McFarland, 2007).

99. Cohen, *Forbidden Animation*.

100. Lee Artz, "Animating Hierarchy: Disney and the Globalization of Capitalism," *Global Media Journal* 1, no. 1 (2002), http://www.globalmediajournal.com/open-access/animating-hierarchy-disney-and-the-globalization-of-capitalism.php?aid=35055; Teju Cole, "The White Savior Industrial Complex," *The Atlantic*, March 21, 2012, https://www.theatlantic.com/international/archive/2012/03/the-white-savior-industrial-complex/254843/.

101. Lee Artz, "Animating Transnational Capitalism," *Journal of Intercultural Communication Research* 44, no. 2 (2015), https://www.researchgate.net/publication/281936654_Animating_Transnational_Capitalism_Journal_of_Intercultural_Communication_Research_442_2015_93-107_DOI_1010801747575920151025817.

102. J. Halberstam, "Animating Revolt/Revolting Animation: Penguin Love, Doll Sex, and the Spectacle of the Queer Nonhuman," *Queering the Non/Human*, edited by Myra J. Hird and Noreen Giffney (New York: Routledge, 2016), 265–280.

103. W.E.B. Du Bois, *The Souls of Black Folks* (Chicago: Dover, 1994), 2; Frantz Fanon, *Black Skin, White Masks* (New York: Grove Press, 1967),123.

104. Angela M. Nelson, "African American Stereotypes in Prime-Time Television: An Overview, 1947–2007," *African Americans and Popular Culture Volume 1*, edited by Todd Boyd (Westport, CT: Praeger, 2008); Richard Delgado and Jean Stefancic, "Images of the Outside in American Law and Culture: Can Free Expression Remedy Systemic Social Ills?" *Critical Race Theory: The Cutting Edge*, editded by Richard Delgado and Jean Stefancic (Philadelphia: Temple University Press, 2000).

105. Glenn A Bowen, "Document Analysis as a Qualitative Research Method," *Qualitative Research Journal* 9, no. 2 (2009): 27–40, https://www.academia.edu/8434566/Document_Analysis_as_a_Qualitative_Research_Method.

106. *Ibid.*, 29.

107. *Ibid.*, 29–31.

Chapter 1

1. Michael Barrier, *Hollywood Cartoons: American Animation in its Golden Age* (New York: Oxford University Press, 1999), 155. Harman and Ising started their careers at Walt Disney's Kansas City studio in the 1920s before Disney moved to California.

2. Scott Thill, "'*Peace on Earth* is 75 years Later-and More Relevant than Ever," *Cartoon Brews*, December 24, 2014, http://www.cartoonbrew.com/ideas-commentary/peace-on-earth-is-75-years-old-and-more-relevant-than-ever-107274.html.

3. Joseph Barbera, *My Life in 'toons: From Flatbush to Bedrock in Under a Century* (Nashville: Turner, 1994), 71–75.

4. Bill Hanna and Tom Ito, *A Cast of Friends* (Dallas: Taylor, 1996), 43.

5. Brian D. Behnken and Gregory D. Smithers, *Racism in American Media: From Aunt Jemima to Frito Bandito* (Santa Barbara, CA: Praeger, 2015), 96.

6. *Ibid.*

7. Lily Rothman, "Columbus Day, Indigeonous Peoples Day and the Problem with Discovery," *Time*, October 10, 2016, http://time.com/4523330/columbus-day-indigenous-peoples-day-history/.

8. Michael Conway, "The Problem with History Classes," *The Atlantic*, March 16, 2015, https://www.theatlantic.com/education/archive/2015/03/the-problem-with-history-classes/387823/.

9. Lawrence D. Bobo, "Inequalities that Endures? Racial Ideology, American Politics and the Peculiar Role of the Social Sciences," *The Changing Terrain of Race and Ethnicity*, edited by Maria Krysan and Amanda E. Lewis (New York: Russell Sage Foundation, 2004), 22.

10. Leonard Maltin, *Of Mice and Magic: A History of American Animated Cartoons* (New York: Penguin, 1987), 238; Michael Rogin, *Blackface, White Noise: Jewish Immigrants in the Hollywood Melting Pot* (Berkeley: University of California Press, 1996), 29; Jennifer L. Barker, "Hollywood, Black Animation, and the Problem of Representation in Little Ol' Bosko and The Princess and the Frog," *Journal of African American Studies* 14 (2010), 483.

11. Terry Lindvall and Ben Fraser, "Darker Shades of Animation," in *Reading the Rabbit*, ed. Kevin Sandler (New Brunswick: Rutgers University, 1998), 126–128.

12. Max Weber, "Politics as a Vocation" [translated lecture], July 1919, http://anthropos-lab.net/wp/wp-content/uploads/2011/12/Weber-Politics-as-a-Vocation.pdf.

13. Nicholas Sammond, *Birth of an Industry: Blackface Minstrelsy and the Rise of Animation* (Durham: Duke University Press, 2015), Location 2034.

14. Renee Montange, "Tom and Jerry Blamed for Violence in the Middle East," NPR, May 9, 2016, http://www.npr.org/2016/05/09/477301514/tom-and-jerry-blamed-for-violence-in-the-middle-east.

15. Viola Sherik, "Rituals of Hegemonic Masculinity: Cinema Torture and the Middle East," *Speaking About Torture*, edited by Julie A Carlson and Elisabeth Webers (New York: Fordham University Press, 2012); Stuart Jeffries, "Animal Magic," *The Guardian*, November 27, 2000, https://www.theguardian.com/media/2000/nov/28/tvandradio.television3.

16. Behnken and Smithers, *Racism in Popular Culture*, 83–100.

17. *Ibid.*

18. "Tom and Jerry Vol. 1," *iTunes*, https://itunes.apple.com/us/tv-season/tom-and-jerry-vol-1/id417551536.

19. William Hanna and Joseph Barbera, dirs., *Mouse Cleaning* (1948, MGM, Culver City, CA). Stepin Fetchit provides the voice of Tom in the film, uncredited.

20. William Hanna and Joseph Barbera, dirs., *Casanova Cat* (1951, MGM, Culver City, CA).

21. William Hanna and Joseph Barbera, dirs., *His Mouse Friday* (1951, MGM, Culver City, CA).

22. Angela M. Nelson, "African American Stereotypes in Prime-Time Television: An Overview, 1947–2007," *African Americans and Popular Culture Volume 1*, edited by Todd Boyd (Westport, CT: Praeger, 2008), 191–192; Richard Delgado and Jean Stefancic, "Images of the Outside in American Law and Culture: Can Free Expression Remedy Systemic Social Ills?" *Critical Race Theory: The Cutting Edge*, edited by Richard Delgado and Jean Stefancic (Philadelphia: Temple University Press, 2000), 226.

23. Jo Johnson, "We'll Have a Gay Old Time! Queer Representation in Prime-Time Animation from the Cartoon Short to the Family Sitcom," *Queers in American Popular Culture*, edited by Jim Elledge (Santa Barbara: Praeger, 2010), 257.

24. William Hanna and Joseph Barbera, dirs., *Puss n' Toots* (1942, MGM, Culver City, CA).

25. Behnken and Smithers, *Racism in Popular Culture*, 100–102.

26. Rebecca "Burt" Rose, "Amazon, iTunes Put Disclaimer on Racist Tom and Jerry Cartoons," *Jezebel*, October 3, 2014, http://jezebel.com/amazon-itunes-put-disclaimer-for-racism-on-tom-and-jer-1641938104.

27. Karl F. Cohen, *Forbidden Animation: Censored Cartoons and Blacklisted Animators in America* (Jefferson, NC: McFarland, 1997), 57.

28. David Pilgrim, "Mammy Two Shoes," The Jim Crow Museum, January 2013, https://www.ferris.edu/HTMLS/news/jimcrow/question/2013/january.htm. They originally redubbed the voice with June Foray to sound Irish in 1966 before African American comedian Thea Vidale redubbed it the shorts again in 1989.

29. Sean Coughlan, "Tom and Jerry Cartoons Carry Racism Warning," BBC, October 1, 2014, http://www.bbc.com/news/education-29427843. Mammy Two Shoes' face was briefly seen in *Part Time Pals* (1947) and *Saturday Evening Puss* (1950) along with several comics and storybooks.

30. Lizzie Crocker, "Is Tom and Jerry Really Racist?" *Daily Beast*, October 2, 2014, http://www.thedailybeast.com/articles/2014/10/02/is-tom-and-jerry-really-racist.html.

31. Michael S. Shull and David E. Wilt, *Doing Their Part, Wartime Animated Short Films 1939–1945* (Jefferson, NC: McFarland, 2004), 62.

32. Eric Avila, "Popular Culture in the Age of White Flight: Film Noir, Disneyland, and the Cold War (Sub) Urban Imaginary," *Journal of Urban History* 31, no. 1 (2004): 3–22.

33. *Ibid.*

34. William Hanna and Joseph Barbera, dirs., *Fine Feathered* (1942, Culver City, CA, Metro-Goldwyn-Meyers); William Hanna and Joseph Barbera, dirs., *Sleepy-Time Tom* (1951, MGM, Culver City, CA). E

35. William Hanna and Joseph Barbera, dirs., *Mouse in Manhattan* (1945, MGM, Culver City, CA).

36. Michan Andrew Connor, "Holding the Center: Images of Urbanity on Television in Los Angeles, 1950–1970," *South California Quarterly* 94, no. 2 (2012): 230–255.

37. Tom VanDerWerff, "10 Episodes That Show Off Leave It to Beaver's Quiet Innovation," *AV Club*, November 11, 2012, https://tv.avclub.com/10-episodes-that-show-off-leave-it-to-beaver-s-quiet-in-1798234600.

38. William Hanna and Joseph Barbera, dirs., *Jerry's Cousin* (1951, MGM, Culver City); Robert Gambone, "George Luks, Hogan's Alley, and Ashcan School Social Thought," *Aurora: The Journal of the History of Art* 6 (2005): 38–79. The term became so synonymous with lower income, dangerous urban areas that the FBI named their urban tactical training ground "Hogan's Alley."

39. Barrier, *Hollywood Cartoons*, 545.

40. Jeff Lenburg, *Who's Who in Animated Cartoons: An International Guide to Film and Televisions Award Winning Animators* (New York: Applause, 2006), 18–19.

41. David Forgacs, "Disney Animation and the Business of Childhood," *Screen* 33, no. 4 (1992): 361–74.

42. Maltin, *Of Mice and Magic*, 304–305.

43. Hanna and Ito, *A Cast of Friends*, 81–83.

44. Carol Stabile and Mark Harrison, "Introduction," *Primetime Animation: Television Animation and American Culture* edited by Carol A. Stabile and Mark Harrison (New York: Routledge, 2003), 8–9.

Chapter 2

1. David Perlmutter, Master's Thesis, University of Manitoba, "Toon In, Toon Out: American

Television Animation and the Shaping of American Popular Culture, 1948–1980" (2010).

2. Michael Barrier, "A Day in the Life," *MichaelBarrier.com*, November 15, 2011, http://www.michaelbarrier.com/Essays/MGMMarch1953/MGMMarch1953.html.

3. Joseph Barbera, *My Life in 'toons: From Flatbush to Bedrock in Under a Century* (Nashville: Turner, 1994), 112–113; Perlmutter, "Toon In, Toon Out," 6–7.

4. Michael Barrier, *Hollywood Cartoons: American Animation in its Golden Age* (New York: Oxford University Press, 1999), 304–307.

5. Scott Thill, "*Peace on Earth* is 75 Years Old—and More Relevant Than Ever," *Cartoon Brews*, December 24, 2014, http://www.cartoonbrew.com/ideas-commentary/peace-on-earth-is-75-years-old-and-more-relevant-than-ever-107274.html.

6. Barbera, *My Life in 'toons*, 215.

7. William Hanna and Joseph Barbera, dirs., *One Droopy Knight* (MGM, 1957, Culver City, CA), Tex Avery, dir., *Senor Droopy* (MGM, 1949, Culver City, CA).

8. Douglas L. McCall, *Film Cartoons: A Guide to 20th Century American Animated Features and Shorts* (Jefferson, NC: McFarland, 1998), 175.

9. Barrier, *Hollywood Cartoons*, 560–562.

10. Hal Erickson, *Television Cartoon Shows: An Illustrated Encyclopedia, 1949–2003* (Jefferson, NC: McFarland, 2005), 224–226.

11. *Ibid.*, 692.

12. Barbera, *My Life in 'toons*, 123.

13. *Ibid.*

14. Bill Burnett, "Limited Animation … Unlimited Imagination," Fred Seibert, http://fredseibert.com/post/71257648/limited-animationunlimited-imagination.

15. Michael Barrier, *Hollywood Cartoons*, 257. Later shows, including early episodes of *The Simpsons*, employed similar strategies.

16. Derek Thompson, "On Repeat: Why People Watch Movies and Shows Over and Over," *The Atlantic*, September 10, 2014, https://www.theatlantic.com/entertainment/archive/2014/09/rewinding-rewatching-and-listening-on-repeat-why-we-love-re-consuming-entertainment/379862/; "Why Toddlers Like Repetition," *Parents Magazine*, http://www.parents.com/toddlers-preschoolers/development/behavioral/why-toddlers-love-repetition/.

17. T.J. Fleming, "T.V.'s Most Unexpected Hit," *The Saturday Evening Post*, December 2, 1961, 62–66.

18. Bill Hanna and Tom Ito, *A Cast of Friends* (Dallas: Taylor, 1996), 77–84.

19. William Hanna and Joseph Barbera, dirs., *Blackboard Jumble* (1957, MGM, Culver City, CA).

20. Barbera, *My Life in 'toons*, 123.

21. *Ibid.*, 124.

22. Todd VanDerWerff, "In *The Flintstones*, Hanna-Barbera Found a Shameless Rip-Off That Worked," *AV Club*, May 12, 2014, http://www.avclub.com/article/flintstones-hanna-barbera-found-shameless-rip-work-204382.

23. Paul Wells, "'Smarter Than the Average Artform: Animation in the Television Era," *Prime Time Animation: Television Animation and American Culture*, edited by Carol A. Stabile and Mark Harrison (New York: Routledge, 2003), 24.

24. "TELEVISION: Stone Age Hero's Smash Hit: TV'S First Cartoon for Grownups Stars the Suburban Flintstones," *LIFE*, November 21, 1960, 57–60.

25. Jason Mittell, "The Great Saturday Morning Exile: Scheduling Cartoons on Television's Periphery in the 1960s," *Prime Time Animation: Television Animation and American Culture*, edited by Carol A. Stabile and Mark Harrison (New York: Routledge, 2003), 42.

26. Blake Edwards, dir., *Breakfast at Tiffany's*, Paramount, Hollywood, CA, October 5, 1961. *Bye Bye Birdie* also included numerous instances of Hanna Barbera product placement through Sidney.

27. "Local Kids' TV," *Pioneers of Television*, http://www.pbs.org/wnet/pioneers-of-television/pioneering-programs/local-kids-tv/ .

28. Jason Mittell, *Genre and Television: From Cop Shows to Cartoons in American Culture* (New York: Routledge, 2004), 69.

29. Paul Wells, *America and Animation* (New Brunswick: Rutgers University Press, 2002), 89.

30. Christopher P. Lehman, *American Cartoons of the Vietnam Era: A Study of Social Commentary in Film and Television 1961–1975* (Jefferson, NC: McFarland, 2007), 27.

31. Jerry Beck and Will Friedwald, *Looney Tunes and Merrie Melodies: A Complete Illustrated Guide to the Warner Bros. Cartoons* (New York: Henry Holt and Co., 1989), 317.

32. Ray Suarez, *Latino Americans: The 500-Year Legacy That Shaped a Nation (London: Celebra, 2013).*

33. Joseph Barbera and William Hanna, dirs., "Cattle Battle Rattled," *The Quick Draw McGraw Show*, 1959, Hanna-Barbera Productions, 1959.

34. Suarez, *Latino Americans.*

35. Leonard Maltin, *Of Mice and Magic: A History of American Animated Cartoons* (New York: Penguin, 1987), 304.

36. Erickson, *Television Cartoon Shows*, 649–650.

37. "11 Famous Actors That Appeared on Both Gunsmoke and the Big Valley," *MeTV*, March 15, 2016, http://www.metv.com/lists/11-famous-actors-who-appeared-on-both-gunsmoke-and-the-big-valley.

38. Jason Mittell, *Genre and Television: From Cop Shows to Cartoons in American Culture* (New York, Routledge, 2004), 72–74.

39. Wells, *Animation and America*, 89.

40. Jesse M. Kowalski, "Hanna-Barbera: The Architects of Saturday Morning," *Illustration History*, January 19, 2017, http://www.illustrationhistory.org/essays/hanna-barbera-the-architects-of-saturday-morning.

41. "Flintstones' Artist Ed Benedict Dies," *USAToday*, October 10, 2006, http://usatoday30.usatoday.com/life/people/2006-10-10-benedict-obit_x.htm.

42. Erickson, *Television Cartoon Shows*, 203–204. H-B Enterprises went on to produce a show based on ancient Rome, *The Roman Holidays*, ten years later. It would only last 13 episodes.

43. Benjamin Svetkey, "The Original Flintstones Pilot: The "Flagstones,"" *Entertainment Weekly*, May 6, 1994, http://ew.com/article/1994/05/06/original-flintstones-pilot-flagstones/.

44. James A. Baughman, *Same Time, Same Channel: The Making of American Television 1948–1961* (Baltimore: Johns Hopkins University Press, 2007), 266.

45. "Miles Laboratories," *AdAge*, September 15, 2003, http://adage.com/article/adage-encyclopedia/miles-laboratories/98776/.

46. Debbie Elliot, "After Bans, Tobacco Tries Direct Marketing," NPR, November 18, 2008, http://www.npr.org/templates/story/story.php?storyId=97136501. This strategy was more directly utilized by the creation of Joe Camel.

47. "First Prime-Time Animated Show," *Guinness World Records*, http://www.guinnessworldrecords.com/world-records/first-prime-time-animation-show.

48. Joseph Barbera, *Archive of American Television*, interview with Leonard Maltin, February 26, 1997, http://www.emmytvlegends.org/interviews/people/joseph-barbera. *The Bugs Bunny Show* premiered in early prime time 10 days later.

49. Jerry Beck, *The Flintstones: The Official Guide to the Cartoon Series* (New York: Running Press, 2011), 74.

50. Poncho Doll, "REEL LIFE / FILM & VIDEO FILE: Music Helped 'Flintstones' on Way to Fame." In 1960, Hoyt Curtin created the lively theme for the Stone Age family. The show's producers say it may be the most frequently broadcast song on TV. *Los Angeles Times*, June 2, 1994, http://articles.latimes.com/1994-06-02/news/vl-64779_1_hoyt-curtin.

51. Barbera, *Archive of American Television*.

52. Barbera, *My Life in 'toons*, 140–141.

53. Lily Rothman, "The Scathing Speech That Made Television History," *Time*, May 9, 2016, http://time.com/4315217/newton-minow-vast-wasteland-1961-speech/.

54. Erickson, *Television Cartoon Shows*, 206.

55. Michael Mallory, *Hanna-Barbera Cartoons*. (New York: Hugh Lauter Levin Associates, 1998), 44.

56. Erickson, *Television Cartoon Shows*, 864–865.

57. Mittell, "The Great Saturday Morning Exile," 41.

58. Erickson, *Television Cartoon Shows*, 864–865.

59. Rothman, "The Scathing Speech."

60. Lehman, *American Animated Cartoons of the Vietnam Era*, 23–24.

61. Linda Brannon, *Gender: Psychological Perspectives* (New York: Routledge, 2016), 159–160.

62. Mallory, *Hanna-Barbera Cartoons*, 116.

63. Megan Mullen, "The Simpsons and Hanna-Barbera's Animation Legacy," *Leaving Springfield: The Simpsons and the Possibility of Oppositional Culture*, edited by John Alberti (Detroit: Wayne State University Press, 2004), 69.

64. Joseph Barbera and William Hanna, dirs., "Yogi in the City," *The Yogi Bear Show*, Hanna-Barbera Productions, November 18, 1961, Hollywood, CA.

65. Joseph Barbera and William Hanna, "The Buffalo Convention," *The Flintstones*, Hanna-Barbera Productions, October 26, 1962, Hollywood, CA.

66. M. Keith Booker, *Drawn to Television: Prime-Time Animation from The Flintstones to Family Guy* (Westport, CT: Praeger, 2006), 35.

67. Lehman, *American Cartoons of the Vietnam Era*, 26.

68. *Ibid.*, 27–28.

69. Michael Heaton, "The Enduring (Gay?) Appeal of The Wizard of Oz: Minister of Culture," Cleveland Plain-Dealer, March 25, 2016, http://www.cleveland.com/ministerofculture/index.ssf/2016/03/the_enduringly_gay_appeal_of_t.html.

70. James Whitbrook, "DC's Latest Hanna-Barbera Comic Will Reimagine Snagglepuss as 'Gay, Gothic Southern Playwright,'" *io9*, January 31, 2017, http://io9.gizmodo.com/dcs-latest-hanna-barbera-comic-will-reimagine-snagglepu-1791836954.

71. Jose Esteban Munoz, *Disidentifications: Queers of Color and the Performance of Politics* (Minneapolis: University of Minnesota Press, 1999), Location 1001.

Chapter 3

1. Joseph Barbera, *My Life in 'toons: From Flatbush to Bedrock in Under a Century* (Nashville: Turner, 1994), 124–125.

2. Bill Hanna and Tom Ito, *A Cast of Friends* (Dallas: Taylor, 1996), 122–123.

3. *Ibid.* Another primetime animated series would not appear on any broadcast network again until December 1989.

4. Hal Erickson, *Television Cartoon Shows: An Illustrated Encyclopedia 1949–2003* (Jefferson, NC: McFarland, 2005).

5. Greg Lenburg, Joan Howard Maurer, and Jeff Lenburg, *The Three Stooges Scrapbook* (Chicago: Chicago Review Press, 2012), 191–193.

6. Rosemarie Truglio, "Sesame Street and Learning through Play." *American Journal of Play* 12, no. 1 (2019).

7. John Rust, dir., *Carved in Stone: The Flintstones Phenomenon* (Baltimore: Taylor Made Entertainment, 2004).

8. Stephanie E. Bor, "Lucy's Two Babies: Framing the First Televised Depiction of Pregnancy," *Media History* 19, no. 4 (2013): 464–478.

9. Erickson, *Television Cartoon Shows*, 206.

10. Rust, *Carved in Stone*.

11. Jeffrey A. Tucker, *It's A Jetsons World* (New York: Laissez Faire Books, 2013), 4.

12. Karen Pinkus, "On Climate, Cars, and Literary Theory," *Technology and Culture* 49, no. 4 (2008), 1008.

13. Jason Mittell, "The Great Saturday Morning Exile: Scheduling Cartoons on Television's Periphery in the 1960s," *Prime Time Animation: Television Animation and American Culture*, edited by Carol A. Stabile and Mark Harrison (New York: Routledge, 2003), 45–46.

14. Barbera, *My Life in 'toons*, 150–151.

15. Hanna and Ito, *A Cast of Friends*, 133–134.

16. Christie Slewinski, "1962: ABC Introduces Its First Color Series 'The Jetson,'" *TV Worth Watching*, September 23, 2012, http://www.tvworthwatching. com/post/THISDAYINTVHISTORY20120923. aspx.

17. Rebecca Farley, "From Fred and Wilma to Ren and Stimpy: What Makes a Cartoon 'Prime Time'?" *Primetime Animation: Television Animation and American Culture*, edited by Carol A. Stabile and Mark Harrison (New York: Routledge, 2003), 160.

18. Michael Eury, *Caption Action: The Original Superhero Action Figure* (Raleigh: Twomorrows, 2002), 16.

19. Christopher P. Lehman, *American Cartoons of the Vietnam Era: A Study of Social Commentary in Film and Television 1961–1975* (Jefferson, NC: McFarland, 2007), 50.

20. "This Is the Saturday Morning Lineup in 1966. Can Anything Top It?" *MeTV*, January 21, 2016, http://www.metv.com/stories/this-is-what-the-saturday-morning-tv-lineup-looked-like-50-years-ago.

21. Sylvia M. Chan-Olmsted, "From Sesame Street to Wall Street: An Analysis of Market Competition in Commercial Children's Television," *Journal of Broadcasting & Electronic Media* 40, no. 1 (1996): 30–44.

22. Mittell, "Saturday Morning Exile," 49.

23. Matt Groening, Commentary for "Bart the Genius," *The Simpsons: The Complete First Season*, 20th Century Fox, 2001, DVD.

24. Rebecca Coyle and Alex Mesker, "Time Warp: Sonic Retro-Futurism in the Jetsons," *Music in Science Fiction Television: Tune-Into the Future*, edited by Kevin J. Donnelly and Phillip Hayward (New York: Routledge, 2013), 28.

25. Tim Brooks and Earle Marsh, *The Complete Guide to Prime Time Network and Cable TV Shows* (New York: Ballantine Books, 2007), 440.

26. Cordelia Fine, "Why Are Toys So Gendered?" *Slate*, April 5, 2014, http://www.slate.com/articles/health_and_science/new_scientist/2014/04/girl_and_boy_toys_childhood_preferences_for_gendered_toys_are_not_innate.html.

27. Darlene Powell-Hopson and Derek Hopson, "Implications of Doll Color Preference Among Black Preschool Children and White Preschool Children," *The Journal of Black Psychology* 14, no. 12 (1988), 57–58.

28. Erickson, *Television Cartoon Shows*, 522–523.

29. Barbera, *My Life in 'toons*, 166–168.

30. Joseph Barbera and William Hanna, dirs., "Carry On, Nurse Fred," *The Flintstones*, Hanna-Barbera Productions, Hollywood, CA, 1963.

31. Nancy Signorielli, "Children, Television, and Gender Roles: Messages and Impact," *Journal of Adolescent Healthcare* 11, No. 1 (1990), 50–58 .

32. Alex Knapp, "The Future We Don't Even Know We Missed," *Forbes*, October 13, 2011, https://www.forbes.com/sites/alexknapp/2011/10/13/the-future-we-dont-even-know-we-missed/#e59a6e658391.

33. Farley, "From Fred and Wilma to Ren and Stimpy," 160.

34. Joseph Barbera and William Hanna, dirs., "Cave Scout Jamboree" (1964, Los Angeles, CA, Turner Home Entertainment, 2006), DVD.

35. Pinkus, "On Climate, Cars, and Literary Theory," 1008; Ian Steadman, "The Jetsons Turns 50: So Where Is All That Cool Stuff?," *Wired*, September 24, 2012, http://www.wired.co.uk/article/jetsons-50th-anniversary.

36. Alana Semuels, "The Parts of America Most Susceptible to Automation," *The Atlantic*, May 3, 2017, https://www.theatlantic.com/business/archive/2017/05/the-parts-of-america-most-susceptible-to-automation/525168/. In this world employees are apparently still paid in spite of the presence of automation.

37. Alana Semuels, "White Flight Never Ended," *The Atlantic*, July 30, 2015, https://www.theatlantic.com/business/archive/2015/07/white-flight-alive-and-well/399980/.

38. Edward Goetz, "Gentrification in Black and White: The Racial Impact of Public Housing Demolition in American Cities," *Urban Studies* 48, no. 8 (2011): 1581–1604.

39. Douglas Holt and Craig Thompson, "Man-of-Action Heroes: How American Ideology of Manhood Structures Men's Consumption," *Harvard Marketing Research*, November 2002, https://papers.ssrn.com/sol3/papers.cfm?abstract_id=386600.

40. Carol Stabile and Mark Harrison, "Introduction," *Primetime Animation: Television Animation and American Culture*, edited by Carol A. Stabile and Mark Harrison (New York: Routledge, 2003), 8–9.

41. Lehman, *American Cartoons of the Vietnam Era*, 26–28.

42. Wulf D. Hund and Charles W. Mills, "Comparing Black People to Monkeys has a Long, Dark Simian History," *The Conversation*, February 28, 2016, https://theconversation.com/comparing-black-people-to-monkeys-has-a-long-dark-simian-history-55102.

43. *Ibid.*

Chapter 4

1. Cynthia Littleton and Geoff Berkshire, "TV's Favorite All-American Families," *Variety*, July 3, 2015, http://variety.com/gallery/all-american-family-tv-shows/#!14/the-donna-reed-show/. *Leave It to Beaver* (1963), *Ozzie and Harriet* (1966), *The Donna Reed Show* (1966) and others were ending their runs.

2. Joseph Barbera, *My Life in 'toons: From Flatbush to Bedrock in Under a Century* (Nashville: Turner, 1994), 152–153.

3. Doug Wildey, "Amazing Heroes #95," *Classic Jonny Quest*, original interview released May 15, 1986, http://www.classicjq.com/info/AmazingHeroes95.aspx.

4. Hal Erickson, *Television Cartoon Shows: An Illustrated Encyclopedia, 1949–2003* (Jefferson, NC: McFarland, 2005), 452–453.

5. *Ibid.*

6. Esther Iverem, "The Real Villains of Jonny Quest," *Washington Post*, May 29, 1996, https://www.washingtonpost.com/archive/lifestyle/1996/05/29/the-real-villains-of-jonny-quest/2f238cd0–44d6–4a47-be45–28950a1e309b/.

7. *Ibid.*

8. Tim Hollis, *Toons in Toyland: The Story of Cartoon Character Merchandise* (Jackson: University of Mississippi Press, 2015), 121.

9. David H. DePatie, "Interview, Part 1," interview by Charles Brubaker, *Baker Toons*, December 19, 2010, http://bakertoons.blogspot.com/2010/12/david-h-depatie-interview-part-1.html?m=1.

10. Ted Sennett, *The Art of Hanna-Barbera: Fifty Years of Creativity* (New York: Viking Studio Books, 1991), 94,137.

11. Barbera, *My Life in 'toons*, 160–161.

12. David A Roach, "Batman," *The Superhero Book: The Ultimate Encyclopedia of Comic Book Icons and Hollywood Heroes,* edited by Renee Misiroglu (Canton, MI: Visible Ink Press, 2004), 103.

13. *Ibid.*, 223.

14. Timothy Burke and Kevin Burke, *Saturday Morning Fever: Growing Up with Cartoon Culture* (New York: St. Martin's, 1999), 152.

15. "7 Things You Might Not Know About Atom Ant," *MeTV*, March 15, 2016, http://www.metv.com/lists/7-things-you-might-not-know-about-atom-ant.

16. Erickson, *Television Cartoon Shows*, 748.

17. Dorothy L. Hurley, "Seeing White: Children of Color and the Disney Fairy Tale Princess," *The Journal of Negro Education* 74, no. 3 (2005): 221–232.

18. Kim Bartel Sheehan, *Controversies in Contemporary Advertising* (Thousand Oaks, CA: SAGE, 2014), 163.

19. Chuck Miller, "Alice in Wonderland: Circa 1966," *Albany Times-Union*, June 11, 2016, http://blog.timesunion.com/chuckmiller/alice-in-wonderland-circa-1966/27418/.

20. Erickson, 348.

21. *Ibid.*

22. Dennis Hevesi, "Alex Toth, 77 Comic Book Artist and 'Space Ghost' Animator Dies," *New York Times*, June 6, 2006, http://www.nytimes.com/2006/06/06/arts/design/06toth.html?mcubz=0.

23. Timothy Burke and Kevin Burke, *Saturday Morning Fever*, 2.

24. Alex McNeil, *Total Television* (New York: Penguin Books, 1996), 777.

25. Mark A. Robinson, *The World of Musicals: An Encyclopedia of Stage and Screen, and Song* (Westport, CT: Greenwood Press, 2014), 345.

26. McNeil, *Total Television*, 721.

27. Erickson, *Television Cartoon Shows*, 560.

28. David Hayes, "'You Guys Are Killing Me with This Dreck': Contemporary Attitudes toward the Golden, Atomic, Silver, and Bronze Eras of Comic Book Production," *Handbook of Cultural Studies and Education*, edited by Peter Pericles Trifonas and Susan Jagger (New York: Routledge, 2018), 255–276.

29. "Biography: Alex Toth," *Illustration History,* http://www.illustrationhistory.org/artists/alex-toth; Graeme McMillan, "The Secret Life of the Other Birdman," *The Hollywood Reporter*, February 23, 2015, http://www.hollywoodreporter.com/heat-vision/secret-life-birdman-775822.

30. "History," *The World of Sid and Marty Krofft*, http://www.sidandmartykrofft.com/about/history/.

31. Erickson, *Television Cartoon Shows*, 60.

32. Les Wedman, "Do Viewers Really Want to See Something New or Different on U.S. Television?" *Vancouver Sun*, October 22, 1968, https://news.google.com/newspapers?id=MjpmAAAAIBAJ&sjid=w4oNAAAAIBAJ&pg=955,2619076.

33. "Was the Animated Series Wacky Races Originally Intended for a Live Action Game Show?" *Entertainment Urban Legends Revealed*, November 29, 2013, http://legendsrevealed.com/entertainment/2013/11/29/was-the-animated-series-wacky-races-originally-intended-for-a-live-action-game-show/.

34. Sarah Deen, "As DC Comics ReVamps Wacky Races-Can You Remember All the Characters?" *Metro*, March 31, 2016 http://metro.co.uk/2016/03/31/as-dc-comics-comics-revamp-wacky-races-can-you-remember-all-the-characters-5785508/.

35. Erickson, 235.

36. Sarah Thomas, "Janet Waldo, the Voice of Penelope Pitstop and Judy Jetson Dead at 96," *Sydney Morning Herald*, June 14, 2016, http://www.smh.com.au/entertainment/tv-and-radio/janet-waldo-the-voice-of-penelope-pitstop-and-judy-jetson-dead-at-96–20160613-gpibkl.html.

37. "The Famous Five," *EnidBlyton.net*, http://www.enidblyton.net/famous-five/.

38. Suzanne Wilson, "Scooby-Doo! How Old Are You?" *ASU Now*, July 26, 2019, https://psychology.asu.edu/content/scooby-doo-how-old-are-you.

39. Joe Ruby and Ken Spears, *The Stu's Show*, interviewed by Stu Shostak, January 16, 2013, http://www.stusshow.com/archives.php?q=spears.

40. Jake Austen, "Rock n' Roll Cartoons," *The Cartoon Music Book*, edited by Daniel Goldmark and Yuval Taylor (Chicago: A Cappella, 2002), 184.

41. Tomasz Żaglewski, "The Impossibles Revived: Hanna-Barbera's Superhero Universe in TV and Comics," *Journal of Graphic Novels and Comics* (2020): 1–17.

42. Donna Mitroff and Rebecca Herr Stephenson, "The Television Tug-of-War: A Brief History of Children's Television Programming in the United States," *The Children's Television Community*, edited by J. Alison Bryant (Mahwah, NJ: Lawrence Erlbaum, 2007), 15–19.

43. Carol Stabile and Mark Harrison, "Introduction," *Primetime Animation: Television Animation and American Culture*, edited by Carol A. Stabile and Mark Harrison (New York: Routledge, 2003), 8–9.

44. Teju Cole, "The White Savior Industrial Complex," *The Atlantic*, March 21, 2012, https://www.theatlantic.com/international/archive/2012/03/the-white-savior-industrial-complex/254843/.

45. Iverem, "The Real Villains of Jonny Quest."

46. Mae M. Ngai, *Impossible Subjects: Illegal Aliens and the Making of Modern America* (Princeton: Princeton University Press, 2004), 42.

47. "The 50 Most Racist TV Shows of All Time," *Complex*, June 3, 2013 http://www.complex.com/pop-culture/2013/06/most-racist-tv-shows/jonny-quest.

48. Edwin C. Hill, Jr., *Black Soundscapes, White Stages: The Meaning of Francophone Sound in the Black Atlantic* (Baltimore: Johns Hopkins University Press, 2013), 130

49. Bryan Thomas, "'Uh, Oh Chongo': Danger Island and the Daredevil Life and Career of Kim Kahana," *Nightflight*, October 8, 2015, http://nightflight.com/uh-oh-chongo-danger-island-and-the-daredevil-life-career-of-kim-kahana/.

50. Erickson, *Television Cartoon Shows*, 748.

51. Courtney Shaw, "Author Codrescu Considers 'Whitewashing' of the Arabian Nights Stories," *Princeton University Press*, June 27, 2011, http://blog.press.princeton.edu/2011/06/27/author-codrescu-considers-the-whitewashing-of-the-arabian-nights-stories/.

52. Frantz Fanon, *Black Skin, White Masks* (New York: Grove Press, 1967), 13.

53. Erickson, *Television Cartoon Shows*, 748.

54. *Ibid.*, 732; Shaw, "Author Codrescu."

55. Erickson, *Television Cartoon Shows*, 709.

56. Stefan Arvidsson, "Aryan Mythology as Science and Ideology," *Journal of the American Academy of Religion* 67, no. 2 (1999), 327–354.

57. Fanon, *Black Skin, White Masks*, 124–126.

58. Sean Clark, "Why Hollywood Drew a Veil Over Sinbad's Arabian Roots," *The Guardian*, July 23, 2003, https://www.theguardian.com/film/2003/jul/23/iraq.world.

59. Walter Rodney, *How Europe Underdeveloped Africa* (Baltimore: Black Classic Press, 2011), 174.

60. Katharine Trendacosta, "Here's How the Scooby-Doo Crew Would Have Dressed through the 20th Century," *io9*, June 19, 2015 http://io9.gizmodo.com/heres-how-the-scooby-doo-crew-would-dress-throughout-th-1712466972.

61. Jose Esteban Munoz, *Disidentifications: Queers of Color and the Performance of Politics* (Minneapolis: University of Minnesota, 1999), Kindle Edition, Location 1001.

62. Kelsey Lueptow, "5 Ways Girls Are Taught to Avoid 'Smart,'" *Everyday Feminism*, July 28, 2014, http://everydayfeminism.com/2014/07/girls-taught-to-avoid-smart/.

63. Burke and Burke, *Saturday Morning Fever*, 52.

64. Anthony Breznican, "'Scooby-Doo' Drops Adult Subcontext," *Topeka Capital-Journal*, June 14, 2002, http://cjonline.com/stories/061402/wee_scoobysubtext.shtml#.Wcp5AdOGMxc.

65. Lueptow, "Five Ways."

Chapter 5

1. Vera Fahlberg, *A Child's Journey Through Placement* (London: Jessica Kingsley, 2012), 48.

2. Michael Lev, "Hanna-Barbera Follows Disney Map," *New York Times*, January 9, 1990, http://www.nytimes.com/1990/01/09/business/hanna-barbera-follows-disney-map.html?mcubz=0.

3. Larry Brody, *Turning Points in Television* (New York: Citadel, 2005), 18.

4. Christopher P. Lehman, *American Cartoons of the Vietnam Era: A Social Commentary of Social Commentary in Film and Television, 1961–1975* (Jefferson, NC: McFarland, 2007), 49.

5. "1970 Oveview," United States Census Bureau, https://www.census.gov/history/www/through_the_decades/overview/1970.html.

6. Rebecca "Burt" Rose, "Amazon, iTunes Put Disclaimer on Racist Tom and Jerry Cartoons," *Jezebel*, October 3, 2014, http://jezebel.com/amazon-itunes-put-disclaimer-for-racism-on-tom-and-jer-1641938104.

7. Amen Oyiboke, "History of Black Entertainment 1960–1970," *Los Angeles Sentinel*, February 10, 2016, https://lasentinel.net/history-of-black-entertainment-from-1960–1970s.html.

8. Lori Takeuchi and Reed Stevens, "The New Co-Viewing: Designing for Learning Through Joint Media Engagement," The Joan Ganz Cooney Center at Sesame Workshop and LIFE Center, Fall 2011, http://www.joanganzcooneycenter.org/wp-content/uploads/2011/12/jgc_coviewing_desktop.pdf.

9. Edward L. Palmer and Shalom M. Fisch, "The Beginnings of Sesame Street Research," *"G" Is for Growing: Thirty Years of Research on Children and Sesame Street*, edited by Shalom M. Fisch and Rosemarie T. Truglio (Mahwah, NJ: Lawrence Erlbaum Associates, 2001), 19.

10. Todd Boyd, *Young, Black, Rich, and Famous: The Rise of the NBA, The Hip Hop Invasion, and the Transformation of American Culture* (New York: Doubleday, 2003), 27.

11. Lehman, *American Cartoons of the Vietnam Era*, 140.

12. Jerry Osborne, "Soundtracks Start with 'Snow White,'" *Chicago Sun-Times*, November 3, 2006, https://www.highbeam.com/doc/1P2-1387100.html.

13. Wilson, "Scooby-Doo! How Old Are You?"

14. Bart Beaty, *Twelve Cent Archie* (New Brunswick: Rutgers University Press, 2015), 178–180.

15. John Wells and Keith Dallas, *American Comic Book Chronicles: 1965–69. Vol. 9* (Raleigh: Twomorrows, 2014).

16. Richard M. Breaux, "It's a Cartoon! The Jackson 5ive as Commodified Black Power and Civil Rights Ideologies," *The Journal of Pan-African Studies* 3 (2010): 84.

17. Kamasi L. Browne, "Brenda Holloway: Los Angeles Contribution to Motown in California Soul," *The Music of African Americans in the West*, edited by Jacqueline Cogdell Djedje and Eddie S. Meadows (Berkeley: University of California Press, 1998), 321.

18. Breaux, "It's a Cartoon!" 84.

19. Hal Erickson, *Television Cartoon Shows: An Illustrated Encyclopedia, 1949–2003* (Jefferson, NC: McFarland, 2005), 283–284.

20. Ted Sennett, *The Art of Hanna-Barbera: Fifty Years of Creativity* (New York, Viking Studio Books, 1991), 179.

21. Paul R. Iverson, *The Advent of the Laugh Track,* Hempstead, NY: Hofstra, 1994.

22. David Mansour, *From Abba to Zoom: A Pop Culture Encyclopedia of the Late 20th Centuries* (Kansas City, MO: Andrews McMeel, 2005), 21–37.

23. Lehman, *American Cartoons of the Vietnam Era,* 142; Greg Ehrbar, "DVD Review: Help! It's The Hair Bear Bunch!" *Cartoon Research,* April 7, 2013, https://cartoonresearch.com/index.php/dvd-review-help-its-the-hair-bear-bunch/. According to Barbera, it was determined Joe Flynn did not sound enough like Joe Flynn. He also most likely commanded a higher salary than Stephenson.

24. Erickson, *Television Cartoon Shows,* 352.

25. Jeff Greenfield, "The Silverman Strategy," *New York Times,* March 7, 1976, http://www.nytimes.com/1976/03/07/archives/the-silverman-strategy-how-fred-silverman-is-helping-abc-get-over.html?mcubz=0. Eisner was an advocate, but the wide ranging quality of shows and scripts may have been due to the (lack of) involvement of Duke Duchovny who was approving scripts for Silverman as his successor. Eisner would go on to guide Disney through their renaissance in the late 1980s and 1990s.

26. Dale Kunkel, "Kid's Media Policy Goes Digital Current Developments in Children's Television Regulation," *The Children's Television Community,* edited by J. Alison Bryant (Mahwah, NJ: Lawrence Erlbaum, 2007), 217.

27. Erickson, *Television Cartoon Shows,* 203–204.

28. Hal Erickson, *Syndicated Television: The First Forty Years, 1947–1987* (Jefferson, NC: McFarland: 2001), 217–218, Depetie-Freleng's *The Barkleys.*

29. "Wait Til' Your Father Gets Home," *TVGuide,* http://www.tvguide.com/tvshows/wait-till-father/205338.

30. Tim Brooks and Earl Marsh, *The Complete Directory to Prime Time Network and Cable TV Shows 1946 to Present* (New York: Ballantine, 2003), 1479.

31. Stu Shostak, "Interview with Joe Ruby and Ken Spears," Stu's Show, May 2, 2012, https://www.stusshow.com/archives.php.

32. Norma Pecora, "The Changing Nature of Children's Television: Fifty Years of Research," *Children and Television: Fifty Years of Research,* edited by Norma Pecora, John P. Murray, and Ann Wartella (Mahwah, NJ: Lawrence Erlbaum, 2007), 18–20.

33. Yunte Huang, *Charlie Chan: The Untold Story of the Honorable Detective and His Rendezvous with American History* (New York: W.W. Norton, 2011), 140.

34. Chuck Miller, "The ABC Saturday Superstar Movie," *Albany Times-Union,* June 21, 2016, http://blog.timesunion.com/chuckmiller/the-abc-saturday-superstar-movie/27324/.

35. Erickson, *Television Cartoon Shows,* 934–935.

36. Miller, "The ABC Superstar Movie."

37. "The Last of the Curlews," *Turner Classic Movies,* http://www.tcm.com/tcmdb/title/319005/Last-of-the-Curlews/.

38. Rick DeMott, "Boomerang to Air, The Thanksgiving That Almost Wasn't," *Animation World Network,* November 23, 2010, https://www.awn.com/news/boomerang-air-thanksgiving-almost-wasn-t.

39. Iwao Takamoto and Michael Mallory, *Iwao Takamoto: My Life with a Thousand Characters* (Jackson: University of Mississippi Press, 2009), 159–160.

40. *Ibid.*

41. *Heidi's Song* (1982), *Once Upon a Forest* (1993).

42. Gene Deitch, "Chapter 28: A Tangled Web," *Animation World Network,* November 19, 2013, https://www.awn.com/genedeitch/chapter-twentyeight-a-tangled-web. Disney famously struggled to obtain rights from living authors like White and P.L. Travers.

43. Karen D'Souza, "The Man Behind the Music of Mary Poppins" *San Jose Mercury News,* May 22, 2012, http://www.mercurynews.com/2012/05/22/the-man-behind-the-music-of-mary-poppins/.

44. Bill Hanna and Tom Ito, *A Cast of Friends* (Dallas: Taylor, 1996), 145.

45. "Baxter!" *British Film Institute,* http://www.bfi.org.uk/films-tv-people/4ce2b6a4c76b7.

46. Michael Hiestand, "Fox Sports Launches Direct Challenge to ESPN Dominance, *USA Today,* March 5, 2013, https://www.usatoday.com/story/sports/columnist/hiestand-tv/2013/03/05/fox-sports-cable-channel-challenging-espn-dominance-catholic-7/1965299/; Kevin Paul DuPont, "NHL Mascot Puck Has Left the Rink," *Boston Globe,* June 9, 2013, https://www.bostonglobe.com/sports/2013/06/08/nhl-mascot-peter-puck-has-left-rink/ix7mlHJHpHmRM6mZzLgqaP/story.html.

47. Peter Aspden, "It's Not Just TV: How HBO Revolutionized Television," *Slate/Financial Times,* September 24, 2011, http://www.slate.com/articles/life/ft/2011/09/its_not_just_tv.html...HBO.

48. Erickson, *Television Cartoon Shows,* 167.

49. Mansour, *From Abba to Zoom,* 454.

50. Erickson, Television Cartoon Shows, 384.

51. *Ibid.,* 425. .She is his niece to possibly avoid questions about conception.

52. Jerry Haggins, "The Andy Griffith Show: U.S. Situation Comedy," The Museum of Broadcast Communications, http://www.museum.tv/eotv/andygriffith.htm.

53. Sennett, *The Art of Hanna-Barbera,* 66.

54. H. Kevin Miserocchi and Charles Addams, The Addams Family: An Evolution (Petaluma, CA: Pomegranate Communications, 2010), 10–13.

55. Or "Wednesday Goes Missing."

56. Steve Inskeep, "The Father of the Addams Family," interview with Linda Davis, NPR, October 31, 2008, http://www.npr.org/templates/story/story.php?storyId=6407492.

57. Robert Cashill, "Unbottling Jeannie: Magic and Mischief on Set of Sitcom Favorite," *Biography,* September 17, 2015, https://www.biography.com/news/i-dream-of-jeannie-facts. Creator Sidney Sheldon did not want a blonde genie to avoid confusion with the blonde Samantha on *Bewitched.*

58. Erickson, *Television Cartoon Shows,* 444.

59. Sennett, *The Art of Hanna-Barbera*, 187–191. *Count of Monte Cristo* (September 1973), *Twenty Thousand Leagues Under the Sea, The Three Musketeers* (November, 1973), *The Last of the Mohicans* (November 1975), *Davy Crockett on the Mississippi* (November 1976), *Five Weeks in a Balloon* (November 1977), *Black Beauty* (October, 1978), *Puss in Boots* (January 1979), *Gulliver's Travels* (November 1979), *Daniel Boone* (November 1981).

60. Marisa Meltzer, "My Dad Lives in a Downtown Hotel: The Subtle Brilliance of the After School Special," *Slate*, July 20, 2006, fhttp://www.slate.com/articles/arts/dvdextras/2006/07/my_dad_lives_in_a_downtown_hotel.html.

61. Scott Collura, Travis Fickett, Eric Goldman and Brian Zoromski, "A History of Batman," *IGN*, July 17, 2008, http://www.ign.com/articles/2008/07/17/a-history-of-batman-on-tv?page=5.

62. *Ibid.*

63. David Perlmutter, *America Toons In: A History of Television Animation* (Jefferson, NC: McFarland, 2014), 128–129.

64. Joseph Barbera. *My Life in 'toons: From Flatbush to Bedrock in Under a Century* (Nashville: Turner, 1994), 176.

65. Michael McAvennie, "1970s," *DC Comics Year by Year: A Visual Chronicle*, edited by Daniel Wallace and Matthew K. Manning (New York: Dueling Kindersley, 2010), 171.

66. Erickson, *Television Cartoon Shows*, 414–415.

67. Mike Fleming, Jr., "Eddie Murphy Lends Voice to Hong Kong Phooey Feature," *Deadline*, August 10, 2011, http://deadline.com/2011/08/eddie-murphy-lends-voice-to-hong-kong-phooey-feature-155977/.

68. Tatiana Siegel, Scott Roxborough, Rhonda Richford, and Clarence Tsu, "Inside the Weird World of International Dubbing," *The Hollywood Reporter*, http://www.hollywoodreporter.com/news/argo-django-unchained-inside-weird-427453. Animated series voices (and songs) could be redubbed even easier than the live-action series.

69. Chris Buchner, "Partridge Family 2200 A.D.," *Saturday Mornings Forever*, August 27, 2016, http://www.saturdaymorningsforever.com/2016/08/partridge-family-2200-ad.html. Teen idol–focused pop led by Shaun Cassidy, David's brother, and Leif Garrett led to a resurgence in the following years.

70. Mansour, *From Abba to Zoom*, 517. *Cars* (2006), may have been inspired by the series.

71. "Legal Guide to Broadcast Law and Regulation," edited by Jean W. Benz, Jane E. Mago, and Jarianne Timmerman, National Association of Broadcasters, https://goo.gl/WiYSZr.

72. Perlmutter, *The Encyclopedia of American Animated Television Shows*, 152–153.

73. Noel Murray, "Hanna-Barbera Dared to Get Real with Its Evel Knievel Riff," *AV Club*, August 16, 2016, http://www.avclub.com/article/hanna-barbera-dared-get-real-its-evel-knievel-riff-240813.

74. "This Is What the Saturday Morning TV Lineup Looked Like in 1975," *MeTV*, August 6, 2016, http://www.metv.com/stories/this-is-what-the-Saturday-morning-TV-lineup-looked-like-in-1975.

75. *TV Guide Guide to TV*, edited by TV Guide (New York: Barnes and Noble, 2004), 351.

76. Ashley Thomas, "Linguistics in Land of the Lost," *Retroist*, August 20, 2016, http://www.retroist.com/2016/08/10/linguistics-in-the-land-of-the-lost/.

77. Hal Erickson, *Sid and Marty Krofft: A Critical Study of Saturday Morning Television, 1969–1993* (Jefferson, NC: McFarland, 1998), 112.

78. Why media companies often wait until the death of the artist to pursue adaptations.

79. Harry Castleman and Walter J. Podrazik, *The TV Schedule Book* (New York: McGraw-Hill, 1984).

80. Lehman, *American Animated Cartoons of the Vietnam Era*, 27.

81. Todd Boyd, *Young, Black, Rich, and Famous*, 27.

82. Breaux, "It's a Cartoon!" 84; A.J. Dent, "Strong Female Character: Valerie of Josie and the Pussycats," *GeekGirlCon*, March 26, 2014, https://geekgirlcon.com/strong-female-character-valerie-of-josie-and-the-pussycats/.

83. Scott Simon, "Hip Hop: Today's Civil Rights Movement?" interview with Todd Boyd, NPR, March 1, 2003, http://www.npr.org/templates/story/story.php?storyId=1178621.

84. Anna Breslaw, "Geena Davis Cites the Feminist Implications of I Dream of Jeannie," *Jezebel*, September 22, 2012, http://jezebel.com/5945463/geena-davis-cites-the-feminist-implications-of-i-dream-of-jeannie.

85. Jordan Calhoun, "18 of the Most Important Voices of Color in Animation," *Black Nerd Problems,* http://blacknerdproblems.com/18-of-the-most-important-voices-of-color-in-animation/; Aaron Barksdale, "23 Black Actors Who Voiced Your Favorite Cartoon Characters," *The Huffington Post*, October 2, 2015, http://www.huffingtonpost.com/entry/black-actors-cartoon-characters_us_560e9be0e4b0af3706e06b23.

86. "The 50 Most Racist TV Shows of All Time," *Complex*, June 3, 2013, http://www.complex.com/pop-culture/2013/06/most-racist-tv-shows/jonny-quest. Important to note that Hong Kong Phooey/Penry is not actually Asian.

87. Huang, *Charlie Chan*, 140.

88. Margeaux Watson and Jennifer Armstrong, "Diversity: Why Is TV So White?" *Entertainment Weekly*, June 13, 2008, http://ew.com/article/2008/06/13/diversity-why-tv-so-white/.

89. Malgorzata J. Rymsza-Pawlowska, "Broadcasting the Past: History Television, 'Nostalgia Culture,' and the Emergence of the Miniseries in the 1970s United States," *Journal of Popular Film and Television* 42, no. 2 (2014): 81–90. *Little House on the Prairie* did have an infamous episode that touch upon racism guest starring Todd Bridges before being cast on *Diff'rent Strokes*.

90. Shumaila Ahmed and Juliana Abdul Wahab, "Animation and the Socialization Process: Gender Role Portrayal on Cartoon Network," *Asian Social Sciences* 10, no. 3 (2014): 44–53; Alana

Semuels, "White Flight Never Ended," *The Atlantic*, July 30, 2015, https://www.theatlantic.com/business/archive/2015/07/white-flight-alive-and-well/399980/.

91. Alison Alexander and James Owers, "The Economics of Children's Television," *The Children's Television Community*, edited by J. Alison Bryant (Mahwah, NJ: Lawrence Erlbaum, 2007), 67.

Chapter 6

1. Nichola Dobson, *Historical Dictionary of Animation and Cartoons* (Lanham, MD: Scarecrow, 2009), 99.

2. George Monbiot, "Neoliberalism—The Ideology at the Root of all Our Problems," *The Guardian*, April 15, 2016, https://www.theguardian.com/books/2016/apr/15/neoliberalism-ideology-problem-george-monbiot.

3. Joseph Barbera, *My Life in 'toons: From Flatbush to Bedrock in Under a Century* (Nashville: Turner, 1994) 194.

4. Les Brown, "Fred Silverman Will Leave CBS-TV to Head to ABC Program Division," *New York Times*, May 19, 1975, http://www.nytimes.com/1975/05/19/archives/fred-silverman-will-leave-cbstv-to-head-abc-program-division.html?_r=0. Silverman had to save *Happy Days*; the show he almost ended with *Good Times* on CBS.

5. Hal Erickson, *Sid and Marty Krofft: A Critical Study of Saturday Morning Television, 1969–1993* (Jefferson, NC: McFarland, 1998), 109.

6. Ted Sennett, *The Art of Hanna-Barbera: Fifty Years of Creativity* (New York: Viking Studio Books, 1991), 257.

7. Lou Scheimer and Andy Mangels, *Lou Scheimer: Creating the Filmation Generation* (Raleigh: Twomorrows, 2012), 124. Isis predated Wonder Woman's debut by two months.

8. Tim Hollis, *Hi, There Boys and Girls! America's Local Children's TV Programs* (Jackson: University of Mississippi Press, 2001), 307.

9. Leonard Maltin, *Of Mice and Magic: A History of American Animated Cartoons* (New York: Penguin, 1987), 70.

10. T.R. Adams, *Tom and Jerry: Fifty Years of Cat and Mouse* (New York: Crescent Books, 1991).

11. Jeff Chang, "Of Course Tom and Jerry was Racist. The Question Is What To Do About That," *Slate*, October 3, 2014, http://www.slate.com/blogs/browbeat/2014/10/03/tom_and_jerry_racist_of_course_warning_on_amazon_and_itunes_is_appropriate.html. It is important to note, however, without the interstitial material and lack of historical knowledge, many children did not recognize this time divide, reintroducing issues discussed in previous chapters.

12. Ben Bertoli, "Pokemon Communication Seems to be Slowly Changing," *Kotaku*, May 30, 2016. http://kotaku.com/pokemon-communication-seems-to-be-slowly-changing-1779485458. Pokemon communicates the same way.

13. "Children's Programming," *The Social History of the American Family: An Encyclopedia*, edited by Marilyn J. Coleman and Lawrence H. Ganong (Thousand Oaks, CA: SAGE, 2014).

14. "Catch Laugh-A-Lympics Fever (All Over Again)," *Wired*, February 19, 2010, https://www.wired.com/2010/02/laff-a-lympic-fever/.

15. Barbera, *My Life in 'toons*, 179–180.

16. Joe Ruby and Ken Spears, "The Stu's Show," interview by Stu Shostak, January 16, 2013, http://www.stusshow.com/archives.php?q=spears.

17. Roger Cormier, "18 Things You Might Not Know About Inspector Gadget," *Mental Floss*, March 27, 2015, http://mentalfloss.com/article/62415/18-things-you-might-not-know-about-inspector-gadget.

18. Fred Silverman, *Archive of American Television*, interview with Dan Pasternack, March 16 and May 29, 2001, http://www.emmytvlegends.org/interviews/people/fred-silverman.

19. Robert T. Bakker, "Dinosaur Renaissance," *Scientific American* 232, no. 4 (1975): 58–79.

20. Hal Erickson, *Television Cartoon Shows: An Illustrated Encyclopedia 1949–2003* (Jefferson, NC: McFarland, 2005), 437–438. Dr. Lo, the villain in the first episode, looks very similar to Dr. Zin in *Jonny Quest*.

21. Michael Mallory, *Hanna-Barbera Cartoons* (New York: Hugh Lauter Levin Associates, 1998), 66–68.

22. Vincent Terrace, *The Encyclopedia of Television Shows: 1925 Through 2010* (Jefferson, NC: McFarland, 2011), 196.

23. Jeff Lenburg, *Encyclopedia of Animated Cartoons* (New York: Facts on File, 2008), 409–411.

24. Cher Martinetti, "Chosen One of the Day: Captain Caveman," *SyFy*, February 16, 2017. http://www.syfy.com/syfywire/chosen-one-of-the-day-captain-caveman. Vernee Wilson played Vy Smith on *The Fresh Prince of Bel Air*.

25. "Catch Laugh-A-Lympics Fever." *Yogi's Yahoos* was completely comprised of anthropomorphic animals.

26. Erickson, *Television Cartoon Shows*, 726.

27. Jack Moore, "The Saga of Superstations and Baseball's Historical Resistence to Technology," *The Hardball Times*, June 29, 2016, http://www.hardballtimes.com/the-saga-of-superstations-and-baseballs-historical-resistance-to-technology/.

28. Brian Philip Webster, "Chapter 29: Barter Syndication," *The Advertising Business: Operations Creativity Media Planning Integrated Communications*, edited by John Philip Jones (Thousand Oaks, CA: SAGE, 1999), 299–309.

29. Tim Lawson and Alisa Persons, *The Magic Behind the Voices: A Who's Who of Cartoon Voice Actors* (Jackson: University of Mississippi Press, 2004), 289.

30. "The Champions Series—A Salute to John Cluster," *Kidscreen*, December 1, 1997, http://kidscreen.com/1997/12/01/20082–19971201/.

31. Erickson, *Television Cartoon Shows*, 193.

32. *Ibid.*

33. Greg Lenburg, Joan Howard Maurer, and Jeff Lenburg., *The Three Stooges Scrapbook* (Chicago: Chicago Review Press, 2012), 238.

34. *Ibid.*; Erickson, *Television Cartoon Shows*, 206.

35. Darran Jordan, *Green Lantern History: An Unauthorized Guide to the DC Comic Book Series* (Sydney: Eclectica, 2015), 416.

36. Joe Ruby and Ken Spears ,*The Stu's Show*.

37. Will Harris, "In 1978, Hanna-Barbera Took to the Ice to Celebrate Fred Flintstone's Birthday," *AVClub*, April 15, 2016, http://www.avclub.com/article/1978-hanna-barbera-took-ice-celebrate-fred-flintst-235288.

38. Anthony Scibelli and Logan Trent, "Why The Flintstones Takes Place in a Post-Apocalyptic World," *Cracked*, June 20, 2012, http://www.cracked.com/quick-fixes/why-flintstones-takes-place-in-post-apocalyptic-future/.

39. Joseph Barbera, *Archive of American Television,* interview with Leonard Maltin, February 26, 1997, http://www.emmytvlegends.org/interviews/people/joseph-barbera.

40. Sennett, *The Art of Hanna-Barbera*, 258–259.

41. Nathan Rabin, "KISS Army AWOL #51: KISS Meets the Phantom of the Park," *AVClub*, December 17, 2015, https://tv.avclub.com/kiss-army-awol-case-file-51-kiss-meets-the-phantom-of-1798287497. The special was parodied in a 2001 episode of *Family Guy* as "KISS Saves Santa."

42. Iwao Takamoto and Michael Mallory, *Iwao Takamoto: My Life with a Thousand Characters* (Jackson: University of Mississippi Press, 2009), 161.

43. Geraldine Fabrikant, "The Fall and Rise of Fred Silverman," *New York Times*, June, 5, 1989, http://www.nytimes.com/1989/06/05/business/the-fall-and-rise-of-fred-silverman.html?pagewanted=all&mcubz=0. *Sanford and Son* (1975–1976), *Little House on the Prairie* (1976–1977, 1977–1978), and *Project U.F.O.* (1977–1978) Also *NBC Monday Night Movie* (1976–1977, 1977–1978).

44. Joe Ruby and Ken Spears, *The Stu's Show*.

45. William Richter, "Action for Children's Television," Museum of Broadcast Communication, http://www.museum.tv/eotv/actionforch.htm.

46. "Census Makes Sense of TV Ownership," *Radio and Television Business Report,* May 30, 2008, http://rbr.com/census-makes-sense-of-tv-ownership/.

47. "Norman Rockwell Museum Presents 'Hanna-Barbera: The Architects of Saturday Morning,'" Norman Rockwell Museum, August 17, 2016, https://www.nrm.org/2016/12/norman-rockwell-museum-presents-hanna-barbera-architects-saturday-morning.

48. Richard B. Haynes, "Children's Perceptions of 'Comic' and 'Authentic' Cartoon Violence," *Journal of Broadcasting & Electronic Media* 22, no. 1 (1978): 63–70.

49. Jason Mittell, *Genre and Television: From Cop Shows to Cartoons in American Culture* (New York, Routledge, 2004), 72.

50. Mathew Klickstein, *SLIMED! An Oral History of Nickelodeon's Golden Age* (New York: Plume, 2013), Kindle Edition.

51. Douglas B. Holt, *How Brands Become Icons: The Principles of Cultural Branding* (Cambridge: Harvard Business Press, 2004), 24.

52. James Allen Smith, *Strategic Calling: The Center for Strategic and International Studies* (Washington, D.C.: Center for Strategic and International Studies, 1993), 80–82.

53. Michael Lind, "How Reaganism Actually Started with Carter," *Salon*, February 8, 2011, http://www.salon.com/2011/02/08/lind_reaganism_carter/.

Chapter 7

1. Amanda D. Lotz, "U.S. Television and the Recession: Impetus for Change?" *Popular Communication* 8, no. 3 (2010): 186–189.

2. Jeff Lenburg, *Encyclopedia of Animated Cartoons* (New York: Facts on File, 2008), 412.

3. Shalom M. Fiske, "Peeking Behind the Screen Varied Approach to the Production of Education Television," *The Children's Television Community*, edited by J. Alison Bryant (Mahwah, NJ: Lawrence Erlbaum, 2007), 96.

4. Maureen Furniss, *Art in Motion: Animation Aesthetics* (London: John Libbey, 2008), 232.

5. "Popeye and Friends, Vol. 1," *DVD Talk*, June 17, 2008, http://www.dvdtalk.com/reviews/33844/popeye-and-friends-vol-1/. Brutus' name was changed back to Bluto after a mistake in the previous series.

6. Hal Erickson, *Television Cartoon Shows: An Illustrated Encyclopedia, 1949–2003* (Jefferson, NC: McFarland,2005), 637.

7. Fred Grandinetti, "When Popeye Was Popular Without His Punch!" *Skwigly*, March 9, 2017, http://www.skwigly.co.uk/popeye-popular-without-punch/. Cartoons in the 1980s became famous for these awkward PSAs including G.I. Joe's "Knowing is half the battle" clips.

8. Vincent Terrace, *The Encyclopedia of Television Shows: 1925 Through 2010* (Jefferson, NC: McFarland, 2011), 13.

9. Erickson, *Television Cartoon Shows*, 637.

10. Steve Ryfle, *Japan's Favorite Mon-Star* (Toronto: ECW Press, 1998), 209.

11. Erickson, *Television Cartoon Shows*, 380–381; Doug Wildey, "Amazing Heroes #95," *Classic Jonny Quest*, original interview released May 15, 1990, http://www.classicjq.com/info/AmazingHeroes95.aspx.

12. *Ibid.*

13. Eric Diaz, "Archie Launches New Josie and the Pussycats Series This Fall," *Nerdist*, June 9, 2016. http://nerdist.com/archie-launches-new-josie-and-the-pussycats-series-this-fall/.

14. https://en.wikipedia.org/wiki/Yogi%27s_Space_Race#/media/File:Yogis_Space_Race.JPG.

15. Lori Kendall, "Nerd Nation: Images of Nerds in U.S. Popular Culture," *International Journal of Cultural Studies* 2, no. 2 (1999): 260–283.

16. Paul Green, *Encyclopedia of Weird Westerns: Supernatural and Science Fiction Elements in Novels, Pulps, Comics, Films, Television, and Games* (Jefferson, NC: McFarland, 2009), 285.

17. Gary H. Grossman, *Saturday Morning TV* (New York: Random House Value Publishing, 1988), 388.

18. Maltin, 229.

19. Green, *Encyclopedia of Weird Westerns*, 47.

20. Marc Tyler Nobleman, "Super '70s and '80s: 'Super Friends'—Darrell McNeil, animator," *Noblemania*, July 29, 2011, https://www.noblemania.com/2011/07/super-70s-and-80s-super-friendsdarrell.html.

21. Kelsey Herschberger, "Black Lightning: 15 Things You Never Knew," *Comic Book Resources,* January 18, 2017, http://www.cbr.com/black-lightning-15-things-you-never-knew/. Electrical manipulation is their main strength.

22. Brian Cronin, "The Super Friends, Ranked," *Comic Book Resources*, November 29, 2016, http://www.cbr.com/all-of-the-super-friends-ranked/.

23. Noel Murray, "Legends of the Superheroes," *AV Club*, February 16, 2011, https://tv.avclub.com/legends-of-the-superheroes-1798225159; Mike Ryan, "Remember This? The Challenge of the Super Friends," *The Huffington Post*, July 18, 2012, http://www.huffingtonpost.com/mike-ryan/remember-this-challenge-of-the-super-friends_b_1683914.html.

24. Terrace, *Encyclopedia of Television Shows*, 8245.

25. Stephen Cox, "The Modern Stone Age Family Has Its Golden Anniversary," *Los Angeles Times,* September 11, 2010, http://articles.latimes.com/2010/sep/11/entertainment/la-et-flintstones-20100911.

26. David Lambert, "The Flintstones—Warner Archive Puts Out 4 DVD Titles with Post-Series Primetime Specials," *TV Shows on DVD*, October 9, 2012, http://tvshowsondvd.com/news/Flintstones-The-Prime-Time-Specials-Collections/17586.

27. Travis Fickett, Eric Goldman, Dan Iverson and Brian Zoromski, "Fantastic Four on TV," *IGN*, July 15, 2007. http://www.ign.com/articles/2007/06/16/fantastic-four-on-tv-2?page=2. Marvel acquired DePatie-Freleng in 1981.

28. David Perlmutter, *America Toons In: A History of Television Animation* (Jefferson, NC: McFarland, 2014), 210.

29. Michael Klosner, *Prehistoric Humans in Film and Television: 581 Dramas, Comedies, and Documentaries, 1905–2004* (Jefferson, NC: McFarland, 2006), 72–73.

30. Yiddish for uterus.

31. Klosner, *Prehistoric Humans in Film and Television*, 72.

32. Erickson, *Television Cartoon Shows*, 341.

33. *Ibid.*, 189–190.

34. Kevin Melrose, "Can DC's Scooby-Doo Apocalypse Redeem Scrappy-Doo?" *Comic Book Resources*, October 10, 2012, http://www.cbr.com/can-dcs-scooby-apocalypse-redeem-scrappy-doo/.

35. Erickson, *Television Cartoon Shows*, 724.

36. Dunbar's alter ego was Gizmo, a hero who held gadgets in his Afro. Nate Branch/Liquid Man (Scatman Crothers), Curly Neal/Super Sphere (Stu Gillam), Twiggy Sanders/Spaghetti Man (Buster Jones), Geese Ausbie/Multi Man (Johnny Williams).

37. Gael Fashingbauer Cooper and Brian Bellmont, *Whatever Happened to Pudding Pops? The Lost Toys, Tastes and Trends of the 70's and 80's* (New York: Perigee, 2011), Kindle Edition. Wade hosted the short-lived Musical Chairs on CBS.

38. "The Old Is New," *Radmar Inc.*, February 12, 2013, https://radmarinc.com/tag/education/.

39. "The Story of Daren the Lion," *D.A.R.E.* https://www.dare.org/the-story-of-daren-the-lion/; Farhad Mirza, "How Mickey Mouse Fought World War II," *Vulture*, October 29, 2015, http://www.vulture.com/2015/10/how-mickey-mouse-fought-world-war-ii.html.

40. Leonard Maltin, *Leonard Maltin's 2009 Movie Guide* (New York: Penguin Group, 2009), 243.

41. "Belle Starr (TV Movie)," Warner Bros., https://www.warnerbros.com/tv/belle-starr-tv-movie.

42. Leonard Maltin, *Of Mice and Magic: A History of American Animated Cartoons* (New York: Penguin, 1987), 273.

43. Jennifer Fickley-Baker, "This Week in Disney History: Oswald the Lucky Rabbit Debuted in 1927," Disney Parks, September 8, 2012, https://disneyparks.disney.go.com/blog/2012/09/this-week-in-disney-history-oswald-the-lucky-rabbit-debuted-in-1927/.

44. Fred M. Grandinetti *Popeye: An Illustrated History* (Jefferson, NC: McFarland, 2004), 142.

45. Terry Kalagian, "Programming Children's Television: The Cable Model," *The Children's Television Community* edited by J. Alison Bryant (Mahwah, NJ: Lawrence Erlbaum, 2007), 149.

46. Vincent Terrace, *Encyclopedia of Television Pilots* (Jefferson, NC: McFarland, 2013), 24.

47. Christopher P. Lehman, *American Cartoons of the Vietnam Era: A Study of Social Commentary in Film and Television, 1961–1975* (Jefferson, NC: McFarland, 2007) 173. *The Simpsons* episode from the second season had the exact same premise, "One Fish, Two Fish, Blowfish, Blue Fish."

48. Jason Motes, "'Young Justice' Pays Homage to The Original Super Hero Cartoon Hit 'Super Friends,'" *ScienceFiction.com*, January 31, 2013, http://sciencefiction.com/2013/01/31/young-justice-pays-homage-to-the-original-super-hero-cartoon-hit/.

49. "Richie Rich," *Comics Through Times: A History of Icons, Idols, and Ideas*, edited by M. Keith Booker (Santa Barbara, CA: Greenwood, 2014), 749.

50. Brian Cronin, "TV Legends Revealed: Was Dr. Who Replaced in a Cartoon by Fonzie?" *Comic Book Resources*, March 16, 2016, http://www.cbr.com/tv-legends-revealed-was-doctor-who-replaced-in-a-cartoon-by-fonzie/. Co-produced with Paramount.

51. Erickson, *Television Cartoon Shows*, 287–288; "Drak Pack: Full Cast and Crew," *Internet Movie Database*, http://www.imdb.com/title/tt0220892/fullcredits?ref_=tt_ov_st_sm.

52. Graeme McMillan, "The Secret Life of the Other Birdman," *The Hollywood Reporter*, February 23, 2015, http://www.hollywoodreporter.com/heat-vision/secret-life-birdman-775822.

53. "The Great Gilly Hopkins," *Turner Classic Movies*, http://www.tcm.com/tcmdb/title/469692/Great-Gilly-Hopkins-The/.

54. "Operation Prime Time Sets Three New Shows," *Broadcasting*, August 29, 1977, http://americanradiohistory.com/Archive-BC/BC-1977/BC-1977-08-29.pdf.

55. Geraldine Fabrikant, "The Fall and Rise of Fred Silverman," *New York Times*, June, 5, 1989, http://www.nytimes.com/1989/06/05/business/the-fall-and-rise-of-fred-silverman.html?pagewanted=all&mcubz=0.

56. Will Harris, "In 1978, Hanna-Barbera Took to the Ice to Celebrate Fred Flintstone's Birthday," *AVClub*, April 15, 2016, http://www.avclub.com/article/1978-hanna-barbera-took-ice-celebrate-fred-flintst-235288.

57. Steve Dale, "Snow White and Greenbacks: Disney's Newest Ice Production Is Nostalgic-and Lucrative," *Chicago Tribune*, January 20, 2015, http://articles.chicagotribune.com/1995–01–20/entertainment/9501200093_1_kenneth-feld-productions-snow-white-dwarfs.

58. Evan Narcisse, "Documentary About Disney's First Black Reveals a Hidden, Turbulent History," *io9*, December 2, 2016, http://io9.gizmodo.com/documentary-about-disneys-first-black-animator-reveals-1789572836.

59. Iwao Takamoto and Michael Mallory, *Iwao Takamoto: My Life with a Thousand Characters* (Jackson: University of Mississippi Press, 2009), 3–9.

60. David Perlmutter, *America Toons In: A History of Television Animation* (Jefferson, NC: McFarland, 2014), 129.

61. Gene Demby, "Who Gets to Be a Superhero? Race And Identity In Comics," *NPR*, January 11, 2014, https://www.npr.org/sections/codeswitch/2014/01/11/261449394/who-gets-to-be-a-superhero-race-and-identity-in-comics.

62. Darran Jordan, *Green Lantern History: An Unauthorized Guide to the DC Comic Book Series* (Sydney: Eclectica, 2015), 508–509.

63. Noel Murray, "Legends of the Superheroes," *AVClub*, February 16, 2011, http://www.avclub.com/article/ilegends-of-the-superheroesi-51932.

64. Michael A. Sheyahshe, *Native Americans in Comic Books: A Critical Study* (Jefferson, NC: McFarland, 2008), 201.

65. Heather Hendershot, *Saturday Morning Censors: Television Regulation Before the V-Chip* (Durham: Duke University Press, 1998), 38–39.

66. Stephen McMillan, "Classic Cartoon Icon: Valerie of Josie and the Pussycats," *Soul Train* March 28, 2012, http://soultrain.com/2012/03/28/classic-cartoon-icon-valerie-of-josie-and-the-pussycats/.

67. Wendy Ashley, "The Angry Black Woman: The Impact of Pejorative Stereotypes on Psychotherapy with Black Women," *Social Work in Public Health* 29, no. 1 (2014): 27–34.

68. "Vulture Asks: What Couple Do You Anti-Ship?" *Vulture*, September 27, 2016, http://www.vulture.com/2016/08/tv-couple-anti-shipping.html.

69. Felicia R. Lee, "Hey, Hey, Hey! Animated Touchstones: Funky Turns 40 Recalls a Seminal TV Moment," *New York Times*, March 19, 2014, https://www.nytimes.com/2014/03/20/arts/design/funky-turns-40-show-recalls-a-seminal-tv-moment.html?mcubz=0&mcubz=0.

Chapter 8

1. Paula Brown Hayton, "United Video, Inc. v. FCC: Just Another Episode in Syndex Regulation," *Loyola Los Angeles Entertainment Law Review* 12 (1992): 251.

2. Adam M. Zaretsky, "I want my MTV ... and My CNN ... The Cable Industry and Regulation," *Regional Economist*, July 1995, https://www.stlouisfed.org/publications/regional-economist/july-1995/i-want-my-mtvand-my-cnn-the-cable-tv-industry-and-regulation.

3. Stephen LaBaton, "Deregulating the Media: The Overview; Regulators Ease Rules Governing Media Ownership," *The New York Times*, June 3, 2003, http://www.nytimes.com/2003/06/03/business/deregulating-media-overview-regulators-ease-rules-governing-media-ownership.html?mcubz=0.

4. Donna Mitroff and Rebecca Herr Stephenson, "The Television Tug-of-War: A Brief History of Children's Television Programming in the United States," *The Children's Television Community*, edited by J. Alison Bryant (Mahwah, NJ: Lawrence Erlbaum, 2007), 15–23.

5. Alison Alexander and James Owers, "The Economics of Children's Television," *The Children's Television Community*, edited by J. Alison Bryant (Mahwah, NJ: Lawrence Erlbaum, 2007), 62–63.

6. Sherille Ismail, "Transformative Choices: A Review Of 70 Years of FCC Decisions," *Federal Communications Commission*, October 2010, https://apps.fcc.gov/edocs_public/attachmatch/DOC-302496A1.pdf, 10–25.

7. C. H. Sterling, "Deregulation," Museum of Broadcast Communication, http://www.museum.tv/eotv/deregulation.htm.

8. Lori A. Brainard, "Television Policy: Economic v. Content Regulation and Deregulation" *Focus on Law Studies,* Fall 2014, https://www.americanbar.org/content/dam/aba/publishing/focus_on_law_studies/publiced_focus_fall04.authcheckdam.pdf.

9. Martha Derthick and Paul J. Quirk, *The Politics of Deregulation* (Washington, D.C.: The Brookings Institute, 1985), 7.

10. Brainard, "Television Policy."

11. "Ownership," FCC Quadrennial Review (2010), https://transition.fcc.gov/osp/inc-report/INoC-30-Ownership.pdf.

12. Michael Z. Newman, *Atari Age: The Emergence of Video Games in America* (Cambridge: MIT Press, 2016), 53.

13. Martin Goodman, "When Reagan Met Optimus Prime" *Animation World Network*, October 12, 2010, https://www.awn.com/animationworld/dr-toon-when-reagan-met-optimus-prime.

14. Cary O'Dell, *Women Pioneers in Television: Biographies of Fifteen Industry Leaders* (Jefferson, NC: McFarland, 1997), 56.

15. David Perlmutter, *America Toons In: A History of Television Animation* (Jefferson, NC: McFarland, 2014), 306. Matty was also sold as a doll.

16. Tim Hollis, *Toons in Toyland: The Story of Cartoon Character Merchandise* (Jackson: University Press of Mississippi Press, 2015), 306.

17. Stuart Fischer, *Kids' TV: The First 25 Years* (New York, Facts on File, 1983), Kindle Edition.

18. Ellen Wojahn, *The General Mills/Parker Brothers Merger: Playing by Different Rules* (Frederick, MD: Beard Books, 1988), 98 .

19. Allen K. Rostron, "Return to Hot Wheels: The FCC, Program-Length Commercials, and the Children's Television Act of 1990," *Hastings Communication & Entertainment Law Journal* 19 (1996): 57.

20. Mitroff and Stephenson, "The Television Tug-of-War," xxx.

21. William D. Crump, *How the Movies Saved Christmas: 228 Rescues from Clausnappers, Sleigh Crashes, Lost Presents and Holiday Disasters* (Jefferson, NC: McFarland, 2017), 226.

22. Peyo's real name Pierre Culliford. He was an animator before moving to comics.

23. Norma Odom Pecora, *The Business of Children's Entertainment* (New York: Guilford Press, 1998), 67.

24. Tara Ariano and Sarah D. Bunting, *Television Without Pity: 752 Things to Love to Hate (and Hate to Love) About TV* (Philadelphia: Quick Books, 2006), 45.

25. Vincent Terrace, *The Encyclopedia of Television Shows: 1925 Through 2010* (Jefferson, NC: McFarland, 2011), 5094., PAL instead of NTSC.

26. Pete Imbesi, "Space Ghost: 15 Weird Facts You Never Knew," *Comic Book Resources*, April 5, 2017, http://www.cbr.com/space-ghost-15-weird-facts-you-never-knew/.

27. Bob Leszczak, *Single Season Sitcoms of the 1980s: A Complete Guide* (Jefferson, NC: McFarland, 2016), 211.

28. Jeff Lenburg, *Encyclopedia of Animated Cartoons* (New York: Facts on File, 2008), Jeff Lenburg, *Who's Who in Animated Cartoons: An International Guide to Film and Televisions Award Winning Animators* (New York: Applause, 2006), 19.

29. "Charlie Brown and Strawberry Shortcake sold for $345M U.S. to Halifax Company", *CBCNews*, May 10, 2017 http://www.cbc.ca/news/business/peanuts-sold-dhx-media-halifax-strawberry-shortcake-children-tv-shows-1.4107903.

30. Brent Staples, "Just a Toaster with Pictures," *New York Times*, February 8, 1987, http://www.nytimes.com/1987/02/08/books/just-a-toaster-with-pictures.html?pagewanted=all.

31. Mark JP Wolf, "Video Games of the 1970s," *The Video Game Explosion: a History from PONG to Playstation and Beyond*, edited by Mark JP Wolf (ABC-CLIO, 2008). Sega produced the motorcycle racing game *Fonz* in 1976.

32. Newman, *Atari Age*, 7–9.

33. Mia Consalvo, *Atari to Zelda: Japan's Videogames in Global Contexts* (Cambridge: MIT Press, 2010), 193–194.

34. Jeffrey L. Wilson "The 10 Most Influential Video Games of All-Times" *PCMag*, June 11, 2010, http://www.pcmag.com/feature/251651/the-10-most-influential-video-games-of-all-time?p=n.

35. Petrina Foli, "Pac-Man Bites Back," *O Say Can You See*, June 11, 2010, http://americanhistory.si.edu/blog/2010/06/pacman-bites-back.html.

36. Ari Voukydis and Marc Sarian, "Did You Know Ms. Pac-Man Is A Feminist Icon?" *HuffPost*, March 27, 2014, https://www.huffpost.com/entry/ms-pac-man-feminist-icon_n_5036619.

37. "What is Pac-Man?" *PacMan.com*, archived November 28, 2010, https://web.archive.org/web/20101128063459/http://pacman.com/en/about.

38. John Corry, "TV: Preview of Saturday Cartoons," *New York Times*, September 14, 1983, http://www.nytimes.com/1983/09/14/arts/tv-preview-of-saturday-cartoons.html?mcubz=0. Frogger, Donkey Kong, Donkey Kong, Jr., Q*Bert, Pitfall. Donkey Kong did feature the rudimentary Mario from the video game before he became the character mascot for Nintendo.

39. Newman, *Atari Age*, 194.

40. David Mansour, *From Abba to Zoom: A Pop Culture Encyclopedia of the Late 20th Centuries* (Kansas City: Andrews McMeel, 2005), 429.

41. "More Care Bears Fun Facts," *Care-Bears.com*, retrieved March 1, 2005, https://web.archive.org/web/20050301073233/http://www.care-bears.com/CareBears/html/history/funfacts.html.

42. Terrace, *Encyclopedia of Television Shows*, 221.

43. Ibid.

44. Jay Bobbin, "Yogi Bear's All-Star Christmas Caper," *Allentown Morning Call*, 2017, http://www.mcall.com/zap-dvd-review-yogi-bears-comedy-christmas-caper-story.html.

45. Hal Erickson, *Television Cartoon Shows: An Illustrated Encyclopedia, 1949–2003* (Jefferson, NC: McFarland, 2005), xxx.

46. David Hofstead, *The Dukes of Hazzard: The Unofficial Companion* (New York: St. Martin's, 1998), 88.

47. Leszczak, *Single Season Sitcoms*, 211. Including Robin Williams, promotional material was very similar to *The Dukes*.

48. Jerry Beck, *The Animated Film Guide* (Chicago: Chicago Review, 2005), 108.

49. Girin Pirnia, "13 Fun Facts About Scooby-Doo," *Mental Floss*, June 2, 2016, http://mentalfloss.com/article/80937/13-fun-facts-about-scooby-doo.

50. Goodman, "When Reagan Met Optimus Prime."

51. Perlmutter, *America Toons In*, 179.

52. Timothy Burke and Kevin Burke, *Saturday Morning Fever: Growing Up with Cartoon Culture* (New York: St. Martin's, 1999), 63.

53. "Margaret Loesch, Executive Chairman of Genius Brands International's Kid Genius Cartoon Channel; Vice Chair," Television Academy Foundation, https://www.emmys.com/foundation/board/110336.

54. Erickson, *Television Cartoon Shows*, 600, 691.

55. Mansour, *From Abba to Zoom*, 318.

56. Mike Burg, *Trial by Fire: One Man's Battle to End Corporate Greed* (Dallas: Benbella, 2016), 200–204.

57. Goodman, "When Reagan Met Optimus Prime."

58. Jake Rossen, "On Smurf Turf: Remembering the Snorks," *Mental Floss*, April 20, 2017,

http://mentalfloss.com/article/94549/smurf-turf-remembering-snorks.

59. Elizabeth Bailey, "Snorks and Popples," *New York Times,* May 1, 1988, http://www.nytimes.com/1988/05/01/books/snorks-and-popples.html?scp=2&sq=snorks&st=cse.

60. Jake Rossen, "Breaking the Mold: Kenner's Super Powers Collection," *Mental Floss,* February 9, 2017, http://mentalfloss.com/article/92022/breaking-mold-kenners-super-powers-collection; Paco Taylor, "The 15 Most Expensive Kenner Super Powers Toys Ever," *Comic Book Resources,* September 24, 2017, http://www.cbr.com/most-expensive-super-powers-toys/.

61. "Children's Educational Television," Federal Communications Commission, https://www.fcc.gov/consumers/guides/childrens-educational-television.

62. "Exclusive Clip, Super Friends: The Legendary Super Powers Show," *MTV,* August 8, 2008, http://www.mtv.com/news/2756496/exclusive-clip-super-friends-the-legendary-super-powers-show/.

63. Michael H. Price, "'Care Bears, 'Gobots,' not Beauty but Likeable," *Chicago Tribune,* April 4, 1988, http://articles.chicagotribune.com/1986–04–04/entertainment/8601250103_1_sleeping-beauty-dark-heart-new-entries.

64. Rob Bricken, "20 Gobots That Remind Us Why the Gobots Sucked So Incredibly Hard," *io9,* January 15, 2013, http://io9.gizmodo.com/5976109/20-gobots-that-remind-us-why-the-gobots-sucked-so-incredibly-hard.

65. Terrace, *Encyclopedia of Television Shows,* 327.

66. Erickson, *Television Cartoon Shows,* 754–756.

67. Gordon Jackson, "13 Superhero TV Shows That It's Hard to Believe Somebody Greenlighted," *io9,* January 25, 2016, http://io9.gizmodo.com/13-superhero-tv-shows-that-its-hard-to-believe-somebody-1754552331.

68. Katha Pollitt, "Hers; The Smurfette Principle," *New York Times,* April 7, 1991, http://www.nytimes.com/1991/04/07/magazine/hers-the-smurfette-principle.html?mcubz=0.

69. Josef Adalian, "10 Episodes is the New 13 (Was the New 22)," *Vulture,* June 12, 2015, http://www.vulture.com/2015/06/10-episodes-is-the-new-13-was-the-new-22.html. Closer to 100 episodes for live- action series syndication.

70. Juliana Menace Horowitz, "Most Americans See Value in Steering Children Toward Toys, Activities Associated with Opposite Gender," *Pew Research,* December 19, 2017, https://www.pewresearch.org/fact-tank/2017/12/19/most-americans-see-value-in-steering-children-toward-toys-activities-associated-with-opposite-gender/.

71. Debra L. Merskin, "Race and Gender Representations in Advertising in Cable Cartoon Programming," *CLCWeb: Comparative Literature and Culture* 10, no. 2 (2008): 10.

72. David J. Fox and Valerie B. Jordan, "Racial preference and Identification of Black, American Chinese, and White Children." *Genetic Psychology Monographs* (1973).

73. Jobia Keys, "Doc McStuffins and Dora the Explorer: Representations of Gender, Race, and Class in U.S. Animation," *Journal of Children and Media* 10, no. 3 (2016): 355–368.

Chapter 9

1. Brent Staples, "Just a Toaster with Pictures," *New York Times,* February 8, 1987, http://www.nytimes.com/1987/02/08/books/just-a-toaster-with-pictures.html?pagewanted=all.

2. Elizabeth Sweet, "Toys are More Divided by Gender Than They Were 50 Years Ago," *The Atlantic,* December 9, 2014, https://www.theatlantic.com/business/archive/2014/12/toys-are-more-divided-by-gender-now-than-they-were-50-years-ago/383556/.

3. Jennifer Mandel, "The Production of a Beloved Community: Sesame Street's Answer to America's Inequalities," *The Journal of American Culture* 29, no. 1 (2006): 3.

4. Nikki Gloudeman, "Why Children's Cartoons Have a Sexism Problem," *The Huffington Post,* October 6, 2014, http://www.huffingtonpost.com/nikki-gloudeman/why-childrens-cartoons-have-a-sexism-problem_b_5924390.html.

5. Martin Goodman, "When Reagan Met Optimus Prime," *Animation World Network,* October 12, 2010, https://www.awn.com/animationworld/dr-toon-when-reagan-met-optimus-prime.

6. "Saturday Morning TV Schedules of the 1980s," *In the 80s,* http://www.inthe80s.com/saturdays.shtml.

7. Darran Jordan, *Green Lantern History: An Unauthorized Guide to the DC Comic Book Series* (Sydney: Eclectica, 2015), 416.

8. David Hofstede, *What Were They Thinking? The 100 Dumbest Events in Television History* (New York: Watson-Guptill, 2004), 190 He returned in the *Scooby-Doo* movie.

9. Jonah Krakow, "TV Playbook: Let's Add a Kid!" *IGN,* December 10, 2008, http://www.ign.com/articles/2008/12/10/tv-playbook-lets-add-a-kid?page=5.

10. David Perlmutter, *America Toons In: A History of Television Animation* (Jefferson, NC: McFarland, 2014), 184.

11. "Saturday Morning TV Schedules of the 1980s."

12. "About the Berenstain Bears," *The Berenstain Bears,* http://www.berenstainbears.com/about.html.

13. Alexis C. Madigral, "The Court Case That Almost Made it Illegal to Tape TV Shows," *The Atlantic,* January 12, 2012, https://www.theatlantic.com/technology/archive/2012/01/the-court-case-that-almost-made-it-illegal-to-tape-tv-shows/251107/.

14. Cathye Kryczka, "Again, Again! Why Your Kid Wants to Do the Same Activity Over and Over," *Today's Parent,* December 14, 2019, https://www.todaysparent.com/toddler/kids-repetition/.

15. "Top Kid Videos," *Billboard Magazine,* February 23, 2002, https://goo.gl/aTi4SR.

16. John Dart, "Biblical Stories Available on Home Video," *Los Angeles Times,* March 29, 1986, http://articles.latimes.com/1986–03–29/

news/mn-1295_1_hanna-barbera-productions, Worldvision was originally owned by ABC before fin-syn rules were enacted in 1971.

17. Stephen Holden, "Movie Review: Film: 'GoBots' TV Spin-Off," *New York Times*, March 22, 1986, http://www.nytimes.com/movie/review?res=9 A0DE5DA143FF931A15750C0A960948260.

18. Hal Erickson, *Television Cartoon Shows: An Illustrated Encyclopedia, 1949–2003* (Jefferson, NC: McFarland, 2005), 934.

19. Claudia Wallace, "The Nuclear Family Goes 'Boom!'" *Time*, October 15, 1992, http://content.time.com/time/printout/0,8816,976754,00.html.

20. Perlmutter, *America Toons In*, 181.

21. Rob Bricken, "12 Cartoons From the 1980s No One Will Ever Have Nostalgia," *io9*, November 11, 2014, http://io9.gizmodo.com/12-cartoons-from-the-1980s-no-one-will-ever-have-nosta-1657410102.

22. Vincent Terrace, *Television Specials: 5,336 Entertainment Programs, 1936–2012* (Jefferson, NC: McFarland, 2013), 154.

23. Josef Adalian, "How Nickelodeon Got America Hooked on Cable," *Vultures*, October 24, 2016, http://www.vulture.com/2016/10/nickelodeon-got-america-hooked-on-cable.html. This strategy was expanded when Nick Jr. premiered in 1988.

24. Jean Ann Wright, *Animation Writing and Development: From Script Development to Pitch* (New York: Focal Press, 2005), 80.

25. Erickson, *Television Cartoon Shows*, 342.

26. Ted Sennett, *The Art of Hanna-Barbera: Fifty Years of Creativity* (New York: Viking Studio Books, 1991), 97.

27. Mark Hughes, "Exclusive: 'Jonny Quest' Could Be Warner's Next Big Franchise," *Forbes*, July 28, 2016, https://www.forbes.com/sites/markhughes/2016/07/28/exclusive-jonny-quest-could-be-warners-next-big-franchise/#754dce16749b.

28. Vincent Terrace, *The Encyclopedia of Television Shows: 1925 Through 2010* (Jefferson, NC: McFarland, 2011), 355.

29. Erickson, *Television Cartoon Shows*, 754–756. *The Smurfs* seasons 6–8 were outsourced to Cuckoo's Nest and the Japanese Toei.

30. Charles Solomon, "Saturday Morning: Good and Bad," *Los Angeles Times*, October 2, 1986, http://articles.latimes.com/1986-10-02/entertainment/ca-3542_1_bad-news.

31. Michael K. Manning, "1970s". *DC Comics Year by Year: A Visual Chronicle*, edited by Daniel Wallace and Matthew K. Manning (New York: Dueling Kindersley, 2010), 201.

32. Erickson, *Television Cartoon Shows*, 638.

33. "Believe It or Not the Cartoon Pound Puppies Was Inspired by Hogan's Heroes," *MeTV*, April 25, 2017, http://www.metv.com/stories/believe-it-or-not-the-cartoon-pound-puppies-was-inspired-by-hogans-heroes.

34. Solomon, "Saturday Morning."

35. Michael Mallory, "Animation's Legendary (Semi-) Lost Film," *Animation Magazine*, November 6, 2017, http://www.animationmagazine.net/top-stories/animations-legendary-semi-lost-film/.

36. Sennett, *The Art of Hanna-Barbera*, 260.

37. John J. O'Connor, "Buddy Ebsen and Joey Cramer Star in Stone Fox," *New York Times*, March 30, 1987, http://www.nytimes.com/1987/03/30/arts/buddy-ebsen-and-joey-cramer-star-in-stone-fox.html?mcubz=0.

38. Jonathan Clements and Helen McCarthy, *The Anime Encyclopedia, 3rd Revised Edition: A Century of Japanese Animation* (Berkeley: Stone Bridge, 2015), 264.

39. "Holders OK $847 Million Deal for Taft," *Los Angeles Times*, September 30, 1987, http://articles.latimes.com/1987-09-30/business/fi-7368_1_buyout.

40. Peter J. Boyer, "Under Fowler F.C.C. Treated as Commerce," *New York Times*, January 19, 1987, http://www.nytimes.com/1987/01/19/arts/under-fowler-fcc-treated-tv-as-commerce.html.

41. Erickson, *Television Cartoon Shows*, 750.

42. Charles Solomon, "Kidvid Reviews: Cartoon Debuts Are All Drawn Out," *New York Times*, October 9, 1987, http://articles.latimes.com/1987-10-09/entertainment/ca-8568_1_cartoon-series.

43. Perlmutter, *America Toons In*, 184.

44. Matt Novak, "50 Years of the Jetsons, Why the Show Still Matters," *Smithsonian*, September 19, 2012, http://www.smithsonianmag.com/history/50-years-of-the-jetsons-why-the-show-still-matters-43459669/.

45. Sennett, *The Art of Hanna-Barbera*, 120.

46. Jeff Lenburg, *Encyclopedia of Animated Cartoons* (New York: Facts on File), 268.

47. *Ibid.*, 317.

48. *Ibid.*, 321.

49. Perlmutter, *America Toons In*, 184–185.

50. Jeff Lenburg, *Encyclopedia of Animated Cartoons*, 349.

51. Douglas Quenqua, "Nancy Reagan's Most Memorable 'Just Say No' Moments," *Campaign*, March 7, 2016, http://www.campaignlive.com/article/nancy-reagans-memorable-just-say-no-moments/1386274.

52. "The Story of Daren the Lion," *D.A.R.E.*, https://www.dare.org/the-story-of-daren-the-lion/.

53. Randall Neece, *Gone Today, Here Tomorrow: A Memoir* (Bloomington: Author House, 2012), 102.

54. Aubrey Whelan, "A Loving Look Back at Double Dare Made-in-Philly TV That's 30 Years Old Today," *Philadelphia Inquirer,* http://www.philly.com/philly/entertainment/television/A-loving-look-back-at-Double-Dare-made-in-Philly-TV.html.

55. Mark McDermott, "Yogi Bear," *The Guide to United States Popular Culture*, edited by Ray Broadus Browne and Pat Browne (Madison: University of Wisconsin, 2001), 944.

56. Anderson Evans, "Fantastic Max, Dirty Diapers All in Your Face," *Gawker*, August 7, 2010, http://gawker.com/5606752/fantastic-max-dirty-diapers-all-in-your-face.

57. "SuperTed," *BBC Wales*, http://www.bbc.co.uk/wales/arts/sites/children/pages/superted.shtml.

58. "Whoopi Goldberg Cartoon Show on Drawing Board," *Jet*, March 21, 1988, 37.

59. Matthew Callan, "'It's All My Fault, Although

I Also Blame Others': The Curious Case of the Ed Grimley Cartoon," *Splitsider*, July 5, 2011, http://splitsider.com/2011/07/its-all-my-fault-although-i-also-blame-others-the-curious-case-of-the-ed-grimley-cartoon/.

60. David Perlmutter, *America Toons In*, 184–185.

61. Teri Schultz, "Smurfs At 50: Ready for a Comeback," *NPR*, February 21, 2008, http://www.npr.org/templates/story/story.php?storyId=18945311.

62. Joseph Lamour, "11 Secrets You Never Knew About Animaniacs, Pinky & the Brain and Freakazoid," *MTV News*, April 14, 2016, http://www.mtv.com/news/2867289/animaniacs-netflix-freakazoid-pinky-brain/.

63. Michael Lev, "Hanna-Barbera Follows Disney Map," *New York Times*, January 9, 1990, http://www.nytimes.com/1990/01/09/business/hanna-barbera-follows-disney-map.html?mcubz=0.

64. James T. Hamilton, *Channeling Violence: The Economic Market for Violent Television Programming* (Princeton: Princeton University, 1998), 339.

65. Brian C. Baer, *How He-Man Mastered the Universe: Toy to Television to the Big Screen* (Jefferson, NC: McFarland, 2017), 184.

66. Nancy Tartaglione, "Michael Bond Dies: Paddington Bear Creator & Author Was 91," *Deadline*, June 28, 2017, http://deadline.com/2017/06/michael-bond-dead-paddington-1202121245/.

67. Justin Caffier, "The 90s Anti-Drug PSA 'Cartoon All-Stars to the Rescue' Didn't Stop Kids from Getting High," *Vice*, April 21, 2015, https://www.vice.com/en_us/article/exqgyk/looking-back-on-cartoon-all-stars-to-the-rescue-421.

68. "Actress Who Originated Judy Jetson Speaks Out," *Orlando Sentinel*, July 13, 1990, http://articles.orlandosentinel.com/1990–07–13/entertainment/9007130666_1_judy-jetson-barbera-robin-hood.

69. Douglas L. McCall, *Film Cartoons: A Guide to 20th Century American Animated Features and Shorts* (Jefferson, NC: McFarland, 1998), 86.

70. Vincent Terrace, *Encyclopedia of Television Pilots* (Jefferson, NC: McFarland, 2013), 334.

71. Nick Sim, "The Top 10 Defunct Universal Studios Florida Attractions," *Theme Park Tourist*, January 27, 2014, http://www.themeparktourist.com/features/20140126/15968/top-10-defunct-universal-studios-florida-attractions.

72. Boyer, "Under Fowler F.C.C. Treated as Commerce."

73. Gretnablue, "The Top 80s Cartoons Analyzed (By Someone Who Wasn't There)," *Observation Deck*, July 21, 2015, http://observationdeck.kinja.com/the-top-80s-cartoons-analyzed-by-someone-who-wasnt-the-1719334081.

74. Jose Esteban Munoz, *Disidentifications: Queers of Color and the Performance of Politics* (Minneapolis: University of Minnesota, 1999), Location 1001.

75. Yasuko Takezawa, "New Arts New Resistance: Asian American Artists in the Post-Race Era," *Racial Representations in Asia*, edited by Yasuko I. Takezawa (Melbourne: Trans Pacific Press, 2011), 213.

76. Sweet, "Toys Are More Divided by Gender."

77. Dr. Monica Brasted, "Care Bears vs. Transformers: Gender Stereotypes in Advertisements," *SocJourn*, February 17, 2009, https://www.sociology.org/care-bears-vs-transformers-gender-stereotypes-in-advertisements/.

78. Matthew Zuras, "Childhood Ruined: 10 Offensive Cartoons of Our Youth," *Refinery29*, November 23, 2013, http://www.refinery29.com/2013/11/57871/offensive-cartoons.

79. Teju Cole, "The White Savior Industrial Complex," *The Atlantic*, March 21, 2012, https://www.theatlantic.com/international/archive/2012/03/the-white-savior-industrial-complex/254843/.

80. Katha Pollitt, "Hers; The Smurfette Principle," *New York Times*, April 7, 1991, http://www.nytimes.com/1991/04/07/magazine/hers-the-smurfette-principle.html?mcubz=0.

81. Soraya Chemaly, "Is Smurfette Giving It Away? What the Smurfette Principle Teaches Your Kids About Girls," *The Huffington Post*, October 19, 2011, http://www.huffingtonpost.com/soraya-chemaly/is-smurfette-giving-it-awy_b_1011329.html.

Chapter 10

1. Michael Lev, "Hanna-Barbera Follows Disney Map," *New York Times*, January 9, 1990, http://www.nytimes.com/1990/01/09/business/hanna-barbera-follows-disney-map.html?mcubz=0.

2. Terry Kalagian, "Programming Children's Television: The Cable Model," *The Children's Television Community* edited by J. Alison Bryant (Mahwah, NJ: Lawrence Erlbaum, 2007).

3. Donna Mitroff and Rebecca Herr Stephenson, "The Television Tug-of-War: A Brief History of Children's Television Programming in the United States," *The Children's Television Community*, edited by J. Alison Bryant (Mahwah, NJ: Lawrence Erlbaum, 2007), 15–19.

4. Digital Electronic Cassette-Headed Kinetic System.

5. Charles Solomon, "TV Reviews: Cartoon Delivers New Twists," *Los Angeles Times*, September 17, 1990, http://articles.latimes.com/1990–09–17/entertainment/ca-482_1_cartoon-series.

6. Brad Middleton, *Un-Dead TV: The Ultimate Guide to Vampire Television* (Pepperell, MA: Light Unseen, 2012), 353.

7. "Good Morning Mickey," *D23*, https://d23.com/a-to-z/good-morning-mickey-television/.

8. Brooks Barnes and Amy Chozick, "New Disney Characters Make It Big in TV's Preschool Playground," *New York Times*, March 31, 2013, http://www.nytimes.com/2013/04/01/business/media/disney-junior-challenges-nick-jr-in-preschool-tv.html?mcubz=0.

9. Matt Schimkowitz, "The Not-So-Excellent Adventures of the 'Bill & Ted's Excellent Adventures' TV Series," *Splitsider*, October 9, 2012, http://splitsider.com/2012/10/the-not-so-excellent-adventures-of-the-bill-teds-excellent-adventures-1992-tv-series/.

10. James B. Stewart, *Disney War* (New York: Simon & Schuster, 2005), 94–95.

11. Denny Angelle, "Fall TV Goes Cartoon Crazy," *Boys Life*, September 1990; Hal Erickson, *Television Cartoon Shows: An Illustrated Encyclopedia, 1949–2003* (Jefferson, NC: McFarland, 2005), 667.

12. Vincent Terrace, *The Encyclopedia of Television Shows: 1925 Through 2010* (Jefferson, NC: McFarland, 2011), 275.

13. *Ibid.*, 688.

14. Associated Press, "TBS Buys Animator Hanna-Barbera Library for $320 Million," October 29, 1991, http://www.apnewsarchive.com/1991/TBS-Buys-Animator-Hanna-Barbera-Library-for-$320-Million/id-e4b7fe7b58573927b9188329b6cd66c1.

15. Al Delugach, "Turner Sells Fabled MGM But Keeps Lion's Share" *Los Angeles Times*, June 7, 1986, http://articles.latimes.com/1986-06-07/news/mn-9950_1_turner-broadcasting.

16. Mark McDermott, "Yogi Bear," *The Guide to United States Popular Culture*, edited by Ray Broadus Browne and Pat Browne (Madison: University of Wisconsin Press, 2001), 944.

17. Dave Trumbore, "Hollywood! Adapt This: The Pirates of Dark Water," Collider, September 9, 2012, http://collider.com/pirates-of-dark-water-movie-adaptation/.

18. Katharine Trendacosta, "Seriously, Another Robin Hood Movie Is Being Written," *io9*, February 27, 2015, https://io9.gizmodo.com/it-did-include-time-bandits-1688413187.

19. AP, "TBS Buys Animator."

20. Jacques Steinberg, "Rivals Unafraid to Borrow, or Steal, From Each Other," *New York Times*, February 23, 2009, http://www.nytimes.com/2009/02/24/arts/television/24nick.html?mcubz=0.

21. Charles Haddad, "Turner Serious About Yogi Bear," *Chicago Tribune*, June 6, 1994, http://articles.chicagotribune.com/1994-06-06/business/9406060008_1_hanna-barbera-joe-barbera-fred-seibert.

22. Joe Strike, "The Fred Seibert Interview—Part 1," July 15, 2003, *Animation World Network*, https://www.awn.com/animationworld/fred-seibert-interview-part-1.

23. *Ibid.*

24. Rebecca Farley, "From Fred and Wilma to Ren and Stimpy: What Makes a Cartoon 'Prime Time'?" *Prime Time Animation: Television Animation and American Culture*, edited by Carol A. Stabile and Mark Harrison (New York: Routledge, 2003), 151.

25. Gregory S. Crawford, "The Impact of the 1992 Cable Act on Household Demand and Welfare," *Rand Journal of Economics* 31, no. 3 (2000).

26. Paul Grainge, *Brand Hollywood: Selling Entertainment in a Global Media Age* (New York: Routledge, 2008), 112. The most racist content was still edited.

27. Jason Mittell, *Genre and Television: From Cop Shows to Cartoons in American Culture* (New York, Routledge, 2004), 79–80.

28. Tom Bierbaum, "The Last Halloween," *Variety Television Reviews: 1991–1992* (New York: Garland, 1994), 17. Crystal Lake is the New Jersey town in the Friday the 13th film series. Mystery Inc. is located in Crystal Cove.

29. Bill Hanna and Tom Ito, *A Cast of Friends* (Dallas, TX: Taylor, 1996), 215

30. Anthony Scibelli, "A Look at The Simpsons Failed Prime Time Competitors," *Splitsider*, November 22, 2011, http://splitsider.com/2011/11/a-look-at-the-simpsons-failed-prime-time-cartoon-competitors/.

31. J. Gordon Melton, *The Vampire Book: The Encyclopedia of the Undead* (Canton, MI: Visible Ink, 2011), 3–5.

32. Charles Solomon, "TV Reviews: Pebbles, Bamm-Bamm Plan Stone Age Wedding in Bedrock," *Los Angeles Times*, February 6, 1993, http://articles.latimes.com/1993-02-06/entertainment/ca-892_1_modern-stone-age.

33. Tom Bierbaum, "Jonny's Golden Quest," *Variety*, April 1, 1993, http://variety.com/1993/tv/reviews/jonny-s-golden-quest-1200432101/.

34. Edward J. Epstein, "How Did Michael Eisner Make Disney Profitable?" *Slate*, September 27, 2005, http://www.slate.com/articles/arts/the_hollywood_economist/2005/04/how_did_michael_eisner_make_disney_profitable.html.

35. Mittel, *Genre and Television*, 83.

Chapter 11

1. Kate Fitzgerald, "Cartoon Network: Betty Cohen," *Advertising Age*, June 28, 1999, http://adage.com/article/news/cartoon-network-betty-cohen/61952/.

2. Cartoon Network Archive, "A Taste of Cartoon Network"—Promos, Intros & Interstitials (1993 Promotional VHS Tape)," *YouTube*, June 22, 2013 https://www.youtube.com/watch?v=l_yTrp-UDc4.

3. Dan Sarto, "Betty Cohen Steps Down as President of Cartoon Network," *Animation World Network*, June 15, 2001, https://www.awn.com/news/betty-cohen-steps-down-president-cartoon-network.

4. "The Banana Splits in TV Comeback," *BBC*, August 18, 2008, http://news.bbc.co.uk/1/hi/entertainment/7567840.stm.

5. Joe Strike, "The Fred Seibert Interview-Part 1," *Animation World Network*, July 15, 2003, https://www.awn.com/animationworld/fred-seibert-interview-part-1.

6. Iwao Takamoto and Michael Mallory, *Iwao Takamoto: My Life with a Thousand Characters* (Jackson: University of Mississippi Press, 2009), 168.

7. "Christian Tremblay—Ask Me Anything," *Reddit*, November 26, 2012, https://www.reddit.com/r/IAmA/comments/140m96/swatkats_the_animated_series_tlak_to_the/c78y3xw/; https://swatkats.info/encyclopedia/interviews/christian-tremblay-ama.

8. Martin Lukacs, "Neoliberalism has Conned us into Fighting Climate Change as Individuals," *The Guardian*, July 17, 2017, https://www.

theguardian.com/environment/true-north/2017/jul/17/neoliberalism-has-conned-us-into-fighting-climate-change-as-individuals.

9. Stuart Heritage, "Captain Planet Returns—to Take Superhero TV Down to Zero," *The Guardian,* March 22, 2017, https://www.theguardian.com/tv-and-radio/2017/mar/22/captain-planet-returns-online-amazon-prime.

10. Jerry Beck, "Once Upon a Forest," *The Animated Movie Guide* (Chicago: Chicago Reader Press, 2005), 184.

11. Joey Anuff, "The Nearly Invisible Animation Genius," *SPIN,* November 1998, 105, ,https://books.google.com/books?id=lgxVa5s7idEC&pg=PA105&lpg=PA105#v=onepage&q&f=false.

12. Strike, "Fred Seibert Interview—Part 1."

13. Becca James, "The Halloween Tree Remains an Adventure in Understanding and Friendship," *AVClub,* October 29, 2016, http://tv.avclub.com/the-halloween-tree-remains-an-adventure-in-understandin-1798253761.

14. William D. Crump, *How the Movies Saved Christmas: 228 Rescues from Clausnappers, Sleigh Crashes, Lost Presents and Holiday Disasters* (Jefferson, NC: McFarland, 2017), 287–288.

15. William D. Crump, *The Christmas Encyclopedia* (Jefferson, NC: McFarland, 2013), 185–186

16. Tom Bierbaum, "Hollyrock-A-Bye Baby," *Variety,* December 1, 1993, http://variety.com/1993/tv/reviews/hollyrock-a-bye-baby-1200435001/. The film had a poster from *Rock Odyssey* in one scene.

17. Catherine Applefeld, "Yogi, The Easter Bear," *Billboard,* March 4, 1995, 72, https://goo.gl/8Appwh.

18. Army Archerd, "Taylor Polishes Cameo for Bedrock," *Variety,* July 23, 1993, http://variety.com/1993/voices/columns/taylor-polishes-cameo-in-bedrock-1117862222/; "The Flintstones: The Best of Bedrock (1994)," *British Film Institute,* http://www.bfi.org.uk/films/tv-people/4ce2b7d6b92c4.

19. Joseph Barbera, *My Life in 'toons: From Flatbush to Bedrock in Under a Century* (Nashville, TN: Turner, 1994), 242–243; "1994 Domestic Grosses," *Box Office Mojo,* http://www.boxofficemojo.com/yearly/chart/?yr=1994. Barbera did appreciate the live-action visuals from the film. Sharon Stone was supposed be played by the actress of the same name, but scheduling conflicts prevented her involvement.

20. Joseph Barbera, *Archive of American Television,* interview with Leonard Maltin, February 26, 1997, http://www.emmytvlegends.org/interviews/people/joseph-barbera.

21. Thor Jensen, "Transmissions from the Ghost Planet: The Definitive History of Space Ghost Coast to Coast," *SyFy,* June 19, 2014, http://www.syfy.com/syfywire/transmissions-ghost-planet-definitive-history-space-ghost-coast-coast.

22. "Scooby-Doo! Arabian Nights," *Warner Bros. UK,* https://www.warnerbros.co.uk/movies/scoobydoo-arabian-nights.

23. Fred Guida, *A Christmas Carol and Its Adaptations: A Critical Examination of Dickens's Story and Its Productions on Screen and Television* (Jefferson, NC: McFarland, 2000), 225–226.

24. Scott Moore, "Dr. Seuss' Daisy-Head Mayzie," *Washington Post,* February 5, 1995, https://www.washingtonpost.com/archive/lifestyle/tv/1995/02/05/dr-seusss-daisy-head-mayzie/70640b5f-322a-4724-ae85-2063d20d3e1c/?utm_term=.50f4b394e407.

25. Kevin S. Sandler, "Synergy Nirvana: Brand Equity, Television Animation, and Cartoon Network," *Prime Time Animation: Television Animation and American Culture,* edited by Carol A. Stabile and Mark Harrison (New York: Routledge, 2003), 96.

26. Martin Goodman, "Deconstruction Zone—Part 1 (Or: Semiotics Means Never Having to Signify You're Sorry)," *Animation World Network,* February 16, 2004, https://www.awn.com/animationworld/deconstruction-zone-part-1-or-semiotics-means-never-having-signify-you-re-sorry.

27. Paul Richter, "General Electric Will Buy RCA for $6.28 Billion," *Los Angeles Times,* December 12, 1985, http://articles.latimes.com/1985-12-12/news/mn-16152_1_general-electric-will.

28. Telecommunication Act of 1996 47 U.S.C. ch. 5, subch. VI § 609, https://transition.fcc.gov/Reports/tcom1996.pdf.

29. Matthew McAllister, "The Financial Interest and Syndication Rules," *Museum of Broadcast Communication,* http://www.museum.tv/eotv/financialint.htm.

30. Larry Stewart "CBS' Downfall: Fox's Money, NBC's Agreement," *Los Angeles Times,* December 24, 1993, http://articles.latimes.com/1993-12-24/sports/sp-5079_1_cbs-personnel.

31. N. R. Kleinfield, "ABC Being Sold for $3.5 Billion-1st Network Sale," *New York Times,* March 19, 1985, http://www.nytimes.com/1985/03/19/business/abc-is-being-sold-for-3.5-billion-1st-network-sale.html.

32. Geraldine Fabrikant, "The Media Business—The Merger—Walt Disney to Acquire ABC in $19 Billion Deal to Build a Giant in Entertainment," *New York Times,* August 1, 1995, http://www.nytimes.com/1995/08/01/business/media-business-merger-walt-disney-acquire-abc-19-billion-deal-build-giant-for.html?pagewanted=all.

33. "The Fallout from the Telecommunication Act of 1996: Unintended Consequences and Lessons Learned," *Common Cause,* May 9, 2005, https://www.worldcat.org/title/fallout-from-the-telecommunications-act-of-1996-unintended-consequences-and-lessons-learned/oclc/60624369.

34. Jamshid Ghazi Askar, "A 15 Failure? Parents Television Council Says TV Content Ratings are Flawed," *Deseret News,* October 18, 2012, http://www.deseretnews.com/article/865564776/A-15-year-failure-Parents-Television- Council-says-TV-content-ratings-are-flawed.html.

35. Bill Mukulak, "Fans vs Warner Bros. Who Owns Looney Toons?" *Reading the Rabbit,* edited by Kevin Sandler (New Brunswick: Rutgers University Press, 1998), 194.

36. Mark Landler, "Turner to Merge into Time Warner in a $7.5 Billion Deal," *New York Times,* September 23, 1995, http://www.nytimes.com/1995/09/23/us/turner-to-merge-into-time-warner-a-7.5-billion-deal.html?pagewanted=all.

37. Heather Hendershot, *Saturday Morning Censors: Television Regulation Before the V-Chip* (Durham: Duke University Press, 1998), 217–218.

38. Kevin Polowy, "Wait, There Was a 'Dumber and Dumber' Cartoon Series?" *Yahoo Movies*, September 29, 2014, https://www.yahoo.com/movies/wait-there-was-a-dumber-and-dumber-cartoon-98763726297.html.

39. Fred Seibert, "Blog History of Frederator's Original Cartoon Shorts. Part 15," *Frederator*, December 30, 2006, http://archives.frederatorblogs.com/frederator_studios/2006/12/30/blog-history-of-frederators-original-cartoon-6/.

40. Fred Seibert, "Blog History of Frederator's Original Cartoon Shorts. Part 17," *Frederator*, September 1, 2007, http://archives.frederatorblogs.com/frederator_studios/2007/09/01/blog-history-of-frederator%E2%80%99s-original-carto-2/.

41. Fred Seibert, "Blog History of Frederator's Original Cartoon Shorts. Part 22," *Frederator*, October 5, 2009, http://archives.frederatorblogs.com/frederator_studios/2009/10/25/blog-history-of-frederator%E2%80%99s-original-cartoon-shorts-part-22/.

42. Strike, "The Fred Seibert Interview-Part 1."

43. Hal Erickson, *Television Cartoon Shows: An Illustrated Encyclopedia, 1949–2003* (Jefferson, NC: McFarland, 2005), 920.

44. Ken P., "An Interview with Seth MacFarlane: The Creator of Family Guy Discusses His Career," *IGN*, July 21, 2003, https://www.ign.com/articles/2003/07/21/an-interview-with-seth-macfarlane.

45. Jeff Lenburg, *Who's Who in Animated Cartoons: An International Guide to Film and Televisions Award Winning Animators* (New York: Applause, 2006), 221.

46. Michael P. Lucas, "Yogi Bear Gets a Bit of the Ren & Stimpy Attitude: The Much-Loved Character and Friends, Created by Hanna-Barbera, are Back—but with John Kricfalusi's Twist," *Los Angeles Times*, September 23, 1999, https://web.archive.org/web/20121026103656/http://articles.latimes.com/1999/sep/23/entertainment/ca-13.

47. "Taste of Cartoon Network 1993 Promo VHS Tape," *Library of Congress*, https://archive.org/details/Taste_of_Cartoon_Network_1993_Promo_VHS_Tape.

48. Sandler, "Synergy Nirvana," 98–99.

49. Seibert, "Blog History—Part 22."

50. Sarah Banet-Weiser, *Kids Rule! Nickelodeon and Consumer Citizenship* (Durham: Duke University Press, 2007), 87.

51. "News: Television," *Animation World Magazine*, November 1998, https://www.awn.com/mag/issue3.8/3.8pages/3.8television.html.

52. The Big Cartoon Database, "The President's Day Nightmare," https://www.bcdb.com/cartoon/10763-Presidents-Day-Nightmare.

53. Andy Swift, "Animaniacs Reboot in Development From Warner Bros., Steven Spielberg," *TVLine*, May 30, 2017, http://tvline.com/2017/05/30/animaniacs-reboot-plans-wakko-yakko-dot-returning/.

54. Thomas S. Mulligan, "Turner-Time Warner Merger Approved by Shareholders," *Los Angeles Times*, October 11, 1996 http://articles.latimes.com/1996-10-11/business/fi-52676_1_time-warner.

55. Tom Sito, "The Late, Great, 2D Animation Renaissance—Part 1," *Animation World Network*, February 13, 2006, https://www.awn.com/animationworld/late-great-2d-animation-renaissance-part-1.

56. Giannalberto Bendazzi, *Animation: A World History: Volume III: Contemporary Times* (New York: Routledge, 2017), 8–9.

57. Alison Alexander and James Owers, "The Economics of Children's Television," *The Children's Television Community*, edited by J. Alison Bryant (Mahwah, NJ: Lawrence Erlbaum, 2007), 60–67.

58. Alan Bunce, "New 'Big Bag' Series Teaches Social Skills to 'Sesame Street' Crowd," *Christian Science Monitor*, May 30, 1996, https://www.csmonitor.com/1996/0530/053096.feat.tv.1.html.

59. Sandler, "Synergy Nirvana," 100–101.

60. Daniel R. Anderson, "Watching Children Watch Television and the Creation of Blue's Clues," *Nickelodeon Nation: The History, Politics, and Economics of America's Only TV Channel for Kids*, edited by Heather Hendershot (New York: NYU Press, 2004), 264.

61. Ed Christman, "Retail Track," *Billboard*, March 1, 1997, 52.

62. Sarah Baisley, "Cartoon Network Launches Tickle U to Humor Preschoolers," *Animation World Network*, August 23, 2005, https://www.awn.com/news/cartoon-network-launches-tickle-u-humor-preschoolers.

63. "Cartoon Network Announces New Action-Adventure Programming Strategy," *Anime News Network*, February 26, 2004, http://www.animenewsnetwork.com/press-release/2004-02-26/cartoon-network-announces-new-action-adventure-programming-strategy.

64. Elijah Watson, "The Oral History of Cartoon Network's Toonami," *Comp.lex*, March 21, 2017, http://www.complex.com/pop-culture/2017/03/oral-history-of-toonami.

65. Jeffrey Tumlin, "City of the Future: Time to Jettison the Jetsons' Vision of Cities," *Journal of Urban Regeneration & Renewal* 8, no. 2 (2015): 152–160.

66. Shinobu Price, "Cartoons from another Planet: Japanese Animation as Cross-Cultural Communication," *The Journal of American Culture* 24, no. 1–2 (2001), 153–169.

Chapter 12

1. Kevin S. Sandler, "Synergy Nirvana: Brand Equity, Television Animation, and Cartoon Network," *Prime Time Animation: Television Animation and American Culture*, edited by Carol A. Stabile and Mark Harrison (New York: Routledge, 2003), 99–100.

2. Irwin Chusid, "Raymond Scott: Accidental Music for Animated Mayhem," *The Cartoon Music Book*, edited by Daniel Goldmark and Yuval Taylor (Chicago: A Cappella, 2002), 159.

3. Jon Krasner, *Motion Graphic Design: Applied History and Aesthetics* (New York: Focal Press, 2008), 43.

4. Sandler, "Synergy Nirvana," 103–104.

5. Sandler, "Synergy Nirvana," 99–100.

6. Daniel Goldmark, *Tunes for 'Toons: Music and the Hollywood Cartoon* (Berkeley: University of California Press, 2005), 18.

7. Neil Strauss, "Tunes for Toons: A Cartoon Music Primer," *The Cartoon Music Book*, edited by Daniel Goldmark and Yuval Taylor (Chicago Review Press, 2002), 5.

8. Pete Imbesi, "The 15 Catchiest Cartoon Theme Songs of the 80s," *Comic Book Resources*, April 30, 2017, http://www.cbr.com/the-15-catchiest-cartoon-theme-songs-of-the-80s/.

9. Andrew Unterberger, "Run the Jewels & Adult Swim: Inside the Hip-Hop/Cartoon Bromance," *Billboard*, January 10, 2017, http://www.billboard.com/articles/news/magazine-feature/7654180/run-the-jewels-adult-swim-bromance.

10. Christina Montford, "When It Comes to Rap Music, Are White Boys Really Doing All the Buying?" *Atlanta Black Star*, November 6, 2014, http://atlantablackstar.com/2014/11/06/really-listening/; Ethan Gach, "Scumbags Harass Woman for Working on Mass Effect: Andromeda's Animations" *Kotaku*, March 18, 2017, https://kotaku.com/scumbags-harass-woman-for-working-on-mass-effect-andro-1793410647.

11. Rebecca Farley, "From Fred and Wilma to Ren and Stimpy: What Makes a Cartoon 'Prime Time'?" *Primetime Animation: Television Animation and American Culture*, edited by Carol A. Stabile and Mark Harrison (New York: Routledge, 2003), 163.

12. Joey Anuff, "The Nearly Invisible Animation Genius," *SPIN*, November 1998, 103–106, https://books.google.com/books?id=lgxVa5s7idEC&pg=PA105&lpg=PA105#v=onepage&q&f=false.

13. Michael P. Lucas, "Yogi Bear Gets a Bit of the Ren & Stimpy Attitude: The Much-Loved Character and Friends, Created by Hanna-Barbera, Are Back—but with John Kricfalusi's Twist," *Los Angeles Times*, September 23, 1999, https://web.archive.org/web/20121026103656/http://articles.latimes.com/1999/sep/23/entertainment/ca-13166.

14. Jason Mittell, *Genre and Television: From Cop Shows to Cartoons in American Culture* (New York: Routledge, 2004), 80–84.

15. Scott D. Pierce, "Conan Can't Shake Off Rocky Start as Host," *Deseret News*, July 17, 1998, http://www.deseretnews.com/article/643555/Conan-cant-shake-off-rocky-start-as-host.html.

16. Martin Goodman, "Talking in His Sheep: A Conversation with Mo Willems," *Animation World Network*, June 25, 2001 https://www.awn.com/animationworld/talking-his-sheep-conversation-mo-willems.

17. David Large and James Farmers, *Modern Cable Television Technology* (San Francisco, Morgan Kaufmann, 2004), 71.

18. Susan King, "Hanna-Barbera Cartoons Return on New Boomerang," *Los Angeles Times*, April 1, 2000, http://articles.latimes.com/2000/apr/01/entertainment/ca-14752.

19. Scott Collins, "Nickelodeon Squeezes 2 Ratings Out of 1 Very Diverse Network," *Los Angeles Times*, March 25, 2004, http://articles.latimes.com/2004/mar/25/business/fi-nick25.

20. Scott Moore, "Fox's King Signals Prime Time Move," *Washington Post*, February 9, 1997, https://www.washingtonpost.com/archive/lifestyle/tv/1997/02/09/foxs-king-signals-prime-move/3ef000f2-e1a9-4f7c-999e-62bf79650b57/?utm_term=.ca8bf34d64af.

21. Thor Jensen, "Transmissions from the Ghost Planet: The Definitive History of Space Ghost Coast to Coast," *SyFy*, June 19, 2014, http://www.syfy.com/syfywire/transmissions-ghost-planet-definitive-history-space-ghost-coast-coast.

22. Daniel Kurland, "When Sealab 2021 Devoted Nearly an Entire Episode to a Single Joke," *Splitsider*, May 10, 2016, http://splitsider.com/2016/05/when-sealab-2021-devoted-nearly-an-entire-episode-to-a-single-joke/.

23. Bryan Menegus, "The History of Adult Swim's Rise to Greatness," *Sploid*, April 11, 2016, http://sploid.gizmodo.com/an-oral-history-of-adult-swim-1770248730.

24. "Adults Only: An Oral History of [adult swim]," *Complex*, February 10, 2012, http://www.complex.com/pop-culture/2010/02/adults-only-an-oral-history-of-adult-swim.

25. Kyle Ryan, "Aqua Teen Hunger Force Sued over Theme Song," *The A.V. Club*, November 10, 2006, http://www.avclub.com/article/aqua-teen-hunger-force-sued-over-theme-song-15851.

26. Jessica Metzger, "Truly They Were an Aqua Teen Hunger Force," *Medium*, June 2015, https://medium.com/on-second-thought/truly-they-were-an-8e7631476c99.

27. Robert Silverman, "'Aqua Teen Hunger Force' Says Goodbye: The Creators on the Influential Animated Sitcom," *The Daily Beast,* June 22, 2015, http://www.thedailybeast.com/aqua-teen-hunger-force-says-goodbye-the-creators-on-the-influential-animated-sitcom.

28. "Adult Swim/CN Split Cement Strategy," *ICv2*, March 3, 2005, http://icv2.com/articles/comics/view/6516/adult-swim-cn-split-cements-strategy.

29. Todd Gitlin, "Media Saturation and the Increasing Velocity of Disposable Feeling," Todd Gitlin, *Media Unlimited: How the Torrent of Images and Sounds Overwhelms Our Lives* (New York: Metropolitan Books, 2001), 142.

30. Whitney Matheson, "Bump It Up: Adult Swim Wants Your TV Teasers," *USA Today*, November 6, 2013, http://www.usatoday.com/story/popcandy/2013/11/06/adult-swim-bump-app/3453467/; "Adults Only: An Oral History of [adult swim]."

31. Evan Elkins, "Cultural Identity and Subcultural Forums: The Post-Network Politics of Adult Swim," *Television & New Media* 15, no. 7 (2014): 595–610.

32. Leah Zitter, "Trending: Black Viewers and Anime" *The Moguldom Nation*, September 27,

2019, https://moguldom.com/229542/trending-black-viewers-and-anime/.

33. C.M. Emmanuel, "How Adult Swim Became a Hip Hop Staple," *XXL Magazine*, October 25, 2013, http://www.xxlmag.com/news/2013/10/adult-swim-made-inroads-hip-hop/.

34. Unterberger, "Run the Jewels & Adult Swim."

35. Dave McNary, "Scooby-Doo Animated Movie Moves Back Two Years to 2020," *Variety*, May 3, 2017, http://variety.com/2017/film/news/animated-scooby-movie-moves-back-2020-1202408718/.

36. Lynne Joyrich, "American Dreams and Demons: Television's "Hollow" Histories and Fantasies of Race," *The Black Scholar* 48, no. 1 (2018): 31–42.

37. Aja Romano, "How Voice Actors Are Fighting to Change an Industry That Renders Them Invisible," *Vox*, July 22, 2020, https://www.vox.com/2020/7/22/21326824/white-voice-actors-black-characters-cartoons-whitewashing.

38. Rupul Parekh, "How Much of The Jetson's Futuristic World Has Become a Reality," *Advertising Age*, September 25, 2012, http://adage.com/article/media/jetsons-world-a-reality/237394/.

Conclusion

1. Kevin S. Sandler, "Synergy Nirvana: Brand Equity, Television Animation, and Cartoon Network," *Prime Time Animation: Television Animation and American Culture*, edited by Carol A. Stabile and Mark Harrison (New York: Routledge, 2003), 99–100.

2. A.J. Katz, "The Top Cable Networks of January 2017," *AdWeek*, January 31, 2017, http://www.adweek.com/tvnewser/the-top-cable-networks-of-january-2017/319137.

3. George Stark, "No Sign of Thawing! Frozen Reaches £800million at the Worldwide Box Office Becoming the Fifth-Highest Grossing Movie of All Time," *Daily Mail*, May 26, 2014, http://www.dailymail.co.uk/tvshowbiz/article-2640043/Frozen-reaches-1–219-billion-fifth-highest-grossing-movie-time.html.

4. Jonathan Gray, *Watching with The Simpsons: Television, Parody, and Intertextuality* (New York: Routledge, 2006), 68.

5. Abby West, "'The Boondocks' (Allegedly) Take on Tyler Perry: Too Far?" *Entertainment Weekly*, June 24, 2010, http://ew.com/article/2010/06/24/boondocks-tyler-perry-made/.

6. Danette Chavez, "Adult Swim Picks up Tyler, The Creator's Cartoon," *AV Club*, May 11, 2017, http://www.avclub.com/article/adult-swim-picks-tyler-creators-cartoon-255154.

7. Yesha Callahan, "Tyler, the Creator Calls Out Lack of Black Cartoon Characters on TV During Comic-Con Q&A: 'We Don't Have Shit,'" *The Grapevine*, July 31, 2017, http://thegrapevine.theroot.com/tyler-the-creator-calls-out-lack-of-black-cartoon-char-1797393694#_ga=2.154717951.610440197.1501537606–1607527215.1458936038.

8. Kevin L. Clark, "10 Twitter Reactions To Marvel Introducing A Black Captain America," *Black Enterprise*, July 17, 2014, http://www.blackenterprise.com/lifestyle/10-twitter-reactions-marvel-a-black-captain-america/.

9. Mihaela Mihailova. "Drawn (to) Independence: Female Showrunners in Contemporary American TV Animation," *Feminist Media Studies* 19, no. 7 (2019): 1009–1025.

10. Sam Barsanti, "Dan Harmon Is Pissed at Rick and Morty Fans for Harassing Female Writers," *AV Club*, September 21, 2017, https://www.avclub.com/dan-harmon-is-pissed-at-rick-and-morty-fans-for-harassi-1818628816.

11. Lauren Rearick, "'Steven Universe' Just Made Queer History with a Same-Sex Engagement," *Teen Vogue*, July 6, 2018, https://www.teenvogue.com/story/steven-universe-is-reportedly-first-cartoon-to-feature-same-sex-engagement.

12. Bill Carter, "Adult Swim Number 1 with Younger Adults, Is Expanding," *New York Times*, February 4, 2014, https://www.nytimes.com/2014/02/04/business/media/adult-swim-no-1-with-younger-adults-is-expanding.html?mcubz=0.

13. Nicolas Ayala, "HBO Max's New Looney Tunes Succeeds Where Scoob Failed," *Screen Rant*, June 14, 2020, https://screenrant.com/looney-tunes-hbo-max-succeed-scoob-fail/.

14. John Hecht, "Mexican Animated Film 'Top Cat' Breaks Record at Box Office," *Hollywood Reporter*, September 20, 2011, http://www.hollywoodreporter.com/news/mexican-animated-film-top-cat-237740.

15. "Turner Rebrands Boomerang Globally," *Turner*, October 14, 2014, https://www.turner.com/pressroom/united-states/boomerang/turner-rebrands-boomerang-globally.

16. "Dorothy & The Wizard of Oz and Wacky Races Headed for Boomerang International," *Turner*, May 11, 2017, http://www.turner.com/pressroom/%E2%80%9Cdorothy-wizard-oz%E2%80%9D-and-%E2%80%-9Cwacky-races%E2%80%9D-headed-boomerang-international.

17. Nellie Andreeva, "'The Jetsons' Live-Action Reboot from Robert Zemeckis Lands at ABC as Put Pilot," *Deadline*, August 17, 2017, http://deadline.com/2017/08/the-jetsons-multi-camera-comedy-reboot-abc-robert-zemeckis-gary-janetti-1202150786/.

18. Nellie Andreeva, "'The Flintstones' Adult Animated Series Reboot in Works at Warner Bros. With Elizabeth Banks Producing," *Deadline*, July 11, 2019, https://deadline.com/2019/07/the-flintstones-animated-series-reboot-warner-bros-animation-elizabeth-banks-1202645055/.

19. Andrea Towers, "DC Entertainment Announces New Slate of Hanna-Barbera Titles," *Entertainment Weekly*, January 29, 2016, http://ew.com/article/2016/01/29/dc-entertainment-hanna-barbera-titles/.

20. Dave McNary, "'Scooby-Doo' Animated Movie in the Works at Warner Bros." *Variety*, August 17, 2015, http://variety.com/2015/film/

news/scooby-doo-animated-movie-warner-bros-1201571538/.

21. Dave McNary, "Scooby-Doo Animated Movie Moves Back Two Years to 2020," *Variety*, May 3, 2017, http://variety.com/2017/film/news/animated-scooby-movie-moves-back-2020-1202408718.

22. Ian Sandwell, "SCOOB! 2: Will there be a SCOOB! Sequel?," *Digital Spy*, July 10, 2020, https://www.digitalspy.com/movies/a33274353/scoob-2-release-date/.

23. Jeff Chang, "Of Course Tom and Jerry was Racist. The Question Is What To Do About That," *Slate*, October 3, 2014, http://www.slate.com/blogs/browbeat/2014/10/03/tom_and_jerry_racist_of_course_warning_on_amazon_and_itunes_is_appropriate.htm.

24. Robert Mitchell, "How Paul Walker Helped Create a Fast and Furious Box-Office Franchise," *CNN*, December 6, 2013, http://www.cnn.com/2013/12/06/business/paul-walker-fast-furious-franchise/index.html.

25. Donald Padgett, "Yes, Velma is a Lesbian in 'Scooby Doo: Mystery Incorporated,'" *Out*, July 13, 2020, https://www.out.com/television/2020/7/13/yes-velma-lesbian-scooby-doo-mystery-incorporated.

26. Hua Hsu, "The End of White America?" *The Atlantic*, January/February 2009, https://www.theatlantic.com/magazine/archive/2009/01/the-end-of-white-america/307208/.

Reference List

"About the Berenstain Bears." *The Berenstain Bears*, http://www.berenstainbears.com/about.html.

Adalian, Josef. "How Nickelodeon Got America Hooked on Cable." *Vultures*, October 24, 2016, http://www.vulture.com/2016/10/nickelodeon-got-america-hooked-on-cable.html.

Adalian, Josef. "10 Episodes Is the New 13 (Was the New 22)." *Vulture,* June 12, 2015, http://www.vulture.com/2015/06/10-episodes-is-the-new-13-was-the-new-22.html.

Adorno, Theodor, and Max Horkheimer. "The Culture Industry: Enlightenment as Mass Deception." *The Cultural Studies Reader*, ed. Simon During. New York: Routledge, 2007.

"Adult Swim/CN Split Cement Strategy." *ICv2,* March 3, 2005, http://icv2.com/articles/comics/view/6516/adult-swim-cn-split-cements-strategy.

"Adults Only: An Oral History of [adult swim]." *Complex,* February 10, 2012, http://www.complex.com/pop-culture/2010/02/adults-only-an-oral-history-of-adult-swim.

Ahmed, Shumaila, and Juliana Abdul Wahab. "Animation and the Socialization Process: Gender Role Portrayal on Cartoon Network." *Asian Social Sciences* 10, no. 3 (2014): 44–53.

Alexander, Alison, and James Owers. "The Economics of Children's Television." *The Children's Television Community*, ed. J. Alison Bryant. Mahwah, NJ: Lawrence Erlbaum, 2007, 57–74.

Altheide, David L. "Media Hegemony: A Failure of Perspective." *Public Opinion Quarterly* 48, no. 2 (January 1984). https://doi.org/10.1086/268844.

Amidi, Amid. "47 Animated Feature Films to Look For in 2017." *Cartoon Brew,* December 28, 2015. http://www.cartoonbrew.com/feature-film/47-animated-feature-films-in-2016-preview-126197.html.

Anderson, Daniel R. "Watching Children Watch Television and the Creation of Blue's Clues." *Nickelodeon Nation: The History, Politics, and Economics of America's Only TV Channel for Kids*, ed. Heather Hendershot. New York: NYU Press, 2004.

Andreeva, Nellie. "'The Jetsons' Live-Action Reboot from Robert Zemeckis Lands at ABC as Put Pilot." *Deadline,* August 17, 2017, http://deadline.com/2017/08/the-jetsons-multi-camera-comedy-reboot-abc-robert-zemeckis-gary-janetti-1202150786/.

Andreeva, Nellie. "'The Flintstones' Adult Animated Series Reboot In Works at Warner Bros. With Elizabeth Banks Producing." *Deadline,* July 11, 2019, https://deadline.com/2019/07/the-flintstones-animated-series-reboot-warner-bros-animation-elizabeth-banks-1202645055/.

Angelle, Denny. "Fall TV Goes Cartoon Crazy." *Boys Life,* September 1990, p. 14, shorturl.at/aekly.

Anuff, Joey. "The Nearly Invisible Animation Genius." *SPIN,* November 1998, 100–106, https://books.google.com/books?id=lgxVa5s7idEC&pg=PA105&lpg=PA105#v=onepage&q&f=false.

Applefeld, Catherine. "Yogi, The Easter Bear." *Billboard,* March 4, 1995, 72, https://goo.gl/8Appwh .

Archerd, Army. "Taylor Polishes Cameo for Bedrock." *Variety,* July 23, 1993, http://variety.com/1993/voices/columns/taylor-polishes-cameo-in-bedrock-1117862222/.

Ariano, Tara, and Sarah D. Bunting. *Television Without Pity: 752 Things to Love to Hate (and Hate to Love) About TV.* Philadelphia: Quick Books, 2006.

Arizpe, Evelyn, and Moag Styles. "Children Reading at Home: A Historical Overview." *Handbook of research on Children's and Young Adult Literature,* eds. Shelby Wolf, Karen Coats, Patricia A. Enciso, and Christine Jenkins. New York: Taylor & Francis, 2011.

Artz, Lee. "Animating Hierarchy: Disney and the Globalization of Capitalism." *Global Media Journal* 1, no. 1 (2002). http://www.globalmediajournal.com/open-access/animating-hierarchy-disney-and-the-globalization-of-capitalism.php?aid=35055.

Artz, Lee. "Animating Transnational Capitalism." *Journal of Intercultural Communication Research* 44, no. 2 (2015). https://www.researchgate.net/publication/281936654_Animating_Transnational_Capitalism_Journal_of_Intercultural_Communication_Research_442_2015_93–107_DOI_101080174757592015102817.

Arvidsson, Stefan. "Aryan Mythology as Science and Ideology." *Journal of the American Academy of Religion* 67, no. 2 (1999): 327–354.

Ashley, Wendy. "The Angry Black Woman: The Impact of Pejorative Stereotypes on Psychotherapy with Black Women." *Social Work in Public Health* 29, no. 1 (2014): 27–34.

Askar, Jamshid Ghazi. "A 15 Failure? Parents Television Council Says TV Content Ratings are Flawed." *Deseret News,* October 18, 2012, http://www.deseretnews.com/article/865564776/A-15-year-failure-Parents-Television-Council-says-TV-content-ratings-are-flawed.html.

Aspden, Peter. "It's Not Just TV: How HBO Revolutionized Television." *Slate,* September 24, 2011, http://www.slate.com/articles/life/ft/2011/09/its_not_just_tv.html.

Associated Press. "Holders OK $847 Million Deal for Taft." *Los Angeles Times,* September 30, 1987, http://articles.latimes.com/1987-09-30/business/fi-7368_1_buyout.

Associated Press. "TBS Buys Animator Hanna-Barbera Library for $320 Million." October 29, 1991, http://www.apnewsarchive.com/1991/TBS-Buys-Animator-Hanna-Barbera-Library-for-$-320-Million/id-e4b7fe7b58573927b9188329b6cd66c1.

Austen, Jake. "Rock n' Roll Cartoons." *The Cartoon Music Book,* eds. Daniel Goldmark and Yuval Taylor. Chicago: A Cappella, 2002, 173–192.

Avila, Eric. "Popular culture in the Age of White Flight: Film Noir, Disneyland, and the Cold War (Sub) Urban Imaginary." *Journal of Urban History* 31, no. 1 (2004): 3–22.

Ayala, Nicolas. "HBO Max's New Looney Tunes Succeeds Where Scoob Failed." *Screen Rant,* June 14, 2020, https://screenrant.com/looney-tunes-hbo-max-succeed-scoob-fail/.

Bailey, Elizabeth. "Snorks and Popples." *New York Times,* May 1, 1988, http://www.nytimes.com/1988/05/01/books/snorks-and-popples.html?scp=2&sq=snorks&st=cse.

Baisley, Sarah. "Cartoon Network Launches Tickle U to Humor Preschoolers." *Animation World Network,* August 23, 2005, https://www.awn.com/news/cartoon-network-launches-tickle-u-humor-preschoolers.

Bakker, Robert T. "Dinosaur Renaissance." *Scientific American* 232, no. 4 (1975).

"The Banana Splits in TV Comeback." *BBC,* August 18, 2008, http://news.bbc.co.uk/1/hi/entertainment/7567840.stm.

Banet-Weiser, Sarah. *Kids Rule! Nickelodeon and Consumer Citizenship.* Durham: Duke University Press, 2007.

Barbera, Joseph. *Archive of American Television,* interview with Leonard Maltin, February 26, 1997, http://www.emmytvlegends.org/interviews/people/joseph-barbera.

Barbera, Joseph. *My Life in 'toons: From Flatbush to Bedrock in Under a Century.* Nashville: Turner, 1994.

Barbera, Joseph, and William Hanna. "The Buffalo Convention." *The Flintstones,* Hanna-Barbera Productions, Hollywood, CA, 1962.

Barbera, Joseph, and William Hanna, dirs. "Cave Scout Jamboree." 1964, Turner Home Entertainment/Hanna Barbera Productions, Los Angeles, CA, 2006, DVD.

Barbera, Joseph, and William Hanna, dirs. "Carry On, Nurse Fred." *The Flintstones,* Hanna-Barbera Productions, Hollywood, CA, 1963.

Barbera, Joseph, and William Hanna, dirs. "Cattle Battle Rattled." *The Quick Draw McGraw Show,* Hanna-Barbera Productions, Hollywood, CA, 1959.

Barbera, Joseph, and William Hanna, dirs. "Yogi in the City." *The Yogi Bear Show,* Hanna-Barbera Productions, Hollywood, CA, 1961.

Barker, Jennifer. "Hollywood, Black Animation, and the Problem of Representation in 'Lil Ol' Bosko' and 'The Princess and the Frog.'" *Journal of African American Studies* 14, no. 4 (2010): 482–498.

Barksdale, Aaron. "23 Black Actors Who Voiced Your Favorite Cartoon Characters." *The Huffington Post,* October 2, 2015, http://www.huffingtonpost.com/entry/black-actors-cartoon-characters_us_560e9be0e4b0af3706e06b23.

Barnes, Brooks, and Amy Chozick. "New Disney Characters Make It Big in TV's Preschool Playground." *New York Times,* March 31, 2013, http://www.nytimes.com/2013/04/01/business/media/disney-junior-challenges-nick-jr-in-preschool-tv.html?mcubz=0.

Barrier, Michael. *Hollywood Cartoons: American Animation in its Golden Age.* New York: Oxford University Press, 1999.

Barsanti, Sam. "Dan Harmon Is Pissed at Rick and Morty Fans for Harassing Female Writers." *AVClub,* September 21, 2017, https://www.avclub.com/dan-harmon-is-pissed-at-rick-and-morty-fans-for-harassi-1818628816.

Bartel Sheehan, Kim. *Controversies in Contemporary Advertising.* Thousand Oaks, CA: SAGE, 2014.

Baughman, James A. *Same Time, Same Channel: The Making of American Television 1948–1961.* Baltimore: Johns Hopkins University Press, 2007.

"Baxter!" *British Film Institute,* http://www.bfi.org.uk/films-tv-people/4ce2b6a4c76b7.

Beaty, Bart. *Twelve Cent Archie.* New Brunswick: Rutgers University Press, 2015.

Beck, Jerry. *The Animated Film Guide.* Chicago: Chicago Review, 2005.

Beck, Jerry. *The Flintstones: The Official Guide to the Cartoon Series* New York: Running Press, 2011.

Beck, Jerry. *The Hanna Barbera Treasury: Rare Art and Mementos from your Favorite Cartoon Classics.* New York: Insight Editions, 2007.

Beck, Jerry, and Will Friedwald. *Looney Tunes and Merrie Melodies: A Complete Illustrated Guide to the Warner Bros. Cartoons.* New York: Henry Holt and Co., 1989.

Begley, Sarah. "Now There's a Class on the Philosophy of The Simpsons." *Time,* November 16, 2016, http://time.com/4573080/simpsons-philosophy-university-class/.

Behnken, Brian D., and Gregory D. Smithers. *Racism in American Media: From Aunt Jemima to Frito Bandito.* Santa Barbara, CA: Praeger, 2015.

"Believe It or Not the Cartoon Pound Puppies Was Inspired by Hogan's Heroes." *MeTV,* April 25, 2017, http://www.metv.com/stories/believe-it-or-not-the-cartoon-pound-puppies-was-inspired-by-hogans-heroes.

Belkhyr, Souad. "Disney Animation: Global Diffusion and Local Appropriation of Culture."

Etudes Caribeenes 22 (August 2012), https://etudescaribeennes.revues.org/5863?lang=en.

Belkin, Lisa. "Why Kids Watch Movies Again and Again." *New York Times,* November 12, 2009, https://parenting.blogs.nytimes.com/2009/11/12/kids-and-movies/.

Belle Starr (TV movie). Warner Bros., https://www.warnerbros.com/tv/belle-starr-tv-movie.

Bendazzi, Giannalberto. *Animation: A World History: Volume III: Contemporary Times.* New York: Routledge, 2017.

Bertoli, Ben. "Pokemon Communication Seems to be Slowly Changing." *Kotaku,* May 30, 2016, http://kotaku.com/pokemon-communication-seems-to-be-slowly-changing-1779485458.

Bierbaum, Tom. "Hollyrock-A-Bye Baby." *Variety,* December 1, 1993, http://variety.com/1993/tv/reviews/hollyrock-a-bye-baby-1200435001/.

Bierbaum, Tom. "Jonny's Golden Quest." *Variety,* April 1, 1993, http://variety.com/1993/tv/reviews/jonny-s-golden-quest-1200432101/.

Bierbaum, Tom. "The Last Halloween." *Variety Television Reviews: 1991–1992.* New York: Garland, 1994.

Biernat, Monica, and Diane Kobrynowicz. "Gender- and Race-Based Standards of Competence: Lower Minimum Standards but Higher Ability Standards for Devalued Groups." *Journal of Personality and Social Psychology* 72, no. 3 (1997), 544–557. http://dx.doi.org/10.1037/0022-3514.72.3.544.

The Big Cartoon Database. "The President's Day Nightmare," https://www.bcdb.com/cartoon/10763-Presidents-Day-Nightmare.

"Biography: Alex Toth." *Illustration History,* http://www.illustrationhistory.org/artists/alex-toth.

Bobbin, Jay. "Yogi Bear's All-Star Christmas Caper." *Allentown Morning Call,* 2017, http://www.mcall.com/zap-dvd-review-yogi-bears-comedy-christmas-caper-story.html.

Bobo, Lawrence D. "Inequalities that Endures? Racial Ideology, American Politics and the Peculiar Role of the Social Sciences." *The Changing Terrain of Race and Ethnicity,* eds. Maria Krysan and Amanda E. Lewis. New York: Russell Sage Foundation, 2004.

Bodroghkozy, Aniko. *Equal Time: Television and the Civil Rights Movement.* Urbana: University of Illinois Press, 2012.

Booker, M. Keith *Drawn to Television: Prime-Time Animation from The Flintstones to Family Guy.* Westport, CT: Praeger, 2006.

Bor, Stephanie E. "Lucy's Two Babies: Framing the First Televised Depiction of Pregnancy." *Media History* 19, no. 4 (2013): 464–478.

Bowen, Glenn A. "Document Analysis as a Qualitative Research Method." *Qualitative Research Journal* 9, no. 2 (2009): 27–40.

Boyd, Todd. *African Americans and Popular Culture.* Westport, CT: Praeger, 2008.

Boyd, Todd. *Young, Black, Rich, and Famous: The Rise of the NBA, The Hip Hop Invasion, and the Transformation of American Culture.* New York: Doubleday, 2003

Boyer, Peter J. "Under Fowler F.C.C. Treated as Commerce." *New York Times,* January 19, 1987, http://www.nytimes.com/1987/01/19/arts/under-fowler-fcc-treated-tv-as-commerce.html.

Brainard, Lori A. "Television Policy: Economic v. Content Regulation and Deregulation." *Focus on Law Studies,* Fall 2014, https://www.americanbar.org/content/dam/aba/publishing/focus_on_law_studies/publiced_focus_fall04.authcheckdam.pdf.

Brannon, Linda. *Gender: Psychological Perspectives.* New York: Routledge, 2016.

Brasted, Dr. Monica "Care Bears vs. Transformers: Gender Stereotypes in Advertisements." *SocJourn,* February 17, 2009, https://www.sociology.org/care-bears-vs-transformers-gender-stereotypes-in-advertisements/.

Breaux, Richard M. "It's a Cartoon! The Jackson 5ive as Commodified Black Power and Civil Rights Ideologies." *The Journal of Pan-African Studies* 3 (2010).

Breslaw, Anna. "Geena Davis Cites the Feminist Implications of I Dream of Jeannie." *Jezebel,* September 22, 2012, http://jezebel.com/5945463/geena-davis-cites-the-feminist-implications-of-i-dream-of-jeannie.

Breznican, Anthony. "'Scooby-Doo' Drops Adult Subcontext." *Topeka Capital-Journal,* June 14, 2002, http://cjonline.com/stories/061402/wee_scoobysubtext.shtml#.Wcp5AdOGMxc.

Bricken, Rob. "12 Cartoons From the 1980s No One Will Ever Have Nostalgia." *io9,* November 11, 2014, http://io9.gizmodo.com/12-cartoons-from-the-1980s-no-one-will-ever-have-nosta-1657410102.

Bricken, Rob. "20 Gobots That Remind Us Why the Gobots Sucked So Incredibly Hard." *io9,* January 15, 2013 http://io9.gizmodo.com/5976109/20-gobots-that-remind-us-why-the-gobots-sucked-so-incredibly-hard.

Brody, Larry. *Turning Points in Television.* New York: Citadel, 2005.

Brooks Tim, and Earle Marsh. *The Complete Guide to Prime Time Network and Cable TV Shows.* New York: Ballantine Books, 2007.

Brown, Les. "Fred Silverman Will Leave CBS-TV to Head to ABC Program Division." *New York Times,* May 19, 1975, http://www.nytimes.com/1975/05/19/archives/fred-silverman-will-leave-cbstv-to-head-abc-program-division.html?_r=0.

Brown Hayton, Paula. "United Video, Inc. v. FCC: Just Another Episode in Syndex Regulation." *Loyola Los Angeles Entertainment Law Review* 12 (1992): 251–274.

Browne, Kamasi L. "Brenda Holloway: Los Angeles Contribution to Motown in California Soul." *The Music of African Americans in the West,* eds. Jacqueline Cogdell Djedje and Eddie S. Meadows. Berkeley: University of California Press, 1998.

Buchner, Chris. "Partridge Family 2200 A.D." *Saturday Mornings Forever,* August 27, 2016, http://www.saturdaymorningsforever.com/2016/08/partridge-family-2200-ad.html.

Bunce, Alan. "New 'Big Bag' Series Teaches Social Skills to 'Sesame Street' Crowd." *Christian Science Monitor,* May 30, 1996, https://www.csmonitor.com/1996/0530/053096.feat.tv.1.html.

Burg, Mike. *Trial by Fire: One Man's Battle to End Corporate Greed.* Dallas: Benbella, 2016.

Burke, Timothy, and Kevin Burke. *Saturday Morning Fever: Growing Up with Cartoon Culture.* New York: St. Martin's, 1999.

Burnett, Bill. "Limited Animation ... Unlimited Imagination." *Fred Seibert,* http://fredseibert. com/post/71257648/limited-animationunlimited-imagination.

Butler, Judith. *Gender Trouble: Feminism and the Subversion of Identity.* New York: Routledge, 1990.

Caffier, Justin. "The 90s Anti-Drug PSA 'Cartoon All-Stars to the Rescue' Didn't Stop Kids from Getting High." *Vice,* April 21, 2015, https://www. vice.com/en_us/article/exqgyk/looking-back-on-cartoon-all-stars-to-the-rescue-421.

Cairns, Bryan. "Scoob! Writer Explains the Maybe-Origins of the Hanna-Barbera Cinematic Universe." *SyFy,* May 20, 2020, https://www.syfy. com/syfywire/scoob-scooby-doo-franchise-screenwriter-free-guy-interview.

Calhoun, Jordan. "18 of the Most Important Voices of Color in Animation." *Black Nerd Problems,* http://blacknerdproblems.com/18-of-the-most-important-voices-of-color-in-animation.

Callahan, Yesha. "Tyler, the Creator Calls out Lack of Black Cartoon Characters on TV During Comic-Con Q&A: 'We Don't Have Shit.'" *The Grapevine,* July 31, 2017, http://thegrapevine. theroot.com/tyler-the-creator-calls-out-lack-of-black-cartoon-char-1797393694#_ga=2. 154717951.610440197.1501537606–1607527215. 1458936038.

Callan, Matthew. "'It's All My Fault, Although I Also Blame Others': The Curious Case of the Ed Grimley Cartoon." *Splitsider,* July 5, 2011, http:// splitsider.com/2011/07/its-all-my-fault-although-i-also-blame-others-the-curious-case-of-the-ed-grimley-cartoon/.

Carey, James W. "Some Personal Notes on US Journalism Education." *Journalism* 1, no. 1 (2000), http://journals.sagepub.com/doi/ abs/10.1177/146488490000100103.

Carter, Bill. "Adult Swim Number 1 with Younger Adults, Is Expanding." *New York Times,* February 4, 2014, https://www.nytimes.com/2014/02/04/ business/media/adult-swim-no-1-with-younger-adults-is-expanding.html?mcubz=0.

"Cartoon Network Announces New Action-Adventure Programming Strategy." *Anime News Network,* February 26, 2004, http://www. animenewsnetwork.com/press-release/2004-02-26/cartoon-network-announces-new-action-adventure-programming-strategy.

Cartoon Network Archive. "A Taste of Cartoon Network"—Promos, Intros & Interstitials (1993 Promotional VHS Tape)." *YouTube,* June 22, 2013 ,https://www.youtube.com/ watch?v=l_yTrp-UDc4.

Cashill, Robert. "Unbottling Jeannie: Magic and Mischief on Set of Sitcom Favorite." *Biography,* September 17, 2015, https://www.biography.com/ news/i-dream-of-jeannie-facts.

Castleman, Harry, and Walter J. Podrazik. *The TV Schedule Book.* New York: McGraw-Hill, 1984.

"Catch Laugh-a-Lympics Fever (All Over Again)." *Wired,* February 19, 2010, https://www.wired. com/2010/02/laff-a-lympic-fever/.

"Census Makes Sense of TV Ownership." *Radio and Television Business Report,* May 30, 2008, http://rbr.com/census-makes-sense-of-tv-ownership/.

"The Champions Series—A Salute to John Cluster." *Kidscreen,* December 1, 1997, http://kidscreen. com/1997/12/01/20082–19971201/.

Chan-Olmsted, Sylvia M. "From Sesame Street to Wall Street: An Analysis of Market Competition in Commercial Children's Television." *Journal of Broadcasting & Electronic Media* 40, no. 1 (1996): 30–44.

Chang, Jeff. "Of Course Tom and Jerry Was Racist. The Question Is What To Do About That." *Slate,* October 3, 2014, http://www.slate.com/blogs/ browbeat/2014/10/03/tom_and_jerry_racist_of_ course_warning_on_amazon_and_itunes_is_ appropriate.htm.

"Charlie Brown and Strawberry Shortcake sold for $345M US to Halifax Company." *CBCNews,* May 10, 2017, http://www.cbc.ca/news/business/ peanuts-sold-dhx-media-halifax-strawberry-shortcake-children-tv-shows-1.4107903.

Chavez, Danette. "Adult Swim Picks up Tyler, The Creator's Cartoon." *AVClub,* May 11, 2017, http:// www.avclub.com/article/adult-swim-picks-tyler-creators-cartoon-255154.

Chemaly, Soraya. "Is Smurfette Giving It Away? What the Smurfette Principle Teaches Your Kids About Girls." *The Huffington Post,* October 19, 2011, http://www.huffingtonpost.com/soraya-chemaly/is-smurfette-giving-it-awy_b_1011329. html.

Chidester, Phil. "'Respect my Authori-tah' *South Park* and the Fragmentation/Reification of Whiteness." *Critical Studies in Media Communication* 29, no. 5 (2012): 403–420. http://nca. tandfonline.com/doi/abs/10.1080/15295036.2012. 676192.

"Children's Educational Television." Federal Communications Commission, https:// www.fcc.gov/consumers/guides/childrens-educational-television.

"Christian Tremblay-Ask Me Anything." *Reddit,* November 26, 2012, https://www. reddit.com/r/IAmA/comments/140m96/ swatkats_the_animated_series_tlak_to_the/ c78y3xw/; https://swatkats.info/encyclopedia/ interviews/christian-tremblay-ama.

Christman, Ed. "Retail Track." *Billboard,* March 1, 1997.

Chusid, Irwin. "Raymond Scott: Accidental music for Animated Mayhem." *The Cartoon Music Book,* eds. Daniel Goldmark and Yuval Taylor. Chicago: A Cappella, 2002.

Clark, Kevin L. "10 Twitter Reactions to Marvel Introducing a Black Captain America." *Black Enterprise,* July 17, 2014, http://www. blackenterprise.com/lifestyle/10-twitter-reactions-marvel-a-black-captain-america/.

Clark, Sean. "Why Hollywood Drew a Veil Over Sinbad's Arabian Roots." *The Guardian,* July 23, 2003, https://www.theguardian.com/film/2003/jul/23/iraq.world.

Clements, Jonathan, and Helen McCarthy. *The Anime Encyclopedia, 3rd Revised Edition: A Century of Japanese Animation.* Berkeley: Stone Bridge, 2015.

C.M. Emmanuel. "How Adult Swim Became a Hip Hop Staple." *XXL Magazine,* October 25, 2013, http://www.xxlmag.com/news/2013/10/adult-swim-made-inroads-hip-hop/.

Cohen, Karl F. *Forbidden Animation: Censored Cartoons and Blacklisted Animators in America.* Jefferson, NC: McFarland, 1997.

Cole, Teju. "The White Savior Industrial Complex." *The Atlantic,* March 21, 2012, https://www.theatlantic.com/international/archive/2012/03/the-white-savior-industrial-complex/254843/.

Collins, Scott. "Nickelodeon Squeezes 2 Ratings Out of 1 Very Diverse Network." *Los Angeles Times,* March 25, 2004, http://articles.latimes.com/2004/mar/25/business/fi-nick25.

Collura, Scott, Travis Fickett, Eric Goldman, and Brian Zoromski. "A History of Batman." *IGN,* July 17, 2008, http://www.ign.com/articles/2008/07/17/a-history-of-batman-on-tv?page=5.

Common Cause Education Fund. "The Fallout from the Telecommunication Act of 1996: Unintended Consequences and Lessons Learned." *Common Cause,* May 9, 2005, https://www.worldcat.org/title/fallout-from-the-telecommunications-act-of-1996-unintended-consequences-and-lessons-learned/oclc/60624369.

Consalvo, Mia. *Atari to Zelda: Japan's Videogames in Global Contexts.* Cambridge: MIT Press, 2010.

Conway, Michael. "The Problem with History Classes." *The Atlantic,* March 16, 2015, https://www.theatlantic.com/education/archive/2015/03/the-problem-with-history-classes/387823/.

Cooper, Gael Fashingbauer, and Brian Bellmont. *Whatever Happened to Pudding Pops? The Lost Toys, Tastes and Trends of the 70's and 80's.* New York: Perigee, 2011.

Corry, John. "TV: Preview of Saturday Cartoons." *New York Times,* September 14, 1983, http://www.nytimes.com/1983/09/14/arts/tv-preview-of-saturday-cartoons.html?mcubz=0.

Coughlan, Sean. "Tom and Jerry Cartoons Carry Racism Warning." *BBC,* October 1, 2014, http://www.bbc.com/news/education-29427843.

Cox, Stephen. "The Modern Stone Age Family Has Its Golden Anniversary." *Los Angeles Times,* September 11, 2010, http://articles.latimes.com/2010/sep/11/entertainment/la-et-flintstones-20100911.

Coyle, Rebecca, and Alex Mesker. "Time Warp: Sonic Retro-Futurism in the Jetsons." *Music in Science Fiction Television: Tune-Into the Future,* eds. Kevin J. Donnelly and Phillip Hayward. New York: Routledge, 2013.

Crafton, Donald. *Shadow of a Mouse: Performance, Belief, and World-Making in Animation.* Berkeley: University of California Press, 2012.

Crawford, Gregory S. "The Impact of the 1992 Cable Act on Household Demand and Welfare." *Rand Journal of Economics* 31, no. 3 (2000).

Crocker, Lizzie. "Is Tom and Jerry Really Racist?" *Daily Beast,* October 2, 2014, http://www.thedailybeast.com/articles/2014/10/02/is-tom-and-jerry-really-racist.html.

Cronin, Brian. "The Super Friends, Ranked." *Comic Book Resources,* November 29, 2016, http://www.cbr.com/all-of-the-super-friends-ranked/.

Cronin, Brian. "TV Legends Revealed: Was Dr. Who Replaced in a Cartoon by Fonzie?" *Comic Book Resources,* March 16, 2016, http://www.cbr.com/tv-legends-revealed-was-doctor-who-replaced-in-a-cartoon-by-fonzie/.

Crump, William D. *The Christmas Encyclopedia,* 3d ed. Jefferson, NC: McFarland, 2013.

Crump, William D. *How the Movies Saved Christmas: 228 Rescues from Clausnappers, Sleigh Crashes, Lost Presents and Holiday Disasters.* Jefferson, NC: McFarland, 2017.

Curtin, Michael. "Beyond the Vast Wasteland: The Policy Discourse of Global Television and the Politics of American Empire." *Journal of Broadcasting and Electric Media* 37, no. 2 (1993), https://doi.org/10.1080/08838159309364211.

da Silvia, Julia. "Children and Electronic Media: How Much is too Much?" *American Psychological Association,* June 2015, https://www.apa.org/pi/about/newsletter/2015/06/electronic-media.

Dale, Steve. "Snow White and Greenbacks: Disney's Newest Ice Production Is Nostalgic-and Lucrative." *Chicago Tribune,* January 20, 2015, http://articles.chicagotribune.com/1995–01–20/entertainment/9501200093_1_kenneth-feld-productions-snow-white-dwarfs.

Dart, John. "Biblical Stories Available on Home Video." *Los Angeles Times,* March 29, 1986, http://articles.latimes.com/1986–03–29/news/mn-1295_1_hanna-barbera-productions.

Deen, Sarah. "As DC Comics ReVamps Wacky Races—Can You Remember All the Characters?" *Metro,* March 31, 2016, http://metro.co.uk/2016/03/31/as-dc-comics-comics-revamp-wacky-races-can-you-remember-all-the-characters-5785508/.

Deitch, Gene. "Chapter 28: A Tangled Web." *Animation World Network,* November 19, 2013, https://www.awn.com/genedeitch/chapter-twentyeight-a-tangled-web.

Delgado, Richard, and Jean Stefancic. "Images of the Outside in American Law and Culture: Can Free Expression Remedy Systemic Social Ills?" *Critical Race Theory: The Cutting Edge,* eds. Richard Delgado and Jean Stefancic Philadelphia: Temple University Press, 2000.

Delugach, Al. "Turner Sells Fabled MGM But Keeps Lion's Share" *Los Angeles Times,* June 7, 1986, http://articles.latimes.com/1986–06–07/news/mn-9950_1_turner-broadcasting.

Demby, Gene. "Who Gets to Be a Superhero? Race and Identity in Comics." *NPR,* January 11, 2014, https://www.npr.org/sections/codeswitch/2014/01/11/261449394/who-gets-to-be-a-superhero-race-and-identity-in-comics.

DeMott, Rick. "Boomerang to Air 'The Thanksgiving That Almost Wasn't.'" *Animation World Network,* November 23, 2010, https://www.awn.

com/news/boomerang-air-thanksgiving-almost-wasn-t.

Dent, A.J. "Strong Female Character: Valerie of Josie and the Pussycats." *GeekGirlCon,* March 26, 2014, https://geekgirlcon.com/strong-female-character-valerie-of-josie-and-the-pussycats/.

DePatie, David H. "Interview, Part 1." Interview by Charles Brubaker, *Baker Toons,* December 19, 2010, http://bakertoons.blogspot.com/2010/12/david-h-depatie-interview-part-1.html?m=1.

Derthick, Martha. and Paul J. Quirk. *The Politics of Deregulation.* Washington, D.C.: The Brookings Institute, 1985.

Diaz, Eric. "Archie Launches New Josie and the Pussycats Series This Fall." *Nerdist,* June 9, 2016, http://nerdist.com/archie-launches-new-josie-and-the-pussycats-series-this-fall/.

Dobson, Nichola. *Historical Dictionary of Animation and Cartoons.* Lanham, MD: Scarecrow, 2009.

Doherty, Thomas. "The Wonderful World of Disney Studies." *The Chronicle of Higher Education,* July 21, 2006, http://www.chronicle.com/article/The-Wonderful-World-of-Disney/9806.

Doll, Poncho "REEL LIFE / FILM & VIDEO FILE: Music Helped 'Flintstones' on Way to Fame: In 1960, Hoyt Curtin Created the Lively Theme for the Stone Age Family. The Show's Producers Say it may be the most Frequently Broadcast Song on TV." *Los Angeles Times,* June 2, 1994, http://articles.latimes.com/1994–06–02/news/vl-64779_1_hoyt-curtin.

"Dorothy & The Wizard of Oz and Wacky Races Headed for Boomerang International." *Turner,* May 11, 2017, http://www.turner.com/pressroom/%E2%80%9Cdorothy-wizard-oz%E2%80%9D-and-%E2%80%9Cwacky-races%E2%80%9D-headed-boomerang-international.

Dow, Bonnie J. *Prime-Time Feminism,* Philadelphia: University of Pennsylvania Press, 1996.

D'Souza, Karen. "The Man Behind the Music of Mary Poppins." *San Jose Mercury News,* May 22, 2012, http://www.mercurynews.com/2012/05/22/the-man-behind-the-music-of-mary-poppins/.

Du Bois, W.E.B. *Black Reconstruction in America, 1860–1880.* New York: Free Press, 1995.

Du Bois, W.E.B. *The Souls of Black Folks.* Chicago: Dover, 1994.

DuPont, Kevin Paul. "NHL Mascot Puck Has Left the Rink." *Boston Globe,* June 9, 2013, https://www.bostonglobe.com/sports/2013/06/08/nhl-mascot-peter-puck-has-left-rink/ix7mlHJHpHmRM6mZzLgqaP/story.html.

Edwards, Blake dir. *Breakfast at Tiffany's,* October 5, 1961, Paramount, Hollywood, CA.

Ehrbar, Greg. "DVD Review: Help! It's The Hair Bear Bunch!" *Cartoon Research,* April 7, 2013, https://cartoonresearch.com/index.php/dvd-review-help-its-the-hair-bear-bunch/.

"11 Famous Actors That Appeared on Both Gunsmoke and the Big Valley." *MeTV,* March 15, 2016, http://www.metv.com/lists/11-famous-actors-who-appeared-on-both-gunsmoke-and-the-big-valley.

Elkins, Evan. "Cultural Identity and Subcultural

Forums: The Post-Network Politics of Adult Swim." *Television & New Media* 15, no. 7 (2014): 595–610.

Elliot, Debbie. "After Bans, Tobacco Tries Direct Marketing." *NPR,* November 18, 2008, http://www.npr.org/templates/story/story.php?storyId=97136501.

Epstein, Edward J. "How Did Michael Eisner Make Disney Profitable?" *Slate,* September 27, 2005, http://www.slate.com/articles/arts/the_hollywood_economist/2005/04/how_did_michael_eisner_make_disney_profitable.html.

Erickson, Hal. *Television Cartoon Shows: An Illustrated Encyclopedia 1949–2003.* Jefferson, NC: McFarland, 2005.

Erickson, Hal. *Syndicated Television: The First Forty Years, 1947–1987.* Jefferson, NC: McFarland, 2001.

Eury, Michael. *Caption Action, The Original Superhero Action Figure.* Raleigh: Twomorrows, 2002.

Evans, Anderson. "Fantastic Max, Dirty Diapers All in Your Face." *Gawker,* August 7, 2010, http://gawker.com/5606752/fantastic-max-dirty-diapers-all-in-your-face.

"Exclusive Clip, Super Friends: The Legendary Super Powers Show." *MTV,* August 8, 2008, http://www.mtv.com/news/2756496/exclusive-clip-super-friends-the-legendary-super-powers-show/.

Fabrikant, Geraldine. "The Fall and Rise of Fred Silverman." *New York Times,* June 5, 1989, http://www.nytimes.com/1989/06/05/business/the-fall-and-rise-of-fred-silverman.html?pagewanted=all&mcubz=0.

Fabrikant, Geraldine. "The Media Business—The Merger—Walt Disney to Acquire ABC in $19 Billion Deal to Build a Giant in Entertainment." *New York Times,* August 1, 1995, http://www.nytimes.com/1995/08/01/business/media-business-merger-walt-disney-acquire-abc-19-billion-deal-build-giant-for.html?pagewanted=all.

Fahlberg, Vera. *A Child's Journey Through Placement.* London: Jessica Kingsley, 2012

"The Famous Five." *EnidBlyton.net,* http://www.enidblyton.net/famous-five/.

Fanon, Frantz. *Black Skin, White Masks.* New York: Grove, 2008.

Farley, Rebecca. "From Fred and Wilma to Ren and Stimpy: What Makes a Cartoon 'Prime Time'?" *Primetime Animation: Television Animation and American Culture,* eds. Carol A. Stabile and Mark Harrison. New York: Routledge, 2003, 147–164.

Fickett, Travis, Eric Goldman, Dan Iverson, and Brian Zoromski. "Fantastic Four on TV." *IGN,* July 15, 2007, http://www.ign.com/articles/2007/06/16/fantastic-four-on-tv-2?page=2.

Fickley-Baker, Jennifer. "This Week in Disney History: Oswald the Lucky Rabbit Debuted in 1927" *Disney Parks,* September 8, 2012, https://disneyparks.disney.go.com/blog/2012/09/this-week-in-disney-history-oswald-the-lucky-rabbit-debuted-in-1927/.

"The 50 Most Racist TV Shows of All Time." *Complex,* June 3, 2013, http://www.complex.com/pop-culture/2013/06/most-racist-tv-shows/jonny-quest.

Fine, Cordelia. "Why Are Toys So Gendered?" *Slate,*

April 5, 2014, http://www.slate.com/articles/health_and_science/new_scientist/2014/04/girl_and_boy_toys_childhood_preferences_for_gendered_toys_are_not_innate.html.

"First Prime-Time Animated Show." *Guinness World Records,* http://www.guinnessworldrecords.com/world-records/first-prime-time-animation-show.

Fischer, Stuart. *Kids' TV: The First 25 Years.* New York: Facts on File, 1983.

Fiske, John. *Television Culture.* New York: Routledge, 2011.

Fiske, Shalom M. "Peeking Behind the Screen Varied Approach to the Production of Education Television." The *Children's Television Community,* ed. J. Alison Bryant. Mahwah, NJ: Lawrence Erlbaum, 2007.

Fitzgerald, Kate. "Cartoon Network: Betty Cohen." *Advertising Age,* June 28, 1999, http://adage.com/article/news/cartoon-network-betty-cohen/61952/.

Fleming, T.J. "T.V.'s Most Unexpected Hit." *The Saturday Evening Post,* December 2, 1961, 62–66.

Fleming, Mike, Jr. "Eddie Murphy Lends Voice to Hong Kong Phooey Feature." *Deadline,* August 10, 2011, http://deadline.com/2011/08/eddie-murphy-lends-voice-to-hong-kong-phooey-feature-155977/.

"The Flintstones: The Best of Bedrock (1994)." *British Film Institute,* http://www.bfi.org.uk/films-tv-people/4ce2b7d6b92c4.

Foli, Petrina. "Pac-Man Bites Back." *O Say Can You See,* June 11, 2010, http://americanhistory.si.edu/blog/2010/06/pacman-bites-back.html.

Forgacs, David. "Disney Animation and the Business of Childhood." *Screen* 33, no. 4 (1992): 361–74.

Fox, David J., and Valerie B. Jordan. "Racial Preference and Identification of Black, American Chinese, and White Children." *Genetic Psychology Monographs* (1973).

Furniss, Maureen. *Art in Motion: Animation Aesthetics.* London: John Libbey, 2008.

Gach, Ethan. "Scumbags Harass Woman for Working on Mass Effect: Andromeda's Animations." *Kotaku,* March 18, 2017, https://kotaku.com/scumbags-harass-woman-for-working-on-mass-effect-andro-1793410647.

Gambone, Robert. "George Luks, Hogan's Alley, and Ashcan School Social Thought." *Aurora, The Journal of the History of Art* 6 (2005): 38–79.

Gelt, Jessica. "200 Years of Authenticity (or lack thereof) in Casting." *Los Angeles Times,* July 13, 2017, http://www.latimes.com/entertainment/arts/la-ca-cm-authenticity-casting-timeline-20170713-htmlstory.html.

Gitlin, Todd. "Media Saturation and the Increasing Velocity of Disposable Feeling." Todd Gitlin, *Media Unlimited: How the Torrent of Images and Sounds Overwhelms Our Lives.* New York: Metropolitan Books, 2001.

Gloudeman, Nikki. "Why Children's Cartoons Have a Sexism Problem." *The Huffington Post,* October 6, 2014, http://www.huffingtonpost.com/nikki-gloudeman/why-childrens-cartoons-have-a-sexism-problem_b_5924390.html.

Goetz, Edward. "Gentrification in Black and White: The Racial Impact of Public Housing Demolition in American Cities." *Urban Studies* 48, no. 8 (2011): 1581–1604.

Goldmark, Daniel. *Tunes for 'Toons: Music and the Hollywood Cartoon.* Berkeley: University of California Press, 2005.

Goldstein, Steve. "ASU Scooby-Doo Scholar Unmasks 51 Years of Mysteries." *KJZZ,* June 5, 2020, https://kjzz.org/content/1589347/asu-scooby-doo-scholar-unmasks-51-years-mysteries.

"Good Morning Mickey." *D23,* https://d23.com/a-to-z/good-morning-mickey-television/.

Goodman, Martin. "Deconstruction Zone—Part 1 (Or: Semiotics Means Never Having to Signify You're Sorry)." *Animation World Network,* February 16, 2004, https://www.awn.com/animationworld/deconstruction-zone-part-1-or-semiotics-means-never-having-signify-you-re-sorry.

Goodman, Martin. "Talking in His Sheep: A Conversation with Mo Willems." *Animation World Network,* June 25, 2001, https://www.awn.com/animationworld/talking-his-sheep-conversation-mo-willems.

Goodman, Martin. "When Reagan Met Optimus Prime." *Animation World Network,* October 12, 2010, https://www.awn.com/animationworld/dr-toon-when-reagan-met-optimus-prime.

Grainge, Paul. *Brand Hollywood: Selling Entertainment in a Global Media Age.* New York: Routledge, 2008.

Grandinetti, Fred. "When Popeye Was Popular Without His Punch!" *Skwigly,* March 9, 2017.

Grandinetti, Fred M. *Popeye: An Illustrated History.* Jefferson, NC: McFarland, 2004.

Gray, Jonathan. *Watching with The Simpsons: Television, Parody, and Intertextuality.* New York: Routledge, 2006.

Gray, Jonathan, and Amanda Lotz. *Television Studies.* Malden, MA: Polity, 2012.

"The Great Gilly Hopkins." *Turner Classic Movies,* http://www.tcm.com/tcmdb/title/469692/Great-Gilly-Hopkins-The/.

Green, Paul. *Encyclopedia of Weird Westerns: Supernatural and Science Fiction Elements in Novels, Pulps, Comics, Films, Television, and Games.* Jefferson, NC: McFarland, 2009.

Greenfield, Jeff. "The Silverman Strategy." *New York Times,* March 7, 1976, http://www.nytimes.com/1976/03/07/archives/the-silverman-strategy-how-fred-silverman-is-helping-abc-get-over.html?mcubz=0.

Groening, Matt. "Commentary for "Bart the Genius." *The Simpsons: The Complete First Season,* 20th Century Fox, Hollywood, CA, 2001.

Grossman, Gary H. *Saturday Morning TV.* New York: Random House Value Publishing, 1988.

Guida, Fred. *A Christmas Carol and Its Adaptations: A Critical Examination of Dickens's Story and Its Productions on Screen and Television.* Jefferson, NC: McFarland, 2000.

Haddad, Charles. "Turner Serious About Yogi Bear." *Chicago Tribune,* June 6, 1994, http://articles.chicagotribune.com/1994-06-06/business/9406060008_1_hanna-barbera-joe-barbera-fred-seibert.

Haggins, Jerry. "The Andy Griffith Show: US Situation Comedy." *The Museum of Broadcast Communications,* http://www.museum.tv/eotv/andygriffith.htm.

Halberstam, J. "Animating Revolt/Revolting Animation: Penguin Love, Doll Sex, and the Spectacle of the Queer Nonhuman." *Queering the Non/Human,* eds. Myra J. Hird and Noreen Giffney. New York: Routledge, 2016.

Hall, Stuart. "Encoding and Decoding." *The Cultural Studies Reader,* ed. Simon During. New York: Routledge, 2007.

Hanna, Bill, and Tom Ito. *A Cast of Friends.* Dallas: Taylor, 1996.

Hanna, William ,and Joseph Barbera, dirs. *His Mouse Friday.* MGM, Culver City, CA, 1951.

Hanna, William, and Joseph Barbera, dirs. *Jerry's Cousin.* MGM, Culver City, CA, 1951.

Hanna, William, and Joseph Barbera, dirs. *Mouse Cleaning.* MGM, Culver City, CA, 1948.

Hanna, William, and Joseph Barbera, dirs. *Mouse in Manhattan.* MGM, Culver City, CA, 1945.

Hanna, William, and Joseph Barbera, dirs. *Casanova Cat.* MGM, Culver City, CA, 1951.

Hanna, William, and Joseph Barbera, dirs. *Fine Feathered Friend.* MGM, Culver City, CA, 1942.

Hanna, William, and Joseph Barbera, dirs. *Puss n' Toots.* MGM, Culver City, CA, 1942.

Harris, Heather E. "Queen Phiona and Princess Shuri—Alternative Africana 'Royalty' in Disney's Royal Realm: An Intersectional Analysis." *Social Sciences* 7, 10, 206, https://doi.org/10.3390/socsci7100206.

Harris, Will. "In 1978, Hanna-Barbera Took to the Ice to Celebrate Fred Flintstone's Birthday." *AVClub,* April 15, 2016, http://www.avclub.com/article/1978-hanna-barbera-took-ice-celebrate-fred-flintst-235288.

Hayes, David. "'You Guys Are Killing Me with This Dreck': Contemporary Attitudes toward the Golden, Atomic, Silver, and Bronze Eras of Comic Book Production." *Handbook of Cultural Studies and Education,* ed. Peter Pericles Trifonas and Susan Jagger. New York: Routledge, 2018, 255–276.

Haynes, Richard B. "Children's Perceptions of 'Comic' and 'Authentic' Cartoon Violence." *Journal of Broadcasting & Electronic Media* 22, no. 1 (1978).

Heaton, Michael. "The Enduring (Gay?) Appeal of The Wizard of Oz: Minister of Culture." *Cleveland Plain-Dealer,* March 25, 2016, http://www.cleveland.com/ministerofculture/index.ssf/2016/03/the_enduringly_gay_appeal_of_t.html.

Hecht, John. "Mexican Animated Film 'Top Cat' Breaks Record at Box Office." *Hollywood Reporter,* September 20, 2011, http://www.hollywoodreporter.com/news/mexican-animated-film-top-cat-237740.

Hendershot, Heather. *Saturday Morning Censors: Television Regulation Before the V-Chip.* Durham: Duke University Press, 1998.

Heritage, Stuart. "Captain Planet Returns—to Take Superhero TV Down to Zero." *The Guardian,* March 22, 2017, https://www.theguardian.com/tv-and-radio/2017/mar/22/captain-planet-returns-online-amazon-prime.

Herschberger, Kelsey. "Black Lightning: 15 Things You Never Knew." *Comic Book Resources,* January 18, 2017, http://www.cbr.com/black-lightning-15-things-you-never-knew/.

Hevesi, Dennis. "Alex Toth, 77 Comic Book Artist and 'Space Ghost' Animator Dies." *New York Times,* June 6, 2006, http://www.nytimes.com/2006/06/06/arts/design/06toth.html?mcubz=0.

Hiestand, Michael. "Fox Sports Launches Direct Challenge to ESPN Dominance." *USA Today,* March 5, 2013, https://www.usatoday.com/story/sports/columnist/hiestand-tv/2013/03/05/fox-sports-cable-channel-challenging-espn-dominance-catholic-7/1965299/.

Hill, Edwin C., Jr. *Black Soundscapes, White Stages: The Meaning of Francophone Sound in the Black Atlantic.* Baltimore: Johns Hopkins University Press, 2013.

"History." *The World of Sid and Marty Krofft,* http://www.sidandmartykrofft.com/about/history/.

Hofstead, David. *The Dukes of Hazzard: The Unofficial Companion.* New York: St. Martin's, 1998.

Hofstead, David. *What Were They Thinking? The 100 Dumbest Events in Television History.* New York: Watson-Guptill, 2004.

Holden, Stephen. "Movie Review: Film: 'GoBots' TV Spin-Off." *New York Times,* March 22, 1986, http://www.nytimes.com/movie/review?res=9A0DE5DA143FF931A15750C0A960948260.

Hollis, Tim. *Hi, There Boys and Girls! America's Local Children's TV Programs.* Jackson: University of Mississippi Press, 2001.

Hollis, Tim. *Toons in Toyland: The Story of Cartoon Character Merchandise.* Jackson: University of Mississippi Press, 2015.

Holt, Douglas, and Craig Thompson. "Man-of-Action Heroes: How American Ideology of Manhood Structures Men's Consumption." *Harvard Marketing Research,* November 2002, https://papers.ssrn.com/sol3/papers.cfm?abstract_id=386600.

Holt, Douglas B. *How Brands Become Icons: The Principles of Cultural Branding.* Cambridge: Harvard Business Press, 2004.

hooks, bell. *Reel to Real: Race, Sex, and Class at the Movies.* New York: Routledge, 2009.

Horowitz, Juliana Menace. "Most Americans See Value in Steering Children Toward Toys, Activities Associated with Opposite Gender." *Pew Research,* December 19, 2017, https://www.pewresearch.org/fact-tank/2017/12/19/most-americans-see-value-in-steering-children-toward-toys-activities-associated-with-opposite-gender/.

Hsu, Hua. "The End of White America?" *The Atlantic,* January/February 2009, https://www.theatlantic.com/magazine/archive/2009/01/the-end-of-white-america/307208/.

Huang, Yunte. *Charlie Chan: The Untold Story of the Honorable Detective and His Rendezvous with American History.* New York: W.W. Norton, 2011.

Hughes, Mark. "Exclusive: 'Jonny Quest' Could

Be Warner's Next Big Franchise." *Forbes,* July 28, 2016, https://www.forbes.com/sites/markhughes/2016/07/28/exclusive-jonny-quest-could-be-warners-next-big-franchise/#754dce16749b.

Hund, Wulf D., and Charles W. Mills. "Comparing Black People to Monkeys has a Long, Dark Simian History." *The Conversation,* February 28, 2016, https://theconversation.com/comparing-black-people-to-monkeys-has-a-long-dark-simian-history-55102.

Hurley, Dorothy L. "Seeing White: Children of Color and the Disney Fairy Tale Princess." *The Journal of Negro Education* 74 no. 3 (2005): 221–232.

Imbesi, Pete. "The 15 Catchiest Cartoon Theme Songs of the 80s." *Comic Book Resources,* April 30, 2017, http://www.cbr.com/the-15-catchiest-cartoon-theme-songs-of-the-80s/.

Imbesi, Pete. "Space Ghost: 15 Weird Facts You Never Knew." *Comic Book Resources,* April 5, 2017, http://www.cbr.com/space-ghost-15-weird-facts-you-never-knew/.

Inskeep, Steve. "The Father of the Addams Family," interview with Linda Davis, NPR, October 31, 2008, http://www.npr.org/templates/story/story.php?storyId=6407492.

Internet Movie Database. "Episode Cast for 'The Tom and Jerry Show.'" http://www.imdb.com/title/tt3559124/epcast.

"Introduction." *Critical Race Theory: The Key Writings that Formed a Movement,* eds. Kimberle Crenshaw, Neil Gotanda, Gary Peller, and Kendall Thomas. New York: The New Press, 1995, xiii–xxxii.

Ismail, Sherille "Transformative Choices: A Review Of 70 Years of FCC Decisions." *Federal Communications Commission,* October 2010, https://apps.fcc.gov/edocs_public/attachmatch/DOC-302496A1.pdf.

Iverem, Esther. "The Real Villains of Jonny Quest." *Washington Post,* May 29, 1996, https://www.washingtonpost.com/archive/lifestyle/1996/05/29/the-real-villains-of-jonny-quest/2f238cd0-44d6-4a47-be45-28950a1e309b/.

Iverson, Paul R. *The Advent of the Laugh Track.* Hempstead, NY: Hofstra, 1994.

Jackson, Gordon. "13 Superhero TV Shows That It's Hard to Believe Somebody Greenlighted." *io9,* January 25, 2016, http://io9.gizmodo.com/13-superhero-tv-shows-that-its-hard-to-believe-somebody-1754552331.

James, Becca. "The Halloween Tree Remains an Adventure in Understanding and Friendship." *AVClub,* October 29, 2016, http://tv.avclub.com/the-halloween-tree-remains-an-adventure-in-understandin-1798253761.

Jeffries, Stuart. "Animal Magic" *The Guardian,* November 27, 2000, https://www.theguardian.com/media/2000/nov/28/tvandradio.television3.

Jensen, Thor. "Transmissions from the Ghost Planet: The Definitive History of Space Ghost Coast to Coast." *SyFy,* June 19, 2014, http://www.syfy.com/syfywire/transmissions-ghost-planet-definitive-history-space-ghost-coast-coast.

Jhally, Sut. "George Gerbner on Media and Culture." *The Electronic Storyteller: Television & The Cultivation of Values,* Media Education Foundation, 2009, http://www.mediaed.org/transcripts/The-Electronic-Storyteller-Transcript.pdf.

Johnson, Jo. "We'll Have a Gay Old Time! Queer Representation in Prime-Time Animation from the Cartoon Short to the Family Sitcom." *Queers in American Popular Culture,* ed. Jim Elledge. Santa Barbara: Praeger, 2010.

Jones, Paul. "The Technology is not the Cultural Form? Raymond Williams Sociological Critique of Raymond Williams." *Canadian Journal of Communication* 23, no. 4 (1998), http://cjc-online.ca/index.php/journal/article/view/1058/964

Jordan, Darran. *Green Lantern History: An Unauthorized Guide to the DC Comic Book Series.* Sydney: Eclectica, 2015

Joyrich. Lynne. "American Dreams and Demons: Television's 'Hollow' Histories and Fantasies of Race." *The Black Scholar* 48, no. 1 (2018): 31–42.

Kalagian, Terry. "Programming Children's Television: The Cable Model." *The Children's Television Community,* ed. J. Alison Bryant. Mahwah, NJ: Lawrence Erlbaum, 2007.

Katz, A.J. "The Top Cable Networks of January 2017." *AdWeek,* January 31, 2017, http://www.adweek.com/tvnewser/the-top-cable-networks-of-january-2017/319137.

Kendall, Lori. "Nerd Nation: Images of Nerds in US Popular Culture." *International Journal of Cultural Studies* 2, no. 2 (1999).

Keys, Jobia. "Doc McStuffins and Dora the Explorer: Representations of Gender, Race, and Class in US Animation." *Journal of Children and Media* 10, no. 3 (2016): 355–368.

Kincheloe, Joe L. "Says Who? Who Decides What Is Art?" *Art, Culture, and Education: Artful Teaching in a Fractured Landscape,* eds. Karel Rose and Joe L. Kincheloe. New York: Peter Lang, 2004.

King, Susan. "Hanna-Barbera Cartoons Return on New Boomerang." *Los Angeles Times,* April 1, 2000, http://articles.latimes.com/2000/apr/01/entertainment/ca-14752.

Kleinfield, N.R. "ABC Being Sold for $3.5 Billion-1st Network Sale." *New York Times,* March 19, 1985, http://www.nytimes.com/1985/03/19/business/abc-is-being-sold-for-3.5-billion-1st-network-sale.html.

Klickstein, Mathew. *SLIMED! An Oral History of Nickelodeon's Golden Age.* New York: Plume, 2013.

Klosner, Michael. *Prehistoric Humans in Film and Television: 581 Dramas, Comedies, and Documentaries, 1905–2004.* Jefferson, NC: McFarland, 2006.

Knapp, Alex "The Future We Don't Even Know We Missed." *Forbes,* October 13, 2011, https://www.forbes.com/sites/alexknapp/2011/10/13/the-future-we-dont-even-know-we-missed/#e59a6e658391.

Kowalski, Jesse M. "Hanna-Barbera: The Architects of Saturday Morning." *Illustration History,* January 19, 2017, http://www.illustrationhistory.org/essays/hanna-barbera-the-architects-of-saturday-morning.

Krakow, Jonah. "TV Playbook: Let's Add a Kid!" *IGN*, December 10, 2008, http://www.ign.com/articles/2008/12/10/tv-playbook-lets-add-a-kid?page=5.

Krasner, Jon. *Motion Graphic Design: Applied History and Aesthetics*. New York: Focal Press, 2008.

Kryczka, Cathye. "Again, Again! Why Your Kid Wants to Do the Same Activity Over and Over." *Today's Parent*, December 14, 2019, https://www.todaysparent.com/toddler/kids-repetition/.

Kunkel, Dale. "Kid's Media Policy Goes Digital Current Developments in Children's Television Regulation in *The Children's Television Community*, ed. J. Alison Bryant. Mahwah, NJ: Lawrence Erlbaum, 2007.

Kurland, Daniel. "When Sealab 2021 Devoted Nearly an Entire Episode to a Single Joke." *Splitsider*, May 10, 2016, http://splitsider.com/2016/05/when-sealab-2021-devoted-nearly-an-entire-episode-to-a-single-joke/.

LaBaton, Stephen. "Deregulating the Media: The Overview; Regulators Ease Rules Governing Media Ownership." *New York Times*, June 3, 2003, http://www.nytimes.com/2003/06/03/business/deregulating-media-overview-regulators-ease-rules-governing-media-ownership.html?mcubz=0.

Lamarre, Thomas. "The Biopolitics of Companion Species: Wartime Animation and Multi-Ethnic Nationalism." *The Politics of Culture: Around the Work of Naoki Sakai*, ed. Richard Calichman and John Namjun Kim. New York: Routledge, 2010.

Lambert, David. "The Flintstones—Warner Archive Puts Out 4 DVD Titles with Post-Series Primetime Specials." *TV Shows on DVD*, October 9, 2012, http://tvshowsondvd.com/news/Flintstones-The-Prime-Time-Specials-Collections/17586.

Lamour, Joseph. "11 Secrets You Never Knew about Animaniacs, Pinky & the Brain and Freakazoid." *MTV News*, April 14, 2016, http://www.mtv.com/news/2867289/animaniacs-netflix-freakazoid-pinky-brain/.

Landler, Mark. "Turner to Merge into Time Warner in a $7.5 Billion Deal." *New York Times*, September 23, 1995, http://www.nytimes.com/1995/09/23/us/turner-to-merge-into-time-warner-a-7.5-billion-deal.html?pagewanted=all.

Laport, Nicole. "Disney and Pixar Fight to Rule the Mouse House." *Fast Company*, June 20, 2016, https://www.fastcompany.com/3060475/disney-andpixar-fight-to-be-the-mouse-house-animation-alpha-pluto.

Large, David, and James Farmers. *Modern Cable Television Technology*. San Francisco: Morgan Kaufmann, 2004.

"The Last of the Curlews." *Turner Classic Movies*, http://www.tcm.com/tcmdb/title/319005/Last-of-the-Curlews/.

Lawson, Tim, and Alisa Persons. *The Magic Behind the Voices: A Who's Who of Cartoon Voice Actors*. Jackson: University of Mississippi Press, 2004.

Lazarsfeld, Paul, and Robert Merton. "Mass Communication, Popular Taste and Organized Social Action." *The Process and Effects of Mass Communication*, revised edition, edited by Wilbur Schramm and Donald F. Roberts. Urbana: University of Illinois Press, 1971, 554–578.

Lee, Felicia R. "Hey, Hey, Hey! Animated Touchstones: Funky Turns 40 Recalls a Seminal TV Moment." *New York Times*, March 19, 2014.

Lehman, Christopher P. *American Cartoons of the Vietnam Era: A Study of Social Commentary in Film and Television, 1961–1975*. Jefferson, NC: McFarland, 2007.

Lehman, Christopher P. *The Colored Cartoon: Black Presentation in American Animated Shorts*, Amherst: University of Massachusetts Press, 2007.

Lenburg, Greg, Joan Howard Maurer, and Jeff Lenburg. *The Three Stooges Scrapbook*. Chicago: Chicago Review Press, 2012.

Lenburg, Jeff. *Encyclopedia of Animated Cartoons*. New York: Facts on File, 2008.

Lenburg, Jeff. *Who's Who in Animated Cartoons: An International Guide to Film and Televisions Award Winning Animators*. New York: Applause, 2006.

Lenburg, Jeff. *William Hanna and Joseph Barbera: The Sultans of Saturday Morning*. New York: Chelsea House, 2011.

Leskosky, Richard J. "The Reforming Fantasy: Recurrent Theme and Structure in American Studio Cartoons." *The Velvet Light Trap* 24 (Fall 1989), https://search.proquest.com/docview/1306639612/citation/6DC307A463004878PQ/1?accountid=14503.

Leszczak, Bob. *Single Season Sitcoms of the 1980s: A Complete Guide*. Jefferson, NC: McFarland, 2016.

Lev, Michael. "Hanna-Barbera Follows Disney Map." *New York Times*, January 9, 1990, http://www.nytimes.com/1990/01/09/business/hanna-barbera-follows-disney-map.html?mcubz=0.

Lind, Michael. "How Reaganism Actually Started with Carter." *Salon*, February 8, 2011, http://www.salon.com/2011/02/08/lind_reaganism_carter/.

Lindvall, Terry, and Ben Fraser. "Darker Shades of Animation." *Reading the Rabbit*, ed. Kevin Sandler. New Brunswick: Rutgers University Press, 1998, 121–136.

Littleton, Cynthia, and Geoff Berkshire. "TV's Favorite All-American Families." *Variety*, July 3, 2015, http://variety.com/gallery/all-american-family-tv-shows/#!14/the-donna-reed-show/.

"Local Kids' TV." *Pioneers of Television*, http://www.pbs.org/wnet/pioneers-of-television/pioneering-programs/local-kids-tv/.

Lotz, Amanda D. "U.S. Television and the Recession: Impetus for Change?" *Popular Communication* 8, no. 3 (2010).

Lucas, Michael P. "Yogi Bear Gets a Bit of the Ren & Stimpy Attitude: The Much-Loved Character and Friends, Created by Hanna-Barbera, are Back—but with John Kricfalusi's Twist." *Los Angeles Times*, September 23, 1999, https://web.archive.org/web/20121026103656/http://articles.latimes.com/1999/sep/23/entertainment/ca-13166.

Lueptow, Kelsey. "5 Ways Girls Are Taught to Avoid 'Smart.'" *Everyday Feminism*, July 28, 2014, http://everydayfeminism.com/2014/07/girls-taught-to-avoid-smart/.

Lukacs, Martin. "Neoliberalism has Conned us into

Fighting Climate Change as Individuals." *The Guardian*, July 17, 2017, https://www.theguardian.com/environment/true-north/2017/jul/17/neoliberalism-has-conned-us-into-fighting-climate-change-as-individuals.

Madigral, Alexis C. "The Court Case That Almost Made it Illegal to Tape TV Shows." *The Atlantic*, January 12, 2012, https://www.theatlantic.com/technology/archive/2012/01/the-court-case-that-almost-made-it-illegal-to-tape-tv-shows/251107/.

Mallory, Michael. "Animation's Legendary (Semi-) Lost Film." *Animation Magazine*, November 6, 2017, http://www.animationmagazine.net/top-stories/animations-legendary-semi-lost-film/.

Mallory, Michael. *Hanna-Barbera Cartoons*. New York: Hugh Lauter Levin Associates, 1998.

Maltin, Leonard. *Leonard Maltin's 2009 Movie Guide*. New York: Penguin Group, 2009.

Maltin, Leonard. *Of Mice and Magic: A History of American Animated Cartoons*. New York: Penguin, 1987.

Mandel, Jennifer. "The Production of a Beloved Community: Sesame Street's Answer to America's Inequalities." *The Journal of American Culture* 29, no. 1 (2006).

Manning, Michael K. "1970s." *DC Comics Year by Year: A Visual Chronicle*, eds. Daniel Wallace and Matthew K. Manning. New York: Dueling Kindersley, 2010, 201.

Mansour, David. *From Abba to Zoom: A Pop Culture Encyclopedia of the Late 20th Centuries*. Kansas City: Andrews McMeel, 2005.

"Margaret Loesch, Executive Chairman of Genius Brands International's Kid Genius Cartoon Channel; Vice Chair." *Television Academy Foundation*, https://www.emmys.com/foundation/board/110336.

Martinetti, Cher. "Chosen One of the Day: Captain Caveman." *SyFy*, February 16, 2017, http://www.syfy.com/syfywire/chosen-one-of-the-day-captain-caveman.

Matheson, Whitney. "Bump It Up: Adult Swim Wants Your TV Teasers." *USA Today*, November 6, 2013, http://www.usatoday.com/story/popcandy/2013/11/06/adult-swim-bump-app/3453467/.

McAllister, Matthew. "The Financial Interest and Syndication Rules." *Museum of Broadcast Communication*, http://www.museum.tv/eotv/financialint.htm.

McAvennie, Michael. "1970s." *DC Comics Year by Year: A Visual Chronicle*, eds. Daniel Wallace and Matthew K. Manning. New York: Dueling Kindersley, 2010, 136–183.

McCall, Douglas L. *Film Cartoons: A Guide to 20th Century American Animated Features and Shorts*. Jefferson, NC: McFarland, 1998.

McChesney, Robert. *The Problem of the Media: U.S. Communication Politics in the Twenty-First Century*. New York: Monthly Review, 2004.

McDermott, Mark. "Yogi Bear." *The Guide to United States Popular Culture*, eds. Ray Broadus Browne and Pat Browne. Madison: University of Wisconsin Press, 2001.

McMillan, Graeme. 'The Secret Life of the Other Birdman." *The Hollywood Reporter*, February 23, 2015, http://www.hollywoodreporter.com/heat-vision/secret-life-birdman-775822.

McNary, Dave. "'Scooby-Doo' Animated Movie in the Works at Warner Bros." *Variety*, August 17, 2015, http://variety.com/2015/film/news/scooby-doo-animated-movie-warner-bros-1201571538/.

McNary, Dave. "Scooby-Doo Animated Movie Moves Back Two Years to 2020." *Variety*, May 3, 2017, http://variety.com/2017/film/news/animated-scooby-movie-moves-back-2020-1202408718/.

McNeil, Alex. *Total Television*. New York: Penguin, 1996.

Melrose, Kevin. "Can DC's Scooby-Doo Apocalypse Redeem Scrappy-Doo?" *Comic Book Resources*, October 10, 2012, http://www.cbr.com/can-dcs-scooby-apocalypse-redeem-scrappy-doo.

Melton, J. Gordon. *The Vampire Book: The Encyclopedia of the Undead*. Canton, MI: Visible Ink, 2011.

Meltzer, Marisa. "My Dad Lives in a Downtown Hotel: The Subtle Brilliance of the After School Special." *Slate*, July 20, 2006, fhttp://www.slate.com/articles/arts/dvdextras/2006/07/my_dad_lives_in_a_downtown_hotel.html.

Menegus, Bryan. "The History of Adult Swim's Rise to Greatness." *Sploid*, April 11, 2016, http://sploid.gizmodo.com/an-oral-history-of-adult-swim-1770248730.

Merskin, Debra L. "Race and Gender Representations in Advertising in Cable Cartoon Crogramming." *CLCWeb: Comparative Literature and Culture* 10, no. 2 (2008).

Metzger, Jessica. "Truly They Were an Aqua Teen Hunger Force." *Medium*, June 2015, https://medium.com/on-second-thought/truly-they-were-an-8e7631476c99.

Meyer, Michaela D.E. "Representing Bisexuality on Television: The Case for Intersectional Hybrids." *Journal of Bisexuality* 10, no. 4 (2010), 366–387. http://www.tandfonline.com/doi/abs/10.1080/15299716.2010.521040.

Meyerson, Collier. "Fighting White Supremacy Means Owning Up to American History." *The Nation*, August 14, 2017, https://www.thenation.com/article/fighting-white-supremacy-means-owning-up-to-american-history/.

Middleton, Brad. *Un-Dead TV: The Ultimate Guide to Vampire Television*. Pepperell, MA: Light Unseen, 2012.

Mignolo, Walter. *The Darker Side of Western Modernity: Global Futures, Decolonial Options*. Durham: Duke University Press, 2011.

Mihailova. Mihaela. "Drawn (to) Independence: Female Showrunners in Contemporary American TV Animation." *Feminist Media Studies* 19, no. 7 (2019): 1009–1025.

"Miles Laboratories." *AdAge*, September 15, 2003, http://adage.com/article/adage-encyclopedia/miles-laboratories/98776/.

Miller, Chuck. "The ABC Saturday Superstar Movie." *Albany Times-Union*, June 21, 2016, http://blog.timesunion.com/chuckmiller/the-abc-saturday-superstar-movie/27324/.

Miller, Chuck. "Alice in Wonderland: Circa 1966." *Albany Times-Union,* June 11, 2016, http://blog.timesunion.com/chuckmiller/alice-in-wonderland-circa-1966/27418/.

Mirza, Farhad. "How Mickey Mouse Fought World War II." *Vulture,* October 29, 2015, http://www.vulture.com/2015/10/how-mickey-mouse-fought-world-war-ii.html.

Miserocchi, H. Kevin, and Charles Addams. *The Addams Family: An Evolution.* Petaluma, CA: Pomegranate Communications, 2010.

Mitchell, Robert. "How Paul Walker Helped Create a Fast and Furious Box-Office Franchise." *CNN,* December 6, 2013, http://www.cnn.com/2013/12/06/business/paul-walker-fast-furious-franchise/index.html.

Mitroff, Donna, and Rebecca Herr Stephenson. "The Television Tug-of-War: A Brief History of Children's Television Programming in the United States." *The Children's Television Community,* ed. J. Alison Bryant. Mahwah, NJ: Lawrence Erlbaum, 2007.

Mittell, Jason. *Genre and Television: From Cop Shows to Cartoons in American Culture.* New York: Routledge, 2004.

Mittell, Jason. "The Great Saturday Morning Exile: Scheduling Cartoons on Television's Periphery in the 1960s." *Prime Time Animation: Television Animation and American Culture,* eds. Carol A. Stabile and Mark Harrison. New York: Routledge, 2003, 33–54.

Mittell, Jason. *Television and American Culture.* New York: Oxford University, 2010.

Mohanty, Chandra Talpade. "'Under Western Eyes' Revisited: Feminist Solidarity through Anticapitalist Struggles." *Signs* 28, no. 2 (2003): 499–535.

Monbiot, George. "Neoliberalism—The Ideology at the Root of All Our Problems." *The Guardian,* April 15, 2016, https://www.theguardian.com/books/2016/apr/15/neoliberalism-ideology-problem-george-monbiot.

Montange, Renee. "Tom and Jerry Blamed for Violence in the Middle East." NPR, May 9, 2016, http://www.npr.org/2016/05/09/477301514/tom-and-jerry-blamed-for-violence-in-the-middle-east.

Montford, Christina. "When It Comes to Rap Music, Are White Boys Really Doing All the Buying?" *Atlanta Black Star,* November 6, 2014, http://atlantablackstar.com/2014/11/06/really-listening/.

Moore, Jack. "The Saga of Superstations and Baseball's Historical Resistance to Technology." *The Hardball Times,* June 29, 2016, http://www.hardballtimes.com/the-saga-of-superstations-and-baseballs-historical-resistance-to-technology/.

Moore, Scott. "Dr. Seuss' Daisy-Head Mayzie." *Washington Post,* February 5, 1995, https://www.washingtonpost.com/archive/lifestyle/tv/1995/02/05/dr-seusss-daisy-head-mayzie/70640b5f-322a-4724-ae85-2063d20d3e1c/?utm_term=.50f4b394e407.

Moore, Scott. "Fox's King Signals Prime Time Move." *Washington Post,* February 9, 1997, https://www.washingtonpost.com/archive/lifestyle/tv/1997/02/09/foxs-king-signals-prime-move/3ef000f2-e1a9-4f7c-999e-62bf79650b57/?utm_term=.ca8bf34d64af.

"More Care Bears Fun Facts." *Care-Bears.com,* retrieved March 1, 2005, https://web.archive.org/web/20050301073233/http://www.care-bears.com/CareBears/html/history/funfacts.html.

Motes, Jason. "'Young Justice' Pays Homage to the Original Super Hero Cartoon Hit 'Super Friends.'" *ScienceFiction.com,* January 31, 2013, http://sciencefiction.com/2013/01/31/young-justice-pays-homage-to-the-original-super-hero-cartoon-hit/.

Motion Picture Association of America. "Theatrical Market Statistics: 2016." http://www.mpaa.org/wp-content/uploads/2017/03/MPAA-Theatrical-Market-Statistics-2016_Final.pdf.

Mukulak, Bill. "Fans vs Warner Bros. Who Owns Looney Toons?" *Reading the Rabbit,* ed. Kevin Sandler. New Brunswick: Rutgers University Press, 1998.

Mullen, Megan. "The Simpsons and Hanna-Barbera's Animation Legacy." *Leaving Springfield: The Simpsons and the Possibility of Oppositional Culture,* ed. John Alberti. Detroit: Wayne State University Press, 2004.

Mulligan, Thomas S. "Turner-Time Warner Merger Approved by Shareholders." *Los Angeles Times,* October 11, 1996, http://articles.latimes.com/1996-10-11/business/fi-52676_1_time-warner.

Munoz, Jose Esteban. *Disidentifications: Queers of Color and the Performance of Politics.* Minneapolis: University of Minnesota, 1999.

Murray, Noel. "Hanna-Barbera Dared to Get Real with Its Evel Knievel Riff." *AV Club,* August 16, 2016, http://www.avclub.com/article/hanna-barbera-dared-get-real-its-evel-knievel-riff-240813.

Murray, Noel. "Legends of the Superheroes." *AVClub,* February 16, 2011, http://www.avclub.com/article/ilegends-of-the-superheroesi-51932.

NAB Legal Guide to Broadcast Law and Regulation, eds. Jean W. Benz, Jane E. Mago, and Jarianne Timmerman. National Association of Broadcasters, https://goo.gl/WiYSZr.

Narcisse, Evan. "Documentary About Disney's First Black Reveals a Hidden, Turbulent History." *io9,* December 2, 2016, http://io9.gizmodo.com/documentary-about-disneys-first-black-animator-reveals-1789572836.

Neece, Randall. *Gone Today, Here Tomorrow: A Memoir,* Bloomington: Author House, 2012.

Nelson, Angela M. "African American Stereotypes in Prime-Time Television: An Overview, 1947–2007." *African Americans and Popular Culture Volume 1,* edited by Todd Boyd. Westport, CT: Praeger, 2008.

Newcomb, Horace. "Television and the Present Climate of Criticism." *Television: The Critical View.* New York: Oxford University Press, 2000.

Newman, Michael Z. *Atari Age: The Emergence of Video Games in America.* Cambridge: MIT Press, 2016.

"News: Television." *Animation World Magazine,*

November 1998, https://www.awn.com/mag/issue3.8/3.8pages/3.8television.html.

Ngai, Mae M. *Impossible Subjects: Illegal Aliens and the Making of Modern America.* Princeton: Princeton University Press, 2004.

Nobleman, Marc Tyler. "Super '70s and '80s: 'Super Friends'—Darrell McNeil, animator." *Noblemania*, July 29, 2011, https://www.noblemania.com/2011/07/super-70s-and-80s-super-friendsdarrell.html.

"Norman Rockwell Museum Presents 'Hanna-Barbera: The Architects of Saturday Morning.'" Norman Rockwell Museum, August 17, 2016, https://www.nrm.org/2016/12/norman-rockwell-museum-presents-hanna-barbera-architects-saturday-morning.

Novak, Matt. "50 Years of the Jetsons, Why the Show Still Matters." *Smithsonian*, September 19, 2012, http://www.smithsonianmag.com/history/50-years-of-the-jetsons-why-the-show-still-matters-43459669/.

O'Connor, John J. "Buddy Ebsen and Joey Cramer Star in Stone Fox." *New York Times*, March 30, 1987, http://www.nytimes.com/1987/03/30/arts/buddy-ebsen-and-joey-cramer-star-in-stone-fox.html?mcubz=0.

Ohmer, Susan. *George Gallup in Hollywood.* New York: Columbia University Press, 2006.

"The Old Is New." Radmar Inc., February 12, 2013 https://radmarinc.com/tag/education/.

"1994 Domestic Grosses." *Box Office Mojo*, http://www.boxofficemojo.com/yearly/chart/?yr=1994.

"1970 Oveview." United States Census Bureau, https://www.census.gov/history/www/through_the_decades/overview/1970.html.

"Operation Prime Time Sets Three New Shows." *Broadcasting*, August 29, 1977, http://americanradiohistory.com/Archive-BC/BC-1977/BC-1977-08-29.pdf.

Osborne, Jerry. "Soundtracks Start with 'Snow White.'" *Chicago Sun-Times*, November 3, 2006, https://www.highbeam.com/doc/1P2-1387100.html.

"Ownership." FCC Quadrennial Review (2010). https://transition.fcc.gov/osp/inc-report/INoC-30-Ownership.pdf.

Oyiboke, Amen. "History of Black Entertainment 1960–1970." *Los Angeles Sentinel*, February 10, 2016 https://lasentinel.net/history-of-black-entertainment-from-1960-1970s.html

P. Ken. "An Interview with Seth MacFarlane: The Creator of Family Guy Discusses His Career." *IGN*, July 21, 2003, https://www.ign.com/articles/2003/07/21/an-interview-with-seth-macfarlane.

Padgett, Donald. "Yes, Velma is a Lesbian in 'Scooby Doo: Mystery Incorporated.'" *Out*, July 13, 2020, https://www.out.com/television/2020/7/13/yes-velma-lesbian-scooby-doo-mystery-incorporated.

Palmer, Edward L., and Shalom M. Fisch. "The Beginnings of Sesame Street Research." *"G" Is for Growing: Thirty Years of Research on Children and Sesame Street*, eds. Shalom M. Fisch and Rosemarie T. Truglio. Mahwah, NJ: Lawrence Erlbaum Associates, 2001.

Parekh, Rupul. "How Much of The Jetson's Futuristic World Has Become a Reality." *Advertising Age*, September 25, 2012, http://adage.com/article/media/jetsons-world-a-reality/237394/.

Pecora, Norma. "The Changing Nature of Children's Television: Fifty Years of Research." *Children and Television: Fifty Years of Research*, eds. Norma Pecora, John P. Murray, and Ann Wartella. Mahwah, NJ: Lawrence Erlbaum, 2007.

Pecora, Norma Odom. *The Business of Children's Entertainment.* New York: Guilford Press, 1998.

Perlmutter, David. *America Toons In: A History of Television Animation.* Jefferson, NC: McFarland, 2014.

Perlmutter, David. "Toon In, Toon Out: American Television Animation and the Shaping of American Popular Culture, 1948–1980." Master's Thesis, University of Manitoba (2010).

Pierce, Scott D. "Conan Can't Shake off Rocky Start as Host." *Deseret News*, July 17, 1998, http://www.deseretnews.com/article/643555/Conan-cant-shake-off-rocky-start-as-host.html.

Pilgrim, David. "Mammy Two Shoes." The Jim Crow Museum, January 2013, https://www.ferris.edu/HTMLS/news/jimcrow/question/2013/january.htm.

Pilling, Jayne. "Intro." *Reader in Animation Studies*, ed. Jayne Pilling. London: John Libbey, 1997.

Pinkus, Karen. "On Climate, Cars, and Literary Theory." *Technology and Culture* 49, no. 4 (2008): 1002–1009.

Pirnia, Girin. "13 Fun Facts About Scooby-Doo." *Mental Floss*, June 2, 2016, http://mentalfloss.com/article/80937/13-fun-facts-about-scooby-doo.

Pollitt, Katha. "Hers; The Smurfette Principle." *New York Times*, April 7, 1991, http://www.nytimes.com/1991/04/07/magazine/hers-the-smurfette-principle.html?mcubz=0.

Polowy, Kevin. "Wait, There Was a 'Dumber and Dumber' Cartoon Series?" *Yahoo Movies*, September 29, 2014, https://www.yahoo.com/movies/wait-there-was-a-dumber-and-dumber-cartoon-98763726297.html.

"Popeye and Friends, Vol. 1." *DVD Talk*, June 17, 2008, http://www.dvdtalk.com/reviews/33844/popeye-and-friends-vol-1/.

Powell-Hopson, Darlene, and Derek Hopson. "Implications of Doll Color Preference among Black Preschool Children and White Preschool Children." *The Journal of Black Psychology* 14, no. 12 (1988).

Price, Michael H. "Care Bears, 'Gobots,' not Beauty but Likeable.'" *Chicago Tribune*, April 4, 1988, http://articles.chicagotribune.com/1986-04-04/entertainment/8601250103_1_sleeping-beauty-dark-heart-new-entries.

Price, Shinobu. "Cartoons from Another Planet: Japanese Animation as Cross-Cultural Communication." *The Journal of American Culture* 24, no. 1–2 (2001): 153–169.

"Public Broadcasting Act of 1967." Corporation for Public Broadcasting, https://www.cpb.org/aboutpb/act/.

Quenqua, Douglas. "Nancy Reagan's Most Memorable 'Just Say No' Moments." *Campaign*,

March 7, 2016, http://www.campaignlive.com/article/nancy-reagans-memorable-just-say-no-moments/1386274.

Rabaka, Reiland. *Against Academic Apartheid*. Plymouth, UK: Lexington Books, 2010.

Rabin, Nathan. "KISS Army AWOL #51: KISS Meets the Phantom of the Park." *AVClub*, December 17, 2015, https://tv.avclub.com/kiss-army-awol-case-file-51-kiss-meets-the-phantom-of-1798287497.

Rearick, Lauren. "'Steven Universe' Just Made Queer History with a Same-Sex Engagement." *Teen Vogue*, July 6, 2018, https://www.teenvogue.com/story/steven-universe-is-reportedly-first-cartoon-to-feature-same-sex-engagement.

"Richie Rich." *Comics Through Times: A History of Icons, Idols, and Ideas,* ed. M. Keith Booker. Santa Barbara, CA: Greenwood, 2014.

Richter, Paul. "General Electric Will Buy RCA for $6.28 Billion." *Los Angeles Times*, December 12, 1985, http://articles.latimes.com/1985-12-12/news/mn-16152_1_general-electric-will.

Richter, William. "Action for Children's Television." Museum of Broadcast Communication, http://www.museum.tv/eotv/actionforch.htm.

Roach, David A. "Batman." *The Superhero Book: The Ultimate Encyclopedia of Comic Book Icons and Hollywood Heroes*, ed. Renee Misiroglu. Canton, MI: Visible Ink Press, 2004.

Robinson, Mark A. *The World of Musicals: An Encyclopedia of Stage and Screen, and Song.* Westport, CT: Greenwood, 2014

Rodney, Walter. *How Europe Underdeveloped Africa.* Baltimore: Black Classic Press, 2011.

Rogin, Michael. *Blackface, White Noise: Jewish Immigrants in the Hollywood Melting Pot.* Berkeley: University of California Press, 1996.

Romano, Aja. "How Voice Actors Are Fighting to Change an Industry That Renders Them Invisible." *Vox*, July 22, 2020, https://www.vox.com/2020/7/22/21326824/white-voice-actors-black-characters-cartoons-whitewashing.

Rose, Rebecca "Burt." "Amazon, iTunes Put Disclaimer on Racist Tom and Jerry Cartoons." *Jezebel*, October 3, 2014, http://jezebel.com/amazon-itunes-put-disclaimer-for-racism-on-tom-and-jer-1641938104.

Rossen, Jake. "On Smurf Turf: Remembering the Snorks." *Mental Floss,* April 20, 2017, http://mentalfloss.com/article/94549/smurf-turf-remembering-snorks.

Rostron, Allen K. "Return to Hot Wheels: The FCC, Program-Length Commercials, and the Children's Television Act of 1990." *Hastings Communication & Entertainment. Law Journal* 19 (1996).

Rothman, Lily. "Columbus Day, Indigeonous Peoples Day and the Problem with Discovery." *Time*, October 10, 2016, http://time.com/4523330/columbus-day-indigenous-peoples-day-history/.

Rothman, Lily. "The Scathing Speech That Made Television History." *Time,* May 9, 2016, http://time.com/4315217/newton-minow-vast-wasteland-1961-speech/.

Ruby, Joe, and Ken Spears. *The Stu's Show,* interviewed by Stu Shostak, January 16, 2013. http://www.stusshow.com/archives.php?q=spears.

Ryan, Kyle. "Aqua Teen Hunger Force Sued Over Theme Song." *The A.V. Club,* November 10, 2006, http://www.avclub.com/article/aqua-teen-hunger-force-sued-over-theme-song-15851.

Ryan, Mike. "Remember This? The Challenge of the Super Friends." *The Huffington Post,* July 18, 2012, http://www.huffingtonpost.com/mike-ryan/remember-this-challenge-of-the-super-friends_b_1683914.html.

Ryfle, Steve. *Japan's Favorite Mon-Star.* Toronto: ECW Press, 1998.

Rymsza-Pawlowska, Malgorzata J. "Broadcasting the Past: History Television, 'Nostalgia Culture' and the Emergence of the Miniseries in the 1970s United States." *Journal of Popular Film and Television* 42, no. 2 (2014): 81–90.

Said, Edward. *Orientalism.* New York: Random House, 1994.

Sammond, Nicholas. *Babes in Tomorrowland: Walt Disney and the Making of the American Childhood, 1930–1960.* Durham: Duke University Press, 2005.

Sammond, Nicholas. *Birth of an Industry: Blackface Minstrelsy and the Rise of Animation,* Durham: Duke University Press, 2015.

Sammond, Nicholas. "*Dumbo,* Disney, and Difference: Walt Disney Productions and Film as Children's Literature." *The Oxford Handbook of Children's Literature*, eds. Lynne Vallone and Julia Mickenberg. New York: Oxford University Press, 2011. https://www.oxfordhandbooks.com/view/10.1093/oxfordhb/9780195379785.001.0001/oxfordhb-9780195379785-e-8.

Sammond, Nicholas. "Who Dat Say Who Dat? Racial Masquerade, Humor, and the Rise of American Animation." *Funny Pictures: Animation and Comedy in Studio-Era Animation,* eds. Daniel Ira Goldmark and Charles Kell. Berkeley: University of California, 2011, 129–152.

Sandler, Kevin. *Reading the Rabbit*, ed. Kevin Sandler. New Brunswick: Rutgers University Press, 1998.

Sandler, Kevin S. "Synergy Nirvana: Brand Equity, Television Animation, and Cartoon Network." *Prime Time Animation: Television Animation and American Culture,* eds. Carol A. Stabile and Mark Harrison. New York: Routledge, 2003, 89–109.

Sandwell, Ian. "SCOOB! 2: Will there be a SCOOB! Sequel?" *Digital Spy,* July 10, 2020, https://www.digitalspy.com/movies/a33274353/scoob-2-release-date/.

Sarto, Dan. "Betty Cohen Steps Down as President of Cartoon Network." *Animation World Network,* June 15, 2001, https://www.awn.com/news/betty-cohen-steps-down-president-cartoon-network.

"Saturday Morning TV Schedules of the 1980s." *In the 80s,* http://www.inthe80s.com/saturdays.shtml.

Scheimer, Lou, and Andy Mangels. *Lou Scheimer: Creating the Filmation Generation.* Raleigh: Twomorrows, 2012.

Schimkowitz, Matt. "The Not-So-Excellent Adventures of the 'Bill & Ted's Excellent Adventures' TV Series." *Splitsider,* October 9, 2012, http://splitsider.com/2012/10/the-not-so-excellent-adventures-of-the-bill-teds-excellent-adventures-1992-tv-series/.

Schultz, Teri. "Smurfs at 50: Ready for a Comeback." *NPR,* February 21, 2008 http://www.npr.org/templates/story/story.php?storyId=18945311.

Scibelli, Anthony. "A Look at The Simpsons Failed Prime Time Competitors." *Splitsider,* November 22, 2011, http://splitsider.com/2011/11/a-look-at-the-simpsons-failed-prime-time-cartoon-competitors/.

Scibelli, Anthony, and Logan Trent. "Why The Flintstones Takes Place in a Post-Apocalyptic World." *Cracked,* June 20, 2012, http://www.cracked.com/quick-fixes/why-flintstones-takes-place-in-post-apocalyptic-future/.

"Scooby-Doo! Arabian Nights." *Warner Bros. UK,* https://www.warnerbros.co.uk/movies/scooby-doo-arabian-nights.

Seibert, Fred. "Blog History of Frederator's Original Cartoon Shorts. Part 15." *Frederator,* December 30, 2006, http://archives.frederatorblogs.com/frederator_studios/2006/12/30/blog-history-of-frederators-original-cartoon-6/.

Seibert, Fred. "Blog History of Frederator's Original Cartoon Shorts. Part 17." *Frederator,* September 1, 2007, http://archives.frederatorblogs.com/frederator_studios/2007/09/01/blog-history-of-frederator%E2%80%99s-original-carto-2/.

Seibert, Fred. "Blog History of Frederator's Original Cartoon Shorts. Part 22." *Frederator,* October 5, 2009, http://archives.frederatorblogs.com/frederator_studios/2009/10/25/blog-history-of-frederator%E2%80%99s-original-cartoon-shorts-part-22/.

Seiter, Ellen. "Different Children, Different Dreams: Racial Representation in Advertising 1." *Journal of Communication Inquiry* 14, no. 1 (1990).

Semuels, Alana. "The Parts of America Most Susceptible to Automation." *The Atlantic,* May 3, 2017, https://www.theatlantic.com/business/archive/2017/05/the-parts-of-america-most-susceptible-to-automation/525168/.

Semuels, Alana. "White Flight Never Ended." *The Atlantic,* July 30, 2015, https://www.theatlantic.com/business/archive/2015/07/white-flight-alive-and-well/399980/.

Sennett, Ted. *The Art of Hanna-Barbera: Fifty Years of Creativity.* New York: Viking Studio Books, 1991.

"7 Things You Might Not Know about Atom Ant." *MeTV,* March 15, 2016, http://www.metv.com/lists/7-things-you-might-not-know-about-atom-ant.

Shah, Dhavan V., Douglas M. McLeod, Melissa R. Gotlieb, and Nam-Jin Lee. "Framing and Agenda Setting." *The Sage Handbook of Media Processes and Effects* (2009): 83–98.

Shaw, Courtney. "Author Codrescu Considers 'Whitewashing' of the Arabian Nights Stories." Princeton University Press, June 27, 2011, http://blog.press.princeton.edu/2011/06/27/author-codrescu-considers-the-whitewashing-of-the-arabian-nights-stories/.

Sherik, Viola. "Rituals of Hegemonic Masculinity: Cinema Torture and the Middle East." *Speaking about Torture,* eds. Julie A Carlson and Elisabeth Webers. New York: Fordham University Press, 2012.

Sheyahshe, Michael A. *Native Americans in Comic Books: A Critical Study.* Jefferson, NC: McFarland, 2008.

Shull, Michael S., and David E. Wilt. *Doing Their Part, Wartime Animated Short Films, 1939–1945.* Jefferson, NC: McFarland, 2004.

Siegel, Tatiana, Scott Roxborough, Rhonda Richford, and Clarence Tsu. "Inside the Weird World of International Dubbing." *The Hollywood Reporter,* http://www.hollywoodreporter.com/news/argo-django-unchained-inside-weird-427453.

Signorielli, Nancy. "Children, Television, and Gender Roles: Messages and Impact." *Journal of Adolescent Healthcare* 11, no. 1 (1990).

Silverman, Fred. *Archive of American Television,* interview with Dan Pasternack, March 16 and May 29, 2001, http://www.emmytvlegends.org/interviews/people/fred-silverman.

Silverman, Robert. "'Aqua Teen Hunger Force' Says Goodbye: The Creators on the Influential Animated Sitcom." *The Daily Beast,* June 22, 2015, http://www.thedailybeast.com/aqua-teen-hunger-force-says-goodbye-the-creators-on-the-influential-animated-sitcom.

Silvio. Teri "Animation: The New Performance?" *Journal of Linguistic Anthropology* 20, no. 2 (2010): 422–438.

Simon, Scott. "Hip Hop: Today's Civil Rights Movement?" interview with Todd Boyd, *NPR,* March 1, 2003, http://www.npr.org/templates/story/story.php?storyId=1178621.

Sito, Tom. "The Late, Great, 2D Animation Renaissance—Part 1." *Animation World Network,* February 13, 2006, https://www.awn.com/animationworld/late-great-2d-animation-renaissance-part-1.

Slewinski, Christie "1962: ABC Introduces Its First Color Series 'The Jetsons.'" *TV Worth Watching,* September 23, 2012, http://www.tvworthwatching.com/post/THISDAYINTVHISTORY20120923.aspx.

Smith, James Allen. *Strategic Calling: The Center for Strategic and International Studies.* Washington, D.C.: The Center for Strategic and International Studies, 1993.

Society of Animation Studies, https://www.animationstudies.org/v3/.

Solomon, Charles. "Kidvid Reviews: Cartoon Debuts Are All Drawn Out." *New York Times,* October 9, 1987, http://articles.latimes.com/1987–10–09/entertainment/ca-8568_1_cartoon-series.

Solomon, Charles. "Saturday Morning: Good and Bad." *Los Angeles Times,* October 2, 1986, http://articles.latimes.com/1986–10–02/entertainment/ca-3542_1_bad-news.

Solomon, Charles. "TV Reviews: Pebbles, Bamm-Bamm Plan Stone Age Wedding in Bedrock." *Los Angeles Times,* February 6, 1993, http://articles.latimes.com/1993–02–06/entertainment/ca-892_1_modern-stone-age.

Stabile, Carol, and Mark Harrison. "Introduction." *Primetime Animation: Television Animation and*

American Culture, edited by Carol A. Stabile and Mark Harrison. New York: Routledge, 2003.

Staples, Brent. "Just a Toaster with Pictures." *New York Times,* February 8, 1987, http://www.nytimes.com/1987/02/08/books/just-a-toaster-with-pictures.html?pagewanted=a.

Starck, Jonathan, and Adrian Hilton. "Surface Capture for Performance Based Animation" *IEEE Computer Graphics and Application* 27, no. 3 (2007), http://ieeexplore.ieee.org/abstract/document/4178157/?reload=true.

Stark, George. "No Sign of Thawing! Frozen Reaches £800 Million at the Worldwide Box Office Becoming the Fifth-Highest Grossing Movie of All Time." *Daily Mail,* May 26, 2014, http://www.dailymail.co.uk/tvshowbiz/article-2640043/Frozen-reaches-1-219-billion-fifth-highest-grossing-movie-time.html.

Steadman, Ian. "The Jetsons Turns 50: So Where Is All That Cool Stuff?" *Wired,* September 24, 2012, http://www.wired.co.uk/article/jetsons-50th-anniversary.

Steinberg, Jacques. "Rivals Unafraid to Borrow, or Steal, From Each Other." *New York Times,* February 23, 2009, http://www.nytimes.com/2009/02/24/arts/television/24nick.html?mcubz=0.

Sterling, C. H. "Deregulation." Museum of Broadcast Communication, http://www.museum.tv/eotv/deregulation.htm.

Stewart, James B. *Disney War.* New York: Simon & Schuster, 2005.

Stewart, Larry. "CBS' Downfall: Fox's Money, NBC's Agreement." *Los Angeles Times,* December 24, 1993, http://articles.latimes.com/1993-12-24/sports/sp-5079_1_cbs-personnel.

"The Story of Daren the Lion." *D.A.R.E.*, https://www.dare.org/the-story-of-daren-the-lion/.

Stossel, Scott. "The Man Who Counts the Killing." *The Atlantic,* May 1997, https://www.theatlantic.com/magazine/archive/1997/05/the-man-who-counts-the-killings/376850/.

Strauss, Neil. "Tunes for Toons: A Cartoon Music Primer." *The Cartoon Music Book,* ed. Daniel Goldmark and Yuval Taylor. Chicago: Chicago Review Press, 2002.

Strike, Joe. "The Fred Seibert Interview—Part 1." *Animation World Network,* July 15, 2003, https://www.awn.com/animationworld/fred-seibert-interview-part-1.

Suarez, Ray. *Latino Americans: The 500-Year Legacy that Shaped a Nation.* London: Celebra, 2013.

Suddath, Claire. "A Brief History of Mickey Mouse." *Time,* November 18, 2008, http://content.time.com/time/arts/article/0,8599,1859935,00.html.

Sun, Chyng Feng, and Erica Scharrer. "Staying True to Disney: College Students' Resistence to Criticism of The Little Mermaid." *Communication Review* 7, no. 1 (2010): 35–55. http://www.tandfonline.com/doi/abs/10.1080/10714420490280189.

"SuperTed." *BBC Wales,* http://www.bbc.co.uk/wales/arts/sites/children/pages/superted.shtm.

Svetkey, Benjamin. "The Original Flintstones Pilot: The 'Flagstones.'" *Entertainment Weekly,* May 6, 1994, http://ew.com/article/1994/05/06/original-flintstones-pilot-flagstones/.

Sweet, Elizabeth. "Toys Are More Divided by Gender Than They Were 50 Years Ago." *The Atlantic,* December 9, 2014, https://www.theatlantic.com/business/archive/2014/12/toys-are-more-divided-by-gender-now-than-they-were-50-years-ago/383556/.

Swift, Andy. "Animaniacs Reboot in Development from Warner Bros., Steven Spielberg." *TVLine,* May 30, 2017, http://tvline.com/2017/05/30/animaniacs-reboot-plans-wakko-yakko-dot-returning/.

"Swim." *Vulture,* November 14, 2016, https://www.vulture.com/2016/11/brett-gelman-explains-his-decision-to-cut-ties-with-adult-swim.html.

Takamoto, Iwao, and Michael Mallory. *Iwao Takamoto: My Life with a Thousand Characters.* Jackson: University of Mississippi Press, 2009.

Takeuchi, Lori, and Reed Stevens. "The New Co-Viewing: Designing for Learning Through Joint Media Engagement." The Joan Ganz Cooney Center at Sesame Workshop and LIFE Center, Fall 2011, http://www.joanganzcooneycenter.org/wpcontent/uploads/2011/12/jgc_coviewing_desktop.pdf.

Taylor, Paco. "The 15 Most Expensive Kenner Super Powers Toys Ever." *Comic Book Resources,* September 24, 2017, http://www.cbr.com/most-expensive-super-powers-toys/.

Telecommunication Act of 1996 47 U.S.C. ch. 5, subch. VI § 609, https://transition.fcc.gov/Reports/tcom1996.pdf.

"TELEVISION: Stone Age Hero's Smash Hit: TV'S First Cartoon for Grownups Stars the Suburban Flintstones." *LIFE,* November 21, 1960, 57–60.

Terrace, Vincent. *Encyclopedia of Television Pilots.* Jefferson, NC: McFarland, 2013.

Terrace, Vincent. *Encyclopedia of Television Shows: 1925 through 2010.* Jefferson, NC: McFarland, 2011.

Terrace, Vincent. *Television Specials: 5,336 Entertainment Programs, 1936–2012.* Jefferson, NC: McFarland, 2013.

Thill, Scott. "'Peace on Earth' is 75 Years Later-and More Relevant than Ever." *Cartoon Brews,* December 24, 2014, http://www.cartoonbrew.com/ideas-commentary/peace-on-earth-is-75-years-old-and-more-relevant-than-ever-107274.html.

"This Is the Saturday Morning Lineup in 1966. Can Anything Top it?" *MeTV,* January 21, 2016, http://www.metv.com/stories/this-is-what-the-saturday-morning-tv-lineup-looked-like-50-years-ago.

"This Is What the Saturday Morning TV Lineup Looked Like in 1975." *MeTV,* August 6, 2016, http://www.metv.com/stories/this-is-what-the-Saturday-morning-TV-lineup-looked-like-in-1975.

Thomas, Ashley. "Linguistics in Land of the Lost." *Retroist,* August 20, 2016, http://www.retroist.com/2016/08/10/linguistics-in-the-land-of-the-lost/.

Thomas, Bryan. "'Uh, Oh Chongo': Danger Island

and the Daredevil Life and Career of Kim Kahana." *Nightflight,* October 8, 2015, http://nightflight.com/uh-oh-chongo-danger-island-and-the-daredevil-life-career-of-kim-kahana/.

Thomas, Sarah. "Janet Waldo, the Voice of Penelope Pitstop and Judy Jetson Dead at 96." *Sydney Morning Herald,* June 14, 2016, http://www.smh.com.au/entertainment/tv-and-radio/janet-waldo-the-voice-of-penelope-pitstop-and-judy-jetson-dead-at-96-20160613-gpibkl.html.

Thomas, Tanja, and Merle-Marie Kruse. "Cultural Studies." *The International Encyclopedia of Political Communication,* January 2016, http://onlinelibrary.wiley.com/doi/10.1002/9781118541555.wbiepc166/full.

Thompson, Derek. "On Repeat: Why People Watch Movies and Shows Over and Over." *The Atlantic,* September 10, 2014, https://www.theatlantic.com/entertainment/archive/2014/09/rewinding-rewatching-and-listening-on-repeat-why-we-love-re-consuming-entertainment/379862.

"Tom and Jerry Vol. 1." *iTunes,* https://itunes.apple.com/us/tv-season/tom-and-jerry-vol-1/id417551536.

"Top Kid Videos." *Billboard Magazine,* February 23, 2002, https://goo.gl/aTi4SR.

Torres, Inés Galiano. "Audience's Perception of Cultural/Ethnic Stereotypes in TV Shows." *European Scientific Journal* 1, no. 10 (2015).

Torres, Sasha. *Black, White, and in Color: Television and Black Civil Rights.* Princeton: Princeton University Press, 2003.

Towers, Andrea. "DC Entertainment Announces New Slate of Hanna-Barbera Titles." *Entertainment Weekly,* January 29, 2016, http://ew.com/article/2016/01/29/dc-entertainment-hanna-barbera-titles/.

Trendacosta, Katharine. "Here's How the Scooby-Doo Crew Would Have Dressed through the 20th Century." *io9,* June 19, 2015, http://io9.gizmodo.com/heres-how-the-scooby-doo-crew-would-dress-throughout-th-1712466972.

Trendacosta, Katharine. "Seriously, Another Robin Hood Movie Is Being Written." *io9,* February 27, 2015, https://io9.gizmodo.com/it-did-include-time-bandits-1688413187.

Truglio, Rosemarie. "Sesame Street and Learning through Play." *American Journal of Play,* 12, no. 1 (2019).

Trumbore, Dave. "Hollywood! Adapt This: The Pirates of Dark Water." *Collider,* September 9, 2012, http://collider.com/pirates-of-dark-water-movie-adaptation/.

Tucker, Jeffrey A. *It's A Jetsons World.* New York: Laissez Faire Books, 2013.

Tumlin, Jeffrey. "City of the Future: Time to Jettison the Jetsons' Vision of Cities." *Journal of Urban Regeneration & Renewal* 8, no. 2 (2015): 152–160.

"Turner Rebrands Boomerang Globally." *Turner,* October 14, 2014, https://www.turner.com/pressroom/united-states/boomerang/turner-rebrands-boomerang-globally.

TV Guide Guide to TV, ed. TV Guide. New York: Barnes and Noble, 2004, 351.

Unterberger, Andrew. "Run the Jewels & Adult Swim: Inside the Hip-Hop/Cartoon Bromance." *Billboard,* January 10, 2017, http://www.billboard.com/articles/news/magazine-feature/7654180/run-the-jewels-adult-swim-bromance.

VanDerWerff, Todd. "In *The Flintstones,* Hanna-Barbera Found a Shameless Rip-Off That Worked." *AV Club,* May 12, 2014, http://www.avclub.com/article/flintstones-hanna-barbera-found-shameless-rip-work-204382.

VanDerWerff, Tom. "10 Episodes that Show Off Leave it to Beaver's Quiet Innovation." *AV Club,* November 11, 2012, https://tv.avclub.com/10-episodes-that-show-off-leave-it-to-beaver-s-quiet-in-1798234600.

Voukydis Ari, and Marc Sarian. "Did You Know Ms. Pac-Man Is a Feminist Icon?" *HuffPost,* March 27, 2014, https://www.huffpost.com/entry/ms-pac-man-feminist-icon_n_5036619.

"Vulture Asks: What Couple Do You Anti-Ship?" *Vulture,* September 27, 2016, http://www.vulture.com/2016/08/tv-couple-anti-shipping.html.

"Wait Till Your Father Gets Home." *TVGuide,* http://www.tvguide.com/tvshows/wait-till-father/205338.

Wallace, Claudia. "The Nuclear Family Goes 'Boom!'" *Time,* October 15, 1992, http://content.time.com/time/printout/0,8816,976754,00.html.

Wartella, Ellen, and Byron Reeves. "Historical Trends in Research on Children and the Media: 1900–1960" *Journal of Communication* 35, no. 2 (1985): 118–135.

"Was the Animated Series Wacky Races Originally Intended for a Live Action Game Show?" *Entertainment Urban Legends Revealed,* November 29, 2013, http://legendsrevealed.com/entertainment/2013/11/29/was-the-animated-series-wacky-races-originally-intended-for-a-live-action-game-show/.

Watson, Elijah. "The Oral History of Cartoon Network's Toonami." *Complex,* March 21, 2017, http://www.complex.com/pop-culture/2017/03/oral-history-of-toonami.

Watson, Margeaux, and Jennifer Armstrong. "Diversity: Why Is TV So White?" *Entertainment Weekly,* June 13, 2008, http://ew.com/article/2008/06/13/diversity-why-tv-so-white/.

Weber, Max. *Politics as a Vocation,* http://anthroposlab.net/wp/wp-content/uploads/2011/12/Weber-Politics-as-a-Vocation.pdf.

Webster, Brian Philip. "Chapter 29: Barter Syndication." *The Advertising Business: Operations Creativity Media Planning Integrated Communications,* ed. John Philip Jones. Thousand Oaks, CA: SAGE, 1999, 299–309.

Webster, Dan. "Hanna Time Bill Hanna Partnered with Joe Barbera, Has Earned the Love of Children of All Ages with His Animated Characters." *The Spokesman-Review,* July 15, 1996, http://www.spokesman.com/stories/1996/jul/15/hanna-time-bill-hanna-partnered-with-joe-barbera/.

Wedman, Les. "Do Viewers Really Want to See Something New or Different on U.S. Television?" *Vancouver Sun,* October 22, 1968.

Wells, John, and Keith Dallas. *American Comic Book*

Chronicles: 1965–69. Vol. 9. Raleigh: Twomorrows, 2014.

Wells, Paul. *America and Animation.* New Brunswick: Rutgers University Press, 2002.

Wells, Paul. "'Smarter Than the Average Artform': Animation in the Television Era." *Prime Time Animation: Television Animation and American Culture,* eds. Carol A. Stabile and Mark Harrison. New York: Routledge, 2003, 15–32.

West, Abby. "'The Boondocks' (Allegedly) Take on Tyler Perry: Too Far?" *Entertainment Weekly,* June 24, 2010, http://ew.com/article/2010/06/24/boondocks-tyler-perry-made/.

"What Is Pac-Man?" *Pac-Man.com,* archived November 28, 2010, https://web.archive.org/web/20101128063459/http://pacman.com/en/about.

Whelan, Aubrey. "A Loving Look Back at Double Dare Made-in-Philly TV That's 30 Years Old Today." *Philadelphia Inquirer,* http://www.philly.com/philly/entertainment/television/A-loving-look-back-at-Double-Dare-made-in-Philly-TV.html.

Whitbrook, James. "DC's Latest Hanna-Barbera Comic Will Reimagine Snagglepuss as 'Gay, Gothic Southern Playwright.'" *io9,* January 31, 2017, http://io9.gizmodo.com/dcs-latest-hanna-barbera-comic-will-reimagine-snagglepu-1791836954.

"Whoopi Goldberg Cartoon Show on Drawing Board." *Jet,* March 21, 1988, shorturl.at/abjsY.

Wickberg, Daniel. "Heterosexual White Male: Some Recent Inversions in American cultural history." *The Journal of American History* 92, no. 1 (2005): 136–157.

Wildey, Doug. "Amazing Heroes #95." *Classic Jonny Quest,* original interview published May 15, 1986, http://www.classicjq.com/info/AmazingHeroes95.aspx.

Williams, Patricia J. "Metro Broadcasting, Inc vs. FCC: Regrouping in Singular Times." *Critical Race Theory: The Key Writings that Formed a Movement,* eds. Kimberle Crenshaw, Neil Gotanda, Gary Peller, and Kendall Thomas. New York: The New Press, 1995, 191–204.

Wilson, Suzanne. "Scooby-Doo! How Old are You?" *ASU Now,* July 26, 2019, https://psychology.asu.edu/content/scooby-doo-how-old-are-you.

Wilson Jeffrey L. "The 10 Most Influential Video Games of All-Times." *PCMag,* June 11, 2010, http://www.pcmag.com/feature/251651/the-10-most-influential-video-games-of-all-time?p=n.

Wojahn, Ellen. *The General Mills/Parker Brothers Merger: Playing by Different Rules.* Frederick, MD: Beard Books, 1988

Wolf, Mark J.P. "Video Games of the 1970s." *The Video Game Explosion: A History from PONG to Playstation and Beyond,* ed. by Mark J.P. Wolf. ABC-CLIO, 2008.

Wolfe, Audra. "Project Troy: How Scientists Helped Refine Cold War Psychological Warfare." *The Atlantic,* December 1, 2018, https://www.theatlantic.com/science/archive/2018/12/project-troy-science-cold-war-psychological-warfare/576847/.

Wright, Jean Ann. *Animation Writing and Development: From Script Development to Pitch.* New York: Focal Press, 2005.

Wright, Megh. "Brett Gelman Explains His Decision to Cut Ties with Adult Swinm." *Vulture,* November 14, 2016, https://www.vulture.com/2016/11/brett-gelman-explains-his-decision-to-cut-ties-with-adult-swim.html.

Young, Kevin. "Schomburg Center for Research in Black Culture Receives James Baldwin Letters." Interview with Audie Cornish, *NPR,* April 13, 2017, http://www.npr.org/2017/04/13/523804448/schomburg-center-for-research-in-black-culture-receives-james-baldwin-letters.

Żaglewski, Tomasz. "The Impossibles Revived: Hanna-Barbera's Superhero Universe in TV and Comics." *Journal of Graphic Novels and Comics* (2020): 1–17.

Zaretsky, Adam M. "I want my MTV ... and My CNN ... the Cable Industry and Regulation." *Regional Economist,* July 1995, https://www.stlouisfed.org/publications/regional-economist/july-1995/i-want-my-mtvand-my-cnn-the-cable-tv-industry-and-regulation.

Zitter, Leah. "Trending: Black Viewers and Anime." *The Moguldom Nation,* September 27, 2019, https://moguldom.com/229542/trending-black-viewers-and-anime/.

Zuras, Matthew. "Childhood Ruined: 10 Offensive Cartoons of Our Youth." *Refinery29,* November 23, 2013, http://www.refinery29.com/2013/11/57871/offensive-cartoons.

Index